CANADA'S UKRAINIANS:

NEGOTIATING AN IDENTITY

CANADA'S UKRAINIANS

Negotiating an Identity

Edited by Lubomyr Luciuk
and Stella Hryniuk

Published in Association with the
Ukrainian Canadian Centennial Committee
by University of Toronto Press
Toronto Buffalo London

© University of Toronto Press 1991
Toronto Buffalo London
Printed in Canada

ISBN 0-8020-5978-3

(∞)

Printed on acid-free paper

Canadian Cataloguing in Publication Data

Main entry under title:
Canada's Ukrainians

Includes index.
ISBN 0-8020-5978-3

1. Ukrainians – Canada – History.
2. Ukrainian Canadians – History.*   I. Luciuk, Lubomyr Y., 1953–   .
II. Hryniuk, Stella M., 1939–   .
III. Ukrainian Canadian Centennial Committee.

FC106.U5L8 1991   971'.00491791   C91-094952-2
F1035.U5L8 1991

This volume is published with the assistance of grants from
the Ministry of Multiculturalism and Citizenship and
from the Ukrainian Canadian Centennial Committee, Inc.

Contents

Foreword

As Governor General of Canada and the representative of Her Majesty The Queen, the responsibilities of my position have evolved in rhythm with the changing structures and moods of the nation. Nevertheless, one element remains constant: the symbolism of the vice-regal office. The milestones of our individual lives, from birth through school graduations, marriages, and anniversaries, are marked by ceremonies and symbols which represent important values as well as a continuum in the history of our nation. In much the same way, the Crown embodies the structures and values of our parliamentary democracy as well as the multitude of political and social ties which bind our country together.

Canadians are heirs to almost four centuries of tradition in the long line of governors since Champlain. Many of my predecessors promoted Canadian unity with the same zest displayed by the first Governor of New France in developing the early colony. Lord Dufferin was the first Governor General to travel across Canada, attending a variety of functions in the provinces and receiving Quebecers at La Citadelle every summer. Lord Tweedsmuir used the prestige of his position to break down the barriers of race and religion that divided Canadians. Speaking in 1936 to a group of Ukrainian Canadians in Fraserwood, Manitoba, he remarked: 'We Scots are supposed to be good citizens of new countries, that is largely because, while we mix well with others and gladly accept new loyalties, we never forget our ancient Scots way, but always remember the little country from which we sprang. That is true of every race with a strong tradition behind it, and it must be so with a people with such a strong tradition as yours. You will all be better Canadians for being also good Ukrainians.' Canada, as a nation made great by its immigrants, has a reputation of welcoming diversity while encouraging its citizens to integrate their customs and values into the fabric of our social character. This has been the strength as well as the joy of the nation we have forged.

The essays in this collection not only commemorate the centenary of Ukrainian settlement in Canada, but also attest to the resilience of spirit and determination of purpose which were essential not only to the success of the Ukrainian community in Canada but also to the very creation of our nation. As Governor General and as a Canadian who cherishes his Ukrainian heritage, I hope that they will serve as a special reminder not only of what we have built but also of what we must continue to nurture.

Ramon John Hnatyshyn

Preface

I remember quite vividly my first serious encounter with Ukrainian Canadians. It took place just over a decade ago, when I immigrated to Canada to accept a professorship at the newly established Chair of Ukrainian Studies at the University of Toronto. Following my inaugural lecture, a public event held in October 1980 with all the pomp and circumstance that both Canada's leading university and traditional Ukrainian society love so much, two students in their early twenties stopped me to express their reactions to my talk. While they seemed pleased with my lecture survey of how and why Ukrainian university chairs had been founded in the past century and a half, they were decidedly less enthusiastic about my optimistic appraisal of the positive financial role played by Canada's federal government in the creation of the Toronto chair.

In short, the young man and young woman began to lecture me about how Ukrainians had been and – so they seemed to imply – still were discriminated against in Canadian society. Despite my entreaties to the contrary, they were determined to convince me that Ukrainian immigrants had always suffered and toiled with only little recompense at the hands of an exploitative Canadian society.

I was dumbfounded. These were not Marxist ideologues from the Soviet Ukraine, or leftist sympathizers from North America. If anything, they were even more adamant about how their Ukrainian homeland was tyrannized by Communist rule. These were clearly angry young people, and I felt somewhat resentful that they would be denigrating a country like Canada where, in contrast to the United States whence I had just come, Ukrainians certainly had a high public profile and were courted with direct governmental support for a whole host of community activities including something even so 'esoteric' as a university chair.

Why were these young people so angry, so anti-Canadian? Clearly by their age it was not they who 'suffered' directly either as pioneer immigrants from the early part of the century or as post–World War II political émigrés. Where, then, did they pick up the cultural baggage that led them to conclude that theirs was a people ill-treated, a people that must somehow be repaid for (Canada's supposed) past injustices? After a decade in this country I am still bothered by these questions, especially since a certain portion of the hundreds of Ukrainian Canadians I have met still express in their own way the anger of the two young students from the night of my inaugural lecture.

I guess the answer lies in the fact that there are two kinds of Ukrainian Canadians. They might be described as (1) Canadians of Ukrainian background and (2) Ukrainians who live in Canada. Whereas scholars have often distinguished Ukrainian Canadians by the time of their arrival in this country, with World War II being a crucial chronological divide, or by place of settlement, with the 'prairie' West and 'urban' East considered key differences, it seems to me that the real distinguishing features derive from the self-perception that is suggested by the dichotomy: Canadians of Ukrainian background versus Ukrainians who live in Canada.

How is one to understand the characteristics of that dichotomy? Canadians of Ukrainian background are those people of whatever generation who consider themselves first and foremost Canadian. Their family ties, education, and general world view are determined by the parameters of this country. They may or may not speak or understand Ukrainian, attend a traditional Eastern Christian Ukrainian church, or belong to a Ukrainian organization. They probably have no interest in or, at best, a passing concern with events either in Ukraine or in the Ukrainian communities outside Ukraine. They simply are Canadians who, like all Canadians, have parents or grandparents who came from somewhere else. That somewhere else on one or both sides of the family is something referred to as Ukraine (even though in actual likelihood it was Austria-Hungary, Poland, Romania, or Czechoslovakia). I would venture to say that perhaps three-quarters of the 800,000 or so Ukrainian Canadians fall into this category, Canadians of Ukrainian background. In essence, they make up the great 'silent majority.'

The second group, Ukrainians who live in Canada, may also come from various generations and they include people born in Canada as well as those born in the old country. Regardless of their place of birth or residence, they consider themselves Ukrainian first and foremost. This means that they prefer to speak Ukrainian (or consider it their mother tongue even if they are more comfortable speaking English); they attend an Eastern Christian church, most especially on major holidays like Easter and Christmas, whether or not they are or ever were believers; and they follow with great concern the fate of the Ukrainian homeland and participate in the activities of what they call diaspora. After all, if one is a member of a diaspora, this implies that one, or one's children or grandchildren, may someday return to a free and independent Ukrainian promised land.

Being a Ukrainian living in Canada is most difficult for those individuals born and educated in Canada. These people often have split personalities, and sometimes suffer from great internal psychological discord. Outwardly, they seemed to have adapted entirely to the host society. They speak English (or in some cases French) with no accent; they have been educated in the same public and private schools as other Canadians; and they hold respectable jobs in the professional and non-professional employment sectors.

Inwardly, however, they have set themselves apart. The result is that they are often torn between what comes more natural – functioning as indistinguishable members in a Canadian host environment – and what has become an intellectualized reality – struggling to be a Ukrainian in a non-Ukrainian world. That struggle may take various forms: speaking Ukrainian wherever possible, marrying only other Ukrainians, attending Ukrainian religious services and secular events, and vicariously transforming themselves into compatriots of Ukraine by following with devotion the fate of those in the homeland who protest the Communist regime. On the diaspora front, the struggle often takes the form of demands upon the Canadian federal, provincial, and local governments for financial and other support for Ukrainian cultural activities, which they insist upon as compensation for the group's sacrifices to Canadian society. More often than not, Canadian politicians are willing to concede to such demands either because of misplaced guilt or, more likely, political opportunism.

It is this category, Ukrainians living in Canada, which has become for most scholars the subject of their research into the Ukrainian-Canadian experience. And it is this same category which has become and remains the concern of the Canadian political world. This is not surprising, because Ukrainians living in Canada are easily identified by scholars looking for subjects and by politicians seeking votes.

However, the category may not have a future. This is because its very existence has depended upon an abnormal political situation in the Ukrainian homeland. For the entire 100 years that Ukrainians have been settling in Canada, Ukrainian territory has been ruled by foreign powers: Austria-Hungary, the Russian Empire, the Soviet Union, Poland, and Romania. Even though the Soviet Union finally united most Ukrainian lands in 1945, it was that same Communist-ruled state that virtually eliminated all normal relations between Ukrainians at home and abroad by restricting travel, family visits, even communication via letter. Stimulated by such inhuman policies, Ukrainians abroad were able to survive and perpetuate a sense of commitment and identity because they had a duty to sustain what they thought was being lost in the homeland.

But as we approach the threshold of the twenty-first century, the Soviet 'stimulus' that contributed toward maintaining a Ukrainian identity abroad is slowly but surely coming to an end in the wake of the revolutionary changes that since the mid-1980s have toppled Communist rule in East Central Europe and now the Soviet Union. In short, as Ukraine becomes a normal country like Germany, or Italy, or France, there will be no need to be a Ukrainian living in Canada. Such Ukrainians will be – and already are – able to travel, live, and work in Ukraine. In the end, there will only be Canadians of Ukrainian descent who comprise the Ukrainian-Canadian community. Ukrainians, moreover, are not unique in this regard, and perhaps it is time to look more systematically at another aspect of the 'Gorbachev revolution': its impact on North American immigrant life among all groups from East Central Europe and the Soviet Union.

It may very well be that the often mechanical chronological units like centennials of settlement have, as in the case of Ukrainian Canadians, more than symbolic significance. We may, indeed, be moving into a new era and not just a second centennial. This may become a time when all Ukrainian Canadians will retain a sense of their heritage not because it is ostensibly or actually threatened in the homeland but because it is simply another aspect of being Canadian.

If and when that time comes, it will be a positive one not only for Ukrainians in the homeland, who for so long have awaited the time when they can rule themselves, but also for the many individuals like those two angry young people I met over a decade ago. In the new reality that promises a Ukraine like any other European country and that allows for easy access to and from the homeland, there will be no reason why some Ukrainian Canadians have to be saddled with internal tensions about whether they are Ukrainians or Canadians. And in the end, Canada will be a better place when the Ukrainian component of its population is made up of Canadians of Ukrainian background and not Ukrainians living in Canada.

Paul Robert Magocsi
Chair of Ukrainian Studies
University of Toronto

Editors' Introduction

Reflection on a hundred years of the Ukrainian-Canadian experience is appropriate in this centennial year. As scholars we felt the best way of accomplishing this would be to strike a committee, to organize public seminars and a symposium, and, most important, to publish a selection of essays dealing with the experience of Canada's Ukrainians from the earliest period of settlement to the present. Our goal was to help Canadians to understand what has happened to Canada's Ukrainians between 1891 and 1991. These considerations led to the incorporation of the Ukrainian Canadian Centennial Committee, affiliated with the Chair of Ukrainian Studies at the University of Toronto.

It is frequently said that a scholar's ultimate goal is the preparation of a comprehensive monograph on the subject at hand. Prefaces to edited collections often contain laments about the lack of primary materials and the inadequate state of existing knowledge and conclude with prescriptions for more research. Here that pattern will not be followed, at least not entirely. This volume was not intended to be a definitive or even exhaustive treatment of the Ukrainian-Canadian experience over the past hundred years. Instead it was our intention to solicit essays exploring primarily the history and geography of Canada's Ukrainians, analyses that would offer new insights into how and why Ukrainians came to be here, how they interacted among themselves, and, perhaps most important, how the larger society, most especially the Canadian state, interacted with them. This basic framework is reflected in our volume's subtitle, *Negotiating an Identity*. By this we mean to suggest that all the papers in this collection share a concern with how Ukrainians came to think of themselves as a people within Canada, affected by events in the old homeland and in this country and by the actions of diverse other players, from the organs of various levels of government to political, religious, and other constituencies. Although Ukrainians came to Canada with cultural baggage reflecting their experiences in Ukraine and elsewhere in Europe, they adapted and transformed themselves in order to conform to changing Canadian realities. In that process a dynamic and distinctive Ukrainian-Canadian community has emerged and is continuing to evolve.

In the course of structuring the Ukrainian Canadian Centennial Seminar Series and compiling this collection, we became aware of several critical elements in the Ukrainian-Canadian experience that have, in the main, been ignored. For one thing, one of the essential factors behind the large-scale assimilation of Ukrainians into Canadian society was the repeated interventions by the Canadian state into Ukrainian-Canadian affairs. These intrusions, direct and indirect, further fragmented the organized component of the Ukrainian-Canadian population and interfered with Ukrainian commitment to organized community life. The Canadian state has at all times been aware of, sometimes anxious about, and often active in, the internal affairs of Ukrainian-Canadian society. From its turn-of-the-century immigration and settlement policies to the internment operations of the First World War, from the covert surveillance activities of the inter-war period to the creation of the Ukrainian Canadian Committee during the Second World War and, in more recent times, the establishment of the Commission of Inquiry on War Criminals, the state has had a formative role in shaping Canadian-Ukrainian society. Governments often made decisions and acted on the recommendations of players centred outside the community, individuals who were sometimes indifferent, ignorant, or even hostile to Canada's Ukrainians, with consequences that could be traumatic. Ukrainian organizations were forced to adapt or, in some cases, disappear.

Identifying oneself publicly as a Ukrainian in Canada in the past has not always been a wise choice. And so the theme of divided political, religious, and social loyalties runs through these essays. After reading them those who have a religious inclination may well ask: are the organized Ukrainians in this country good Catholics, or is it more important for them to be good Ukrainian Catholics? Those of a political bent may wonder: are these Ukrainians good Canadians or good Ukrainian nationalists, and which comes first? These are questions of no mean importance, particularly in times of international or domestic crisis, as Canada's Ukrainians have learned more than once and often at their cost. For the moment all we can say is that not many seem to have affirmed Governor-General Lord Tweedsmuir's 1936 exclamation to the effect that Ukrainians in Canada 'would all be better Canadians for being also good Ukrainians.' Being Ukrainian in Canada has meant negotiating with the larger society, not only about the group's collective identity but also about its place within Canada. Such negotiation has been going on from the pioneer years to our own days.

The structure of the book reflects the organizing principle suggested in the title. The three sections, all of more or less equal length, deal with immigration and settlement, internal community politics, and Canada's Ukrainians and the state. With regard to the state, the organized Ukrainian community in Canada has yet to resolve long-standing issues related to its collective status within the larger society. Why should this be the case? We believe that the nature of scholarship in Canada has much to do with it.

Until very recently, the Canadian academic establishment has not welcomed studies of Canada's Ukrainians or, for that matter, of this country's other ethnic, religious, and racial minorities. This is not to say that important books on Ukrainian-Canadian themes did not appear. But, for the most part, they were descriptive or filiopietistic accounts highlighting the accomplishments of selected individuals or groups within the community or advancing particular ideological or religious concerns. The few non-Ukrainian commentators supposedly addressing Ukrainian-Canadian themes actually focused on 'Old World' issues, like ties between Canada's Ukrainians and the struggle for Ukrainian independence, or the attraction of Soviet communism for some in the community, all in the belief that such homeland-oriented attitudes had a retarding effect on the assimilation of Ukrainians and their progeny into mainstream Canadian society. For these Anglo-Canadian writers complete integration was the most desirable of all possible outcomes for these immigrants. Non-Ukrainian writers tended, otherwise, to ignore the Canadian-Ukrainian experience as irrelevant or peripheral, save for acknowledging the hardships of the pioneer Ukrainian settlers who opened up the prairie West.

Ukrainian and Ukrainian Canadian Studies achieved recognition only with the founding of the Canadian Institute of Ukrainian Studies at the University of Alberta, the Centre for Ukrainian Canadian Studies at the University of Manitoba, and the Chair of Ukrainian Studies at the University of Toronto. Modest financial support became available for research and publications, and a new generation of Canadian-born students, representing several academic disciplines, could draw support from a small but growing community of like-minded scholars. In turn this fuelled a search for archival, oral, and other primary sources, a quest facilitated by grants and support from the Secretary of State for Multiculturalism, the Social Sciences and Humanities Research Council of Canada, the National Archives of Canada, the Canadian Institute of Ukrainian Studies, the Multicultural History Society of Ontario, and the Ukrainian community. Where only a few years before many primary materials remained undiscovered or locked away in private or public repositories, either uncatalogued or deliberately closed, many important collections (although far from all) became available by the early 1980s. It was at this point that important publications in the area of Ukrainian Canadian Studies began to appear. Less self-congratulatory about Ukrainian-Canadian achievements than most earlier writings, books like *A Heritage in Transition* were a first attempt to bring together scholarly analyses of the Ukrainian experience in this country. That volume's greatest contribution, however, was in stimulating future research. In its concluding essay Frances Swyripa predicted that further Ukrainian-Canadian studies would focus on the organized community, defined as 'that narrowing sector of the ethnic group consciously propagating Ukrainian cultural traditions, promoting the Ukrainian language and culture in Canada, and actively concerned about the fate of Ukraine.'

The present collection attests to just how prescient that statement was. But it also goes further by offering investigations of several pivotal episodes in the Canadian-Ukrainian experience, based on new data and approaches by a cohort of writers and scholars. Several of these studies are, we contend, at the 'cutting edge' of research in the field. More remains to be done, of course, but, significantly, only four of the twenty-one authors included in this collection were published in *A Heritage in Transition*. The fact that several of them are not of Ukrainian origin suggests that important links are developing between Canadian and Ukrainian Canadian Studies, ties that, until recently, did not exist. We view that as a positive development. Ukrainian Canadian Studies, a healthy if still small field, seem to be growing. As for the demographic, social, political, and religious trends in this population and the varied experiences of Canada's organized Ukrainian communities in the past, these would seem to suggest the need for new thinking about community organizational efforts and infrastructural systems. Perhaps the time has come for a new commonality to evolve, uniting Canadian Ukrainians of varied backgrounds on the basis of their shared interests rather than on the less flexible bonds of linguistic ability or organizational and religious affiliation. Some of the structures of the past have been crippling rather than constructive.

This volume demonstrates that the study of Canada's Ukrainians involves the study of Canada. Once the immigrants got off the proverbial boat they began accommodating to, and being shaped by, the society, church, and state they encountered. Well before the Second World War most Ukrainians in this country were Canadian-born, and by the end of this century over 90 per cent will fit into that category. Their history, their geography, and their sociology are all basically Canadian. Students of the Ukrainian-Canadian experience, we contend, are not 'doing ethnic history.' Whether they consider immigration policies, internal security measures, the evolution of Canadian-Ukrainian ideologies, or independent Canadian-centred churches among the Ukrainian faithful, they are dealing with an intrinsic aspect of the evolution of the Canadian nation. Most Canadian historians and other social scientists have yet to appreciate this point, confining Ukrainian Canadian Studies to the periphery. This says more about them, and the Canada of the past, than it does about Canada's Ukrainians or the future of this confederation.

As the editors of this volume, we bear responsibility for the selection of its major themes and of the papers that have been included here. However, each paper presents the individual author's perceptions of the Ukrainian-Canadian experience. Not every author will necessarily agree with the conclusions put forward by the others, and not all members of the public will find this book to their liking. The willingness to consider, debate, and learn from others is essential to academic life. We hope this book will help foster understanding of Canada's Ukrainians and their place in this country.

A few words of thanks. This book would not have been possible without the scholars who presented or submitted papers to our Ukrainian Canadian Centennial Seminar Series. Not every paper, regrettably, could be included in this volume, but we thank all those who worked with us for the energy, thought, and commitment they demonstrated. We are also indebted to Professors Paul R. Magocsi of the Chair of Ukrainian Studies and Wsevolod Isajiw of the Department of Sociology at the University of Toronto. Both served capably as academic advisers to the Ukrainian Canadian Centennial Committee from its inception to the conclusion of its work with the appearance of this volume. Members of our board of directors supported our committee's work across Canada, often sharing their thoughts about appropriate ways for commemorating the Ukrainian Canadian Centennial. Marco Carynnyk copy-edited the manuscript, and Jeff Picknicki helped locate missing references. Judy Young, Aldean Anderson, and Cliff Yumansky of the Ministry of Multiculturalism and Citizenship helped us with our grant applications.

Without that ministry's generous support this volume would not have appeared during the centennial of Canada's Ukrainians. We are also grateful to the Social Sciences and Humanities Research Council of Canada and the Ukrainian Canadian Congress for their support of our conference on the Ukrainian experience in Canada. Sally Jones of the Chair of Ukrainian Studies and Dr Lillian Petroff of the Multicultural History Society of Ontario helped to organize that conference and to co-ordinate the seminar arrangements. Eugene Cholkan, our committee's accountant, kept its funds in order, no mean accomplishment. Special thanks are also due to Dr Ron Schoeffel, editor of the University of Toronto Press. His enthusiasm and sage counsel made working with the Press a joy.

Finally, we wish to thank our spouses, Alexandra Luciuk and Fred Stambrook. Their good cheer and support kept us happy as we set up the Ukrainian Canadian Centennial Seminar Series, secured papers from our contributors, and juggled our hectic schedules over the past three years. Their contribution is not easily gauged, but we recognize that our debt to them is substantial.

Our one regret is that Professor Robert F. Harney, whose interest in our work never flagged even when he had more pressing personal concerns, is not with us. He would have voiced pithy observations about this book and what it is we Ukrainian Canadians are doing in observing this centennial. His death in 1989 robbed the Ukrainian community in Canada of a friend. It is to his memory that we dedicate this book.

Lubomyr Y. Luciuk   Stella Hryniuk

Part 1

TO CANADA:
IMMIGRATION AND
SETTLEMENT

'Sifton's Pets':
Who Were They?

A considerable literature has accumulated on the background to the immigration of Ukrainians to Canada at the turn of the century and on their early history in this country. With varying degrees of emphasis various authors have maintained that Ukrainians were victims of social, political, and even religious oppression, suffering from lack of economic and educational opportunities, fleeing from a stagnant, backward, and impoverished society. Such gloomy accounts are to be found in both popular and scholarly writings and are due, perhaps, to limited knowledge of the appropriate sources for the history of Eastern Galicia and Bukovyna.[1] That recent scholarship should uncritically reiterate such interpretations can lead to different questions: Do the authors like a 'rags-to-riches' explanation, which contrasts supposed poverty and backwardness in Western Ukraine to the gains subsequently made in Canada? Do they minimize the homeland experience because of their inadequate grasp of a rural society's dynamics? Have they failed to observe that the most damning indictments of Galician conditions in the last quarter of the nineteenth century were written by observers who had political or economic grievances particular to their subgroup in that society? Among the latter were Polish publicists who were concerned with the fate of the Polish nation and its gentry class, especially during a time of agricultural depression.[2] Others with such grievances were contemporary Ukrainian radical publicists like Ivan Franko and Mykhailo Pavlyk, whose gloomy views of Western Ukrainian society grew out of their socialist convictions.[3] In the light of newer, wider-ranging research in the past decade, the centenary year of the first immigration invites a re-examination of Galician and Bukovynian conditions before and during the first immigration.

Such a study is necessary in itself, especially as the literature suggests that immigrants were generally not the poorest of their society; as a historian of another immigrant society has written: 'Weak, beaten men and women do not undertake transoceanic journeys to far-off lands unless they are herded aboard ship at gunpoint.'[4] The individual and societal experiences of the immigrants – their 'cultural baggage' – were to have a considerable bearing on their own and their descendants' lives in their new homeland. A closer examination of conditions in rural Eastern Galicia and Bukovyna is therefore indicated, especially as their agrarian history has hitherto been neglected.[5]

The Ukrainians who came to Canada between 1891 and 1914 were, with few exceptions, citizens of the Austrian Empire and resided in the villages and towns of the crownlands of Galicia (Halychyna) and Bukovyna. They began to emigrate to Canada in very small numbers in 1891, setting out as individuals or in groups of a few families. The large numbers, variously estimated at between 128,000 and 170,000, came after 1895, following the scouting visit that year by the Galician agronomist Dr Osyp Oleskiv and the publication of his pamphlets on emigration to Canada. Two groups of settlers, groomed for this experience by Oleskiv, came in May and July 1896 and formed the nuclei of settlements in Manitoba, to add to the already existing settlement at Edna-Star in the Northwest Territories. These three groups and the areas along the railway line in between formed the targets for the chain migration before the First World War.

The first point to be noted in any reinterpretation of the background to emigration is that between 1880 and 1910 Eastern Galicia and Bukovyna were provided with modern communications. By 1872, main railway lines connected both regions with other parts of the Austrian Empire and with Western Europe. In the 1880s the Austrian state provided funds for the construction of a second railway across Galicia; in the 1890s and early 1900s the Galician Seim and the Bukovynian Landtag raised money for local railways, which connected at Zalishchyky in 1898, but which were not fully completed until the railway reached Sokal in 1910. The volume of goods carried and the amount of passenger traffic rapidly increased. Many small towns and villages were now on a railway line, others often no more than a few kilometres from a station. Roads, previously the main transportation arteries, took on the character of feeders for the railways; although they were often still in poor condition, their state was also improving. Postal services benefited from the new transportation systems and were inexpensive, especially for printed matter such as newspapers. Telegraph services were widespread by the turn of the century, either as an adjunct to the railways or as part of the Austrian postal service. Chernivtsi had electric trams by 1897.[6] And although only twenty-two towns in Galicia had telephone service in 1900, by 1909 telephones had penetrated even remote southeastern rural regions.[7]

The railways, now spread out over rural Bukovyna and Eastern Galicia, brought peasant emigrants to the north German and other ports. Improved transportation made possible many other developments, not the least of which was speedy access to Austrian and Western European markets for the agricultural produce of Eastern Galicia and Bukovyna. They also made it easier and quicker for people to move around, thereby facilitating the contacts with the greater world that were increasingly important for rural populations. Newspapers and journals also contributed to the greater information base available in the villages, mainly from the 1880s onwards.

Ukrainians have long held that they suffered great historical injustices in the sphere of education. So they did, especially in Galicia. Their access to secondary education was limited; they were grossly underrepresented in post-secondary education, and in the village and small-town schools, instruction was often given in Polish. It may be noted that before about 1900 Galician villagers did not regard it as a hardship to have their children taught in both Ukrainian and Polish. No doubt their experience of bilingual education in the homeland helped them to adjust to the pre-1916 education system in Manitoba.[8]

There were other positive developments in respect of education. Ukrainians lived in a country that had compulsory school attendance laws. Initially these were much ignored. But elementary education for their children was important to many Ukrainian villagers in both Bukovyna and Galicia, and large numbers of schools were built between 1880 and 1910. By 1900, most of the elementary schools in Eastern Galician villages had two or more teachers.[9] Although there began to be some pressure from crownland authorities, it was the villagers themselves, through their school district councils, who decided to tax themselves in order to build schools and pay for their upkeep and for the salary of the teachers and who contributed labour and materials during the construction. Again, this experience was invaluable to Ukrainian settlers in Canada, and the speed with which they set up school districts and built their first schools often surprised the school inspectors. The very high rates of illiteracy of the Ukrainian regions of Bukovyna and Galicia improved only gradually, as more and more children attended school.[10] It was not until the Austrian census of 1910 that more than half of the Ukrainian population over the age of ten declared itself to be literate. The same data also showed clearly that in that year each ten-year age cohort was better educated than its predecessor: 67.68 per cent of Ukrainian males and 54.59 per cent of Ukrainian females aged eleven to twenty were literate; the equivalent percentages for the twenty-one to forty age cohort were 44.41 and 23.12.[11] Clearly, much had been achieved, though much remained to be done, particularly in Bukovyna, which lagged behind Eastern Galicia in literacy. Especially after the turn of the century, Ukrainian voluntary associations built residential accommodations (*bursy*) in the towns to assist children to get a secondary education; they would also get some tutoring there.[12] Both the school councils and the enlightenment societies concerned themselves increasingly with the provision of Ukrainian primers and other books in the elementary schools. Education was thus not a neglected field, as many writers have suggested. Rather, it was taken very seriously, and more knowledge came to be imparted to more children in the two decades when the pre-1914 emigration was taking place.

And not only in the public education system. A growing network of informal educational institutions supplemented elementary schooling. In Galicia the two major enlightenment associations were the Prosvita Society (founded in 1868) and the Kachkovsky Society (1874). Initially seen as complementary, they came from the 1890s onwards to be increasingly in competition with each other, for they represented respectively the populist Ukrainophile and the Old Ruthenian orientations in the Ukrainian nationalist movement. Their rivalry probably redounded to the advantage of Ukrainian villagers. They provided an impressive array of materials ranging from primers to pamphlets and books on health measures, cultural development, civic rights, and improved agricultural practice. Between 1869 and 1898 the Prosvita published 224 books in a total of 1,392,155 copies; by 1914 each of the two societies had published over 2.5 million copies, most of which had been mailed to members. The titles included *Facts about the Soil*, *Practical Education for a Peasant Farmer*, *How to Care for the Sick*, *Cultivation of Barley and Oats*, *About the Profitable Use of Wastelands*, and *On the Rights and Duties of Citizens at the Village, District, Province, and State Level*. In 1895 each enlightenment society published a brochure by Dr Osyp Oleskiv on emigration to Canada – *Pro vilni zemli* (About free lands) and *O emigratsii* (On emigration).[13] There were other enlightenment societies in Eastern Galicia, such as the Narodnyi Dim (People's Home) and the society whose specific goal it was to promote the rural co-operative movement, Narodna Torhivlia (People's Commerce).[14] In Bukovyna the first Ukrainian voluntary association, Ruska Besida (Ruthenian Dialogue), was established in 1869 to conduct cultural-educational work, though with far fewer resources than its Galician counterparts. Later other societies were founded, such as the student organization Soiuz (Alliance, 1875) and Samopomich (Self-Help, 1888).[15]

Usually closely associated with one (and occasionally more than one) of the enlightenment societies were village reading clubs. Although the drive to establish reading clubs dates back to the early 1870s, the movement got under way in the 1880s and gathered pace in the 1890s. By 1895, 233 reading clubs in Eastern Galicia were affiliated with the Prosvita Society; by 1900, 924, by 1905, 1,550, and by 1910 their number had grown to 2,376.[16] This was not the total number of Ukrainian reading clubs in Eastern Galicia, for many continued to be affiliated with the Kachkovsky Society, while in Bukovyna the Ruska Besida and for a time the Soiuz took the lead, although both the Kachkovsky and the Prosvita societies were also active there. It is thus clear that a dense network of reading clubs covered rural Eastern Galicia and Bukovyna. Priests often played a leading role in establishing village reading clubs, but the secular intelligentsia, such as teachers and lawyers, might at times be their principal founders, and sometimes enlightened villagers would take the lead.[17]

In their simplest form, reading clubs were places where villagers could come to read weekly newspapers or other publications and to read them aloud to others. Discussion would often follow. There can be no doubt that as a result of the reading of the press and of the ensuing discussions villagers came to be better informed about the wider world around them. But the newspapers did not only give them news about political events in the land, the empire, and the continent. As the press was usually associated with one of the Ukrainian nationalist movements, it provided the population with political education. In a narrow sense this meant a focus on the political struggles of the day, but it also involved civic education, thereby providing the villagers with a regular alphabet of their rights as Austrian citizens.[18] And because the enlightenment societies were concerned with the welfare of the Ukrainian people generally, the publications that were associated with them ran articles on Ukrainian culture and provided their readers with practical knowledge through didactic features on such topics as crop production, animal husbandry, beekeeping, manuring, maximizing of income, and health education.[19] The new knowledge, especially when augmented by the exhortations and particularly the example of the village priests, was put to good practical use.[20]

The number of Ukrainian-language publications for village reading halls and other readers increased over the years. There were fourteen titles in 1880, twenty-six in 1890 (twenty-one in Eastern Galicia, two in Bukovyna, and three in Vienna), and thirty-eight in 1900 (thirty-two in Galicia, three in Bukovyna, two in Hungary, and one in Vienna).[21] Many of them were weeklies, and some were published two or three times a week. *Dilo* became a daily; *Batkivshchyna*, the newspaper most widely read in the villages during its lifespan of 1879–96, appeared fortnightly at the beginning and end but was a weekly in 1883–92. Their press runs were not large: *Batkivshchyna* printed fifteen hundred copies, *Dilo* thirteen hundred, and *Nauka* six hundred per issue in 1885.[22] But they were read by many people in each reading club, and in addition many individual subscribers allowed others to read their copies.[23] Many village reading clubs subscribed to two or at times more newspapers. *Batkivshchyna* gave much space to news from the villages, written by villagers themselves; seeing their own news and that of people like themselves in print helped develop in the peasants a sense of self-worth.[24]

The opening of a reading club was a significant occasion in the lives of villagers, often drawing people from many surrounding villages. The opening of the club in Chornohuzy, Vyzhnytsia county, Bukovyna, was attended by visitors from Vyzhnytsia, Byzhenka, Ispas, Bahna, Myliv, and elsewhere. Several priests were in attendance, as were the head of the county court, academics from Chernivtsi, two teachers, and three cantors. 'The school room [where the opening ceremony was held] was too small to hold all the people, and many had to stay outside and watch and listen through the windows.'[25] Typically, a religious service formed part of the festivities.[26]

Apart from reading and discussion of newspapers, the reading clubs featured a host of other activities. Reading clubs received the publications of the enlightenment society with which they were affiliated and might be the recipient of donations of books.[27] Some built up considerable libraries in this way: the reading club in Chornohuzy reported receiving 115 books from Prosvita in Lviv, 30 from the Kachkovsky Society, and 12 from Soiuz.[28] By 1897 the club in Skala, Borshchiv county, Galicia, boasted that it had 320 books that 'were read diligently' by its 270 members.[29] Other activities also came to be associated with the reading clubs or were initiated under their aegis. The club in Skala owned its stone building, valued at several thousand gulden, which included a hall used for meetings, concerts, and theatrical performances;

it also had a grain-storage facility and a savings and loan society with an annual turnover of forty thousand gulden.[30] In size the Skala club may have been atypical, but not in the range of its activities. Many village reading clubs organized savings and loan societies or credit unions, communal grain storage facilities, and shops (whose activities were also supported by the Narodna Torhivlia). The clubs also organized social events (*vechernytsi*) and sponsored lectures that featured visiting speakers on all sorts of topics as well as local talent: in the village of Verbivtsi, Terebovlia county, Galicia, in 1886 a teacher from a nearby village 'gave a clear and understandable lecture on the theme of the history of printing'; at Tsyhany, Borshchiv county, Galicia, Dr Roman Iarosevych lectured his audience in 1895 on progress in the nineteenth century.[31] Annual commemorations of Taras Shevchenko and his works were a feature of all reading clubs affiliated with Prosvita.[32]

It may thus be seen that village reading clubs, though not always accepted by all villagers,[33] brought considerable changes to the village. Women were allowed to be members – an innovation in a hitherto traditionalist world. Choirs began 'to sing from notes,' and one village in Terebovlia county claimed in 1900 to have the first village brass band in Galicia. In many places the reading hall replaced the tavern as the hub of village life. It enabled people to retain and even enhance reading skills they had learned at school. It provided a forum for civic education and for discussion on a host of issues. It played a significant role in bringing knowledge to the village.[34] The knowledge entering the village was both general and specific. The specific knowledge that was of most concern to villagers was that pertaining to agriculture. The government also played some part here by providing horticultural and agricultural courses in the elementary school curricula and through the activities of the state-subsidized Galician Agricultural Association and its local branches. The enlightenment societies paid considerable attention to raising agricultural productivity and published booklets on a whole range of topics from beekeeping to animal raising. The press ran articles on drainage, improved seed, implements, co-operatives, orchards, animal diseases, and so on. But 'mere urging of farmers to change their methods isn't enough'; it is the demonstration that new methods work that is important in getting farmers to change their ways.[35] As the newspaper *Hospodar i promyshlennyk* stated in 1886, 'It is the example of the priest that is best accepted and copied by the peasants.'[36] Numerous instances can be found of enterprising priest-farmers who led by example as well as by exhortation. Some, like Father Dudykevych of Shyshkivtsi, Borshchiv County, gave parishioners 'information about various

branches of agriculture from the pulpit.'[37] Others experimented successfully with new varieties of seed, raised good quality livestock, concerned
themselves with improved agricultural implements such as ploughs,
and introduced new fruits into orchard cultivation. They spread their
good news through constant teaching and example, through the press,
and in Eastern Galicia through a network of Greek Catholic priests.
Other agricultural education came from village schoolteachers and from
itinerant teachers hired by enlightenment societies.[38]

The historical literature on Western Ukraine has focused on rural
ignorance, declining sizes of peasant landholdings, and low agricultural
productivity.[39] The first of these was being overcome, and there are
many indications in the contemporary press that by the 1890s peasants
no longer deemed themselves to be as ignorant as they had always been
told they were.[40] The issue of the size of landholdings is a complex one.
Contemporaries claimed that to be viable, a peasant holding had to be
at least six hectares in size. This may have been true earlier in the
nineteenth century, when an extensive rather than an intensive mode
of agriculture was practised, but as will be seen, it was no longer true.[41]
The average size of Western Ukrainian landholdings did decline in the
nineteenth century, largely as a result of inheritance customs. However,
it did not decline as much as has sometimes been thought. In part this
is due to the complexity of the land-tax data that contemporary authors
used to establish the average sizes of holdings.[42] Furthermore, these
same authorities seemed oblivious of the fact that although husband
and wife were officially registered as individual owners for land-tax
purposes, they in fact operated one peasant farm.[43] Contemporary
authors also usually failed to take into account the leasing of land and
the value to peasants of grazing rights on communal land (a right
possessed by 30 to 40 per cent of the peasants in some counties).

Most Western Ukrainian smallholdings, except in the mountain
regions, were very small, with most of them being in the range of one
to five hectares.[44] However, it is the use made of the land and not its
mere size that is significant. Peasants in fact followed the advice of
agricultural experts to cultivate every part of their holdings, to plant
second crops such as buckwheat or clover after the first crop on a plot
had been harvested, and to replace fallow in favour of crop rotation.[45]
As a Canadian visitor observed in 1898, 'In the cultivation of their
respective locations, not even the width necessary for the furrow of a
plough is wasted ... crops may be seen at any stage of growth.'[46]

Annual yields of wheat, rye, and potatoes in Eastern Galicia increased
appreciably, more than keeping pace with population increases.

TABLE 1
Average yields per hectare in metric centners in Eastern
Galicia

	Wheat	Rye	Potatoes
1886–1895	8.8	7.5	95.7
1896–1905	10.5	8.5	108.7

Source: Podręcznik statystyki Galicyi, VII, pt. 1: 160; VIII, pt. 1:
169.

There were lesser increases in yields of other grain crops in Eastern
Galicia, though some regions, such as Podillia, recorded increases in
yields of barley and oats that were well above the average. Yields of
grain crops in Bukovyna tended to be appreciably higher than those in
Eastern Galicia.[47] Yields on peasant holdings were generally somewhat
lower than on large landholdings, but peasants did share in the general
increase in productivity per hectare.[48] By Western European standards,
yields were low, but from the perspective of Western Ukrainian villagers
the important feature was the upward trend.

Peasant production was also more diversified. Legumes, fodder crops,
and cash speciality crops were cultivated. In parts of southeastern Galicia
and in Bukovyna tens of thousands of peasant smallholders profitably
grew tobacco: a quarter of a hectare devoted to tobacco could show a
profit of two hundred to three hundred crowns in 1905.[49] New commercial crops such as aniseed, fennel, linseed, and poppy seed began to be
cultivated. The villagers' gardens produced a variety of food for their
own consumption or barter,[50] and orchards began to assume a commercial importance. Intercrops (crops planted between the rows of other
crops, sometimes by day labourers on a large landowner's land but with
the produce belonging to the labourer) and second crops were not
recorded in the official data on agricultural production, but they too
augmented the worth of peasant production.[51]

Of great importance was the increase in the area of land devoted to
the cultivation of clover,[52] with which is connected the very significant
and much neglected topic of animal husbandry. The numbers of cattle
and pigs raised by peasants in Eastern Galicia increased significantly in
the 1880s and especially the 1890s, and improved breeds of animals
made their appearance, first on the larger holdings but gradually also
on some of the smaller ones. Peasants owned 75 to 80 per cent of Eastern
Galicia's cattle and oxen, 90 per cent of the pigs, and most of the declining
number of sheep. Significantly, peasants with holdings of less than five
hectares owned the preponderance of these animals, and almost half

the horses. Even some of the dwarf holdings of less than half a hectare had at least one farm animal, and sometimes more.[53] In the 1880s and 1890s peasants became animal raisers as well as grain growers. Franciszek Bujak, one of the few contemporary experts who noted this development, estimated that by the turn of the century peasant income from animal husbandry was at least as great as that from crop production.[54] This was a significant transition, made possible by improved transportation. Peasant livestock could now be readily marketed. Austrian statisticians noted, with some surprise, that for Galicia in 1900 'the export of cattle is quite significant. Stock cattle and milk cows are exported to Russia, Siberia, Moravia, and Bohemia, fattened cattle to Vienna, Prague, Olmütz, and Germany.'[55] Some parts of southeastern Galicia were by now renowned for their milk-fed veal, and had thus become a source of Wiener Schnitzel.[56] Improved railway wagons for the transportation of animals helped to ensure that they arrived in good condition.[57] The railways also allowed for the speedy transportation of perishables: fruit, eggs, milk, butter, cheese, and poultry. Associated small-scale industries, such as egg sorting and packing plants and jam-making factories, made their appearance in small rural towns. Ukrainian marketing co-operatives sprang up and grew in the late 1890s and early 1900s, for the benefit of village economies.[58]

Improved agricultural productivity and an improving quality of nutrition were in part responsible for another significant development, the decline in the death rate. Government vaccination programmes against smallpox were also important in this regard, as was a general pro-cleanliness campaign and health education provided by Ukrainian newspapers.[59] Alcoholism was not nearly as great a problem as has generally been supposed.[60] In some parts of Western Ukraine the death rate declined by about one-third between 1880 and 1900. For whatever reason, there was also a 15 to 20 per cent decline in the high birth rate. These are indications of modernizing trends.

The peasant society of Western Ukraine was thus on the move. Peasants were indeed exploited by the large landowners for whom many of them worked at seeding and harvest times. At times there was not enough such work for those who sought it,[61] and isolated work stoppages on large landowners' properties were apt to be broken by the gendarmerie.[62] The widespread agrarian strike of 1902 in Eastern Galicia, however, did lead to increased day cash wages or improved payments in kind for seasonal labourers,[63] at a time when villagers knew very well from the press that prices for grain on the European markets had risen.

Peasants also suffered from arbitrary acts on the part of the authorities. Regularly in Galicia but somewhat less so in Bukovyna there was intimidation at election times.[64] Ukrainians in Galicia were systematically discriminated against in education, especially beyond the elementary school level.

There were thus dark sides in the picture, too, and not everyone shared in the modest increase in material prosperity that agricultural progress and better organization brought about. But there were material and cultural improvements for the majority of the population of Western Ukraine.[65] There was also a growing self-confidence in the villages from the 1890s onwards. Peasants acquired expertise in local government and became more aware of their rights as Austrian citizens.[66] In Galicia they stood up to the landowners' bullies at elections (and at least on occasion were acquitted in court when subsequently brought to trial).[67] People's assemblies (vichi) were held, sometimes in major towns and sometimes in the countryside, attended by three hundred or four hundred people or more, and often focusing at least in part on issues that were important to villagers, such as elections to commune and county councils and the formation of agricultural co-operatives.[68] The first assembly was held at Lviv in 1880; the spread of assemblies throughout the region, despite some harassment of villagers who attended, showed rising peasant self-awareness and confidence.[69] So did incidents like the refusal of peasants to allow two large landowners to speak at an assembly in Husiatyn county in 1897 and the demand – unsuccessful, it is true – that the Narodna Rada, the Ukrainophile political organization in Lviv, hold a special meeting to discuss economic issues of concern to peasants after the regular meeting had spent all the available time on political questions.[70]

The improvements, however modest, in their material conditions, hard work, civic self-help, and new feelings of human dignity and of a Ukrainian consciousness brought the Eastern Galician and Bukovynian peasants from a psychological bondage to tradition into a more modern world.[71] Why then, if conditions were getting better, did a wave of emigration to Canada begin in the mid-1890s?

Some historians have found a very simple answer to a slightly but significantly different question, namely, why did they emigrate? A leading Soviet historian bluntly asserted that 'socio-economic and political circumstances gave rise to moods of depression among the bereaved Galician peasants – the most deprived stratum of the population – and caused their firm determination to force their way out of a vice of misery and hunger.'[72] Others have put the matter still more bluntly: they were 'men and women who were driven by poverty, oppression and hopelessness.'[73]

The answer is not likely to be so simple; indeed, the answer is a many-layered one. The peasantry was not a homogeneous unit. Different motivations worked in varying degrees in different people. But one major motive may be confidently set out: it was precisely because conditions had improved and people's expectations for themselves and even more so for their children had increased that they were willing to entertain the idea of uprooting themselves. One Manitoban told the author that her family was 'pretty well-to-do' in the old country, but 'there were better prospects in Canada.'[74] In respect of Bukovyna it was reported at the time that people were leaving for Canada because they wanted 'a better future for their children.'[75]

It may be that some perceived, however faintly, that increases in crop yields and in animal husbandry and other improvements in the village could not go on indefinitely. The amount of village land was finite; land was in much demand and commanded high prices, and although many gentry landowners were in financial trouble and had to sell or lease land, the amount available for purchase by Ukrainian peasants was small. Having been initiated into a market economy, the peasants looked for more land on which to grow more crops and raise increasing numbers of animals and thereby augment their incomes. If necessary, they would look for that land overseas.

The first mass migration from Western Ukraine was in fact not to Canada but to Brazil. Peasants were lured by propaganda and by agents working on behalf of the Brazilian government, which was so anxious to settle 'empty' lands that it paid for the voyage from an Italian port to Brazil.[76] It was in large part because of reports of the bad experiences of the Ukrainian settlers in Brazil that Oleskiv in 1895 published his two pamphlets O emigratsii and Pro vilni zemli, which mark the real beginning of the mass emigration from Western Ukraine to Canada.[77]

Emigrants from Western Ukraine may not have seen any Canadian immigration literature because of its poorly organized distribution.[78] The governments of central and eastern European countries were actively opposed to emigration agents,[79] but booking agents for steamship companies had been operating legally throughout Europe on behalf of Canada for decades. The Austrian government was slow to comprehend the dimensions of the activities of steamship company agents and to try to curtail them.[80] The distinction between an emigration agent and a booking agent for a steamship company, although important in law, was in practice often a very small one. And brochures like those of Oleskiv were published legally. The lure of land, with almost seventy hectares available for fifty gulden (ten dollars), was very strong. Once the first few dozen emigrants had settled in Canada, there was a constant stream of information back home, which sometimes painted an overly positive picture of Canadian conditions and which served to attract more migrants.[81]

As V.J. Kaye pointed out a quarter century ago, a considerable proportion of the Ukrainian immigrants to Canada were 'peasants of means,' modest no doubt by many standards, but among the more successful of the peasants.[82] Most of the immigrants, in fact, appear to have been peasants whose Western Ukrainian smallholdings were of between two and five hectares in size. Unlike emigration to Brazil, that to Canada required the peasant to pay the fare for himself and his family. It is no wonder, then, that Vasyl Stefanyk characterized the emigrants to Canada as moderately wealthy, free of debt, owners of land, and possessing between five hundred and eight hundred gulden when they emigrated. Their motive for emigrating was 'the good of the children.'[83]

This profile of the society from which the pre-1914 Ukrainian immigrants came to Canada is very different from the one that others have presented.[84] Peasant responses to socio-economic changes in the last quarter of the nineteenth century brought into being in Eastern Galicia and Bukovyna a different kind of society and with it, often, a different kind of peasant. Changes in health and nutrition were producing a strong and resilient population able to respond to the prospects of the late nineteenth and early twentieth centuries. Peasants took advantage of education and technical advances to improve both the quantity and the quality of their agricultural produce, and improvements in communications provided them and their produce entry into the wider world. Their enhanced earning capacities imbued them with feelings of dignity and worth. Achievements in learning and in organizing themselves for local economic and political activities beneficial to themselves contributed to their self-confidence. They began to take pride in their distinctiveness, though this feeling was in most cases not yet the Ukrainian nationalism that the urban propagandists hoped for.

These changes, dramatic in their entirety and 'internal' to their rural society,[85] gave the resilient, hard-working people a sense of control over their thoughts, their labour, their productivity, and ultimately their lives. Discrimination remained, of course, but there was no real political oppression as in tsarist Russia. The late Ivan Rudnytsky perceived much of this when he wrote, in an essay first published in 1963, that 'Austria was a constitutional state, and this enabled the Galician Ukrainians to apply civic self-help. In this they achieved signal successes. The country was covered with a dense and ever-expanding network of economic, educational, and gymnastic associations, branching out to every village. The peasant masses ... owed to this work not only an improvement of their living conditions, but also a new feeling of human dignity and civic pride.'[86] No longer were the Western Ukrainian peasants mired in ignorance and poverty, resigned to 'the ultimate arbitrariness of fate.'[87] Tens of thousands of them, the more adventurous and risk-taking segment of the peasantry, chose to leave their homeland and to realize in Canada the rising expectations for their own and their children's future betterment that their recent experiences had engendered.

Sifton's Immigration Policy

JAROSLAV PETRYSHYN

Standard historiography has it that under the astute direction of Clifford Sifton, minister of the Department of the Interior between 1896 and 1905, the Laurier administration embarked upon an enormously successful campaign to secure agriculturists for the settlement and development of the Northwest. In particular, Sifton has been credited with devising a policy to satisfy the economic requirements of the prairies by encouraging immigrants who hitherto had been deemed only 'marginally acceptable.' Focusing his attention on the Ukrainians of Galicia and Bukovyna, Sifton argued that these 'stalwart peasants' would make desirable settlers and that their economic value outweighed negative social and cultural considerations. In this context, he has been portrayed as a great benefactor of the Ukrainians who facilitated the beginnings of their mass immigration into Canada.

The evidence for this thesis rests on the obvious observation that during Sifton's term as minister of the interior Ukrainians started to immigrate to Canada at an unprecedented rate.[1] Those who attribute this development to Sifton most often cite his encouragement of the activities of Osyp Oleskiv, the Ukrainian professor of agriculture who first proposed directing a mass migration of Ukrainian farmers to Canada, and his agreement in 1899 with the mysterious North Atlantic Trading Company, or NATC, which, it has been contended, successfully recruited Ukrainians and other Eastern European peasants en masse to Canada.[2] This paper suggests that such an unreserved interpretation of Sifton's role vis-à-vis the Ukrainians is only partially correct at best because it does not address a number of anomalies in Canadian promotional efforts regarding the Ukrainians and does not consider the role played by the immigrants themselves. A closer examination of the record reveals that the commitment of the Department of the Interior to Ukrainian immigration has been exaggerated – that in fact immigration officials exhibited a troubled ambiguity, if not outright hostility, to the spectre of a substantial influx of Galicians and Bukovynians.[3] As a result, the department's relations with Oleskiv were less fruitful than has been generally assumed. Far from recruiting Ukrainians, the NATC simply sought to profit from what already was a dynamic, independently driven Ukrainian movement to Canada.

Dr Osyp Oleskiv first articulated the prospects of Ukrainian immigration to Canada.[4] Distressed by the deteriorating economic status of the Ukrainian peasants in Galicia and the disastrous consequences of the ensuing emigration to South America,[5] this progressive member of the Ukrainian intelligentsia conducted a study of conditions in Canada and wrote a popular pamphlet, *Pro vilni zemli* (About free lands), which identified Canada as infinitely more suitable for Ukrainian emigrants than Brazil. Published by the Prosvita Society in the spring of 1895, the pamphlet was distributed to the society's 351 village reading halls across Galicia and became the topic of wide discussion.[6]

Having resolved to visit Canada in order to acquire detailed information on settlement opportunities and having established contact with the Department of the Interior and obtained a letter of introduction from Sir Charles Tupper, the Canadian high commissioner in London, Oleskiv undertook an exhaustive coast-to-coast tour of Canada in August and September 1895.[7] He was impressed with what he found and on his return published a second pamphlet, *O emigratsii* (About emigration), in which he reaffirmed his earlier research and again urged his countrymen to consider Canada as a destination.

While he was in Canada, Oleskiv aroused the interest of the Canadian government. He met with Thomas Daly, the Conservative minister of the interior, on 16 August in Edmonton and on 1 October in Ottawa. Daly asked him to prepare a memorandum regarding large-scale Ukrainian immigration and promised to submit it to cabinet. Oleskiv did so, but before anything of substance could be achieved, the Conservatives were voted out of office and he had to deal with Sifton and the Liberal administration. It appeared that he and Sifton could come to a mutually beneficial agreement. Oleskiv claimed that he could bring to Canada an organized stream of diligent, thrifty peasant-farmers, each with a reasonable amount of capital. Although the government seemed to promote exactly that type of immigrant and although there was clear evidence that Oleskiv could deliver what he promised, from the initial negotiations with him in 1896 to the final settlement of accounts in 1900, the Department of the Interior avoided placing Ukrainian immigration in his care.

A key ingredient in Oleskiv's proposal was that he be given direct control of a Canadian immigration agency in Lviv where immigrants could be screened and organized into appropriate groups acceptable to Canadian officials. He assured the Department of the Interior that 'the government have decided to give me the concession for the sole emigration agency in this country [Galicia] ... which will give the agency under my direction practically the monopoly for issuing of tickets for railways and ocean passage to the emigrants.'[8] Oleskiv planned for orderly and controlled immigration to Canada, where the emigrants would be 'gathered in parties and conducted by experienced travellers to embarkation' and where they would be serviced by 'selected sea-port agents' paid through him.[9] However, for this scheme to work Oleskiv needed official authority and financial support from the Canadian government; thus, he asked to be appointed as Canada's emigration commissioner for Austria-Hungary and to be paid the bonus for the immigrants he had secured.

The Department of the Interior bandied Oleskiv's proposals in inter-departmental memos but procrastinated in formulating a direct response.[10] A frustrated Oleskiv wrote to the department in December 1896: 'I commenced the work on my means in spring 1896: in due sense by sending out an organized party of settlers of desirable sort ... and I have patronized several consequent small parties. But as I saw, that the Government does not take any serious steps towards securing of such an emigration and has shown no signs of will to support my efforts, so I have retired in a more passive position.'[11] Oleskiv continued to act as an 'unofficial' Canadian immigration organizer and promoter in Galicia, but the Department of the Interior never fully utilized his services.

The strain in Oleskiv's relations with the Canadian government can be garnered from a meeting he had in Cracow on 19 June 1899 with W.T.R. Preston, the newly appointed inspector of Canadian immigration agencies in Europe, and Professor James Mavor, a political economist from the University of Toronto who had been retained by the Department of the Interior. Oleskiv gave an overview of his activities, emphasizing that through his personal contacts, pamphlets, newspaper articles, and lectures thousands of Ukrainians had learned about the benefits of emigrating to Canada. Then, pointing out that he was not a wealthy man and that he had paid for most of his expenses out of his own pocket, he proceeded to present a claim against the Department of the Interior for 'services rendered.' Of the approximately ten thousand Galicians who had emigrated to Canada in 1898 and 1899,[12] Oleskiv contended, five thousand had done so as a consequence of his efforts. On the basis of his understanding of a $2.50 bonus per head he therefore concluded that he was entitled to a payment of £2,380 (about $12,500).[13]

Mavor, in his report to Sifton, was less than sympathetic to Oleskiv's claim, wryly commenting that 'it was as difficult for us to disprove the validity of this claim as it was for him to prove it.'[14] It should be noted, however, that officials in the immigration branch readily acknowledged Oleskiv's role in initiating the 'Galician movement' into Canada. Superintendent of Immigration Frank Pedley, for example, believed that 'the bulk of Galicians have come out ... as a result of Oleskiv's work.'[15]

Oleskiv was prepared to come to an amicable settlement on the account and to continue sending Galician emigrants to Canada if the government further funded his activities. To Mavor and Preston he proposed a sliding scale of 'capitation grants.' For 1900 and 1901 he suggested a grant of $2.50 per head if three thousand immigrants arrived from Galicia in a year; $2.00 if the figure reached five thousand; $1.50 for seventy-five hundred; down to $1.00 per immigrant in the event that ten thousand or more came.[16] Again, it should be emphasized that Oleskiv's request for a funding formula was not at all unreasonable considering that since 1895 he had conducted and borne most of the cost of emigration activity himself.[17]

In the end, Oleskiv could make no suitable arrangement with the Canadian government. Mavor in his correspondence with Sifton did not leave a favourable impression of Oleskiv.[18] He was blunt about Oleskiv's proposition: 'even if Galician emigration were wholly desirable the proposal of Mr. Oleskow is out of the question.' Mavor suggested that 'a smaller sum might be offered to him by way of compromise [for services previously rendered] and the matter closed up.'[19] This was, in fact, what occurred.[20]

Misunderstandings and personality clashes aside, the larger question still remained: why, at a time when Canada fervently desired agriculturists, could not Sifton's department and Oleskiv come to terms? The answer is twofold. First, by 1899 Sifton and his officials were not convinced that Canada needed more Galicians and Bukovynians. Second, Oleskiv (along with many other promoters and booking agents throughout Europe) was suddenly redundant. In the latter part of 1899 a new organization, the NATC, was granted a monopoly on government bonuses for continental immigrants arriving in Canada.

By the spring of 1899 Sifton was under growing pressure to curtail the continuing increase of Ukrainians. W.F. McCreary, the commissioner of immigration, wrote to Sifton in April 1899: 'There are now almost 20 thousand Galicians, the natural increase of which should be about two thousand per year ... There is no doubt whatever that the general impression exists among our opponents and even among a great many of the friends of Government, that we have sufficient for the present, as many as we can assimilate for some years.'[21]

McCreary's main objection to the arrival of more Ukrainians in Canada was their 'penniless' state. Placing and providing for these 'destitute immigrants,' he said, would cost the government 'a large amount of money.'[22] He laid the blame on booking agents and the government's bonus system: 'just as long as we continue to pay a bonus to the steamship agents ... they will ship to Canada in droves immigrants [who have] sufficient money to pay their actual transportation [but] would not have a dollar on arrival.' McCreary suggested to Sifton that the government stop paying bonuses to steamship agents for Galicians and Bukovynians and that those who did come should possess a specified sum of money.[23]

Sifton agreed with his commissioner of immigration. In a memo to James A. Smart, the deputy minister of the interior, a short time later he stated: 'There is apparently an accumulation of testimony that it is going to be difficult to handle any large number of Galician immigrants ... It is doubtful policy to encourage any more to come ... I incline to the view that we should stop the European bonuses [for the Galicians] ... for the present.'[24]

Sifton may have sincerely believed that the Ukrainians were desirable citizens whom the government should continue to encourage. But he was also a practical and pragmatic politician who, while publicly defending the government's immigration policy, took into account the concerns of his officials.[25]

Thus, the government did attempt to put restrictions on the number of Ukrainians coming to Canada. On 1 June 1899 the system of bonuses was suspended, and a money standard was imposed. According to James A. Smart: 'We undertook to say that a Galician on arriving at Halifax or any seaport town should be possessed of a certain amount of money and if he were not the steamship company would have to take him back.'[26]

Opposition to such a policy, however, came from an unexpected source – the Austrian government. Like other European states, Austria-

Hungary had restrictive emigration legislation, but in such overcrowded areas as Galicia, Vienna was quite willing to permit its excess peasants to emigrate. Indeed, it was pleased that Canada had been opened as an avenue for them. Thus, as Smart explained: 'As soon as it was known [that Canada was about to restrict Ukrainian immigration] the government communicated with their Consul at Montreal who visited Ottawa and wished to know on what grounds the Canadian government acted in restricting immigration.' According to Smart: 'The Austrian government reported these people as good, law-abiding citizens and they did not see any reason why a country should undertake to prevent them from emigrating to it.'[27] In the end, it threatened to stop all movement from Austria-Hungary to Canada if Ottawa curtailed Galician and Bukovynian immigration.[28]

After some consideration, the Department of the Interior decided to reinstitute the bonus system and to withdraw the money restrictions on Galicians and Bukovynians. However, it did so under conditions directly related to the clandestine contract it made with the NATC in October 1899.

The Canadian government had had since 1882 a policy of granting bonuses to booking agents who sent immigrants to Canada. For a myriad of reasons this policy was not working; although people were emigrating from Europe, insufficient numbers were coming to Canada. When he became the minister of the interior, Sifton determined to remedy this situation. W.T.R. Preston[29] and his small staff in London were charged with making Canadian immigration efforts more successful than they had been.[30] Armed with a list of all the booking agencies on the continent whose addresses he could secure in London, Preston set off on an 'inspection and investigation' tour that took him to all parts of Europe. He found that the promotion of immigration to Canada on the continent was in chaos. A large part of the reason for this state of affairs, according to Preston, was that restrictive immigration laws made it exceedingly difficult for agents to operate. Although the authorities in Germany, Austria-Hungary, and the Scandinavian countries did not prohibit their citizens from emigrating, they did discourage those who would induce them to leave their country.[31] To complicate matters, Preston discovered that emigration laws and police regulations were, in many instances, mutually exclusive. Even if agents were operating in accordance with the legislation respecting immigration advertising, local police regulations left them open to the 'most summary action on the part of the police.'[32]

To find a solution to this problem, Preston held a number of meetings in Bremen and Hamburg in May 1899 with 'influential individuals' who were willing to 'promote the interests of Canada.' A consensus was reached: a syndicate could be established to carry on emigration propaganda throughout Europe if the Canadian government gave it a monopoly and redirected its bonus system to the syndicate and undertook not to reveal the names of the members of the syndicate.[33]

Preston cabled this information to Ottawa, representing the syndicate as 'a combination of people who would make a success of immigration work because they had representatives in practically every country in Europe and they would make such a combination as would make a successful propaganda.'[34] Sifton cabled his approval in principle and suggested that a provisional agreement be drafted. He also sent his deputy minister, James A. Smart, to London in September 1899 to aid Preston in the negotiations and to make final recommendations. Through September and October, Preston and Smart conferred with representatives of the proposed syndicate, officially designated the NATC. On 20 October they concluded an intriguing agreement. The company would supply Canada with families from continental Europe whose heads were agriculturists and possessed at least one hundred dollars. In return, the Canadian government agreed to pay an annual fee of five hundred pounds for promotional literature and a bonus of five dollars for each suitable immigrant over twelve years of age who registered in a Canadian port and who intended to settle on agricultural land.[35]

The three contracts that the NATC and the government concluded between 1899 and 1906 covered virtually every country in Europe. For the purposes of this paper, however, we will concentrate on how the NATC contracts affected Ukrainian immigration to Canada.

One major item that the NATC found unsatisfactory from the outset was the money standard required for Ukrainians. Apparently, those who arrived in Canada made a poor showing: the records indicated that 'only 1,165 out of 7,342 for the year 1901–2 and 1,114 out of 9,168 in 1902–3 had the necessary cash.'[36] The company insisted that these immigrants were not telling the truth and that most possessed considerably more than the required amount but were reluctant to inform government officials.[37] Nevertheless, the result was that the NATC was not receiving the bonus of five dollars per head on the majority of Galicians and Bukovynians disembarking at Canadian ports. The company thus sought to have the money standard on these particular immigrants removed.

That is precisely what the government did. On 15 August 1904 Smart proposed that the NATC be granted 'the bonus without any restriction whatever on all those classes which were formerly under the financial restriction up to 5,000 [per annum] and to make this arrangement applicable to the three past years as well as to the future.'[38] Sifton quickly approved this generous retroactive offer to the NATC, and an order in council was passed on 20 September 1904 which stipulated in part that 'in respect of settlers from Galicia, Bukovinian and Poland, excepting Germans ... the bonus under this agreement shall not be paid on any immigrants in excess of 5,000 coming from these 3 countries in any one year and this provision shall be made applicable to all accounts between the Department and the Company in respect of past services which are as yet unsettled.'[39]

Two questions arise from the above. How was it that the deputy minister of the interior suddenly became the NATC's chief lobbyist? And why was the contract so readily amended to accommodate the company? Testifying before the Select Standing Committee on Agriculture and Colonization in 1906, Smart explained in somewhat muddled fashion that 'when the first contract was made a money standard was put upon these people for the reasons that ... there were too many Galicians of the poorer class coming ... But since then it is much easier to get these people to Canada and it was only fair to the government to limit the number upon whom we should pay and do away with the money standard altogether.' He further elaborated that 'Galicians, Poles and Bukowinians ... were not perceived as the most desirable and the limit of 5,000 encouraged the NATC to continue its work in other parts of continental Europe.'[40]

Smart's explanation gave the impression that the limit of five thousand immigrants was more advantageous to the government than the company. However, in reality it was much more lucrative for the NATC to be guaranteed payment on five thousand Ukrainians per year than to leave it to a head count subject to the money requirement. This, in a somewhat skewed way, brings us to the role played by Preston and Smart in the formation of the NATC and in its subsequent dealings with the Department of the Interior.

From the start Preston and Smart were exceedingly partial to the NATC. They initiated governmental negotiations with it, consummated the agreement, and then insisted that the company's activities be kept secret from the Canadian public and Parliament. And with good reason: there is a substantial amount of evidence to indicate collusion between the two men whereby while officially acting as government representatives, they were conducting their own profitable business as close associates (if not outright proprietors) of the NATC.[41] Indeed, in December 1904, Smart officially resigned his office in the government of Canada to become an officer of the NATC. Several months before he left the department he informed Preston that it would be 'agreeable to you to know that I am prepared to recommend some very important concessions in favour of the Company.'[42] The concessions he referred to are the aforementioned changes in the contract regarding the Ukrainians. In speedily agreeing to Smart's recommendations, Sifton, for his part, seems to have acted in good faith, accepting the judgment of his old political friend from Manitoba.[43]

The question of whether the NATC was an outright fraud cannot be fully addressed here, but certainly Preston, Smart, and a select combination of booking agents in Europe stood to make a great deal of money on immigrants bound for Canada. A case in point were the Ukrainians. A large Ukrainian exodus to Canada was well under way by 1900 regardless of the promotional activities the NATC may have carried out. Since the immigrants were coming anyway, the NATC sought to maximize its profits from their numbers. This explains Smart's proposal to do away with the money standard and retroactively set a limit of five thousand per annum. He would have preferred undoubtedly to impose no limit on the numbers, but that was not possible given the department's reservations about the Ukrainians. Later, as an official representative of the NATC, Smart did complain that 'because of the 5,000 limit on Galicians, Bukowianians and Poles the company had lost between $30,000 and $40,000 between 1903 and 1905.'[44]

The full extent of the NATC's contract with the government did not come to light until July 1905, when the information was leaked from the auditor general's account. A Select Standing Committee on Agriculture and Colonization was assembled in April 1906 to investigate the NATC-government connection. During the investigation an aura of 'scandal' and 'fraud' prevailed. Only Preston and Smart knew the principals in the company, and both refused to disclose any names. As the committee hearings proceeded the integrity of Preston and Smart was put into question. Smart, for example, had burned all his 'private' correspondence with the company. Further, as noted above, he resigned his position as deputy minister of the interior to be the 'representative' of the NATC in Canada. He steadfastly declined to state the terms of his engagement with the company or his remuneration, which was considerably more than the three thousand dollars a year that he had received as deputy minister.[45] Preston, for his part, profited handsomely from his role as the financial intermediary between the department and the NATC.[46]

Finally, it was discovered that the NATC did not have a corporate existence until 3 June 1905. On that date it was officially registered on the Island of Guernsey, where, unlike in England or continental Europe, registration required only seven signatures of 'shareholders' to the articles of incorporation.[47] The solicitor of the company was E.A. Alexander, who, it was revealed, was Preston's son-in-law. It was obvious that the belated incorporation was an attempt to legitimate the NATC with token shareholders.

Under intense scrutiny from the parliamentary opposition and adverse public opinion, Frank Oliver, who replaced Sifton as the minister of the interior, cancelled the NATC-government contract on 30 November 1906 on the grounds that the NATC had not fulfilled its 'special work' mandate in Norway, Sweden, Denmark, and Finland.[48] However, it can be safely suggested that the issue had become too hot politically and that further probes into the company would have embarrassed the government.

Once the NATC-government agreement was exposed to public and parliamentary scrutiny Sifton and his Liberal supporters argued vigorously that the NATC was not a fraud, that it carried out its obligations faithfully and provided extensive promotional work on behalf of the Canadian government, and that the Department of the Interior received full value for the cost – value which continued to be translated into immigrants long after political pressure forced cancellation of the contract.[49] Preston, for example, averred that 'we have got from 100 thousand to 125 thousand people, who, but for this company would not have known about Canada.'[50] Sifton in defending his officials and the department believed that the arrangements with the NATC were 'satisfactory' because it acted as a screening agency with regard to the quality of immigrants.[51] Implicit was the notion that the immigrants for whom the government paid five dollars per head to the company – including the over seventy thousand Ukrainians the company claimed it was directly responsible for enticing to Canada – were indeed inspected and found to be of good quality.[52]

Nevertheless, compelling arguments can be put forth to establish that Ukrainian immigration to Canada had less to do with Canadian efforts (in fact, as we have seen, these were often counter-productive) and more to do with what was occurring in the homeland. In the 1880s Ukrainians started to emigrate from the Austro-Hungarian Empire at an accelerated pace. At a conservative estimate about 800,000 left Galicia and Hungarian Transcarpathia between the mid-1880s and the First World War.[53] This emigration was but part of a massive shift of some ten million eastern European peasants from their native lands to the United States, Canada, Brazil, Argentina, and parts of Western Europe.[54]

The reason for such a dramatic movement of humanity was, by and large, economic or, as Ivan Franko aptly put it, 'the bread question.' A case in point was the province of Galicia. It seemed that every patch of good soil was replete with redundant peasants preoccupied with the realities of life – overpopulation, shortage of land, unemployment, political and social oppression, and starvation. For hundreds of thousands, emigration was 'an absolutely natural, indispensable, and inevitable phenomenon.'[55]

Once the decision to emigrate had been taken (either individually or collectively as a group or a village) the question became one of destination. After the lamentable experience of those who went to South America came to light, prospective emigrants and philanthropic societies concerned with the welfare of the peasants adopted the practice of sending scouting parties. Thus when Ivan Pillipiw and Wasyl Eleniak came to Canada in September 1891 from the small Galician village of Nebyliv, they were investigating reports that they had heard from Germans about the vast, uninhabited stretches of fertile land in western Canada. Their arrival – and the subsequent arrival of their families and friends – was the best possible endorsement of Canada as a destination.[56] The approval of Canada by one of their own trusted representatives gave the peasants a greater incentive to emigrate than did unreliable promotional literature or deceitful booking agents. Similarly, when Oleskiv came to Canada, he was on a scouting mission supported by the Prosvita Society. A noted soil expert, Oleskiv was the obvious choice to collect first-hand information and to write pamphlets about Canada and the United States.[57]

The Ukrainians who had settled in Canada also played an important role in the emigration process. In effect, they acted as immigration agents when they wrote home to their relatives and friends, describing conditions in the country, encouraging them to come, and often providing financial assistance for the journey. Statistics of steerage passengers with prepaid tickets for North America are not available, and the Canadian government kept no record of immigrants brought over by relatives and friends already in the country, but a bank in Winnipeg reported in 1905 that it had received nearly one million dollars from its Slavic clients in the Northwest to send to the 'old country.'[58] This was a substantial sum, which, as Smart observed, 'would bring out quite a number of people.'[59]

Booking agents and sub-agents, of course, were important in the emigration process. A veritable army of agents in Eastern Europe worked for steamship companies, earning their livelihood from the commissions they received on the ocean tickets they sold and the railway fares they booked. As noted above, some of these agents were retained by the Canadian government and received a bonus (on top of their ordinary commission) for the people they sent to Canada. The advent of the NATC did not alter this process of obtaining immigrants. The independent local booking agents were simply replaced by a syndicate of selected agents who now had the monopoly over the government's bonus system. The question thus arises, what improved service did the NATC offer over that of the local booking agents?

There is no evidence to support Sifton's contention that the NATC screened the immigrants to ensure quality or Preston's assertion that up to 125,000 came as a direct result of the NATC's efforts. Since the company was paid not for direct bookings, but for the 'propaganda work' it performed, no mathematical or empirical formula was instituted for the bonuses other than a head count of the emigrants disembarking at Canadian ports. The company was not obliged to prove that it had induced the immigrants to come to Canada. In all probability, the vast majority of immigrants for whom the NATC received bonuses arrived in Canada totally ignorant of the NATC.

The procedure for ascertaining the amount owed to the company was simple. Officers of the Department of the Interior met all 'continental immigrants' who landed in Canadian seaports, gave them a medical examination, and questioned them about their occupation and their intentions in coming to Canada. If they indicated that they were agriculturists or domestic servants, they were credited to the NATC, provided all other stipulations of the contract were fulfilled. Afterwards the reports of American immigration officers were checked to see who had applied to cross the border into the United States; those immigrants were then deducted from the credit of the company. W.P. Scott, the superintendent of immigration, was in charge of counting immigrants and deciding which fulfilled the requirements of the contract. When Scott had been satisfied as to the number, he sent a cheque (usually once a month) to Preston, who signed it over to the NATC.[60]

Preston and Smart's most compelling argument for the existence of the NATC was its ability to operate with impunity in countries with restrictive emigration laws. This assertion, too, can be challenged.

Despite restrictive laws local booking agents had no difficulty in practising their trade. As one critic of the NATC pointed out: 'You cannot find anyone on the continent who knows how to evade the laws better than steamship agents, who have been in the business all their lives ... Hundreds of thousands [are] coming from Europe every year to North America so that the agents get inside the regulations and laws and police surveillance.'[61]

The picture that emerges is that the NATC did not do anything that local agents could not have accomplished just as well. Indeed, these agents were doing most of the company's work with the difference that Preston, Smart, and their friends and not the agents were receiving the governmental bonuses. Oleskiv's activities provide a good illustration. As a promoter of Ukrainian immigration to Canada and an Austrian civil servant, he could expect to attract the attention of the authorities. And indeed the landed gentry of Galicia (mostly Poles) were hostile to any depletion of their peasant labour reserve.[62] Yet the government in Vienna encouraged a certain 'moderate' emigration from overcrowded provinces;[63] Austrian law guaranteed the right to emigrate; and although local officials frowned on those who engaged in propaganda work, Oleskiv was not molested.

It is, therefore, difficult not to conclude that the NATC reaped the benefit of the work done by Oleskiv and the local booking agents and that an overwhelming portion of these immigrants would have come to Canada if the NATC did not exist. This is particularly true of Ukrainians. As Smart freely admitted, because of the limit of five thousand per year on Galicians, Bukovynians, and Poles, the NATC began concentrating on the 'Northern countries' and Scandinavia, where there were no restrictions. It is doubtful if the NATC retained any representatives in Galicia after 1905.[64]

Thus, the Sifton years were not the boon to Ukrainian immigration that Canadian historians have assumed. The Department of the Interior did attempt to diminish, if not severely restrict, the flow of Galicians and Bukovynians. This was evident in its dealings with Oleskiv and in the monetary and later numerical stipulations that it sought to impose on the immigrants. Mitigating against the government's efforts, however, were two factors. First, it was difficult, if not impossible, to curtail the Ukrainian wave once it had begun. And second, it was not in the interests of the NATC and its government spokesmen – Preston and Smart – to encourage such a course of action. For purely pecuniary reasons they wished to see an unrestricted flow of immigrants to Canada.

Peopling the Prairies with Ukrainians

JOHN C. LEHR

Between 1892 and 1914 Ukrainian immigrants from Galicia and Buko-vyna settled large tracts of the plains of western Canada.[1] The immi-grants seldom dispersed themselves among settlers of different ethnic backgrounds but settled adjacent to one another on quarter-section homesteads, with the result that extensive areas of agricultural land in the West became almost totally Ukrainian in character. This type of settlement also occurred among other ethnic groups, but it generally arose when the government set aside land for the exclusive settlement of a specific group as in the case of the Mennonites, Icelanders, and Doukhobors.[2] The Ukrainians were not accorded this privilege, yet they established some of the largest bloc settlements in the West. These Ukrainian blocs were remarkable for their extent and were a reflection of a pronounced natural tendency to settle next to relatives and kinsmen.

Ukrainian settlement in western Canada was also distinct in terms of its location. The Ukrainian pioneers were noted for their avoidance of the open grasslands of the Canadian prairies and their settlement in the bush country of the northern parkland of the three prairie provinces. From an agricultural standpoint they took out their homesteads on some of the poorest land opened to settlement in western Canada. The land they chose was often wooded, stony, sandy, or marshy. In many cases it had been ignored, rejected, or abandoned by more discriminating pioneers who elected to settle on the more open lands to the south, which proved to be exceptionally fertile and admirably suited for the development of commercial wheat farming. For the Ukrainians settle-ment in the 'bush country' of the northern parkland was little short of disastrous and retarded both their economic progress and their assimilation into Canadian society.

This apparently inept environmental appraisal by a people with long-standing agricultural traditions is not easy to explain. So glaring was the discrepancy between the lands settled by Ukrainians and the lands settled by German, English, and American settlers that it gave rise to the accusation that at the time of settlement the Canadian government had discriminated against the Ukrainian immigrants and by controlling access to homesteads had forced them to accept marginal lands on the fringe of the ecumene.[3] This paper traces the process of Ukrainian settlement in western Canada during the pioneer era. It argues that its geography cannot be explained by the charge of governmental discrimination and was a product of complicated relations between the immigrants, the officers of the Department of the Interior responsible for the settlement of the West, the Ottawa politicians, and the largely Anglophile Canadian public.

Ukrainian Immigrants

Over 120,000 Ukrainians came to Canada between 1892 and 1914.[4] Although the character of immigration changed during the twenty-two years of this first phase of Ukrainian settlement in Canada, the vast majority of Ukrainian immigrants throughout this period were peasants whose goal was to secure a homestead.[5] Almost all of them came from the westernmost limits of the Ukrainian ethnic area, the provinces of Galicia and Bukovyna, which until 1918 were part of the Habsburg empire (fig. 1). About 5 per cent came from Hungarian Transcarpathia. Less than 1 per cent came from Greater Ukraine, which then fell under the dominion of the Russian tsarist regime.

In the 1890s peasants in Austrian Western Ukraine were emerging from quasi-feudal conditions. Absentee landlords, mainly Austrian or Polish in Galicia and Romanian or German-Austrian in Bukovyna, controlled most of the land. Despite emancipation from serfdom in 1848, the mass of the peasantry remained poor, oppressed, and exploited. Land rents and prices for timber were high, but wages for labour were low. Farms were small and often fragmented. In Galicia almost half of all peasant holdings consisted of fewer than two hectares at a time when about five hectares were necessary to achieve self-sufficiency.[6] Self-sufficient farms, those ranging from five to ten hectares, accounted for only 14.6 per cent of all holdings. In Bukovyna the situation was worse.

Figure 1. Galicia and Bukovyna.

There 16 per cent of the peasants were landless, 42 per cent had less than two hectares, and 25 per cent had less than three hectares.[7] In Transcarpathia one feudal landowner alone held 20 per cent of the territory and, according to one historian, kept the Ukrainian peasantry 'in virtual serfdom, illiterate, ignorant, and financially dependent.'[8] Although it was changing for the better, agricultural technology in most areas of Western Ukraine was backward; farm operations were labour-intensive, and productivity was low.[9] The situation gave little hope for improvement. The Austrian government was content to maintain its Ukrainian territories as economic colonies, captive markets for Austrian manufactured goods. Economic betterment was beyond the reach of the average peasant, for the usurious interest rates charged on mortgages made farm consolidation or expansion difficult.[10]

Social and political repression exacerbated the economic woes of the peasantry. Although Galicia was under Austrian rule, it was under a de facto Polish administration.[11] Polish and German were the languages of administration; Ukrainian was relegated to vernacular status. In Bukovyna and Transcarpathia the situation was similar, for there civil administration was the preserve of Romanian and Hungarian minorities.[12]

Seasonal migration to work on the estates of Prussia or in the oilfields of Boryslav ameliorated the economic situation for some peasants.[13] But by the 1870s Ukrainian peasants were working further afield, in the factories and mines on the eastern seaboard of the United States. For the most part they went as temporary workers, not as settlers, and although many eventually remained, their movement, at least initially, was that of migrants rather than emigrants.[14]

For many peasants such seasonal or short-term movements were a palliative, not a cure. They looked to emigration as a way for their children to escape from a depressing social and economic future. By the late 1880s peasants from Galicia were settling on the frontiers of Brazil; the dawn of the 1890s saw their first tentative steps towards free homesteads in western Canada.[15]

Most of those who contemplated emigration came from the middle stratum of the peasantry. The wealthy peasants had no pressing economic reason to emigrate, and the poorest peasants could not afford to do so. The peasants who left their homeland in search of a new life were those who feared that the future would see their children's well-being decline and who had sufficient property to raise the fare for a transatlantic journey.

Ukrainian Immigration

The first immigrants from Western Ukraine to Canada were not ethnically Ukrainian. Volksdeutsche (ethnic Germans) from Kryvulia near Belcha Volytsia in Galicia settled at Josephburg, near Edmonton, Alberta, in 1890.[16] Correspondence between Volksdeutsche from Galicia and their former neighbours initiated the mass migration of Ukrainians to western Canada.[17] The first Ukrainians to migrate to Canada left the village of Nebyliv, in the Kalush district of Galicia, in 1892. Those who immediately took up homesteads did so in Alberta, where they settled adjacent to former neighbours, seeking opportunities for work from established settlers conversant in Ukrainian. For the next four years word about settlement opportunity in Canada diffused slowly from Nebyliv through the Kalush district. The few score Ukrainians who emigrated to Canada in this period were almost all from around Nebyliv, and virtually all gravitated to the solitary Ukrainian settlement at Star, near Josephburg, in Alberta (fig. 2).[18]

In light of the considerable migration of Ukrainians to the mines and factories of the United States it is curious that few Ukrainians entering Canada chose to remain in the urban centres. Nevertheless, not all

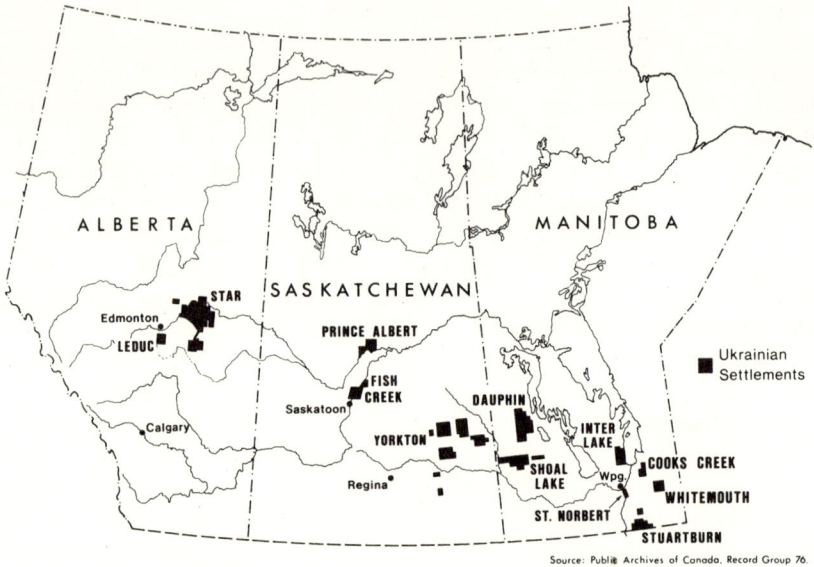

Source: Public Archives of Canada. Record Group 76.

Figure 2. Ukrainian settlements in western Canada ca 1905.

Ukrainians went on the land; Osyp Oleskiv, the Galician educator and agricultural expert who visited Canada in 1895, reported that ten Ukrainian families were living in Winnipeg; all of them were from the Kalush district and had elected to stay in the city and to pursue trades or to work as labourers.[19] For most Ukrainian immigrants the chance to obtain land was the primary lure; most, but by no means all, had no skill in a trade and no experience of living in a large city and so had little incentive to remain in any of the cities or towns through which they travelled en route to the frontier.[20]

The Canadian government had no desire to see its settlers remain in urban centres, and immigration officers went to some lengths to discourage them from remaining in Winnipeg even for a short time.[21] The government regarded immigrants who decided to remain in a city as a direct loss to its programme for settling the West. Those Ukrainians who took manual jobs in the industrial and mining areas of the east coast such as Sydney, Nova Scotia, were most likely remigrants from the Pennsylvania mines rather than immigrants from Ukraine.[22] Nevertheless, by 1900 the demand for labour in Canadian industries, and the immigrants' need for capital, led many arrivals to seek work in factories

and mines. Many later moved out and took up homesteads, but a proportion remained as urban dwellers.

The choice of the Star area for settlement established a pattern that
later arrivals followed with little deviation and ultimately created a
distinctive geography of Ukrainian settlement across the Canadian West
(fig. 2). Initially the attraction of Star was the Volksdeutsche. Later, it
was fellow Ukrainians from Galicia. No less important was the setting
of Star in the aspen parkland belt, which the Ukrainian immigrants
found well-suited to their needs, since it provided the wood, water, and
meadow that they craved.

From a tiny settlement of less than five families in 1893 the Ukrainian
settlement in Alberta grew to a modest thirty-eight families at the beginning of 1896.[23] They attracted little attention. The government regarded
them as Austrian nationals and hence ethnic Germans.[24] Indeed, their
origin came to government notice only in 1895, when Osyp Oleskiv
sought information about settlement in Canada.[25]

Oleskiv was concerned about the growing Ukrainian emigration to
Brazil. There in the rain forests of Parana Ukrainians were being decimated by disease and reduced to penury. Realizing that emigration was
inevitable given the socio-economic situation in Western Ukraine, he
hoped to redirect it to more favourable regions.

Early in 1895 Oleskiv published a pamphlet for intending emigrants,
Pro vilni zemli (About free lands), which reviewed the alternatives open
to them.[26] It was based on secondary sources and materials solicited
from countries then seeking immigrants. Its message was one of caution,
but suggested that western Canada was the most promising destination.
After a subsequent reconnaissance of western Canada as a guest of the
Canadian government in July 1895, Oleskiv threw aside his reservations
and in two further pamphlets enthusiastically recommended Canada.
Rolnictwo za Oceanem a Przesiedlna Emigracja (Agriculture across the ocean
and the emigration movement), in Polish, received little attention,[27]
but his pamphlet in Ukrainian, *O emigratsii* (On emigration), circulated
throughout the Ukrainian areas of Galicia and Bukovyna. Oleskiv hoped
to obtain a monopoly on the organization of Ukrainian emigration to
Canada, so as to prevent rapacious steamship agents from extorting a
profit from naïve emigrants. He also wished to ensure that all emigrants
were well provided for and were adequately prepared for the rigours
of pioneering. He failed to do this, partly because the Canadian government distrusted his motives and refused his request for total jurisdiction
in the promotion of Canada in Western Ukraine, but mainly because the
success of his publications so spurred emigration to Canada that he

was swept aside by the rush of emigrants. Although he organized and dispatched many parties, his major influence lay in popularizing Canada and reinforcing the patterns of decision-making that had already been manifested by those who had emigrated before 1896.

In *O emigratsii* Oleskiv purveyed a good deal of practical advice to immigrants. Knowing that most Ukrainian peasants lacked the means and experience to settle on the open prairie, he advised against moving beyond the shelter of the parkland and intimated that soils would be more fertile in wooded areas. He also implored them to follow the example of the Galician Volksdeutsche and Ukrainian settlers already established in the West.[28] Oleskiv stressed the advantages of settling near such settlers along river banks and by freshwater lakes.[29] His advice carried substantial weight with the peasants, who respected him for his integrity and expertise as a professor of agriculture.

Oleskiv's writings and instructions to departing emigrants had the effect of entrenching the pattern of spatial behaviour already manifested in the selection of Star for settlement by those who had emigrated before 1896. In the eyes of the Ukrainian immigrants timber was vital for building, fencing, and fuel. They were anxious to avoid a replication of the circumstances in their homeland, where timber was strictly controlled and often expensive.[30] Their obsession surprised even the government colonization officers, who were aware that settlers of all nationalities wanted some timber on their land: 'The Galicians [Ukrainians] are a peculiar people; they will not accept as a gift 160 acres of what we should consider the best land in Manitoba, that is first class wheat growing prairie land; what they want is wood, and they care but little whether the land is heavy soil or light gravel; but each man must have some wood on his place.'[31]

But the Ukrainian settlers were concerned with more than the presence of timber. Most of them had little capital and appraised the land from the perspective of the peasant farmer intent on attaining self-sufficiency. Few contemplated entering the market economy immediately. In consequence, the Ukrainian settlers prized aspects of the physical environment that facilitated self-sufficiency. Whereas commercially oriented farmers would try to avoid slough or swamp, the penurious Ukrainians saw in them materials for thatching, water for stock, and fish and game for dietary supplements.[32]

The land that best fulfilled the Ukrainians' needs was found in the aspen parkland belt.[33] The best lands along the southern fringe of this belt had been settled before the onset of massive Ukrainian immigration, but large tracts along its northern edge still awaited settlement in the late 1890s.[34] Ukrainian immigrants soon made clear their aversion to settlement on the prairie, and Crown agents acknowledged the wisdom of their predilection for the timbered environments of the northern parkland, but considerable friction arose from the Crown's attempt to modify the pattern of settlement that immediately began to emerge. Left to their own devices, Ukrainian immigrants headed for the existing Ukrainian settlements, hoping to obtain the benefits of a familiar social, religious, and linguistic milieu. Even though in 1896 Crown agents established some Ukrainian settlers on homesteads at Cook's Creek and Stuartburn in southern Manitoba and a few others settled independently on river lots along the Red River at St Norbert close to Winnipeg, the main flow of Ukrainians was to Star in Alberta.[35] This was administratively undesirable. To have large numbers of settlers searching for homesteads within a limited area caused squabbles between settlers and led to chaos. Furthermore, and far more serious, it raised the spectre of the Star colony expanding into a massive ethnically homogeneous settlement – a virtual Canadian Ukraine – in east-central Alberta, a potential development that the government viewed with apprehension, if not alarm.

The government found it difficult to halt or break up the patterns emerging in 1896 and 1897. Under the terms of the Dominion Lands Act all settlers were free to go where they chose in the West, so long as the land they selected had not been alienated under the terms of a land grant or set aside for use as a timber lease or Indian reserve. The function of the Crown officials in the field was intended to be purely advisory. They were responsible for placing immigrants in locations that would facilitate agricultural progress and ensure permanent and successful settlement. They had no authority to order immigrants into specific locations and were thus obliged to achieve their ends by persuasion and accommodation to the wishes of the incoming settlers. Hence, although the government could to some extent channel Ukrainian immigrants, it could not coerce them into specific areas.[36]

This lack of authority immensely complicated the Crown's task of administering the efficient and orderly settlement of Ukrainians. As of 1896 a system had been established whereby the commissioner of immigration organized incoming Ukrainians into parties at Winnipeg and placed them under the guidance of a colonization agent. These parties were then dispatched to various centres in the West, where land guides led them to areas open for homestead settlement.[37] Immigrants with specific destinations were sent wherever they wished to locate, but those without a destination in mind were assigned one by the commissioner.[38]

The success of this system depended upon the co-operation of the immigrants, most of whom were amenable so long as their wishes were accommodated but were not disposed to accept government decisions that would place them in isolated locations away from their fellows or on lands they regarded as unsuited to their requirements. But in the case of the Ukrainians the government was unable to maintain its laissez faire policy of settlement administration in the West, for the immigration of 1896 had brought the Ukrainians to public notice. By the summer of 1897 they were at the centre of a national debate on the wisdom of the government's policy of encouraging Slavic immigration.[39] Emotions ran high. Clifford Sifton, the minister of the interior, stoutly defended the Ukrainians as good material for pioneer settlement: 'I think a stalwart peasant in a sheepskin coat, born on the soil, whose forefathers have been farmers for ten generations, with a stout wife and half a dozen children is good quality. We do not want mechanics from the Clyde – riotous, turbulent and with an insatiable appetite for whiskey. We do not want artisans from the southern towns of England who know absolutely nothing about farming.'[40]

Sifton's opponents rejected this view. Through the Anglophone Conservative press they vilified the Ukrainians as the scum of Europe – 'physical and moral degenerates not fit to be classed as white men.'[41] For five years the debate over the merits of Ukrainians raged in the western press. It ceased only when the Conservatives realized in 1902 that it was politically unwise to alienate a segment of the population that was acquiring the franchise.

During this crucial formative period of Ukrainian settlement in Canada the government found its actions in the field subject to the scrutiny of the public and the press. Its critics refrained from demanding the immediate and total cessation of Slavic immigration only long enough to insist that the Slavs be segregated from immigrants from Western Europe, yet be dispersed throughout the West so as to ensure their rapid assimilation into the mainstream of Britannic culture. As the government was painfully aware, the two latter demands were essentially irreconcilable, for segregation implied the growth of massive ethnic bloc settlements, which, even if on the edge of the ecumene, were unacceptable to both the Liberal and the Conservative parties.

The question of bloc settlement was more than a matter of administration. The bureaucrats charged with settling immigrants in the West favoured their placement in bloc settlements for administrative convenience and because settlers located together demanded less governmental aid.[42] But the press saw the issue as one that affected the very nature of the society that was emerging in the West. On 20 July 1897, the *Nor'Wester* launched a sustained vitriolic campaign against the 'colony system' of Ukrainian settlement in the West:

It is a positive misfortune for an enlightened community to be handicapped by having a cargo of these people settled in or near it. Both economically and socially they will lower the standard of citizenship. If they are put in colonies by themselves, they will be still less susceptible to progressive influences; and the districts where the colonies are located will be shunned by desirable immigrants. Not only are they useless economically and repulsive socially, but they will constitute a serious political danger. They are ignorant, priest-ridden and purchasable. In the hands of a practical politician, a few thousand of such votes will decide the political representation of the province ... All who are interested in the progress of Manitoba should protest more vigorously against the further importation of such a dangerous element.'[43]

The question soon transcended regional interest and became the subject of national debate. The Anglophone press manifested a rare unanimity when it insisted that immigrants must not be permitted to dilute the British character of the West through creation of foreign enclaves resistant to assimilation. The only correct policy, editorialized the *Winnipeg Telegram*, was the complete assimilation of all foreigners: 'The Government is making a great mistake in establishing these exclusively foreign colonies. The proper policy is to mix the foreigners up with the rest of the population as much as possible. It is only in that way that they will be assimilated. The colony system tends to perpetuate their own language and peculiar customs. It prevents their observation of improved methods of cultivation and keeps them out of touch with British institutions and ideas.'[44]

Most anglophones in the West subscribed to the view that 'Canada is British, and Canada is English,' and undoubtedly many were sympathetic to the claims of Frank Oliver, the Liberal member of Parliament for Edmonton, who argued that the creation of large blocs of Ukrainian settlers would 'lower levels of intelligence and civilization and cause native-born Canadians to leave in favour of the United States.'[45] The *Winnipeg Telegram* expressed the fears of many English-speaking settlers:

It must be thoroughly disheartening to any respectable English speaking settler to find himself surrounded by a colony of Russian serfs [Ukrainians], and to know that, if he remains on his homestead, he is likely to have no other neighbors for himself and his family all his natural life. He has braved all the difficulties of a pioneer in the hope of building up a comfortable home for himself and his children. He has selected for his home the Canadian Northwest because the British Flag flies over it, and because, as a Canadian, an Englishman, an Irishman or a Scotsman, he wants to remain a Britisher among British people ...

The unfortunate settler finds himself hemmed in by a horde of people little better than savages – alien in race, language and religion, whose customs are repellent and whose morals he abhors. Social intercourse is impossible, all hopes of further British settlement in the neighborhood vanishes; he becomes an alien in his own country. There is nothing left for him but a galling life-long exile on British soil equivalent to deportation to a Siberian settlement.[46]

Although the Liberal, staunchly pro-Sifton *Manitoba Free Press* rejected the negative assessment of the Ukrainians, it did not take issue with the assumption that Canadianization of the immigrants was vital for the welfare of the West.[47] The failure of the *Free Press* to support the denunciation of the colony system may be attributable to fear of embarrassing its owner – Clifford Sifton – and the government rather than to any sympathy for the immigrants' preference for settling together.[48]

The controversy surrounding Ukrainian immigration undoubtedly had an impact upon the Crown. It never articulated a formal policy for the guidance of its agents in the field, but the extensive correspondence between James A. Smart, the deputy minister of the interior in Ottawa, and William F. McCreary, the commissioner of immigration in Winnipeg, suggests that the government was apprehensive of adverse public reaction to its actions in the West.[49] At a time when the press was decrying bloc settlement and when some newspapers were labelling the Ukrainians 'Sifton's pets,' alleging that they received preferential treatment, it was politically imperative that the government's actions refute such charges.[50] This heightened the need to check the growth of large bloc settlements and to place Ukrainian immigrants in locations where they could fend for themselves and be independent of governmental aid.

It was ironic that the most expeditious approach to minimizing immigrant reliance upon governmental assistance in settlement was to allow the settlers to pursue the collective security of the bloc settlement. As noted, it was an approach fraught with political dangers, and one that the Crown could not openly promote. Indeed, from 1897 onwards the Crown made determined efforts to deflect settlers from the largest bloc of Ukrainian settlement at Star, Alberta. It did this by attempting to establish new settlements elsewhere in the West that would serve as attractive alternative destinations for incoming Ukrainians. The Crown's agents in the field were well aware that the complete dispersal of Ukrainian immigrants was impractical. It ran counter to the wishes of the immigrants, and the government lacked the authority and personnel to implement it. There was no enthusiasm for a course of action that would lead to direct confrontation with incoming settlers.

Apart from political considerations, the government colonization officers working in the field were generally well-disposed to the concept of bloc settlement. Planning and administration were greatly simplified when immigrants of the same ethnic background were settled together.[51] Social and religious needs were more easily provided for and co-operation between settlers was usually better than in ethnically mixed areas. There were fewer crises in settlement, fewer cases of destitution requiring government assistance, and a concomitant decrease in the work load of the Crown agents responsible for their welfare. Indeed, in the early days of mass immigration Commissioner McCreary had advocated bloc settlement: 'These people [Ukrainians] at least for the first few years should be settled in colonies; each colony will need an Interpreter who will also act as a Farm Instructor, Purchasing Agent and so forth. They should have in each colony a Priest or spiritual advisor who will also act as Teacher ... In each colony there should be reserved by the Crown a piece of land suitable for a Church, Cemetery, School house, Store building and so forth. This piece of land to be devoted to the general interests of the entire colony.'[52]

This practical advice was seldom, if ever, followed in full, for expediency and financial constraints dictated otherwise. But colonization officers found that once they had placed Ukrainian settlers in an area opened for settlement they experienced little difficulty in locating further immigrants alongside them. Established settlers attracted their kinfolk and compatriots and enabled them, in the words of the commissioner for immigration, to 'drop into their place without a tithe of the trouble hitherto experienced.'[53]

Creation of New Settlements

The great difficulty facing the Crown was the creation of new nodes of settlement. No Ukrainians with friends or relatives already settled in the West wanted to miss the opportunity to settle adjacent to them. They were reluctant frontiersmen and hesitated to be the first of their group to settle in a new area. Indeed, much of the time and energy of McCreary and his staff at Winnipeg was devoted to the vexing question of inducing incoming settlers to go to pioneer areas remote from other Ukrainians. McCreary appealed without success for the legal authority to direct immigrants into specific areas as he saw fit.[54] Denied this authority, he harangued, cajoled, and even tricked incoming Ukrainians in a sustained effort to channel them into new areas.[55] At times his procedures contravened the Dominion Lands Act, but in the main they provoked little opposition from Ottawa, the western press, or the Ukrainians themselves.

McCreary strove to settle Ukrainians in areas where the physical environment satisfied their marked predilection for wood, water, and meadows. Prospective sites were also evaluated in terms of their ability to absorb large numbers of immigrants, the opportunities for capital generation through resource development, the availability of off-farm employment, the presence of Ukrainian-conversant Volksdeutsche settlers, and accessibility by railway or all-weather trails.[56]

Since few Ukrainian settlers contemplated the immediate organization of a commercial farming operation, acquisition of prime wheat-growing land was not an overriding concern. The range of the resource base was of greater interest than the quality of one aspect of it. From the standpoint of both the government and the immigrants the lands on the northern fringe of the parkland, usually regarded as of second quality by settlers who were orientated towards commercial farming, afforded the range of resources vital to the penurious settlers bent upon subsistence farming. On such lands capital could be generated by exploiting the non-agricultural resources. By cutting and marketing cordwood new settlers could raise sufficient capital to establish themselves in farming. In most districts with a market for cordwood, an industrious settler could earn 70 cents a day. This was a reasonable return on labour at the turn of the century, when heavy labour on the railway section gangs brought only $1.25 for a ten-hour day, from which the railway companies deducted 75 cents for board, while farm labourers in the Brandon area were receiving a maximum of $15.00 a month in addition to their board.[57] In the bush country a family could also earn over a dollar a day by digging snakeroot (*Polygana senega*).[58] Other features of the northern parkland that had no commercial potential were prized as aids to survival, and colonization officers encouraged new settlers to supplement their diets with wild fruits, berries, fungi, game, and fish.[59]

Areas of this type adjacent to established Volksdeutsche from Ukraine were always viewed as excellent sites for settlement of Ukrainians.

Government agents had high regard for these Ukrainian-conversant Germans, and after several years of settlement most were in a position to employ new immigrants as farm help.[60] The Volksdeutsche, furthermore, played an important psychological role in ameliorating the sense of dislocation experienced by the Ukrainian settlers cut off from contact with their countrymen. Oleskiv, too, in *O emigratsii* had advised settlement near 'older [Ukrainian] colonists or at least near Germans,' arguing that those striking out alone without the benefit of advice from experienced settlers would come to grief.[61]

In evaluating potential sites for settlements the government had to consider their accessibility. The logistics of mass settlement demanded that immigrants be carried by rail as close to their destination as possible; it was undesirable to have settlers walking fifty miles or more to reach the area opened for settlement. Colonization trails were cut into areas not reached by the railway, but they were liable to become impassable during wet weather.[62] But uninterrupted access was vital: the government could not afford, either financially or politically, to have angry and often destitute settlers crowding the immigration halls in the major distribution centres of the West.

McCreary was further constrained in his choice of areas for the establishment of new Ukrainian colonies. Areas not yet surveyed could not be opened to settlement. Nor could areas wherein the railway companies were still eligible to select lands under the terms of a land grant.[63] Despite these formidable obstacles, by 1900 the government had managed to create a series of Ukrainian settlements across the northern fringe of the parkland belts, running from Leduc, near Edmonton, to Stuartburn, southeast of Winnipeg (fig. 3).[64]

The government attained this only by making determined efforts to minimize immigrant resistance towards pioneering new areas and taking great pains to select lands for new colonies that accommodated the immigrants' needs: wooded environments offering access to settlements of Volksdeutsche or other nationalities with potential for off-farm employment. When such tactics were adopted with well-led groups which had been exposed to the influence of Oleskiv and which were not determined to join relatives at all costs, the government easily established new nodes of settlement. In 1896, for example, a new settlement was established without difficulty at Stuartburn in southeastern Manitoba. The initial party of settlers had been dispatched by Oleskiv. They were well organized, well led by Kyrylo Genik, and had some knowledge of the character of the lands in southeastern Manitoba from the description in *O emigratsii*.[65] Like the government officials accompa-

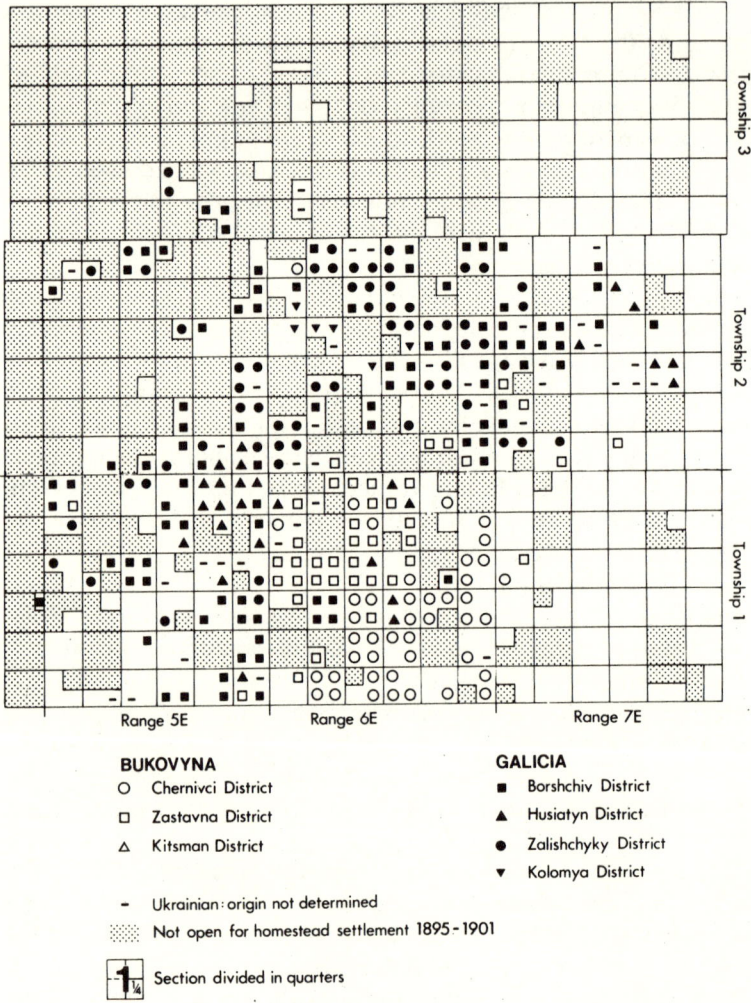

Figure 3. The Stuartburn Colony by district of origin in 1900.

nying them, they hoped to obtain land near the Mennonite reserves, 'where stock, food and other necessities, required for a new settler could be had on very reasonable conditions and where employment is plenty at any time of the year.'[66]

Although the settlers failed to find sufficient land for a colony alongside the Mennonite reserves, they were favourably impressed by the large tracts of vacant homestead land in the Stuartburn district only forty-eight kilometres from the Mennonite West Reserve and less than thirty kilometres from the East Reserve. The land was officially described as 'for the most part of inferior character' and not such as to attract much attention from the Canadian settler, being 'to a good extent very rough and hard to clear and improve,' although it was still thought to be 'well adapted for mixed farming.'[67] It was eagerly settled by Ukrainian immigrants impressed by the presence of wood and water and the closeness to the Mennonite reserves and the railway at Dominion City.

An attempt to establish a new settlement near Dauphin, Manitoba, early in 1896 ran into difficulties when the colonization road into the area became impassable after the spring thaw. Late in the year some eight Ukrainian families moved into the area, following advice that their leader had solicited from Oleskiv.[68] After the completion of the railway into Dauphin in 1897 the Crown was able to direct more settlers into the district and to establish a solid basis for further expansion. All of these early settlers were induced to go to the Dauphin district by Oleskiv, hence the ease with which the nucleus of settlement was established. Significantly, it was these early settlers sent by Oleskiv who showed the greatest concern for soil quality and who were prepared to strike out into new areas in order to secure lands in a setting reminiscent of their Carpathian highland home.[69]

In 1897 Crown agents also experienced little difficulty in planting a nucleus of eleven families in the Manitoba Interlake district, which appealed to the first Ukrainians to homestead there because it offered good timber, hay meadows, easy access to Winnipeg, and, perhaps, the psychological comfort provided by the nearby long-established Icelandic settlements along the shores of Lake Winnipeg.

Coercion

It was only when colonization officers failed to accommodate the wishes of immigrants and attempted to direct them away from their fellows and into districts which the Crown saw as fine wheat-growing areas that conflict erupted. The most notable example of this occurred in 1898 when the minister of the interior suggested the creation of a Ukrainian settlement at Fish Creek in Saskatchewan. The Crown agents at first disregarded the ministerial instruction to settle the next group of immigrants there, arguing that the immigrants then in their charge 'had made up their minds to go to certain parts, and it would have been very difficult to get them to change this decision, in fact, impossible ... A large number had friends in the Edmonton district ... and would go nowhere else.'[70] Nevertheless, it was resolved to locate 'several families at least of the next large party at that point.'[71]

Shortly thereafter a large consignment of Ukrainian immigrants, mostly from Bukovyna, arrived in Winnipeg. Some two years of experience with Ukrainian immigrants had convinced McCreary that 'it is simply an impossibility, by persuasion, to get a number of these people to go to a new colony, no matter how favoured, and some ruse has to be played, or lock them in the [railroad] cars.' The immigrants were therefore told that they were bound for Edmonton or Dauphin and were dispatched to Fish Creek under the control of Colonization Agent Speers. When they learned of their true destination, open revolt broke out, and all but a few began walking back to Regina. Unable to cope, Speers telegraphed McCreary in Winnipeg:

Almost distracted with these people, rebellious, act fiendish, will not leave cars, about seventy-five struck off walking [to] Regina, perfectly uncontrollable. Nothing but pandemonium since leaving Regina. Have exhausted all legitimate tactics with no avail. Policeman here assisting situation – eclipses anything hitherto known. Edmonton, Dauphin or die. Will not even go [to] inspect country, have offered liberal inducement, threatened to kill interpreter. Under existing circumstances strongly recommend their return Edmonton and few Dauphin and get another consignment people special train leaving this afternoon. Could take them [to] Regina. Answer immediately am simply baffled and defeated – quietest and only method will be their return. Waiting reply. Mostly have money and will pay fare. They are wicked.[72]

Faced with the possibility of an armed revolt by hundreds of Ukrainians determined to walk to where they wished to settle, the government decided to transport the dissidents to Edmonton or Dauphin and drew some consolation from Speer's success in persuading seven families to locate at Fish Creek. In essence it mattered little whether seven or seventy families had been established. The nucleus of a new colony had been set in place, and the Crown could afford to acquiesce to the demands of the notoriously stubborn Bukovynian settlers, whom

McCreary described as 'an obstreperous, obstinate, rebellious lot [who] all want to go where the others have gone.'[73]

It is noteworthy that the triumphant dissidents of the Fish Creek incident congratulated themselves on having settled on the open prairie, saying 'Hey, if it wasn't for us stubborn Bukovynians you'd be eating gophers in Siniboia [Assiniboia].' To which the Galicians would respond, 'That's why we stuck with you Hutsuls, because Hutsuls know where are the woods and meadows.'[74] Woods and meadows settled by their kinfolk exerted a seemingly irresistible pull upon the newly arrived Ukrainian immigrants. It was certainly sufficient to cause them to disregard even the advice of the government agents and interpreters of their own nationality; it caused them to overlook obvious shortcomings in the land upon which they could settle, and it led them to endure years of adversity on lands clearly less promising than others still open to settlement.[75]

Resource Appraisal

Although the new immigrants may have lacked the experience of North American conditions necessary to evaluate homestead lands, it is difficult to accept that they could have been oblivious to the shortcomings of the lands they enthusiastically settled in the Interlake and Stuartburn regions of Manitoba and in the Sniatyn area of Alberta. In the former case homesteaders waded waist-deep to their homesteads, while in the latter new immigrants settled eagerly on land described as 'mostly covered by water' and 'all sand and bush and not fit for farming.'[76] That they did so was partially a reflection of the nature of their experiences in the homeland. Certainly the Ukrainian peasants valued resources differently. Equally important was their experience of working tiny fragmented farms in Galicia and Bukovyna. Many assumed that even on an extremely poor homestead they would find a dozen acres of arable land, which, if supplemented by a few acres of meadow or marshland, would permit the kind of farming operation of which they had experience. Some even thought their 160-acre homesteads were too large and tried to achieve denser settlement by requesting permission to subdivide them into 80-acre units.[77]

Kinship Linkages

The determination to settle alongside others of the same nationality may also have been a major factor in leading Ukrainian settlers to homestead on lands of inferior character. It is important to note that the initial groups of settlers farming the nucleus of colonies selected lands that fulfilled their needs in settlement. If the land was not the 'finest wheat growing land,' at least it suited their needs. Indeed, it was in the interests of the government that it be so, for it had no wish for the Ukrainians to perform poorly as farmers and have charges that they were poor material for settling the West borne out. The surge in the volume of Ukrainian immigration after 1896 saw a concomitant expansion of settlements. In some instances, this led to a gradual movement of the settlement frontier on to progressively poorer land.

When the first Ukrainians settled in Stuartburn in southeastern Manitoba, they selected a locale endorsed by Oleskiv that promised to be well-suited to their intended purpose of stock rearing.[78] What neither the immigrants, Oleskiv, nor the government agents realized was that the quality of the land declined rapidly as one moved east of the initial area of settlement. In 1896 the first Ukrainian settlers on Township 2, Range 5E, obtained land that was satisfactory to them and, it should be added, to English stock raisers who had moved into the area several years earlier. Subsequently, as immigrants sought land adjacent to their established kinfolk and compatriots, the tide of settlement in the Stuartburn area was funnelled eastwards, away from the fertile Red River clays on to stony beach ridges and areas of poor drainage, marsh, and swamp. Successive newcomers traded off a progressive decline in land quality against the advantages of a familiar social, religious, and linguistic milieu. For many, if not most, of those homesteading in the Stuartburn district, emotional factors clearly determined the decision. Within the colony members of extended families and former neighbours settled together, effectively re-creating elements of their former society in Ukraine. The settlement of Bukovynians in this area showed the extent to which family, village, and regional ties influenced the choice of homestead land within an area of settlement.[79] By 1900 Ukrainian settlers had occupied over five townships (180 square miles) in the Stuartburn area. This area of contiguous settlement was characterized by a marked separation of immigrants in a settlement on the basis of their province of origin and a clustering on the basis of their district and village of origin (fig. 3).

Immigrants from Galicia settled alongside but separately from those from Bukovyna. In part this arose from a natural inclination of all immigrants to seek out the company of those who shared a similar cultural heritage, religion, and outlook.[80] At the time of settlement in Canada the Ukrainians from the two provinces were divided on the basis of religion. Those from Galicia were almost all of the Greek Catholic (Uniate) church; those from Bukovyna of the Greek (Russian) Orthodox church. Adherents of each church regarded the other with distrust. The Uniates held the Orthodox as agents of Russian imperialism who were preaching a gospel of Russification and oppression of Ukrainian culture. The Orthodox thought the Uniate clergy was bent on the absorption of Western Ukraine into the Polish sphere.[81] These religious differences, which have political undertones, were heightened by other minor cultural and linguistic differences between the two groups.

This intra-ethnic division was manifested in the pattern of Ukrainian settlement across the West.[82] Wherever the two groups settled in the same locale, they segregated themselves according to province of origin. Though puzzled at first by their determination to avoid mixing, Crown agents willingly accommodated their requests when it became evident that those from Bukovyna were 'somewhat different from regular Galicians; their chief difference however, being in their religious persuasion. They do not affiliate and, in fact, are detested by the Galicians.'[83]

The attitude of the immigration officials was one of amusement rather than annoyance. One colonization officer reported an incident when he was settling Ukrainians in the Yorkton district of Saskatchewan: 'after a little trouble which arose, the Galicians, not wishing to go with the Bukowinians – verily the Jews not wishing to deal with the Samaritans – I assured them that they were all Canadians now under free institutions and they were well satisfied as we agreed to colonize them in different parts of the Township.'[84] Thus the actions of Crown agents who were anxious to avoid intra-group conflict contributed to the division of Ukrainian settlements on the basis of the province of origin.

The Stuartburn area is therefore typical of Ukrainian bloc settlements in this regard and illustrates the intensity of old-country groupings in Ukrainian settlement on the Canadian frontier (fig. 3).[85] Among the settlers from both Galicia and Bukovyna who settled in the Stuartburn area there was a further clustering according to the district of origin. For example, settlers from the Zalishchyky district of Galicia settled in two discrete groups, and those from the Chernivtsi and Zastavna districts of Bukovyna showed a strong tendency to cluster in settlement.[86] This extended even to the level of village of origin. Families from the village of Bridok in the Zastavna district intermixed with families from the village of Onut, also in the Zastavna district. Settlers from the village of Lukivtsi in the Chernivtsi district of Bukovyna settled alongside them but did not intermix to any great extent (fig. 4).

The determination of Ukrainian immigrants to settle alongside their

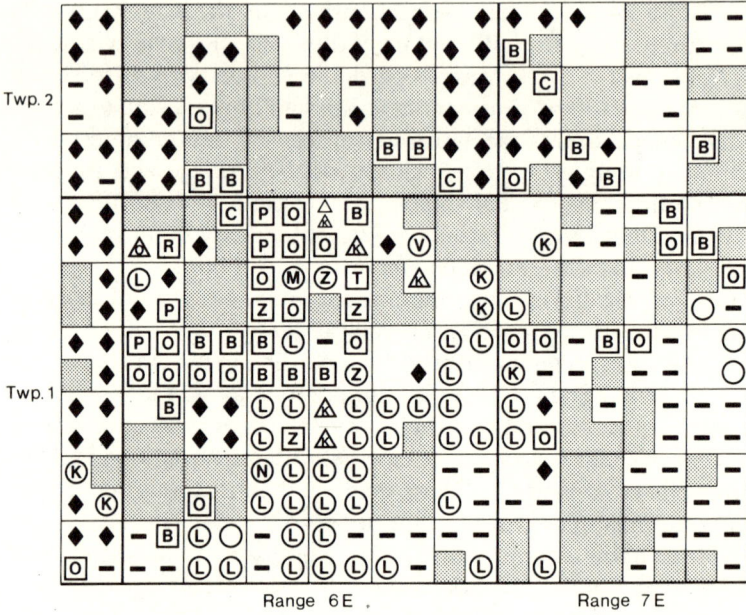

Twp. 2

Twp. 1

Range 6 E   Range 7 E

○ **CHERNIVCI DISTRICT**   □ **ZASTAVNA DISTRICT**   △ **KITSMAN DISTRICT**
     villages   villages   villages

L Lukivci	O Onut	K Khuvyshche
Z Zuchka	B Bridok	O Ozhekhlib
M Molodia	Z Zastavna Town	
V Kuchuriv Velykyi	T Tovtry	
K Kotul Biansky	P Pohorylivka	
N Nova Zuchna	R Borivci	
	C Chornyi Potik	

◆   Galician Settler

—   Ukrainian: origin not determined

▨   Not open to settlement

Section divided into quarters

Figure 4. Bukovynian settlement in the Stuartburn Colony by village of origin.

former neighbours and kinfolk was undoubtedly a major factor in perpetuating old-country village and district ties. Eleven of thirty-eight families from Lukivtsi, Chernivtsi district, had the surname Kossawan; several were related to the Kossawans by marriage; three had the surname Zyha, and three Shypot. This is not conclusive evidence of strong kinship ties, but it certainly points in that direction. It is almost impossible to determine kin linkages created through marriage, yet it is probable that such ties played a role comparable to ties of blood in maintaining closely clustered patterns of settlement.[87]

The social structure of Ukrainian pioneer settlements shows that Ukrainian immigrants who sought homesteads were strongly influenced by their determination to attain a familiar linguistic, religious, and social milieu. The consistency in their appraisal of any prospective homestead had an important geographical effect. It led to the re-creation of the geography of Western Ukraine in microcosm across the lands that they settled, perpetuating old-country ties and relationships in the new land. But those ties, so comforting to disoriented and fearful settlers, bound many of them to a life of hardship and penury on land that they would never have settled had they evaluated it on its agricultural merits alone.

In some areas – at Pakan, Alberta, on the southern slopes of the Riding Mountains, or at Stuartburn, Manitoba, for example – the newcomers' determination to settle near friends and kin led them to squat on lands not open to homestead settlement.[88] But squatters ran awesome risks. There was no guarantee that they would ever obtain title to the land on which they had made improvements, no certainty that their improvements lay completely within one quarter-section or that their houses and building did not lie on land found to be a road allowance. And the lands for which such risks were taken were by no means first class; some were even designated as 'swamp lands.' Such homesteads derived their attraction from their location adjacent to kinfolk and compatriots and not from their agricultural qualities.

Conclusion

The Ukrainian immigrants who sought homesteads in the West were remarkably consistent in their behaviour. A desire for timber and a wide resource base, proximity to Volksdeutsche, an emotional affinity for the topography, fear of the open prairie, lack of mobility, and ignorance of alternative areas open to homesteading influenced their decision to locate in a specific area. The willingness of later arrivals to rank cultural factors above economic or environmental ones determined the perpetuation and expansion of settlement. This the immigrants did, according to one official, 'regardless of their own welfare.'[89] Less desirable sites were occupied because of a perceived superiority of location. The tide of settlement rolled on to marginal lands, and immigrants made formal application to take out homesteads on land they would have probably rejected if their assessment of it had been more dispassionate and based only on its long-term agricultural potential. Thus the Ukrainians came to settle increasingly larger areas of marginal land. They did so not because of incompetence at environmental appraisal, but because they valued the company of their fellows and because the bush country presented a far better prospect for immediate survival than the more fertile prairies. This pattern of Ukrainian settlement in the West was sketched by 1900, cast by 1905, and firmly entrenched by 1914, when the war curtailed immigration from Europe and ended the period of massive frontier settlement in western Canada. During the following decade Ukrainians remigrating from the industrial centres and the resource frontiers of Canada and others fleeing from the turmoil of war and revolution in Europe extended the margin of settlement but had negligible impact upon the established geography.

With the passing of the frontier, the tastes and inclinations of the Ukrainian settlers veered towards cash flow and entry into the market economy, and the marginal homestead came to be seen as less than satisfactory. As the Ukrainian pioneers assimilated Anglo-Canadian agricultural goals, old-country values declined and social ties were weakened. Resource perception thus came to reflect more clearly the qualities of the land rather than those of the cultural milieu. The passing of old-country values and regional loyalties marked the beginning of a new phase of Ukrainian life in Canada, one dominated by the Canadian-born, in which actions and attitudes revealed an attachment to the values of the New World and a loosening of ties with the Old. It was in this context that the mythology of governmental responsibility for the plight of those Ukrainians struggling to survive on marginal farmsteads found fertile ground.

The Ukrainian Impress
on the Canadian West

JAMES W. DARLINGTON

A journey through the western interior of Canada, in the zone where the grasslands mix with the aspen-poplar forest, reveals extensive districts that stand out as one of the most distinct ethnic landscapes to be found anywhere in Canada and indeed in all of North America. They are the areas settled by Ukrainian immigrants and their descendants who began arriving in western Canada one hundred years ago. To uninitiated travellers, the onion-domed churches with their detached bell towers provide perhaps the strongest clue that they have entered a different ethnic environment. Closer inspection reveals additional features found predominantly, if not exclusively, in the Ukrainian districts. The more prominent elements include clusters of whitewashed crosses that mark the numerous graveyards, a preponderance of log buildings of various kinds, the frequent occurrence of houses and other structures painted pale blue and light green both on the farms and in the small communities, and a disproportionately high number of crossroad hamlets containing a church, a general store, a community hall, and a house or two. These and other features that set the areas of Ukrainian settlement apart from the surrounding districts have not gone unreported in both the popular and the academic press.[1]

As distinctive as the present-day Ukrainian-Canadian settlement landscape is, there is ample evidence that it was even more distinct in times past. 'When less than five miles of our journey [from Lamont] was covered,' wrote a visitor to the Edna-Star district of Alberta in 1911, 'we entered a district as typically Russian [sic] as though we dropped into Russia [sic] itself. Here and there beside the winding trail loomed up groups of buildings, low browed, and heavily thatched. These always faced south. The houses were all of rough logs, rough hewed and chinked with a mortar made of clay and straw. Some were plastered on the exterior, and almost all of them had been lime-washed to a dazzling whiteness.'² Although this description is of a rural area in Alberta, it could just as easily apply to contemporary Ukrainian districts in Manitoba or Saskatchewan.

But the visual presence of Ukrainian immigrants and their descendants in western Canada extends beyond the individual cultural elements in the landscape. For example, one of the most impressive aspects of the Ukrainian landscape is its geographic extent. With few exceptions, Ukrainian immigrants settled among their countrymen in what came to be extensive, nearly homogeneous, and often densely inhabited tracts. The Ukrainians were not the only ethnic group to settle in this manner. Throughout North America, immigrants and other long-distance migrants commonly settled among people of similar background, so much so that such behaviour was more conspicuous by its absence than by its presence. In western Canada, the Mennonites and Icelanders were two of the groups that established large, ethnically exclusive settlements.³ But the federal government facilitated the establishment of bloc settlements by both these groups by setting aside sizeable reserves for their exclusive use.⁴ In contrast, the Ukrainians received no such government assistance. The development of their settlements was essentially voluntary, the result of a combination of related concerns.

The economics of survival was one of these. With few exceptions, the Ukrainian immigrants arrived in Canada with limited financial resources and were not able to purchase improved farmland in previously settled areas of the prairies.⁵ They had little choice but to seek out free homesteads, the bulk of which were located at or near the settlement frontier.⁶ But rather than consider unclaimed sections of prime wheat-growing land in the extensive grasslands of the southern prairies, most new arrivals, to the consternation of immigration agents, turned instead to the wooded, moderately to extremely poor lands within the parkland.⁷ The decision to settle on such marginal land, which other settlers had rejected or bypassed, led to economic disaster, but at the time it made eminent sense to a financially destitute people.

The parkland belt, where the vast majority of Ukrainians settled, held a number of advantages in the form of raw materials that the open prairies could not supply in equal abundance. Among these items were timber for building, fuel, and fencing, marsh grass for roofing, water for stock, and wild game and fish to supplement a limited diet.⁸ All of these were put to immediate use by the Ukrainian immigrants, who were well acquainted with log-building and roof-thatching techniques.[9] Further, the parkland provided an opportunity to earn much-needed cash from seasonal work in nearby lumber camps or from the sale of cordwood or seneca root cut or dug on the homestead.[10]

Like other immigrants, the Ukrainians arrived with preconceived ideas as to what constituted valuable and productive land. Coming as they did from a part of Europe where woodland was the prized possession of the upper class, it is not surprising that these people of peasant stock would be attracted to treed land. And if they perceived the lack of trees on the prairie as a sign of infertility, then certainly they were not alone. Many farmers from the forested eastern half of the continent or from northwest Europe came to the same conclusion, only to change their minds later.[11] Their logic was as consistent as it was straightforward: 'bareness equals barrenness equals infertility equals uselessness for agriculture.'[12] Even if the Ukrainian immigrants did perceive the true potential of the grasslands and bush, the logic of their choice of the woodland remains unchanged when one takes into account their limited knowledge of commercial agriculture as practised in North America at the time. Peasant farms in Western Ukraine were marginal at best. The average farm in Galicia had less than twelve acres (five hectares) and still less in Bukovyna.[13] So, even if the wooded land did hold less agricultural promise than the prairie land, surely all but the meanest 160 acres of Canadian woodland could be made to outproduce the average farm in Western Ukraine. From this perspective it is small wonder that many Ukrainian settlers during the early period tried to subdivide their allotments.[14] Further, since few of the immigrants had experience with commercial agriculture, it is unlikely that they foresaw the economic consequences of their locational decision.

For some, nostalgia played a role in the selection of land. John Lehr cites a group of Hutsuls, or Carpathian highlanders, who chose to homestead in the wooded country near Hafford, Saskatchewan, because it reminded them of their homeland.[15] Another group of Ukrainian highlanders who came from three neighbouring villages in the Galician district of Kolomyia selected land south of Dauphin, Manitoba, and several townships removed from the principal area of Ukrainian settlement for the same reason. In the words of one member of the group, 'We chose to settle in that part of the district because the mountains, woods, streams, and meadows very much resembled our native Carpathian scenery.'[16] In the second instance, the land chosen was part of the Riding Mountain Timber Reserve and therefore not open to homesteading, a fact the settlers were soon made aware of. But they nonetheless persisted and after six years of debate with the government managed to gain title to their farms.[17] The point suggests the strength of the settlers' emotional attachment to the land.

New immigrants were guided by more than their own instincts and perceptions in their efforts to select land. In 1895, Dr Osyp Oleskiv, professor of agriculture at Lviv, Galicia, visited the Canadian prairies in order to identify areas suitable for Ukrainian settlement. Impressed with what he had seen, Oleskiv returned to Lviv, where he immediately published a pamphlet entitled *O emigratsii* (On emigration) in which he offered encouragement and advice to prospective emigrants. The publication quickly achieved wide circulation among the Ukrainian rural population in the Austrian provinces of Galicia and Bukovyna. In this and subsequent publications, Oleskiv, cognizant of the emigrants' limited financial resources and the advantages of woodland, advised them to select land in the parkland as opposed to the open prairie.[18] Oleskiv also served as an unofficial emigration officer for many groups of Ukrainians bound for western Canada and in that capacity at times urged emigrants to select homesteads in specific locales.[19]

Once the vanguard of Ukrainian settlers became established in an area, an additional set of factors entered into the decision making of subsequent immigrants. With rare exception, later arrivals tried their utmost to settle among family or friends or, if this was not possible, among people from the same district or province of Western Ukraine.[20] In many instances the desire to locate near friends or relatives overrode any concern about the quality of the land with the result that large tracts of marginal land were occupied.[21] From an economic perspective this pattern of behaviour was disastrous. Not only was this the case on the poorer lands where entry into commercial agriculture was seriously delayed, but the resultant high density also restricted expansion into areas of better land. On the other hand, the fact that the Ukrainians did settle close to family and friends meant that strong social ties existed within the new communities from the very beginning. Ironically, the marginal conditions the settlers faced only served to strengthen those ties and to enhance social support structures, which in turn made it more difficult for these people to leave the area and thus alleviate the situation.[22]

The combination of a marginal agricultural base that hindered economic success and an exceptionally strong social structure that encouraged the population to look inward was a major cause of a third characteristic of the Ukrainian-Canadian landscape, its persistence over time. Whereas other cultural groups accepted the Anglo 'norm,' the

Ukrainians resisted it. And whereas the reasons for this resistance are numerous and include forces internal and external to the Ukrainian culture itself, from the perspective of landscape the result is a series of regions within the parklands of the Canadian prairies that remain today decidedly different from the surrounding countryside.

As the citations referred to above indicate, many aspects of the Ukrainian-Canadian cultural landscape have been examined individually or in combination. Yet there have been few attempts to consider these various elements as they have persisted or evolved over the years within a single bloc settlement. The remainder of this paper will examine the development of the cultural landscape created by Ukrainian settlers and their descendants in the area north of Dauphin, Manitoba.

The Initial Wave of Settlers

In the late summer and early fall of 1896, eight Ukrainian families from the Austrian province of Galicia stepped off the train in Dauphin. They came on Oleskiv's advice to file homestead claims in the area. Following the lead of one of the first arrivals, Basil Ksionzik, all eight families filed a homestead claim in the western half of Township 26, Range 20 W, approximately a dozen miles northwest of Dauphin village (fig. 1).[23] The quarter-sections, clustered along the Drifting River, were, aside from some small scattered areas of marsh, mostly covered with stands of good-sized poplar and willow. Although a few patches of trees had been killed by fire several years earlier, the supply and quality of the timber was adequate for use as logs in house and barn construction. In addition, the quarter-sections were all close to a cart-track that led back to Dauphin.[24]

Shortly after their arrival, the settlers began calling the rural neighbourhood Terebowla, after the district of Galicia from which Ksionzik and several of the others had come. Over the course of the winter several more Ukrainian families arrived, and by the early spring of 1897 the settlement had grown to fifteen families. Father Nestor Dmytriw, a touring priest who visited the growing community that April, reported that seventy-eight Ukrainian immigrants were living there.[25] This modest group of Ukrainian settlers grew rapidly in the months and years that followed. Between 30 April and 22 May of that year, for example, three steamships carrying over a hundred Ukrainian families bound for the Dauphin region docked in eastern Canada.[26] By the end of the summer, more settlers had arrived, and the government was prompted to order the construction of an immigration shed at Dauphin. The stream

58   James W. Darlington

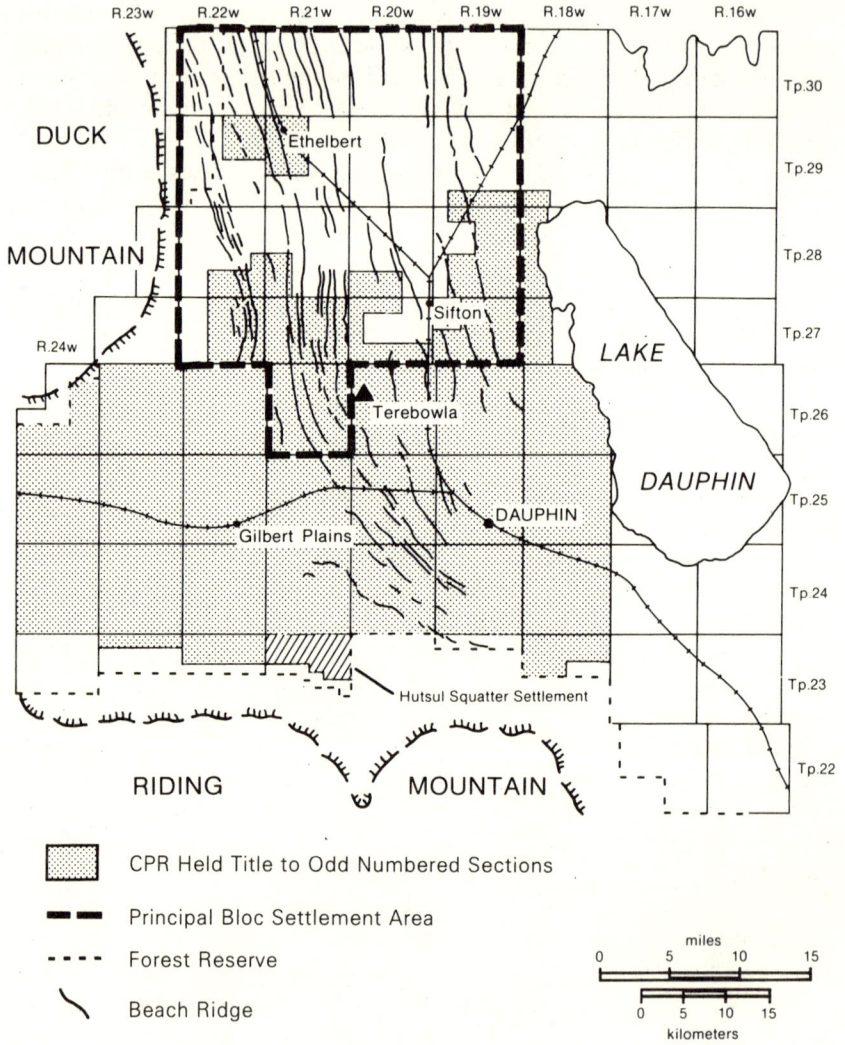

Figure 1. Ukrainian bloc settlement, Dauphin region.

of Ukrainian migrants into the region continued unabated during the next several years, and in 1901 J.O. Smith, the commissioner for immigration in Winnipeg, estimated the Ukrainian population in the greater Dauphin district to be 5,500 and growing.[27]

The vast majority of these immigrants filed for quarter-sections north or west of the original settlement at Terebowla. And, although Ukrainian settlement eventually extended from the shores of Dauphin Lake on the east to the lower elevations of the Duck Mountain escarpment in the west and to the end of the arable land in the north, settlement activity concentrated in townships 26, 27, 28, and 29 and ranges 19, 20, 21, and 22 W. The land immediately to the south of this bloc was of better quality, but much of it was already in the hands of English and Scottish homesteaders who had moved into the area several years before the first group of Eastern Europeans arrived.

Physical Setting

The country the Ukrainians chose to occupy in the Dauphin region is similar in many ways to that found in the other areas of extensive Ukrainian settlement. The eastern two-thirds or more of the Dauphin bloc settlement are flat and low-lying and as a consequence poorly drained. A major contributing factor to the poor drainage is an extensive series of gravel ridges that cut across the area in a northwest-southeast trending fashion. Composed primarily of sand and gravel, the ridges are remnant beach lines of glacial Lake Agassiz. Within the area where they exist, these modest ridges provide the only recognizable relief aside from some localized downcutting of the streams that flow east across the area. In contrast, the western third of the area is gently to moderately rolling country that stands roughly two hundred feet higher in elevation than the area to the east and is as a result better drained (fig. 1).

At the time of initial occupancy the better-drained portions of the entire area of Ukrainian settlement were largely covered by stands of poplar and willow intermixed with occasional bluffs of spruce. Sizeable patches within these areas were reported by government surveyors in the years immediately before settlement as having been recently burnt over, and other areas that had presumably burnt some years earlier were, at the time of survey, covered with bush. The wettest areas were covered with marsh grass and occasional stands of tamarack and black spruce.

From an agricultural standpoint, the quality of the land within the bloc settlement varies considerably. The soils that offer the greatest potential in the district are confined almost exclusively to a strip four to eight miles wide on the broad shoulder of elevated ground that extends along the base of the Duck Mountain escarpment. And, while many of the soil associations within this portion of the bloc settlement are classed as being of high or good productivity, a notable proportion of these soils is also stony. East and west of this band of better agricultural land, indeed throughout the rest of the bloc settlement, the soil is of moderate quality or worse. Today extensive areas are deemed suitable only for hay production or grazing.[28]

Land Selection

Its limited agricultural potential notwithstanding, much of the land within the bloc settlement was ultimately homesteaded. A section-by-section examination of the land taken by Ukrainians reveals that ultimately only the very worst land failed to attract settlers. There is nothing to suggest that this behaviour was the result of indifference. New immigrants did not take the first piece of land available for settlement. Indeed, some spent a considerable amount of time checking conditions before selecting a quarter-section. Jacob Maksymetz, for instance, arrived in the region in late April 1898 and checked possible homestead sites for over a month before filing a claim in early June.[29] New arrivals sometimes traversed considerable amounts of territory looking for the right combination of environmental factors before deciding where to locate. For example, Dmytro Romanchych was a member of a party of Hutsuls who set off on foot from Dauphin in search of land the day after their arrival in the spring of 1897. Spades and axes in hand, they headed cross-country in a northwesterly direction, stopping occasionally to dig a pit so as to check the quality of the soil. Proceeding in this fashion, they reached the vicinity of the present-day village of Ethelbert on the second day. Not satisfied with what they had seen, most of the group decided to turn back south and investigate the higher ground nearer the base of the Duck Mountain escarpment. Several members of the group found homestead sites to their liking near the hamlet of Venlaw, but most continued on and eventually selected land much further to the south in Township 23, Range 20, along the north slope of Riding Mountain. For these individuals the exploratory trek took the better part of a week and covered at the very minimum 70 miles (112 kilometres) and in all likelihood much more.[30]

The actions taken by this group of highlanders to settle together also illustrate the importance of social ties in the selection of land. The mutual support members of this party of Ukrainian settlers must have felt for one another undoubtedly influenced their decision to settle away from the principal bloc settlement and to risk the possible consequences of squatting. This desire to settle among relatives, friends, or, at the very minimum, persons from the same district or region was also repeatedly demonstrated within the main settlement bloc. Besides the initial group of settlers from Terebowla, immigrants from other Galician districts including Borshchiv, Sokal, and Husiatyn showed the same tendency.[31] Kinship ties were understandably stronger than community ties in most cases, and in numerous cases throughout the Dauphin bloc settlement relatives settled near or even next to one another. One example that stands out in this regard is the Negrych family. In 1897 six members of the family settled on quarter-sections located on three contiguous sections of Township 27, Range 22. Four family members filed homestead claims in section 14 alone.[32] As part of the initial wave of settlers in the area, the Negryches were in a reasonably good position to fulfil the twin desires of reasonable quality land and proximity to other family members. Later arrivals had fewer options. More often than not one or the other concern could be met but not both.[33]

External forces, primarily government regulation, played a critical role in determining the pattern of settlement. The federal government placed definite restrictions on where these people could settle. With rare exception new arrivals were not in a position to buy land. This left them with the options of filing a homestead claim or squatting. At the time of initial occupancy lands of a typical township were designated as follows: even-numbered sections, with two exceptions, were designated by the government as homestead land; odd-numbered sections, with two exceptions, were reserved for selection as railway grants; the Hudson Bay Company held title to section 8 and all but the northeast corner of section 26, which was available for homesteading; and sections 11 and 29 were reserved as school lands. Thus, sixteen and a quarter of the thirty-six sections contained in a standard township were set aside for homesteading and therefore available for a ten-dollar registration fee. The rest of the lands in a township were either held in reserve or available for purchase. These conditions resulted in a checkerboard pattern of settlement with alternate sections of land standing vacant until such time when additional lands were made available for home-steading or the settlers had established themselves well enough to purchase more land. The year-by-year sequence of land alienation in two adjoining townships in the western portion of the Dauphin bloc settlement illustrates this process (fig. 2).[34] All of the appropriate railway lands

James W. Darlington

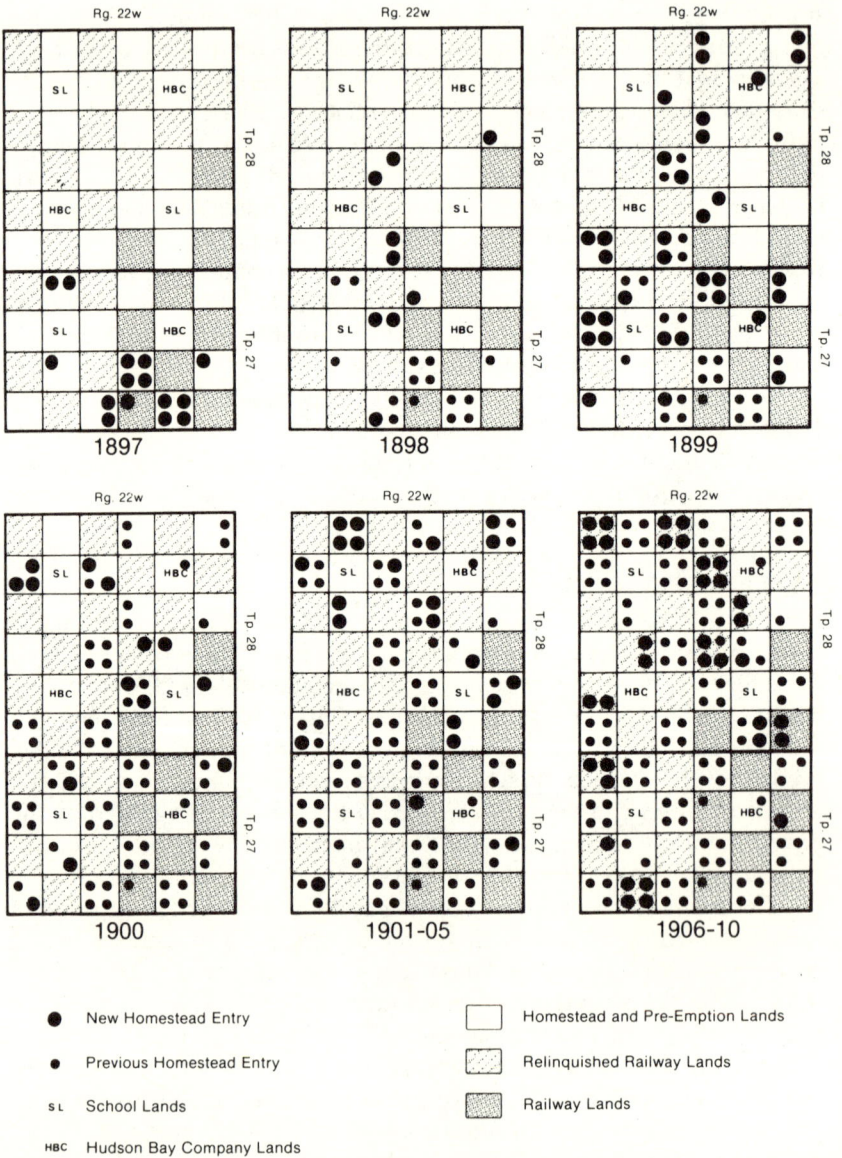

Figure 2. Land disposition, Mink Creek–Venlaw area, 1897–1910.

were held in reserve until 1903, when, by order of the Privy Council, the Canadian Pacific Railway relinquished its claim to all sections except those in the southeast corner.[35] Between settlement in 1897 and 1903 eighty-five quarter-sections were occupied, all but two of them homestead land. In the seven years that followed, the trend continued. An additional forty-two quarter-sections were occupied; four were purchased, the rest homesteaded.

Clearly the locational decisions made by the Ukrainian immigrants were based on a number of factors. Some had to do with the physical or social environment; others were imposed by governmental and other agencies. Although the multi-dimensional concerns and restraints were no doubt present throughout the period of initial land alienation, it should be pointed out that the examples cited all occurred during the first wave of settlement in the region.

Creating a Farm

Having selected a quarter-section of land, the immigrant family faced an immediate need for shelter. Normally a lean-to of sorts was erected to serve that purpose for a few weeks until a more substantial structure could be built. Most often this second shelter was a simple sod-roofed dug-out modelled after the *staia*, a type of hut used by Hutsul shepherds in the Carpathians. Crude and cramped as this structure was, it provided many a newly arrived family with modest protection from the elements through the first Canadian winter or until such time when a more substantive home could be built.[36]

Within a year or two, a modest log house reminiscent of those found in the builder's home region was built near the *staia*. A large majority of these were of horizontal log construction with saddle or dovetail corner notching. Occasionally, when the quality of timber necessitated, frame and fill, or Red River Frame, was used instead. Vertical log construction or *poteaux-en terre*, a building technique used by Ukrainian settlers elsewhere in the province, appears to have been rarely used in the Dauphin district.[37] Once the walls were in place, the building was covered with a thatched roof made from marsh grass gathered from nearby sloughs.[38] The walls were covered, inside and out, with a plaster made of mud mixed with straw or dung. In turn, the plaster was covered with a coat of lime-wash, which Galicians often tinted by adding laundry bluing. The dirt floor was also coated with a layer of mud and animal urine, which made it hard and easy to keep clean. With rare exceptions, the resultant one-storey, rectangular house was oriented with its roofline running east-west and the single entryway and most of the windows located on the southern exposure. Inside, the house was commonly divided into two or sometimes three rooms. These were known as the *velyka khata*, or 'big room,' the *mala khata*, or 'little room,' and the *seeny*, or entry hallway.[39] The *mala khata* contained a massive earthen stove, or *peech*, used for both cooking and heating. Besides serving as kitchen, the *mala khata* was also both common meeting room and children's bedroom. The *velyka khata* traditionally occupied the eastern half of the house and served as the parents' bedroom, but was otherwise reserved for use on special occasions. The east wall of this room was normally decorated with icons, family photographs, and religious calendars.

On many farms, these initial log houses were replaced later by larger and more carefully constructed log structures. These second-generation houses were more apt to be made of hewn timber held in place with wooden pegs and dovetail corner notching. The first of these second-generation dwellings were otherwise very similar to the old. But as the economic situation improved the Ukrainian settlers began to introduce different materials: sawn lumber was used for doors, window frames, and plank floors; wood shingles replaced thatch; a cast-iron stove replaced the *peech*; and brick replaced wattle chimneys. Despite the changes, these second-generation farmhouses remained very much a reflection of Ukrainian culture. In room arrangement, general orientation, and wall treatment the houses remained as before. Upon completion of the new farmhouse, the old one was invariably relegated to use as a summer-kitchen, storage shed, or animal shelter.

Before a second-generation log house could be contemplated many other tasks had to be carried out. Land had to be cleared and broken; crops had to be planted and harvested; barns and other outbuildings had to be raised; a well needed to be dug; and fences had to be erected. Homestead inspection reports and other scattered evidence make it possible to discern the rate at which individual farms took form. In June 1898, one year after the group of Ukrainian highlanders squatted on the timber reserve lands south of Dauphin, a survey was made of their progress. Of the twenty-three families that had settled in the area the previous June, all had built a house; seventeen had erected a stable; the same number had dug a well. Each family was reported to be cultivating between one and six acres, the average being slightly less than three.[40] In the spring of 1901 a number of these families petitioned the government in an attempt to gain legal title to the land. In that document the petitioners described the status of each farm. In nine cases the descriptions can be traced back to the previous list, and comparisons can be made. During the two and a half years the average number of acres broken rose from approximately 2.7 to 7.6. The number of outbuildings on the nine farms increased from seven to twenty-four, the number of cattle from fifteen to fifty.[41] Progress was clearly being made.

The rate at which land was cleared increased once the essential structures were in place and more time and effort could be devoted to clearing operations. This pattern is demonstrated by three of the original families that homesteaded in the Terebowla area in 1896. According to the colonization report of 1899, these three families had, in addition to erecting several essential buildings, cleared or ploughed eight, five, and one acre on their farms.[42] Three years later, in 1902, a similar report identified these same families as having respectively 32, 32, and 18 acres under cultivation. By that date, the first two families had also seen fit to purchase an additional 160 acres of land, thus doubling the size of their farms.[43] These two families were not the only ones to experience enough prosperity to invest in more land. A more extensive record exists for Jacob Maksymetz, who filed a homestead claim on a quarter-section (SW 34–27–22) in the Venlaw region in June 1898. Five years later, a growing family, a modest amount of financial success, and some keen foresight prompted him to purchase an adjoining quarter-section (NW 27–27–22) from the CPR. The family continued to prosper, and in 1918, encouraged by high commodity prices brought on by the First World War, purchased two quarter-section farms from neighbours (SW 4–28–22 and SE 4–28–22). Two years later two more farms came under family control, one of 60 acres (SW 27–27–22) and another of 160 (NE 28–27–22). In 1921 the family purchased yet another quarter-section (SW 26–27–22), thereby bringing its total holdings to 1,020 acres.[44] The Maksymetz family was not the only one to buy land with the profits made during the war years. The combination of hard-won financial success and population pressure led a number of Ukrainian families to purchase Anglo farms located on the better lands along the southern margin of the Ukrainian settlement tract.[45] The post-war recession cut this venture short for some, but most who made the move managed to survive and ultimately gained from their decision.[46] Others responded differently to the heightened population pressure. Rather than seek to expand their acreage, they subdivided their quarter-section homesteads in an effort to accommodate more families. This latter practice appears to have been most common on the worst lands, where only subsistence agriculture was possible.[47]

Under both scenarios, however, the amount of cleared land rose and with it farm production. As crop acreage expanded and livestock multiplied, the need for ancillary farm buildings increased accordingly. By 1910, for example, the Wasyl Negrych farmstead, settled in 1897, contained nine buildings: a substantial, three-room house, two barns, two granaries, a chicken coop, a hog shed, a summer-kitchen, and a storage shed.[48] The progress made by the Ukrainian settlers in the area and their imprint on the farm landscape was noticed by a Manitoba school inspector who wrote in 1900, 'I drive from Ethelbert across to Sifton, through the heart of Galician settlements. I was impressed with [the] prosperous appearance of most of the farms. The country is flat and uninviting – once the ridge upon which Ethelbert is situated is left – but in spite of the apparently unfertile nature of the soil, the little homesteads are surrounded by patches of wheat, rye and hemp and invariably a good vegetable garden. Most of the houses are small but with their thatched roofs and heavy overhanging eaves, on plastered walls, they are quite picturesque. I saw some quite large houses too.'[49]

Although farmsteads were springing up everywhere, not all the Ukrainian settlers met with success. Among 425 known homestead claims filed by Ukrainian settlers in the Dauphin region between 1896 and 1899, 350, or approximately 82 per cent, were granted patent.[50] Of those individuals or families who failed to receive patent, some purchased land elsewhere in the region. A few, it seems, filed a second homestead claim in the area. Others left the area.[51]

Creating the Sacred Landscape

The landscape beyond the homestead was also being transformed during this period, as various social groups established facilities to meet community needs and service centres containing a variety of commercial enterprises appeared in response to actual and projected opportunities. Of all the social institutions, none was more important than the church. The prominent role religion played in the lives of Ukrainians before and after immigration to Canada is well documented.[52] Churches invariably appeared within a few years of settlement,[53] and the first Ukrainian parish in the bloc settlement north of Dauphin was established at Sifton in 1900.[54] The following year St Michael's Ukrainian Catholic Church was erected seven miles west and two miles north of the present village of Sifton. Although very modest in size, the structure was centrally located within the Ukrainian district. More churches appeared throughout the region during the following decade. The dates of construction of many of them have been lost, but at least five were built before 1910. In the years that followed the residents of the area organized more congregations, and by 1940 at least thirty-four Ukrainian churches existed in the area (fig. 3). The structures themselves exhibit various levels of architectural sophistication and design, cultural transfer, and monetary expenditure.[55]

Distributed throughout the bloc settlement, standing in rural isolation and small urban centre alike, these houses of worship with their distinct onion-shaped domes offer tangible evidence of the importance of religion in the lives of the Ukrainian immigrants and their descendants. Their number, however, reflects more than unbending religious faith, and is certainly greater than population size or poor travel conditions would warrant. The Ukrainians who settled in the Dauphin district mostly came from Galicia and were, with few exceptions, members of the Uniate, or Ukrainian Catholic, faith.[56] The majority of the churches built in the area give credence to that fact, but the significant number of Orthodox churches suggests that the religious homogeneity that characterized Galician society did not survive the journey to Canada intact. Indeed, the Ukrainian community was buffeted by religious turmoil during the first several decades of settlement. The history of the various religious denominations that attracted a following among the Ukrainian settlers during the early years is long and complex and goes well beyond the scope of this paper. Suffice it to say that the early settlers were thwarted, largely through no fault of their own, in their efforts to attract Ukrainian Catholic clergy. Out of frustration, and at times despair, many Ukrainian settlers in the Dauphin region, as elsewhere on the Canadian prairies, turned to other religious groups. The Roman Catholic church, the Russian Orthodox church, and the Independent Greek church were all involved in this competition for souls. In the case of the Independent Greek church, an organization founded in Winnipeg in 1905 with the surreptitious moral and financial support of the Presbyterian church, the intent went beyond religious conversion to include deliberate efforts to acculturate or 'Canadianize' the Ukrainian population.[57] All of these religious denominations established congregations and erected churches in the area around Sifton during this early period of settlement.

By the outbreak of the First World War the Independent Greek church was defunct, the Russian Orthodox church was in rapid decline, and some Ukrainian Catholics increasingly disapproved of the Roman Catholic church's powerful influence on Ukrainian Catholic affairs. This dissatisfaction among a sizeable segment of the Ukrainian population

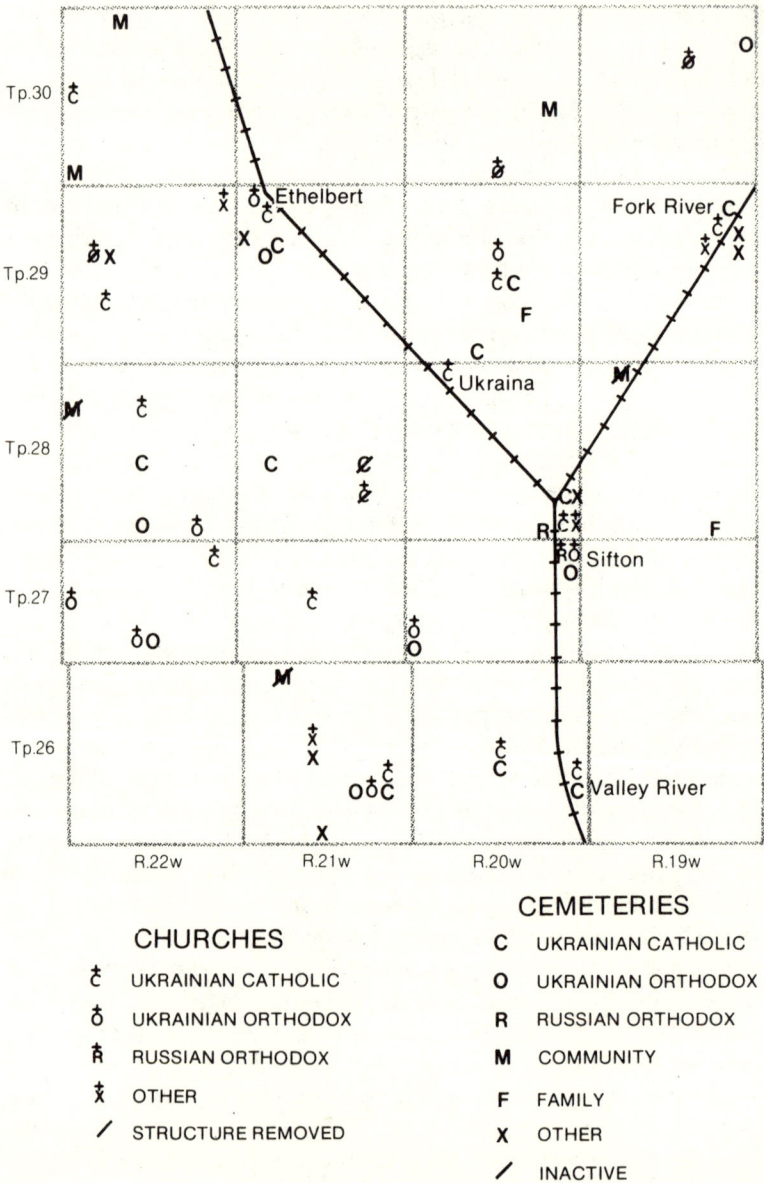

CHURCHES

☩	UKRAINIAN CATHOLIC
☩	UKRAINIAN ORTHODOX
☩	RUSSIAN ORTHODOX
☩	OTHER
/	STRUCTURE REMOVED

CEMETERIES

C	UKRAINIAN CATHOLIC
O	UKRAINIAN ORTHODOX
R	RUSSIAN ORTHODOX
M	COMMUNITY
F	FAMILY
X	OTHER
/	INACTIVE

Figure 3. Religious landscape: churches and cemeteries.

led to the formation of the Ukrainian Greek Orthodox Church of Canada in 1918. Across the prairies as a whole, the new church drew most of its adherents from the Bukovynian settlers, who were, by tradition, followers of the Orthodox faith. In the Dauphin district, however, most members came from the dissolved Independent and Russian churches or were dissatisfied members of Ukrainian Catholic congregations. In regard to the latter, a number of congregations split in dispute over church ritual and calendar.[58] In several instances these schisms resulted in the construction of a new church building, at times within sight of the old. Indeed, in the case of the congregation north of Ashville, the second church was built immediately across the road from the first. Ironically, the large number of churches in the Dauphin bloc settlement was a manifestation not only of profound religious feeling but also of a social fabric that had been deeply torn. A legacy of bad feeling remains to this day.

Cemeteries constitute another major element of the religious landscape of a region. As on most frontiers, the earliest burials in the Dauphin district took place near the family farmstead. But within a few years of settlement, as the community developed, a farmer would donate a portion of his land for use as a community cemetery. Both Catholic and Orthodox church law requires that a burial site be consecrated by a priest before a member of the faith can be interred there. As a consequence, many of the cemeteries in the area became tied to a specific church congregation. Where this is the case, the church and graveyard are frequently situated adjacent to or within a short distance of each other. More often than not the cemetery was in existence some time before the church was built. Thus the site of the cemetery influenced the location of the church.[59]

The most conspicuous display of the religious character of Ukrainian cemeteries is not their association with specific churches, but with the symbolism displayed on the individual grave markers. The cross stands out in this regard. Regardless of their religious background, Ukrainian settlers brought with them the long-standing tradition of denoting graves with free-standing crosses that were of Eastern, Latin, or, in a few cases, Greek form.[60] The earliest of these were made of wood, but the impermanence of that material soon led to the use of wrought iron and cast cement. By the 1920s a modest number of carved stone monuments had begun to appear. A large majority of these monuments maintained the same free-standing or at least partially free-standing cross form. In a few cases, however, the stone or cast-cement monument was in the shape of an obelisk or block, and the cross was displayed in bas-relief rather than in silhouette. These adjustments in grave monument material and style reflect more than changing tastes among the Ukrainian settlers. The material from which the monument is made mirrors the economic well-being of the family of the interred, and the basic change in design indicates an acceptance of Anglo grave monument design and thus a desire to acculturate.[61]

Creating the Social Landscape

Within a few years of settlement secular features that reflected the growing social cohesion in the region began to appear in the public landscape. Some of the resulting facilities were more distinctly Ukrainian than others, but all fulfilled critical social needs. The most obvious of these were schools. Shortly after their arrival in the area, the Ukrainian settlers began agitating the provincial government for educational facilities. Unfortunately for the Ukrainian districts in the province, a lack of local funding and a shortage of qualified instructors who could speak Ukrainian slowed the government's response.[62] Aware of the situation, the Presbyterian Home Missionary Society financed the construction and staffing of the first school in the district. Located at Terebowla, the one-room school opened around 1900. By 1903 the Presbyterians had opened additional schools at Sifton and Ethelbert.[63] Before the end of the decade, publicly funded schools were also operating across the region, and more were being added annually. By the early 1920s at least twenty-eight primary, principally one-room, schools were serving the Ukrainian area (fig. 4). The school buildings looked the same as school buildings found elsewhere in the province and thus were not culturally distinct. But in some instances they were given Ukrainian names, such as 'Bohdan,' 'Halicz,' 'Kulish,' 'Zelena,' and 'Zoria,' which came to identify rural neighbourhoods and which remain in use today long after the schools have closed and in some cases have disappeared from the landscape.[64]

The Prosvita, or community hall, was another important element that first appeared in the public landscape during these early years. With the establishment of a *chytalnia*, or reading hall, at Sifton in 1903, Ukrainian settlers throughout the area began to organize enlightenment or reading societies. Modelled after the self-help associations established in Ukraine in 1868, these societies had the purpose of cultivating education and cultural identity. In 1905 a reading hall was established at Venlaw. The following year two more were organized in the district, and in the year after that another two. By 1910 there were at least nine cultural societies

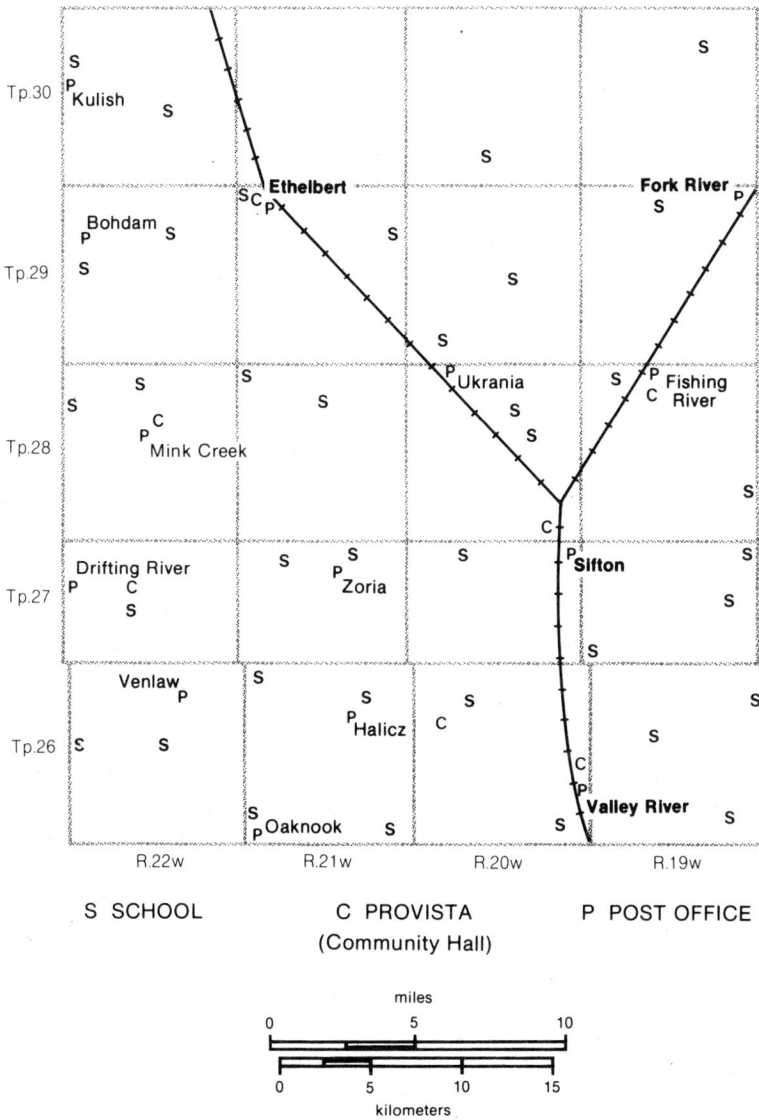

Figure 4. Public landscape: schools, reading halls, and post offices, ca 1925.

with their respective community halls scattered across the area, and more would be built in the years to come (fig. 4).[65] Throughout the early years and into mid-century these community halls and the reading clubs, drama societies, and other organizations affiliated with them helped maintain Ukrainian culture and encouraged public interchange of ideas.

Creating the Commercial Landscape

Commercial enterprise followed close on the heels of settlement in the Dauphin region as it did in the other Ukrainian settlements on the prairies. In 1897 a railway line was built through the eastern portion of what was to become the Ukrainian bloc settlement, extending north from Dauphin to Winnipegosis. The stations along it became the site of almost instant commercial development. In the same year the railroad was built, for example, John Kennedy opened a general store at the site of the present-day village of Sifton. A year later the village of Ethelbert came into existence when a branch line was extended northwest from a point near Sifton. The other train stations in the area also attracted commercial activity. Valley River, Fork River, Dnieper (later Fishing River), and Ukraina all owed their location, if not their very existence, to the railroad. Besides a store or two, each of these places soon had a post office and, with the exception of Ukraina, eventually one or more grain elevators. Dnieper and Ukraina stand out in another way. Modest though they were, they constitute the largest centres in the region with names that reflect the Ukrainian presence in the area.

Not all of the region's commercial activity took place along the railroad. Soon after settlement, enterprising farmers began to open small general stores. Basil Ksionzik, for example, is reported to have been operating a store (which was probably nothing more than a room in his house) in the Terebowla neighbourhood in 1899, just three years after his arrival.[66] Unfortunately, few details are available concerning the number or location of the other stores that operated in the Dauphin region. But what occurred in the Ukrainian bloc settlement of east-central Alberta suggests that Ksionzik's store was not the only one established during this pioneer period. More came into existence in the 1910s, after some of the more entrepreneurial settlers had managed to accumulate a bit of savings.[67]

Like the store and the railroad station, the post office marked a community's social and commercial links with the larger world. Postal services within the Ukrainian tract north of Dauphin expanded in a fashion parallel to that of country stores. Sifton received mail service in 1898, and by 1905 all of the railroad communities aside from Ukraina had a post office, as did the rural community of Venlaw in the southwest corner of the bloc. In response to a growing population and increased demand, six more post offices were opened between 1911 and 1915, all in the western or central portions of the district (fig. 4). The similarity in the pattern of post offices and stores was in at least some instances more than just coincidence. A store proprietor often doubled as the postmaster, thereby assuring the store customer traffic. In the early years, the sites of the central place functions not anchored to a train stop tended to shift from time to time. Some began as part of a private farmhouse. Later it became common for the country store and the post office to be located at a crossroads, frequently in conjunction with some other central place function such as a church, school, or community hall. The result was a hamlet containing three to six establishments that constituted a tangible manifestation of Ukrainian community life. In Ukraine community life centred around the *selo*, or village, where farmers lived and churches and various services were located. In Canada the township and range survey system and the federal government's refusal to suspend the section of the Homestead Act that stated that each homesteader must reside on his or her homestead hampered the immigrants' attempts to re-create their traditional settlement pattern. Rather than acquiesce entirely to the situation, the settlers located rural central place functions at the corners of four adjoining survey sections, thereby achieving the maximum amount of clustering possible given the circumstances. Sometimes a less compact settlement form evolved. In either case, however, the result was a hamlet that served as the focus for both social and economic activities in the neighbourhood.

A more detailed picture of the economic growth of the bloc settlement during the first few critical decades can be gained by examining the commercial expansion of the village of Sifton. At the turn of the century, the community consisted of a train station, a general store, and a post office. By 1902 a second general store had been added along with a farm implement dealership and a livery stable. A grain elevator was built in 1905, and the next year the village could boast of its own newspaper, the *Sifton Gazette*. As the name of the paper implies, the early residents and businessmen of the budding community were Anglo. One of the first exceptions to this trend was the Ruthenian Trading Company (Ruska Torhovelna Spilka), which opened for business shortly after the turn of the century.[68] In 1919, according to a fire underwriters' map, Sifton had a population of approximately 250 persons and contained two flour mills, two grain elevators, two lumberyards, a Bank of Commerce, numerous stores, a Presbyterian mission hospital, several schools, and at least three churches – a Ukrainian Catholic, a Ukrainian Orthodox, and a Presbyterian (later United) mission church. The last served mostly the merchants and businessmen of the community.[69] By this time more of the businesses were in the hands of Ukrainians, who now constituted a majority of Sifton's population.

By 1920 the Ukrainian settlers' imprint on the cultural landscape in the Dauphin bloc settlement was at or near its greatest extent. Land alienation had for all intents and purposes ceased. The population in the original area of Ukrainian settlement had reached its peak of 7,587 persons, a 128 per cent increase over the figure for 1901.[70] Clearly the pioneer stage had passed, and the social and economic infrastructures of the district were in place. On the farms, second-generation log houses had been erected and the farmsteads expanded to include sizeable clusters of special use buildings. Substantial acreages of land stood clear of trees and bush, and much of that acreage was under crop. The majority of the region's churches, schools, and community halls were in place, as were most of the economic institutions.

The Inter-war Years and Later

The 1920s and 1930s were a period of gradual economic and social adjustment for the Ukrainians in the bloc settlement north of Dauphin. The population declined slightly from its high of 1921, but overall remained stable. This was also a time of transition within the local economy. The production capabilities of individual farms continued to increase during the 1920s as more of the previously alienated land was cleared and planted. The First World War had provided many of the area's farmers with the opportunity to enter into the agricultural market economy for the first time. Having enjoyed the high commodity prices of those years, many Ukrainian farmers invested in new equipment in an effort to improve their efficiency. The more venturesome expanded operations by purchasing additional land from their Ukrainian neighbours or from Anglos residing on better land directly to the south of the bloc settlement. Some farmers found themselves overextended when the post-war recession struck and as a result suffered a setback, but most managed to weather the economic downturn and were in a more advantageous position when the commodity markets improved a few years later.

By the late 1920s and early 1930s evidence of this shift away from a self-sufficient farm economy and towards a market-oriented one could be seen in the landscape. Besides investing in more modern farm equipment, many farmers took the opportunity to make improvements to their homes. Thatch roofs were replaced by shingle roofs of lower pitch. Additions of various sorts were built on existing houses using milled lumber rather than logs. Existing log structures were sheathed in wood siding. In some instances entirely new houses were erected using milled lumber. These new buildings often deviated in other ways besides building materials from the traditional Ukrainian houses built a generation earlier. Sometimes the house form or room arrangement was modified, and even when the basic form was maintained, traditional features like large overhanging eaves were no longer incorporated in the design since the building's wooden siding did not need to be protected from rain the way mud-plastered walls did.[71] Builders became less concerned with orienting the front of the house to the south and more with orienting it to the road. The outbuildings constructed at this time were also frequently built with milled lumber. New barns sported gambrel roofs that allowed farmers to store feed hay in the loft rather than under a hay barrick or out in the open.[72] This innocuous change in a barn's roofline was clear evidence of a desire to make the farm operation more efficient and cost-effective.

Not everyone was in a position to benefit from the upscale farm prices of the war years. This was most decidedly the case for the farmers who occupied the more marginal lands. For them full integration into the market economy remained more a hope than a reality. For many in this position, off-farm employment remained an important, if not essential, activity. Not surprisingly, it was most frequently these marginal farm operations that were the first to be sold or abandoned.

This was also a time of technological transition. The radio and the telephone helped to break down the barriers of physical and social isolation and expedited the process of acculturation. But it was the internal combustion engine that had the greatest impact on the region, just as it did throughout North America. The internal combustion engine did two things for the farmer: it put him on a tractor that allowed him to farm more efficiently with fewer hands, and it put him behind the wheel of an automobile that allowed him and his family to travel greater distances for everyday goods and services. The impact of this technology was not felt overnight, of course, but by 1940 a third of the post offices in the bloc settlement had been closed, no doubt in part because of improved travel conditions.

The high farm commodity prices during the Second World War brought greater prosperity for those living in the Dauphin bloc settlement. Even the most marginal farmland in the region could be used to turn a profit. Outstanding debts could be retired, and by the war's end some farmers had accumulated enough savings to make major investments in their farms or to move their farming operations elsewhere. The war-time economy and the limited supply of labour meant that those without savings could leave the region feeling confident they would find employment. By the end of the Second World War the Dauphin region had been drawn into the national economy, and the people of Ukrainian heritage in the settlement were in a position to become fully integrated into Canadian life.[73]

The Dauphin Bloc Settlement Today

Today the Ukrainian settlement north of Dauphin is far different from what it was nearly a hundred years ago, when the first Ukrainian immigrant stepped off the train in that town, or even at mid-century. The population has declined precipitously in recent years; many of the local residents, especially the younger ones, have left for better opportunities elsewhere. Depopulation is writ large on the land in the form of vacant and abandoned houses and farm buildings. Agriculture remains the mainstay of the economy, but aside from some of the better land in the southern and particularly southwestern portion of the original settlement district, farming has shifted almost entirely away from grain farming to livestock raising – principally cattle. Average farm size has increased, but the Manitoba government has bought extensive areas of what were once private farms for use as community pasture. The more prosperous farms can be identified by modern houses, many of which were built in the 1960s or 1970s, when the farming economy was particularly strong. Once again the former farmhouse was recycled, so that it is now possible to see three generations of farmhouse on at least a few of the farmsteads.

Most of the churches stand vacant, some in a very sad state of repair. Several have been completely removed from the scene. The Ukrainian Catholic churches at Sifton and Mink Creek are the only ones in the entire area that remain active, and then only on a biweekly and monthly basis. Anyone who wishes to hear mass more frequently must travel to Dauphin or Winnipegosis. The rural schools have long been abandoned, and two years ago the elementary school at Sifton was closed. Now all the children in the region are bussed outside the original bloc settlement to Dauphin, Gilbert Plains, or Winnipegosis. The community halls are all boarded up, and the rural post offices have closed. The country stores at Mink Creek and Venlaw remain open but only on an irregular basis since the owners of both have essentially retired. A drive down the main street of the once bustling town of Sifton reveals more of the same. Of the dozen or so commercial and public buildings, only the post office, the credit union, and Kennedy's general store remain open. The last also serves as the local gas station. The only other commercial functions that continue to operate are a grain elevator and a lunch counter that doubles as a beer parlor. All the other commercial buildings and some of the houses stand derelict. The population, now about two hundred, is a third of what it was at its peak in the late 1940s. Most of the residents who are not retired commute to Dauphin to work. In the face of all of this decline the community has experienced a small amount of new construction. A twelve-unit retirement home has gone up in the past few years, as have half a dozen new houses in a small housing tract recently laid out on the edge of town.

Most of the cemeteries in the region remain active, and it is here that the most complete picture of the area's social transition during the past forty years can be seen. A survey of the grave markers reveals a number of important changes that extend well beyond the graveyard. The typical grave marker erected in the mid-1940s was made of cement in the shape of a cross inscribed in the Cyrillic alphabet. Today stone, most notably granite, has all but completely replaced cement, a clear sign of improved economic conditions. The style of the monument has also shifted from a free-standing cross to a block essentially identical in size and shape to those found in Anglo cemeteries. Simultaneously, the crosses have diminished greatly in size and are now shown in bas-relief on the face of the monument. All of this points to a decline in the importance of religion within Ukrainian society. Perhaps the most telling transition has been the dramatic drop in the use of the Ukrainian language. In the mid-1940s well over 80 per cent of the monuments were inscribed in Ukrainian. That figure remained over 50 per cent until the 1960s, but by the mid-1970s, Ukrainian had all but disappeared. The acculturation process was, for all intents and purposes, complete.

Conclusion

The creation and evolution of the cultural landscape in the Ukrainian bloc settlement north of Dauphin, Manitoba, like cultural landscapes everywhere, has been a long and involved process. The incidents and decisions that transformed this region from an unsettled wilderness to an entrenched ethnic community to a relic agricultural district are, of course, unique, but the general pattern by which the landscape of the Dauphin bloc settlement evolved is not unlike that of many of the other tracts of marginal land settled by Ukrainian immigrants at the end of the nineteenth century.

Considered from hindsight, the Ukrainian settlers' occupation of the treed lands of the parkland proved to be a mixed blessing. Given their financial constraints, environmental perceptions, and economic expectations, the decision to occupy less than ideal – but nonetheless arable – farmland seems to have been a prudent one for the first wave of Ukrainian pioneers. For those who came later, the decision to settle on what was at times clearly sub-marginal land in order to be close to relatives and acquaintances turned out to be extremely shortsighted in most instances.[74]

Regardless of where they settled, powerful forces of acculturation confronted Ukrainians upon their arrival in western Canada. The disruptive effects of migration and exposure to a dominant culture that spoke a different language, practised a different religion, and functioned under different social, economic, and political systems induced the settlers to modify and ultimately abandon many of their traditional practices and cultural traits. Many of these practices were not given up easily. At times acculturation was simply imposed, as in the basic settlement system, which disallowed the creation of traditional farm villages. The overall lack of economic landscape features that are distinctly Ukrainian within the region lends support to the contention that acculturation was most rapid in those aspects of life that were most closely linked to commercial activity. Buffered though they were by an environment that allowed them to remain partly self-sufficient, when it came to making a living the Ukrainian settlers had little choice but to adapt as quickly as possible to the Canadian system.[75] They were better able to retain their identity in those aspects of culture that were further removed from the marketplace. In the public landscape this was evident in the establishment of community halls, which served a social function within the community, and even more pronounced in the construction of churches, which functioned as symbols of ethnic as well as religious identity. An analogous situation developed around the ethnic landscape features erected on the basis of personal or familial decisions. The design and construction of the first- and second-generation Ukrainian farmhouse are the most obvious statement of ethnic identity of this sort. Grave markers comprise a second set of features that display personal attitudes as they relate to social and economic as well as religious matters.

Research on immigrant communities elsewhere in North America suggests that several factors slowed the rate of loss of cultural traits. One was the physical size of the ethnic community: the larger an ethnic community's territorial base the greater its ability to resist assimilation.[76] A second factor was the isolation imposed by the cultural distinctiveness of the ethnic group. A third was a strong sense of cohesiveness among the minority group in regard to common community or family background. Finally, strong ties between the immigrant church and the community encouraged the retention of some cultural traits.[77] All these factors certainly came into play among the Ukrainians who settled in the Dauphin district. Indeed, the factors reinforced one another, thereby increasing the immigrants' will to resist acculturation. Add to these the settlement district's limited potential for commercial agriculture, which not only restricted external economic influences but also helped bind the Ukrainian community together in the face of economic adversity, and it is small wonder that the Ukrainian cultural landscape remains to this day as extensive and conspicuous as it is.

This landscape remains visible to all who wish to see. Most of the old farmhouses are gone, many bulldozed to make room for other things, but a scattering of second-generation houses can still be found, along with some log outbuildings. A larger proportion of the public structures has survived. The situation is much the same in Ukrainian bloc settlements elsewhere. There have been modest efforts to preserve old Ukrainian buildings in the Dauphin area by moving them to a common site in an effort to create a 'theme' park.[78] Unfortunately, although a few buildings are preserved by such efforts, the geographical setting within which the collected buildings are displayed is totally artificial, a gross distortion of the actual settlement environment as it existed. Instead of moving a few select buildings to a designated site, the buildings, along with their associated artifacts, need to be preserved *in situ*, thereby capturing a far more comprehensive and authentic perspective not just of the buildings but of the cultural landscape as well. Historic landscapes can be protected only by creating rural preservation districts. None at present exist in Canada, but heritage conservation districts are in place in the United States and Europe.[79] There is no reason why such an arrangement could not be used to preserve representative cultural landscapes in one or more of the Ukrainian blocs of western Canada. The fact that this type of preservation effort need not require immense amounts of government funds adds a further incentive. However, a critical time is rapidly approaching in regard to the Ukrainian ethnic landscapes of the region. Unless something is initiated within the next few years, much of what is worth preserving will be lost, and the whole of Canada will be the poorer for it.

'Non-Preferred' People: Inter-war Ukrainian Immigration to Canada

BRIAN OSBORNE

I wonder who was the last Ukrainian off the last boat in 1914? That year marked the outbreak of the Great War and also the end of the 'Great Canadian Migration.' Some 2.5 million immigrants had entered Canada during the Laurier-Sifton years, 1896–1914. Among them were over 170,000 'Ukrainians.'[1] Armistice Day, 1918, marked the cessation of hostilities, and Canada, faced with the possible renewal of the pre-war mass migration, re-evaluated its immigration policy. My apocryphal Ukrainian of 1914 had made it just in time.

Ultimately, another 1.6 million persons were admitted during the 1919–39 period, including 68,000 Ukrainians.[2] But the immigration experience of those entering Canada during the inter-war years differed in many ways from that of the previous generation. Both the European and Canadian contexts of the inter-war immigration had changed. In fact, they would never be the same again.

For a start, Europe had changed. The Ukrainians who entered Canada during the Laurier-Sifton migration were primarily from the Habsburg-controlled regions of Eastern Galicia and northern Bukovyna, with relatively few from Greater Ukraine, which was in the tight grip of the Russian tsars. But following the First World War, the political map of Europe had been redrawn, although President Wilson's concern for 'national self-determination' did nothing for the cause of Ukrainian nationalism. The independent Ukrainian republic proclaimed in 1919 was short-lived. Greater Ukraine fell under the control of the Soviets, and Western Ukraine was partitioned between three political neologisms. Thus, Poland acquired Eastern Galicia, Kholm, Polissia, and western Volhynia; much of Bukovyna and Bessarabia fell to Romania; and the 'Ruthenians' of Carpatho-Ukraine were assigned to Czechoslovakia.

Ukrainians constituted large minorities in all these new states, the seven million in Poland amounting to some 25 per cent of the national population and 91 per cent of that of Eastern Galicia. Moreover, the other Wilsonian idealistic premise, the 'protection of the rights of minorities,' was realized only in Czechoslovakia. In both Poland and Romania, nationalist zeal was directed at the cultural and economic oppression of the Ukrainian population. Not surprisingly, therefore, the bulk of the Ukrainian immigration to Canada and elsewhere during the inter-war years emanated from Poland, Romania, and to some degree, Czechoslovakia. The main destinations for the estimated 200,000 who left were Argentina (44,000), France (36,000), the United States (12,000), and Belgium (8,000). The largest contingent, 67,578, moved to Canada, but it was a Canada markedly different from that of the pre-war immigrant experience.[3]

Many of the Laurier-Sifton Ukrainians had been located in large bloc settlements throughout the brush-covered northern prairies from southeastern Manitoba to east-central Alberta. They served as nuclei for the inter-war arrivals. Much land had been cleared; the railways were established and expanding; and a system of cities, towns, and villages served the rural areas. The major districts of Ukrainian settlement all hosted Ukrainian Catholic, Orthodox, and Protestant churches and a well-established Ukrainian community structure in the process of developing a network of regional, national, and international linkages. By the commencement of the post-war period, the development of the Canadian West was well under way.

But there was still a demand for more settlers. Dr W.J. Black, the director of the CNR's Department of Colonization and Agriculture, argued that although railways needed four hundred people per mile of track to be economically viable, Canada had about three hundred per mile overall, and only one hundred per mile in the prairies.[4] However, it was estimated in 1921 that some 190,000 vacant homesteads amounting to 30 million acres were still available along the northern edge of the prairies. Of these, 100,000 were in the Athabasca, Grande Prairie, and Peace River districts of Alberta, 40,000 in the northern fringe of the Saskatchewan parklands, and 34,000 in northwest Manitoba and the Interlake region. Another 34 million acres of abandoned homesteads were dispersed throughout the settled areas and within fifteen miles of rail.[5] Further, other immigrants were needed as agricultural labourers and domestics in a farming economy that had heavy demands for man-power in the fields and woman-power in the homesteads.

These were the essential parameters of the inter-war Ukrainian migra-tion: a movement to Canada of 67,578 Ukrainians, mostly from Poland, Romania, and Czechoslovakia. Intended for rural destinations through-out the prairie West, many moved to farms in established areas of Ukrainian settlement or pioneered in new areas of frontier development. But others – especially the labourers – gravitated to cities, industry, and non-agricultural pursuits. Furthermore, all Ukrainians were becoming more visible and sensitized to the need for cultural and political survival. The very migration of the newcomers was a product, directly or indi-rectly, of their concept of Ukraine and being Ukrainian. Accordingly, many welcomed the establishment of societies that nurtured their ideol-ogy of patriotic nationalism such as the United Hetman Organization and the Ukrainian National Federation of Canada. For those of more radical bent, left-wing organizations such as the Ukrainian Labour-Farmer Temple Association (ULFTA) flourished during the depression years.[6]

The Canadian reaction to this reality, and to immigration in general, was remarkable and was reflected in the new assumptions, new priorit-ies, and new processes in immigration policy. The new assumptions were a formalization of long-held views regarding ethnic differences and their significance for Canadian nation building. In 1919–39, these assumptions were implemented as explicit criteria for establishing priori-ties in the immigration policy. And these assumptions and priorities were administered by new procedures for inspecting, admitting, and monitoring the subsequent progress of immigrants – or at least some of them. Henceforth, the new concerns were with 'selection' and 'quotas.'

Establishing Priorities, 1918–1925

For the first few years following the First World War, continental immi-gration continued to be interrupted by unsettled conditions throughout much of Central Europe and by post-war economic adjustments. Accord-ingly, Canada did not reactivate an aggressively pro-immigration pos-ture. Immigration was regulated by the terms of the Immigration Act of 1910, and only particular categories of immigrants were encouraged to enter, categories that reflected historical links, ethnographic assump-tions, economic conditions, and ideological concerns.

One of the first post-war priorities was the reception and settlement of thousands of Canadian and British ex-servicemen and their families. Assistance was afforded by passage grants from the Imperial Government and assistance in land settlement through the Soldier Settlement Board.[7] Commenced in 1917, its scope and powers extended in 1920, this Canadian initiative was but a part of a grand design of post-war imperial restructuring. The passage of the Empire Settlement Act on 31 May 1922 formalized co-operation between Britain and her dominions in the field of emigration and colonization, to the mutual benefit of both. One prominent initiative introduced in 1924, 'the 3,000 Families scheme,' attracted 3,349 families and resulted in the final establishment of 1,981 operating farms.[8]

Preoccupied as it was with integrating the returning soldiers into Canadian society according to grand designs of imperial development, Canada did not return to pre-war immigration levels. Further, a post-war economic recession in Canada, together with social and political unrest in Europe, argued against large-scale international movements. Not until the normalization of the economic and political contexts did immigration pick up. Thus, by 1920, dependents of immigrants established in Canada were allowed to enter, provided they passed muster in terms of health, ideology, and documentation.[9] These flows were regulated by the terms of the Immigration Act of 1910. The interpretation of this legislation, however, crystallized around two important imperatives concerning the Canadian economy and society.

First, Canada favoured those immigrants who would advance agricultural settlement and contribute to the development of natural resources. With improved prospects for agriculture in 1922, C.A. Stewart, the acting minister of immigration and colonization, commented: 'I know that Canada needs between 3,000,000 and 4,000,000 more citizens, I am anxious to bring in people.' He added a cautionary note: 'the people we bring in must be able to establish themselves and they must be farmers,' care being taken 'not to swell the ranks of the unemployed.'[10] A year later, the Immigration Act was amended by order in council PC 183: British and United States immigrants were allowed virtually unrestricted entry; other nationals were admitted only if they had sufficient means to establish farms or were farm labourers or domestic servants.[11] Thus was established the economic profile for permissible immigration from the continent during the inter-war years: farmers, farm labourers, and domestics.

It was more complicated than this, however. Other assumptions in the air at the time also coloured the selection process. A reputable authority of the day contextualizes the underlying attitudes that were closing the gates in the United States and Canada:

A line drawn across the continent of Europe from northeast to southwest, separating the Scandinavian Peninsula, the British Isles, Germany, and France from Russia, Austria-Hungary, Italy, and Turkey, separates countries not only of distinct races but also of distinct civilizations. It separates Protestant Europe from Catholic Europe; it separates countries of representative institutions and popular government from absolute monarchies; it separates lands where education is universal from lands where illiteracy predominates; it separates manufacturing countries, progressive agriculture, and skilled labour from primitive hand industries, backward agriculture, and unskilled labour; it separates an educated, thrifty peasantry from a peasantry scarcely a single generation removed from serfdom; it separates Teutonic races from Latin, Slav, Semitic, and Mongolian races.[12]

During and after the First World War, such views were exacerbated by a surge of patriotic 'nativism.' A 'red scare' combined with hostility to nationals from the Central Powers of the First World War engendered antagonism to the European immigrants who had settled in blocs in the West. Not surprisingly, therefore, Canada beefed up its already stringent immigration restrictions. Section 38, clause (c), of the 1910 Act prohibited 'immigrants belonging to any race deemed unsuited to the climatic requirements of Canada, or of immigrants of any specified class, occupation, or character.'[13] In 1919, this clause was made even more restrictive to exclude 'immigrants belonging to any nationality or race or of immigrants of any specified class or occupation, by reason of any economic, industrial or other condition temporarily existing in Canada or because such immigrants are deemed unsuitable having regard to the climatic, industrial, social, educational, labour or other conditions or requirements of Canada or because such immigrants are deemed undesirable owing to their peculiar customs, habits, modes of life and methods of holding property, and because of their probable inability to become readily assimilated or to assume the duties and responsibilities of Canadian citizenship within a reasonable time after their entry.'[14]

In 1919, special orders in council prevented the admission of subjects of Austria-Hungary, Germany, Bulgaria, and Turkey (PC 1203) and Doukhobors, Hutterites, and Mennonites (PC 1204). Such groups were excluded because of their 'peculiar customs, habits, modes of living and methods of holding property' and also because of their unfortunate location in states that had been hostile during the recent war.[15] Another immigrant official was even more blunt: 'At the present moment, we are casting about for some more effective method than we have in operation to prevent the arrival here of many of the nondescript of Europe, whose coming is regarded more in the light of a catastrophe than anything else.'[16]

These actions and attitudes were diagnostic of the sentiments of the day. In fact, during these years, immigrants were unofficially classified as 'preferred,' 'non-preferred,' and 'special permit.' Though never used in immigration legislation, regulations, or annual reports, this terminology was common in correspondence between officials and was central to the conduct of immigration up to the Second World War and even after.

Those considered to be 'suited' to the requirements of Canada were the residents of the British Isles, the United States, Norway, Sweden, Denmark, Iceland, France, Belgium, Holland, Switzerland, and, eventually, Germany. Those said to be 'unsuited' or 'non-preferred' were nationals from the rest of Europe: Austria, Hungary, Poland, Romania, the Baltic States, Yugoslavia, Czechoslovakia, and Germany (for a period after the First World War). The 'special permit' immigrants included Albanians, Arabians, Armenians, Bulgarians, East Indians, Greeks, Hebrews, Italians, Japanese, Maltese, Negroes, Persians, Portuguese, Spanish, Spanish-Americans, Syrians, Turks – and many others. These required special permission to enter Canada.[17]

But the growing demand for agricultural labour, and the failure of the 'preferred' countries to provide it, necessitated that at least some 'non-preferred' peoples be allowed to enter. In 1923, James A. Robb, the newly appointed minister of immigration and colonization, recognized the need to 'encourage the migration of those ... able and willing to settle on the land and assist in agricultural development.' The policy was still one of 'Imperial and British preference' for those 'in the cradle of the British Empire to proceed to and successfully settle in the Dominion.'[18] But, henceforth, at least some of the 'non-preferred' had to be tolerated.

The railway companies welcomed the prospect of increased traffic. The CPR's interests transcended traffic alone, and it had long been involved in parlaying its twenty-five million acres into settlements, and promoting immigration into, and development of, its territories. It embarked on an even more aggressive colonization mission with the establishment in 1916 of its Department of Colonization and Development.[19] The motives for this were clear at least to President E.W. Beatty: 'We have huge railway systems which can only be maintained by traffic and increased traffic can only be secured by agricultural expansion in the West, the proper utilization of our resources in mines and timber and consequent industrial expansion in the East.'[20]

The CPR's competitor, the newly formed CNR, held similar views. Having acquired the colonization interests of the Grand Trunk Pacific and the Department of Industrial Resources of the Canadian Northern, the new president of the CNR, Sir Henry Thornton, urged a more dynamic and comprehensive view of his company's activities in immigration, colonization, and settlement. Accordingly, on 20 February 1923, the CNR Department of Colonization and Development came into being. A set of progressive and patriotic principles underscored the fit between corporate and national priorities: 'the immigration and satisfactory settlement in Canada of the largest possible number of people of productive capacity which the country can absorb and assimilate'; the dissemination of information concerning the 'vast and extensive natural resources of the Dominion'; the promotion of the settlement of new Canadians 'to enjoy such social and religious institutions as are necessary to individual happiness and contentment'; 'the immigration of young people of desirable type and character, especially from Great Britain'; the development of 'effective means of selecting immigrants physically fit and anxious for work'; and the promotion of 'all measures calculated to contribute toward an increase in immigration of adaptable people and in their settlement under the most favourable conditions possible.'[21]

References to 'people of productive capacity,' 'absorb and assimilate,' 'young people of desirable type and character,' and the selection of 'immigrants physically fit and anxious to work' all sent out the signal that the CNR would play the immigration game by the rules of the day. The central message was clear: national and corporate views of immigration and settlement were compatible – at least initially.

Thus, in June 1924, the government authorized the '650 Continental Families Scheme,' and in the following year the '1,000 Continental Families Scheme' and the '200 Families Scheme' were launched.[22] Families from all of the 'preferred' countries were eligible, but for the rest of the continent, selection was restricted to those from Hungary, Yugoslavia (excepting Dalmatians, who were too dark in complexion), Germany, Poland, and Czechoslovakia.[23] All three schemes met with limited success: only nine families for the '650 scheme,' eighty-eight for the '1000 scheme,' and thirty-eight for the '200 scheme.' However, some 3,600 farm workers from Yugoslavia, Czechoslovakia, and Hungary had also been admitted in 1924, another 6,727 arriving in 1925.[24]

Others were exploring more elaborate initiatives. Thus, Albert Dubuc, a Winnipeg lawyer, succeeded in interesting Bishop Budka of the Ukrainian Greek Catholic church, representatives of the French Line, Major John Barnett of the Soldier Settlement Board, and the government of Quebec in locating thousands of Ukrainians throughout Manitoba and Quebec.[25] Barnett stated his interests clearly: 'We have a great problem in resettling these particular lands on account of the pioneer difficulties involved, and because we cannot hope to put on them Anglo-Saxons ... I feel quite sure that Ruthenian peasant people, if selected carefully, with the aid of Greek priests, can be successfully established to their own advantage, and to the advantage of the Board and the country.'[26]

Dubuc was nothing if not ambitious. His grandiose estimates were based upon the somewhat questionable premises that if the 5,000 parishes in Western Ukraine would yield a mere three families each, they would generate 15,000 families or some 120,000 persons! Dubuc spoke of using Eastern Galician priests to screen out the 'Bolshevik influence' and was confident that Poland would co-operate in ridding itself of its seven million Ukrainians, 'who form a big Ireland' there.[27] Dubuc ultimately delivered only two families, but he did succeed in mobilizing Ukrainian interest, establishing contacts with leading figures in the Ukrainian Greek Catholic church, and demonstrating the need for overseas networks.

Ultimately, some 700,000 immigrants entered Canada between 1919 and 1924, with the low of 64,224 in 1922 more than doubling to 133,729 persons in 1923 and 124,163 in 1924. But only 3,700 Ukrainians entered during these years as continued unrest in Europe and discriminatory legislation kept the doors tightly closed.[28] But times were changing. Clearly, the agricultural sector of the 1920s economy required labour. The areas favoured for cultural-historical reasons were not providing it in sufficient numbers, and so an active promotion of 'continental' immigration was initiated. 'Non-preferred' they may have been, but needed they very definitely were.

1925–1930: Dividing Responsibilities

By 1925, therefore, there were signs of increased immigration activity, and the two railway companies were refining their organization to handle it. In that year, the CPR and CNR prepared a proposal for co-operation between the government and their respective colonization departments regarding immigration from the 'non-preferred' nations.[29] Although they recognized the importance of continued immigration from Great Britain, they advocated a more efficient system whereby they and not government immigration officers would recruit, inspect, and approve immigrants from 'non-preferred' areas.

The 'Railways Agreement' signed on 1 September 1925 granted authority to the CNR and CPR to select, transport, and locate certain categories of immigrants. The ones to be so favoured were 'agriculturalists, agricultural workers, and domestic servants from countries provided for by existing laws and regulations.'[30] It was also noted that the railways had a vested interest and expertise in this process 'by reason of their special interest in the early settlement of available unoccupied lands and their transportation facilities by land and sea.' Ominously, the agreement also stipulated that the railways would return to their home states those immigrants who, 'refusing to engage in agriculture, agricultural labour or domestic service in Canada, shall become public charges within the period of one year from the date of their admission to Canada.'[31]

Deputy Minister F.C. Blair of the Ministry of Immigration and Colonization outlined the workings of the system: 'The Railways will each place accredited agents with Canadian experience and free from the control of steamship companies in the various countries from which immigrants are drawn. These accredited agents will issue the certificate ... The certificates will have to do with occupation ... On the presentation of the certificate our officer, if satisfied that the immigrant complies with the regulations, will issue a visa and the immigrant will come forward to be placed by the company that started him from Canada.'[32] Accordingly, Dominion government inspection officers were established at such main points as Riga, Danzig, Hamburg, Rotterdam, Antwerp, and Paris. Henceforth, inspection to ensure compliance with rules concerning economic resources, occupational type, ethnicity, literacy, and health was effected prior to departure rather than on arrival in Canada.

The terms of the Railways Agreement required the railways to operate a parallel set of structures. Both companies managed their European colonization affairs from offices in London. They also maintained district offices in London, Liverpool, Glasgow, and Belfast and ran their continental business from offices in Oslo, Gothenburg, Copenhagen, and Rotterdam. These were well placed for serving immigrants from the 'preferred' countries. Following the 1925 Railways Agreement, however, arrangements had to be made to service the 'non-preferred' countries. Central to this function were the 'certificate issuing officers,' who issued certificates guaranteeing employment as agriculturalists and carried out preliminary checks for literacy and health. With these in hand, prospective immigrants could then be processed expeditiously by Dominion officers issuing visas. The CNR located two CIOs in Warsaw, one each in Prague and Zagreb, and part-time officers in Paris, Antwerp, and Rotterdam.[33]

Although employment criteria were the primary basis of selection, ethnic prescriptions were also made explicit. In the first month of the Railways Agreement, Deputy Minister W.J. Egan listed the countries to which 'it is understood it applies': the British Isles, the United States, France, Belgium, Holland, Switzerland, Denmark, Norway, Sweden, Finland, Estonia, Latvia, Lithuania, Russia, Poland, Germany, Czechoslovakia, Yugoslavia, Austria, Hungary, and Romania. Although no reference was made to 'preferred' and 'non-preferred' immigrants, the need for careful selection was not neglected: 'It is understood and agreed that care will be taken to secure only the best types of settlers. All the countries contain people that Canada cannot absorb, and some of them contain very large numbers. For example, we do not want all classes from Russia. In fact, the classes in Russia now wanted in Canada are comparatively few. From Rumania, we want especially the German and Hungarian types.'[34]

This preference for 'German types' was a leitmotif of the inter-war years. Thus, Black communicated that 'the Minister's attitude, and as a matter of fact his statement was that outside the countries originally listed as preferred we should not take anybody excepting those of German race.'[35] This preference within the 'preferred' and 'non-preferred' system had long been implemented. Thus, at the height of the Railways Agreement, 1,520 families were handled by the CNR's colonization department in 1928. Of these, only 259 were 'preferred,' 32 coming from Germany. But of the 1,269 'non-preferred' families admitted that year, 633 were categorized as 'German non-preferred,' a much larger group than the 381 Ukrainians or 225 Poles.[36] Increasingly, therefore, the colonization business throughout Poland, Czechoslovakia, and Hungary continued, but with a priority given to those of 'German race.'

By 1929, the terminology, if not the underlying philosophy of immigration, was being sanitized. In that year, Black advised his regional officers throughout the Western District that the Dominion Department of Immigration had decided to discontinue entirely the terms 'preferred' and 'non-preferred.' Henceforth, Northwestern Europe was to be used for the 'so-called preferred' countries; Central Europe was to be used for the 'former non-preferred'; all other European states were henceforth Southern Europe; and the Near East was to be used for the part of Asia that adjoined Europe.[37] Clearly, there were sensitivities about the matter.

During the years 1925–30, over 800,000 immigrants entered Canada, with 166,783 entering in the peak year of 1928. The large numbers recruited from Central and Eastern Europe were made up of many farm families, but more were unattached labourers and domestics. Among them, were some 55,000 Ukrainians, who constituted the largest national group admitted during these years. The numbers tell the story. Only 2,245 Ukrainians were admitted in 1925. This increased to 9,534 in 1926 and to 16,000 in 1928.[38]

The Railways Agreement also required that once the immigrants had been approved and admitted, 'distribution, placement and such supervision as the new settlers may require after their arrival in Canada, shall be undertaken by the Parties to this Agreement on the basis of joint responsibility.'[39]

Both the CPR and the CNR had well-developed organizations in place ready for the commencement of the Railways Agreement.[40] In many ways, they were very similar. Although both maintained corporate headquarters at Montreal, the centre of their colonization enterprises was Winnipeg, with district offices located in all of the western provinces and the midwest United States. Moreover, each railway's colonization enterprise had developed liaison organizations to manage the interface between the railway and settlement businesses: the Canadian Colonization Association and the Canadian National Land Association served as land brokers and estate managers for the CPR and CNR respectively.

But there were differences in the companies' modes of operation. Thus, initially the CPR made use of a well-developed network of affiliated organizations and 'settlement clubs' whose members helped sponsor and settle friends and relatives throughout their sponsors' territories. By 1928, there were 25 federally chartered colonization associations supported by 138 local colonization boards. The ethnic profile of the CPR's southern prairie settlement field was dominated by British, Ontario-British, American, and Scandinavian settlers, although contacts were also maintained with Mennonites, Hungarians, German Roman Catholics, and German Lutherans. Although its contacts with the 'non-preferred' nations were relatively weak, it did bring in some Czechs, Slovaks, Austrians, and Ukrainians.[41] Ukrainian staff were appointed to assist in this area, but increasingly the CPR relied upon three regional settlement agencies: the Confederation Land Corporation in Edmonton, the Greek Orthodox Ukrainian Colonization Board in Saskatoon, and the Greek Catholic Ukrainian Settlers Aid Association in Winnipeg. Between them, they accounted for more than half of the CPR's allocation of continental immigrants.[42]

Unlike the CPR with its system of affiliated agencies, the CNR relied upon some 400 part-time field operatives who surveyed settlement possibilities, met immigrants, and assisted in locating them. There were also 2,221 station agents throughout Canada who participated in the colonization effort by acting as contact points for new settlers. Another difference was that whereas the CPR benefited from its co-operation with its affiliate, the CP steamship line, the CNR had developed contacts with no fewer than a dozen major transatlantic carriers of the day. The CNR's 'Allied Steamship Companies' reads like an inventory of the age of transatlantic ocean travel. However, despite this diversity of carriers, some 77 per cent of a total of 739 families settled by the CNLSA in 1927 were carried by four lines: the Baltic-American (153), the Scandinavian-American (149), the Cunard (144), and the White Star (122).[43]

Further, the principal continental bloc settlements were in the CNR's settlement field, and the company enjoyed particularly strong links with Ukrainian groups. Ukrainians were appointed to the colonization staff, and links were forged with community leaders.[44] In 1924, the CNR was instrumental in establishing the St Raphael's Ukrainian Immigration Welfare Association in Canada with Bishop Budka, the leader of the Ukrainian Greek Catholic church, as its first president.[45] The association established links with the Ukrainian Emigration Aid Association in Lviv, worked closely with the CNR and the Cunard line, and attained a semi-official status as an immigration agency. Four years later, the CNR's colonization people could comment about the Ukrainian Catholic church that 'our Department has been very closely associated with this Church organization in the past, and we feel safe in predicting that the very best co-operation may be counted on from them during the coming year.[46]

An insight into the CNR's system may be gained from a consideration of its several categories that further refined the ethnic-economic priorities of the day. Table 1 displays the specifications for the Cunard Line's quota for 1929. The 'nationalities' referred to were from the 'non-preferred' countries, categorized by the capital possessed by each family. All were required to travel directly to Winnipeg and be 'fully experienced agricultural people.' There were other specifications as well.

Scheme 'X' families had no restrictions other than having to arrive between 15 March and 31 October. Scheme 'A' families were to be

TABLE 1
CNR's 1929 allocation under the 'Continental Family Settlement
Programme' (numbers of families)

| | Schemes (minimum capital requirements) | | | | |
| | 'X' | 'A' | 'B' | 'C' | 'J' |
Nationalities	$1,000	$500	$250	$100	$100
German-speaking	100	140	17	17	15
Ukrainian	100	70	26	12	12
Polish	100	35	8	5	3
Hungarian	100	8	–	–	–
Lithuanian	100	–	–	–	–

Source: 'Continental Family Settlement, Western Canada, 1929,'
RG 30, vol. 8400, NAC.

parents of mature age and with not more than one or two children
under six years, had to be 'prepared to take up pioneer propositions in
outlying districts,' and had to arrive between 15 April and 1 September.
Scheme 'B' families constituted parents of mature age, with no more
than two or three children under twelve years and no children under
five or six, and were to be advised that they would be placed in outlying
districts, under pioneer conditions, and would probably have to erect
their own buildings and work out for a number of years. They were to
arrive between 1 May and 1 August.

Scheme 'C' and 'J' families had even more stringent requirements
imposed on them. Because of their poor capital resources, it was stipulated that they had to be 'agriculturalists without previous residence in
Canada or the United States, accustomed to manual labour,' and would
be required to sign an agreement, written in their own language, to
accept farm employment under the CNR's direction on arrival. Moreover, these families were to be told that they would be placed in 'outlying
districts, under pioneer conditions,' and would probably have to 'erect
their own buildings and work out for a number of years.' Both 'C' and
'J' families were expected to arrive between 15 March and 15 May, and
preferably in April. Additional restrictions and demands were placed on
the 'J' scheme: families were to consist of parents between twenty-one
and forty years of age, with no more than three children under fifteen,
and none under three years; parents were to be prepared to take separate employment if necessary.

There were several other schemes during this period: 'L' and 'M' for
German Lutherans, 'T' for German Baptists, 'P' and 'K' for German
Catholics, 'S' for families with less than fifty dollars in capital who were

proceeding to employment with friends and relatives. Nothing better demonstrates the degree to which the new principles of selection and monitoring of immigrants were implemented during these inter-war years – but only for the 'non-preferred' farming families. Less care was taken in overseeing and regulating the immigration of labourers. They proved to be a very vexatious element of the Railways Agreement migration.

At first, there was little public reaction and even a degree of measured support as evidenced by the report on the CPR colonization activities for 1927: 'Notwithstanding some adverse criticisms of a too large per-centage of other than Anglo-Saxon stock in the immigration totals for the year, it may safely be said that by far the larger majority in the West are favourable to increased immigration, and are favourable to the Central Europeans of selected agricultural type to undertake the pioneering work necessary for the agricultural development of the West, to lay a sound foundation of largely increased British immigration for industrial pursuits made possible by the agricultural development.'[47]

Such corporate rhetoric was predictable: But 1927 saw the beginnings of a public concern that was to intensify throughout the rest of the decade. The perennial 'red scare,' claims of the dilution of Anglo-Saxon stock by foreigners, and the droughts and economic trauma of the late twenties all served to foment a public outcry against immigration. Furthermore, an oversupply of farm labourers resulted in the very visible presence of Europeans looking for work in cities, logging camps, and industrial sites. But if the government was concerned that immigrants were moving from the country to the cities, some were concerned that too many were staying on the farms. The resolution from the Craigmyle branch of the United Farm Workers of America may be taken as repre-sentative of the popular economic and cultural concerns:

We understand that practically all the new settlers coming here are brought in by the Canadian Colonization Company and are from Central and Southern Europe. We very strongly object to such large numbers of these people coming into our district with practically no Anglo-Saxons. Last year there were over thirty families and this year we understand double that number will come to the Craigmyle-Hanna district. Kindly let us know if there is no way to arrange that at least an equal number of Anglo-Saxons be sent with them to this district as we are unable to assimilate so many of foreign extraction and they will soon dominate our district which is not the desire of those of us who wish to make permanent homes here and which is surely not the desire of our Government.[48]

Such pathetic cries did not lack champions. The ridiculous posturings of the KKK were directed against 'the uncontrolled influx of garlic-smelling, Catholic immigrants from Eastern Europe; Ukrainians, as the largest such group, were ... a prime target of attack.'[49] The RCMP turned its attention to the Ukrainian Labour-Farmer Temple Association, which was reported as being 'well known to us as a definite communist organization.'[50] In 1928, the peak immigration year, the House of Commons referred the problem to a Select Standing Committee on Agriculture and Colonization, and its recommendations addressed the abuses perpetrated by the system, the public's fears, and the worsening economic conditions.

The writing was on the wall. In 1929, Gardiner's pro-immigration Liberal government was defeated in Saskatchewan. Public protests intensified as the economy worsened. The federal government responded by lowering its annual immigration quotas. In 1930, with the victory of Bennett's Conservatives, who had campaigned on a strong anti-immigration platform, European immigration to Canada came to a virtual stop.

Understandably, the railways looked back on the previous five-year experiment from a different perspective. The CNR's performance in settling continental agriculturalists, and the degree to which it monitored the programme, are demonstrated in table 2.

Perhaps attempting to draw attention away from the disastrous programme that had introduced thousands of single male labourers, the two railway companies reported that, under the terms of the Railways Agreement, they had brought to Canada 10,302 families from the 'non-preferred' countries. These had brought with them some $2.74 million in 'recorded' capital, the real figure probably being much higher. And, assuming that each family settled on the land would generate $746.33 in traffic earnings per annum, the bottom line was that 'the above families will produce an annual revenue for the Railways of $7,688,691.66.' The figure was right down to the last sixty-six cents! Families from the British Isles and the 'so-called preferred countries' numbered 4,537 in the same period, the estimated railway revenue from this group amounting to $3.4 million. Further, the presidents reported that no less than 5,758,431 acres of 'new breaking' had taken place on lands adjacent to their railway lines throughout the prairie provinces. They recognized that although not all of this was effected by new settlers, much had been cleared 'either by Continental farm labour or [by] settlers from Continental countries. The stimulation to agricultural

TABLE 2
Families settled by the CNR under the Railways Agreement

	1926	1927	1928	1929	1930	Total
Purchased lands	–	181	377	425	244	1,227
Rented lands	–	36	62	62	46	213
Homesteads	–	75	136	259	230	700
Farm employment	–	25	108	240	63	436
Settled, no details	–	–	–	–	42	42
Settlement pending	–	45	129	54	248	476
Returned east	–	37	49	41	38	165
In cities	–	11	28	15	8	62
In USA	–	–	2	–	–	2
Returned to Europe	–	–	3	1	1	5
Government families	200	93	–	–	–	293
German refugees	–	–	–	–	33	33
Disappeared	–	82	45	103	62	292
Nominated families	84	117	86	56	–	343
Totals	284	702	1,032	1,256	1,015	4,289

Source: J.S. McGowan to Dr W. Black, 11 December 1930, RG 30, vol. 8337, file 3070–31, NAC.

production from this class of colonization effort has been one of the major factors in our immigration. The facts recited, we consider, prove conclusively that the families referred to are a real asset to Canada.'[51]

However, no amount of corporate boosterism could reverse the decision to cut back immigration. The Railways Agreement was over, and Black, the head of CNR's colonization department, recognized the implications: 'The outlook for this year has never been at all bright, and it is even less so now than at any previous time. In fact, you may practically take it for granted that no immigrants of any kind, other than wives and children, will be admitted to Canada from those countries which in times past were classified as "non-preferred." The Railways Agreement is a thing of the past and we have no longer any need for Certificate Issuing Officers because there will be nothing whatever for them to do until times change.'[52]

1930–1939: Regulating the Flow

The Railways Agreement was allowed to run out on 31 August 1930. Moreover, in March 1931, 'having regard to the unemployment conditions now temporarily existing in Canada,' a new order in council, PC 695, amended section 38 of the Immigration Act yet again. After 18

March 1931, 'the landing in Canada of immigrants of all classes and occupations' was prohibited, excepting British and United States subjects, wives and children of Canadian residents, and agriculturalists 'having sufficient means to farm in Canada.'[53]

A mere 130,000 immigrants entered Canada in the 1930s, with a low of 11,277 in 1935. The doors were closed to all 'non-preferred' immigrants, except those with sufficient resources to establish farms, and fewer than 7,000 Ukrainians entered Canada during these years. The major slackening occurred in 1931–5. The movement of large numbers of single labourers had been terminated, and since only agricultural families with capital were admitted, the intake of qualified Ukrainians dropped to mere dozens per annum. Another factor was the intransigence of the Polish government.[54] The Piłsudski regime wanted to maximize the benefits of outmigration by shedding itself of excess population and unwanted groups and by developing Poland's shipping and ports. The ensuing conflict resulted in Canada's withdrawal of immigration inspection officers from Poland in 1931, all potential travellers to Canada having to be cleared at Hamburg, Rotterdam, Amsterdam, or another location. While this measure had little impact on ethnic Poles, most of whom favoured emigration to the United States, it did serve to cut off Poland's Ukrainians from their preferred destination as was reflected in the immigration figures.

For W.A. Gordon, the minister of immigration and colonization in the new Bennett government, the facts spoke for themselves: it was anticipated that there would be some 200,000 unemployed in Canada by the end of 1930; that some 221,561 immigrants had entered Canada in the sixteen months ending 31 July 1930, including 99,367 males over sixteen years of age; and that 'it is clear, therefore, beyond peradventure that either substantial numbers of immigrants who have recently arrived in Canada are in the ranks of the unemployed, or conversely, they have displaced Canadians who are now unemployed.'[55]

Given these data, the new concern was 'the task of assimilation and absorption of these people.' Rather than international immigration, therefore, Gordon urged the railways to consider 'a comprehensive colonization plan for settlement on land of Canadian citizens.'[56] With international immigration slackening, attention was directed to internal redistributions by the 'back to the land' programme, by transferring large numbers of farmers from drought areas, and by opening up new agricultural frontiers. In the summer of 1930, an agreement was struck between the Dominion government and the colonization departments of the two railways to mount a programme of 'internal colonization' and population redistribution to alleviate the worst of the pockets of poverty.[57]

The railway companies directed attention to the task of resettling the overcrowded bloc settlements, particularly in southern drought areas. The agreement between the federal, provincial, and railway agencies provided the logistical support for this diaspora, and, in 1931 alone, 1,868 carloads of stock, equipment, and household effects and some 45,000 people were moved north in Saskatchewan and Alberta. In east and central Alberta, the CNR was helped by priests of the Basilian Order who scouted lands in Athabasca and Peace River.[58] Similar northward transfers moved farmers to the Swan River region of northwest Manitoba and the Prince Albert, St Walburg, and Meadow Lake areas of Saskatchewan.

Another exercise in internal colonization, the 'back-to-the-land' movement, was a strategy composed of social idealism and economic pragmatism. To help cope with the rampant unemployment among immigrants and native Canadians alike, federal, provincial, and municipal governments co-operated with the railways in inducing people to leave cities and industrial centres. It was thought that by establishing self-sufficient farms the unemployed would become gainfully employed and relieve pressure on the welfare rolls. Saskatchewan made the first move in this policy in 1931: Saskatoon settled 54 families in the Loon Lake area, Moose Jaw moved 74 families to the Pelly district, and by the close of 1931 some 124 unemployed families had been relocated. The Relief Settlement Plan and Manitoba's Rural Rehabilitation Commission also contributed to these major schemes of relocating families and communities.[59] The railways' colonization organizations were very active in this, and CNR agents attempted to persuade Ukrainians and others to leave western cities, mining camps, and other resource industries and to locate in the open farmlands in the north of the province.[60]

There was, however, another, less benign approach to alleviating Canada's pressing unemployment rate and pressure on available sources of relief. The Dominion and provincial governments, together with the railways, turned to the deportation of unwanted immigrants because of the putative economic, social, and security threat that they posed.[61] There were thousands of unemployed immigrants on the relief rolls in the 1930s, and between March 1930 and March 1934 over 24,000 were deported. Nativist anti-immigration groups had long charged that many of Canada's economic and social ills were attributable to immigrants in general and Central European immigrants in particular. The statistics of deportation are revealing. Of the 14,579 deportations between 1 April

1929 and 31 March 1932, 10,364 were British. Or again, 13,268 (4.6 per cent) of the 288,232 British who had been admitted in 1926–31 had been deported, and only 5,822 (1.5 per cent) of the 369,905 non-British immigrants had shared that fate.[62]

Given the general fears of the nativists and the specific accusations of the RCMP, it is reasonable to ponder on how these draconian measures impacted upon Ukrainians. Indeed, in a confidential letter to the London office in charge of the CNR's European operation, Black reported that 'when we held our meeting at Ottawa we found the officers of the department [Immigration and Colonization], together with the Minister, unanimous in their opposition to Ukrainians.' Black went on to explain the government's position:

During the past two months especially, Ukrainians who are avowed Communists, have given the authorities more trouble than the Reds of all other nationalities put together and they have created at Ottawa decidedly bad feeling against people of this race. We have endeavoured to combat this as best we could by emphasizing the loyalty and soundness of a large section of the Ukrainian people of Canada. At first we were of the opinion that all Ukrainians living on farms and resident in country districts were reliable, but we were immediately faced with reports of activities checked by the Royal Canadian Police showing subversive influences emanating from the country. It is altogether too bad that this has occurred, but there it is, and the influence of good Ukrainians must suffer in consequence.[63]

Nevertheless, Ukrainians do not appear to have been singled out for particular attention. To be sure, the records were categorized by 'country of origin' rather than by nationality, but it would appear that despite the claims of some, Ukrainians did not bulk large in the statistics as in 1934 only two hundred persons were repatriated to Poland, the country of origin of many inter-war Ukrainians.[64] Indeed, many noticed that it was not a continental-immigrant phenomenon as 'the difference in the percentage deported as compared with the deportation of British cannot be regarded as other than significant, and is contrary to much that has passed as considered public opinion.'[65]

Large-scale deportation ceased in 1934 because of growing public opposition to its excesses. Indeed, these years had witnessed other programmes more concerned in celebrating ethnic diversity than in vilifying it. These initiatives reflected how corporate interests in shipping, railways, land, farm-equipment, and all others involved in moving people and establishing them on the land were anxious to diminish the xenophobia of Canadian society. Thus, both the CNR and the CPR developed their own radio stations that broadcast concerts and poetry readings, the CNR's historical drama series, 'The Romance of Canada,' being designed to 'encourage Canadian national consciousness' among listeners.[66] The prospectus of the CNR's more grass-roots scheme, the 'Community Progress Competitions,' tells its own story: 'To the encouragement of progress towards Canadian Ideals in Home, Community and National Life, in Communities of European Origin in Western Canada, this plan of Community Competitions is dedicated.'[67] For its part, the CPR sponsored a series of 'festivals of culture' to bring the various ethnic organizations together to 'create a more mutual understanding between the ... racial groups.'[68]

Others have recognized that these ventures were prompted by more prosaic corporate concerns such as proselytizing pro-immigrant viewpoints in the minds of the public and, it was hoped, policy-makers, and the stimulation of hotel and rail business during the slow spring and autumn seasons. Perhaps even more important, the ultimate and more subtle goal was to engender a social and political environment and national stability and unity that would be conducive to corporate health and vitality.[69] Nevertheless, such developments were another dimension of the way in which Canada was struggling with the questions of immigrants and immigration and nativism and pluralism.

The whole context of the immigration policy changed yet again after 1935 as economic recovery favoured less stringent Canadian immigration regulations and as fear of the approaching war encouraged many to leave. The CNR's Black advised his contacts in shipping that quotas for continental families had been removed for 1938, 'the whole arrangement being wide open and permitting the freest possible action on the part of each Steamship Line concerned.'[70]

Ukrainian immigration, however, still faced restrictions emanating from within Poland. Canadian immigration authorities were well aware of the problem: 'Ukrainian farmers who have land and want to sell it and leave Poland are encouraged to do so by Poland. The Government sets the price and sees that the amount paid is very little more than will pay passage and allow $1,000 to be taken out of the country. They also see that the land sold by the Ukrainian farmer falls into the hands of a Polish settler. By one operation they therefore, get rid of a Ukrainian, replace him on the land by a Pole, and by routing this business into the hands of the Polish Lines get back from the Ukrainian a considerable part of the price of his land by selling him transportation on the National Line.'[71] Even in the face of such obstructionism, Ukrainian immigration climbed steadily from a mere 300 or so in 1935 to a high of 1,905 in 1938.[72]

Ironically, towards the close of the decade, the new concern was that the CNR's colonization department would not be able to find sufficient immigrants. Black aired his fears thus: 'it does appear to me that we are going to have a hard time to get many immigrants out of Europe during the next few years, and as we are going to need as many as we can secure from anywhere, we haven't much ground on which to speculate. Canada will need a heavy influx of people to enable her to hold her domain. If she does not get them, someone else will be in charge of this British Dominion, and we will be told what to do by some gang that has little regard for the traditions according to which we have been reared to responsibility.'[73]

Indeed, in 1939, while the rest of the world was preoccupied with the promise of yet another international conflict, railway land settlement agencies looked forward to new business: 'In many respects the year just concluded has been a noteworthy one for our Department. It marked the commencement of the second World War with its effect on immigration from South Eastern Europe, and it opened what may prove to be an entirely new phase of settlement activity for the Dominion.'[74] But that's another story.

Writing in 1909 in his famous study *Strangers within Our Gates*, J.S. Woodsworth commented on the qualities of the people he called 'Little Russians,' 'Ruthenians,' and 'Galicians.' His somewhat inconsistent and certainly bigoted view of these peoples is important to note. For Woodsworth, they were illiterate, ignorant, despised, unskilled, grimy, stolid, animalized, quarrelsome, dangerous, and unrefined, if also patient, industrious, and eager to become Canadianized.[75] A generation later, Robert England recognized them as Ukrainians and provided a different perspective: 'We now know enough to realize the qualities which the best of the Ukrainian people have brought to Canada, and it is certain that when the history of Western Canada widens out in the coming decades there will be a high place on the scroll for the achievement of the Ukrainian people.'[76]

By the time immigration was closed off again in 1939, Ukrainian communities were firmly established throughout Canada. In 1945, V.J. Kaye produced a document for the Citizenship Division of the Department of National War Services, 'for departmental use only.' The Citizenship Division had been established 'to create among Canadians of French and British origin a better understanding of Canadians of recent European origin and to foster among the latter a wider knowledge and appreciation of the best traditions of Canadian life.[77] Basing its data on the 1941 census, the report recorded that in that year, Canada's population of 11.5 million included 305,929 Ukrainians by 'racial origin,' 313,273 Ukrainians by 'mother tongue,' and 324,894 of 'Ukrainian descent.'[78] Further, this community was served by fifteen Ukrainian newspapers, over a dozen organizations, and some 1,429 cultural centres.

The 1919–39 period had been a challenging one for the generations who had arrived during the Laurier-Sifton years as well as for those who came in the inter-war years. A combination of economic, social, political, and – it must be admitted – 'racist' concerns had resulted in new policies. Henceforth, all immigrants – but especially some – were scrutinized to determine their suitability for assimilation, absorption, and compatibility with the Canadian polity. Canada had embarked on the age of planned society and social engineering.

The debate as to whether Canada is pluralistic and cosmopolitan or nominally bicultural and essentially xenophobic is still with us. One analyst, commenting on the combination of fear of strangers and fear of economic stress, has coined the term 'xeconophobia.'[79] It precisely defines the sentiments of those opposed to the migration of the Ukrainians and other 'non-preferreds' during the 1920s and 1930s. Ironically, the descendants of these Ukrainians now find themselves part of a Canadian establishment that is guarding the gates against the new strangers from Central and Eastern Europe and, once again, from Asia. The faces are the same, the issues are familiar, but perhaps the public and policy makers are better informed.

'This Should Never Be Spoken or Quoted Publicly': Canada's Ukrainians and Their Encounter with the DPs

LUBOMYR Y. LUCIUK

Millions of Ukrainians became refugees during the Second World War. No one foresaw just how important Canadian servicemen of Ukrainian descent would be in providing relief and resettlement assistance to hundreds of thousands of these displaced persons (DPs). Yet it was these soldiers who in January 1943 set up the Ukrainian Canadian Servicemen's Association (UCSA), around which they subsequently formed the Central Ukrainian Relief Bureau (CURB).[1] At first, the bureau was 'a strictly Canadian venture.'[2] Later, Ukrainian Americans came to play an important role in financing its operations, although the Ukrainian Canadian Committee (UCC) in Winnipeg continued to provide much of the funding through its Ukrainian Canadian Relief Fund (UCRF).[3] The committee, established as an 'umbrella group' that would co-ordinate the activities of the leading Ukrainian-Canadian organizations of the Centre and Right, had been intended to last no longer than the war. However, the unexpected refugee crisis and the committee's increasing involvement in providing aid to the DPs furnished a ready-made reason to extend its mandate into the post-war period.[4]

Despite their enthusiasm for helping their fellow Ukrainians, many of the CURB's staff and those of its successor, the Canadian Relief Mission for Ukrainian Victims of War (CRM), and even some of those in the executives of the UCC and UCRF, eventually became disillusioned with the tangled politics of the refugees. Themselves divided by the secular and religious factionalism that had fractured inter-war community affairs, the Ukrainian Canadians were also circumscribed by the political considerations that informed the refugee policies adopted by the governments of the United Kingdom, the United States, and

Canada. Finally, they were debilitated by the disillusionment and even hostility that emerged as the encounters between previously established Ukrainian Canadians and newly arriving refugees multiplied.[5] Seeking, at first, to do little more than secure asylum for the DPs and help supply food, housing, clothing, and protection against persecution, the Ukrainian Canadians later turned from welfare work to resettlement operations, placing their charges in Western Europe, North and South America, and Australasia. This post-war emigration of political refugees would have profound, and largely unanticipated, consequences for the social, religious, and especially political life of Ukrainian communities in the West, including Canada.

After detailing the internal and external constraints that encumbered the work of the CURB and related Ukrainian-Canadian organizations, this paper will trace how Ukrainian-Canadian attitudes towards the DPs changed between 1943 and 1951. A markedly negative attitude towards the Ukrainian refugees developed as the Ukrainian Canadians who were involved with them became more familiar with, and alarmed about, their political attitudes. This opinion came to be ever more widely shared as other Ukrainian Canadians came into contact with the newcomers and realized that they were not getting immigrants of the kind they had hoped for or been told to expect. Exploring why this occurred, and how the in-migrating group's integration into an established community of similar ethnic background often failed, will highlight a little-known chapter in Ukrainian-Canadian history and help inform the process of model building in the field of refugee studies.[6] It will also reveal historical reasons that explain the contemporary community life of one of Canada's major ethnic minorities.[7]

Characterizing the Refugees: 'All Liberal-Minded People'

At the first Ukrainian Canadian Committee congress, held in Winnipeg on 22–24 June 1943, most of the 496 delegates were preoccupied with demonstrating their community's undivided support for the Anglo-American war effort. Not only did the committee's leaders understand that their organization had been brought into being through the direct intervention of the federal government in November 1940, but they were gravely concerned over what might happen if the government came to doubt their loyalty in wartime.[8] The congress gave the question of aid to Ukrainian DPs only passing mention. Knowledge of a refugee problem in Europe was all but missing.

The situation changed quickly after the invasion of Nazi-occupied

Europe in June 1944. Among the Canadians who landed on the beaches of Normandy was Bohdan Panchuk, a young Ukrainian-Canadian teacher and member of the Ukrainian Self-Reliance League. By June 1944 Panchuk was also president of the British-based Servicemen's Association and an RCAF intelligence officer. Shortly after D-Day, he began writing to friends about the growing numbers of Ukrainian DPs he was finding in liberated Europe.[9] It was imperative that Ukrainian Canadians give them aid and comfort, for many of the DPs, he presciently observed, might later be allowed to emigrate to Canada. There, he felt sure, they would help buoy up existing Ukrainian-Canadian organizations. As for any political or religious factionalism among the DPs, Panchuk and, indeed, the other Ukrainian Canadians who wrote about them either missed it or ignored it when they penned their first impressions. In fact, the Ukrainian Canadians shared the view that the DPs were all 'Western-minded, Christian, educated, religious, hard-working, liberal-minded people.'[10] This idealized description would be promulgated for several years in the literature the CURB and its support groups distributed in Europe and North America, even after many of those who worked with the DPs in the field or back in Canada had taken a rather different view. Boosters advocating Ukrainian-Canadian community aid for the DPs continued, then, to stress the benefits that a migration of the Ukrainian refugees would guarantee, emphasizing that once they were resettled they would strengthen established Ukrainian-Canadian secular and religious groups. After visiting a DP camp near Heidenau, Germany, Panchuk described it as a 'miniature state' in which the Ukrainians had formed a united group motivated by the most humanitarian of concerns. For him this proved that the DPs were capable of achieving unity on the principle of the greatest good for the greatest number, much as the Ukrainians of Canada had come together to form the UCC.[11] Such assessments of the DPs motivated Panchuk and his co-workers to urge Winnipeg to send an 'authoritative person' overseas to 'apply some pressure' to organize all of the Ukrainian DPs in Western Europe along the lines of the Ukrainian-Canadian model.[12] At this time, Panchuk and most other Ukrainian Canadians serving overseas were unaware of the pivotal role the British and Canadian governments had played in the creation of the committee and had no idea of the repercussions their efforts on behalf of the refugees were having on official levels. Furthermore, their overly confident vision of how Ukrainian refugees could be guided into establishing a united body to represent themselves in the diaspora revealed an incomplete understanding of the competing political forces at work among them. Still, confident that they had proven their loyalty to Canada through active service overseas during the war and convinced that Canada and the other Western powers would support their efforts, the Ukrainian Canadians went ahead with their work among the DPs. They could not have been more wrong.

'Mechanical Unity' versus Reality

Early in January 1946, partially in response to the CURB's requests, the chairman of the committee and fund, the Reverend Dr Wasyl Kushnir, a Ukrainian Catholic priest, visited Western Europe on a 'fact-finding tour.' Altogether he would spend several months touring DP camps in the British, French, and American zones of Germany and Austria. Kushnir had apparently been briefed about the divisiveness of political life among the DPs, for he was not slow in instructing the spokesmen of their various organizations how to behave if they wished to continue receiving Ukrainian-Canadian support. At a meeting between CURB staff members and several refugee group representatives, held in London in early February 1946, Kushnir stressed that although Ukrainian Canadians were not interested in a 'mechanical unity' brought about through the consolidation of all refugee groups into one organization, they were firm in rejecting even the possibility that the DPs might import any of their internal political differences with them, should they ever be resettled to Canada. Any refugees who emigrated there, Kushnir said, would be expected to join one of the existing constituent organizations of the committee. There was no need for the DPs to bring anything 'new' with them to Canada, for within the UCC the complete range of religious and political persuasions was already present, excluding only the pro-Soviet Left, which would not, of course, attract any of these anti-Communist refugees. Finally, Kushnir told his London audience that any formations still active among the DPs must conceal 'even the least political activity' from outside observers, since the Allied governments disapproved of any manifestations of anti-Soviet or Ukrainian nationalist sympathies.[13] He knew this because he had been repeatedly advised that the British and Canadian governments were concerned that DP anti-Communist activism might undermine cordial relations with the USSR. Senior government officials in England had underlined this point to Kushnir during several formal briefings, and they would repeat it under similar circumstances to other Ukrainian Canadians active overseas immediately after the war. The Anglo-American powers would not tolerate any behaviour that the Soviet authorities might misconstrue as Western support for exile groups intent on destabilizing or dismembering the Soviet Union.[14]

After proselytizing the DPs for several weeks about the importance of unity, Kushnir and his CURB colleagues were able to announce, in March 1946, that they had succeeded in creating an 'umbrella group' that combined all the major political parties then active among the Ukrainian DPs. The new body, based in Munich, was to be known as the Co-ordinating Ukrainian Committee (CUC); perhaps coincidentally, its Ukrainian acronym, KUK (for Koordynatsiinyi ukrainskyi komitet), was the same as that of the Ukrainian Canadian Committee (Komitet ukraintsiv Kanady). The list of organizations that Kushnir brought together to form the CUC provides a glimpse into the diversity of the post-war emigration: it included competing nationalist factions, social-ists, and democrats.

Kushnir's motives in helping to establish the committee are not entirely clear, but it appears that he hoped, at least in part, to limit the influence that Stepan Bandera's faction of the Organization of Ukrainian Nationalists was gaining within the refugee camps.[15] Distressed at find-ing such a militantly nationalistic movement among the DPs, particularly one that was largely unknown to Ukrainians in Canada, Kushnir attempted to mute its influence by structuring the CUC on a modified version of the UCC model he was familiar with. Whereas in the latter a veto privilege ensured Ukrainian-Canadian unanimity, the Co-ordinat-ing Ukrainian Committee accorded one vote to every organization, regardless of its numerical strength, representativeness, or political rele-vance. Just as the Canadian committee would be thwarted, time and again, by its essentially undemocratic governing rules, so the CUC's structure would prove unworkable. Obviously, that was not to Kushnir's liking. But he may not have foreseen the difficulties that would befall the CUC. At least until the end of the war, the UCC had been able to cope with most of its tasks. It is possible that Kushnir sincerely believed that the organizational model he was imposing upon the DPs would work. Then, too, Kushnir's efforts may have reflected the influence that the president of the Ukrainian National Federation (UNF), Volodymyr Kossar, had over him. Kossar was not only a leading executive member of the committee but a man whose political sympathies lay not with the Banderites but with the rival Melnykites. Whatever its provenance, this effort by the Ukrainian Canadians to circumscribe the influence of those refugees whom they deemed to be the most uncontrollable and militant of the nationalists within the post-war Ukrainian diaspora failed. The numerically preponderant Banderites soon made it clear that they believed their movement was far more important than any other group in the co-ordinating committee. Arguing for 'representation by population' and against the 'one group, one vote' principle, they pointed out that their movement represented a majority of the DPs, yet their proposals kept being obstructed. As a result they began boycotting the CUC and finally left it altogether. They would continue to have nothing to do with it even after it had been renamed the Ukrainian National Council (Ukrainska Natsionalna Rada). This would later become a major point of contention between those who supported the Banderites and the many influential Ukrainian-Canadian leaders who did not, an argument that lasted at least until 1959. Thus, even though the abandonment of the council by the Banderites dealt it a crippling blow, it also set the stage for political infighting between a significant and well-organized subgroup within the post-war emigration and the leaders of the organized community. Factionalism had begun to creep into their relations well before any large number of DPs were resettled in Canada.

The mounting tension between Ukrainian-Canadian expectations about the DPs and the DPs' understanding of their own needs had become evident, as we have seen, as early as the meeting in London in February 1946, when a spokesman for the Banderites bluntly stated that although the DPs appreciated the help extended to them by North America's Ukrainians, they had their own ideas about how to put this aid to use. Curiously, most of the Ukrainian Canadians who were working in Europe then seem to have discounted or ignored what they should have taken as a signal about crucial differences between their views and those of the DPs. More significantly, the CURB workers did nothing to communicate these facts to the community at large. In time, of course, it would become abundantly clear to most Ukrainian Canadians that few of the DPs were willing to conform to Ukrainian-Canadian rules of behaviour. This was to become the principal cause of factionalism within post-war Ukrainian-Canadian society, with repercussions to the present.

But these problems were as yet in the future. At the February 1946 meeting Kushnir not only tried to ignore the importance of the Banderites but also failed to appreciate their plans for what their spokesman referred to as a protracted national liberation struggle. One of their representatives at the meeting, Pavlo Shumovsky, even explained to Kushnir that not only must Ukrainian Canadians not try to impose an unnatural union upon the DPs but that they should be prepared to accept the continuation of nationalist organizational efforts in North America. Shumovsky predicted that should the Ukrainian nationalist movement be frustrated in Europe, 'political activities on a grand scale' would be transplanted to the American continent. 'With this in view a principle of selection of new settlers in North America must be applied, whereby only the most constructive and best people would migrate there.'[16]

Of course, defining who those 'best people' were would not be easy, but Shumovsky's forthrightness should, at a minimum, have alerted everyone present to the fact that at least one nationalist group was planning to take advantage of the temporary asylum granted by the DP camps in order to prepare for a relocation of its covert cells throughout the emigration, including Canada. Yet instead of reacting to this information, Kushnir and his CURB colleagues marked the minutes of the meeting 'strictly confidential' and 'not to be published.' No one in Canada was given any indication about the factionalism within the DP population or about the nationalists' stated intentions to rebuild their networks in North America. Whether the Ukrainian Canadians in London took such statements at face value or simply wrote them off as bluster is uncertain. Yet, as archival evidence and oral accounts make clear, in the years following this meeting many Banderites were ordered, encouraged, and helped to resettle in Canada, where they went on to play a major role in maintaining the organizational integrity of their faction. Other Ukrainian DPs, such as the rival Melnykites, took similar steps, although their integration was somewhat easier because they found a sympathetic infrastructure in Canada in the form of the UNF and its affiliated women's, veterans', and youth groups. Eventually, semi-covert nationalist networks were re-created throughout the West, the strongest centres being developed in Britain, West Germany, France, Canada, and the United States. In all these places the refugees continued their often intense infighting, in the process achieving little more than the alienation of their hosts and, in time, even of many of their offspring.

No small measure of skulduggery was involved in this relocation, as the competing factions did whatever they could to steal a march upon their opponents. For example, one disillusioned UNF member who had transferred his loyalties to the Banderites advised their chief organizer (known as the *terenovyi providnyk* or *rezydent*) in Canada not only about how easy it would be to take over the federation but about how important it was for the new wave of nationalists to place supporters in key cities throughout the country: 'I don't think it would be very difficult to take over their organization [the UNF] ... by sending our own people into the cities ... The whole issue comes down simply to having a few of our own people on the spot. That is why I am so concerned about having an answer to my question as to whether a planned settlement of our own is taking place. And I'd also like to know if we're going to get any of our own people here ... Is there anything being done along these lines; if so, what should we be doing locally?'[17] The *rezydent* for Canada assured him that there was such a plan. Unfortunately, its details remain secret.

At the second UCC congress, held in Toronto on 2–4 June 1946, refugee issues were, for the first time, deliberated at considerable length in a national Ukrainian-Canadian forum. In their addresses to the 405 delegates and 412 guests who attended the congress Father Kushnir and Panchuk referred to the scale of the Ukrainian refugee situation in Europe and its relief needs. Yet, despite their own growing misgivings about the political beliefs and behaviour of many DPs, neither Kushnir nor Panchuk attempted to acquaint the congress with their politics or to discuss the impact that their immigration might have on the Ukrainian-Canadian community. Left ignorant of these matters, the delegates voted overwhelmingly to prolong the existence of the UCC and mandated it to continue doing everything possible to help the DPs. The committee was also specifically instructed to continue lobbying the government to ensure that as many DPs as possible would be admitted to Canada.[18] So it was that Ukrainian Canadians were left unprepared for the arrival of a politicized refugee population that would not readily integrate into the framework of Ukrainian-Canadian society.

'Conspiratorial Activity': Dissent within the CURB

When Panchuk left London for Canada in early May 1946, Stanley W. Frolick took charge of the CURB's operations, serving as its first executive secretary and then, between May and mid-October 1946, as its director. Posted overseas with the Allied Control Commission for Germany, Frolick soon left its employ to work for the CURB, on Panchuk's invitation. Born in Hillcrest, Alberta, in 1920, Frolick had spent his teenage years attending school in Western Ukraine. Influenced by nationalist instructors there, he had joined a youth group affiliated with the OUN and, after barely managing to leave the Soviet Union by heading east through Siberia in June 1941, had returned to Canada, where he was welcomed into the ranks of the UNF, the main nationalist Ukrainian organization in Canada at the time. But after he joined the CURB, Frolick quickly realized that his sympathies lay with the revolutionary nationalists, or Banderites. Although he played an important role in the CURB, helping to orchestrate protests against the forcible repatriation of refugees to the

Soviet Union and serving as an effective spokesman in explaining their plight to Allied governments, he also became increasingly caught up in trying to help the Banderites reconstitute and expand their undercover networks throughout the post-war diaspora.[19] His political sympathies soon came to irritate those members of the Winnipeg committee's national executive who rejected the platform of the Banderites, particularly men like Frolick's former supporter, the UNF president Kossar, who held a high rank among the Melnykites at this time. Frolick's contrary political sympathies required his removal from the bureau post. To do so the committee dispatched Panchuk and a group of Ukrainian-Canadian veterans to London to take over the bureau. The process was accomplished, not without some unpleasantness, during the late fall and early winter of 1946.

Upon the return of Panchuk, his wife Anne, Anthony J. Yaremovich, and Ann Crapleve – the group was known as the Canadian Relief Mission for Ukrainian Victims of War (CRM) – Frolick was forced to resign. By 19 October 1946 Panchuk was formally reinstated as the director of the bureau. When he returned to Canada later that year, Frolick discovered that he was no longer welcome as a member of the UNF and had become a persona non grata at the UCC. Convinced that it could prevent the disruption of the status quo in Ukrainian-Canadian society simply by refusing to recognize the new political formations active among the DPs, the UCC had decided that Frolick's association with the Banderites was unacceptable. In its view so, too, was he.

There were several reasons for the committee's abhorrence of Frolick's allegiance and his advice. Being all too familiar with the crippling effect of internal dissent within the Ukrainian-Canadian community during the inter-war period, the UCC leaders were intent on ensuring that any in-migrating DPs conformed to their ideas about how Ukrainian life in Canada should be organized. They were not about to tolerate a highly nationalistic organization that might challenge their domination of organized Ukrainian-Canadian society. Nor would they accept one of their own who had adopted the novel and, to them, foreign world-view of the Banderites, even if he and the DPs were all fellow Ukrainians. And, having experienced censure at government hands because of their allegedly 'divided loyalties,' the committee's executive members knew that if they appeared to be too interested in Ukrainian affairs, they might once again be exposed to repression. They were therefore anxious about how both their own community and the larger host society would view the arrival of such militantly nationalistic Ukrainians as the Banderites. In fact, they were convinced that things would go much better for everyone concerned if only they could somehow disguise the national-ism of the newcomers. All these factors militated against their acceptance of Frolick's admonitions about the need to revise their positions to accommodate and build upon the nationalist movement as represented in the DP camps by the Banderites. The federation's leaders branded Frolick a 'traitor' and subjected him to a 'smear' campaign.[20]

That Frolick had indeed become an active supporter of the Banderites is evident from the materials Panchuk uncovered in the CURB's London offices. For example, letterheads that he found in Frolick's desk indicate that from 2 December 1945 he had served in Britain as the representative of the Ukrainian Supreme Liberation Council, a body closely identified with the Banderites. Panchuk reported to the UCC that, in his view, there had been 'a lot of conspiratorial activity' going on before the mission's return to Britain.[21] Frolick himself made little effort to disguise his involvement with the nationalists. Indeed, for him, co-operation with the Banderites was perfectly in consonance with his mandate to represent the DPs before the Allied powers. By supporting the Bander-ites he was taking the side not only of the leading political movement within the diaspora but of the majority of the DP population that Ukrai-nian Canadians had come overseas to help.

No one in Winnipeg saw things quite that way. For example, Teodor Datzkiw, a member of the United Hetman Organization and of the UCC executive, noted that there had been hints for some time that Frolick had close ties with the Banderites. Datzkiw added that the UCC was opposed to Frolick's ties with the movement. For the committee's mem-bers, the bureau's director must not, under any circumstances, be, or even be thought to be, a spokesman for any particular political group, the two functions being 'mutually exclusive.'[22] Although meritorious in principle, this attitude did not reflect the real reasons behind the committee's annoyance with Frolick's activism. It was the group that he was working for rather than political action that it decried. Certainly it would place no similar constraints on the activities of Dmytro Andriev-sky, a high-ranking member of the Melnyk faction who was receiving financial support from Ukrainian-Canadian coffers while on the bureau's payroll. In reality, and at least some of the committee's members must have known this, Andrievsky was busily engaged in political activi-ties in support of his faction, not coincidentally the same one that the federation's president, Wladimir Kossar, supported. Once Frolick sided with the Banderites, he found himself without a patron in Winnipeg and was left exposed to criticism that ensured that he would be dismissed.

Whether Panchuk realized, before he went overseas, how dissatisfied the executives of the committee and fund were with Frolick's political activities, or whether he was instructed to remove Frolick as the CURB director, remains unclear. Once back in England, Panchuk did write to several of his most trusted friends about the difficulties he was having with Frolick's political involvements, but this personal correspondence did not become public knowledge. What makes the clash between Frolick and Panchuk at all relevant, then, is not its personal dimensions but the way in which their antagonism echoed fundamental differences between two groups about their definitions of themselves and their roles as Ukrainians outside their homeland. Ukrainian Canadians, content to be living in Canada, thought their principal duty was to rescue as many Ukrainian DPs as possible. Their motive was straightforward. An infusion of new DP blood would revive Ukrainian-Canadian society. In contrast, most DPs were seeking only temporary asylum in the refugee camps, hoping that there they could mobilize their own people and the Ukrainian-Canadian community in support of the national liberation movement. The much-heralded success of the movement would then allow all displaced Ukrainians to go home to Ukraine. The DPs could not, as yet, accept the fact that for many Ukrainian Canadians Ukraine was a distant place and Canada had become their home. Indeed, although it lauded the goal of independence in principle, in practice the Ukrainian-Canadian community dismissed it as untenable, for it had come to appreciate that if it forcefully put forward such a platform it would only court Canadian government and public disapproval, to say nothing of that of the other Anglo-American powers. Not wishing to risk such a reprimand, the community aligned itself with those officials whose responsibility it was to ensure that nothing done by the Ukrainian Canadians, or any of the refugee newcomers, jeopardized Canadian domestic or foreign policy.[23] Thus, although the Ukrainian-Canadian press frequently wrote about the 'Ukrainian question,' the community did little to support any of the political movements struggling for independence. What modest efforts the resettling DPs could themselves manage also proved to be far from enough. In the end many of the refugees concluded that Ukrainian-Canadian society had been generous with material aid and resettlement advice but meek when called upon to underwrite the political and military struggle for independence. That realization prompted some of them to rededicate their energies to taking control of the internal life of the DP camps, a 'struggle for the minds of the masses' that would shape the world-view of many of those who lived in the post-war refugee camps. As for the Ukrainian Canadians, the militant refugees threatened their Canadianized way of thinking; indeed, contrary to all expectations, they might even prove to be a liability. And so, the Ukrainian Canadians and the DPs rapidly grew disenchanted and embittered with one another, a fact that official watchers on both sides of the Atlantic took note of. Some of them even voiced the hope that, with the passing of time, this internal divisiveness would help erode the community to the point where all the problems caused by the presence of non-assimilated Ukrainians would disappear from Canadian politics.

'A Source of Considerable Embarrassment': External Constraints on Canada's Ukrainians

Although the newly constituted relief mission arrived in England in October 1946, ready to begin work among the Ukrainian DPs, none of its members were allowed to proceed to the continent until December. Both the British and Canadian governments were reluctant to grant a go-ahead to a Ukrainian-Canadian project about whose purpose they remained uneasy. This was not a unique reaction on the part of Anglo-American governments. For example, when the Ukrainian Canadian Relief Fund was authorized by the Canadian government on 18 January 1945, the community felt that permission had been granted almost automatically. In fact, the Canadian Department of External Affairs regarded the suggestion that a distinctly Ukrainian refugee fund be set up as a very grave matter. In the early fall of 1944, when the committee first raised the proposal, one of External's mandarins, Norman A. Robertson, indicated to George Pifher, the director of voluntary and auxiliary services in the Department of National War Services, that although the government was 'absolutely certain of the loyalty of the UCC to Canada,' authorization for the proposed fund would likely 'prove to be a source of considerable embarrassment to the Canadian government.'[24] Indeed, some of External's bureaucrats believed that the Polish and Soviet governments would misconstrue the establishment of such a fund as tacit Canadian recognition of Ukrainian demands for independence, a political agenda they wanted everyone to understand they had no intention of endorsing.

Dana Wilgress reported to Ottawa from the Canadian embassy in Moscow that, as of late January 1945, the Soviets had 'shot 20,000 Ukrainian Nationalists [and are] probably biding their time before taking energetic steps to suppress these guerrillas.'[25] It would therefore be inopportune, Wilgress noted, for the government to suggest that it was sympathetic to the nationalist insurgents. And setting up a Ukrainian relief fund, Wilgress argued, would be tantamount to approving 'relief for enemy agents.'[26] Supported by such opinions, Robertson replied to Pifher's inquiry regarding approval for a Ukrainian-Canadian fund with the suggestion that the committee be persuaded 'to abandon this project.'[27] It was not the first time, nor would it be the last, that high-ranking government officials attempted to influence developments within Ukrainian-Canadian society.

To its credit, the committee remained so persistent in its appeals for the creation of a relief fund that by January 1945 General L.R. LaFleche, the director of the Department of National War Services, granted it the right to proceed. Outwardly this may have appeared to be a victory for the committee. But it was only partly so. External Affairs had insisted on placing several checks upon the fund's organizers. They were not permitted to refer to their new body as the 'Canadian Ukrainian Refugee Fund.' The word 'refugee' was deleted from the title presumably because it was politically loaded. The fund was allowed to operate only under the condition that its collected monies be made available to anyone of the 'Ukrainian race,' regardless of status or citizenship. Soviet Ukrainians and non-refugees were eligible, at least technically, for financial assistance. This lame cover was intended to give Canadian officials something to say to anyone who inquired about the fund's purpose. And not only was an upper limit set on the amount that could be gathered but all funds were to be entrusted to a Canadian bank account before being forwarded to the Canadian Red Cross for disbursement. The Ukrainian Canadians who gathered these monies were not, it seems, to be trusted with spending them. Even with these limitations in place some of the bureaucrats involved remained uncomfortable with the prospect of the fund's monies getting into the hands of members of the anti-Soviet groups known to be sheltering in the DP camps. Thus, several months after permission was granted for the setting up of the UCRF, an External Affairs official suggested that the government reconsider its decision and 'block' the fund's account so as to prevent money from being sent to help Ukrainian refugees. Although he had no evidence to support his view, these Ukrainian DPs, he wrote, were all 'pro-Nazi' and, as such, undeserving of any consideration.[28]

'War Criminals of the Worst Type': The Anti-DP Lobby

Xenophobia caused some of the Canadian public's objections to the admission of DPs. Other obstacles were placed in the way of immigration by organizations that were ideologically indisposed to Ukrainian nationalism. The pro-Soviet Ukrainian Left in Canada orchestrated a public and, at times, vicious campaign to dissuade the government from admitting DPs. Appreciating the anti-Soviet character of the refugees, they correctly concluded that a large influx of them would jeopardize the functioning of such Communist groups as the Association of United Ukrainian Canadians. To prevent this they engaged in lobbying and propaganda efforts aimed at depicting the DPs as nothing more than 'war criminals' and 'fascists.'[29] So loudly was this clarion sounded that its echoes were sometimes heard in the mainstream Canadian press. For example, Peter Lazarowich, a UCC supporter, wrote to the national executive to call its attention to an article that he said had appeared in a February 1945 issue of the *Edmonton Journal*. The article condemned plans for the admission into Canada of 'Ukrainian Quislings.' In a not very oblique reference to some of the UCC's constituent organizations, the article suggested that Ukrainian 'nationalist' organizations in Canada were urging the government to intercede on behalf of 'pro-Nazi' Ukrainians then stranded in Germany, both to prevent their forced repatriation to Ukraine and to get them into Canada.[30]

The article, Lazarowich wrote, also claimed that the DPs were 'war criminals of the worst type.' He cited its caveat to the effect that 'the admission of these Nazi zealots to Canada would be nothing less than a national disaster. They could no more be expected to be loyal citizens of this country than they were of their own native land.'[31] Echoes of this theme would be heard again in Canada from the middle to the late 1980s with much the same kind of constituency doing the chousing.[32]

'A Noticeable Deterioration':
Ukrainian-Canadian Perceptions of the Refugees Change

Although they rejected all such 'war criminal' allegations as spurious and correctly pointed to the ignorance or political biases that lay behind them, more than a few Ukrainian Canadians who worked with the DPs were themselves becoming discouraged both by their politics and by the government's ever more obvious misgiving about permitting a massive influx of them into Canada. Reviewing why this might be so, they concluded that much of the problem lay with the DPs themselves, for their nationalistic fervour was clearly disconcerting the Anglo-American authorities. As the Canadian Ukrainians became aware of the bureaucrats' displeasure with the political activism of the Ukrainian refugees they began to fear that negative perceptions of them might be translated into a stronger disapproval of what they were doing, overseas and in Canada. And so those working in the field redoubled their efforts to suppress all public manifestations of Ukrainian nationalism within or outside the DP camps. Not surprisingly, this placed them on a direct collision course with the political leadership of the Ukrainian nationalist movement, which was busily rebuilding its war-tattered networks. For the nationalists, mobilizing the DPs in support of an insurgency in Ukraine was a crucial aim that they would allow neither friend nor foe to thwart.

The Ukrainian Canadians' discomfort was only heightened by the knowledge that their activities, not to mention those of the DPs, were the subject of systematic and intense government surveillance. As Vladimir Kaye (Kysilewsky), an inter-war immigrant to Canada who later became one of the leading historians of the Ukrainian-Canadian community, wrote, everything being done overseas was 'watched with a telescopic magnifying glass.'[33] He advised friends in the Ukrainian-Canadian contingent overseas to take care that the DPs did nothing that might be perceived as running counter to Canada's domestic or foreign interests. He also urged them to make certain that the DPs scrupulously avoided 'the luxury of politics.'[34] To ensure conformity to Canadian wishes, Kaye advised the bureau's workers to distract the refugees by channelling their energies into such 'safe' activities as the production of folk handicrafts. If these measures were not taken, he warned, the lobbying to persuade the government to admit Ukrainian DPs into Canada would be seriously impeded. Since he was at the time working for the federal government in Ottawa, his counsel was taken seriously. And so, for the Ukrainian Canadians who were working with the displaced persons, it became axiomatic that, if they were to succeed, the 'political nonsense' that kept 'popping up' in the DP camps would have to be thoroughly controlled or even eradicated altogether.[35]

At about the same time as Kaye was insisting upon circumspection, Panchuk was independently revising his earlier uncritical perceptions of the DPs:

As far as our own people on the continent are concerned things are not what they were when the war ended or when I was there before. They are certainly not what Dr. Kushnir saw and remembers. For one reason or another there has been a noticeable DETERIORATION in type and character. The camps are full of 'politicians' who are forever playing politics and games of God knows what instead of getting down to earth and realizing their true position – THAT THEY ARE DISPLACED PERSONS AND NOT WANTED BY ANY COUNTRY EXCEPT PERHAPS THE

USSR. Instead of rolling up their sleeves and getting down to work and learning something and making something of themselves, they find politics, black-marketeering and even banditry and looting, stealing, beating up those they don't like, etc. etc. etc. more 'entertaining.' This should never be spoken or quoted publicly. We must defend the PRINCIPLE OF THE REFUGEES AND THE DPS ... AND VICTIMS OF WAR, but in actual fact, God forbid and protect us if some of these parasitic bandits ever get into Canada.[36]

Increasingly made aware of official anxieties over the DPs' politics, Panchuk also began to grow concerned about the impact the resettlement of such refugees would have on the Ukrainian-Canadian society he had known as a young man. This problem so troubled him that he began urging friends at home to push for the development of community structures that would be more suitable for coping with the 'danger' that the DPs might pose to the 'unity' of Canada's Ukrainian society. Unless a 'common and solid foundation' was in place before the refugees began arriving, Panchuk wrote, they would bring havoc to the community.[37]

Other Ukrainian Canadians underwent a similar change of heart. The letters and reports of Ann Crapleve, written from the British zone of Germany, bear evidence of a growing frustration with the political activities of the DPs.[38] Eustace and Anne Wasylyshen, who took over the UCRF mission from Crapleve, also felt uncomfortable with the attitudes of many DPs. Ukrainians in Canada would likewise find themselves unable to accommodate to the immigrants' politics. Even so, such were the momentum and scale of the Ukrainian-Canadian refugee relief operation that it was not until 1951 that it ground to a halt. Well before then, however, much of the goodwill that had fuelled it had dissipated.

'Locking Horns on Canadian Soil'

A number of prominent Ukrainian community figures in Canada, like Joseph Choma in Fort William and Dmytro Gerych in Winnipeg, kept those posted overseas informed about the tensions that were arising in Canada between the newcomers and the established community.[39] Kaye summed up the apprehensions in early 1949 when he reported that a 'definite rift' had emerged between the refugees and the 'old-timers,' primarily as a result of the politics of the new immigration. In many Ukrainian Canadians' minds there was 'no room in Canada for bickering [about] who is greater, Bandera or Melnyk. We are not interested.'[40] Tempers flared when the Bandera faction founded its own newspaper, *Homin Ukrainy* (Ukrainian Echo), with Frolick as the publisher. Antagonism grew acute when many of the same people set up the pro-Bandera League for the Liberation of Ukraine in Toronto on 1 May 1949. Reading about these developments in Canada, Panchuk wrote that he was encountering 'the same difficulties' in England and warned that similar organizations were springing up in every country in which DPs were resettling.[41] His own forbearance ended when, in March 1949, a group of Banderites allied with the Hetmanites successfully expelled him from his position as the second president of the Association of Ukrainians in Great Britain, a body he had helped constitute.[42] There seem to have been few instances of steadfast co-operation between 'newcomers' and 'old-timers.' The two groups belonged to different worlds.

By the spring of 1949 many community leaders shared the disillusionment felt by Panchuk and others who had worked with the DPs. They had realized that their hopes that these DPs would be ideal settlers who would conform to the pattern of Ukrainian-Canadian community life were unjustified. Understandably, the Ukrainian Canadians tried to make sense of why this had occurred. The more perceptive came to appreciate that they had been correct in their early evaluations of the DPs but that the latter had changed during the DP camp phase of their refugee experience. Within these enclaves, where DPs spent several years cloistered together, exposed to the daily proselytizing of a militant nationalist minority and feeling threatened by the nearby Soviet power, the majority had come to share in a revolutionary and nationalistic world-view. This, from the Ukrainian-Canadian viewpoint, was a most unpalatable development. Panchuk summed up what many Ukrainian Canadians felt in the spring of 1949 when he wrote:

ALL refugees and DPs whatever their nationality, consider themselves POLITICAL REFUGEES (although many of them are far from that) and therefore feel that their prime and most important duty and mission as 'emigres' is to carry on political work and activities, for the liberation of, and their own ultimate return to, their native land ... The MAJORITY, however, are really and in actual fact ECONOMIC REFUGEES as most people who have had to deal [with them] ... have learned, as I did. Most of them have always been in search of a place to live where they will be better off ... The so-called 'political refugees' have often and at every opportunity IMPOSED and forced their influence on the economic refugees and the real and actual WAR VICTIMS, and thus 'coloured' all refugees and displaced persons ... The hardest problem that we had to solve was HOW TO ELIMINATE POLITICS from relief and welfare work.[43]

This penetrating appreciation of the formative influence of the refugee experience came too late to have much practical value for the management of Ukrainian-Canadian relief and resettlement efforts. Panchuk's insight, however, suggests important research themes. Sociological analyses of the nature and impact of migration have indicated that migrant attributes can change as a result of the migration experience.[44] An earlier case study dealing with post-war Ukrainian refugee migration to Canada confirmed Panchuk's view that during the camp phase of the refugee experience the political consciousness of many Ukrainian DP camp inhabitants was transformed and described the effect that this had on their subsequent resettlement and integration in Canada.[45] Such observations recommend the study of historical and contemporary refugee populations in order to determine the extent to which other forcibly displaced populations have been influenced by their refugee experience.

Faced with refugees who would not accept Ukrainian-Canadian rules of behaviour, the UCC executive decided that the time had come to call another national congress, a major purpose of which was to 'iron out the differences' between the immigrants and the organized community.[46] As Anthony Yaremovich, who had served as the bureau's director and so knew the DP situation, wrote at the time: 'The Banderites and Melnykites are locking horns on Canadian soil. They certainly are going at each other with typical Ukrainian vigour. No quarter is given by any side ... We who are on the sidelines have quite a bit of fun watching them. There is spying and counterspying ... It seems that the Ukrainians have some years to grow before they start reaching the age of maturity. This is not concealed from other people.'[47]

The third congress, held in Winnipeg from 7 to 9 February 1950, was almost entirely given over to debating how Ukrainian-Canadian society should contain the unwelcome influences being generated by the 'newcomers.' The proceedings were turbulent, and – with the apparent blessing of the congress chairman, none other than Father Kushnir – some refugee delegates were evicted from the meeting hall amidst catcalls.[48] Passions were inflamed by allegations that the Banderites, now allied in Canada with the supporters of the late Hetman Pavlo Skoropadsky, had infiltrated the fund and committee offices and were working mischief against their political foes while channelling funds to compatriots who were still living as émigrés in Europe.[49]

Panchuk would later claim that it was at this third congress that the 'dissident' element among the resettled DPs was 'reminded that Canada was NOT GALICIA and Winnipeg not Lvow,' but the vigour with which DP-based groups like the League for the Liberation of Ukraine spread across Canada suggests that its members were quite capable of establishing a niche for themselves in Canada, even in the face of the wishes of the established community.[50]

'Not a Voluntary Immigration'

Motivated by a humanitarian concern for the welfare of the their fellow Ukrainians and hoping that a large number of them would resettle in Canada, Ukrainian Canadians had mobilized to help them even before the Second World War ended. However lofty their motives, many nevertheless brought a naîve and even smugly paternalistic attitude to these efforts. In the months immediately after the war they seem to have overlooked, whether deliberately or otherwise, the political opinions many DPs held about their refugee experience and the steps they had to take to rectify their situation. Many of the refugees were convinced that if they persevered in their support of the national liberation struggle, they would, sooner rather than later, expel Soviet occupation forces from Ukraine and be able to go home. They therefore deliberately put off resettlement, preferring to stay in the often uncomfortable DP camps rather than give up the hope of returning to their homeland. They were encouraged in this attitude by the militant Ukrainian nationalists among them who needed them as a source of material support and political power.

When it became impossible to ignore the resulting widespread anti-resettlement and irredentist activism of the refugees, the Ukrainian Canadians tried to wrestle them away from the control of those whom one student of the refugee experience has termed 'homeward-oriented' revolutionary activists.[51] The effort was largely unsuccessful. Most Ukrainian Canadians failed to appreciate that the essence of the refugee experience is to be *displaced*. The DPs had not gone searching for a new homeland and were not economic migrants like the overwhelming majority of the pre-war Ukrainian immigrants to Canada. Instead they had been forcibly ejected from a place to which, as an Allied psychological study group described it, they felt 'a compulsive need to return.'[52] For Ukrainian Canadians the desire of many DPs to go back to Ukraine and the belief that their refugee existence was only temporary were almost incomprehensible. For their part, many of the refugees refused to accept resettlement, believing that to seek a new home would be to admit that their struggle for an independent Ukraine had failed. Even after they had been resettled in Canada for decades, many could not accept the likelihood that they would never go home. To this day, a minority claims that it still feels this way.[53]

Such a world-view informed the efforts of some DPs to re-create in emigration the organizational structures that had served them well in their homeland and in their exodus. Just as the Ukrainians who had settled in Canada before the war had created a distinctly Ukrainian-

Canadian cultural and material landscape, particularly on the prairies, so the post-war refugees brought with them their own cultural baggage, reflective of the life they had known in Ukraine and the DP camps. Between thirty-five thousand and forty thousand Ukrainian DPs resettled in Canada and found places for themselves primarily within the urban-industrial centres of Ontario and Quebec.[54] Since their refugee experience was markedly different from the experience of immigration and settlement familiar to most Ukrainian Canadians, fissures between the two populations emerged within a few years and have continued to fragment Ukrainian-Canadian society. Although time has diminished the cleavages, they are still evident – a telling indicator of the long-term impact a refugee immigration can have.[55]

After working for many months with the Ukrainian refugees Ann Crapleve wrote a report in which she cautioned her fellow Ukrainian Canadians to remember that 'the D.P. population is not a voluntary immigration. This fact must never be overlooked.'[56] If her insight had been more widely appreciated, then some of the hostility and disappointment that arose out of the encounter between the DPs and the Ukrainian Canadians may have been avoided. Before they came to know each other both groups had believed that, since they were all Ukrainians, they would get on well together. They came to realize how very different they were. And in the process the 'fashion to help the refugees' passed.[57]

The Resettlement of Ukrainian Refugees in Canada after the Second World War

IHOR STEBELSKY

Post-war refugees comprised the third and most recent wave of Ukrainian immigration to Canada.[1] The previous two groups had consisted chiefly of economic immigrants from Western Ukraine (Austria-Hungary before the First World War and Poland, Czechoslovakia, and Romania between the wars). By contrast, the post-war refugees, who were part of the 2.5 to 3 million Ukrainians who found themselves in war-torn Germany in 1945, came from all parts of Ukraine.[2] Among them were young people who had been pressed to work in the German military-industrial complex, prisoners of war who had served in the Polish and Soviet armies, nationalists who had been incarcerated in Nazi concentration camps, and political refugees who had suffered oppression in Soviet Ukraine or had escaped arrest and execution when the Soviets occupied Western Ukraine in 1939–41. Towards the end of the war, Nazi Germany had even formed a division of Ukrainian volunteers to fight the Red Army. After the division was defeated in battle and its remnants were redeployed to rearguard action, it surrendered to the Western allies in Austria and was interned in Italy.[3]

When Soviet forces occupied eastern Austria and Germany, they identified over five million 'Soviet citizens,' including Balts, Belorussians, and Ukrainians from pre-war Poland. All were promptly repatriated. The Western allies delivered almost all the 'Soviet citizens' in their zones of occupation to the Soviet authorities in the spring and summer of 1945.[4] Of an estimated two million Ukrainians in the zones of Austria and Germany occupied by the Western allies, only a quarter of a million remained by the time mass repatriations had ceased.[5] This small core of refugees who had avoided repatriation by hook or crook found relief in

the displaced persons' camps of Austria and Germany and later emigrated overseas.

Among the destinations that the Ukrainians sought was Canada,
which already had a sizeable Ukrainian community. Between 1947 and
1957, over thirty-five thousand Ukrainian refugees made their way into
Canada. They differed from the Ukrainian Canadians in their political
outlook (for they sought a refuge from which they could liberate Ukraine
from Communist oppression and then return home), and these differences generated considerable stress in the Ukrainian-Canadian community.[6] The refugees were also not mostly peasants, as were the pre-war
Ukrainian immigrants, but represented a broad socio-economic mix of
the Ukrainian population, with a large admixture of intelligentsia. It was
the refugee intelligentsia, professionals, and businessmen who contributed to a restructuring of the Ukrainian-Canadian community and the
emergence of a new urban profile within it.

This paper will detail the numbers of Ukrainian refugees who immigrated to Canada after the Second World War, their demographic, socio-
economic, and political characteristics, the routes they took, and the
experiences they had along the way. The effect of Canadian immigration
policy on the selection of immigrants, their destination within Canada,
and their initial employment contracts will also be considered. Finally
an attempt will be made to assess the demographic, economic, and social
impact of the refugees on the Ukrainian-Canadian community.

Ukrainian Refugees in Europe

At the end of the war Ukrainian displaced persons (DPs) were encountered in many parts of Europe that had been occupied by Nazi Germany.
The largest concentration was in Austria and Germany.[7] Their numbers
were not at first apparent, for the occupying forces had agreed at the
Yalta conference in February 1945 to return displaced persons to their
home countries – a policy that led those who feared repatriation to the
Soviet Union to conceal their identities or even to resort to suicide.[8]
Since Soviet policy aimed at retrieving all DPs who had resided on
territories that became part of the USSR during and after the war, even
Ukrainians from pre-war Poland were targets of Soviet agents agitating
for return to 'the workers' paradise.' By contrast, the United States
emphasized former citizenship and, after protests against forced repatriation from Ukrainian organizations in the United States, issued reassuring statements with regard to Ukrainians who were not Soviet citizens

on 1 September 1939.[9] As a result the Ukrainians who came from pre-war Poland (often registered as 'Polish Ukrainians') began to declare themselves openly. Ukrainians from eastern Ukraine, however, were still fearful of repatriation and tried to conceal their identities. Many availed themselves of Ukrainian Red Cross documents (issued in Geneva) on which they gave a place of birth in pre-war Poland.[10] Only after the International Refugee Organization (IRO) replaced the United Nations Relief and Rehabilitation Administration (UNRRA) in July 1947 and a policy of resettlement replaced repatriation did the declared numbers of Ukrainians increase and even the new category 'Ukrainian SSR' was not used. Nevertheless, the Western allies preferred to use citizenship rather than ethnic origin to classify displaced persons. Since Ukrainians came from the pre-war territories of Poland, Czechoslovakia, and Romania as well as the Soviet Union, their former citizenship varied accordingly. Even the stateless, or Nansen passport, category was employed. As a result, many Ukrainians were counted as 'Poles' and other nationalities or included in the 'undetermined nationality' category. Thus, an IRO report for 30 November 1947 recorded that only eighty thousand Ukrainian refugees in the Western zones of Germany, over seven thousand in Austria, and over three hundred in Italy were receiving IRO care and maintenance.[11]

The true number of Ukrainian refugees was in fact considerably greater. Bohdan Panchuk, a flight lieutenant in the RCAF and director of the Central Ukrainian Relief Bureau in London who maintained close contact with refugee organizations, frequently visited Ukrainians in the DP camps and collected information on their numbers, location, morale, and living conditions. According to Panchuk, Ukrainian organizations, which knew their own people and their locations, estimated that in January 1947 there were 250,000 Ukrainian refugees in Western Europe.[12] In late 1947, about 200,000 Ukrainian refugees were recorded in the Western zones of Austria and Germany. Their distribution and the decline in their numbers caused by immigration overseas are presented in table 1.

While they were under IRO care, about half of the Ukrainian DPs in Austria and over three-quarters of those in Germany resided in camps known as assembly centres (map and table 2). The remainder, especially those classified as Ukrainian SSR, received IRO services in private homes away from camps (where agents would be less likely to approach them for repatriation). At first, military and UNRRA officials showed little concern for national differences among the DPs and preferred multina-

UKRAINIANS IN D.P. CAMPS OF WEST GERMANY AND AUSTRIA 1946-1950

by

Ihor Stebelsky

BOUNDARIES

---·---·--- INTERNATIONAL

—·—·—·— OCCUPATION ZONES

--------- PROVINCIAL

○ CITY

APPROXIMATE UKRAINIAN POPULATION IN CAMP OR SETTLEMENT

● More than 1,000

● 501 to 1,000

• 100 to 500

· UNSPECIFIED

SOVIET

Dresden

Berlin

Fr.
Br.
US

Potsdam

Leipzig

Halle

Magdeburg

G.D.R.

Karl Marx Stadt

Erfurt

Rostock

D

Flensburg

SCHLESWIG-HOLSTEIN

Kiel

Preetz

Neustadt

Itzehoe

Lübeck

Hamburg

Wentorf

Seedorf · Buchholz

Heidenau

Münster-Lager

NIEDERSACHSEN

N

Bremerhaven

Oerel

Wilhelmshaven

Varel

Oldenburg

Papenburg

Delmenhorst

Bremen

BREMEN ENCLAVE
Under US and
BRITISH control

BRITISH

Haren

Lingen

Bathorn

Rheine

Osnabruck

Bielefeld

Münster

Haltern

Dorsten

Bocholt

Dinslaken

Essen

Duisburg

Mülheim-Ruhr

Lintorf Velbert

Düsseldorf

Solingen

Köln

NORD RHEIN WESTFALEN

Dortmund

Bochum

Menden

Paderborn

Neukirchen

Kolbach

Landau

Ziegenberg · Furstenwald

Kassel

Correberg

Herxfeld

Burgdorf

Hannover

Lichtenberg

Hildesheim

Godenau

Gandersheim

Hameln

Barum

Goslar

Osterode

Northeim

Gottingen

Braunschweig

Hollendorf

Sulzgitter

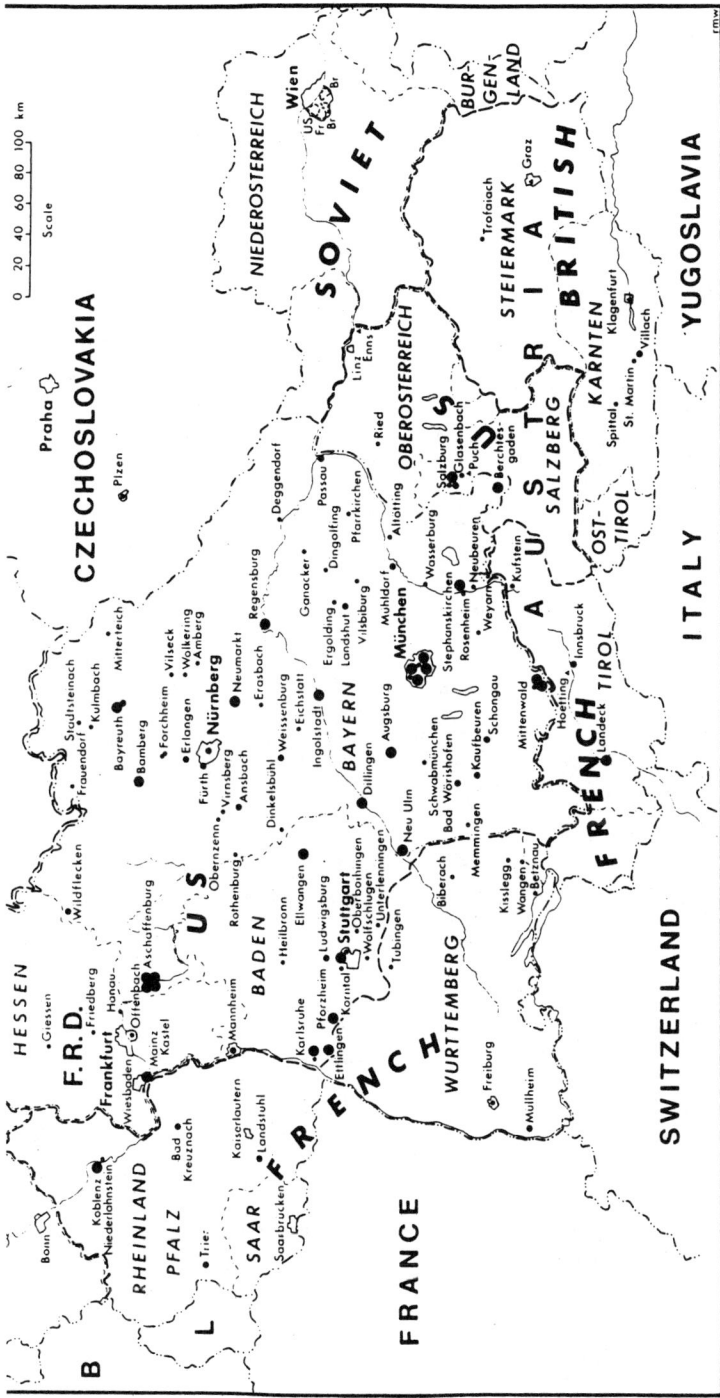

B

HESSEN
F.R.D.
Giessen
Friedberg
Hanau
Frankfurt
Wiesbaden
Mainz
Kastel
Offenbach
Aschaffenburg
Mannheim

L
Bonn
RHEINLAND
Koblenz
Niederlahnstein
PFALZ
Bad Kreuznach
Kaiserlautern
Landstuhl
SAAR
Trier
Saarbrucken

FRENCH

FRANCE

SWITZERLAND

Praha
CZECHOSLOVAKIA
Plzen

Wildflecken
Stadtsteinach
Frauendorf
Kulmbach
Mitterteich
Bayreuth
Bamberg
Forchheim
Erlangen
Vilseck
Wolkering
Amberg
Nürnberg
Furth
Virnsberg
Ansbach
Neumarkt
Erasbach
Regensburg
Obernzenn
Weissenburg
Eichstatt
Ingolstadt
Dinkelsbuhl
Rothenburg
Ganacker
Deggendorf
Heilbronn
Ellwangen
Ludwigsburg
Stuttgart
Korntal
Pforzheim
Ettlingen
Karlsruhe
BADEN
Oberboihingen
Wolfschlugen
Unterlenningen
Tubingen
WURTTEMBERG
Neu Ulm
Dillingen
BAYERN
Augsburg
Schwabmunchen
Bad Worishofen
Kaufbeuren
Memmingen
Biberach
Kisslegg
Wangen
Betznau
Schongau
München
Ergolding
Landshut
Vilsburg
Dingolfing
Pfarrkirchen
Muhldorf
Altotting
Passau
Stephanskirchen
Rosenheim
Weyarn
Neubeuern
Wasserburg
Kufstein
Mittenwald
Hoefing
Innsbruck
Landeck
FRENCH
OST-TIROL
TIROL
Freiburg
Mullheim

US

OBEROSTERREICH
Ried
Linz
Enns
AUSTRIA
Glassenbach
Salzburg
Puch
Berchtesgaden
SALZBURG

SOVIET
NIEDEROSTERREICH
Wien
US Fr Br
BUR-GEN-LAND
STEIERMARK
Trofaiach
Graz
BRITISH
KARNTEN
Klagenfurt
Spittal
St. Martin
Villach

ITALY

YUGOSLAVIA

0 20 40 60 80 100 km
Scale

TABLE 1

Ukrainian refugees and displaced persons in the western zones of
Austria and Germany

	Mar. 1946	Aug. 1947	Feb. 1948	Jan. 1949
Austria	29,241	26,422	17,786	10,680
Germany	177,620	140,555	119,742	85,608
British Zone	54,580	44,987	35,108	24,923
French Zone	19,026	9,922	6,130	4,074
US Zone	104,024	85,646	78,504	56,611
Total	206,861	167,977	137,528	96,288

Source: Data compiled by the Central Representation of the Ukrainian
Emigration in Germany, the Ukrainian Central Consultative Commit-
tee of the British Zone, and the Ukrainian Central Aid Alliance of
Austria and summarized in a table in a Central Ukrainian Relief
Bureau (CURB) report. CURB Reports, 1948–9, MG 28 V9, vol. 17, NAC.

TABLE 2

Ukrainians and Ukrainian SSR categories registered by the IRO in the western zones
of Austria and Germany, 31 December 1949

	Ukrainians		Ukrainian SSR		Total	
	no.	%	no.	%	no.	%
Austria						
Receiving care						
in camps	3,093	53.4	354	41.2	3,447	51.9
Outside	73	1.3	30	3.5	103	1.5
Services only	2,619	45.3	476	55.3	3,095	46.6
Total	5,785	100.0	860	100.0	6,6645	100.0
Germany						
Receiving care						
in camps	34,097	80.0	1,483	41.8	35,580	77.1
Outside	161	0.4	20	0.6	181	0.4
Service only	8,346	19.6	2,041	57.6	10,387	22.5
Total	42,604	100.0	3,544	100.0	46,148	100.0

Source: International Refugee Organization, 'Schedule of Refugees Receiving IRO Assistance, 31 December, 1949,' AJ 43:1097, Archives Nationales de France, Paris.

tional camps. Through the efforts of the Ukrainian committees, however,
UNRRA and IRO officials agreed to place the Ukrainians in separate
camps.[13]

Each camp was soon allowed to establish its own government, or
'camp republic.'[14] A council elected by the residents held the highest

authority, and an appointed commandant and his executive officers handled daily affairs. These posts offered refugees an opportunity to hone their skills in administering culture, education, labour, and finance. Enjoying a broad latitude of self-administration and supplied with adequate food, clothing, shelter, and health care, the camps became hearths of intense cultural and political activity. The larger camps, which housed a thousand or so residents, boasted an elementary school, high school, and vocational school or adult education programme. They invariably had both a Catholic and an Orthodox parish and supported community organizations.[15] Contact among the writers, artists, and scholars who resided in various camps improved to the point where it was possible to convene conferences and establish various associations, all of which began to publish newsletters, bulletins, and books. Munich, which had several large Ukrainian camps on its outskirts and accommodated many Ukrainians in private residences, emerged as a major Ukrainian cultural and political centre. It housed the Ukrainian Free University, the Ukrainian Technical Economic Institute, and several newspapers. The last provided a forum for the competing political parties: nationalists, democrats, socialists, and monarchists. The two factions of the Organization of Ukrainian Nationalists, the Banderites and the Melnykites, formed the nationalist camp. The middle-of-the-road democrats consisted of the Ukrainian National Democratic Union, which had existed in Galicia before the war, and two newly formed groups. The socialists (chiefly refugees from Soviet Ukraine) were organized in the Ukrainian Revolutionary Democratic Party, which was split into a moderate majority and a radical minority. The small group of monarchists, supporters of the Hetman regime of 1918, belonged to the Union of Hetmanites-Patriots.[16] Thus the Ukrainian DP experience was highly charged both culturally and politically and had a profound impact on the people who were to emigrate to Canada.

The demographic characteristics of the Ukrainian refugees were quite favourable for the purposes of emigrating and establishing a new life. Except for the nine thousand men in the First Ukrainian Division, the population in the DP camps of Austria and Germany was reasonably well balanced by sex. According to a survey of the Ukrainians in DP camps and hospitals in the British zone of Germany, the male-female ratio was 48:52 in March 1948, 45.1:54.9 in December 1950, and 44.6:55.4 in November 1951.[17] The trend indicated a decline in the number of men, as more of them departed on labour contracts overseas, often on group resettlement schemes, with the hope that their families would join them later.

TABLE 3
Age structure of the Ukrainian population in
post-war Germany

Age cohort	Jan. 1946 (%)	Oct. 1948 (%)
0–4	6.2	15.2
5–9	4.3	4.9
10–14	3.8	4.2
15–19	8.5	4.0
20–29	31.8	26.0
30–39	26.0	21.6
40–49	13.5	14.9
50–59	4.6	6.9
60 +	1.3	2.5
Total	100.00	100.00

Source: V. Kubiiovych, 'Z demohrafichnykh problem ukrainskoi emigratsii (na prykladi taboriv u
Mittenvaldi),' *Sohochasne i mynule* 1–2 (Munich,
1949), 15–17, as reproduced in V. Maruniak, 'V
25ty-littia ukrainskoi emihratsii v Nimechchyni ta
Avstrii po druhii svitovii viini: 1943–1951–1967'
(PhD dissertation, Ukrainian Free University,
1968), 68.

TABLE 4
Age structure of Ukrainian DPs in the camps and hospitals of the British zone
of Germany

Age cohort (approximate)	31 Mar. 1948		31 Sept. 1949		31 Dec. 1950		15 Nov. 1951	
	no.	%	no.	%	no.	%	no.	%
0–4	4,763	16.9	2,053	15.8	481	8.7	320	9.5
5–9	2,218	7.9	1,127	8.7	816	14.7	444	13.2
10–14	1,089	3.9	482	3.7	219	3.9	135	4.0
15–19	914	3.2	302	2.3	178	3.2	91	2.7
20–29	9,014	31.9	3,465	26.7	1,051	18.9	671	19.9
30–39	5,165	18.3	2,374	18.3	1,120	20.2	668	19.8
40–49	2,955	10.5	1,637	12.6	837	15.1	527	15.6
50–59	1,521	5.4	1,032	7.9	541	9.8	319	9.5
60 +	570	2.0	520	4.0	308	5.5	202	5.8
Total	28,209	100.0	12,992	100.0	5,551	100.0	3,367	100.0

Source: Central Ukrainian Relief Bureau, 'Material for CURB Commemorative
Book 1945–1952,' 34, MG 28 V9, vol. 17, NAC.
Note: Age cohorts have been adjusted to correspond to those used by Kubijovyč.

TABLE 5
Occupational structure of the Ukrainian refugee
population in parts of Germany and Austria in 1946

| | Germany | | Austria |
	US zone (%)	British zone (%)	(%)
Farmers	30	44	41.5
Workers	34	35	22.5
Professionals	23	8	14.0
Other	13	13	22.0
Total	100	100	100.0

Source: Compiled from data collected by the Central Representation of the Ukrainian Emigration in Germany.
Summarized in Maruniak, 'V 25ty-littia ukrainskoi emihratsii,' 68.

The population was relatively young. It had a high concentration in
the 20 to 29 age cohort, a fair number of middle-aged (30–49) adults, and
only a small number of the elderly (over 60). According to Volodymyr
Kubijovyč, who conducted a survey in Germany, the age cohort composition for January 1946 and October 1948 revealed not only a young
population, but also one that was experiencing a burst of growth (table
3). This trend was confirmed by a repeated survey of the Ukrainian DPs
in the camps and hospitals of the British zone of Germany from 1948
until 1951 (table 4). After the war had ended and the refugees found
food and shelter in the DP camps of Austria and Germany, the young
people married and began to raise families. In 1948 the youngest age
cohort (0–4) became prominent; by 1950 the baby boomers had moved
into the second age cohort (5–9). Meanwhile, the young adults were
being siphoned off by emigration overseas, and the elderly cohort (60
and over) was gaining importance.

The occupational structure of the Ukrainian refugees was diverse and
broadly based. Surveys conducted by the Central Representation of
the Ukrainian Emigration in Germany indicated both a wide diversity
and a concentration of professionals in the American zone of Germany
(table 5). Another tabulation for 1948 revealed the diversity of workers
and professionals in greater detail (table 6). Both tables suggest that
farmers and workers each represented at least a third of the employable
population and that professionals were a significant group, especially
in the American zone of Germany. Indeed, the Ukrainian refugees in
Germany had a larger proportion of skilled workers and professionals

TABLE 6
Occupational structure of Ukrainian refugees in the US and British zones of Germany
in 1948

	US zone		British zone	
	no.	%	no.	%
Farmers	14,402	23.8	7,082	24.7
Workers	14,481	24.6	8,839	30.8
unskilled	3,497	5.8	4,329	15.1
skilled	4,292	7.1	2,826	9.8
skilled tradesmen	7,052	11.7	1,684	5.9
Professionals of lower qualifications	4,328	7.2	952	3.3
nurses and orderlies	267		104	
forest rangers	122		0	
teachers (primary)	1,382		423	
clerks	1,779		211	
businessmen	778		214	
Professionals of higher qualifications	3,159	5.2	517	1.8
engineers	225		134	
economists and accountants	91		4	
foresters and agronomists	151		15	
veterinarians	41		2	
medical doctors	248		36	
pharmacists	34		2	
dentists	31		5	
priests	206		48	
scientists	652		27	
lawyers	310		40	
teachers (secondary, university)	829		125	
artists (visual, musical, etc.)	191		58	
journalists	110		10	
writers	40		11	
Others and housewives	23,683	39.2	11,259	39.3
Subtotal	60,413	100.00	28,669	100.00
Children and students	18,641		5,884	
Total of survey	79,054		34,553	

Source: Based on data collected by the Central Representation of the Ukrainian Emigration in Germany. Adapted from Maruniak, 'V 25ty-littia ukrainskoi emihratsii,' 67.

than did male Ukrainians in Canada in 1941 (table 16), and the proportion of skilled workers and professionals in this group in turn would
have been even greater than among the Ukrainian immigrants to Canada before the Second World War.

Migration of Ukrainian Refugees from Europe to Canada

The war-torn economy in Europe could not support a large body of refugees, and the Ukrainians themselves sought safety from the Communist foe across the Atlantic. On the other hand, there were resource-rich countries in the West that could accommodate additional labour force. One of the latter, Canada, also had the advantage of a viable Ukrainian community, towards which many of the Ukrainian refugees gravitated, whether they had relatives there or not.

The UNRRA sought to resolve the refugee problem by means of repatriation and to a large degree succeeded. Meanwhile, in the West, the Inter-Governmental Committee for Refugees (IGCR) started to assist some refugees to emigrate, but at first this scheme did not affect Ukrainian DPs. By 1946, however, the IGCR signed an agreement with Belgium, the Netherlands, France, and French Tunisia for workers, among whom were a number of Ukrainian DPs. Since the IGCR did not possess an operational budget, however, it could not finance group migration, and the numbers involved were small. Only with the creation of the IRO was a mechanism set in place to expedite the migration of DPs overseas.[18]

Migration, however, also depended on the will of the potential host countries to implement measures that would facilitate immigration. Although some countries moved quickly, others moved very cautiously or not at all. Each government set its own guide-lines as to the number and kinds of immigrants desired. Group schemes could accommodate the largest number of refugees, but they were open only to those who possessed the specified qualifications. Individuals or families were allowed to join relatives who would sponsor them, but the process was slow.

Mass migration of DPs assisted by the IRO was associated with group schemes. Between July 1947 and December 1951, the IRO assisted 14,877 Ukrainian DPs, or 13.1 per cent of all the Ukrainian DPs assisted in resettlement, to come to Canada. Approximately as many were assisted to Britain, an even larger number to Australia, and three times as many to the United States (table 7). Smaller numbers were sponsored to Belgium, France, Brazil, Argentina, and Venezuela. Other recipient countries took in few Ukrainian DPs.

The first countries to respond with schemes for the Ukrainian DPs were in Western Europe itself. France offered a short-lived agricultural worker scheme, and Belgium recruited workers for the coal-mines.[19]

TABLE 7
Ukrainian refugees assisted by the IRO for resettlement, 1 July 1947–31 December 1951

Country of destination	Ukrainian refugees		All refugees (no.)	Ukrainian refugees as % of all refugees
	no.	%		
Western Europe				
Belgium	5,650	5.0	22,477	25.1
France	3,342	2.9	38,455	8.7
United Kingdom	15,001	13.2	86,346	17.4
Other	296	0.3	11,500	2.6
North America				
Canada	14,877	13.1	123,479	12.0
USA	45,044	39.6	328,851	13.7
South America				
Argentina	2,283	2.0	32,712	7.0
Brazil	4,609	4.0	28,848	16.0
Venezuela	1,887	1.7	17,277	10.9
Other	563	0.5	18,838	3.0
Australasia				
Australia	19,607	17.2	182,159	10.8
New Zealand	179	0.2	4,837	3.7
Israel	35	0.0	132,109	0.0
Other	230	0.2	9,393	2.4
Not reported	74	0.1	1,469	5.0
Total	113,677	100.0	1,038,750	10.9

Source: International Refugee Organization, Office of Statistics and Operational Reports, *The Final Statistical Report of IRO: With Summaries Covering the 54 Months of Its Operations, July 1947 to December 1951* (Geneva, nd), 12–13.

Britain provided by far the largest migration scheme for Ukrainian refugees. Even before the initiation of mass migration, Britain was instrumental in removing the First Ukrainian Division from its POW camp in Rimini, Italy, to work camps in Britain, where the men retained POW status until the end of 1948.[20] The mass movement of some fourteen thousand civilian Ukrainian refugees to Britain in 1947–8, assisted by the IRO, was part of a major scheme, called 'Westward Ho,' which helped reduce the burden of maintaining large refugee populations in the British zones of Austria and Germany while providing labour for the undermanned British industries. By the end of May 1951 nearly thirty thousand Ukrainian refugees came to reside in Britain.[21] The demographic structure of the refugees in Britain, who were mostly working-age men, facilitated their further immigration, when opportunity arose, to Australia, the United States, and Canada.

Brazil, Argentina, and Venezuela also responded quickly to accept refugees. Of these, Brazil took in the largest number of Ukrainian DPs, for it maintained a policy of acceptance and had an established Ukrainian community in Curitiba that provided assistance in settlement through its committee.[22] The small, though poorer, Ukrainian community in Argentina also extended a helping hand, but in late 1948 the government switched its immigration policy to the sponsorship of first-degree relatives only, which sharply curtailed the inflow of Ukrainian refugees. Venezuela lacked a Ukrainian community, and in November 1948 a new government came to power and virtually halted further refugee immigration. In effect, Brazil provided reasonable conditions for Ukrainian refugee settlement, Argentina less so, and Venezuela had no basis for a sustained Ukrainian community and hence lacked the attraction for Ukrainian intelligentsia to stay.

The overwhelming majority of the Ukrainian refugees immigrated with the assistance of the IRO to the United States, Australia, and Canada. The largest number, some forty-five thousand, migrated to the greatest and wealthiest power in the West, the United States. A quota system that did not favour immigrants from Eastern Europe at first restricted the movement, but in July 1948 Congress passed the Displaced Persons Act, which allowed 'quota mortgaging' so that four times as many immigrants from those areas, including Ukrainian refugees, were permitted to enter.[23] Through such organizations as the United Ukrainian American Relief Committee the established and sympathetic Ukrainian community in the United States also assisted Ukrainian refugee movement. Ultimately, some eighty-five thousand to one hundred thousand Ukrainians immigrated into the United States after the Second World War.[24]

Australia, which initiated a vigorous immigration policy for Europeans after the war, hosted the second largest migration of Ukrainian refugees assisted by the IRO. As group labour recruitment increased in 1948 and 1949, the intake of Ukrainian refugees increased rapidly, and some twenty-one thousand Ukrainians immigrated to Australia, forming a new and viable community centred in the two largest cities, Sydney and Melbourne.[25]

Canada was both quick to respond to the refugee problem and possessed a substantial Ukrainian community that extended assistance to the refugees through the Central Ukrainian Relief Bureau.[26] Although

TABLE 8

Ukrainian refugees assisted by the IRO for resettlement in Canada, 1 July 1947–31 December 1951

Year	Ukrainian refugees (no.)	All refugees (no.)	Ukrainian refugees as % of all refugees	Ukrainian immigrants to Canada (no.)	Ukrainian refugees as % of Ukrainian immigrants
1947	1,287[a]	7,448	17.3	2,044	63.0
1948	7,328	41,092	17.8	10,011	73.2
1949	3,235	28,650	11.3	6,570	49.2
1950	2,049	16,568	12.4	3,769	54.4
1951	978	29,721	3.3	6,894	14.2
Total	14,877	123,479	12.0	29,288	50.8

Source: International Refugee Organization, Office of Statistics and Operational Reports, Statistical Report on PCIRO Operations, December 1947 (Geneva, n.d.), 18; ibid., December 1948, 42; ibid., May 1949, 30; ibid., June 1949, 63; ibid., July 1949, 36; ibid., August 1949, 37; ibid., September 1949, 48; ibid., October 1949, 37; ibid., November 1949, 33; ibid., December 1949, 48; ibid, January 1950, 28; ibid, February 1950, 28; ibid., March 1950, 38; ibid, April 1950, 31; ibid., May 1950, 31; ibid., June 1950, 39; ibid., July-September 1950, 23; ibid., October-December 1950, 22; ibid., The Final Statistical Report of IRO: With Summaries Covering the 54 Months of Its Operations July 1947 to December 1951, 12-13. a For the six-month period of 1 July to 31 December 1947.

Canada did not pursue as vigorous an immigration policy as Australia and hence did not accept as many IRO-assisted Ukrainian refugees on group schemes, it did take in over thirty-five thousand Ukrainian refugees and immigrants between 1947 and 1957. A comparison of the two categories for the period during which the IRO functioned is provided in table 8.

Although the number of IRO-assisted Ukrainian refugees accepted into Canada was small in 1947, it rose to a peak in 1948, and then declined towards the end of the programme in 1951. The proportion of the IRO-assisted refugees entering Canada who were Ukrainian exceeded 17 per cent in the first two years, indicative both of early support for the Ukrainians and of their desire to come to Canada. As opportunities to migrate to Australia and the United States increased, however, the proportion of Ukrainians among the IRO-assisted refugees entering Canada declined.

Group migration schemes involved the selection of certain kinds of people who were needed in the labour force and distorted the sex ratio of the immigrants. The Canadian government, however, sought workers for the lumber industry and the mines (which called for healthy young males) as well as for the garment industry and domestic labour (which required chiefly women). Employment on the farms, such as sugar-beet harvesting, involved labour of both sexes. Even so, the hiring of males prevailed so much that, when combined with the influx of some of the men from the former First Ukrainian Division, almost two-thirds of all the Ukrainian adults who arrived in Canada between 1947 and 1951 were men.[27] This sex imbalance promoted exogamous marriages. Group migration schemes also discriminated against the infirm and the elderly. The exacting medical standards set by the Canadian immigration authorities excluded many Ukrainian refugees who would have otherwise qualified.[28] Finally, group schemes did nothing for the immigration of refugees with professional and technical qualifications. Special sponsorship by the Ukrainian Canadian Committee (involving guarantees of rail transportation, housing, and employment) secured the admission of a number of such families.[29]

The other mode of immigration into Canada was through sponsorship by a 'close relative.' The large Ukrainian community in Canada provided a good opportunity for Ukrainian refugees in Europe, especially those who could not meet the group migration criteria, to re-establish contact with their relatives and seek entry into Canada. Assuming that all those who did not come as IRO-assisted refugees were individually sponsored by 'close relatives,' already in the first two years a significant number (717 in 1947, 2,683 in 1948) immigrated on that basis. Their numbers, however, increased in both absolute and relative terms, reaching a peak of 5,916 (or 95.8 per cent) in 1951. This happened in part because the definition of 'close relatives' was broadened beyond immediate relatives, so long as the applicant could support them financially. Even more important was the fact that a male refugee worker who came on a group migration scheme could, within three years, sponsor his family to Canada.[30] Thus the peak in Ukrainian refugee group migration in 1948 gave rise to an echo (this time a peak for 'close relatives') in 1951.

The intake of Ukrainians from 1946 to 1952, classified according to intended occupation, reflected the Canadian immigration policy. As a result, the composition of the Ukrainian immigrants to Canada by intended occupational groups was significantly different from the Ukrainian DPs surveyed in Austria and Germany (tables 5 and 6). The main difference was the sharply reduced share of the professional class (including the clerical and merchant class), but it also involved a slightly

TABLE 9
Ukrainian immigrants to Canada, 1946–52, classified
according to intended occupation

	no.	%
Farmers	7,660	29.6
Workers	9,078	35.2
Professionals	466	1.8
Housewives and others	8,613	33.4
Subtotal	25,817	100.0
Children	6,406	
Total	32,223	

Source: Canada, Department of Citizenship and Immigration, Statistics Section, 'Immigration to Canada by Ethnic
Origin from Overseas and Total from the United States
by Intended Occupation, Calendar Years 1946 to 1955,
Inclusive,' MG 31 D69, vol. 47, file 8, NAC.

lower share of the farming class, a slightly higher share of the worker
class, and a significantly lower share of housewives and people of other
occupations (table 9).

Following the initial massive influx of Ukrainian refugees, there was
a continuing but declining immigration for at least one decade (table
10). Immigration in excess of two thousand Ukrainians per year occurred
only between 1947 and 1952, dropping to below one thousand in 1953,
below five hundred in 1957, and below two hundred in 1961. The points
of departure of the immigrants also changed. Initially, these were mostly
IRO-supported refugees from the DP camps in the Western zones of
Germany and Austria as well as some workers and their families relocating from Belgium, France, and Britain. By 1952 the IRO mandate had
ended. The refugees who were acceptable for immigration had left, and
the DP camps in Austria and Germany were closed or transferred to
other jurisdictions (such as the United Nations High Commissioner for
Refugees) and then phased out.[31] Most of the remaining Ukrainian
refugees were absorbed into the West German economy. Ukrainians
who continued to immigrate into Canada represented in most cases the
final stage in the migration process: adjustment in the selection of a
permanent country of residence.

A sample of consecutive years from 1956 to 1961 is indicative of the
variety of countries from which Ukrainians came to Canada (table 11).
The largest contingent (42 per cent) came from Britain. Germany was a

TABLE 10
Ukrainian immigration to Canada, 1945–61

Year	Ukrainian immigrants	All immigrants	Ukrainian immigrants as % of all immigrants	Ukrainians in given year as % of all Ukrainians for 1945–61
1945	12	22,722	0.1	0.03
1946	114	71,719	0.2	0.31
1947	2,044	64,127	3.2	5.60
1948	10,011	125,414	8.0	27.43
1949	6,570	95,217	6.9	18.00
1950	3,769	73,912	5.1	10.33
1951	6,894	194,391	3.5	18.89
1952	2,821	164,498	1.7	7.73
1953	908	168,868	0.5	2.49
1954	692	154,227	0.4	1.90
1955	516	109,946	0.5	1.41
1956	540	164,857	0.3	1.48
1957	494	252,164	0.2	1.35
1958	351	124,851	0.3	0.96
1959	295	106,928	0.3	0.81
1960	298	104,111	0.3	0.82
1961	165	71,726	0.2	0.45
1945–61	36,494	2,069,678	1.8	100.00

Source: Employment and Immigration Canada, *Immigration Statistics 1896–1961* (Ottawa: Unpublished government tables for library use only, 1973), 5–7, 26.

distant second (12 per cent), followed by the United States (9 per cent), Poland (7.5 per cent), Australia (7 per cent), France (6 per cent), Belgium (3.5 per cent), and various countries of South America. Only the influx from Poland, which became noticeable in 1958–60, and the slight dribble from the USSR consisted of new refugees or individuals who were allowed to join their families. The other movements represented locational adjustments of the Ukrainian post-war refugees. Such adjustments reflected the significant pools of Ukrainian immigrants who came to reside in Britain, Germany, France, Belgium, Brazil, Argentina, Venezuela, Australia, and the United States, as well as the vitality of the Ukrainian community in Canada. In many cases the Ukrainian refugees, finding themselves isolated in the small and backward communities of South America or seeking a higher standard of living than was available in Britain, France, or Belgium, immigrated to Canada to satisfy their socio-economic needs.

TABLE 11

Ukrainian immigrants to Canada according to country of last permanent residence, 1956-61

Region or country of last permanent residence	1956 no.	1956 %	1957 no.	1957 %	1958 no.	1958 %	1959 no.	1959 %	1960 no.	1960 %	1961 no.	1961 %	1956-61 no.	1956-61 %
USSR and Eastern Europe														
USSR	3	0.5	0	0	3	0.7	3	1.0	15	4.3	16	9.7	40	1.7
Poland	3	0.5	8	1.5	24	5.9	83	28.1	39	11.2	17	10.3	174	7.5
Yugoslavia	4	0.7	2	0.4	6	1.5	4	1.3	2	0.6	0	0	18	0.8
Czechoslovakia	1	0.2	0	0	2	0.5	0	0	1	0.3	0	0	4	0.2
Other, Eastern Europe	0	0.0	2	0.4	0	0	0	0	0	0	0	0	2	0.1
Western Europe														
Austria	4	0.7	9	1.7	4	1.0	0	0	1	0.3	3	1.8	21	0.9
Germany	84	14.5	64	12.1	29	7.2	12	4.1	40	11.5	46	27.9	275	11.8
Belgium	30	5.2	33	6.2	9	2.2	5	1.7	4	1.1	0	0	81	3.5
France	60	10.4	23	4.3	16	4.0	8	2.7	16	4.6	15	9.1	138	5.9
United Kingdom	279	48.3	276	52.1	164	40.5	113	38.3	117	33.5	18	10.9	967	41.7
Other, Western Europe	12	2.1	1	0.2	0	0	2	0.7	5	1.4	1	0.6	21	0.9
South America														
Brazil	7	1.2	5	0.9	39	9.6	12	4.1	10	2.9	3	1.8	76	3.3
Argentina	3	0.5	2	0.4	13	3.2	2	0.7	4	1.1	0	0	24	1.0
Other, South America	29	5.0	19	3.6	8	2.0	13	4.4	22	6.3	3	1.8	94	4.0
Australasia														
Australia	17	2.9	47	8.9	34	8.4	38	12.9	20	5.7	5	3.1	161	6.9
New Zealand	3	0.5	3	0.5	0	0	0	0	0	0	0	0	6	0.3
United States	38	6.6	36	6.8	54	13.3	0	0	51	14.6	37	22.4	216	9.3
Other	1	0.2	0	0	0	0	0	0	2	0.6	1	0.6	4	0.2
Total	578	100.0	530	100.0	405	100.0	295	100.0	349	100.0	165	100.0	2322	100.0

Source: Department of Citizenship and Immigration, Statistics Section. Immigration Statistics, 1956 (Ottawa, 1957), 15; ibid., 1957 (Ottawa, 1958), 17; ibid., 1958 (Ottawa, 1959), 17; ibid., 1959 (Ottawa, 1960), 17; ibid., 1960 (Ottawa, 1961), 17; ibid., 1961 (Ottawa, 1960), 17; ibid., 1960 (Ottawa, 1961), 17; ibid., 1961 (Ottawa, 1962), 17. MG 31 D69, vol. 47, files 4, 6, NAC.

Destination and Settlement of Ukrainian Refugees in Canada

At the start of the war Ukrainians in Canada were concentrated in the farm belt of the prairie provinces and in the adjacent cities of Winnipeg and Edmonton. Industrially based outliers had formed elsewhere, such as Kenora, Thunder Bay, and Sudbury in northern Ontario. In the industrial heartland of southern Ontario the Ukrainian communities were still small, having grown predominantly during the economic expansion of the 1920s. Small Ukrainian communities were also emerging in British Columbia in association with mining, railway maintenance, and sawmilling. Since most Ukrainians were residing in the prairie provinces, one would have expected that the post-war refugees would have joined the established communities in proportion to the existing pattern. Such was not the case. Over 47 per cent of the Ukrainian refugees migrated to Ontario; the next largest group, over 20 per cent, went to Quebec (table 12). Only 29.6 per cent migrated to Manitoba, Saskatchewan, and Alberta, where the largest Ukrainian communities were located. When the distribution of Ukrainian immigration is compared to the distribution of Ukrainian Canadians by province in 1941, the difference becomes quite clear. The outstanding gain in immigration went to Ontario and a major one to Quebec. The greatest deficiencies in migration occurred with respect to Saskatchewan, Manitoba, and Alberta.

Canadian immigration policy and the group schemes it supported brought about this change in the pattern of intended destination. The group schemes were largely designed to bolster the development of raw material resources: mining and forestry in northern Ontario and Quebec, railway construction and maintenance (again, in the less hospitable places of northern Ontario), coal-mining and sugar-beet harvesting in southern Alberta, and other extractive and agricultural activities elsewhere. This meant that for the duration of the labour contract (usually one year) the immigrant was obliged to reside in an isolated small town where the extractive industry was located.

By contrast, sponsorship by 'close relatives' reinforced the existing settlement pattern of Ukrainians in Canada. This was, however, modified by the rapidly industrializing economy of Canada and the new opportunities for employment that arose in industry, notably in southern Ontario, as opposed to labour in agriculture, especially on the rapidly mechanizing grain farms of western Canada. Moreover, the Ukrainian Canadians were undergoing a locational change themselves, as many left farming for urban employment and migrated from the

TABLE 12
Ukrainians in Canada by province in 1941 and Ukrainian immigration to Canada by
province of intended destination, 1946–55

Province	Ukrainians in 1941		Ukrainian immigration 1946–55		Differences in distribution
	no.	%	no.	%	
Newfoundland	0	0.0	1	0.0	0.0
Prince Edward Island	2	0.0	58	0.2	+0.2
Nova Scotia	711	0.2	182	0.5	+0.3
New Brunswick	22	0.0	62	0.2	+0.2
Quebec	8,006	2.6	7,013	20.4	+17.8
Ontario	48,158	15.7	16,282	47.4	+31.7
Manitoba	89,762	29.3	4,131	12.1	−17.2
Saskatchewan	79,777	26.1	2,127	6.2	−19.9
Alberta	71,868	23.5	3,867	11.3	−12.2
British Columbia	7,563	2.5	593	1.7	−0.8
Yukon and NWT	60	0.0	11	0.0	0.0
Canada	305,929	100.0	34,329	100.0	0.0

Sources: Canada, Dominion Bureau of Statistics, Eighth Census of Canada, 1941 (Ottawa:
Printer to the King's Most Excellent Majesty and Controller of Stationery, 1946) 8:
128–70; Employment and Immigration Canada, Immigration Statistics 1896–1961
(Ottawa: Unpublished tables for library use only, 1973), 10–19.

prairies to the industrial centres of Ontario and British Columbia. A
simple simulation model of inter-provincial shift of Ukrainian population between 1941 and 1951 demonstrates that at least as many Ukrainian
Canadians who migrated from province to province in that period contributed to the inter-provincial shift of Ukrainian population in Canada
as did the new influx of immigrants (table 13). It demonstrates a huge
shift from the prairie provinces (and a small one from Quebec) to
Ontario and British Columbia. Therefore the immigration component
sponsored by 'close relatives' only partly coincided with the existing
settlement pattern of Ukrainians in Canada. In fact, it tended to reflect
within that broad pattern the shift taking place within the Ukrainian-
Canadian population and was heavily weighted towards the areas with
the best job opportunities, which were mostly in industrial central
Canada.

Locational readjustment was particularly strong among those who
entered Canada on contract in group schemes. This was, in part, related
to the inherent instability of the extractive industries (such as gold-
mining in Kirkland Lake, Ontario, or Val d'Or, Quebec) and to their
remoteness from other population centres generally and larger Ukrai-

TABLE 13
Ukrainian immigration and inter-provincial shifts, 1941–51

	Ukrainians in 1941[a]	Ukrainian immigration 1946–51[b]	Ukrainians in 1951[c]	Ukrainians expected in 1951[d]	Inter-provincial shift[e]
Newfoundland	0	0	20	0	+20
Prince Edward Island	2	58	47	60	−13
Nova Scotia	711	163	1,235	1,013	+222
New Brunswick	22	58	129	84	+45
Quebec	8,006	6,029	12,921	15,598	−2,677
Ontario	48,158	13,647	93,595	71,206	+22,389
Manitoba	89,762	3,520	98,753	110,806	−12,053
Saskatchewan	79,777	1,933	78,399	97,285	−18,886
Alberta	71,868	3,479	86,957	89,377	−2,420
British Columbia	7,563	492	22,613	9,531	+13,082
Yukon and NWT	60	11	374	83	+291
Canada	305,929	29,392	395,043	395,043	0

a Canada, Dominion Bureau of Statistics, *Eighth Census of Canada*, 1941 (Ottawa: Printer to the King's Most Excellent Majesty and Controller of Stationery, 1946) III:128–70.
b Employment and Immigration Canada, *Immigration Statistics 1896–1961* (Ottawa: Unpublished tables for library use only, 1973), 10–19.
c Canada, Dominion Bureau of Statistics, *Ninth Census of Canada. 1951* (Ottawa: Queen's Printer and Controller of Stationery, 1953) I:33–1–10.
d A simple model based on the assumption that the total in 1951 is the result of the Ukrainians in 1941 plus Ukrainian immigration, 1946–51, plus the difference, which is natural increase (19.52 per cent over a ten-year period), here assumed to be totally attributable to the Ukrainian population in 1941.
e Ukrainians in 1951 − Ukrainians expected in 1951.

nian communities specifically. In part this instability was also related to the fact that there were numerous single men and members of the Ukrainian intelligentsia (such as teachers, artists, and professors) who resorted to group schemes in order to come to Canada. Some even faked their socio-economic background when they were being screened by the Canadian immigration officials in order to score more points. When their contracts with the resource-extracting companies expired, they joined Ukrainian communities in larger urban centres, such as Winnipeg, Edmonton, Vancouver, and Montreal, but especially in Toronto and other cities in Ontario. By 1981, of the surviving 28,750 individuals who had immigrated to Canada between 1945 and 1954, 62.2 per cent were residents of Ontario.[32]

Relocation for permanent settlement was not related only to opportunities for stable employment and personal preference. Some individuals who chose to serve the Ukrainian community as priests or as political leaders were directed by their organizations to locate in places that were considered to be in need of them. Their responsibilities were to develop a viable church or political community in an area where there was a significant number of Ukrainians. The headquarters of the organizations that the immigrants brought with them were usually located in Toronto, and this is where the leadership and administrative apparatus concentrated.

The Impact of the Refugees on the Ukrainian-Canadian Community

The post-war immigrants had a significant impact on the Ukrainian-Canadian community. First, they provided a demographic enlargement and linguistic rejuvenation of the Ukrainian population in Canada. Second, they brought a powerful new political dynamic that clashed with some Ukrainian-Canadian institutions and modified others. Third, they included a rich component of skilled and professional people who changed the occupational profile of the Ukrainian-Canadian urban community.

Demographically, the influx of post-war refugees was significant, but it was not great. Of the three waves of Ukrainian immigration to Canada (about 170,000 before the First World War, 68,000 in the inter-war period, and 35,000 in the post-war period), it was the smallest. Overall, it was equivalent to about 11 per cent of the Ukrainian population in Canada at the time of the last group's arrival. By province, however, the significance varied greatly (table 14). In the prairie provinces, the influx amounted to only 3 to 5 per cent of the Ukrainian-Canadian population. This was somewhat higher in British Columbia (8 per cent) and the Yukon and Northwest Territories (18 per cent). The post-war immigrants had the greatest significance in Ontario (34 per cent), Quebec (88 per cent), and the Maritimes (41 per cent). Nevertheless, the numbers going to the Maritime provinces were too small to establish viable communities. By contrast, the numbers destined for Ontario, Quebec, and the prairie provinces, together with initial migration and subsequent readjustment into British Columbia and the cities of central and western Canada, allowed for the formation or strengthening of Ukrainian communities that emulated the political and social activities the refugees had experienced in the DP camps of Austria and Germany.

The language of communication in the Ukrainian DP camps was

TABLE 14
Ukrainian immigrants in 1946–55 in comparison with the Ukrainian-Canadian
population in 1941, by province

Province	Ukrainians in 1941 (no.)	Ukrainian immigrants in 1946–55	
		Total no.	As percentage of Ukrainians in 1941
Maritime Provinces	735	303	41
Quebec	8,006	7,013	88
Ontario	48,158	16,282	34
Manitoba	89,762	4,131	5
Saskatchewan	79,777	2,127	3
Alberta	71,868	3,867	5
British Columbia	7,563	593	8
Yukon and NWT	60	11	18
Canada	305,929	34,329	11

standard Ukrainian. It was used not only in the intimate surroundings
of a family, but for all the social and economic needs of the camp. Young
people learned standard Ukrainian in the schools. Audiences thrilled to
plays or choirs staged by some of the best Ukrainian artists. Ukrainian
could be heard on the street and seen on the signs. The refugees brought
this highly visible level of Ukrainian-language use to Canada and hoped
to perpetuate it, for in Ukraine itself the language was being suppressed
in favour of Russian.

Upon arriving in Canada, the immigrants sought places where they
could communicate in Ukrainian, for few knew English or French. They
often rented rooms with Ukrainian families and sought employment
with Ukrainian employers. Larger concentrations of Ukrainians made
the immigrants feel at home and allowed for the Ukrainian language to
assume a high external profile. The use of Ukrainian with such a high
profile was possible only in such larger cities as Toronto or in working-
class neighbourhoods of smaller towns where high concentrations of
Ukrainians could be found within a short distance of a Ukrainian church
or meeting hall. There, youth organizations, Saturday or Sunday schools,
dance groups, choirs, and sports teams were organized or rejuvenated
in order to provide the youth with opportunity for socialization. Such
instruments of socialization helped retain the Ukrainian language
among the immigrant youth, and the standard Ukrainian that they

brought improved the Ukrainian spoken by Ukrainian-Canadian youth (which was coloured with an English accent and words derived from English).

In areas of lower concentrations, where non-Ukrainian neighbours frowned on hearing a 'foreign' language, by contrast, Ukrainian was restricted to domestic use. This also tended to limit the subject of discussion to household matters (and a 'kitchen' vocabulary) and hindered the diffusion of Ukrainian to partially assimilated Ukrainian Canadians. Greater isolation also allowed for the internal household factor to play a more prominent role. Since most immigrants did not know English (a handicap that loomed even larger in more isolated areas), many made an extra effort to learn it. Some even preferred that their children not speak Ukrainian to them so as to provide an English immersion environment in their home. Such children lost their knowledge of Ukrainian within two to three years. Parents who were determined that their children retain the Ukrainian language and insisted on a 'Ukrainian only' policy at home were successful. Nevertheless, even in the latter cases, exogamous marriages made Ukrainian-language retention in the households of the newly-weds virtually impossible.[33] Thus, although the use of Ukrainian among Ukrainian post-war immigrant adults and youth was universal, the retention of the language among immigrant children, notably in the more dispersed areas, was not. Indicative of this spatial trend was the distribution by province of the percentage of Ukrainian Canadians speaking Ukrainian at home (table 15). Quebec, Ontario, Manitoba, Saskatchewan, and Alberta, where Ukrainian urban concentrations were high, registered high percentages; the Maritime provinces, British Columbia, and especially the Yukon and the Northwest Territories, where the Ukrainians were dispersed, showed low values. Quebec, however, stood out particularly high, possibly because social attitudes and the French language served as barriers for the Ukrainians, who tended to prefer English to French.[34]

Retention of the Ukrainian language by the Canadian-born children of the post-war immigrants became even more difficult. The diffusion from tightly knit neighbourhoods into suburbia, the weakening links with Ukrainian institutions, the growing dominance of the mass media at the expense of home and community activities, and increased exogamous marriages were responsible. The last stemmed, in part, from a desire of the children of the post-war immigrants for social mobility. They de-emphasized the importance of ethnicity and shifted from a first-generation Ukrainian or Ukrainian-Canadian identity to a second-generation Ukrainian-Canadian or simply Canadian identity.[35] Thus,

TABLE 15
Ukrainian Canadians speaking Ukrainian at home by province in 1971

Province	Total no. of Ukrainian Canadians	Persons speaking Ukrainian at home	
		no.	%
Maritimes	3,215	170	5.3
Quebec	20,325	7,622	37.5
Ontario	159,880	41,889	26.2
Manitoba	114,410	31,119	27.2
Saskatchewan	85,920	22,768	26.5
Alberta	135,510	24,663	18.2
British Columbia	60,145	4,330	7.2
Yukon and NWT	1,245	45	3.6
Canada	580,660	132,606	22.8

Source: Adapted from I. Tesla, 'The Ukrainian Canadian in 1971,' in A. Baran, O.W. Gerus, and J. Rozumnyi, eds., The Jubilee Collection of the Ukrainian Free Academy of Sciences in Canada (Winnipeg: UVAN, 1976), 515.

although the post-war immigrants rejuvenated the language and cultural activity of Ukrainian Canadians, their children succumbed to assimilation, especially in those areas where Ukrainians constituted a small fraction of the population and support for language retention was lacking.

The influence that the post-war immigrants exerted on Ukrainian Canadians came from their strong political convictions. As refugees from Communist oppression who had also experienced persecution from Nazi Germany and pre-war Poland and Romania, the new immigrants were staunchly nationalistic and anti-Communist in their outlook. Their chief aim was the independence of Ukraine. They viewed Canada as a temporary refuge from where support could be gained for the destruction of the Soviet Union and the liberation of Ukraine. Towards that end they set up a network of political organizations and institutions that replicated the ones they had established in Europe.[36]

Part of the reason for this replication was that the Ukrainian organizations that the refugees encountered in Canada would not serve their political purposes. When refugees joined an existing Catholic or Orthodox parish, they were dismayed to discover that Ukrainian Canadians condoned the use of English in their churches and related youth associations, schools, and credit unions. While the immigrant Ukrainian Catholics disliked the Romanization of the Ukrainian Catholic church in

Canada, the Ukrainian Canadians viewed the newcomers' organizations with suspicion. On these points there were heated debates. In large cities where there were several churches of the same denomination, the refugees concentrated in the church where the pastor was also a refugee and shared their political sentiments. To the refugees, most secular Ukrainian-Canadian organizations (even the Ukrainian National Federation, which had been established by the second wave of immigrants) seemed too carefree, for they focused on social activities and folk dancing. Their members, in turn, viewed the refugees as political fanatics who were disrupting their established way of life and tarnishing their image as loyal and grateful citizens of the Dominion. The refugees also clashed with Ukrainian Canadians of Communist ideology. The latter, organized in the Association of United Ukrainian Canadians (formerly the Ukrainian Labour-Farmer Temple Association), harked back to the radicals who came from Galicia before the First World War. Having fallen under the influence of Soviet propaganda, they accused the refugees (and especially members of the Ukrainian Division) of war crimes and opposed their admission into Canada.[37] But eyewitness accounts by the refugees and travel to Ukraine by the pro-Communists proved more convincing about Soviet reality, and the AUUC lost its membership.

Within ten years of their arrival, the refugees had established organizations that came to dominate Ukrainian activities in Canada. The Bandera faction of the nationalists attracted the largest following among the refugee population in Canada.[38] It created the Canadian League for Ukraine's Liberation, its weekly newspaper *Homin Ukrainy* (Ukrainian Echo), the bookstore Arka, the Ukrainian Youth Association of Canada (which attained the largest membership among the Ukrainian youth groups in Canada), schools at both the elementary and secondary levels, the Mikhnovsky Ukrainian Student Association, and several commercial enterprises, such as the UBA Trading Company and the credit union Buduchnist, which supported publishing and education from their proceeds. The Melnyk faction of the nationalists took over and revitalized the Ukrainian National Federation and its affiliated organizations, the Ukrainian War Veterans' Association, the Ukrainian Women's Organization of Olha Basarab, the Ukrainian National Youth Federation, its affiliated Ukrainian schools, the newspaper *Novyi shliakh* (New Pathway, published in Winnipeg and since 1977 in Toronto), and the Ukrainian Credit Union (the largest Ukrainian credit union in Toronto). That faction also established the Ukrainian Academic Society Zarevo and held influential positions in the politically unaffiliated youth organization Plast and the secondary-school-level Hryhorii Skovoroda Courses in

Toronto. The Ukrainian Revolutionary Democratic Party, composed largely of refugees from Soviet Ukraine, formed the Association of Ukrainian Victims of Russian Communist Terror and its youth wing, the Ukrainian Democratic Youth Association. In smaller centres, such as Windsor, where their numbers were too small to form separate chapters, the Eastern Ukrainians, being Orthodox, joined and helped revitalize the Ukrainian Orthodox church and its associated organizations, the Ukrainian Self-Reliance League of Canada, the Ukrainian Women's Association of Canada, and the Canadian Ukrainian Youth Association. They also helped support the affiliated weekly *Ukrainskyi holos* (Ukrainian Voice) in Winnipeg, the Ilarion Society of Orthodox Students, and university residences for students (the Mohyla in Saskatoon, the St John's in Edmonton, and the St Vladimir's in Toronto). The small group of monarchists temporarily replenished the ranks of the declining United Hetman Organization. The middle-of-the-road democrats from Galicia, being Catholic, often joined the Ukrainian Catholic organizations – the Brotherhood of Ukrainian Catholics, the Ukrainian Catholic Women's League of Canada, the Ukrainian Catholic Youth of Canada, and the student association Obnova – and supported the affiliated institutions at the parish levels: the supplemental Ukrainian schools and credit unions. The new immigrants reversed the Latinization of the Ukrainian Catholic church and started publishing the Catholic weekly *Nasha meta* (Our Aim) in Toronto in 1949, increased the readership of the Catholic monthly *Svitlo* (Light, also published in Toronto), and supported Ukrainian Catholic private schools, monasteries, and their publications.[39]

Ukrainian refugee scientists and scholars brought with them two learned organizations, the Shevchenko Scientific Society (which had been founded in Lviv in 1873) and the Ukrainian Free Academy of Sciences (which had been founded as the Ukrainian Academy of Sciences in Kiev in 1918 and then renewed as the Ukrainian Free Academy of Sciences after the war in Western Europe).[40]

Youth organizations played an important role in the political socialization of Ukrainian youth in Canada and in the activation of young Ukrainian Canadians. The Ukrainian Youth Association of Canada Plast and the Ukrainian Democratic Youth Association maintained high political profiles by jointly staging anti-Soviet rallies in Toronto, Montreal, and Ottawa and supporting action to convince Canadian politicians to implement multiculturalism. By organizing cultural and sports programmes and summer camps, these organizations also attracted the largest share of organized Ukrainian youth in Canada. The secondary schools associated with these youth organizations provided advanced language training and imparted a knowledge of Ukrainian geography, history, literature, and culture. This education and socializing activity left a lasting imprint on the organized Ukrainian refugee youth and the young Ukrainian Canadians who joined their ranks.

As we have seen, the post-war refugees brought with them a high level of political dynamism and a greater share of skilled workers and qualified professionals. This characteristic, however, did not immediately change the employment pattern of male Ukrainians in Canada (table 16). Initially, both skilled workers and professionals accepted employment in farming, physical labour, and industry. In this way, they increased the Ukrainian share of the labourers in the logging, manufacturing, and construction occupational groupings and strengthened the Ukrainian relative share of the farming, mining, and quarrying occupational groupings. Nevertheless, the professionals learned English, sought Canadian accreditation or supplemental training, and within a decade many obtained work in their fields. This is reflected in the rapid rise of the Ukrainian share and relative share of the professional, the technical, and, to a lesser extent, the owners, managers, and clerical and sales occupational groupings.

Priests, writers, journalists, and some artists and teachers (whose service or end-product was in the Ukrainian language) had to rely on low-paying employment with Ukrainian institutions, such as churches, newspapers, and schools. Economists and accountants sometimes obtained government positions, but were seldom accepted by the Canadian establishment in private business. People with academic backgrounds in the arts or Slavic languages earned degrees in library science and became librarians at universities. Those with a background in education and other arts or sciences retrained in English for positions as teachers. Those with the appropriate professional qualifications sought employment as university professors, scientists, engineers, physicians, veterinarians, dentists, and pharmacists. The engineers, doctors, librarians, and journalists even established their own professional organizations. Thus, whether placed within the Ukrainian community or outside it, the new immigrants contributed to the rapid growth of professional and technical occupations among the Ukrainians in Canada.[41]

Some immigrants ventured into business. Those who had managerial experience in co-operatives and industrial enterprises in Galicia started small firms with the help of loans from Ukrainian credit unions. The former managers of Maslosoiuz, a dairy co-operative in Lviv, for example, started the MC and Green Vale dairies in Toronto.[42] Both companies

TABLE 16
Change in the share of occupational groupings among male Ukrainian Canadians and
all male Canadians, 1941–71 (U = Ukrainian Canadians; A = all Canadians)

Occupational groupings		1941	1951	1961	1971
Owners, managers	U	nd	5.0	7.1	3.9
	A	nd	9.0	10.2	5.5
	U as % of A	–	55.6	69.6	70.9
Professional, technical	U	1.5	2.6	5.8	8.8
	A	3.5	5.1	7.6	9.9
	U as % of A	42.9	51.0	76.3	88.9
Clerical and sales	U	4.8	5.6	9.2	13.5
	A	14.4	11.2	12.5	17.5
	U as % of A	33.3	50.0	73.6	77.1
Service, transportation,	U	10.6	14.1	13.7	18.8
and communication	A	13.5	15.8	16.0	18.4
	U as % of A	78.5	89.2	85.6	102.2
Farming	U	54.6	35.3	23.0	13.2
	A	31.7	19.4	12.2	7.1
	U as % of A	172.2	182.0	188.5	185.9
Mining and quarrying	U	2.9	2.3	1.8	1.4
	A	2.1	1.6	1.4	1.0
	U as % of A	138.1	143.8	128.6	140.0
Logging, manufacturing,	U	16.0	23.6	30.2	28.3
and construction	A	25.5	27.5	30.5	28.2
	U as % of A	62.7	85.8	99.0	100.4
Labourers	U	9.2	10.5	6.9	3.5
	A	7.5	8.0	6.2	3.5
	U as % of A	122.7	131.3	111.3	100.0
Others, not specified	U	0.4	1.0	2.3	8.6
	A	1.8	2.4	3.4	8.9
	U as % of A	22.2	41.7	67.6	96.6
Total	U	100.0	100.0	100.0	100.0
	A	100.0	100.0	100.0	100.0

Source: Derived from tables in Wsevolod W. Isajiw, 'Occupational and Economic Development,' in Manoly R. Lupul, ed., A Heritage in Transition: Essays in the History of
Ukrainians in Canada (Toronto: McClelland and Stewart, 1982), 76–9.
Note: Because definitions of occupational groupings were not consistent from one year
to another, the shares of occupational groupings should be considered only as approxi-
mations. A more reliable measure is the relative share of an occupational grouping,
expressed in terms of the share of Ukrainian Canadians as a percentage of all
Canadians.

provided food-processing and truck-delivery employment to their fellow immigrants for a number of years, until they could no longer compete with the giants of the dairy industry and had to close. A number
of retail fuel oil companies carved out a niche for themselves in Toronto
and still remain in business. In fact, Ukrainians tended to stay in the
service-related low-risk family-run businesses. These included real
estate, hotels and motels, general stores, grocery stores, gas and auto
repair shops, and barber and beauty shops.[43] This reflected their dependence on a Ukrainian clientele, the lack of financial security for undertaking large risks, and the difficulty of raising large amounts of capital
for starting major enterprises. To support their efforts, they organized
themselves into Ukrainian business and professional clubs. In effect,
although the refugees brought with them a pool of talent for professional
and even entrepreneurial endeavour and were generally successful in
finding appropriate professional employment, they lacked the capital
with which they could launch major enterprises and were thus less
successful in this area.

The post-war immigrants also brought with them a penchant for
education. This was related, in part, to the larger percentage of the
immigrants possessing professional education than the Ukrainian Canadians generally and in part to the immigrants' stronger political purpose.
This background and inner drive provided them with the will to learn
English or French, to upgrade their professional skills, to seek better
positions, and to educate their children in their chosen professions.
Many immigrant youths took up the challenge, pursued higher education, and became engineers, doctors, dentists, lawyers, scientists, university professors, and teachers. The contribution of this age cohort became
apparent by 1971 (table 16), but whether this group outdid the Canadian-
born Ukrainians, and to what extent, needs further exploration. Nevertheless, they are actively participating in Ukrainian business and professional clubs to enhance the cultural vitality of the community. With
revolutionary changes occurring in Ukraine itself, these members are
also assisting it in its economic and political restructuring.

The post-war refugees comprised the third wave of Ukrainian immigration into Canada. Consisting of over thirty-five thousand immigrants,
this wave represented only half the number that came in the inter-war
period and one-fifth of the number that came before the First World
War. Yet it contained an above-average component of skilled workers
and intelligentsia, had a significant number of refugees from eastern
Ukraine, and was by far the most politicized and best organized group

of the three waves. The composition of the refugees and their strong political convictions were conditioned by the events of the Second World War, the persecution, repression, and forced repatriation they experienced, and the interpretation of the events they shared through Ukrainian political organizations and their communications organs in the post-war DP camps.

Ukrainian immigration to Canada was encouraged in part by the assistance that the Ukrainian-Canadian community extended to the refugees in Europe and in part by Canada's favourable immigration policy. The group schemes, which brought over large numbers of IRO-supported refugees, however, distorted the demographic balance of the immigrants. Nearly half the Ukrainian post-war immigrants came via such schemes. This, combined with the arrival of some of the former Ukrainian Division men from Britain, meant that nearly two-thirds of the Ukrainian immigrant adults arriving in Canada between 1947 and 1951 were male. Soon, however, the men who were married but came alone were able to sponsor their wives and children to join them, which somewhat rectified the imbalance. The remaining imbalance tended to promote exogamous marriages.

The bulk of the post-war Ukrainian migration originated in the DP camps of Germany and Austria between 1947 and 1951. However, since refugees were also given temporary relief in other countries first, such as Belgium, France, and especially Britain, many Ukrainian immigrants came from these countries as early as the main influx, but continued to immigrate (in gradually declining numbers) into the late 1950s. Some immigration could also be observed from other countries of the New World, where the Ukrainian refugees had landed with IRO assistance, suggesting a final period of adjustment in the selection of the permanent country of residence, which was, in this case, Canada.

The settlement of the refugees in Canada was determined not so much by the existing pattern of Ukrainian settlement in Canada as by group schemes and opportunities for employment. Therefore, at variance with the pre-war patterns, over 47 per cent of the Ukrainian refugees migrated to Ontario, and over 20 per cent migrated to Quebec. Less than 30 per cent migrated to the three prairie provinces, where the Ukrainian-Canadian population was concentrated. This migration reshaped the distribution of Ukrainians in Canada, although Ukrainian Canadians themselves were undertaking inter-provincial migration in the same direction (mostly from the prairie provinces to Ontario and British Columbia). The selection of a permanent place of residence was determined by job opportunities and quality of life, which to a politically committed Ukrainian refugee often meant location in a viable Ukrainian community. Some who chose to serve the Ukrainian community were even directed by their religious or political organization to towns where their services were needed.

The post-war refugees had a profound impact on the Ukrainian Canadians. They provided a demographic increment for the Ukrainian-Canadian community in excess of 10 per cent. Although this effect was not more than 5 per cent in the prairie provinces, it was much higher in other parts of Canada, notably Ontario (34 per cent) and Quebec (88 per cent). Moreover, with the arrival of a larger proportion of Ukrainian intelligentsia and young people recently educated in Ukrainian schools came an infusion of standard Ukrainian into the Ukrainian-Canadian community. However, linguistic improvement was only temporary and limited to the largest Ukrainian concentrations. Assimilation affected the children of the immigrants, particularly in isolated locations, and spread with time to the larger urban centres, notably affecting the second generation. The highly politicized refugees also brought with them political organizations that provided strong support for urban Ukrainian communities. The new organizations became the dominant players in the Ukrainian-Canadian community. They set a more aggressive political agenda (anti-Soviet and pro-multiculturalism) and helped maintain the ethno-linguistic vigour for at least one generation. Finally, the refugees contributed to the growth of the share of professional and technical occupations among the Ukrainians, contributed to the establishment of businesses, and fostered the organization of professional and business associations and clubs, which have become important loci of support for the Ukrainian-Canadian community.

160 акрів = 130 моргів австр. ❋ ВІЛЬНОЇ ЗЕМЛІ ❋ 200 мільонів акрів під управу в західній КАНАДІ ДЛЯ КОЖДОГО ОСЕЛЕНЦЯ

A Ukrainian-language leaflet advertising free land available in Canada (National Archives of Canada)

The land rush, 1909 (Western Canada Pictorial Index)

Passport holder provided by immigration agent F. Missler, of Bremen, Germany (Private collection of Jeff Picknicki, Winnipeg)

Arriving at the immigration sheds, Quebec City, 1911
(Western Canada Pictorial Index)

Ukrainian settlers at Pine Creek, Manitoba
(Ukrainian Cultural and Educational Centre, Winnipeg)

Ukrainian women at the plough in Alberta, 1900
(Western Canada Pictorial Index)

First shelter of a Ukrainian pioneering family in the LaCorey district of Alberta, 1929 (National Archives of Canada)

The same family's first home, LaCorey district, Alberta, 1929
(National Archives of Canada)

Bishop A. Langevin and other Roman Catholic priests in Edmonton, 1902 (Ukrainian Cultural and Educational Centre, Winnipeg)

SOUVENIR DE LA CONSECRATION DE MGR. BREYNAT EVEGUE D'ADRAMYTE 6 AVRIL 1902
PHOTO BY MATHERS EDMONTON N.W.T.

Consecration of the Ukrainian Greek Catholic Church of St Nicholas
in Kenora, Ontario, by Bishop Nykyta Budka, 1917
(Multicultural History Society of Ontario)

ALIEN INVESTIGATION BOARD
CARRY THIS CARD ON YOUR PERSON

PROVINCE OF MANITOBA   This is to Certify that   OUR FLAG

Mr. _____ P. Russin _____ 2764 _____ now

residing at _____ Wpg. Beach _____

within Manitoba, born in _____ Poland,
one of our Allied Countries, and is a **Naturalized British Subject** and
has proved to the satisfaction of this Board that he has been faithful and
borne true allegiance to His Majesty and the Allied Cause and has been a
good law-abiding citizen of Canada, deserving the goodwill of the people.
   The lawful holder of this card may be identified by the endorsements.
   Note.—Employers will please give **Returned Soldiers** preference of
employment.

SEAL   Signature of the Commissioners,

_____ T. Neil Myers _____   _____
                     Chairman   _____ Sutherland _____

Alien Investigation Board card of P. Russin
(Ukrainian Cultural and Educational Centre, Winnipeg)

OPPOSITE

Ukrainian-Canadian internees at the Castle Mountain camp, near
Banff, Alberta, in 1915 (Whyte Museum of the Rockies, Banff,
Alberta)

Ukrainian-Canadian internees hauling in stove wood at the Spirit
Lake, Quebec, internment camp (Private collection of Yurij Luhovy,
Montreal)

Bishop Nykyta Budka in Lviv, Western Ukraine, 1923
(Ukrainian Cultural and Educational Centre, Winnipeg)

Michael and Myroslav Stechishin in Vancouver, British Columbia, 1906 (G. Dragan Collection, National Archives of Canada)

Wasyl Swystun, 1919
(G. Dragan Collection, National Archives of Canada)

Convention at the P. Mohyla Institute, Saskatoon, Saskatchewan, 1918
(G. Dragan Collection, National Archives of Canada)

Sixth Convention of the Ukrainian Labor Farmer Temple Association, in Winnipeg, Manitoba, 26–28 January 1925
(G. Dragan Collection, National Archives of Canada)

Part 2

AMONG OURSELVES: COMMUNITY POLITICS AND RELIGION

Consolidating the Community: The Ukrainian Self-Reliance League

OLEH W. GERUS

In November 1940 the nationally conscious Ukrainians of Canada became consolidated in the form of the Ukrainian Canadian Committee (Komitet ukraintsiv Kanady). An umbrella organization, the committee (renamed the Ukrainian Canadian Congress in 1989) has represented the majority of the non-Communist Ukrainian community associations in Canada and has claimed to speak on behalf of all Ukrainian Canadians. That such a body came into being was in itself a major achievement on the part of the highly individualistic and factious Ukrainians, who in 1940 constituted the largest Slavic group and fourth largest minority (305,000) in Canada. Concerned with the preservation of their ethnic identity in an Anglo-Celtic environment that was both assimilatory and discriminatory, Ukrainian Canadians had always been sensitive to a need for a representative body that could present their views to provincial and federal government authorities. However, although the ideal of community solidarity was first on the agendas of all Ukrainian organizations, profound religious and political differences mitigated against the formation of an acceptable and effective representative body.

It is the contention of this paper that of all community organizations in the inter-war period, the Ukrainian Self-Reliance League (Soiuz ukraintsiv samostiinykiv or SUS) was the most influential. Its indelible imprint on Ukrainian society in Canada and its role in community consolidation will be examined. Special attention will be paid to the origins of the USRL, to its relations with its chief rival nationalist organization, the Ukrainian National Federation, and to its input into the establishment of the Ukrainian Canadian Committee.

Origins of the Ukrainian Self-Reliance League

The Ukrainian Self-Reliance League was formed in December 1927.[1] Its roots and ideology lay in the personalities, ideas, and activities of the tiny intelligentsia that was part of the much-studied pioneer history.[2] It evolved through three distinct yet related stages: the weekly *Ukrainskyi holos* (Ukrainian Voice), the Mohyla Institute of Saskatoon, and the Ukrainian Greek Orthodox church. To understand this process, a brief historical overview is first necessary.

The overwhelming majority of Ukrainian immigrants before the First World War came from Galicia. Among them were several dozen *gymnasium*, seminary, and university students who, for either economic or political reasons, had been unable to complete their education at home. Most of this small but dynamic and zealous village intelligentsia became teachers in western Canada, where they formed the first national and political elite of the Ukrainian community.

The Ukrainian-Canadian nationalist intelligentsia had been imbued with the social and political ideas of Galician radicalism. This involved elements of Ukrainian nationalism (anti-Polish and anti-Russian sentiment), agrarian socialism (the ideas of Mykhailo Drahomanov and Ivan Franko), and anti-clericalism.[3] The anti-clericalism, which was politically and not theologically motivated, was most relevant to the Canadian experience. Although the radicals attacked the conservative ecclesiastical establishment of the Ukrainian Catholic church (then known as the Greek Catholic or Uniate church), including Metropolitan Andrei Sheptytsky, for its alleged failure to defend the interests of the Ukrainian people, they deeply appreciated the historical importance of the church.[4]

When mass emigration from Galicia began, the strained relations between the 'Godless' radicals and the church were transferred to Canada, where they were intensified by organized socialist and Protestant influences aimed at the immigrants. The ideological outlook of the intelligentsia and the peculiar circumstances of pioneer life in Canada combined to make the religious issue of paramount importance in the formative phase of the immigrant community.

In the first decade, the mainly Catholic pioneers were served and exploited by a variety of religious sources: several Ukrainian Catholic missionaries and Latin priests who switched to the Byzantine rite,[5] a Russian Orthodox mission, and proselytizing Presbyterians, who assumed that the only dependable immigrant was an English-speaking Protestant. A major, albeit a short-lived, success of the Presbyterians was the creation of the Independent Greek church, Ukrainian in appearance and Protestant in content, which appealed to those who favoured rapid assimilation.[6] The Roman Catholic hierarchy in Canada eventually realized that a separate ecclesiastical province was essential for the preservation of Ukrainian Catholicism in the new land. Concerted lobbying resulted in the formation of the Ruthenian (Ukrainian) Catholic church of Canada in 1912. Bishop Nykyta Budka, a young and energetic but very conservative man, was placed in charge of the growing Ukrainian Catholic community.[7] The bishop, who made Winnipeg his home, had many virtues but did not grasp the critical difference between Canada, with its democracy and church-state separation, and Galicia, with its established and privileged church.

Since it had taken a long time for the resolution of the Ukrainian Catholic church question in Canada, the secular intelligentsia began to fill the community leadership vacuum, which in Galicia had been occupied largely by the clergy. These young men, individuals like Taras Ferley, Orest Zerebko, Peter Svarich, Wasyl Swystun, and the Stechishin brothers, mainly in their early twenties, possessed a strong sense of purpose and community concern. Above all, they wanted to help their bewildered countrymen, who were largely ignored by the Canadian authorities upon their arrival, to succeed in Canada. The problem was that Eastern Europeans could not blend immediately into the majority population.[8] They appeared as a visible alien element (the original visible minority) that typified the potential danger of the new migration for the British majority. All agreed that if Eastern Europeans were allowed into Canada, they had to be assimilated.

Of course, assimilation, particularly in the bloc settlements, would not be easy. But to the radical-nationalist intelligentsia, assimilation was an immediate and direct threat to Ukrainian identity. They responded by organizing community institutions that would sustain the settlers in their traditional culture. The missionary zeal of the intelligentsia, however, acquired real significance only when they took advantage of the bilingual education available in western Canada.[9] The educational system unexpectedly allowed them to exert their influence over the growing Ukrainian community in an organized and concerted way. As early as 1907 several dozen teachers formed the Ukrainian Teachers' Association in Winnipeg as the first clearly nationalist Ukrainian organization in Canada.

In 1910 the teachers' association initiated the formation of the independent Ukrainian National Publishing Company, later known as the Trident Press. The teachers believed with some justification that the existing Ukrainian newspapers, published in Winnipeg, the emerging centre of Ukrainian life, were unduly influenced by non-Ukrainian interests.[10] The *Kanadiiskyi farmer* (Canadian Farmer) was associated with the Liberal party. *Ranok* (Morning) was a proselytizing vehicle of the Presbyterian church. The *Kanadyiskyi rusyn* (Canadian Ruthenian) was initially identified with the Roman Catholic church. The weekly that the teachers' association began to publish, the *Ukrainskyi holos*, was destined to become one of the most influential Ukrainian papers in Canada.[11] The use of the word 'Ukrainian' rather than the traditional 'Ruthenian' clearly reflected the populist-nationalist ideology of the paper's founders. At the beginning, the *Ukrainskyi holos* identified itself with the broad national interests of the Ukrainian people rather than with any specific religious or political interests.

Wasyl Kudryk, the thirty-year-old editor,[12] Taras Ferley, the twenty-eight-year-old manager,[13] and Jaroslav Arsenych, the twenty-three-year-old president of the Ukrainian Publishing Company,[14] spoke on behalf of this crusading and nationalistically minded intelligentsia. Their task was simple in its intention but most difficult in its implementation. They were determined to Ukrainianize and modernize the arriving peasant masses, most of whom, they believed, were destined for assimilation. The *Ukrainskyi holos* had to convince the immigrants of the virtues of cultural retention and at the same time impress upon them the need to adopt positive Canadian attitudes like the work ethic and temperance, which, in the view of the paper, many Ukrainian peasants lacked. The *Ukrainskyi holos* frequently urged its readers to 'participate in trade and industry [and] to inculcate thrift, punctuality, and self-reliance.'[15]

The *Ukrainskyi holos* attracted to its affirmative philosophy those self-aware immigrants who quickly learned English and were 'making good' in Canada soon after their arrival. Individuals like the entrepreneur Peter Svarich understood the Canadian capitalistic system and modified their Galician radicalism into liberal and middle-class values. They took advantage of the available opportunities to become small businessmen and farmers or to acquire professional status as teachers, municipal officials, and later lawyers. They represented the socio-political stratum that stood in direct opposition to the socialists.

The *Ukrainskyi holos* through its journalism and the bilingual teachers through their individual and group activities demonstrated remarkable dedication to the task of transforming both the substance and the stereotype of Ukrainians as primitive and undisciplined people. The initial demonstration of public support and encouragement for the *Ukrainskyi holos* indicated that a situation was being created in which the intelligentsia would indeed become indispensable in the community life of Canada.

However, the intelligentsia's definition of a good Ukrainian as an independently minded nationalist was at serious odds with that of the Catholic clergy, which preferred an obedient and loyal flock. The question of community leadership would turn the *Ukrainskyi holos* and the majority of the lay intelligentsia against their traditional church and its primate, Bishop Nykyta Budka, and create the first serious crisis in the Ukrainian community.

Budka brought with him a deep suspicion of the lay intelligentsia, a suspicion that characterized the hierarchy of the Ukrainian Catholic church in Galicia and was reflected in its official organ, the *Kanadyiskyi rusyn*. In Winnipeg he encountered the *Ukrainskyi holos*, the self-appointed and confrontational guardian of the Ukrainian people and their national dignity. It quickly became apparent that Budka's traditional view of the nature of the church was incompatible with the democratic and nationalist notions advocated by the *Ukrainskyi holos*.[16] The deepening mutual distrust made the coexistence of traditional Catholicism and populist nationalism in the same church impossible. By the summer of 1918 a series of events, including Budka's threat to excommunicate the dissidents, had led to a serious schism in the Ukrainian Catholic church.

The immediate cause was the Peter Mohyla Institute. This residential school was established in 1916 in Saskatoon by the lay intelligentsia and students to train high school and university students as community leaders.[17] Two students, A. Kibzey and Wasyl Swystun, are credited with the initiative. The Mohyla Institute became the focal point of the struggle between the nationalist intelligentsia, which had incorporated the institute as a non-denominational body, and Bishop Budka, who demanded that the Mohyla be a Catholic school. The *Ukrainskyi holos* threw its influential support behind the nationalists who refused to submit to the authority of their church: 'We place Ukrainianism first and religious upbringing second because all Ukrainians are members of one nationality and not exclusively Greek Catholic or Orthodox.'[18]

In July 1918 the Mohyla–*Ukrainskyi holos* bloc convened a special council of 150 laymen at Saskatoon. In a revolutionary but logical decision the council not only separated from the Catholic church but undertook to organize a rival church: the Ukrainian Greek Orthodox Church of Canada (UGOC).[19] Why did the Saskatoon meeting, consisting of people who had advanced the concept of interdenominationalism, decide on Orthodoxy? The church founders were all laymen with no theological expertise, and they were motivated by nationalistic and jurisdictional reasons and not by theological differences with the Catholic church. According to one of the participants, Semen Sawchuk, they rationalized the formation of the UGOC as a conscious and patriotic return to the faith of their ancestors, who had been obliged to renounce Orthodoxy and unite with Rome in 1596. They no longer saw themselves as Catholic dissidents but as 'born again' Orthodox because to them Ukrainian Orthodoxy now represented their national identity and their cultural heritage.[20] By equating Ukrainian nationalism exclusively with Orthodoxy, they effectively but unfairly implied that a Catholic could not be a genuine Ukrainian patriot because of his allegiance to an alien power, Rome.

The UGOC, with its democratic structure and Ukrainian-language liturgical services, attracted the bulk of the Bukovynian settlers and part of the free-thinking Catholic intelligentsia. Nominally headed by an American-based hierarch, the new church was administered by an elected consistory of laity and priests. By 1941 the UGOC claimed nearly a quarter of the Ukrainian population of Canada.

The Orthodox nationalists maintained their secular organizational cohesiveness in the 1920s by means of the *Ukrainskyi holos* and regular annual conventions (*narodni zizdy*). These conventions were hosted by the Mohyla Institute in Saskatoon, its affiliate in Winnipeg, and the Hrushevsky Institute (now St John's) in Edmonton and normally drew hundreds of delegates from parishes and community centres (*narodni domy*). But such an arrangement was deemed unsatisfactory by the leadership of the institutes. A series of private discussions in Saskatchewan and Alberta led to a meeting in Winnipeg at the end of October 1927. Julian Stechishin, I. Ruryk, Wasyl Swystun, Father Semen Sawchuk (the administrator of the UGOC), Jaroslav Arsenych, Myroslav Stechishin, and General Vladimir Sikevych (a former emissary of the Ukrainian People's Republic to Hungary) agreed on the need to form a national organization that would unite the Ukrainian people of Canada.[21] The success of the Ukrainian Labour-Farmer Temple Association, a pro-Soviet group, in establishing itself throughout Canada both frightened and inspired the Orthodox nationalists to action. It seems that it was Myroslav Stechishin, the oldest of the Stechishin brothers, who had initiated a campaign for a Canada-wide organization to counter the Left.[22]

The founding fathers had a difficult time in deciding on the appropriate name for the new organization. According to Julian Stechishin, 'Some proposed the name "populists" [narodovtsi], others "nationalist."

Both names were disputed because one was too vague and the other too militant.' After a long discussion the name Soiuz ukraintsiv samostiinykiv or, in shortened form, Samostiinyky was accepted. The participants agreed to the name because it clearly reflected their objectives, which were to conduct cultural and educational work completely independently, without any foreign commands or influences. Finally, such a name could not antagonize anyone even in its English version – Ukrainian Self-Reliance League.[23] The name of the new organization, credited to Myroslav Stechishin, proved to be an intelligent choice as it had just enough ambiguity in both languages to appear positive and strong, yet not threatening.

The eleventh national convention was held in Edmonton on 24–26 December and in Saskatoon on 28–30 December 1927. The convention voted to form the Ukrainian Self-Reliance League, 'an organization that would unite those Ukrainians who have as their ideal an independent Ukrainian state and who value independence of political thought and self-reliance in community life.'[24] Wasyl Swystun, the dynamic and combative co-organizer of the UGOC, was elected the first president of the USRL.[25] The birth of the USRL signified the completion of the organizational process of a part of the community that had begun in 1910 with Ukrainian bilingual teachers and the *Ukrainskyi holos* and moved by various stages to the Mohyla Institute, the formation of the Orthodox church, and the staging of annual national conventions.

Based on the parish level, the USRL grew into an integrated organization that consisted of men's clubs, the Tovarystvo ukrainskykh samostiinykiv or TUS, ladies' auxiliaries, the Soiuz ukrainok Kanady or SUK, and a youth wing, the Soiuz ukrainskoi molodi Kanady or SUMK. With 180 locals, the youth wing was the largest and most active component of the USRL in the 1930s. The Ukrainian Women's Association excelled at cultural and educational work and local fund-raising. An important component was added in the form of the Union of Ukrainian Community Centres. Of course, not every Orthodox Ukrainian became a member of the USRL, but, judging from published convention reports, a number of those with a sense of Ukrainian consciousness did.

For the next several years, the USRL was a dynamic and imaginative organization zealously promoting its vision of Ukrainian interests in Canada and the cause of Ukraine's independence. Until the formation of the Ukrainian National Federation in 1932, the USRL was the dominant nationalist organization in Canada and vigorously competed with the ULFTA for the allegiance of the politically uncommitted Ukrainians.[26] The USRL was particularly effective in promoting community protest meetings in Winnipeg, Saskatoon, and Edmonton to denounce Stalinist terror in Soviet Ukraine and Polish repression in Western Ukraine.[27] Such target-oriented unity, however, was always short-lived. Although the prairie provinces remained the bastion of the USRL, it also established locals in British Columbia, Ontario, and Quebec. The exact number of members in the inter-war period is not known, but a reasonable estimate of activists and sympathizers of the USRL (excluding the SUMK) is around six thousand. The bulk of the membership in the 1930s comprised small town and rural Ukrainians. Their economic condition had a bearing on the capacity of the USRL to carry out its agenda. While the ideology gave the USRL its raison d'être, the quality of its leadership gave it vision and strength. It seems that the sense of idealism and dedication was more intense and the political skills were sharper among the senior members of the USRL than in other organizations.

The USRL ideology crystallized the Mohyla spirit in a slogan that emphasized the ideal of ethnic pride, dignity, and independence: 'self-respect, self-reliance and self-help.'[28] This philosophy was to be applied to the personal, community, and national activity of the membership of the USRL. It was presented in detail to the founding convention in 1927. Swystun, Julian Stechishin, and Myroslav Stechishin were the keynote speakers. Here two distinct currents, seemingly contradictory but in the view of the USRL very complementary – Ukrainian nationalism and Canadian patriotism – were synthesized as the basic ideological ingredients of the organization.[29] In its public pronouncements the USRL stressed its nationalism and gave the impression that its membership was limited to Ukrainian patriots. In the words of Myroslav Stechishin, 'the USRL unites within itself all sincere Ukrainians who want and can work for the well-being and enlightenment of the Ukrainian people. Whenever there appears a member who is not 100 per cent but only 75, 50, or 25 per cent Ukrainian ... the USRL must have the courage to expel such a member.'[30] It is highly unlikely that Stechishin's stringent criteria were ever used in membership recruitment, but they helped in image building.

It was religion that prevented the USRL from becoming an all-embracing nationalist organization. Because the USRL was formed by the same people who had undermined the Catholic church and organized the rival Ukrainian Greek Orthodox church, the religious factor was a major deterrent to the USRL's aspirations to unify the community. It was Julian Stechishin, an educator and one of the key people at the Mohyla Institute, who became a frequent spokesman on the sensitive and divisive question of religion and the USRL. Stechishin stressed the importance of religion and church in general. 'Where there is no church there is no morality, and this leads to social disintegration and the demise of a community or a nation ... The USRL appreciates the formidable significance of the church and supports that church which works for the benefit of the Ukrainian people and is under their exclusive control.' In Stechishin's view, Catholicism and Protestantism were foreign ideologies and thus represented negative influences on Ukrainian history and people. Hence, 'to be Orthodox is to be Ukrainian; to be non-Orthodox is to be non-Ukrainian.'[31] It was clear that such an extreme position was unacceptable to the majority of Ukrainian Canadians, and on occasion Stechishin added moderating qualifiers: 'We do not mix religious and political issues. It so happens that only the UGOC has the qualities to be called a truly Ukrainian church ... but this does not mean that the UGOC ought to remain the only truly Ukrainian church.'[32] Stechishin hinted that when other churches became 'genuinely Ukrainian,' the USRL would support them as well. He implied that the USRL support of religious institutions hinged on their Ukrainianism, not on their theology. The USRL official position on religion, however, remained consistently pro-Orthodox and thus discouraged the nationally conscious and liberal-minded Catholics and Protestants from joining it. But because the USRL activities were occasionally applauded in the English press as examples of how the 'loyal Ukrainians' were enriching Canada, the USRL often presumed to represent the majority of Ukrainian Canadians.

In the short period of 1926 to 1929 the bulk of the inter-war Ukrainian immigration arrived in Canada from Galicia and Volhynia, then under Poland. Canada's restrictive immigration policies made the second immigration of around 70,000 much smaller than the original wave of nearly 180,000. In further contrast with the pioneers, the inter-war emigrants were better educated and more nationally conscious. Although agriculturalists and labourers continued to predominate, several hundred political émigrés and veterans of the failed wars of independence, 1917–21, represented an important component of the new immigrants. Manitoba continued to boast the largest Ukrainian population in Canada with nearly 30 per cent of the three hundred thousand Ukrainians in Canada living there. Winnipeg became the centre of Ukrainian community life in Canada.

The USRL leadership had assumed, perhaps naïvely, that many of the newcomers, especially the nationalistic war veterans, would join it en masse. That this did not happen is partly explained by the religious situation. Most of the immigrants were Catholics, and although they had a progressive religious outlook and held that religion was a personal matter, they felt uncomfortable with the prominent Orthodox label attached to the USRL and chose to form their own groups.[33] In 1928 the first of several Ukrainian War Veterans' Association cells (*striletski hromady*) was set up in Winnipeg.[34] Initially there was some co-operation between the veterans and the USRL, but it quickly became apparent that, in addition to the contentious religious factor, serious differences about the nature of nationalism divided the USRL and the UWVA.

The USRL's brand of nationalism was of the old-fashioned liberal variety while the UWVA espoused the new integral nationalism that had emerged in Central Europe and among Ukrainian political exiles in the aftermath of the defeat of Ukraine's brief independence. The USRL was firmly committed to the democratic process, a concept that the integral nationalists rejected in favour of authoritarianism as a superior form of political organization. The UWVA members brought with them a sense of political bitterness which blamed liberalism and socialism for the Ukrainian failure. The veterans, mainly former Sich Sharpshooters, considered themselves as a political extension of the European-based Ukrainian Military Organization (UVO). This was a militant, underground, and right-wing group led by Colonel Evhen Konovalets. In 1932 the UVO merged with the Organization of Ukrainian Nationalists (OUN), a mass revolutionary organization, dedicated to an uncompromising armed and political struggle against the Soviet, Polish, Romanian, and Czechoslovak regimes occupying various regions of Ukraine.[35] Headed by Konovalets, the underground OUN dominated political life in Polish-occupied Western Ukraine and found strong support among the inter-war immigrants in the diaspora.

The difference in approach to Ukrainian issues between the USRL and the UWVA was as divisive as the difference in ideology. It became obvious in the 1930s that although the USRL saw itself as an activist organization, it actually represented a cautious approach. The veterans, on the other hand, tended to consider themselves émigrés rather than settlers and were prepared to 'rock the boat' on behalf of Ukraine. This militant behaviour embarrassed the USRL, which was cultivating in Canada an image of moderation and respectability acceptable to the Anglo-Celtic majority. Thus a clash on issues and methods between the Canadian-educated and the European-educated intelligentsia, between Canadian citizens and Ukrainian émigrés, was all but inevitable.

Increasing friction among old and new nationalists in Canada notwithstanding, the European leadership of the OUN was so impressed with the organizational potential of the USRL that it initiated serious discussions about co-operation and amalgamation. The OUN overtures caused dissension within the leadership of the USRL. Although its president, Wasyl Swystun, was prepared to consider affiliating with the OUN, providing the OUN met certain conditions that would have given the USRL a major voice in the ideology and leadership of the OUN, the Stechishin brothers insisted on the independence of the USRL. Given the ideological outlook of both organizations, the informal discussions were doomed to failure.

The first meeting between three leading USRL representatives, Father Semen Sawchuk, Julian Stechishin, and Wasyl Swystun, and Colonel Konovalets of the OUN took place in New York in May 1929 when the Canadian trio was attending a general council of the Ukrainian Orthodox church in the United States.[36] The initiative for a meeting came from Konovalets, who was promoting the OUN among the Ukrainian communities of North America. During these preliminary discussions, according to Sawchuk, Swystun indicated greater readiness to co-operate with Konovalets than his more cautious colleagues. Stechishin and Sawchuk warned Swystun not to divulge too much about the USRL. Konovalets insisted on further talks in Winnipeg in June during his trip through western Canada. There the USRL leaders (Myroslav Stechishin, Swystun, Woycenko, Arsenych, Burianyk, and Bachynsky) showed that they were more interested in getting Konovalets to exercise greater discipline over the 'disruptive' UWVA than in joining the OUN.[37] He promised to mediate the differences between the two groups. However, a face-to-face meeting of the USRL and UWVA executives failed to ease the tensions. On 19 June, following his trips to Saskatoon and Edmonton, where he had met with both the UWVA and the USRL, Konovalets held his final inconclusive discussions with the Winnipeg USRL.[38]

The USRL leaders in 1930 remained ambivalent towards a formal arrangement with the OUN, stating that their main reason for talking was to understand better the nature of the OUN. Yet they saw co-operation with the OUN as a means of asserting their control over the UWVA. But to reach an agreement, the two sides had to resolve their differences of opinion on the vital question of the OUN tactics. The USRL would not condone the violent activities of the Ukrainian Military Organization in Galicia in 1930, which were causing Polish counter-terror. The USRL was also concerned about the OUN's foreign policy, notably its German orientation, and its implications for Ukrainian Canadians. The lawyer Jaroslav Arsenych put the USRL position as follows: 'We in Canada can help the Ukrainian cause only in the framework of our Canadian and British citizenship. An international situation could emerge in which enemies of Ukraine would be on the same side as Britain. Such a situation, however, can never change our loyalty to Canada and the British Empire.'[39]

When Konovalets asked the USRL for a regular subsidy of five hundred dollars a month, a sizeable sum in those days, in support of the OUN activities, several USRL leaders lost their enthusiasm for affiliation. Nonetheless, the USRL president, W. Swystun, personally supported affiliation and in January 1931 sent a confidential memorandum to Konovalets, outlining the USRL conditions for a working arrangement with the OUN. Briefly, the USRL demanded that the OUN change its tactics and abandon its reliance on sabotage and terror in the liberation struggle before the USRL could co-operate with it. The USRL wanted a direct voice for the USRL in the OUN leadership and the recognition of the USRL as the exclusive OUN representative in Canada.[40] The last demand was apparently aimed at severing relations between the UWVA and the OUN and placing the war veterans under the USRL. Such an arrangement would have assured the USRL its desired role as the pre-eminent voice of Ukrainian nationalism in Canada. For the OUN, however, the USRL demands meant unacceptable changes to its ideology, tactics, and organization.

The USRL memorandum of conditions was a brave but naïve attempt to change the OUN into a democratic organization. In January 1932 the OUN emissary to Canada, Colonel Roman Sushko, verbally informed the USRL executive of the rejection of the memorandum.[41] The OUN now moved vigorously to consolidate and expand the UWVA. The result would be a serious struggle within the ranks of Ukrainian nationalists in Canada.

Coincidental with the rise of Ukrainian integral nationalism in Canada was the beginning of the Great Depression. The implications of the depression – unemployment and poverty – were grave for all Ukrainian organizations except the ULFTA. The pro-Communist Ukrainian Labour-Farmer Temple Association skilfully exploited the economic crisis by its propagandistic accounts of the 'good life' in the USSR and attracted many of the urban unemployed to its ranks. The small farmer and the semi-skilled urban labourer represented the majority of the Ukrainian-Canadian society and had provided the bulk of financial support for Ukrainian organizations and institutions.[42] Now even the USRL institutes, the Mohyla and Hrushevsky, faced hard times as rural students on whom they so depended could no longer afford higher education.[43] The reduced economic resources of the Ukrainian community in Canada made organizational competition for membership and support very intensive. This is the climate in which the USRL competed with the ULFTA on the left and the new Ukrainian National Federation on the right.

The formation of the Ukrainian National Federation (Ukrainske natsionalne obiednannia) in 1932 was the direct outcome of the failure of the USRL and the OUN to compromise. During the USRL-OUN negotiations, Professor Tymish Pavlychenko, an OUN member who had arrived in Canada from Czechoslovakia a few years earlier, had been actively promoting in Saskatoon the formation of a nationalist umbrella organization.[44] The proposed all-Ukrainian body was tentatively called the Union for the Independence of Ukraine.[45] The initiative committee received support from prominent USRL people in Saskatoon, including the rector of the Mohyla Institute, Julian Stechishin. But this promising co-operation between the Saskatoon nationalists did not last long because Saskatoon was an exception to the general pattern of the UWVA-USRL hostilities. When the *Ukrainskyi holos* alleged that Polish repression in Galicia was at least in part provoked by the terrorist activities of the UVO,[46] the UWVA reacted with rage and decided to establish its own newspaper to refute such negative publicity and to promote the OUN ideology. In Edmonton the UWVA established the *Novyi shliakh* (New Pathway), edited by Mykhailo Pohorecky, an experienced journalist and war veteran.[47] Later it would be transferred to Saskatoon, then to Winnipeg, and finally to Toronto. In the *Novyi shliakh* Stechishin and the *Ukrainskyi holos* now had a new and aggressive rival.

On 17 July 1932 the UWVA with assistance from the OUN formed in Edmonton the Ukrainian National Federation as the Canadian arm of the OUN. A strictly secular body, it was conceived as a medium of political consolidation in Canada on a nationalistic platform ('Ukraine above all'), and its Canadian orientation was at first largely symbolic. Unlike the USRL, the UNF considered religion a personal matter and preached religious toleration and respect. This approach proved to be highly successful in winning support from those Ukrainians who had a sense of nationalism but resented continuous religious bickering. With the UWVA as its base, the membership in the 1930s consisted of men's, women's, and youth components. It was drawn predominantly from the inter-war emigration, but it did have a sprinkling from the pioneer era and some Canadian-born, like Paul Yuzyk, the future member of the Canadian Senate.[48] Although the first president, Alexander Gregorovich, was from the pioneer emigration, the real power in the new organization was in the hands of the UWVA. Tymish Pavlychenko and Wolodymyr Kossar,[49] both war veterans with university educations, dominated the

UNF executive. Pavlychenko was the UNF ideologue, and Kossar became the principal organizer. Largely through their efforts, the organization grew, despite the depression, and clashed head on with existing USRL locals. The UNF also established itself in the new mining and lumbering towns of northern Canada (Sudbury, Kirkland Lake, and Timmins in Ontario, The Pas in Manitoba, Rouyn Noranda in Quebec), where only the Communists had had an organized Ukrainian presence. Direct and occasionally violent confrontations characterized relations between the Ukrainian Left and Right in Canada.[50]

In addition to the UNF, the USRL was faced with an organizational resurgence from the Catholic side. In 1932 the Bratstvo ukraintsiv katolykiv, or Brotherhood of Ukrainian Catholics (BUC), was organized. Modelled on the militant Catholic Action and partly on the USRL, the BUC espoused a mixture of conservative Ukrainian nationalism, Catholicism, and Canadian patriotism. Like the USRL, it was based on the parish level and co-ordinated women's and youth activities, but unlike the USRL, it was strongly influenced by the clergy. Potentially the largest Ukrainian organization in Canada, the BUC did not acquire national prominence until the Second World War.[51]

In the escalating feud between the USRL and the UNF, ideology and personalities combined to accentuate the existing divisions in the community. As expressed in their respective organs, the *Ukrainskyi holos* and the *Novyi shliakh*, both organizations had a deep commitment to Ukrainian statehood but differed on the nature of that commitment and on the tactics of the struggle for independence. In the 1930s Myroslav Stechishin developed for the USRL a distinct Ukrainian-Canadian ideological position that featured unconditional rejection of the emerging quasi-fascist characteristics of the OUN and their adoption by the UNF.[52]

The UNF leaders, Pavlychenko and Kossar, were committed to the OUN liberation philosophy and to its organizational goal, which called for the UNF to consolidate and lead the entire nationalist movement in Canada.[53] The USRL stood in the way of those objectives and had to be pushed aside. According to *Novyi shliakh* editor Pohorecky, anyone who did not accept the uncompromising nationalist position of the OUN (one country, one nation, one leader) was nothing short of a traitor (*khrun*).[54] Indiscriminate name calling and mud slinging would become the unfortunate trade-mark of the USRL-UNF competition, especially in the late 1930s.[55]

As the 1930s unfolded, varieties of fascism and nazism began to sweep Europe at the expense of the demoralized democracies. The OUN sought support for the Ukrainian cause in Germany and Italy. However, the

OUN never subscribed to the Nazi ideology, although it praised Hitler's strong leadership in turning Germany into an industrial and military power. The OUN was also in the revisionist camp, denouncing the 1918 Paris peace settlement and demanding territorial changes that would bring about a united independent Ukrainian state. Since such a drastic redrawing of borders could not be achieved by peaceful means, the OUN favoured a general European war. Accordingly, the *Novyi shliakh* carried admiring stories about the growth of German militarism and of positive German interest in Ukraine. Evhen Onatsky, the OUN representative in Rome, contributed flattering accounts about Mussolini's Italy.[56] The UNF was thus tainted with fascism. In the late 1930s the *Ukrainskyi holos* began a steady ideological attack on both the OUN and the UNF, reflecting Stechishin's passionate abhorrence of totalitarianism as well as his efforts to undermine the UNF's growing popularity in Canada.[57] Stechishin repeatedly denounced the OUN-German connection and accused the UNF of fostering anti-democratic sentiments in Canada.

The escalating conflict with the UNF was further compounded for the USRL by a serious internal problem caused by the irrepressible Swystun. In the 1930s Father Sawchuk, the administrator of the UGOC, was trying to reduce the traditional role of the USRL in church matters, which on occasion amounted to direct interference, but without losing its vital support. As a key member of the USRL himself, Sawchuk was striving to strike a balance. Swystun, who had resigned earlier from the presidency of the USRL over policy and personality differences, rose to champion the secular power over the church but in the guise of defending canon law.[58] In 1935 Swystun lost his fight and was ostracized by the Orthodox church that he had helped to create. In 1938 he joined the UNF on the grounds of nationalism.[59] Swystun argued that the UNF had become what the USRL had been under his leadership – a dynamic leader of the Ukrainian people in Canada. For a true Ukrainian nationalist there was only the UNF.

For both the UNF and the USRL, Swystun's move was a mixed blessing. While some considered this a coup for the UNF and a blow to the USRL, it seems that Swystun's unpredictability and well-known ambition (his detractors called him 'Vasilini') caused understandable consternation for the UNF executive. For the USRL, the defection of one of its founders was a bit of an embarrassment, but it was outweighed by the fact that Swystun was now clearly in the enemy camp. There was no longer any doubt about his relationship with the USRL or the UGOC. As the newly elected vice-president of the UNF, Swystun launched a Canada-wide speaking tour promoting Ukrainian nationalism and

attacking the USRL. Swystun's cross-over to the UNF further intensified
the polemical warfare between the *Novyi shliakh* and the *Ukrainskyi holos*
and strengthened Myroslav Stechishin's resolve to isolate the UNF from
the mainstream of the community, an impossible task. The *Ukrainskyi
holos* kept hammering the OUN-German connection while the USRL
accelerated its own cultural and political activities. Thus the USRL-
sponsored speaking tours of several prominent Ukrainians from Europe,
such as the eminent historian Dmytro Doroshenko. More importantly,
the USRL concentrated on developing greater awareness among the
Anglophones. It published an English translation of Dmytro Doroshenko's history of Ukraine,[60] and the Ukrainian Women's Association
organized cultural displays. The USRL proudly held up Governor-General Tweedsmuir's much-quoted remark in 1937, 'You will all be better
Canadians for being good Ukrainians,' as an official Canadian endorsement of its philosophy. The subsequent editorial in the *Winnipeg Tribune*
lavishly praised the USRL's contributions 'to the upbuilding of the Canadian nation' and helped to soothe the organization's collective ego,
which had been badly bruised by the UNF.[61]

In the 1930s Polish and Romanian repression of cultural and religious
institutions in Western Ukraine and Stalin's famine and the bloody
purges in Soviet Ukraine captured the attention of Ukrainians in Canada, in part because many had relatives who were directly affected. Both
the USRL and the UNF staged demonstrations to raise general public
awareness and to draw Ottawa's attention to Ukraine. The USRL's
annual conventions regularly passed resolutions affirming support for
the Ukrainian liberation struggle and stressing that the Ukrainians in
Ukraine and not in Canada must determine the nature of the struggle
and the future Ukrainian social and political order. Ukrainian Canadians, it was said, could only act in a supplementary capacity. The UNF,
on the other hand, advanced the OUN programme, emphasizing one
leadership, one liberation policy, and one predetermined political order.
According to Pavlychenko, 'Ukraine will be nationalistic because it cannot be any other.'[62] Both organizations, however, were in agreement
that the Soviet Union would collapse in the anticipated conflict with
Germany.

The Formation of the Ukrainian Canadian Committee

It was the Czechoslovak crisis of 1938–9 that demonstrated to the Ukrainians in Canada the urgency of having a national co-ordinating and

representative body. Approximately half a million Ukrainians had been included in Czechoslovakia in 1918. They lived in the region of Subcarpathian Ruthenia. When Hitler and the Western powers pressured Czechoslovakia into ceding the German-populated part of the country in 1938, the remainder of the country was reorganized. The Ukrainians profited from the Munich Agreement and Prague's misfortune by winning political autonomy for their region, now renamed Carpatho-Ukraine. To Ukrainian nationalists everywhere, tiny Carpatho-Ukraine appeared as the first step towards the long-awaited liberation and unification of all Ukrainian lands. The UNF greeted these developments with enthusiastic public rallies, fund raising, and talks about organizing Canadian volunteers to go to Carpatho-Ukraine. The USRL also welcomed the 'birth of the Ukrainian autonomous state,' but the *Ukrainskyi holos* was more reserved in its evaluation of Carpatho-Ukraine's chances, being sceptical about German intentions towards Ukraine.[63] Indeed, the *Ukrainskyi holos* published a series of articles and even a booklet entitled *Germans and Ukraine,* warning that German interests in Ukraine were exclusively imperialistic.[64] Hitler's invasion of Czechoslovakia in March 1939 and his transfer of most of Carpatho-Ukraine to Hungary led to a largely symbolic declaration of Carpatho-Ukrainian independence and a brief military struggle before a total Hungarian victory. The demise of Carpatho-Ukraine justified the scepticism of the *Ukrainskyi holos.*

As the events in Carpatho-Ukraine were unfolding, a number of local committees, often independent of the USRL and the UNF, sprang up in Canada to collect funds to assist Carpatho-Ukrainians.[65] The press raised questions about lack of co-ordination and misappropriation of funds.[66] Winnipeg, with its numerous cultural and social organizations, became a centre of community activity. An important precedent for co-ordinated action had been set on the eve of the Carpatho-Ukrainian crisis. In September 1938, in response to the Polish destruction of Orthodox churches in the Kholm region, the Ukrainian National Home, which was one of the oldest Winnipeg institutions, had initiated the formation of a community protest committee.[67] The Orthodox and Catholic churches temporarily overcame their antagonism and were represented through the USRL and the BUC. The fact that the BUC participated in this action was due to Father Wasyl Kushnir, the pastor of the largest Ukrainian parish in Canada, Sts Vladimir and Olga Church, and the vice-president of the BUC.[68] Kushnir, who had sharp political instincts, represented the nationalistic wing of the Ukrainian Catholic clergy, which, in opposition to the ultra-Catholic Basilians, placed Ukrainian national concerns above denominational interests. Kushnir, as it turned out, strongly believed in national unity and even in the highly unlikely possibility of reconciling the USRL with the UNF.

The tortuous and confusing route leading to the formation of the Ukrainian Canadian Committee began in November 1938. This route consisted of formation of tentative structures, which were combinations of the existing organizations and which would change membership as the understanding grew in all of them of the need to co-operate in one co-ordinating body. In November 1938 the Committee to Aid the Native Land, a body struck to collect and disperse funds for Carpatho-Ukraine and to lobby Ottawa to place the Ukrainian issue on the international agenda, was initiated in Winnipeg by Taras Ferley on behalf of the Ukrainian National Home, a pro-USRL body.[69] It included the USRL, the BUC, and a variety of local groups such as Prosvita and the Ukrainian Fraternal Society but deliberately excluded the UNF. The committee performed reasonably well. It collected several thousand dollars and provided public fiscal accountability. Within it, informal discussions began about the need for a national representative body, especially in the light of the unfolding European affairs.

That process of building a consensus was hampered by a virulent vendetta between the editors of the *Ukrainskyi holos* and the *Novyi shliakh*, and it would require the intervention of the Canadian government to end it. Within the leadership of the USRL the question of the degree of involvement with Ukrainian concerns in Europe was constantly debated. The USRL stressed its commitment to 'broad nationalism' while rejecting the 'narrow' or integral nationalism of the UNF.[70] Jaroslav Arsenych, the first Ukrainian lawyer in Canada to be awarded the prestigious title of King's Counsel, repeatedly cautioned the USRL to approach European affairs from a Canadian perspective and not to antagonize the Canadian government. 'We are Canadians and Ukrainians inseparably. We face questions that must be answered from both positions – Canadian and Ukrainian – and we must have one answer from both positions.'[71] The course of events dictated the urgent need for united action, and Stechishin called for a 'congress of all Ukrainian groups in Canada' except, of course, the UNF and the Communists.

Excluded from the Winnipeg-based Committee to Aid the Native Land, the UNF executive spearheaded in Saskatoon the formation of a rival ad hoc group, the Representative Committee of Ukrainian Canadians, or RCUC. The local branch of the USRL, which was headed by Julian Stechishin, brother of the intransigent editor of the *Ukrainskyi holos*, participated in it.[72] The task of the Saskatoon committee was to solicit the support of prominent Canadians for Carpatho-Ukraine. The strident opposition of the Winnipeg USRL to the UNF was clearly at odds with the more moderate Saskatoon USRL, which was prepared to co-operate with its rival on specific common interests. Julian Stechishin's subsequent election to the presidency of the USRL would have a positive influence on the relations between his organization and the UNF. The *Ukrainskyi holos* ignored the existence of the committee.

Early in 1939, the Ukrainian press in Canada concluded that a general European war was inevitable. Both the *Ukrainskyi holos* and the *Novyi shliakh* assumed that Britain would play a determining role in the settlement of post-war Europe. Both the USRL and the UNF separately tried to convince Ottawa that Ukrainian independence would be of geopolitical importance to the British Empire. In the process of lobbying the Canadian government the need for a central agency to represent Ukrainian interests more effectively was strikingly obvious. But the question was how and what to do in the face of the existing political and religious hostilities.

The leaders of the three major organizations – the USRL, the UNF, and the BUC – undertook a number of initiatives. It is important to note that the original anti-Catholic attitudes of the USRL were moderating in the late 1930s. Indeed, the Orthodox leaders were prepared to discuss seriously the idea of a representative committee based on the Catholic and Orthodox churches and their secular affiliates.[73]

An opportunity for real church co-operation occurred in June 1939. Wasyl Burianyk, one of the USRL activists and a Liberal party worker in Saskatchewan, was unexpectedly invited to Ottawa to brief Prime Minister Mackenzie King and Secretary of State O.D. Skelton on Eastern Europe and Ukraine.[74] Burianyk saw this as an opportunity for a major community presentation to Ottawa, and the matter was discussed at a USRL cabal in Winnipeg. The USRL decided to invite the BUC to sponsor a joint Orthodox-Catholic delegation because it would be more prestigious and perhaps even more influential, especially given that Ottawa was aware of the factionalism within the community.[75] Father Kushnir agreed with this purpose on behalf of the BUC and Bishop Ladyka, who personally was ambivalent about inter-church co-operation.

The delegation consisted of Burianyk and Theodor Humeniuk, a lawyer from Toronto, representing the UGOC and the USRL respectively, and Fathers Wasyl Gigeychuk of Ottawa and Mykhailo Olenchuk of Hamilton, representing the Catholic church and the BUC. Between them the two blocs could claim the allegiance of the vast majority of Ukrainian Canadians. However, when the USRL members of the delegation arrived in Ottawa on 6 July, they discovered that the Catholic delegates knew nothing about the mission. Father Olenchuk did not even show up. Kushnir never explained his failure to contact the BUC delegates, but the USRL suspected interference from the Basilian Order, which apparently opposed Orthodox-Catholic co-operation.[76]

Burianyk nonetheless prevailed upon Father Gigeychuk to join the USRL representation and thus preserve the facade of unity.[77] The joint delegation was well received and presented its memorandum on behalf of Ukrainian independence to Mackenzie King and Skelton. Burianyk also treated them to long discourses on Ukrainian, Polish, and Russian history. Lester Pearson, then the senior secretary to Canada's high commissioner to Britain, advised the Ukrainians to establish a permanent representation in London in order to lobby the British government more effectively. The USRL, as a result, commissioned Vladimir Kaye (Kysilewsky), who had been working in London in the privately funded Ukrainian Bureau, as its temporary representative there.[78] There is no evidence of Kaye's activities on behalf of the USRL.

The outbreak of the Second World War on 1 September 1939 pitted the British Empire, including Canada, against Nazi Germany. By virtue of its non-aggression pact with Germany the Soviet Union sided with Hitler. As long as Nazi Germany and the Soviet Union were enemies of the West, the issue of Ukrainian independence was quite acceptable to Ottawa and the Ukrainian organizations could pursue it without hindrance. However, when in June 1941 Germany invaded its partner and the Soviet Union became an overnight ally of Canada, the 'Ukrainian question' became a political embarrassment to Ottawa and the government discouraged the Ukrainians from raising it in order not to upset the Soviet government.

The war made the question of a Ukrainian-Canadian central co-ordinating body critical. Public opinion as expressed in the letters to the Ukrainian press demanded community harmony and co-ordination of community objectives. Both the USRL and the UNF reaffirmed their Canadian patriotism, pledging undying loyalty to Canada and the British Empire.[79] Both strove to unite the community around them. The success of Burianyk's mission to Ottawa encouraged the USRL in Winnipeg to push for the formation of a formal joint council composed of the Orthodox and Catholic churches and their lay organizations, the USRL and BUC. The USRL continued to reject the UNF and the small conservative United Hetman Organization as unworthy partners in such a council because of their political connections with Berlin.[80] However, when Kushnir called an informal gathering, the USRL did send three of its leaders, A. Pawlyk, N. Bachynsky (the Manitoba MLA), and J. Arsenych. Swystun was among the UNF representatives at the meeting. Kushnir's proposal called for a central committee composed of representatives of the four major organizations – the BUC, the USRL, the UNF, and the UHO. The proposed committee would enjoy complete independence from its component organizations. The USRL rejected the proposal outright, favouring the simpler Orthodox-Catholic bloc.[81]

In September the UNF executive decided to transform the ad hoc RCUC into a national committee resembling Kushnir's proposal.[82] While Peter Lazarowich, an Edmonton lawyer and president of the USRL, sent mixed signals about the USRL's attitude towards the UNF initiative, the turning point came in November. The USRL was now prepared, albeit reluctantly, to tolerate its rival in a joint committee, but only if the UNF publicly confessed its 'errors' and renounced its alleged pro-Nazi position. Unofficial and official discussions among the USRL, the BUC, and the UNF representatives continued in Saskatoon, Edmonton, and Winnipeg in a stifling atmosphere of distrust and suspicion. The USRL steadfastly regarded the UNF as an evil and irresponsible organization and blamed it for the failure to achieve community unity. Stechishin still alleged that the UNF 'defiled democracy and praised dictatorship as an ideal form of government. These people neither repented nor demonstrated in any way that they changed their outlook ... The USRL worked long and hard to earn for itself a good name, and now it cannot afford to splatter its face by stretching out its hand to the UNF.'[83]

The USRL leaders were becoming increasingly suspicious of Kushnir's collaboration with the UNF. At the annual USRL convention held in Saskatoon on 26–28 December 1939 the delegates overwhelmingly rejected the invitation to join the proposed RCUC. Instead, the convention approved the formation of its own three-man initiative committee (Arsenych, M. Stechishin, and J. Solomon, the future Manitoba MLA) to organize an alternative 'democratically structured' representative body.[84]

The UNF–BUC-sponsored RCUC was formally proclaimed in Winnipeg on 3 February 1940. Its constitution provided for the eventual inclusion of the USRL, which refused the invitation. Headed by Kushnir in Winnipeg and Pavlychenko as secretary-general in Saskatoon, the RCUC began to act as the long-awaited central committee. It quickly organized a network of committees and issued a series of unity newsletters. The RCUC activity reports were published in all Ukrainian papers except the *Ukrainskyi holos* and the *Ukrainskyi robitnyk* (Ukrainian Worker), the organ of the UHO, which gravitated towards the USRL.

The RCUC bombarded Ottawa and London with memos on Ukraine. It generated enthusiasm for Canada's war effort (appeals for enlistment and fund raising for ambulances and the Red Cross) in the *Novyi shliakh*, the Catholic papers, the *Ukrainski visti* (Ukrainian News), and *Buduchnist natsii* (Future of the Nation) and at cross-Canada public rallies. The inclusion of two known and sympathetic Anglo-Canadian academics, Professors George Simpson in Saskatoon and Watson Kirkconnell in Winnipeg, as well as several Canadian politicians, on the advisory committee helped to enhance the RCUC's credibility as a representative of a somewhat consolidated community. The UNF itself worked hard to democratize its maligned image and to demonstrate its Canadian patriotism. For a time the *Novyi shliakh* even refrained from responding to provocative attacks by the *Ukrainskyi holos* in order to cool the polemical warfare and thus appear statesmanlike. Ties with the OUN were played down. The UNF campaigns to enlist young Ukrainians in the armed forces drew applause from the Anglo majority.

However, the USRL refused to accept the obvious change in the UNF as real and continued to insist on a public confession of its political sins as a prerequisite for co-operation. Stechishin still dearly wanted to humiliate the UNF and kept alleging that it was fascinated with fascism. But in 1940 not all USRL leaders shared Stechishin's bias. At the Winnipeg USRL meeting on 6 March, it became clear that the Saskatoon people, including the general secretary of the USRL, Ivan Danylchuk, and the president of the Ukrainian National Home Association, Hawrylo Slipchenko, had concluded that the USRL had to compromise its position on the UNF. They saw co-operation with the RCUC as a political necessity. Otherwise, they feared that the USRL would become isolated.[85] However, the USRL-Orthodox position, as presented by Father Sawchuk in the *Vistnyk* (Herald), the organ of the UGOC, was that although unity was desirable, the RCUC could not be its vehicle because it had an authoritarian ambition to usurp control over the existing organizations. Sawchuk proposed yet another loosely structured co-ordinating committee that would be based on the Orthodox and Catholic churches and would not interfere with the existing organizations.[86] Kushnir's commitment to the UNF and Bishop Ladyka's reluctance to get involved with the Orthodox doomed Sawchuk's scheme.

The USRL thus began a search for other partners. M. Stechishin convinced Teodor Datskiw, the vacillating editor of the popular weekly *Kanadiiskyi farmer* (Canadian Farmer) and the leading member of the United Hetman Organization, to join the USRL committee.[87] This was a setback to the RCUC because it had been assumed that the United

Hetman Organization, because of its conservative and largely Catholic membership, would join the UNF-BUC coalition. Curiously, the *Ukrainskyi holos*, in praising its new partner, omitted the fact that the supreme leader of the UHO, Hetman Pavlo Skoropadsky, resided in Berlin. The USRL arranged an even more surprising partnership with the little known, rather small Soiuz ukrainskykh orhanizatsii (League of Ukrainian Organizations). This was a splinter group from the Communist Party of Canada, which under the leadership of Danylo Lobay had turned away from communism but retained a socialist outlook. Because of its past, the LUO continued to be perceived in the community with considerable distrust. In the eyes of the UNF, Lobay's group remained a Communist organization whose purpose was to infiltrate and destroy nationalist groups from within.[88] Since the UNF was so vehemently opposed to the LUO, the USRL's sponsorship of this mini-organization would become one more stumbling block on the road to consolidation. One cannot help but wonder whether M. Stechishin, who knew Lobay well, deliberately flirted with the LUO in order to frustrate the UNF. Lobay, incidentally, later became an associate editor of the *Ukrainskyi holos*.

On 7 March 1940 the new bloc, consisting of the USRL (Sawchuk, Ferley, and Arsenych), the UHO (Datskiw and Zahareychuk), and the LUO (Kashchak), drafted a public position vis-à-vis the RCUC. The document denounced the RCUC as unrepresentative and illegitimate and proposed its own version of a committee, one that would at last include the BUC and the UNF. The USRL proposal, which called for a joint committee consisting of the USRL, UHO, LUO, BUC, and UNF in which all organizations would be equal, was skilfully designed to assure the USRL a dominant position.[89] In a committee of five equal organizations the USRL with its two small allies would prevail over its two major partners – the UNF and the BUC. It was obvious that the USRL's acceptance of the UNF would be at the cost of the UNF's influence in the proposed central committee. Furthermore, the RCUC would have to be dissolved and Winnipeg rather than Saskatoon would have to be the headquarters of the new representative committee. The choice of Winnipeg seemed logical because it was the centre of Ukrainian life in Canada. But the USRL had a more sinister motive. Since Kossar and Pavlychenko resided in Saskatoon, they would be obliged to leave the centre stage to the USRL activists in Winnipeg.

The USRL proposal was discussed in Saskatoon on 12 March 1940 at a special meeting hosted by Professor Simpson in his house.[90] The discussions between the UNF and the USRL were heated, especially on the participation of the LUO, which Pavlychenko denounced as a 'Trotskyite-Communist' gang. It was Simpson who persuaded the quarrelling participants to minimize their hostilities, pointing out that the Ukrainian squabble was making a negative impression on the rest of Canada. On his urging the participants agreed to cease public hostilities for two weeks while unity discussions continued.[91] But nothing was achieved because the USRL treated the Simpson meeting as informal and not binding. Moreover, the USRL insisted on dealing separately with the UNF and BUC executives rather than with the RCUC.

The failure of both sides to reach an understanding on a common representative body in the first part of 1940 was due largely to the lack of will to do so. The USRL suffered from extreme 'UNF-phobia,' which often blurred the difference between perception and reality. Also it simpiy did not trust the UNF to negotiate in good faith. Nor did the Winnipeg USRL hardliners trust Kushnir, whom they accused of duplicity, and thus insisted on everything being written down.[92] On the other side, the UNF became increasingly obstinate in its rejection of the LUO. Much as the USRL had previously identified the UNF with fascism, the UNF now portrayed the LUO as a Communist fifth column.

In the meantime the RCUC had expanded its activities throughout Canada and designated Swystun as its representative to London. Kaye, who had briefly represented the USRL in Britain, was returning to Canada, and there was a need for an authoritative Ukrainian-Canadian voice in London to help shape British policy towards the 'Ukrainian question.' The RCUC nominated Swystun as its 'ambassador' and immediately sparked a new controversy.[93] The Catholic clergy had not forgiven Swystun his role in the formation of the Orthodox church and objected to his fraternization with the BUC. In fact, Father M. Pelech of the BUC had to plead with his fellow priests to tolerate Swystun in the RCUC because 'it is much better for us to have Swystun with us than against us.'[94] The BUC executive itself was upset at the rumours of Swystun's desire to return to Catholicism. Bishop Ladyka, wisely, would have nothing to do with Swystun, but Kushnir was in deep trouble for treating Swystun's intending reconversion seriously. Arsenych further embarrassed Swystun and by implication Kushnir by leaking to the *Ukrainskyi holos* semi-confidential information about Swystun's legal difficulties with the local mutual benefit association. Swystun, as it turned out, did not see London. He encountered emigration difficulties, attributed to the influence of the USRL, and remained in Canada.

The USRL meanwhile had proceeded to form a rival representative committee. At the founding meeting on 7 May in Winnipeg the RCUC was denounced and a constitution was drawn up for a new representative and co-ordinating body, the Ukrainian Central Committee in Canada (UCCC). The constitution, however, included a provision for the eventual addition of the BUC and the UNF upon their withdrawal from the RCUC. Several local cultural groups also joined. The executive, approved by a public meeting on 24 May 1940, was headed by Arsenych.[95] Lobay's public renunciation of all forms of communism made the contentious LUO more acceptable to the nationalist camp. However, the formation of the UCCC failed to generate any noticeable public enthusiasm. The public, it seems, favoured the RCUC as the Ukrainian representative, largely because it was already well-known and had a network of nearly thirty affiliates throughout Canada. Pavlychenko and Kushnir provided competent and responsible leadership that strengthened the consolidation process. At the same time, Stechishin's continuing attacks on the RCUC ('the Kushnir-Swystun committee') and its leaders ('disgraceful') in a series of polemical columns entitled 'Mymokhodom' (By the Way) were becoming counter-productive and caused growing concern among the USLR moderates, especially in Saskatoon. Public pressure to bring the two committees together, including threats to cancel subscriptions to the *Ukrainskyi holos*, intensified.[96] Even the Ukrainian Women's Council offered its services in mediating the differences.

As a recent study of Ukrainian Canadians during the Second World War confirms, the Canadian government was also concerned about the sharp factionalism among the Ukrainians.[97] The Department of National War Services, headed by J. Thorson, an MP from Selkirk, Manitoba, deemed unity among the more than two million Canadians of non-British and non-French ancestry essential to the war effort. RCMP reports suggest that Ukrainians rated highly on the list of priorities for unity. Ottawa was thus anxious to play a part in the consolidation process and engaged Tracy Philipps, a British specialist on Eastern European affairs, to analyse the Ukrainian community in Canada and to make recommendations to the government.

By September both camps concluded that strong mediation by a third party was needed to break the impasse between the UCCC and the RCUC. At the Winnipeg USRL meeting in September Arsenych raised the need to approach Ottawa to act as a broker.[98] Myroslav Stechishin and Wasyl Burianyk conveyed the USRL proposal to their Ottawa contacts.[99] At the same time Swystun was entertaining a similar proposal to the government on behalf of the RCUC, probably suggested by Professor Kirkconnell, who was the committee's adviser and who worked with the Department of National War Services.

Ottawa responded with uncharacteristic speed to take advantage of the willingness of the two groups to resolve their differences and to unite. Philipps and Simpson were dispatched to Winnipeg. Philipps, who had been touring Ukrainian communities in western Canada on behalf of the RCUC, informed both committees that they must work towards reconciliation. Anxious not to antagonize the government during the uncertainty of wartime, the USRL agreed to meet with the RCUC. Simpson was an adviser to the UCCC and enjoyed a great deal of prestige among Ukrainians while Philipps was an unknown quantity. The emissaries arrived into a situation in which the Ukrainian leaders were desperately searching for a face-saving way to amalgamate their conflicting organizations. The task at hand was not to proclaim the principle of unity but to find a formula for unity that all could agree to.

The fateful gathering was held on 6 and 7 November 1940 in Swystun's large law office in Winnipeg. This was a meeting of the two central committees, the UCCC and the RCUC, rather than of their respective organizations.[100] Both committees had mandates from their member organizations to unite. Most participants, however, did not know that Simpson and Philipps would be involved in the proceedings and were surprised and intimidated when the two joined them during the second session. On the surface the meeting of the UCCC and the RCUC appeared to be a surprise, considering the record of acrimony between the UNF and the USRL. But the numerous private encounters over the previous months had prepared much of the ground. Ottawa's direct involvement signalled its seriousness about Ukrainian unity, and the participants were prepared to accept directions from Philipps and Simpson. The USRL had always insisted that co-operation with Ottawa was essential to maintain the positive image of the community that the USRL had been cultivating for years. The USRL agreed to co-operate with the 'reformed' UNF while the UNF reluctantly accepted the socialist LOU as a legitimate Ukrainian organization. Once this major hurdle to co-operation was overcome, the remaining disagreements revolved around the nature of the proposed central committee and power sharing, that is, the specific functions of the five organizations in it.

The two committees met four times on 6 and 7 November. J. Arsenych, T. Ferley, T. Datskiw, A. Zahareychuk, M. Mandryka, P. Barytsky, M. Stechishin, T. Kobzey, N. Bachynsky, and J. Stechishin represented the UCCC. Father Sawchuk's absence was due to church commitments outside Winnipeg. The RCUC had a smaller delegation consisting of W. Kushnir, W. Kossar, T. Pavlychenko, and W. Swystun. Later, Father Semchuk, E. Wasylyshyn, and W. Topolnytsky joined it. The sketchy minutes of the proceedings reflect considerable tension between the UNF and the USRL. Arsenych and Kushnir took turns chairing. Both committees readily agreed on the urgent need for a common front to help the Ukrainian cause in Europe and to assist the Canadian war effort. They agreed that the new committee would speak on behalf of all Ukrainians, not merely the member organizations. The new central co-ordinating body, the Ukrainian Canadian Committee (UCC), was finally born in the late afternoon of 7 November with Simpson and Philipps acting as midwives. The UCC was the accepted replacement for the feuding representative blocs, which agreed to dissove them- selves. The main purpose of the UCC was to help meet the exigencies of Canada's war effort; its secondary function was to speak out on behalf of Ukrainian Canadians and Ukraine.

Structurally, the UCC consisted of a fifteen-member executive, a co- ordinating commission, and an advisory council, which included Simp- son and Kirkconnell. Their presence ensured that Ottawa's views would be clearly represented. The nature of the UCC and of power sharing in it took up the most time in the struggle between the USRL and the UNF. The USRL had always insisted on a co-ordinating rather than an executive committee and successfully foiled the UNF proposal for a highly centralized executive committee that would claim to represent all Ukrainians in Canada. In other words, the new UCC had no power over the existing member organizations except persuasion. The UCC could co-ordinate only those activities that were approved of by the committee. Although not apparent immediately, the long-standing USRL proposal for an all-Canadian congress of Ukrainians would become a fact of life in 1943 and would evolve into a regularly scheduled triannual parliament of sorts.

The debate over executive positions took up much time and emotion. Kossar of the UNF prevailed in his view that the five organizations should not be treated as equal. The BUC, the UNF, and the USRL would receive senior positions; the UHO and the LUO, as junior partners, would have lesser responsibilities. Arsenych was determined to prevent the offices of the president and the secretary-general, the two most important positions, from going to the UNF and the BUC. Kossar wanted the executive to be divided between Winnipeg and Saskatoon. Such a division would have allowed the UNF, whose national executive was located in Saskatoon, to be more influential. Arsenych was determined to prevent the key positions of president and secretary from going to the RCUC. In the USRL view, Kushnir was an unsuitable candidate because he did not speak English and had not been naturalized yet.[101] Swystun wanted to be secretary, but this was unacceptable to the USRL, and Arsenych declared that his group did not have 'the slightest degree of confidence' in him.[102]

The failure of both committees to agree on the distribution of offices resulted in a request to Philipps and Simpson, who were in the next room, for binding arbitration. They ruled that the president would be from the BUC (Kushnir), the first vice-president and chairman of the executive from the USRL (Sawchuk), the second vice-president, rapporteur, and chairman of the co-ordinating committee from the UNF (Swystun), the secretary-general from the USRL (Arsenych), and the treasurer from the UHO (Datskiw). The outcome of the arbitration obviously favoured the USRL as it received two of the five key positions. Furthermore, the fact that the new committee would be based in Winnipeg also strengthened the the hand of the USRL as the majority of its power brokers lived there.

As the events of the next several years demonstrated, the USRL tended to dominate the UCC, and Kushnir increasingly became a figure-head. The transcripts of the early UCC executive meetings show that, although long-standing personal and ideological antagonisms occasionally surfaced, the meetings were conducted in a businesslike manner.[103] The task at hand was to generate support for the war effort.

The long-awaited unity (excluding the Communist organizations) was not only hailed by the Ukrainian and western Canadian press, but met with financial support from the Ukrainian community. The UCC, operated exclusively by volunteers in their free time, depended on the goodwill and generosity of its component organizations and the public at large. Ottawa's involvement in its establishment notwithstanding, there were no government grants. All member organizations proudly claimed credit for the successful completion of the consolidation process.[104] However, the 'made-in-Ottawa' label did cause some embarrassment.[105] It was the determination of the UCC to demonstrate its independence that moved the UCC to convene the first national congress of Ukrainian Canadians in 1943 despite Ottawa's strong political reservations. The government was in a bit of a quandary, on the one hand trying to placate UCC concerns about the future of Ukraine and on the other remaining supportive of its Soviet ally. It was clear that the Ukrainians would not influence Canada's foreign policy. The question of Ukrainian independence would repeatedly fall victim to international power politics. But that is another story.

For many years the UCC carried the imprint of the USRL.[106] Its organizational structure and political focus reflected the ideas and personalities of the USRL members (including some younger people like J. Solomon, J. Syrnick, and P. Kondra) who were involved in the UCC.[107] At the same time, a constant and occasionally stormy interaction with other organizations convinced the USRL that it no longer had a monopoly on Ukrainian-Canadian nationalism. It had taken the USRL twenty years to evolve from an idea into a powerful and influential national organization. Until the formation of the UNF, the USRL had epitomized Ukrainian nationalism in Canada. With a membership of several thousand capable and dedicated people, the USRL assumed that it spoke on behalf of the entire Orthodox community as well as the non-Orthodox nationalists. Of course, the rise of the UNF made the USRL an exclusively Orthodox organization. Yet the relations between the church and the USRL remained ambivalent. On the surface the USRL, like the BUC, appeared to be a secular arm of a church. In reality, the Orthodox church was a religious extension of the USRL. It was the secular origin of the Orthodox church in Canada that determined the relations in favour of the USRL. For years the same people sat on the executive of the USRL and on the governing board (consistory) of the church. Although tensions arose occasionally, the USRL and the church pursued a policy of Orthodox isolationism or, as they saw it, self-reliance. This attitude was reflected in the long-standing refusal of the Canadian church to establish a binding relationship with any other Orthodox church for fear of losing its independence.[108]

The same people who created the USRL inadvertently contributed to its decline. As so often happens in successful organizations, the leaders began to consider themselves indispensable to the organization's well-being and overstayed their usefulness. Much of the history of the USRL was dominated by the same people. The Stechishin brothers, Swystun, Ferley, Arsenych, Lazarowich, Kudryk, Sawchuk, Syrnick, Burianyk, Pawlyk, Sawchuk, Solomon, and Kondra were synonymous with the Orthodox church, the USRL, and later with the Ukrainian Canadian Committee. Although they provided effective leadership, their monopoly as power brokers in the USRL discouraged younger members with new ideas from dedicating themselves to the increasingly conservative USRL.[109] The reluctance of the post-1945 immigration to enter the ranks of the USRL compounded the problem. The new Orthodox immigrants readily joined the Canadian church but refrained from becoming members of the USRL, preferring to remain with their own organizations such as the Association of Ukrainian Victims of Russian Communist Terror (Suzhero). In part, then, the decline of the USRL as a major force in Ukrainian life can be attributed to the aging of its membership.

But perhaps the most important reason for the decline of the USRL was its success in fulfilling the Canadian dimension of its original agenda. The founding fathers of the USRL had called for full Ukrainian integration into Canadian society as equal citizens. To them integration meant rejection of assimilation and preservation of Ukrainian identity in Canada. They knew that the realization of this ideal was contingent on the constitutional transformation of Canada into a land of cultural diversity and equality. As the USRL persisted in this objective, other Ukrainian organizations followed, and in 1962 the UCC adopted multiculturalism as its objective. Finally, in 1971, for better or for worse, Canada officially became a multicultural society. The consolidated nature of the Ukrainian community as epitomized by the UCC influenced the reshaping of Canada. Formally at least, the wishful thinking of the pioneer nationalists was realized.

Swallowing Stalinism: Pro-Communist Ukrainian Canadians and Soviet Ukraine in the 1930s

MARCO CARYNNYK

When the National Committee of the Association of United Ukrainian Canadians met in Toronto on 10–12 November 1989, it adopted a resolution in which it announced that the time had come for 'an honest, frank, and objective appraisal of some particular periods and practices in our history ... in light of revelations brought out by the processes of reconstruction, openness, and democratization in the Soviet Union.' During the era of Stalinism, the AUUC said, 'monstrous crimes and disastrous errors' had been committed. 'The atmosphere of defending everything Soviet without question led us into serious errors: embracing the cult of Stalin; accepting lies about and stoutly defending monstrous crimes like forced collectivization and the manufactured 1932–33 famine in Ukraine and other Soviet territories; disowning our own members who, upon returning to Ukraine to help build socialism, fell victim to Stalinist repression; not recognizing the chauvinistic policy aimed at the destruction of non-Russian nations through massive, sometimes brutally forced shifts of populations ... All this, and much more, we stoutly and earnestly defended in our daily activities, our conventions, and especially in our press. We defended in good faith what we sincerely believed to be the truth.'[1]

Questioned about their defence of what they now consider to be a lie, pro-Communist leaders also plead ignorance. William Kardash, a member of the Ukrainian Labour-Farmer Temple Association who sat in the Manitoba legislature from 1941 to 1958, used that argument when he was interviewed by the *Globe and Mail*: 'When you hear it first, you don't believe it. You say, it's a bunch of lies – the bureaucracy and the graft, the killing of people who were innocent, putting them into concentration camps.' Then he began to realize that the reports were true. 'Of course I am upset,' he said. 'These things were going on that I never suspected. I feel bad. I wasn't aware of it, and I don't think our party was aware of it. We weren't told.'[2]

George Hewison, the general secretary of the Communist Party of Canada, speaks in similar terms. 'You can't make such a radical break in human development – a Communist revolution – without a lot of experimentation,' he says. 'What we've seen is a distortion of socialism and cult leadership in economically poor countries, where they've used and abused socialist principles. And we were wrong because we accepted with an uncritical eye a lot of things, going way back to Stalin. Now, it's time to throw out the mistakes, the distortions, the crimes. And there's a large bill that Communists are going to have to pay for having been wrong.'[3]

And Peter Krawchuk, the head of the National Committee of the AUUC, took the floor at the conference 'The Famine of 1933 in Ukraine,' held in Kiev in September 1990, to explain 'how tens of thousands, perhaps even hundreds of thousands, overseas Ukrainians fell victim to a great lie and fraud':

When news reached the West and was published in the capitalist press, we thought it was all slander, lies, and fabrications. Thus it went until 1933, the terrible year of the terrible famine. All the more because the first article about the famine appeared in the Lviv newspaper *Dilo* in February 1933. The author of the article was Ewald Ammende, a spokesman for the Hitlerite Ministry of Foreign Affairs. How could we believe such a source? At the same time letters were reaching our newspaper, *Ukrainski robitnychi visti*, from workers and peasants in Ukraine who denied that there was famine. They said that this was all capitalist propaganda ... There were also the reports of the prominent journalist Walter Duranty in the *New York Times*, who wrote that he had visited the southern regions of Ukraine and not seen famine. On the contrary, at train stations between Rostov and southern Ukraine ... he saw chickens, eggs, and butter being sold at very low prices. When it became known that there had been a famine and we demanded through the Communist Party of Canada to be told the truth, the Communist Party of the Soviet Union, as late as mid-1987, categorically denied that anything of the sort had happened ... Are we to be blamed then for falling victim to a lie, or are those who deceived us? If we had known about the famine in Ukraine, about the need for aid, you can be certain that we would have rushed to help as actively and generously as we did after the Second World War ... We greatly regret that because of our loyalty to the ideals of socialism we allowed ourselves to become involved in such an unpleasant situation. So we in Canada have our own accounts to settle with the bloody

Stalinist regime ... We paid a high price for being friendly and sincere with the Soviet government because we believed that this was the government of our people ... And so it is unpleasant when people here in Ukraine accuse us of lying. We simply repeated lies. You can be certain that if we had known [the truth], we would have made our position clear.[4]

Yet the pro-Communist Ukrainian Canadians did know. And if the reports in the Western press were not enough to convince them, they had the words of their trusted party comrades. Let us look, therefore, at the Ukrainian-Canadian Left and its relations with Soviet Ukraine in the age of Stalin.[5]

Although we speak about the 'famine of 1932–3,' the origins of that catastrophe can be traced back at least to 1928, when the First Five-Year Plan was adopted in the Soviet Union and a bad harvest and a campaign of enforced grain collection denuded the southern regions of Ukraine of their food supplies. Almost immediately reports began to reach the West about the spread of shortages and hunger across the countryside and purges of Ukrainian Communists and cultural leaders in the cities. On 11 October 1928 the American consul in Riga, Latvia, advised the secretary of state in Washington that an American woman who had just visited her relatives in Ukraine had told him that the population was 'again on the verge of a dreadful famine.'[6] Two days later the American chargé d'affaires in Finland informed Washington that according to official Soviet reports seventy-six Ukrainian regions with a total population of about three million were suffering from crop failure, but that foreign correspondents in Moscow were estimating that eight to ten million people were suffering from starvation.[7] In December 1928 the American chargé in Latvia reported to the State Department that an American who had travelled through Ukraine had concluded that 'the shadow of hunger' was resting upon the country.[8]

Several weeks later the American consul in Tallinn wrote that 'the situation in the Ukraine, where the 1928 harvests were very poor, is described as being very, very bad, as respects good supplies for the towns and cities. In some places, the shortage of foodstuffs is so marked that conditions similar to those which existed during the famines of 1921-1922, are said to prevail. The general impression is that this situation will not improve, but that it will become much more serious during the remaining months of the present winter.'[9]

And an executive of the American Export Lines who visited Ukraine in May–July 1929 apprised the State Department that 'the crop is said to be good, and the Government claims that there will be a considerable amount of grain available for export. From other sides I have heard. different tales, and I am unable to judge who is right and who is wrong, but I am safe in saying that the next few months will be very critical months for the Government, because the living conditions in Southern Russia have reached an extremely low point. All Ukrania, one of Russia's main granaries and larders, has been stripped of everything that could possibly be exported and turned into a cash balance abroad, and outspoken dissatisfaction was general. In some places where I had to make a stop, f. i. Kieff, which is the capital of the Ukranian Republic and the third largest city in Russia, I could not get anything but a poor quality of black bread and no butter, and in Odessa a chemical analysis of the bread which could be obtained would hardly let the bread pass under that name.'[10]

Similar reports soon made their way into the Western press. The pro-Communist Ukrainian Canadians, however, either ignored them or denounced them as anti-Soviet slander. In December 1930 the *Farmerske zhyttia* reviled the anti-Communist *Ukrainskyi holos* for writing that there was famine in the Soviet Union even as Soviet wheat was being dumped on world markets. 'Either there is a poor crop in the Soviet Union and famine and no wheat for export or there is a good crop, no famine and wheat for export,' the *Farmerske zhyttia* argued speciously.[11] When the French radical politician Edouard Herriot visited the Soviet Union in August–September 1933 to obtain support for an anti-German alliance and was given a carefully staged trip across Ukraine, the *Ukrainski robitnychi visti* approvingly quoted his findings: 'When I travelled across Ukraine, lengthwise and crosswise, I did not see anything resembling a famine. Of course, here and there problems of supply or unsatisfactory production exist. But this is the result of laziness or wrecking. I did not find any famine anywhere.'[12] And in 1934 *Farmerske zhyttia* published a letter from a reader who indignantly denounced non-Communist newspapers for writing about famine and cannibalism in Ukraine: 'Perhaps only editors with underdeveloped animal intelligence could write such lies ... Every serious-thinking worker and farmer laughs at these fairy tales about famine in Soviet Ukraine.'[13]

The pro-Communist Todovyrnazu – the Tovarystvo dopomohy vyzvolnomu rukhovi na Zakhidnii Ukraini, or Association to Aid the Liberation Movement in Western Ukraine, which had been founded in March 1931 and of which Peter Krawchuk was an executive – responded to the publicity that these events received by publishing a series of brochures in which it ridiculed all reports of famine.[14] In *Whom Should We Help?* it

asserted that 'the Ukrainian landlords and priests and their organizations are working hand in glove with the Polish aristocracy in starving
and terrorizing the famished Western Ukrainian worker and peasant
masses and instead of providing them with relief are waging a fierce
campaign of lies about the "famine" in Soviet Ukraine and the Soviet
Union, thus helping German fascism and the Polish aristocracy to prepare an armed attack on the first workers' and peasants' state and to
divert the attention of the working masses from the struggle against the
real famine that exists in Western Ukraine.'[15]

In *Down with the Occupiers and the Ukrainian Military Organization in
Western Ukraine* Todovyrnazu again charged that the regions of Ukraine
under Polish, Romanian, and Czechoslovak rule were being decimated
by famine, dysentery, and typhoid fever and Ukrainian cultural institutions were being persecuted. In Soviet Ukraine, by contrast, 'workers
and peasants are assured of bread, have clothes – and good clothes at
that – to put on, live in well-lit and warm houses, visit theatres, cinemas,
and concerts, are developing their country, and are living a new and
happy life.' Reports of peasant uprisings, mass executions, and famine
were lies put out by the Ukrainian bourgeoisie. Had not the defendants
in the trial of the League for the Liberation of Ukraine admitted that
they wanted to hand over Right-bank Ukraine to Poland and Left-bank
Ukraine to Germany? Were not the Czechoslovak government and the
Ukrainian Military Organization preparing to take control of the Ukrainian economy? Were not Hitler and Goebbels spreading reports of famine
and cannibalism in Ukraine so that they could seize the country for
themselves? The real cannibals were the Ukrainian counter-
revolutionaries.[16]

One man who knew better was Ivan Navizivsky. Born in Galicia in
1888, he studied at a teachers' seminary and then, proscribed as a teacher
for his socialist views, emigrated to the United States, where he adopted
the name John Navis. In 1911 he accepted an invitation to work as a
typesetter for *Robochyi narod* in Winnipeg and moved to Canada. Within
a year he was elected editor-in-chief.[17] Along with Matthew Popovich
and John Boychuk, Navis was a leader of the Red Ukrainians. He was
a member of the first Central Committee of the Communist Party of
Canada and remained a member for thirty years almost without inter-
ruption and was also the secretary of the Bureau of the Ukrainian
Section of the CPC. One student of the radical movement calls him 'the
personification of the old leader, the "father of his people."'[18] When
Navis died in 1954, Peter Krawchuk eulogized him as a man who loved
people, an honest and principled man, a great teacher and humanist,

an exemplary patriot of Canada, and a faithful son of the Ukrainian people.[19]

On 11 April 1931 Navis, who had already made several trips to the Soviet Union,[20] led a Ukrainian-Canadian delegation to Moscow and Ukraine. He was regarded as the ideal choice to head the delegation because, as Matthew Popovich pointed out to Tim Buck, 'he can talk to the delegates on their way to the USSR and prepare them psychologically for the visit. He can give them the proper interpretation of everything they will see there. We want the delegates to come back with a unanimous opinion about the achievements in the USSR and utilize their experiences for propaganda purposes.'[21] The delegation spent more than a month in Ukraine, visiting factories, collective farms, coalmines, hospitals, scholarly institutions, schools, and theatres. 'The delegates were filled with admiration for the great economic and cultural achievements,' writes Navis's biographer Krawchuk. 'Everything that they saw moved them to the bottoms of their hearts. They left Ukraine with great enthusiasm and inspiration. Before leaving Soviet Ukraine Ivan Navizivsky made a statement on behalf of the delegation for the newspaper *Proletarska pravda* in which he said, "During our stay in the land of the Soviets we have been convinced that you are successfully building and will build socialism. Your successes, both on the economic and cultural front, are enormous. This is the result of the unwavering implementation of the Communist party's general line and of the creative enthusiasm that is characteristic of all the proletarians and workers of the land of the Soviets." On their return to Canada the members of the delegation arranged hundreds of meetings at which they spoke to many thousands of Ukrainian workers about their impressions of what they had seen in the first workers' and peasants' country in the world.'[22]

But Krawchuk fails to mention that on his return to Canada Navis stopped off in Toronto to attend a meeting of the party executive. Brigadier-General Denis Draper, the Toronto chief of police, had placed an informer in the ranks of the party. 'Our inside man,' as Draper referred to him, prepared daily reports on Communist activities in and around Toronto. Draper's 'inside man' seized the opportunity to question Navis. On 11 July 1931 Draper relayed to the Ontario Provincial Police information from his 'inside man' about Navis's disclosures: 'Things are not so wonderful as is presented in the Labor News, or the Worker, the people living in Russia say that about 25% are in a bad way, some of them starving, 40% are facing near starvation this winter, 5% are dying from hunger, and only 15 to 20% are well off. Conditions are next to bad and the Five Year Plan is collapsing ... If conditions can not be improved by the end of the year they fear that a revolution will break out on a large scale and that will be the end of Bolshevism. The Bolshevist and Communists only hope of survival is in the strength they may develop in Poland, Germany, China, U.S.A., and the Canadian Workers.'[23]

Another Ukrainian-Canadian Communist who had first-hand knowledge of what was happening in the Soviet Union was John Hladun, who studied at the Lenin School in Moscow in 1931–2. When a British delegation came to visit the lumber camps on the Moscow-Arkhangel railway, a GPU (secret police) officer instructed Hladun how and what to interpret. Britain was buying enormous quantities of lumber from the Soviet Union, and British conservatives were protesting that it had been produced by slave labour. The inmates of the camps, the GPU officer explained to Hladun, were political prisoners and as such class enemies. If he heard any of them complain, either among themselves or in the presence of the British delegation, Hladun should at once report them to the GPU officer who would accompany the party. When he was interpreting, Hladun had to phrase the questions and answers so as to give the impression that the inmates were happy and well cared for. Above all he had to make it clear that they acknowledged their guilt and were eager to expiate it by serving their sentences. To the inmates he had to give the impression that the British delegates were sympathizers of the Communist party and had come not to investigate injustices but to learn how to build an efficient socialist state.

At the first camp that the delegation visited, camp officials produced a set of records which indicated that the minimum monthly pay for the workers was 140 roubles. The delegates were not shown a second set of books which showed that deductions for board, lodging, clothing, and miscellaneous services exactly equalled wages. Afterwards the delegates talked to the inmates for an hour. Hladun's job proved to be easy: the inmates had been at least as well briefed as he had been, and the conversation consisted of stilted pleasantries. Only when he got away from the GPU officials and talked to inmates on his own, did Hladun learn who they were.

One elderly man, when he was finally convinced that Hladun was a Canadian and was not connected with the GPU, said that he was from Cherkasy in Ukraine. 'They picked me up, tortured me in Kiev and finally sent me here.'

'What for?' Hladun asked.

'They said I was a kulak, but I am not. When will they let us out? I hope my family is well,' the old man said, and started to cry.

30 ∠ 0756

ADDRESS ALL CORRESPONDENCE TO
THE CHIEF CONSTABLE

REPLYING REFER TO N°_____

OFFICE OF CHIEF CONSTABLE

POLICE DEPARTMENT

TORONTO, CANADA

SECRET AND CONFIDENTIAL

July 11th, 1931.

Major Gen. V.S. Williams,
Commissioner of Ont. Prov. Police,
Parliament Buildings,
Toronto.

Sir,

Communist activities in Toronto from
our inside man, dated, July 7th,

Last evening a meeting of the executive leaders of the
Toronto Communists was held here and reported by Nawowsky,
secretary of the Ukrainian Labor Farm Temple of Winnipeg,
who has just returned to Canada after attending a convention
in Moscow, Russia. The following is a portion of his statements (given to our man).

Things are not so wonderful in Russia as is presented in
the Labor News, or the Worker, the people living in Russia say
that about 25% are in a bad way, some of them starving, 40%
are facing near starvation this winter, 5% are dying from hunger,
and only 15 to 20% are well off. Conditions are next to bad and
the Five Year Plan is collapsing, which is due to the fact that
the Russian workers are not trained in the line of manufacturing
machinery.

If conditions can not be improved by the end of the year
they fear that a revolution will break out on a large scale and that
will be the end of Bolshevism. The Bolshevist and Communists only
hope of survival is in the strength they may develop in Poland,
Germany, China, U.S.A., and the Canadian Workers.

To my question is it possible to raise the workers of Canada
in revolution against the Government he said it is possible, but
impracticable at the present time because of the lack of trained
forces and most important the lack of ammunition, and without these
two things it is impossible to do anything at present.

After the convention of the Communist Party to be held in
Toronto at the same time as the convention of the Y.M.C.A. Congress,
we will see what to do in the future, and some plan will be made to
draw in large masses of foreigners into the Communist organization.

Russia will be informed of the conditions that exist here
continually, by Boychuk, of Toronto, who recently returned from
Russia and has been instructed to take charge of the Province of
Ontario for the Bolshevist. He will keep in close touch with the
Armtorg in New York, and will get his daily instructions from the
Central Headquarters in Winnipeg.

30 ∠ 0757

OFFICE OF CHIEF CONSTABLE

POLICE DEPARTMENT

TORONTO, CANADA

(2)

This year Russia will spend $175,000 to promote their cause in Canada and about $500,000 in the U.S.A.

The orders from Russia concerning Canada is as follows:
1. To hold meetings wherever and whenever possible.
2. To enlarge the strength for propaganda purposes.
3. To educate the workers generally in Bolshevism.
4. To start training the former soldiers of the last war as far as possible.
5. To draw in all foreigners and immediately start training.
6. Then await further orders from Russia.

The Toronto Communists recently received $7,000 and Boychuk is to pay each leader his back salary. Winnipeg will also get $11,000 at the same time, it will be spent on propagand work only. When the Canadian Communists are short of cash the Armtorg will pay monthly through the Winnipeg, Headquarters.

This is the first report we have had of any meeting of this kind since the return of the last delegation from Russia and from it we gather a general idea of what is in the mind of the Communist Party.

About the end of this week a search warrant visit will be made to these headquarters and it is expected that more informatio will be secured.

Yours truly,

DcDraper

Chief Constable.

'Can't he write to his family?' Hladun asked a bystander.

'We are not allowed to write or receive letters,' the man explained.

After talking to several other groups, Hladun learned that none of the inmates had had a public trial. They had all been sentenced by three-man GPU collegiums.[24]

In May 1932, Hladun used a ten-day recess at the Lenin School to visit a commune that had been established near Kryvorizhzhia in southern Ukraine by a group of Ukrainian-Canadian Communists from Lethbridge, Alberta. They had sold their belongings in Canada and on their return to their homeland had been allotted a large tract of land. Within six months of its formation the Canadian commune began to disintegrate. Some of those who still held Canadian passports returned to Canada; others fled to various countries in Europe. Hladun learned why when he visited the commune. Practically all of the farm implements lay in disrepair. They were of several makes and it was impossible to interchange their parts. Of six tractors only one was in working order. But the ruined machinery was only a fragment of a larger and more bitter tragedy. The communards' lives had been ruined. They made their regret at having left Canada perfectly clear, and they begged Hladun to warn friends back in Canada against believing anything they might hear about the resurrection of Ukraine.[25]

The arrests of Ivan Sembay and Myroslav Irchan constitute a further episode that deeply touched Ukrainian-Canadian Communists. Sembay, a leader of the ULFTA, had been deported from Canada as a Communist and had gone to Soviet Ukraine. Irchan, a Galician who had joined the Communist party in 1920, had come to Canada in 1923 to edit the magazine *Robitnytsia*. In the five and a half years that he spent in Canada he maintained close ties with Soviet Ukraine (he established a Canadian branch of the writers' organization Hart) and came to know most of the Ukrainian-Canadian Communists, and his tale of immigrant life *Karpatska nich* drew heavily on the experiences of his friend John Navis.

In May 1929 Irchan went to Soviet Ukraine to edit the journal *Zakhidna Ukraina* (Western Ukraine), but kept up his contacts with Canada. He corresponded with Navis, accompanied him and the delegation that toured Ukraine in 1931, and wrote an article about the trip for Ukrainian-Canadian newspapers.[26] Then, like so many others at the time, Irchan and Sembay were arrested in 1934 on charges of being 'foreign agents.' The subsequent furor, led to a split in the ranks of the Ukrainian-Canadian Left.

The chief dissident was Danylo Lobay, the long-time editor of the

Ukrainski robitnychi visti. According to Lobay's account of the split, he had become convinced of the validity of the reports of famine conditions and persecution of Ukrainian Communists by the autumn of 1933 and proposed to certain members of the central committees of the organizations affiliated with the party that they make a public protest against 'Muscovite Communist terror in Ukraine.' But none of the people Lobay approached supported him, and he thought it unwise to speak out individually for fear that he would be accused of having sold out to the nationalists. The following year came the news that Irchan had been arrested and Sembay had been executed. In response to inquiries from readers the *Ukrainski robitnychi visti* began to label Irchan a 'counter-revolutionary,' although without offering any proof or explaining what had happened to him. To quell the unrest that the reports evoked, Stewart Smith, a member of the party's Politbureau in Toronto, arrived in Winnipeg in the summer of 1934. The bureau of the Ukrainian fraction held a meeting at which Lobay expressed his views about the situation in Ukraine. He was supported by Mykhailo Smyt from Transcona. Stewart Smith denounced their views, said that party members could not question Soviet policy in Ukraine, and demanded that Lobay and Smyt submit written statements to that effect. The two dissidents refused to do so. At a meeting a week later Smith proposed that Navis be sent to Ukraine to determine what had happened to Irchan and Sembay. Until his return, Lobay, as a disciplined party member, would have to keep quiet. Navis, writes Lobay, 'came back from Ukraine in the second half of December 1934, but did not bring back any information about Irchan and Sembay. He did not keep other promises that he had made before his departure. His report failed to satisfy even those members of the party fraction bureau who knew about his "mission" to Ukraine.'

The following March, at a secret conference of party delegates to a congress of the ULFTA, Lobay expressed his concerns about Soviet policies in Ukraine to close to a hundred delegates. In his speech, writes Lobay, 'I sharply criticized the Russophile policies in Ukraine and said that prominent people in Ukraine were being arrested and destroyed for being Ukrainians. I mentioned the suicides of Khvylovy, Skrypnyk, and Hirniak, the arrest and deportation or execution of Irchan, Sembay, and many other Ukrainian scholars and writers ... I spoke out against the ULFTA press, which was groundlessly attacking and defaming Irchan without explaining the matter factually, as members and readers were demanding. I also spoke out against the absence of freedom of speech within the organizations and the demand that members agree with the party leadership. If this continued and there were no change for the better, I said clearly, I was prepared to leave my work as an editor of the *Ukrainski robitnychi visti*, because I did not agree with such a party policy.'

The ULFTA retaliated the following day by passing a resolution in which it denounced Lobay for his 'counter-revolutionary-nationalist deviation.'[27] Lobay, in turn, published a vehement counter-attack in which he claimed that in a speech at a ULFTA conference on 11 March 1935 Shatulsky admitted that 'the exposure and arrest of Irchan and Sembai made more of an impression on some members of our organizations than any other arrests in Ukraine.'[28] He also quoted Stalin: 'A party that conceals the truth from the people, a party that is afraid of light and criticism, is not a party, but a gang of impostors fated to perish.'[29]

Finally Lobay said that in private conversations Popovich had told him that all of Navis's close friends in Ukraine had been arrested and convicted as 'wreckers.' Only Navis had escaped arrest, even though he had been in close contact with the arrested men during his trips to both Soviet and Western Ukraine. Shatulsky and Navis, wrote Lobay, 'have the greatest responsibility for the failure to clarify the situation in Soviet Ukraine. The former because all the Soviet press passed through his hands and he selected from it only what he liked, deliberately concealing the rest from the readers. The latter because he visited Soviet Ukraine most often and never told the truth.'[30]

John Hladun gives a similar account of the revolt, but adds the interesting detail that even Navis was prepared to break with the party over the arrests of Irchan and Sembay. 'These reports came so abruptly and had such a stunning effect on the many Canadian admirers of Irchan and Sembay,' wrote Hladun in 1947, 'that the central committee's hastily contrived "explanation" for once wasn't acceptable. The Central Committee of the ULFTA, sensing a serious threat to the party's hold over the ULFTA, sent its head, John Navis, to Moscow to make his own investigation. Navis returned with a vague report which satisfied neither the rank and file nor many of the leaders of the ULFTA. A general conference of the ULFTA was called and, just before the conference began, the ULFTA officials met secretly and decided to make a clean break with the Communist Party. Even Navis, hitherto an unwavering Communist, fell in with this decision. The whole uprising blew up as abruptly as it began. Tim Buck heard about the impending defection, brought pressure to bear on Navis and one other official of the ULFTA, and the upshot was that the party loyalists triumphed and the rebels were expelled.'[31]

In 1935 Lobay, Hladun, and Toma Kobzey, the former national secretary of the ULFTA, established a non-Communist labour and cultural organization, the Workers' and Farmers' Educational Association, with branches in Winnipeg, Transcona, and Portage la Prairie, and began publishing *Pravda*, which openly criticized Stalin and his new anti-Ukrainian policies.[32] But the organization remained small, and its influence did not extend beyond Winnipeg. The ULFTA, by contrast, almost doubled its membership – from 8,080 in 1932 to 15,000 in 1938.[33]

Irchan was 'rehabilitated' in the late 1950s, but the only reference to the circumstances of his death, even in the era of *glasnost*, was the phrase 'Died in 1937.'[34] In an article about Irchan that first appeared in the Soviet Ukrainian literary journal *Vitchyzna* in 1957, Krawchuk said nothing about Irchan's death.[35] As late as 1986 Krawchuk referred to the split in the party without revealing its cause and dismissed Lobay's charges as 'renegade fabrications.' In discussing Matthew Popovich's friendship with John Navis, Krawchuk wrote that 'there was a short period when their friendship cooled, after Matthew Popovich came out of Kingston prison in 1934 and visited Winnipeg, where a battle had begun with a renegade grouping headed by Danylo Lobay. This group descended to a nationalist position and tried to split the Ukrainian progressive movement. It directed its fire against John Navis and Matthew Shatulsky. Not oriented in the situation, Matthew Popovich made several comments that were used by the renegades against John Navis and Matthew Shatulsky, as well as against members of the leadership who had remained on a correct organizational position. When Matthew Popovich made his remarks, his friend John Navis was in Soviet Ukraine and could not effectively rebutt the renegade fabrications. But when Matthew Popovich later understood the situation and sharply condemned the renegades, they began a dishonourable and slanderous campaign to defame his character. He was forced to take them to court and to use legal means to exonerate himself from the renegade lies.'[36]

Krawchuk broke his silence only in 1989 when he published an article about Sembay in which he admitted that his arrest, as well as the famine of 1933, led Lobay's group to pose 'legitimate questions about the famine, the arrests and other events, but the ULFMO [Ukrainian Labour-Farmer Mass Organizations] leadership rejected them *a priori*, branding them fictions, lies and slander. The tragedy is that all this was done in good faith, for the leadership was completely blinded by fanatical loyalty to Communist ideas and Party discipline.'[37]

And in an article about the writers' association 'Western Ukraine' Krawchuk wrote that for Ukrainians abroad 'the arrest and defamation of Myroslav Irchan as a nationalist and traitor were a great blow. Out

of loyalty and respect for the first workers' and peasants' state in the
world, Ukrainian toilers, particularly those who were united in progressive organizations and who had great trust in the workers' and farmers'
press, swallowed the bitter pill with deep pain in their hearts ... It is
time to tell the truth, and only the truth, about the Association of
Revolutionary Writers 'Western Ukraine' and the fate of its members.'[38]

In the post-war period, pro-Communist attacks on the historicity of
the 1933 famine were sporadic.[39] In the early 1980s, however, a more
concerted campaign was mounted in response to the commemorative
programmes, articles, books, and films that appeared on the fiftieth
anniversary of the famine.[40] The issue with which these attacks began
was the photographs with which the famine was being illustrated. One
reason why the famine has remained such a secret is the paucity of
visual documentation for it. In the early 1930s, few Soviet citizens could
afford to own a camera; the photographing of famine scenes was strictly
forbidden, and foreign visitors often had their film confiscated as they
were leaving the country.[41] Today we have only a handful of genuine
and authentic photographs from 1933. Yet nothing draws attention to
an iniquity like a picture – the Holocaust has made such an indelible
impression on us in part because we have all seen the photographs that
Allied troops took in the death camps in 1945 – and one of the more
embarrassing aspects of the effort to publicize the 1933 famine has been
the misuse of photographs that purport to show its horrors, but were
taken during the 1921–2 famine, when the Soviet government welcomed
foreign aid and placed no restrictions on the taking of pictures.[42]

Like most of the American and Canadian press, the Hearst newspapers
paid scant attention to the events in Ukraine in 1932–3. In January 1935,
when the famine was long over, however, William Randolph Hearst
attacked Franklin D. Roosevelt's Soviet policy in a radio speech in which
he painted a picture of hunger and ruin in Ukraine and predicted that
five to ten million people would starve to death in the coming year.
Shortly afterwards, Hearst's papers published several long series on
famine and desolation in the Soviet Union. One series was ascribed to
Thomas Walker, a 'noted journalist and traveler' who had supposedly
visited Ukraine in 1934. His account was illustrated with gruesome
photographs of corpses and of people in advanced stages of starvation.[43]

Louis Fischer, the prominent pro-Soviet correspondent, assailed
Hearst in the Nation. He had never heard of a Thomas Walker, he said,
and could find no one who had. Moreover, Walker's photographs could
have been taken on the Volga in 1921 or even outside the Soviet Union.

They were also taken at different seasons of the year: one picture showed trees or shrubs with large leaves that could not have grown by the 'late spring' of Walker's alleged visit; others depicted winter and early autumn backgrounds.[44] Fischer had his own reasons for attacking Hearst – he would get around to an unequivocal admission of the famine only in 1950 – but he was probably right when he implied that Walker was a fiction.[45] No such journalist is listed in the standard biographical dictionaries. And the articles attributed to him had appeared in August 1934 in the London *Daily Express*, where the anonymous author was described as a tourist who had broken away from a guided tour in order to see the real state of affairs.[46] Fischer also had a point when he said that Walker's photographs were taken on the Volga in 1921–2 and not in Ukraine in 1932–3.

The issue became even more tangled when Ewald Ammende, a Baltic German who had been campaigning on behalf of the famine victims, published *Muss Russland hungern? Menschen- und Völkerschicksale in der Sowjetunion*.[47] The book contained twenty-one pictures, which were described as having been taken by an Austrian technical specialist in Kharkiv in the summer of 1933. They are for the most part shots of streets and show shops that did not exist in 1921. Unless evidence to the contrary is presented, these twenty-one pictures are the only photographs of the famine that may be accepted as both genuine and authentic.[48] When Ammende's book was translated into English, however, only twelve of these pictures were reprinted, and fourteen others were added.[49] Most of these additional pictures also appeared in the *Daily Express*, the Hearst newspapers, and Nazi propaganda publications.[50] Ammende died before the English translation was published, and so we do not know whether he himself made the claim, but the book does assert that this second group of pictures had been taken in the summer of 1933 by the manager of a German agricultural concession in the North Caucasus. Yet neither the *Daily Express* nor the Hearst series mentioned the North Caucasus, and the German propagandists, for all their desire to discredit the Soviet regime, carefully labelled the same photographs as 'Famine in the Soviet Union' and refrained from identifying the region or the year.

In the early 1980s these spurious photographs turned up in several documentaries, in Robert Conquest's *Harvest of Sorrow*, in the *Encyclopedia of Ukraine*, on the cover of Roman Serbyn and Bohdan Krawchenko's *Famine in Ukraine, 1932–1933*, and in dozens of newspaper articles and reviews. In Conquest's *Harvest of Sorrow*, for example, a photograph showing a pile of corpses at a graveyard, which Conquest identifies only as 'famine victims,' was taken in the Volga region and first appeared on a Russian poster in the early 1920s. A picture of homeless children seated in a row was taken in Berdiansk, Ukraine, in 1921 or 1922. And a picture of a young woman with a naked child in her lap, whom Conquest, following Walker, describes as a girl of fourteen and her brother, appeared in Nazi publications as a picture of a mother and her child and dates back to the 1920s.[51] The author may argue that because he discusses both famines the photographs are justified here. But since they have often been published as visual evidence of the 1932–3 famine, since he says nothing about their origin and since he treats the Walker series as an authentic account and frequently cites it in his text, some readers will conclude that he has validated the pictures as documentation of the 1932–3 famine. And those who want to cast doubt on the famine will unfortunately be strengthened in their argument that the evidence is fraudulent.

One of those eager to cast doubt was Douglas Tottle, a former steel-worker and trade-union activist who published several articles and letters to editors in which he charged that talk about a 'man-made famine' in 1932–3 was nothing more than an attempt to divert attention away from Ukrainian participation in crimes against Jews during the Second World War.[52] In his book *Fraud, Famine and Fascism: The Ukrainian Genocide Myth from Hitler to Harvard* Tottle stepped up the attack by arguing that most of the photographs used to illustrate the horrors of 1933 were mislabelled.[53] He had a point here, and he would have performed a useful service if he had re-examined the history of the disputed photographs, but his arguments were largely paraphrases of those used by the American Communist party's *Daily Worker* in 1935.[54] Even more disturbing was Tottle's claim that 'right-wing allegations of a 1932–1933 deliberate "famine-genocide"' were nothing more than 'attempts at covering up the wartime record of a national fascist move-ment which collaborated with Hitler.'[55]

That Tottle had the support of the pro-Communist Ukrainian Canadi-ans in this endeavour was evident from the approving review that Wilfred Szczesny, the editor of the *Ukrainian Canadian*, published. Tottle 'sets out to debunk a big lie and does a creditable job of it,' he wrote. 'For the most part, [the book] is compelling reading ... Teachers required to teach about the famine of 1932–33, school trustees, schoolboard offi-cials considering its inclusion in the program of study, and Ministry of Education officials having to make a decision on this issue will find this book very revealing and relevant. Members of the general public who want to know about the famine, its extent and causes, and about the motives and techniques of those who would make this tragedy into something other than what it was will find Tottle's work invaluable.'[56]

Thus the famine photographs, like the famine victims themselves, became a political football that was kicked back and forth in newspaper articles, book reviews, and letters to the editor. One side argued that since the famine was a historical fact, it did not matter what photographs were used to convey its horrors. The other side replied that the famine, at least as a premeditated, genocidal onslaught against Ukrainians, was not a historical fact, and the fraudulent photographs were proof of this.

Throughout the 1930s and until the late 1980s, pro-Communist Ukrainian Canadians ignored the famine, executions, and deportations in Ukraine and failed to speak up even for imprisoned party colleagues. When they could not remain silent, they denounced the victims or tried to divert attention first to the oppressions practised by Poland, Romania, and Czechoslovakia and then to the crimes of the Nazis and their 'bourgeois-nationalist collaborators.' When it came to evaluating events in the Soviet Union, the Communists' will to believe prevailed over public information and firsthand reports by their own comrades.

Why, then, the difference between what Peter Krawchuk, for example, said in 1984, when he called a proposal to introduce the famine into the Toronto school curriculum 'political axe-grinding,'[57] and what he said in 1990, when he expressed satisfaction that Ukrainian scholars can now study the famine and future generations will be able to learn the truth about this 'real genocide' and 'terrible national tragedy'? The obvious answer is that the Soviet policy of *glasnost* that has been in effect for several years has allowed writers and scholars to question virtually every aspect of the Stalinist past. The decision to collectivize agriculture in the late 1920s and the subsequent famine in the early 1930s, the radical shift in the nationalities policy that led to the destruction of the Ukrainian Autocephalous Orthodox Church, the attacks on the non-Communist Ukrainian intelligentsia and the trial of the League for the Liberation of Ukraine in 1930, the purges of the Communist intelligentsia, the destruction of the Communist Party of Western Ukraine, the mass purges and executions of the late 1930s, the arrests and deportations in Western Ukraine in 1939–41, the famine of 1946–7 – all these and many other sensitive questions have undergone fundamental re-evaluation.[58] In some cases Soviet writers are simply restating what people in the West have been saying for many years.[59] But in other cases Soviet scholars are bringing to light new documents and interpretations that enrich our knowledge of the 1920s and 1930s. They are re-evaluating the nature of Soviet rule and asking disturbing questions about its moral – and hence political – legitimacy.

The obvious answer, correct though it is, raises a larger question: why did the Ukrainian-Canadian Left not dissociate itself from Stalin's crimes sooner? Here, too, obvious answers can be offered. As a historian of the Canadian Communist movement has put it, 'After 1928 the party leaders were completely under Soviet domination. Their first loyalty was to the USSR, their main objective revolution in Canada ... Cynical and opportunistic in their campaigns on behalf of the working classes, the Communist leaders recognized the advantages of martyrdom and played the politics of provocation. Whenever the powers-that-be acted humanely, instead of welcoming such actions the Communists tried to find ulterior motives. They maligned and undermined other groups who were seeking ways to alleviate the suffering of the jobless. The party leaders deceived themselves and their followers about Stalin's Russia.'[60]

Or we may consider the implications of Bruno Ramirez's remarks about the relations of Italian Canadians with fascism. 'For many Italians – whether in Montreal or elsewhere in Canada,' Ramirez has written, 'their search for an ethnic identity could hardly be divorced from the political developments that had occurred in their old motherland. For an immigrant population in which two out of three adult persons had left Italy before the advent of fascism, in which an overwhelming proportion had little or no formal education, and whose image of the Italy they had left was one of oppression and political exclusion, the transformations that fascism advertised could not but be perceived as signs of progress. For many of those Italians, then, fascism was seen less as a political ideology and form of government, and more as synonomous with a renewed *italianitö*.'[61]

If we make several substitutions – Ukrainians for Italians, Ukraine for Italy, communism for fascism, and *ukrainstvo* for *italianitö* – we can begin to see the significance of communism for Ukrainian Canadians. Although they had reshaped the Galician, Bukovynian, or Ruthenian identity that they had brought to Canada into a Ukrainian one, Ukraine itself was a distant and even alien place for them. It had been divided among four powers, three of which repressed the emerging Ukrainian national movement and one of which offered a semblance of statehood, a programme of Ukrainization, a promise of unification of all Ukrainian lands, and a dream of universal brotherhood.

Yet these answers, true though they are, also fail to be fully satisfying. Perhaps we must wait until the Ukrainian-Canadian Left completes the 'honest, frank, and objective appraisal' of its history that it has called for and opens up its records to scholarly inspection. But even now one thing is certain. Caught between loyalty to their party comrades and solidarity with their persecuted kinfolk on the one hand and obedience to the dictates of Moscow, on the other, Ukrainian-Canadian Communists chose the latter. Befuddled and unwilling to make the effort to sort out the truth, they are, to paraphrase Peter Krawchuk, still trying to swallow the pill of Stalinism.

Between a Rock and a Hard Place: Francophone Missionaries among Ukrainian Catholics

ANDRII KRAWCHUK

The first chapter in the religious history of Ukrainian Canadians, which set the stage for the split that occurred in 1918, has been examined in many ways – from the secularizing and democratizing effects of the prolonged shortage of priests to the pluralizing effects of proselytizing by denominations that were not part of the Ukrainian Christian tradition. Recently opened archival materials of the Ukrainian Greek Catholic church at the Central State Historical Archives in Lviv, Ukraine, shed light on yet another important dimension of this story – the missionary work of francophone Roman Catholics among the Ukrainian immigrants to Canada.

The connection between the Latin-rite church in Canada and the Eastern-rite Greek Catholic church in Austrian Galicia was established very early at the archiepiscopal level. In March 1901 the Oblate archbishop of the ecclesiastical province of St Boniface, Louis-Philippe-Adélard Langevin, wrote to Metropolitan Andrei Sheptytsky in Lviv with an urgent invitation to come to Canada 'as soon as possible in order to prevent the danger that threatens hundreds of souls ... *Veni, Domine, veni*. May the good angels bring you to us very soon; we will receive you as God's emissary.'[1] But Sheptytsky was not able to travel to Canada until nine years later. Meanwhile the Canadian Catholic church pondered the pastoral implications of the continuing influx of Catholic immigrants from Europe, a major part of whom were Greek Catholic Ruthenians from Austrian Galicia.[2]

Roman Catholic concern for the spiritual welfare of Ukrainians at the turn of the century was centred in Manitoba, where many of them first settled. It was Archbishop Langevin in St Boniface who would urge every Latin-rite seminary and diocese in Canada to provide at least one priest to minister to the Ukrainian Greek Catholics.[3] The first encounters between these priests and Ukrainian immigrants shed light upon a basic fact – that Roman Catholic priests who wanted to serve in the Ukrainian missions needed a special formation, in addition to the seminary, that would enable them to bridge the immense socio-cultural, linguistic, and liturgical divide between them and the Galician immigrants.

Among the earliest Roman Catholic priests from Manitoba who would try to bridge that cultural gap was the Belgian-born Redemptorist Achilles Delaere. By the time he first wrote to Metropolitan Sheptytsky from Brandon on 28 December 1901, he did so not only as a pastor who celebrated liturgies for and preached to the Ukrainians; he also informed Sheptytsky that he had spent a year in Galicia, where he had learned the Polish language.[4]

Another French-Canadian priest who found his way to Galicia was J. Adonias Sabourin. A secular priest from the diocese of St Boniface, he came to Lviv in the summer of 1906 after a year of studies in Rome. It was from the Basilian Fathers' church on Folkievska Street in Lviv that he wrote to Metropolitan Sheptytsky (who was then in Rome) in order to introduce himself and to declare that he intended to devote his priestly life to the Galician people in his home diocese.[5] With that aim in mind he had obtained Archbishop Langevin's permission to spend his summer holidays in Lviv and there to study the language and customs of the Ukrainian people. Moreover, Sabourin sought permission to be admitted into the Ruthenian College in Rome; for this special privilege he appealed to the Basilian provincial, the Reverend Platonid Filas, OSBM, and to Metropolitan Sheptytsky to intercede on his behalf at the Vatican.[6] Later, preparing for his return to Canada, Sabourin on Sheptytsky's advice wrote to Archbishop Langevin to request permission either to transfer to the Ukrainian rite or to become biritual.[7]

By January 1910 both Delaere and Sabourin were serving in Manitoba as priests with biritual privileges that were granted for five years.[8] Later that year Archbishop Langevin told Metropolitan Sheptytsky in Montreal of three more French-Canadian priests who were set to go to Galicia for a time and to return to Canada after transferring to the Greek Catholic rite – Arthur Desmarais, Joseph Gagnon, and François-Joseph Jean.[9]

These early efforts by French-Canadian clerics to enter into the Ukrainian cultural and liturgical tradition appear to have been sincere and not mere covers for Latinization. Archbishop Langevin's expression of concern for the spiritual welfare of Ukrainian immigrants reflected his

understanding of the educational import of the Eastern Christian liturgical heritage: 'these dear children are without the benefit of the divine
services; nor do they hear the melodic chants, the sublime prayers,
many of which were written by such fathers of the church as St Basil
the Great and Gregory of Nazianzus and which constitute an eloquent
homily directed to the spirit and the heart, since they express Catholic
dogma in its entirety.'[10]

Moreover, biritualism in this case was by no means limited to a super-
ficial comprehension of the Eastern rite. In celebrating the distinctive
Eastern liturgy of St John Chrysostom, French-Canadian priests consciously had to 'step outside' the Latin liturgical tradition. The biritual
priests also adapted themselves to the sacramental tradition of the Ukrainian Greek Catholics and thus departed from accepted Latin practices;
for example, although only a bishop may administer the sacrament of
confirmation to Roman Catholics, the biritual priests followed the Eastern practice with the Ukrainians and themselves administered this sacrament.[11] For his part, Delaere also showed a keen sensitivity to values
close to the heart of the Ukrainian people when he asked Metropolitan
Sheptytsky to answer one of his letters in Ukrainian, so that he could
read and show it to his people.[12]

The main reason why French-Canadian priests felt called to serve in
the Ukrainian missions was that this large Catholic immigrant constituency had far too few of its own priests. There is every basis for believing
that, in their decision to dedicate their lives to the Ukrainian people,
Delaere, Sabourin, and those who followed in their footsteps were motivated by a sincere concern for the spiritual well-being of the people.[13]
Yet, along with that fundamental pastoral concern, a variety of additional factors was also at play.

The French-Canadian priests saw themselves not only as missionary
priests but also as defenders of the Catholic faith. In addition to active
proselytizing by established Protestant and fledgling Russian Orthodox
denominations, an array of suspended priests, apostates, and outright
impostors had declared open season on the Ukrainian settlements, challenging the symbols of religious authority to which the immigrants still
clung.[14] To counter that spiritual threat, a strong Catholic mission was
seen as vital. But for all their dedication, the French missionaries did
not always grasp that the people wanted their own priests, from their
homeland, in their own church, one that they had built with their own
hands.[15] And when the people specifically asked for married priests
from Galicia, the Roman Catholic clerics' first response, regardless of the
time they had spent in Galicia (where 96 per cent of the Greek Catholic

clergy were married), was to close ranks and defend the established western Catholic practice. Thus, Sabourin, suspecting that the Ukrainian bishop for the United States, Soter Ortynsky, opposed the idea of biritualism and hearing that he was poised to send married priests to Canada, raised an urgent alarm. 'The situation is grave,' he wrote. 'Married priests are about to be introduced into Canada!'[16] When a Reverend Slivinski from the United States presented himself to the bishop of Montreal in early 1910, the latter asked him in Latin whether he was married: 'Estne mariatus?' Slivinski's response, 'Non sum solus,' was at best ambiguous. As Delaere, who knew he was indeed married, noted wryly, 'It remains to be determined whether [Slivinski] intended to put a comma after the word "non."' But Delaere was truly concerned that Slivinski should not be accepted either in Montreal or in Toronto. As he put it, 'That would be *a breach in the defence* and moreover a dangerous precedent that could have enormous consequences for us and for Canada.'[17] Thus when Delaere and Sabourin wrote to Metropolitan Sheptytsky with assurances that they would heartily welcome 'good' Ruthenian priests from Galicia, it appears that they really meant celibate priests.[18]

Another dimension of the biritual Catholic missions to Ukrainian immigrants concerns the respective approaches of the anglophone and francophone sectors of the Canadian Catholic church. Contemporary documents indicate that there was a competitive rivalry between French and English Catholics over 'the question of the day – the Ruthenian Canadian question.'[19] Differences of opinion between the French and the English occasionally arose over the handling of Ukrainian church affairs. For example, when the married Reverend Slivinski presented a letter of introduction from Alfred Burke, the president of the Catholic Church Extension Society in Toronto, Delaere commented to his colleague Sabourin, 'If we don't watch out, this Mr. Burke will cause us more mischief.'[20]

But there were also indications that a much broader tug-of-war was taking place. Dr Schwegel, the Austro-Hungarian consul in western Canada, gave a unique perspective on the subject when he commented on Archbishop Langevin's efforts to develop a cadre of French-Canadian priests familiar with the language and culture of Galicians:

It seems as is it were a determined purpose not to allow the business to go out of French hands ... The chief point seems to me to be, not the question of the difference of rite, but the question of French domination of the Catholic church in western Canada. I can assure anyone, however, who is working in that direction that he is working at a hopeless task, and that our people, who are coming to this country, are of different stock from the half-breeds of Louis Riel. If the Ruthenian people in their large colonies through western Canada have their own priests, children of their own blood, able to speak their language, to read the service exactly as the people were used to having it read abroad, these priests will exercise a beneficial influence on our immigrants, and will be instrumental in making good Canadians of them – not one-sided and prejudiced supporters of the French idea in western Canada.[21]

Thus, in the larger picture, the importance of supplying Canadian priests for Ukrainian immigrants was tied not only to the salvation of their souls but also to their future place within the religious and socio-political fabric of Canada. Consul Schwegel, for one, seemed confident that, given the chance, Ukrainians would find their own creative path for integrating their traditional sense of religious and social identity with the new reality in Canada.

No account of the francophone pastoral ministry to Ukrainian immigrants can be complete without a consideration of the various difficulties that the non-Ukrainian priests encountered in their work. When Metropolitan Sheptytsky met Archbishop Langevin at the Montreal Eucharistic Congress in September 1910, he tempered his statement of enthusiasm for francophone pastoral assistance with a strong measure of realism about the hardships that would be an inevitable part of such a ministry: 'You will be of assistance to our compatriots, who are threatened by schism and heresy, if you provide them with priests who can understand them and who adopt their rite, regardless of the many difficulties to which they will be exposed, and in spite of the defiance of our people, who will not at first understand this type of dedication.'[22]

Ukrainian resistance to non-Ukrainian pastors was characterized by a strong sense of self-righteousness. It was so elevated that it even affected the relations of the Ukrainian Catholic immigrants with the episcopal authority back home. 'If the French bishops impose their priests upon us,' a group of sisters in Winnipeg wrote to Sheptytsky in 1910, 'they will stir us up, and then you will have to answer for our actions. We are holding on to what our forefathers held fast to and died for.'[23] And when a Ukrainian priest in Canada was suspended by Sheptytsky, opposition to the French ministry was mobilized in the form of assemblies that passed a resolution to disregard such suspensions in Canada.[24] For a variety of reasons, personal no less than social, many Ukrainian parishes boycotted Sabourin's ministry. From the Winnipeg community came the firm declaration that 'every church has renounced the Reverend Sabourin.'[25] The differences of perspective encompassed the religious community as well as laymen. When in November 1910 Sabourin asked for and was sent two Sisters Servants from Mundare for assistance in Winnipeg, their superior, Sister Ambrose Lypkevych, felt compelled to point out to Sheptytsky that she had consented to this arrangement only out of monastic obedience and in order to avoid trouble with Archbishop Langevin. Although the sisters were concerned about the future of their order and its role in the community (they were especially interested in teaching religion and the Ukrainian language, in order to counteract both types of assimilation), they were instead being recruited as maids (*naimychky*) at Sabourin's residence. They were particularly offended by the argument that 'a monastic person does everything much better and costs less' than lay hired help.[26]

The vulnerability of the French missionaries to such resistance centred on the perception of them as agents acting on behalf of the French bishop. Despite their effort to absorb the Ukrainian language and culture in Galicia and regardless of their change of rite and regular communication with the metropolitan archbishop of Lviv, the francophone clerics' most immediate recourse to episcopal authority was the Latin-rite diocesan office in St Boniface. The missionaries themselves were quick to realize that such recourse had virtually no impact on the Ukrainians and only undermined their pastoral authority. As Delaere expressed it, 'In any other place, the zealous missionary finds natural solace and support in the authority of his legitimate bishop. The situation is clear and simple. Among the Ruthenians, however, the missionary cannot invoke the authority of the Latin bishop because that authority is not recognized. The less the priest refers to the Latin bishop, the more favourably he is viewed by his [parishioners].'[27]

So suspicious were Ukrainians that the francophone priests were out to Latinize them that when the latter offered financial assistance to the impoverished immigrants, such funds were flatly refused as a matter of principle. The crisis of authority at the pastoral level was compounded by differences of opinion inside the Ukrainian community as well. In such questions, too, no authority was recognized in the francophone priests. Delaere gave a concrete example: 'What fasts must the Ruthenians observe? One group will say, "the same ones as in Galicia." Others say, "no, those customs were local, and since we have left that place, that law no longer binds us." Try telling the people that they are not obliged to observe the fasts and they will raise a cry of "scandal" and "treason." Thus the position of the priest in the confessional becomes very precarious; he does not know what to say or what to advise. And you have exactly the same situation with a thousand other liturgical, canonical, and ceremonial questions.'[28]

Of all the issues and questions that the francophone priests faced in their Ukrainian ministry, the most divisive and emotionally charged was the question of the registration of churches. Delaere referred to it as 'the central issue around which the battle lines have been drawn.' In legal terms the matter was quite simple. According to Manitoba law, a contract to purchase or lease land for church use had to be filed at the provincial registry within two years of the transaction. Otherwise such a contract was null and void.[29] In ecclesiastical terms, registration also involved submission to a recognized diocesan authority. But to the Ukrainian mind, possession was nine-tenths of the law. Most parishes therefore refused to register their church except with a Ukrainian bishop. Those that did register, whether under Roman Catholic diocesan authority or under the Ukrainian Basilian fathers, did so on the condition that the church would be transferred to a Ukrainian bishop once one was appointed in Canada.[30]

From the francophone priests' point of view, the essential issue was to keep the Ukrainians within the Catholic fold and the church building out of the hands of Protestants.[31] But whereas Delaere seemed to focus attention on external threats in this regard, Sabourin was more concerned about the danger within: 'To differ on [the question of] putting churches under ecclesiastical authority is excessively dangerous ... Once a contract is registered and it puts the church in the hands of the population, it is practically impossible to change. What we have is a Catholic church with a Protestant administration.'[32]

Sabourin's concern about the urgency of the registration issue and his worry about the future of the Ukrainian Catholic polity in Canada led him to adopt an uncompromising stance in favour of registration. But when Metropolitan Sheptytsky urged him to exercise more discretion and pastoral prudence, Sabourin promised to be less intransigent in his handling of the issue.[33]

So sensitive were the Roman Catholic priests to the broad implications of the registration issue that it way well have been the decisive factor in their strong support for the establishment of a Ukrainian Catholic episcopal see in Canada. Anticipating precisely the type of crisis of authority that Sabourin had described, Archbishop Langevin wrote to the apostolic nuncio in Canada with assurances that he and his colleagues Légal and Pascal fully supported the idea of nominating a Ukrainian bishop for Canada. Langevin explained that, in the view of the French bishops, although it would not resolve everything, this was 'the only way to settle the question of the registration of Ruthenian churches under ecclesiastical authority, whereas the majority wants to place or to leave church properties in the hands of lay or cultural committees.'[34]

The French priests serving the Ukrainian church took essentially the same view. They were aware that most Ukrainians believed them to be opposed to the nomination of a Ukrainian bishop. In fact, they were convinced that such a nomination would be a tremendous boost to the French-Canadian missionary effort. Conversely, 'if, after Monsignor Sheptytsky's visit [to Canada in 1910], a Ruthenian bishop is not named, all the people will be convinced that it was we and the Latin-rite bishops who prevented it. And if the Protestants and the independents catch on to this accusation, the reaction could be terrible ... If we want to keep these people in the Catholic church, the nomination of a Ruthenian bishop is an absolute necessity.'[35]

Thus, whether focusing on the internal, organizational danger of Protestant-like tendencies among Ukrainian Catholics or on the external threat of proselytizers, the francophone clergy and episcopate in Canada expected that a Ukrainian bishop would not only solve the registration issue but would also rehabilitate the francophone clerics' credibility within the Ukrainian community.

Another factor that lay behind the Ukrainian resistance to French Catholic pastoral resistance was national fervour. In the Ukrainian missions, two very different conceptions of the church were competing with one another: a universal, transnational model and a national model. On the one hand, those priests who had decided to devote their lives within a completely alien cultural and liturgical tradition of Christianity did not seem in the least interested in denationalizing the Ukrainian immigrants to Canada. Rather, their practical dedication to a pluralistic view of catholicity seems to have been remarkably far in advance of its time. On the other hand, Ukrainian resistance to the biritual experiment in Canada was quite clearly informed by varying degrees of national and even nationalist sentiment. Delaere, a keen observer of the Ukrainian psyche and its historical roots, clearly saw the linkage between the Ukrainian defiance towards the Latin-rite priests and bishops in Canada and the historic Polish opposition to the Union. In Delaere's opinion, there was nothing at all surprising in the Ukrainians' fears and suspicions, since 'with the flow of time, the Ruthenian people came to regard anything Polish or Latin as the enemy of their religion and their nationality.'[36] In fact, the linkage between religion and national sentiment was so powerful, Delaère believed, that even though the Catholic church condoned patriotism, any priest serving the Ukrainian people would have to recognize that their sense of national identity was bound up with the question whether or not to be Catholic: 'The Ruthenians, although Catholic and belonging to the universal church have not yet developed to the stage of imagining a church without a large dose of national sentiment. Whoever would want to make Catholics of these Ruthenians in one fell swoop, while neglecting or opposing this spirit, is bound to fail.'[37]

Moreover, the particular socio-ecclesiastical conjuncture in Canada heightened the national sensitivity among Ukrainians to the extent that even secular priests from Galicia who submitted to the jurisdiction of the Latin ordinary could expect to be rejected by their own people.[38] But the Ukrainians' full fury was reserved for the non-Ukrainian priests. For example, on the registration issue, he was inevitably perceived as a promoter of religious denationalization. From Winnipeg, one group wrote to Metropolitan Sheptytsky: 'Father Sabourin wants us to register the church with him. We will gladly register, but only with our Ruthenian priests or a Ruthenian bishop, when we will have one – not with the French. We want not independent priests but Greek Catholic ones, and we want to remain Greek Catholics, faithful to the Holy See of Rome.'[39]

In another instance, Sabourin himself cited an example of national prejudice. When a Ukrainian priest, the Reverend Barysz, left Sifton after a brief tour of duty, Sabourin wrote that 'despite many fine qualities, this fine man is terribly prejudiced against everything non-Ruthenian and in particular against what is French.'[40] National exclusivism was not limited to individual Ukrainian Catholics. In September 1910 Metropolitan Sheptytsky received a petition signed by more than two thousand Ukrainian Canadians. Article 4 of the petition called on him to 'withdraw all priests of foreign nationality and to bar them from entering our parishes in the future.'[41] The petition went on to explain that Ukrainian-Canadian 'ecclesiastic and national life' had become one and that foreign priests could not live up to the ideal of a nationally committed clergy.

For their part, the francophone missionaries were guided by a point made in Kraus's *History of the Church*: that the popes had always instructed Catholic missionaries to accommodate, preserve, and Christianize national customs and that this to a large measure accounted for the rapid growth of the faith.[42] In principle, then, they affirmed the need for the Catholic church in Canada to support the national traditions and values of the Ukrainian people. As Delaere expressed it, 'To the extent that it is possible and licit, it is necessary to yield [accorder] to the Ruthenians what remains. In fact, that is the only effective way to take charge of the mass and to establish it within the body of the Catholic church, where it wants to be but only while remaining Ruthenian. It is up to us to put this mass into the body [of the church], and then the serious and effective work on the whole may begin.'[43]

Thus, despite even the most unreserved support for national values, and regardless of the lengths to which francophone missionaries were prepared to go to become Ukrainian priests for Ukrainian people, the trump card in this complex relationship was always in the hands of the Ukrainian pioneers. Even if the missionaries understood that differences often centred not on principles but on tactical posturing by Ukrainians who wanted their way, there was little they could do when Ukrainians questioned their authority and sincerity.[44]

By the end of the first decade of the century, substantive steps were taken that appeared to herald a new and more promising phase in the Roman Catholic pastoral and organizational assistance to the Ukrainian church. Integration of Ukrainian Catholics into the Canadian Catholic scene occurred in a significant way in the area of education. In January 1910 several Ukrainian girls who were completing studies in the Roman Catholic convents of St Boniface, St Norbert, Ste Anne, St Jean Baptiste, and St Charles prepared to write their final exams. Ukrainian candidates for the priesthood also began to study in Canadian Roman Catholic seminaries. In November 1909 Vasyl Ladyka reported to Metropolitan Sheptytsky from the Grand Séminaire in Montreal on the studies of three Ukrainians there.[45] And in June 1913 Petro Kamenetsky wrote to the metropolitan from St Augustine's Seminary in Toronto about the progress of seven Ukrainian seminarians.[46] Thus, the process of cultural adaptation that the first francophone missionaries had started by travelling to Galicia for study had come full circle. The emergence of a Canadian-educated Ukrainian clergy had begun.

In October 1909 Archbishop Langevin, Bishops Légal and Pascal, and Apostolic Delegate Sbarretti met in a plenary council in Quebec City to discuss pressing issues of the Ukrainian religious community. Responding to a request from the Sisters Servants in Galicia, the bishops assigned to Sozont Dydyk OSBM (the provincial of the Ukrainian Basilian Fathers in Canada) the task of modifying the statute of that women's community, making its Canadian wing distinct and autonomous and its raison d'être teaching in primary schools.[47] Another issue was the need of a Ukrainian newspaper that would 'promote and defend the truth and

Catholic interests among Ruthenians.'[48] The bishops contributed four thousand dollars towards the purchase of a printing press and sent money to Galicia to cover the travel expenses for a Ukrainian editor to come to Winnipeg.

Archbishop Langevin convoked a second meeting in St Boniface on 4 January 1910. Present were four Eastern-rite priests: the francophone missionaries Delaere and Sabourin, Sozont Dydyk, and the priest of St Nicholas parish in Winnipeg, the Reverend A. Fylypiw. The meeting discussed a broad range of problems and concerns and led to what was termed a 'fraternal entente,' or agreement in principle, between Ukrainian and non-Ukrainian clergy on how best to unify their pastoral work.[49] In an effort to achieve a degree of solidarity, existing parish jurisdictions were affirmed, and it was decided that settlements would be visited only by the priest in charge or with his permission.[50]

On the question of ensuring a priest's financial needs, it was recognized that such practices as tithes and the renting of pews were repugnant to Ukrainians and that fees for baptism would be waived if they were keeping Ukrainian parents from bringing their infants to church.[51] Instead, some standard fees were suggested, and priests serving in Ukrainian missions were cautioned that although it was their prerogative to withhold sacraments for chronic non-payment of fees, such measures could backfire and lead Ukrainians into schism and heresy.[52] Similarly, with a view to preventing apostasy, priests were urged to exercise pastoral prudence on the question of fasts and feast days; in particular, former Latin-rite priests were reminded that they were dealing with 'an uneducated and defiant people' and that discretion was especially important.[53] However, in dealing with direct instances of the perceived evils of schism and heresy, an uncompromisingly hard line was set out: parents who insisted on sending their children to Protestant Sunday schools were to be barred from the sacraments, and there was to be no burial of heretics and schismatics in Catholic cemeteries.[54]

The challenges facing the francophone priests were great and would mount as the numbers of Ukrainian Catholic immigrants rose without a commensurate increase in priests of their own kind. Of their dedication there can be little doubt. Over the course of a decade they had learned many things about their charges. Now an institutional framework was beginning to be put in place for the Greek Catholic church in Canada, though its true implementation awaited the arrival of a Ukrainian bishop in 1912. The 'fraternal entente' of 1910 was an attempt to overcome some of the more painful differences and uncertainties that arose out of the francophone missionary work among Ukrainians, to achieve a unity of pastoral action, and thereby 'to save thousands of souls from spiritual ruin.'[55]

In resisting non-Ukrainian missionary priests, the Ukrainian immigrant was driven by national values more than by religious concerns. The francophone Catholic priest was all too ready to cater to both needs and to recognize the historical factors that had fused them together within the Ukrainian psyche. But he could not change his ethnic background, and that remained the main stumbling block between him and his parishioners. For his part, the Ukrainian immigrant, whether out of a historically cultivated defence mechanism or out of sheer prejudice, was susceptible to the notion that a non-Ukrainian priest was an agent of denationalization. Ukrainian national concerns were also a decisive factor that prevented the contentious issue of registration from being resolved. To the Ukrainian mind, registration under a Latin-rite bishop was akin to a renunciation of church property in favour of a foreign church. Consequently, the Canadian Catholic perspective on registration as a defence against Protestantism did not enter into the Ukrainian position. The Ukrainians' organic rejection of the francophone pastoral ministry was thus an important indicator of the nature and degree of their national sentiment. The issue also served as an early opportunity to formulate and mobilize support for objections by the laity that would become a key factor in the creation of a new church in 1918.

'A Portion for the Vanquished': Roman Catholics and the Ukrainian Catholic Church

MARK G. MCGOWAN

The future of the Ruthenian [in Canada] will be in the hands of those who know how to stir up and direct a great social movement, at once national and religious, which will carry along the whole Ruthenian population ... Scant indeed will be the portion left to the vanquished.[1]

The words of Metropolitan Andrei Sheptytsky of Lviv offered a challenge to the Latin Catholics of Canada to help build a strong Uniate church in this country. For Ukrainian Catholics, Sheptytsky's comments offered hope and confidence that a Greek Catholic church could be built in Canada. For Latin Catholics his words could have served as warning to those who confused their own burgeoning nationalism with the interests of the Catholic faith. Throughout much of their early history in Canada, Ukrainian Catholics found themselves squarely in the midst of a struggle between the two host cultures for control of the Canadian Catholic church. In this position, the Ukrainians became the object of a major 'Saving and Reclamation Effort' underscored by a French and English Roman Catholic desire to enlist Ukrainian allegiance in the larger national struggle within the Canadian church. In the end, the Ukrainians saved themselves, developing an indigenous clergy and a solid record of episcopal leadership after 1930. By the end of the Second World War, Ukrainian refugees from Europe would find a reasonably strong Uniate presence in Canada, the product of decades of institutional and organizational development, amidst bitter ethno-cultural struggle.

The attempts of Ukrainian Catholics to reconstruct and practise their distinctive form of Christianity in Canada were difficult. It is surprising that, faced by a dearth of clergy, Vatican restrictions, and the competing visions of French- and English-speaking Roman Catholics, the Uniate church was able to survive its first half-century in Canada. This paper explores the often tenuous relationship between Ukrainians and their anglophone and francophone Catholic brethren, from the arrival of the first Ukrainians in 1891 until the establishment of regional exarchates in 1948. The relations between the Greek and Latin rites that emerged in this period manifested distinctive historical phases: 1891–1912, the period of Latin control; 1912–29, the struggle for Ukrainian autonomy; and 1929–48, a period of survival and expansion for Ukrainians in the Canadian Catholic mosaic. Within these phases, three primary issues underscored the often troubled relations between Uniates and Latins: the question of jurisdiction, the struggle over clerical formation, and the Roman Catholic efforts to assimilate the newcomers. Relations between the rites became focused on a struggle between three competing visions of the Canadian community – the Ukrainians' determination to retain their cultural integrity; the French Canadians' belief in the *Gestae Dei Per Francos*, their divine mission to evangelize the West; and the English-speaking Catholics' vision of a loyal, imperialist, and anglophone Catholic Canada. The story of the Ukrainian church in Canada to 1948 is, in part, a story of the struggle of these visions and of the continuing challenge of creating cultural harmony under the canopy of Canadian Catholicism. Neither the anglophones nor the francophones succeeded in their plans, yet their struggle inadvertently produced a vibrant pluralism in the Canadian church.

From 1891 to 1912, Ukrainian Catholics were heavily dependent on their Latin-rite hosts for chapels, clergy, and the sacraments. The decisions made on such issues as jurisdiction, clergy, and assimilation would establish precedents for subsequent periods of Ukrainian religious life in Canada. When Ukrainians first arrived in the resource-rich northern regions of Ontario, the industrial centres in the St Lawrence–Great Lakes corridor, and the agricultural belt of the Canadian prairies, they brought neither clergy nor the capital to rebuild their distinctive religious traditions. In the Austro-Hungarian monarchy, the state had provided for their religious needs, supplying the clergy and church buildings, and as such, the religious rites of passage considered integral to Ukrainian life. In the voluntarist and religiously pluralistic environment of North America, however, Ukrainian Catholics were left to fend for themselves. As a result, most struggling Ukrainian colonies depended either on the goodwill of the local Latin ordinary or on the services of an itinerant Orthodox priest or Protestant minister. The latter became a frequent refuge when the local Latin clergy were sometimes less than cordial or failed to appreciate the Greek-rite liturgy and married clergy.[2]

In Canada, French- and English-speaking Catholics were unprepared for the thousands of Catholic immigrants arriving weekly from Europe after 1897. For Canadian Catholics, these new arrivals could not have come at a worse time. Still smarting from the loss of separate schools in Manitoba and the fallout from the Riel crisis and Jesuit Estates affair, French- and English-speaking Catholics were becoming more vocal about their own linguistic jurisdictions and control in the Canadian church. Since language was quickly replacing religion as the focus of Canadian identity, the linguistic debate within the church made the immigrant question seem secondary in importance. For these and other reasons, bishops, priests, and laity appeared woefully uninformed about southern and eastern European Catholics entering the country. In Toronto, for example, Ukrainian and other migrants set up temporary services in Roman Catholic churches, only to find that they were subjects of curiosity to the hosts, susceptible to being locked out of churches, rudely scrutinized by local children, and taken advantage of by 'sham priests' and con artists.[3] Eventually, when the numbers of new Canadian Catholics became too overwhelming to ignore, and as these new Catholic communities made demands, or Protestant missionaries converted the newcomers, the local Latin ordinaries provided some material and financial aid. By 1910, for example, Bishop David Scollard of Sault Ste Marie, Ontario, had helped to finance two Ukrainian Catholic churches, one near the mining centre of Coppercliff and the other near the rail yards and docks of Fort William.[4] Similar ventures had been jointly sponsored by local clergy and Ukrainian migrants in Montreal (1908),[5] Toronto (1910), Brantford (1911), Oshawa (1910), Winnipeg (1899), and in other prairie settlements.

It was the French-Canadian hierarchy on the prairies that set many precedents in the relations between the Latin and Greek rites in this first phase of Ukrainian Catholicism in Canada. Louis-Philippe-Adélard Langevin, the Roman Catholic archbishop of St Boniface, was the most powerful Catholic prelate on the prairies and was chiefly responsible for formulating church policy towards the Ukrainians. Preoccupied with the decline of the francophone presence on the prairies, Langevin was slow to respond to the needs of the Greek-rite Catholics. He was not happy with the 'belligerent' Uniate priests who moved in and out of his diocese and, protective of his own authority, refused to entertain the idea of special status for Ukrainian Catholics. He adamantly rejected the idea of a separate Ukrainian bishop, for fear of jurisdictional disputes and the possible migration of married priests to North America.[6] In concert with Cardinal Ledóchowski, the Polish-born prefect of the Propaganda Fide, Langevin supported a policy of Latinization of Ukrainian Greek Catholics. Pursuant to this policy, the apostolic delegate, Diomede Falconio, sought the appointment of a Uniate priest as apostolic visitor, who, when under the control of the delegate, would facilitate the Latinization.[7] For Langevin, the Ukrainians were part of his vision that the French were divinely ordained to convert and administer the church in the Canadian West.[8]

The francophone hierarchy's most serious problem was finding suitable clergy for the Ukrainians. Petitions from the American hierarchy in the early 1890s had resulted in the Vatican prohibiting the migration of married clergy from Europe to America after 1894. American and Canadian bishops were afraid that the presence of married clergy might damage the uniformity and discipline of the Latin-rite clergy, which had been officially celibate since the Fourth Lateran Council. For those interested in securing Ukrainian clergy, the Vatican ban provided a formidable obstacle, since less than 5 per cent of the Uniate clergy in Galicia were celibate and had no desire to emigrate. In the 1890s, Langevin did not seek Ukrainians exclusively, but put Ukrainians in Winnipeg under the care of two Polish priests at Holy Ghost parish. Given the traditional conflicts between the Ukrainians and Poles, it is not surprising that Ukrainian Catholics were insulted by such a move.[9]

The rising numbers of Ukrainian migrants to the West and the growing success of Protestant and Orthodox proselytizers among dissatisfied Ukrainian Catholics forced a complete reassessment of Langevin's policy after 1900. In response to the request of the apostolic delegate, Metropolitan Andrei Sheptytsky of Lviv sent his secretary Vasyl Zholdak to Canada to assess the situation of the Greek rite in 1901. The fact that Orthodox priests were undercutting the authority of the Uniate itinerants and were spreading rumours about Latinization was sufficient cause for alarm. Moreover, the American newspaper *Svoboda* continually criticized the work of the Roman Catholic and Uniate leaders, adding to the Ukrainians' fears that they were being Latinized. With perhaps as many as sixty thousand Ukrainian Catholics being served by less than ten priests,[10] Langevin faced a veritable crisis. From 1901 to 1910, he executed a multi-faceted strategy that included a more zealous attempt to recruit Ukrainian celibates, an effort to bring Belgian Redemptorists to the missions, and an attempt to have some French Canadians translate to the Greek rite. In 1902 Zholdak and Sheptytsky arranged for three celibate Basilian monks, one brother, and four Sisters Servants of Mary

Immaculate to journey to Canada.[11] By 1906, several Belgian Redemptorists, including Achilles Delaere, who had served in the field since 1898,
were translated to the Greek rite, an act which the Vatican had rejected
until that point. By 1912, Langevin and Bishop Émile Légal of St Albert
had roughly 150,000 Ukrainian adherents, with only twenty-one clergy,
many of whom were Belgian or French-Canadian.[12]

The Ukrainian people were not entirely receptive to these new priests.
Father Henrich Boels, a Belgian Redemptorist, complained that Ukrainians would not confess to a former Latin priest for fear they might
themselves be Latinized.[13] Many Ukrainians simply refused to attend
services offered by a non-Ukrainian priest. In Sifton, Manitoba, for example, William Zaporzan reported that Ukrainians were not satisfied with
the French and Belgian clergy there because they could not speak Ukrainian well; as a result many of Zaporzan's countrymen were turning to
the 'schismatics and Presbyterians.'[14] Worse still, one Ukrainian priest
commented that many Ukrainians did not respect the celibate Basilians
recruited in Galicia, because many of the monks were drawn from the
lowest ranks of Galician society.[15] Unhappy with the priests provided,
Ukrainian Catholics turned elsewhere. After 1904, immigrants could
seek spiritual guidance from several Ukrainian-born priests in the new
Independent Greek church, which drew from the followers of Seraphim
Stefan Ustvolsky and was financed by the Presbyterians. In addition,
desertions to the Russian Orthodox fold caused a number of court battles
over church property between Uniate and Orthodox factions within
existing Catholic congregations. The negative Ukrainian response to
Langevin's effort to keep the Greek Catholics under his control was
understandable, given the historical resistance offered to Latinizers, be
they Polish or Austrian. By 1912, Langevin's ability to retain the loyalty
of Ukrainian Catholics and, ironically, the confidence of his fellow Latin-
rite brethren to the East was in serious trouble.

Langevin's English-speaking Catholic colleagues had been slow in
their response to the Ukrainian presence for a number of reasons. First,
the Anglo-Celtic Catholic presence on the prairies at the turn of the
century was weak, particularly since all of the episcopal sees were under
the control of francophone bishops. Even in the anglophone-controlled
dioceses of Ontario, where most Ukrainians outside the prairies settled,
the immigrant assistance programmes did not commence in a meaningful way until after 1905. Most bishops found it difficult to find celibate
Uniate priests; most of the priests they did acquire came via Bishop
Ortynsky in the United States.[16] Although the evidence is fragmentary,

it would appear, too, that the distinctiveness of the Greek rite made some clergy wary of formalizing a liturgy and priesthood that was not uniform with their own. The question of immigration by Latin-rite Catholics seemed to be far easier to handle, since their order of the mass and clerical discipline were in harmony with the charter Catholics of the province. Congregations for Poles, Italians, Slovaks, and Germans had been established as early as the mid-nineteenth century. Ukrainians were not accorded the same speed in delivery of services. Archbishop Denis O'Connor of Toronto, for example, was reluctant to build any new churches, preferring to consolidate and lower the church debt rather than expand the Catholic position in the city.[17]

The most significant and controversial anglophone response to the Ukrainian Catholic presence was the Catholic Church Extension Society. Founded in 1908 by Father Alfred E. Burke, Archbishop Fergus McEvay of Toronto, and Supreme Court Chief Justice Charles Fitzpatrick, the Extension Society attempted to raise funds and Catholic consciousness about immigrants and the need for home missions in Canada. The Canadian Extension Society was entirely independent of the American Extension Society (founded by Canadian expatriates in 1905) and received its own pontifical constitution in 1910. Its executive, largely anglophone, brought together some of the richest and most influential Catholics in the country, while its women's auxiliaries marshalled rank-and-file Catholics behind the home mission effort. Through its control of the *Catholic Register and Canadian Extension*, the CCES secured a national audience for its financial drive to aid Catholic immigrants, especially Ukrainians, whom it identified as most in need of Latin-rite assistance.

Father Alfred Burke, the president and a noted British imperialist, launched a zealous drive to resolve the 'Ruthenian crisis.' In 1909, during the first phase of his campaign, Burke used the pages of the *Catholic Register* to alert English-speaking Catholics to the Ukrainian rite and its problems:

The first difficulty the Church in Canada had to face in connection with the Ruthenians was the fact that she had no priests of the Rite to serve them ... They have a few little chapels and churches; only a few – not enough. Worse still the sects have spied out their chance, and the 'soul chasers' of the Protestant societies have been trying to win the people. The schismatic Greeks, with the money of the Czar, are working to win them over to the Greek Church ... This is the glorious call of God to His workers. Catholic Canada must act promptly and effectively. Dear friends: because we knew you we have dared to act for you.

We want it now, and you will not refuse ... Can you turn a deaf ear to the cry of these little ones, children of those from far-off lands, strangers to your shores, now in danger of losing their most precious Faith?[18]

These 'consciousness raisings' were followed by blistering attacks on Presbyterian missionaries and officials who were supporting the Independent church. Burke denounced the Protestant-inspired 'sham priests' as 'wolves in sheep's clothing,' and he would claim partial credit when the Independent Greek church collapsed in 1912. In a third operation, Burke with the assistance of Uniate clergy and Bishop Légal launched a plea for the Ukrainians at the First Canadian Plenary Council of Bishops in 1909. The appeal eventually engendered a resolution by the hierarchy to collect ten thousand dollars a year for ten years for the Ukrainian missions.[19] Within five years Burke made the Extension Society the front and centre of the Ukrainian mission movement and in the process sharpened the hostilities between the rival English- and French-speaking arms of the Catholic church.

The Catholic Church Extension Society and many of its leaders also had a hidden agenda. Many English-speaking Catholics in Canada entered the twentieth century with a new confidence in themselves as loyal citizens of the British Empire and with a vision of an anglophone and Catholic Canada. In addition to the vestments, altarplate, clergy, literature, and chapels that it would supply the Ukrainians, the Extension Society promised to be 'purely and simply Canadian and Patriotic as well as religious.'[20] For Burke and his anglophone colleagues, the introduction of the English language was critical to the survival of Ukrainians in the job market and for Canadianization in general. To this end Burke sponsored English-instruction programmes for immigrants and encouraged anglophone clergy to interest themselves in the home missions. Although clergy who spoke the Ukrainian language were clearly preferable in the home missions, both Burke and Archbishop McEvay knew how hard such priests were to recruit and so actively sought priests who could speak both English and Ukrainian.[21] Leaders of the Extension Society recognized the need to save the Catholic church in the West and the need to recognize that English was destined to dominate in that region. Thus, English-language instruction was regarded as good both for Ukrainians and for the preservation of Anglo-Canadian society. Burke considered the evangelization and Canadianization of immigrants as integral parts of the home missionary programme; the immigrant question had to be solved for the 'good' of Canadian society, because according to Burke: 'The way of our statesmen and Churchmen is bestrewn with difficulty, but it must be kept clear for the advance of British civilization and effective religion.'[22]

For Langevin and the French-Canadian hierarchy, Burke and his Extension Society were a formidable threat to *Gestae Dei Per Francos* in the West. Langevin's fears were heightened by the fact that Burke was on excellent terms with Légal, Langevin's French-born suffragan. Worse still, Burke had the ear of the apostolic delegate Donatus Sbarretti, who had helped organize the Extension Society. Langevin resented the intrusion into his territory and informed several of his priests that the Extension Society was an Irish and 'imperialist' plot to destroy the work he had done with immigrants and to undermine the francophone presence in the West.[23] Much of this ill will was reciprocated by Burke and his colleagues, one of whom referred to Langevin as a 'large overblown archiepiscopal (———)' – the blank allowed Burke to fill in any word he deemed fit.[24] Not surprisingly, by 1910 all francophones except Légal had abandoned the Extension Society, recognizing in it an anglicizing institution, inimical to French-Canadian interests in the church.[25] Somewhere in this bitter internecine squabble, the Ukrainian missions became a secondary issue to the assertion of control over the Canadian church by one of its two charter groups.

One negative side-effect of the Langevin-Burke struggle on the Ukrainian church was in the recruitment of clergy. Langevin's difficulties in attempting to recruit celibate Uniate clergy were repeated when the Extension Society sought Ukrainian priests. Burke, however, seemed to be less discriminating on the question of clerical celibacy. In 1909, he co-operated with Father Lev Sembratovych, a Uniate priest serving in Buffalo, in securing priests from Galicia. The latter was upset by what he judged to be the poor quality Basilian priests and the French Uniates, whom the Ukrainian people considered as Latinizers.[26] Sembratovych informed Burke that he could return to Galicia and recruit from nearly three hundred young seminarians there. Burke requested episcopal support but was blocked by several bishops. It is likely that Sembratovych, himself married and separated, did not have the confidence of either Langevin, Delaere, or Bishop Paul Bruchesi of Montreal, who feared he would bring in married clergy.[27] When his efforts to recruit Ukrainian clergy were thwarted, Burke blamed the French hierarchy and bitterly told Archbishop McEvay: 'The Extension Society is ready to do something – everything to win the esteem of the "most reverent [sic] high and mighty seigneurs of the plains." '[28] If the French feared disruption of the Latin clergy by allowing some of the Greek-rite customs, their fears may have been sustained by Burke's alliance with

Sembratovych. Moreover, unknown to most concerned except Burke, the Extension Society's two agents to the West, Fathers Roche and Canning, had already expressed a preference for the Greek rite, which they thought 'a big advance over the Latin.'[29]

English- and French-speaking advocates of home missions also disagreed on the issue of a separate Ukrainian bishop to administer the Greek rite in Canada. Langevin had consistently opposed such an appointment, which he felt would be the prelude to serious jurisdictional disputes between the Latin and Greek bishops in the West. Burke and the Extension Society, on the other hand, advocated the appointment of a 'Ruthenian' bishop, indicating that the missionaries and Ukrainians interviewed desired one.[30] Burke's position probably further estranged him from Langevin and widened the chasm between the parties they represented. As the numbers of Ukrainian immigrants increased and the recruiting of clergy stagnated, however, those opposed to a separate Ukrainian eparchy almost reversed their positions. At a meeting of the Canadian hierarchy in Quebec City in 1911, Langevin and four of his suffragans decided to leave the matter of an appointment in the hands of Rome. These prairie bishops did caution that there were the potential dangers of married clergy, jurisdictional disputes, and prejudice against the French and Belgian Uniates if an independent Ukrainian bishop was appointed.[31] By 1912, the Ukrainian Catholic population was still starved of clergy; Protestant and Orthodox missionaries were still working in the Catholic colonies, and titles to church property were still being contended by Uniate and Orthodox laypersons.[32] For the French prelates involved, however, acquiescence to the appointment of a Ukrainian bishop was an admission that the policies employed by the Latin rite, English and French sections, from 1891 to 1912, were clearly insufficient to build a strong Ukrainian Catholic church in Canada.

The appointment of Nykyta Budka as the Ukrainian bishop of Canada in 1912 brought temporary hope that Ukrainians could free themselves from the domination of French, Polish, and Anglo-Celtic outsiders. Unlike his American contemporary, Bishop Ortynsky of Philadelphia, Budka was not required to report to the Latin episcopacy in any particular diocese. Instead, he answered directly to the apostolic delegate, the pope's representative in Canada. Although he was responsible for one of the world's largest dioceses, Budka could rest assured that he did not have to consult with local Latin ordinaries every time controversy erupted among the various rites of a given district. Upon arrival in

Canada, he quickly consolidated his control and independence by a federal act of incorporation for the 'Ruthenian Greek Catholic Church in Canada.'[33] Budka, however, faced four enormous challenges to his leadership and to the integrity of the Uniate church: the First World War, resurgent Ukrainian nationalism, the rise of Ukrainian Orthodoxy, and assimilatory Catholic nationalism in Canada.

From the outset, Archbishop Langevin demonstrated only luke-warm support for his Uniate colleague. By 1912, Langevin was fighting French-Canadian Catholicism's last stand on the prairies, and although Budka's appointment relieved him of some practical burdens, it further eroded the authority of the See of St Boniface in the region. Langevin went so far as to instruct at least one of the French-Canadian Uniate priests to remember that his primary loyalty was to Langevin, even if it conflicted with Budka's decisions.[34] Father Josaphat Jean, one such priest who had transferred to the Greek rite, reported that some of the French-Canadian Uniates continued to fuel Ukrainian fears that they were Latinizers. Jean claimed that one of the most prominent of these priests, Father Sabourin, 'chantant partout et toujours qu'il est Canadien-Français, et nous reprochant lorsque dans nos sermons nous nous disions Ruthenes.'[35] Despite continued Ukrainian fears of Latinization at the hands of the French, Budka attempted to remain on amicable terms with Langevin and his suffragans. He realized only too well that he still depended on the francophone priests – Québecois, French, or Belgian – who comprised over one-third of his twenty-seven clergymen.[36]

Archbishops Langevin and Beliveau of St Boniface and Bishop Paul Roy of Quebec were concerned about the new powers exercised by Budka. Simultaneously, they continued to combat the 'anglicization' tactics of the Extension Society, which posed a formidable threat to the French stewardship of the Ukrainians west of Ontario. This cultural animosity was only exacerbated by French-English tension over the demolition of bilingual schools in Ontario in 1912 and the Conscription Crisis during the Great War. When Thomas O'Donnell, who had succeeded Burke as CCES president in 1915, attempted an approchement with the prairie bishops in 1918, he was supported by all but Arthur Beliveau, who had succeeded Langevin in St Boniface. Beliveau felt that he could not taint the memory of his beloved predecessor by acknowledging the Extension Society's wish to elevate the faith over all considerations. Furthermore, an attempt to found a branch office of the society in Montreal failed, and Roy in Quebec maintained that his dioceses would contribute to the Ukrainians without the intermediary role of the Extension Society. The continued estrangement of French and English

Catholics on the Ukrainian question damaged the effectiveness of Catholic aid after 1918 and seemed to bear out Sheptytsky's prediction that the portion to the 'vanquished' would be small. From 1914 to 1929, while Budka struggled to keep his flock, French power in the West disintegrated dramatically, as most of the principal sees in Alberta, Saskatchewan, and Manitoba fell to the Anglo-Celts. For Bishop Budka and the Ukrainians, it was clear that it was the Anglo-Celts with whom they would have to deal west of the Ottawa River.

From the earliest days of his episcopate, Budka diligently pursued a close working relationship with the Catholic Church Extension Society. It was the CCES that had paid for his passage to Canada and offered him generous financial aid. With Budka in close contact with the board of governors, the CCES accentuated its efforts to raise funds for the Ukrainian church, build educational institutions, construct chapels for Ukrainian worship, and help finance the cash-starved *Kanadyiskyi rusyn* (Canadian Ruthenian), which was renamed the *Kanadyiskyi ukrainets* (Canadian Ukrainian) in 1919. From 1919 to 1927, the society poured over $250,000 – an annual outlay of 15 to 25 per cent of its national budget – into the Ukrainian church.[37] In 1916 alone, the CCES and the *Catholic Register* launched a three-month fundraising drive for Ukrainian Catholics. Making his presence felt, Toronto's Archbishop Neil McNeil, chancellor of the Extension Society (1912–34), highlighted the urgency of the Ukrainian appeal to Latin Catholics: 'The Catholic Church Extension Society is the only organization in Canada through which our home missions can be regularly and effectively aided by the Catholic laity. The work of Bishop Budka among the Ruthenians calls urgently for help. Delay in this case may easily mean disaster.'[38] The campaign steamrolled through the spring, and despite the financial hardships inflicted on Canadians by the war, CCES supporters raised nearly seventeen thousand dollars, a figure that exceeded every annual tally since 1909, save one (1911–12).[39]

The effort of the Extension Society and its leaders, however, still bore an assimilatory edge in this second phase of Uniate-Latin relations. Although they maintained that they would defend and nurture the Catholicity of the Ukrainian people, Anglo-Celtic leaders were still intent on making Ukrainians become upstanding, law-abiding Canadian citizens. With the support of the Anglo-Celtic episcopate, the society initiated several educational ventures to integrate a new generation of Ukrainian Catholics into the English Canadian mainstream. In 1919, the Extension Society, Budka, and the Christian Brothers founded St Joseph's College for Boys in Yorkton, Saskatchewan. In keeping with the Canadianizing aim of the society the school intended to 'bring these people in touch with our ordinary Canadian customs.'[40] The boys would follow courses in English, and the *Catholic Register* concluded that all of the Ukrainian lads would be 'taught loyalty to their faith and to the country into which they have come to build up a future for themselves.'[41] In addition to St Joseph's, the Extension Society supported similar schools for Ukrainians boys and girls in Edmonton, Vegreville, Vilna-Radway, Yorkton, Sifton, and Morden. The Sisters of Service, founded in 1922, operated several rural hospitals in Ukrainian prairie settlements.[42] Budka himself was not unaware of the dual mission of the schools, as he publicly praised 'the benefits of an English-language education' for the Ukrainian people.[43]

Similar clerical support was offered for Extension Society efforts to educate Ukrainian Catholic adults in English. In Toronto, Father Charles Jermy praised the women's auxiliary of the Extension Society for running an English-language night school for his parish. In a few cases, Anglo-Celtic women brought Ukrainians into their homes for instructions. Likewise, anglophone Catholic men in Toronto used the Holy Name Society to acclimatize the Ukrainians to Canadian cultural mores and solid citizenship. Under the auspices of the Holy Name Society not only would Ukrainian souls be secured for the church, but the 'foreigners' would be taught the 'conditions, customs, and tongue' of other Anglo-Canadians.[44] Like other Catholic migrants in the city, however, Ukrainians failed to sustain their interest in these societies after the Great War. Seasonal employment in natural resource industries took them far afield from Toronto, and those who remained regarded the Holy Name societies as alien to their culture.[45]

For English-speaking Catholics 'Canadianization and Catholicization' were a double-edged sword to win the battle for Ukrainian immigrants. Redemptorist Father George Daly, an ardent supporter of the Church Extension Society, asserted that English would have to become the dominant language in the mission field. 'The sooner our Ruthenians know English well, the better they will be equipped for the struggle of Canadian life and the preservation of our Catholic faith,' he contended in 1920.[46] One way to assure this was to recruit Ukrainian clergy who were fluent in English, or vice versa. In any event the priest was the key to success. The hierarchy made arrangements for Ukrainians to study at St Augustine's Seminary in Toronto. In 1914, the seminary hired the Reverend Dr Amvrozii Radkevych (or Ambrose Radkiewicz) to direct the spiritual formation of fourteen Ukrainian candidates.[47] Five of these candidates graduated that same year. By 1917, when Radkevych left his teaching post in metaphysics, six more candidates had graduated.[48] The Ukrainian episcopate did not invest all of its hopes in St Augustine's, as it still kept strong ties to the College St Boniface and the Grand Séminaire in Montreal.

Despite these numerous programmes by Anglo-Celtic Catholics during and after the war, the urgency of the Ukrainian crisis never seemed to abate. Although the Extension Society's coffers were filling at an unprecedented rate after 1919, and the religious artifacts and chapels supplied to the Ukrainians kept pace, neither the hierarchy nor the society saw this effort as enough. In 1923, Thomas O'Donnell complained that even though the Extension Society had raised almost $150,000 that year, Presbyterian missionaries had almost $700,000 at their disposal. Throughout the 1920s, Bishops McNally of Calgary and McNeil of Toronto launched several appeals for the Ukrainian mission, none of which ever matched the astonishing success of 1916.[49] Even the 'bursa' programme, which had financed Ukrainian schools and the education of missionary priests, began to decline. The inability of the Extension Society to mend its fences with French Canada seriously weakened its ability to help the Ukrainians and other immigrants. More interesting, however, is the fact that by the late 1920s English-speaking Catholics seemed to be losing interest in the Ukrainian missions. Even some of the Latin bishops were beginning to doubt that Ukrainian immigrant aid was having any impact.

Some of this Anglo-Celtic Catholic indifference may be attributed to the maelstrom whirling within the Uniate church, with Budka at the centre. The hostility to Budka on the part of Canadian imperialists during the war, the crash of the Ukrainian Catholic press, and the success of the Ukrainian Orthodox movement were taking a dramatic toll on the vitality of the Uniate church. In 1914, for instance, Budka issued a pastoral letter to his flock urging them to support Austrian emperor Franz Josef in his impending struggle with Russia. Unfortunately for Budka, Britain declared war within the week, the Austro-Hungarian monarchy was now the enemy, and Budka had the appearance of being a traitor to the British cause, of which most Anglo-Celtic Catholics considered themselves a part. Budka recalled his pastoral letter and called upon his flock to defend their new home and rally about the Union Jack. Despite the support of the Latin bishops and particularly the *Catholic Register*, which vociferously defended Budka, a cloud hung over him throughout the war. At war's end he faced eleven counts of sedition, all of which were dropped for lack of evidence.[50] Latin Catholics may have rallied to his aid, but there is little evidence to account for the silence of Catholic leaders and laity when Ukrainian Catholics were disenfranchised and some were incarcerated as enemy aliens during the war. In Vancouver, for example, the Catholic Children's Aid refused to help a Ukrainian internee at Vernon who wanted to see his children, despite the support of the latter by the chair of the camp committee.[51] Thus, there is little to suggest that the attitudes of English-speaking Catholics differed appreciably from those of other Canadians when the issue of 'enemy aliens' arose.

Budka's leadership suffered repeated crises in the closing phases of the war. With the collapse of the Russian empire and the birth of the long-sought Ukrainian republic, Ukrainian nationalism spread throughout the colonies of Galician expatriates after 1917. Part and parcel of this renewed Ukrainian confidence was the emergence of the Ukrainian Orthodox church of Canada in 1918. The new church expressed its disdain for the Uniate church, which it felt existed 'according to the wishes and under the rigid control of the French Roman Catholic Church, in contradiction to our national interests.'[52] The Orthodox presence directly threatened Catholic membership, so much so that by 1931 it could claim the allegiance of one-quarter of Canada's Ukrainians.[53] Ukrainian Catholic efforts to fight the incursion of the Orthodox led to the collapse of the *Kanadyiskyi ukrainets* in 1927, after it lost a libel suit launched against it by the Orthodox. With all of these crises in the 1920s, Budka still had personal credibility problems to solve. As early as 1921, his lawyer had reported to Archbishop McNeil that the Uniate prelate had few organizational skills and lacked the confidence of his priests. Finally in 1927, faced by problems of confidence and failure against the Orthodox, Budka, in ill health, returned to Europe.

Correspondence between the Extension Society and the Anglo-Celtic hierarchy indicates that Latin-rite Catholics were well aware of the problems within the Uniate church from 1914 to 1928. The presence of the Orthodox, the Ukrainian Labour-Farmer Temple Association, the socialists, and Budka's apparent weakness caused alarm among Catholic leaders and were chiefly responsible for the urgent pleas for financial aid for the Ukrainians throughout the 1920s. Behind the scenes, however, one suspects that many bishops were prepared to implement extraordinary measures to ensure Ukrainian Catholicity without a formal Uniate church. As early as 1923, Father George Daly tabled a 'confidential report' to the Canadian bishops, outlining in detail the problems facing the Greek rite in Canada. Daly, a well-travelled founder of the Sisters of Service, a home missionary order, praised the Ukrainians as 'a strong, energetic, thrifty and prolific race,' but concluded that the

Protestant missionaries, public schools, Budka's weakness, and the 'inherent tendency of the Greek to schism' threatened Catholicism among Ukrainians. He proposed to the Canadian episcopate the 'supreme remedy' of the 'gradual, prudent, systematical absorption of the Ruthenian Catholics into the Latin Church.'[54] Although the Latin hierarchy did not execute the 'remedy,' its very existence indicates Latin dissatisfaction with the minimal success of Ukrainian aid campaigns and the loss of confidence in the Greek-rite leadership in Canada.

By 1929 the fate of the Ukrainian Catholic church was in serious question. The bishop had resigned, leaving behind a shattered Ukrainian Catholic press, a dismayed priesthood, and a laity that was increasingly under pressure from the Protestant and Orthodox proselytizers, the socialists, and the Latin-rite forces of assimilation. One of the few successful pillars of the Uniate community was the monarchist-dominated 'Canadian Sitch,' a popular fraternal movement founded by the Ukrainian patriot Volodymyr Bossy.[55] Nevertheless, the Anglo-Celtic Catholics who had been the mainstay of the Uniate presence in Canada witnessed an erosion of support for recurrent Ukrainian appeals. The Extension Society survived its estrangement from francophone Catholics, but it could not continue if its vital anglophone support in Ontario and the Maritimes evaporated. Even the society's showcase project, St Joseph's College in Yorkton, was burdened by a staggering debt of sixty thousand dollars in 1928 and was being hounded by creditors.[56] A crisis of confidence permeated all levels of the Latin church, with Archbishop McNeil of Toronto admitting that the home missions had reached a veritable crisis, particularly since the church was losing an average of ten thousand souls per year in the prairie West.[57] Under these circumstances it is not hard to understand the Anglo-Celtic Catholic concerns about the Eastern rite that had been outlined in the 'confidential report.'

The era of the Great Depression and the Second World War was a period of rebuilding for the Ukrainian Uniates of Canada as well as a time of renewed tensions between the sister rites in Canadian Catholicism. Vasyl Ladyka, the new Ukrainian bishop who was consecrated in 1929, spearheaded a renewal in the Uniate church, while at the same time Roman Catholics made a new effort to fight what they believed to be the forces of communism at work among Eastern European Catholics. Although it was faced by fewer new arrivals and growing support for socialism and Orthodoxy in the Ukrainian population, the Uniate church witnessed unprecedented growth in terms of clergy and congregations. This renewal, however, was not without problems, and disputes between the rites over jurisdiction and married clergy persisted through-out this period.

The 1930s witnessed remarkable changes in the Uniate church. Although many of the transformations within it could be attributed to the solid leadership offered by Ladyka, the first fruit of his episcopate was actually the long-awaited harvest sown by his predecessor in the 1920s. When Budka retired in 1927–8, he left behind approximately 47 priests, 299 missions and churches, 26 night schools, 5 orphanages, and between 160,000 and 200,000 adherents.[58] By the early years of Ladyka's episcopate the programme of training secular Ukrainian priests in Montreal, St Boniface, and Toronto had matured. The bishop could rely on at least one hundred priests, 58 per cent of whom were seculars. Concurrently with the increase in clergy, the Uniates also experienced an expansion of parish facilities with now over 350 parishes.[59] The flood of displaced Ukrainians, including refugee clergy, into North America after the Second World War prompted a drastic redrawing of the episco-pal map of the Ukrainian church in Canada. On 3 March 1948, Ladyka's transcontinental diocese was divided into the smaller exarchates of Edmonton, Winnipeg, and Toronto, with Ladyka in Winnipeg assuming the role of titular archbishop. Ladyka's new episcopal colleagues included Isidore Borecky in Toronto, Nil Savaryn in Edmonton, and, after the creation of a fourth exarchate in 1951, Andrei Roborecki in Saskatoon. By November 1956, Ladyka's successor, Maxim Hermaniuk, assumed the title of metropolitan of the Ukrainian Catholic church, and the other exarchates became eparchies, equivalent to Latin dioceses. To fill the gap left by the demise of the previous Ukrainian Catholic newspapers Ladyka also established the *Ukrainski visti* (Ukrainian News). Given these new directions and the more pronounced control by the Ukrainians over their own affairs, it appeared that the formerly high levels of material assistance of the Latin rite would not be needed.

The growth and gradual success of the Ukrainian Catholic church in this period coincided with a pulling away from immigrant aid by the Extension Society. During the drastic economic dislocation of the 1930s, the society concentrated on distressed church communities and native missions in the West. The *Catholic Register* in the 1930s did not maintain the earlier high profile of Ukrainian news in its pages. The gradual withdrawal of the Extension Society, however, did not signal the with-drawal of the interest of the Latin rite per se. Such issues as the 'Red Menace' and the married clergy prompted the Latin-rite bishops and laity to keep a 'watchful eye' on their Ukrainian brethren.

During the 1930s Canadian Roman Catholics were deeply concerned about the spread of communism, particularly among the recent Eastern European immigrants. After the Russian Revolution in 1917, Canadians had considered Eastern Europeans to be susceptible to the lure of socialism, bolshevism, and communism. The harsh economic climate of the 1930s and the inept political solutions offered by traditional political parties provided a fertile environment for the growth of more radical options to deal with the inequality and poverty of Canadian society. Both English- and French-speaking Roman Catholic prelates sponsored programmes to eliminate the Communist menace among Catholics. West of the Ottawa River, Anglo-Celtic Catholic leaders scrambled to 'save' their Poles, Ukrainians, and other Slavs from communism. Archbishop James McGuigan, McNeil's successor in Toronto, openly encouraged the Holy Name Society as a 'bulwark against communism.'[60] Throughout the depression and war Roman Catholics organized study clubs, labour schools, and co-operatives to offer Christian alternatives to the Communists. Similarly, Henry Somerville, editor of the *Catholic Register*, used the weekly as an organ of social Catholicism and anticommunism.[61] Such anti-Communist activities dovetailed nicely with similar anti-Communist activities within the Uniate church itself and within the Sitch network across the country.

A link between the Greek and Latin rites in the area of anticommunism came in the person of Catherine de Hueck Doherty, an expatriate Russian baroness. A fervent anti-Communist, de Hueck had fled Russia during the Revolution and subsequently dedicated her life to working with immigrant communities, rooting out bolshevism. In 1934, Archbishop McNeil invited de Hueck to Toronto to work among the Eastern European Catholics of the inner city, who, in his mind, seemed particularly susceptible to communism and the labour temple movement. In Toronto she founded Friendship House, an urban settlement for men and women, with the twofold purpose of upholding the Catholic faith and fighting communism. The reading-room and soup-kitchen were located on Portland Street in the heart of Toronto's Slavic neighbourhoods and within a hurling distance of Communist halls and clubs. De Hueck boasted that amidst the thousands of meals served every month, many immigrant men were restored to the faith from communism.[62] In addition to her linguistic acumen and activism, de Hueck brought her strong Eastern Christian spirituality to her pastorate, thus providing a valuable bridge between the Latin and Greek traditions. Although the Friendship House movement spread to Hamilton and Ottawa in 1936, the movement collapsed when questions were raised about her canonical status in each archdiocese and her character was attacked by some clergy and laity.[63] By 1937 the Friendship House experiment was dead, an ironic casualty of a Latin-rite church dedicated to eliminating the 'communists,' yet unwilling to allow an Eastern European lay woman the direction of a venture that seemed to undercut the authority of local Latin-rite priests.[64]

Such experiments and failures as de Hueck's were peaceful compared to the struggle over married clergy. The issue had persisted from the earliest years of the Ukrainian migration without suitable solution in the minds of the Ukrainian Catholics in North America. In the mid-1930s, several clergy and their congregations in Canada and the United States grew tired of what they considered 'Roman' control in their affairs. One particular case, the rebellion at St George's Ukrainian Catholic parish in Oshawa, demonstrates the tension between the rites over the issue of married clergy. Founded in 1910, St George's was one of the oldest Ukrainian Catholic parishes in Ontario. As with so many other Ukrainian parishes, the local Latin-rite institutions had a strong hand in its early life: its first pastor, Andrei Sarmatiuk, was trained at St Augustine's Seminary and ordained in Toronto in 1916. The church building and hall provided a debt load, which by the time of the depression had to be assumed by the archdiocese of Toronto, because as a local Uniate priest asserted, 'the majority of the parishioners is on relief.'[65]

In 1935, however, the debt problem appeared minor compared to the controversy created when Father Sarmatiuk disclosed that he was married with children. In January, Sarmatiuk was suspended by 'an order from the Holy See,' a fiat supported by Bishop Ladyka and McNeil, who held the parish mortgage.[66] The *Catholic Register* offered its support to Bishop Ladyka, and the local Latin clergy debated the idea of foreclosing on the mortgage, but, fearing nasty publicity, rejected it. Nevertheless, Sarmatiuk, who refused to leave his marriage, rallied both his parishioners and the press to his defence. From the former he secured a petition of three hundred names, some of which were those of children and of local Orthodox Ukrainians,[67] who protested that the old country custom of married clergy was not honoured in Canada. By February the Toronto press carried news of the schism and demonstrated some sympathy for the Ukrainians in their struggle against the imposition of Roman authority.[68] One parishioner gleefully claimed that Sarmatiuk's supporters were weeding out the Catholics 'who wish to stay under the power of the pope,' and Sarmatiuk himself declared that he was forming a branch of the Independent Ukrainian Catholic church with the remnants of his flock. Sarmatiuk and his followers subsequently formed St John's Orthodox congregation, leaving the St George's Uniate community in ruins. The Oshawa 'schism,' as it was referred to by local Latin clergy, impacted on several other communities, as Uniate congregations in Brantford, Hamilton, and London were shaken by the 'Roman authority' issue.[69]

The Oshawa crisis crystallized the long-standing issue of Roman authority over the Ukrainian Catholics in Canada. Sarmatiuk was probably correct when he reported to the *Toronto Star* that Ukrainians resented the imposition of Latin authority in Canada.[70] The issue of married clergy persisted without solution throughout the first five decades of the Ukrainian establishment in Canada. It is still a point of contention between the Latin and Greek rites in Canada, as the recent controversy about ordination in the Toronto eparchy demonstrates. It appears that while Ukrainian Catholics expanded their institutional and episcopal networks, incorporated their own fund-raising networks, and secured an indigenous secular clergy among Canadian-born generations, certain issues, such as married clergy, exacerbated old tensions and confirmed that the Latin rite was still very much in control on some issues. By 1948, the Ukrainian Catholic church in Canada had come a long way from its early dependence on the goodwill of Latin-rite Catholics. Yet even in the post-war period jurisdictional problems could easily shatter co-operation between the rites.

The relation between the Greek and Latin rites in Canada has consistently been focused on matters of jurisdiction, clerical celibacy, and Ukrainian acculturation. In the first phase of the Ukrainian Canadian church, Ukrainians were powerless under the Latin rite, which restricted their clergy, refused them a bishop, and exerted incredible assimilatory pressures. Even though the Ukrainians had assured themselves of independence with the appointment of Budka in 1912, the next seventeen years were marked by repeated crises of leadership in the church. Pressures within the Ukrainian community and the Canadianizing tactics of the Anglo-Celts weakened Budka's leadership. English-speaking Catholics emerged as the primary force in the Catholic home missions and became presumptuous in their treatment of Ukrainian culture. Anglo-Celts were prepared to defend a different rite, but were unwilling to let the Ukrainians halt the march of Canadian progress. In the 1930s, even after anglophone assimilatory motives were toned down, the Ukrainian bishop was firmly in place, and the French presence vastly reduced, Ukrainians and Latins still battled on the issue of married clergy. The Latin desire to ensure uniformity in the priesthood, and perhaps in language, remained in all the phases of Ukrainian Catholic church growth.

For Sheptytsky the vanquished would receive little. The Latin-rite activists did not assimilate the Ukrainians as they had hoped; the Ukrainians remained devoted to their culture and language. Neither charter group could stir up a 'national' movement sufficiently enticing to the Ukrainians before 1948. Had the French and English united on their home missions, the Ukrainians may have suffered fewer defections and found it easier to get to their feet. Nevertheless, it was perhaps that very division between the French and English that helped Ukrainian survival. With the assimilatory efforts of the host church bitterly divided, Ukrainians, who regarded their religion and culture as integrally related, strengthened themselves as a third force in the church. Divided, the French and English could not prevail over the will of the Ukrainian people to survive as a distinctive community. In the process, the Latin-rite failure and Greek-rite persistence may have helped pave the way to a formalized cultural pluralism in the Canadian Catholic church.

Wedded to the Cause:
Ukrainian-Canadian Women

FRANCES SWYRIPA

The 1970s saw women's history emerge as a legitimate discipline in Canada. Critics of conventional male-dominated scholarship resolved to rescue the 'second sex' from invisibility and trivialization by making women independent actors and subjects of enquiry. Individual achievers or 'Great Women' to complement the 'Great Men' of nation building, together with female participation in such landmark events as two world wars, incorporated women into the traditional framework of Canadian history. More importantly, women's historians demanded recognition of the female experience on its own terms, liberated from the restrictions and distortions of patriarchal criteria. The mass of ordinary women – and the political, economic, socio-cultural, and intellectual forces shaping their lives – attracted much of the new research. Appreciation of a distinct women's world, accompanied by integration of the female experience and a feminist perspective into mainstream scholarship, would give women a past and challenge accepted tenets of Canadian history to enrich understanding of the nation's development.[1]

Like their political counterparts in the feminist movement, whose agenda was acknowledged as the motivation behind their work, the first generation of Canadian women's historians was predominantly of British and French origin. Ideological roots and goals shared with the feminist movement combined with personal roots in the dominant culture to dictate the assumptions they applied to their discipline, the framework they imposed, and the themes they identified and pursued. The result was a perception of the proper subject matter of Canadian women's history, and of the boundaries of the national experience, that left the non-British and non-French on the fringes – marginal, faceless, and passive. Ethnic women appeared in the literature as part of an undifferentiated mass, in an emphasis on common female experiences and problems, or as the objects of concern to the mainstream suffragists, prohibitionists, missionaries, and educators who constituted historians' real subjects.[2] Moreover, emphasis on traditional mainstream interests and concerns – prairie settlement, immigrant adjustment, assimilation, the economy – confined ethnic women to their relations with the larger society to the neglect of their relations with their own communities.[3] Reducing the experience of ethnic women to that of 'all' women, and to issues familiar and historically important to the dominant 'national' culture, said much about the acceptance of ethnicity as a positive or valid force in Canadian life.

Indifference to ethnicity stemmed partially from the demands of the feminist movement. Historians' present-mindedness, with their wish to mobilize women against gender-based discrimination, channelled them towards female oppression – its causes, forms, and effects – and women's efforts to conform or resist. This decision, politically motivated, made women's relations with men and male systems an inevitable and major focus. Women's history in Canada also owed a debt to the pioneering ideas of the American historian Gerda Lerner, who insisted that female criteria determine structure and content.[4] 'To view women as persons in their own right,' it was claimed in placing Canadian women at the centre of their past, 'as human beings of reason, will, and feeling, is a feminist perspective, and obviously the only correct one. That feminist perspective is what legitimizes women's history as a field of study.'[5] The primacy of gender, whether positive or negative, as a conceptual and organizing principle necessarily subordinated factors like ethnicity to women's unique and common condition, either alone in the world of women or as women in the world of men. It applied to historical scholarship the feminist notion of all-encompassing and dominating sisterhood. But feminist politics alone account inadequately for the inattention to ethnicity as other factors cutting across gender – class and regional differences, for example – escaped the same fate. Historians' dominant-culture outlook must also be considered.

In 1977, Margaret Andrews argued that in English Canada the purpose of women's historiography had always been to improve women's position in society, while in French Canada it was to propagandize for women's traditional roles in the interests of *la survivance*. The converging of the two streams in the 1970s as French Canadians turned increasingly to feminist issues she saw as a sign of unity during escalating French-English tensions.[6] A second interpretation is perhaps more illuminating.

By the 1970s the psychological framework for many French Canadians had shifted from the French-Catholic province of Quebec struggling for survival in an unsympathetic English sea to the Quebec nation controlling its own destiny. As group survival against outside pressures receded in importance, the 'woman question' could become an internal matter directly concerned with women's needs and divorced from their relation to *la survivance*. The situation in English Canada has been entirely different. Secure in their membership in the dominant culture (politically, socially, and economically), Anglo-Canadian women have never been faced with basic group survival, in spite of unfounded fears in the early twentieth century that 'foreign' immigration would swamp their race and way of life. Unlike French-Canadian women, they have been free to concentrate on improving women's position in society without having to debate whether women's rights or group rights should take priority.

Group security, regardless of their inferior status as women in their society, not only determined the interests and perspective of mainstream women's historians in English-speaking Canada. It also made the French-Canadian perspective – and that of ethnic women as members of distinct national-cultural entities – at best irrelevant or secondary, at worst alien and threatening.[7] Erring in generalizing from the Anglo-Canadian experience, both the women's movement and mainstream women's historians failed to appreciate that for many ethnic women the problem was not simply to improve women's position in society. It was to improve their position in an Anglo-dominated society (as women and as non-Anglo-Canadians) while simultaneously addressing their position (as women) within their group. Complicating their options were the latter's status and interest in survival, as well as their own feelings towards the retention of all or part of their heritage. If they belong to a group that has historically considered women inferior to men, or assigned their sex specific roles and responsibilities in the name of the group, ethnic feminists must either choose between ethnicity and personhood or work to reconcile the two.

No discussion of Ukrainian women in Canada can afford to ignore their origins. Although they could and often did manoeuvre to modify the effects of membership in a much maligned minority harbouring a strong sense of identity, being Ukrainian (and female) prejudiced women's mobility as Canadians in Canadian society. It also imposed behaviour models and obligations, whether solicited or not, that tied them to Ukraine and to the Ukrainian-Canadian group. Women's ethnicity in the first instance, not willingly chosen or understood to be a positive aspect of their identity, represented external forces beyond their control: Ukrainians' low immigrant entrance status, the position of women in traditional Ukrainian peasant society, the nativism shared by Anglo-Canadian men and women alike, and Canadian attitudes to women's roles in both public and private spheres. Women's ethnicity in the second instance was also involuntary. Upset at their group's negative stereotype, and anxious for acceptance from Anglo-Canada, community leaders insisted that all Ukrainian Canadians had a responsibility towards their people's image and status.[8] They equally insisted that the predicament of twentieth-century Ukraine, following its failure to secure political independence in 1917–20, obliged Ukrainians in Canada to preserve the language and culture threatened in the homeland and to extend to the latter material and moral aid.

Given the complex pressures that ethnicity has exerted on Ukrainian-Canadian women, the 'woman-oriented' and 'woman-defined' approach to the female experience that a Canadian women's historian described as writing 'directly about the experience of women in the past for its own sake rather than as part of some broader or other subject'[9] must be rejected as too narrow and restricting. This is not to belittle the value of women's own story, although ethnicity touches it at every point. But an approach that puts the Ukrainian-Canadian group first, defining women in terms of their group membership and what a community elite has declared is the group's collective will and needs, is equally if not more rewarding. It is also justified for the simple reason that Ukrainian Canadians, with and without the co-operation of their women, have put the group first in the past and continue to do so in the present. Placing Ukrainian-Canadian women within the context of their group membership permits examination of the impact of minority status and 'frustrated nationalism'[10] on women's choices and roles, both those imposed by the community at large and those women define for themselves. Expressed another way, how community historians and spokespersons, male and female, have seen women as factors in the Ukrainian-Canadian experience has been a direct product of the group's reception in Canada and its identification with the fate of Ukraine abroad.

The primacy of the group subordinated not only female issues and perspectives to Ukrainian ones but also individual women and their sex to the agenda of the organized Ukrainian-Canadian community. Ukrainian-Canadian women merited attention because they had specific needs and obligations *as Ukrainians*; because their attitudes and behaviour impinged upon the group image and group objectives; and because they shared a common mission with Ukrainian men that overshadowed narrowly female or individual interests. At the same time, women became automatic and indispensable participants in the Ukrainian-Canadian experience, both actors in their own right and objects of community mobilization, cultivation, and exploitation; this fact modified the effects of their inferior status as women while imposing an arbitrary group tie with its own constraints. The group concerns responsible for the dominance of nationality over gender – recognition and acceptance in Canadian society, national-cultural survival because of oppression in Ukraine, and obligation to the homeland – also resulted in a perception of women that at once embraced and transcended their procreative function and socially prescribed roles of mothering and home-making. Because Ukrainian-Canadian women were Ukrainians as well as women, their traditional functions acquired new meaning with peculiar Ukrainian nuances: on the values mothers transmitted to their offspring rested the quality of Ukrainian-Canadian life and the commitment of future generations to things Ukrainian. But Ukrainian-Canadian women have also had additional roles, as public figures and group symbols, in which femaleness has often been secondary to Ukrainianness.

Agitation for women's traditional maternal, domestic, and cultural roles on behalf of group survival and Ukrainian identity evokes the roles historically prescribed for French-Canadian women to ensure *la survivance*. But there are significant differences. Whereas *la survivance* was long inward-looking, limited to Quebec, Ukrainian survival looked outward, and their citizenship in the Ukrainian 'nation' gave Ukrainian-Canadian women a perspective well beyond the local parish or village and even beyond the borders of Canada. Then, too, major French-Canadian figures long propagandized for a rural lifestyle and values, convinced that North American urbanization, industrialization, and materialism would erode the foundations of their society. Ukrainian Canadians and their leaders, in contrast, sought full integration into Canadian life as the equals of 'the English,' leaving their peasant origins and cultural baggage behind. In committing their group to 'progress,' they not only strained, extended, and changed women's roles, but also altered women's expectations in ways not always conducive to furthering community objectives, as education and upward mobility encouraged both assimilation and careers other than homemaking. Finally, unlike either French or English Canada, where women had to justify their presence in the public sphere, Ukrainian Canadians placed their women outside as well as inside the home. The Ukrainian cause required women who were both knowledgeable about the issues and politics of

their group and prepared to contribute actively and directly to community and national life.

Ukrainian Canadians' reluctance to conceive of women independent
of the group emerges in the work of community historians. Responsible
for arranging the players on the stage and assigning them their parts,
they decide what is significant in the past and what is not and why this
should be so. Ultimately, the criteria for women's inclusion in Ukrainian-
Canadian history (or their exclusion from it) had less to do with being
female than with being Ukrainian. But it is precisely because they were
Ukrainian that they were included at all, and in the implications of
group membership lie the reasons for the different treatment of mainstream and Ukrainian-Canadian women in their respective historiog-
raphies. An interpretative framework to serve nationalists' twin goals
of full participation in Canadian life and survival as a viable national-
cultural community explains the more equitable consideration given
Ukrainian-Canadian women in their group's development. It also
explains how and why they have been painted in the literature as they
have.

If Ukrainian-Canadian women have always enjoyed a niche in their
group's history, that niche did not preclude an overall male perspective
that saw Ukrainian-Canadian development as an essentially male experience: men were the ones who took homesteads, found jobs, earned
money, made decisions, erected schools and churches, and gave their
society shape.[11] Women's contribution was restricted to sketches of
immigrant pioneer life, prominent or successful individuals, and wom-
en's organizations. The female experience outside the popular group
preoccupations these three phenomena represented was important neither in its own right nor in the group's history. Nor were issues that
challenged or repudiated community objectives and comfortable self-
perceptions to be acknowledged or addressed. It was more important
to present Ukrainians in a positive light, for example, than to probe
male-female relations in Ukrainian peasant society for the truth behind
the Anglo-Canadian image of Ukrainian women as 'domestic drudges'
and 'beasts of burden,' or of their menfolk as unloving and insensitive
'wife-beaters.'[12] One community historian who mentioned the well-
publicized murder of a Ukrainian woman by her husband in 1901 did
so not to comment on the treatment of women but to stress the bad
impression such actions created among outsiders.[13] Inspired not by the
feminist goal of improving women's position in society but by equally
politically motivated Ukrainian goals that imposed their own constraints, community historians subordinated questions of women's con-

dition and status as women to the needs of the group to which they belonged. Ukrainian-Canadian feminists like Vera Lysenko and more recently Myrna Kostash and Helen Potrebenko were more willing to criticize. 'When the land was plowed for sowing,' Potrebenko wrote, 'whatever manure was available was scattered on the field by women ... My father says you wouldn't expect men to get shit on their hands.'[14]

The desire for recognition and acceptance by Anglo-Canadian society that deflected nationalist historians from the potentially negative and unpleasant made them equally eager to exploit the 'firsts' and success stories that attested to progress and integration and were proof of Ukrainian Canadians' potential. The sex of the individuals whose accomplishments were celebrated as the collective achievement of the group was irrelevant. As notable Ukrainian Canadians, women have lagged behind men, showing better in the arts and letters (where the 'child prodigy' violinist Donna Grescoe has symbolized Ukrainian talent and success for fifty years) than in the long-time male preserves of business, the professions, and politics.[15] Nevertheless, the exceptional existed, and well before her appointment as lieutenant-governor of Saskatchewan, Sylvia Fedoruk was heralded as 'the first woman physicist actively engaged in cancer research in Canada' and 'undoubtedly one of Canada's most brilliant women.'[16] Individuals recognized for their achievement in the larger Canadian context are primarily symbols and models of success and integration, in which Ukrainianness is a secondary quality. Yet they are claimed by the group because of their Ukrainian origins – whether or not they welcome the association, see themselves as hyphenated Canadians, or identify with community goals.

The majority of women profiled by community historians have been known and active only or primarily within Ukrainian-Canadian circles. Their ranks include organizational figures, writers representing immigrant generations and producing only in the Ukrainian language, and performers who owe their reputations to community audiences. Individuals recognized for their activities within the ethnic group alone act as symbols and models of Ukrainian consciousness and service, in which their identification with the Ukrainian-Canadian community is voluntary. But again, sex is often irrelevant. Women who make a Ukrainian statement through their art, for example, are as important as their male colleagues, for group function not gender is the criterion.

Concern for Ukrainianness, with the organized community as its formal expression, also guaranteed as a matter of course a place in historians' works for Ukrainian-Canadian women's organizations and their leading personnel, albeit in a subordinate capacity to their male counterparts.[17] Yet the larger issue of women's relation to community goals failed to generate interest – despite the importance of Ukrainian women as mainstays of culture preservation and transmission. Language discussions, for example, were never related to the women whose changing roles and attitudes were so crucial to loss or maintenance.[18] And while historians identified embroidery, Easter eggs, and food – all representing female activities – as among the best preserved and most popular expressions of Ukrainianness, they ignored the women on whose skill, labour, interest, and free time the manufacture of these symbols depended.[19] Such omissions imply indifference to women's work and the private realm, even when it impinges on group survival and identity. But they say more about the need to reaffirm popular assumptions about the group's vitality, which precludes examining these assumptions as a reflection of Ukrainian-Canadian reality.

The guiding hand of community concerns behind the treatment of women and women's issues in Ukrainian-Canadian history – to cultivate or endorse a particular view of the past and collective self-image – is one way of showing how women have been used for group purposes. The relation between gender and ethnicity that it reveals, however, is impersonal, passive, and almost accidental. It has no effect on women's lives as such and says nothing about what women themselves think. Arbitrator and policy maker of the present rather than recorder and interpreter of the past, the organized community offers greater insight into the impact of ethnicity on Ukrainian-Canadian women. As the means for female participation in community life and as the vehicles through which women propagandize other women, women's own organizations are especially worthy of attention. They illustrate how ethnicity, or group membership, has acted as a direct force in the lives of Ukrainian-Canadian women, dictating their roles in both public and private spheres and colouring their perceptions of women's rights and duties as citizens of the nation. But the impact of ethnicity extends beyond the propaganda and programmes that an organizational elite aims at its sex. Ukrainianness accounts for the very existence of Ukrainian-Canadian women's organizations, while their fortunes have been tied not only to the popularity of specific religious or political creeds but also to non-ideological factors like the changing demographic character of the Ukrainian-Canadian population. The remainder of the paper explores the relation between ethnicity, or group membership, and gender by examining three distinguishing features of Ukrainian-Canadian women's organizations.

The first point establishes the dominance of Ukrainianness at the

outset. Women's organizations were formed not because Ukrainian-
Canadian women had specific concerns, needs, and duties as women,
but because they had specific concerns, needs, and duties as *Ukrainian*
women. This thinking immediately targeted all Canadian women of
Ukrainian origin as potential members. It also demanded separation
from mainstream Canadian women and their organizations, while insisting that ties be cultivated. Such contacts, the president of the Ukrainian
Canadian Women's Committee argued in 1950, enabled Ukrainian-
Canadian women to meet the wives of influential men and through
them influence Ukrainian affairs.[20] Increased participation by organized
Ukrainian-Canadian women in mainstream women's organizations
since the Second World War is in part a sign of growing confidence and
maturity, of 'Canadianization.' But it also reflects their long-standing
recognition of the need for a larger platform than the Ukrainian community from which to publicize and win sympathy for the Ukrainian cause.
In 1976, for example, when the Ukrainian Women's Association of Canada was a host organization at the Vancouver meeting of the International Council of Women, it spoke to delegates about Russification and
political oppression in Soviet Ukraine, presented a resolution protesting
the treatment of female dissidents, and called upon all women in the
free world to stand in their defence.[21]

Women's organizations have functioned as an integral part of the
Ukrainian-Canadian community since their pioneer beginnings in
church sisterhoods and secular groups formed around local *narodni domy*
(national halls), *chytalni* (reading halls), and *prosvita* (enlightenment)
societies. Large-scale organization among both sexes was an inter-war
phenomenon, stimulated and shaped by events in Ukraine that split
the community into hostile camps. While the Communist minority
extolled the Soviet experiment in the homeland and supported the
workers' struggle elsewhere in the world, nationalists mourned the
collapse of the Ukrainian People's Republic and opposed all foreign
regimes on Ukrainian soil. Despite a common enemy, however, nationalist ranks were divided. Catholics and Orthodox, émigré monarchists
and republicans, and the Canadian children of pre-war immigrants
disagreed over both the solution to Ukraine's problems and the proper
course of action for Ukrainians in Canada. Following the Second World
War, the displaced persons immigration would inject a new divisiveness,
together with a new vitality, into the Ukrainian-Canadian community.

The passions aroused by Ukrainian politics prohibited women from
organizing simply as women within their community. Instead, they
replicated its ideological factionalization. Communists created the

Women's Section of the Ukrainian Labour-Farmer Temple Association (ULFTA) in 1922,[22] while four main rivals emerged to represent the nationalists. Conceived in 1926 as non-denominational, the Ukrainian Women's Association of Canada (UWAC) soon gravitated to the new Ukrainian Greek Orthodox church.[23] Ukrainian Catholic sisterhoods were restructured as the Ukrainian Catholic Women's League (UCWL) in 1944 and, like the UWAC, drew on a pre-war base.[24] Inter-war immigrants politicized by the revolutionary struggles in Ukraine formed women's branches of the monarchist Canadian Sitch Organization and its successor, the United Hetman Organization, and spearheaded the militantly nationalistic Ukrainian Women's Organization of Canada (UWOC), which had its roots in female branches of the republican Ukrainian War Veterans' Association.[25] The Women's Association of the Canadian League for Ukraine's Liberation (1949) was the largest of the various organizations established by the displaced persons. If Ukrainianness has united women through a common focus and purpose, it has also divided them into antagonistic and competing groups.

Ukrainianness was also perceived to unite women and men, working together for the general good. But male dominance in community structures and male interference in the internal affairs of individual women's organizations suggest that a common goal was not enough to overcome traditional sex-role stereotyping and divisions of power. Although motivated by class, not service to the nation, the Women's Section of the ULFTA provides the best example of reliance on male initiative and guidance: men played a prominent role in its creation, edited its official organs, wrote much of its educational and discussion literature, and acted as organizers and instructors – often at women's request.[26] In the nationalist camp, war veterans provided the initiative for several UWOC branches, while the local Orthodox priest more than once encouraged women in his parish to organize under the UWAC umbrella.[27] Catholic women have always acknowledged the practical and inspirational assistance of the clergy, including authorship of the UCWL constitution, which requires the permission of the church hierarchy for the organization to disband.[28]

The Women's Section of the ULFTA never existed independently of the main 'male' body. Nationalist women's organizations, with the partial exception of the UCWL, have enjoyed independence in their own sphere, but they function as affiliates of the male organizations that give the Ukrainian-Canadian community its definition and official profile. More importantly, these male organizations have controlled community decision making and acted as community spokespersons. When in 1940 they created the Ukrainian Canadian Committee to co-ordinate the Ukrainian-Canadian war effort and speak for Ukraine with a single voice, women's organizations, to their chagrin, were excluded as independent participants.[29] They formed their own Ukrainian Canadian Women's Committee in 1944, which continued to function when the co-ordinating superstructure was retained after the war to represent Ukrainian-Canadian interests. Those interests had been responsible for the organization of nationalist women *as Ukrainians*, within their community, but gender was responsible for their separate sphere within its structures.

The second distinguishing feature of Ukrainian-Canadian women's organizations takes the implications of ethnicity, or group membership, beyond the relation between nationality and gender. In that the evolution and fortunes of the organized community and its institutions have been influenced by trends among the Ukrainian-Canadian population at large, women's organizations mirror in miniature the broad strokes of the history of their group. They register two phenomena in particular: widespread assimilation, the result of both conscious and unconscious pressures, and settlement and migration patterns that show Ukrainian Canadians responding to the same socio-economic stimuli as other Canadians. Organizational membership figures attest to the greater or lesser appeal of divergent ideologies; shortly before the Second World War, for example, the UWAC had 4,000 members compared to 2,400 for the Women's Section of the ULFTA and a modest 610 for the UWOC.[30] The distribution of organizations' members, however, is not simply a carbon copy of the numerical distribution of Ukrainian women across Canada. Ukrainians' 'Canadian' experience, reflecting interacting class, immigrational, and generational factors, has worked in conjunction with ideology to complicate things. The strength of a single organization has varied across Canada just as the popularity of different organizations has varied in different regions of the country, and in both cases the picture has changed over time. Two examples will suffice.

Between the wars some 80 per cent of Ukrainian-Canadian women lived in the prairie provinces, yet 30 of 78 branches and 749 of 1,923 members of the Women's Section of the ULFTA were located in Ontario, another 289 members and 14 branches in Quebec and British Columbia.[31] The relevance of the Communist message to a Ukrainian urban proletariat was partly responsible for such 'over-representation,' but it equally reflected the settlement patterns of that proletariat, putting down and pulling up roots in factory towns and on resource frontiers according to the dictates of the marketplace. In contrast to the ULFTA, both the

UWAC and UCWL derived their initial strength from the pre-1914 peasant immigration homesteading in the prairie provinces. Most branches existed in the bloc settlements, outside the largely Anglo-Canadian towns and villages, at rural points dominated by their Ukrainian church and hall. In 1983, however, almost half of the UCWL branches in Manitoba existed in the greater Winnipeg area, where they were no longer clustered in the city core. Alberta, meanwhile, had suffered a net loss of four hundred members and twenty-eight branches over the two previous decades. The casualties were the rural areas of the Vegreville bloc as the focus of Ukrainian organizational life moved into nearby towns and villages, young women and families abandoned farming for opportunities elsewhere, members grew old and inactive (or retired to Vegreville and Edmonton), and assimilation with alienation from things Ukrainian prevented new recruits from replenishing rosters depleted by deaths. Concurrent with these developments, and paralleling Ontario's post-war challenge to prairie dominance in community life, the number of UCWL branches in the Toronto eparchy rose to forty-one, more than even the archeparchy of Winnipeg boasted. This increase was due in part to the presence of Catholic displaced persons arriving after 1945, but it owed much to the economic boom that drew migrants from across Canada and helped make Ontario the most populous Ukrainian province.[32]

The post-war profiles of women's organizations with inter-war roots reflect demographic trends among Ukrainian Canadians that testify both to large-scale 'progress' by members of the group and to the push and pull of forces in Canadian society. These trends are urbanization, movement from the prairies to the West Coast and central Canada, and relocation from immigrant reception areas in Canadian cities to more affluent suburbs. The profile of an organization like the Women's Association of the Canadian League for Ukraine's Liberation, with its some thousand members and twenty-one branches limited to large Canadian cities (the majority in Ontario),[33] reflects the geographical preferences of the displaced persons. The recent history of the 'old' organizations also comments on assimilation, although community activists never mobilized more than a fraction of their sex. In the inter-war years, traditionally heralded as the heyday of organizational activity, perhaps one-tenth of women over nineteen belonged to the major national organizations or local Ukrainian Catholic sisterhoods. Improved economic prospects and the cold war subsequently undercut the Communists, so that only eighteen branches (male and female) of the ULFTA's successor marked the fiftieth anniversary of women's organized activity in 1972.[34] Fourteen branches sent reports when the UWOC celebrated its golden jubilee in 1980; evidence of the growing irrelevance of old-country politics, this was almost half the number active twenty-five years earlier.[35] Measures to attract younger (often career) women and to accommodate non-Ukrainian speakers, whether members' own daughters or the non-Ukrainian wives of their sons, demonstrate organizations' concern.[36] But declining and aging memberships, language loss, and intermarriage evoke the tensions inherent in the nationalist blueprint; it has been impossible to encourage integration into Canadian life without inadvertently encouraging assimilation too. The consequences of alienation from the Ukrainian heritage that a leadership elite says it is women's duty to preserve and defend are serious. Assimilation jeopardizes the future not only of women's organizations but also of the cause they promote.

The third distinguishing feature of Ukrainian-Canadian women's organizations builds upon this final point and returns to the relation between ethnicity and gender. 'Ukrainian nationalism,' for better or worse, has dictated what women can and cannot do. On the one hand, Ukrainian group needs promoted female emancipation and equality: women were assured a niche in Ukrainian-Canadian history, were considered full citizens of the nation, active in both public and private spheres, and were encouraged in and applauded for the education and careers that reflected positively on all Ukrainian Canadians. On the other hand, regardless of the voluntary acceptance of their roles by many women, Ukrainian group needs precluded choice (being born Ukrainian imposed certain obligations) and made emancipation and equality often more illusory than real. Despite the command to be 'active on every front' and to march 'arm in arm with men,' women's freedom of movement was limited. The Ukrainian cause demanded co-operation between the sexes, and women who agitated for 'rights' said to represent narrow and selfish female interests could be accused of betraying the group interest that took priority.[37] Moreover, that group interest reinforced women's traditional roles as mothers in the home to ensure that Ukrainian-Canadian children, raised in a Ukrainian spirit, would carry the torch in their turn. And if motherhood and home-making remained women's primary concern, their public activities stressed traditional 'female' nurturing qualities and competencies – children, education, charity, the church, handicrafts, and bake sales and bazaars to maintain community institutions and programmes.

The liberation implied in the admonition for women to join men as intelligent and active members of the community had as its goal the benefit of Ukraine, not the improvement of women's position in society or women's personal development for the sake of the individual alone. 'Emancipated' Ukrainian women were necessary for the good of the Ukrainian people, inter-war UWAC circles and men close to them said, and 'emancipated' Ukrainian women were nationally conscious patriots – mothers who raised 'free citizens not slaves.'[38] The UWOC also called for women's emancipation, realizing their full potential to aid in the emancipation of the Fatherland. Centuries of national subjugation had made women feel inferior to men, it was explained, unprepared to shoulder equal (although not necessarily identical) burdens and responsibilities: 'Ukraine's conquerors knew that as long as the Ukrainian woman remained oppressed and degraded, they had nothing to fear. They knew that an enslaved woman could not rear her children to be good patriots who could be expected to fight for their nation.'[39] Clearly, motherhood was not just women's greatest function in national life but the key to national liberation itself, for on the quality of the Ukrainianness of mothers rested the fate of Ukraine.

Saying that the preparation of Ukrainian women to be good mothers was 'a matter of far greater importance than politics, electoral rights or office-holding,' one of the UWAC's founders elaborated: 'Today, when our homeland, church and schools are in the hands of foreign conquerors, the women of ... [Galicia] and central Ukraine must pay attention to the upbringing of children. Only the home remains in our hands, and the home must provide a national upbringing.'[40]

The same caution held true for Canada, where an Anglo-Canadian majority strove to assimilate the first Ukrainian immigrants and their children to so-called British standards and ideals. When the abolition of bilingual schools on the prairies during the Great War eliminated the one state mechanism that had assisted an emigrant community in the Ukrainization of youth, pressures on the home to defuse the denationalizing influences of Canadian society increased.[41] Ukrainian-Canadian women's organizations recognized that the family was to be the primary bastion of Ukrainianness in Canada, and the preparation of women to be good Ukrainian mothers and homemakers dominated their agenda. Instructions have changed little over the past seventy years. They focus on the mother as teacher – of the language, customs, history, songs, politics, and national aspirations of her people – reinforced by a home environment that immerses the family in a Ukrainian patriotic, cultural, and religious atmosphere.[42]

Defined in terms that emphasized their sex's 'maternal' and 'feminine' nature, women's public role was in essence an extension of their domestic one. Just as they bore responsibility for the well-being of their immediate biological families, Ukrainian-Canadian women were informed, so they had a duty towards their larger blood tie and family, the nation.[43] This equation of the nation with the family both obliged women to take an active part in community life and justified their involvement. But it pushed them into stereotyped 'women's work' – training youth, cooking for community functions, helping the poor and sick, raising money, preserving the handicrafts that were the most visible expression of Ukrainian identity. Through the form their public activities took, Ukrainian-Canadian women's organizations acknowledged that they perceived gender to guarantee them a separate sphere, specific roles and obligations as members of their group, and special talents to bring to their work.

Emigration and minority status in Canada, which emasculated Ukrainian men in the world of male power politics, exaggerated the importance of women's traditional volunteer and auxiliary functions, as Ukrainians' social, cultural, and educational needs had to be met solely by the community. Many UWAC branches on the prairies, for example, withdrew from *ridni shkoly*, or Ukrainian vernacular schools, only when the introduction of Ukrainian-language courses and bilingual programmes in the public schools after the Second World War removed some of the responsibility for the formal socialization of youth from their shoulders.[44] 'Women's work' has also had a concrete focus and relevance, with visible results, that the politicking and rhetoric of male organizations lacks. It has given organized women a strong sense of accomplishment as builders, in a very real way, of the Ukrainian-Canadian community.[45] A genuine and positive expression of self-worth and value, this legitimization of traditional 'female' activities and traditional 'female' roles performed through separate women's organizations, by women who perceive themselves as full members of their community, is also a rationalization of political powerlessness.

Recently, calls for a reassessment of women's relation to the Ukrainian-Canadian community have come from both inside and outside establishment circles, and from both men and women. Younger, career-oriented women and feminist activists have grappled with the problems of being female and Ukrainian while seeking a meaningful role for themselves within a community that is sensitive to the realities of late twentieth-century North America.[46] In 1984, a representative of the existing women's organizations criticized the arrangement that gave the major male organizations, through the Ukrainian Canadian Committee, the authority to decide everything for everyone; she also criticized the sex stereotyping that allowed men to play politics while women worked and raised money, which gave the male organizations their finances but which provided no mental stimulation.[47] In 1986, *Building the Future*, a blueprint for the twenty-first century prepared for the Ukrainian Canadian Committee, identified 'the very limited impact of the women's movement in mainstream society ... on our organizations and their members' as a major reason for women's historical and continued subordinate role in community life. Recommendations for community renewal in the face of 'critical' assimilation and worrisome trends (low fertility, increasing intermarriage, high divorce) included making women equal partners. 'By excluding women from decision-making structures,' the report stated, 'we fail to recognize issues that are of particular concern to women. This limits the involvement of women in our community's development, since many women choose to work in the mainstream women's movement where their specific concerns are addressed. Nor, moreover, should women's issues be of concern only to women. They must be addressed by all of us to ensure the full development of our community. Accordingly, specific initiatives that include a broad educational programme need to be implemented to deal with the central issue of equal opportunity for women.'[48]

How such recommendations, largely the work of a small number of intellectuals and professionals (drawn from western Canada), will be received in the long run by the male-dominated organizations comprising the Ukrainian Canadian Committee (now Congress) or by the existing women's organizations remains to be seen. Whether their implementation will induce the great majority of women now outside formal Ukrainian networks to gravitate to them is also uncertain. But one thing is not in doubt. Rewriting the rules for women's participation in Ukrainian-Canadian community life, taking into account their changing profile and needs, has been identified as crucial to the future.

The Changing Community

WSEVOLOD W. ISAJIW

Has the Ukrainian community in Canada changed in any significant way in the past twenty years? Do new issues occupy it, and what difference do they make to its character and structure? The following discussion does not answer these questions completely or even adequately. It simply tries to suggest a way of looking for the answer.

I am focusing on the last twenty years for a variety of reasons. The last 'good' census of Canada was conducted in 1971, and since then only the 1986 20 per cent sample census has produced a set of published data useful to my purposes. Any comparison of 1981 or 1986 census data with those of previous years, however, should be done with caution. The different phrasing of the ethnic origin question from 1981 on makes the data not directly comparable. Further, it takes about twenty years for a new generation to emerge. Although this new generation may not immediately alter the character of a community, it often raises new questions and issues for the community that in the long run may make a difference. Twenty years is also the minimum period for a meaningful long-range perspective. Finally, the events of the last twenty years in both Canada and Ukraine warrant an assessment of the community.

The question of what has happened to the Ukrainian community must also be put into a broader conceptual framework that includes the following questions: (1) the relation of the minority group to the majority ethnic group of the society and to the society at large, including other minority ethnic groups; (2) the relation of the minority ethnic group to its home society; (3) the relation between different sectors or subgroups within the minority ethnic group itself; and (4) the relation between the minority groups of the same ethnicity in different larger societies as, for example, in Canada and the United States. It is also important not only to describe the changes taking place in the ethnic community, but to offer some theory explaining them or, at the very least, to subsume them under an existing theory or theories. This paper will discuss only selected aspects of the first two types of relations. A complete study would require greater length.

Ukrainians and Canadian Society

The question of the relation of the Ukrainian community to Canadian society has at least four aspects: the attitude of Ukrainians, particularly the younger generations, towards the society at large and towards their own ethnicity, the attitude of the majority Canadians towards Ukrainians, the socio-economic incorporation of Ukrainians into Canadian society, and the loss of Ukrainian identity or, inversely, its retention.

Much sociological research has been directed at the second generation and to a lesser extent the third generation. This includes a number of studies of the Ukrainian generations.[1] The prevalent sociological theory is that the second generation rebels against its ethnic group and has a strong desire to become part of the society at large. Yet it is also indebted to its ethnic group for much of its socialization. That is, typically, the second generation goes through a process of double socialization, within its community and within the society at large. It often feels itself to be a natural part of both. This, of course, produces problems of cognitive inconsistencies and dissonance and divided feelings, desires, and loyalties.[2]

In regard to Ukrainians, although research on generations has begun, it has not progressed very far. One interesting study of some of the issues involved is Nadia Skop's study of a sample of Ukrainian second-generation singles in Toronto.[3] Her study shows that Ukrainian second-generation males and females have a high degree of hostility to one another but at the same time express a desire to marry within the Ukrainian community. The study also indicates that second-generation Ukrainian females are more emancipated from the Ukrainian community and take their models from Canadian society in general more often than Ukrainian males. Nevertheless, the study also shows the respect both sexes have for Ukrainian language, customs, and traditions.

A current theory in regard to the third generation points to its need to rediscover its ethnic identity.[4] Alexander Roman attempted to apply the theory of third-generation rediscovery to the Ukrainian community. He offered fascinating insights into small groups of Ukrainian young people whose mother tongue is English and who strongly identify with Canada as their own country but who have developed a great interest in their Ukrainian heritage.[5]

An important issue arises when we talk about the ethnic community's world of doubleness. This has to do with ethnic culture not as a heritage produced 'back home,' but as something new produced by creative persons in the country of settlement. This cultural production refers particularly to visual, literary, and musical art. To what extent does new cultural production within the community reflect attitudes towards the society in general, and to what extent does it interpret the ethnic experience in relation to this society? Over the past twenty years, there has been no empirical research on this subject, but the artistic production that is publicly known indicates that there are different trends within the community. Some artists do not reflect the Canadian ethnic experience in their art production. Others, such as William Kurelek or Natalka Husar, have shown a strong concern with the question of doubleness and attempt to bring into unity the Ukrainian and Canadian experience.

Thus the Canadian-born generations of Ukrainians show in their attitudes a decided attempt to integrate their Ukrainian and Canadian identities as complementary to each other. Being Canadian does not exclude being at least to some extent Ukrainian. The majority of Canadians, particularly those of British background, do not necessarily share these attitudes.

One may study both government policies and the attitudes of the general population in order to ascertain the societal attitudes of the majority towards the minority. The Canadian government has traditionally seen immigrants as a way to develop the labour force. At times the role given to Ukrainians was even more specific. At the turn of the century, Ukrainians were admitted to Canada as farmers or agricultural workers. After the Second World War, refugees were allowed into the country as a means of labour force recruitment. In other words, until recently the possibility of acceptance into the labour force was the only promise that the government extended towards the immigrant minorities. No political or cultural obligations to the groups, as ethnic groups, were intended. It is only within the last twenty years that the government of Canada has recognized the claims of some ethnic groups to be compensated for injustices done to them, as in the cases of the native peoples and Japanese Canadians. Again, it is only in the last twenty years that the policy of multiculturalism has given some official recognition to cultural claims by minorities. However, it should also be remembered that the government has given such recognition largely because of the political pressure exerted by the French in Canada in defence of their own cultural rights. Yet over the past twenty years the government's attitudes in regard to the objectives of the policy of multiculturalism have fluctuated. On the one hand, the government has seen the policy as a means of giving ethnic groups permanent recognition, and on the other hand, as a temporary means of helping the 'adjustment' and integration of current immigrants into the host society.

In terms of the attitudes of the general population towards minority groups, it is generally known that there are often widespread prejudices against some ethnic groups in society, particularly against racial groups. One of the oldest types of research in sociology has been the attempt to measure the prevalence and degree of ethnic prejudices. Such research can show the prestige that an ethnic group is given within the society, which can then be used, though only indirectly, as an indicator of the degree of discrimination against the group. For this purpose, sociologists have invented such instruments as the Bogardus social distance scale and the ethnic social standing scale. When measured by these scales, the groups that appear at the top of the scale enjoy the most prestige and are least discriminated against whereas the groups that appear at the bottom enjoy the least prestige and are most discriminated against. In North America, the groups most different racially from the dominant Anglo groups usually end up at the bottom of the scale, even if their socio-economic level is high.

The question for us is, what place do the Ukrainians hold on the prestige ladder of our society, and have they been moving upward in the past twenty years? For Ukrainians, this is an unresearched question in virtually all countries of their settlement, except Canada. Even in Canada, however, only a few sociological studies give some information on Ukrainians in this respect. The most important study is that of Peter Pineo, of McMaster University, who tried to determine the prestige status of some thirty ethnic groups in Canada, among them Ukrainians. His results have divided the prestige continuum roughly into three categories: top, middle, and bottom. Ukrainians were in the middle category, but among the eleven ethnic groups in this category, they were at the bottom. Below them were the groups most prejudiced against.[6] In other words, the prestige of Ukrainians in southern Ontario was low. There may be some regional differences in the prestige of Ukrainians in Canada. In the prairies, where the Ukrainian community is older and more visible than in other provinces, its prestige may well be higher.

TABLE 1
Ukrainian Canadians by highest level of schooling,
15 years of age and older

	no.	%
Total (single and multiple origin)	714,205	100
Less than grade 9	114,390	16
Grades 9–13		
without secondary certificate	206,295	29
with secondary certificate	81,035	11
Trades certificate or diploma	15,715	2
Other non-university education only		
without certificate	47,105	7
with certificate	106,205	15
University		
without degree	72,695	10
with degree	70,135	10

Source: Statistics Canada, 1986 Census, vols. 93–154, *Profile of Ethnic Groups*, tables 2–20; single and multiple origins combined.

The attitudes of the majority society towards Ukrainians in Canada are not absolutely clear. There seems to be a basically positive recognition by the government, much of it tied up with the policy of multicultural-ism. But the policy itself has had fluctuating objectives and has never received complete support from the general population, particularly from the societal elites. It is therefore difficult to say whether the atti-tudes of the general population towards Ukrainians in Canada have substantially improved over the last twenty years.

Socio-economic Incorporation into Canadian Society

The concept of social incorporation differs from the notion of integration in that it does not assume the idea of a harmonious whole or of complete equality. Nor does it assume the idea of cultural assimilation. In other words, it leaves open the questions of how much cultural assimilation and ethnic identity retention there is, and to what extent members of an ethnic group are dispersed throughout the socio-economic structure. It retains only the notion of movement into the structure of society and, therefore, offers a better way to measure the degree of any of the above.

Table 1 presents the educational achievement of Ukrainian Canadians, fifteen years of age and over, from the 1986 Canadian census. It shows that the single largest category is that of persons with nine to thirteen years of education (40 per cent). The British have a similar distribution

TABLE 2
Occupational distribution of Ukrainian labour force

Occupational category	no.	%
Managerial	49,045	10
Professional	81,840	17
Clerical	96,970	20
Sales	48,330	10
Service	58,420	12
Primary	38,055	8
Processing	21,075	4
Product fabricating	28,720	6
Construction	28,995	6
Other	40,695	6
Total (experienced labour force)	492,345	100

Source: Statistics Canada, 1986 Census, vols. 93–154, *Profile of Ethnic Groups*, tables 2–22; single and multiple origins combined.

in educational achievement in this category (44 per cent). At the higher level of education, about 20 per cent of Ukrainians had at least some university education in 1986. About half of these had attained a university degree by that year. This is also almost exactly the same for the British group in Canada for that year, but much lower than the achievement of Jewish Canadians. Of this group 44 per cent of those fifteen years of age and over had some university education, and more than two-thirds of these already possessed university degrees. Chinese Canadians were also higher in their attainment of university degrees. Thirty per cent had some university education, and close to two-thirds of these had university degrees. Thus, as far as university education is concerned, the Ukrainians in Canada have caught up with the general population, particularly the British ethnic group, over the past twenty years, although they lag behind several other groups. An important difference is in the percentage of those who have less than grade nine education. Sixteen per cent of all Ukrainians age fifteen and over had less than a grade nine education, as compared with only 11 of the British and 9 of the Jewish. This can be partially explained by the presence in the Ukrainian population of those who immigrated before 1946 and who received little education in Ukraine.

Table 2 presents the 1986 census data on the occupational distribution of the Ukrainian-Canadian labour force. The single largest category of occupations in which Ukrainians were engaged in that year was clerical, followed by professional and service occupations. This is much the same pattern as for the Canadian labour force as a whole, except that for all three types of occupation the percentage of Ukrainians was slightly higher than that in the general labour force. Thus, 20 per cent of the Ukrainian labour force was in clerical occupations as compared with 18 per cent of the Canadian force as a whole, 17 per cent in professional occupations, as compared with 16 per cent in the general labour force, and 10 per cent in managerial occupations, as compared with 8 per cent in the general labour force. However, a slightly higher percentage of the British (11 per cent) is involved in managerial occupations in general. The bigger difference with the British comes in the higher level managerial occupations. Ukrainians are not well represented in managerial occupations at the level of big business. The highest concentration of Ukrainians in the management category is in teaching administration, followed by post-office management and government inspectors. Another difference from both the general and the British populations is in the agricultural sector. More Ukrainians are still involved in agriculture than either the British or the general population, although the difference has been decreasing over the past twenty years.

How can these statistics be interpreted? An analysis of the Ukrainian occupational structure in Canada was done in 1980, comparing the 1971 and 1961 censuses.[7] The analysis concluded that Ukrainian upward mobility in Canadian society has been significant, with the exception of mobility into the managerial, financial, and higher business occupations. The study also concluded that Ukrainians, like several other ethnic groups (particularly the French), rely heavily on the public sector for their social mobility. This analysis still holds true today with some significant modifications. For one thing, Ukrainians have continued moving out of agricultural occupations into white collar occupations. In 1941, more than 55 per cent of the Ukrainian male labour force was in agriculture; by 1971, this had dropped to 13 per cent, and by 1986 (if the census is comparable) it had dropped to 8 per cent. Similarly, in 1941 18 per cent of the Ukrainian labour force was in white collar occupations; by 1971 the percentage increased to 33, and by 1986 to 57 (taking into account the comparability problem). Reliance on the public sector for social mobility has continued as the statistics on involvement in managerial occupations indicate. Movement into managerial occupations in general has continued, and unlike in 1971 or before, Ukrainians in 1986 appear to be better represented in the managerial category than the general Canadian labour force. This is a significant change. However, as mentioned above, they remain underrepresented in the higher managerial occupations, which seems to have remained a constant. There seem to be some structural blockages for this step.

In 1970 I introduced a theory of stages of ethnic-group mobility in Canadian society.[8] According to this theory, ethnic groups that come into the country with low entrance status – i.e., those that are overrepresented in low status occupations at the time of their entry into the country, particularly in agriculture – go through three stages, or patterns, of occupational mobility. The first is a shift out of the low status occupation, in our case, agriculture. The second is a pattern of rapid increase in participation in service, clerical, and manufacturing occupations, with the largest increases in the last. The third pattern appears when the participation in labouring occupations decreases below the point of equal representation with the rest of the labour force, participation in the manufacturing occupations either remains constant or decreases below the point of equal representation, but significant increases in the sales, managerial, and professional categories reach the point of overrepresentation and continue in that direction. These patterns are not necessarily stages of one process. Although interdependent, they can vary independently. An ethnic group can receive its entrance status by means of the second or even the third pattern of occupational participation. On the other hand, there is no guarantee that all ethnic groups will reach the third pattern.

These patterns of ethnic mobility are sociologically significant because they represent different relations of the ethnic group to the mainstream society. The first pattern reflects the process of educational-cultural assimilation of the group, that is, the fact that the members of the group are learning the occupational skills available through the educational or other institutions in society and are taking over the values and behaviour of the society. The second pattern reflects the process of structural assimilation. It seems to represent a move towards equality so as to accommodate itself and its interests in it.

In the 1960s, Ukrainians, like many other groups, were in the second stage, i.e., engaged in the process of structural assimilation, in finding, as it were, their equal place in the society. In the 1980s, Ukrainians by and large completed this process and entered into the third pattern. They are, of course, not the only minority in Canadian society that has reached this point. For the Ukrainians, however, this is a new and limited experience since it does not extend to the higher – or 'strategic' – level of the higher status occupations, but only to their lower or middle level. Nevertheless, they appear to have arrived at the stage where there are structural conditions for a 'reach' for some rights of the establishment.

Social Incorporation and Retention or Loss of Identity

Do Ukrainians who are mobile retain a significant degree of their identity, or is mobility into the higher status levels predicated upon relinquishment of ethnic identity and complete assimilation into the mainstream culture? This question has been one of the more controversial issues in the sociology of ethnic group relations. A number of sociologists have claimed that ethnic identity and culture are an obstacle to social mobility.[9] Before attempting to answer this question in regard to the Ukrainian Canadians, it will be useful to look at some empirical data to ascertain if there is much identity loss or retention from one generation of Ukrainian Canadians to another.

In 1979 a sociological survey of nine major ethnic groups in Metropolitan Toronto was completed.[10] It included a comparative study of ethnic identity retention and loss of three generations of five ethnic groups, among them Ukrainians. The purpose of the comparative study was to ascertain ethnic identity loss or retention on the basis of as many different indicators as practically possible. These indicators were divided into those measuring the external and those measuring the internal aspects of ethnic identity. The former included such observable behaviour patterns as consumption of ethnic food, possession of ethnic ornamental or artistic articles, practice of ethnic customs, possession of ethnic friends, knowledge and use of the ethnic language, and participation in ethnic functions. The latter included feelings of closeness with the ethnic community, importance placed on one's ethnic background, feelings of obligation to marry within the group, to support ethnic causes, and to teach children the language. The results differed for different ethnic groups, but they also showed definite patterns.

If we average the percentages of respondents who retain each indicator of identity used in the study, then external aspects of identity are retained by 78 per cent of the first-generation Ukrainians, 57 per cent of the second-generation, and 26 per cent of the third-generation. In regard to language, 71 per cent of the second generation state that Ukrainian is their mother tongue, but only 12 per cent of the third generation do so. Yet 56 per cent of those in the second and 48 per cent of those in the third generation who state that their mother tongue is English report that they still have some knowledge of Ukrainian. Of all the Ukrainian second-generation respondents in the sample, 58 per cent used the language every day or frequently, and 23 per cent used it occasionally. For the Ukrainian third-generation respondents, however, the percentages were 9 for daily or frequent use and 24 for occasional use.

In regard to retaining friendship with other Ukrainians, the study showed that 46 per cent of the second and 35 per cent of the third generation have one or two close friends who are also of Ukrainian background. Furthermore, 49 per cent of the second and 33 per cent of the third Ukrainian generation participate in some Ukrainian community functions, but only 20 per cent of the second and 1 per cent of the third generation read Ukrainian newspapers or magazines.

The most frequently retained pattern of ethnic identity is consumption of ethnic food: 92 per cent of the Ukrainian second and 82 per cent of the third generation consume Ukrainian food more often than on holidays and special occasions. This is true of other ethnic groups as well. The observance of ethnic customs and the possession of ethnic objects of art are also highly retained patterns of external identity. Among the Ukrainian second generation, 67 per cent of the respondents have maintained observance of Ukrainian customs, and 80 per cent possess some Ukrainian objects of art. Among the third generation, 47 per cent still observe some customs, and as many as 64 per cent possess objects of Ukrainian art.

In regard to the internal aspects of ethnic identity, of the indicators used in the study, those retained in the highest percentages are the feelings of obligation to help group members find a job and to teach children the Ukrainian language. In the second generation, 54 per cent felt that they have an obligation to help other Ukrainians find a job, and 66 per cent felt an obligation to teach Ukrainian to their children. In the third generation, 53 per cent felt the former and 37 per cent the latter. Supporting Ukrainian group needs and causes was also felt to be an obligation: 49 per cent of the second and 36 per cent of the third generation considered this to be so. What is interesting is that marrying other Ukrainians was not felt to be important: only 20 per cent of the second generation and 5 per cent of the third considered it to be important. Finally, in response to a combined measure of the degree of the internal aspects of identity, 27 per cent of the Ukrainian second-generation and only 10 per cent of the third-generation respondents could be classified as possessing a 'high' intensity of Ukrainian identity; 38 per cent of the second- and 35 per cent of the third-generation respondents were classified as having a 'medium' intensity of identity.

What is the significance of these percentages, and how do they bear on the problem of incorporation into the larger society? Do they indicate

a large degree of loss or a large degree of retention of identity? One
could answer either way. A better answer depends on further analysis
of the data and on what theoretical direction one takes. The study
suggests that there are different types of ethnic identity. One can distinguish: (1) an identity revolving around concrete objects with symbolic
value, such as food and artistic articles; (2) an identity revolving around
the practice of customs and community participation; (3) an identity
revolving around the language itself; (4) an identity revolving around
friends of the same ethnicity; and (5) an identity related to the support
of group causes or needs.[11] All these types can be combined together
into one, of course, but it appears that for the second or third generation
they tend to separate into these more specialized forms with one or
another gaining primacy for different persons or categories of persons.
Numbers 1 and 4 appear to be more pronounced among the third
generation. We can hypothesize that these types of identity may be more
functional for the third generation's incorporation into the mainstream
society.

Whether ethnic identity retention is a drawback to social mobility also
varies according to the ethnic group and the generation. Analysis of the
data from the study reported above has shown that for the Germans
ethnic identity is a drawback in the first generation but not in the second
or third. For the Jewish group, it is not a drawback in any generation.
In fact, it can be seen as a resource, and persons who identify with their
group highly are also socially highly mobile. For the Italians, it is a
resource, especially for the second generation. For the Ukrainians, ethnicity is a drawback for the first generation, but has no influence on
the social mobility of the second or third generation. That is, those
Ukrainians in the first generation who are high on their identity are less
socially mobile than those whose identity is of medium intensity. Yet in
the second and third generation it does not matter: those whose identity
is high are just as mobile as those whose identity is of medium or low
intensity.[12]

Ukrainian Canadians, New Immigration, and Ukraine

An important development in the Ukrainian-Canadian community in
the past twenty years has been the arrival of new immigrants from
Poland and to a lesser extent Czechoslovakia, Romania, and Ukraine
itself. Although this has not been a major wave of immigration, the
numbers and the character of these immigrants are significant enough
to make a difference in the life of the community. The exact number of

these new immigrants is difficult to ascertain; one estimate places the figure at around eight thousand.[13]

The new immigrants have been settling in the cities of large Ukrainian concentration, particularly Toronto. They have been predominantly young people, in their twenties and thirties. Most of them are children of the Lemko people whom the Polish government deported from their age-old settlements along the Polish-Ukrainian border to northern Poland immediately after the last world war. They have fulfilled two roles in the Ukrainian community, one economic, the other cultural. They have provided a labour force for Ukrainian-owned enterprises as labourers, drivers, sales clerks, waiters, bank tellers, and the like, and some of them have become teachers in Ukrainian weekend schools or secretaries and staff members in Ukrainian organizations and institutions.

The post-war wave of immigration made a strong impact on the Ukrainian-Canadian community, primarily by developing cultural life and scholarship and by reviving the use of the Ukrainian language in community functions. No such impact can be foreseen from this new, small influx of immigrants. The post-war immigrants came to Canada to a large extent with their own organizations, which dated back to the displaced persons camps in Germany and Austria and to community life in pre-war Ukraine. No such organizations are being transplanted with the new group of immigrants. For one thing, they are on the average younger than the post-war immigrants were at the time of their arrival, and very few have been coming with families. Furthermore, their educational and occupational background is not as high or as differentiated as was that of the post-war immigrants, and their knowledge of Ukrainian is often weaker. Nevertheless, even during their short stay in Canada they have had an impact on Ukrainian-Canadian cultural life. This impact is visible in the avant-garde theatre established by the young immigrants and in the art brought over by immigrant artists. More research, however, is needed to assess the significance of this new immigration.

The policies of *glasnost* and *perestroika* in the Soviet Union have changed the relations between Ukrainian Canadians and their home country and have already affected the community. For one thing, both the government and the people of Soviet Ukraine have taken an increased interest in the Ukrainian Canadians. In general, the interest by home governments in their emigrants has been on the increase in the past ten years or so. Some governments – Italy and Japan, for example – have established agencies to keep liaison with their emigrants, particularly those who have gone to North America. The government of Greece has created a separate ministry for this purpose. The main reason for this has been economic. Many immigrants, both first and subsequent generations, have done well in their country of settlement. Many who came to the country at the bottom of the socio-economic ladder and who might have been an employment liability in the home country have become solid members of the middle class in the new country. At the same time the economies of the home countries have often faltered. Thus the interest in the emigration has been to a large extent an attempt to direct some resources from the emigrants back to the home country. This has also been true in the case of Ukraine. The difference is that the emigrant resources are potentially useful in assisting the process of democratization and sovereignization in Ukraine, much of which is not covered by the public purse.

The changes that have taken place in Ukraine since 1985 have galvanized much of the Ukrainian community in Canada and in the other countries of the diaspora. This, however, has revealed several differences within the Ukrainian community. For example, the pre-war and the post-war immigrants and the first, second, and third generation of the post-war immigrants all show different attitudes towards Ukraine and towards visits to Ukraine as well as different relations with visitors from Ukraine.

Current changes in Ukraine seem to fulfil the intellectual orientation and the expectations of the post-war immigration. Much of the work of this wave of immigrants has consisted of activities that were not allowed in Soviet Ukraine. Thus many scholarly institutions, and journals and other periodicals, in the diaspora published articles and books that could not appear in Ukraine. Students studied such subjects as Ukrainian history that were excluded for a long time from university programmes in Ukraine. The rationale was that these books and articles and this knowledge would be needed some day in Ukraine. Indeed this has been the case. Many institutions in Ukraine today request such materials from the diaspora. The post-war immigrants who have cultivated Ukrainian culture and scholarship may feel vindicated.

A significant change has taken place in the attitude towards contacts with people from Ukraine. Until *glasnost* and *perestroika*, Soviet contacts with the West were maintained almost exclusively by officially designated persons, and Ukrainian Canadians, particularly the post-war immigrants, were reluctant to enter into relations with them. In fact, such relations were by and large socially proscribed, and persons engaging in them were often looked at with suspicion. Since 1985, however, the Soviets have relaxed their policy of prohibiting their citizens from travelling to the West. Most imprisoned dissidents have been released; relatives have been allowed to visit their kin outside the Soviet Union, and scholars and professionals have been permitted to travel and to develop professional relations with their colleagues in the West. Accordingly, attitudes in the Ukrainian diaspora have also changed. The new attitudes emphasize the importance of exposing persons raised in the Soviet Union to Western culture and of bringing to Ukraine the ideas and values from which Soviet citizens have been removed for so long.

The 'glasnost generation' in Ukraine, however, appears to have more in common with the post-war first and second generations than with the pre-war second and third generations. This is understandable historically. Yet the orientation of the third generation, pre-war or post-war, is interesting even if it is not yet completely clear and requires more detailed study. The pre-war immigrants' interest in Ukraine appears to be motivated by a desire to re-establish family ties more than by ideology. The third generation, however, is involved, at least to some extent, in the roots phenomenon and wants to learn about its culture and to rediscover its identity.

There is, however, another sector of the third, as well as some of the second, generation whose interest in their cultural background and in Ukraine is purely recreational. That is, Ukraine is seen as a place to travel to in the summer and the Ukrainian community in Canada as a place to meet friends on weekends. This, unlike for the first and second post-war generations, does not include an ideological commitment to help with the processes taking place in Ukraine. This does not mean that there are no persons committed to the Ukrainian cause among the third generation of whichever immigrant wave. On the contrary, there are outstanding examples of third-generation individuals who are committed, but in terms of total numbers, they are only a small sector of the third generation. This, however, needs a much closer empirical study.

To sum up, significant changes have taken place in the structure of the Ukrainian community in Canada in the past twenty years. These changes have involved a decided move into the middle class to the point – and in some degree beyond the point – of equality with most ethnic groups in Canada. The community has developed more widely differentiated attitudes towards the society as a whole and towards itself. But the community's subjective status in Canada, its prestige in the eyes of the general Canadian population, does not seem to have changed much. The community has been influenced by the events taking place in its home country, and its relation to it has changed. Many of these changes, however, are still taking place and require more careful study.

Part 3

OF CANADA?
UKRAINIAN CANADIANS
AND THE STATE

Divided Loyalties:
The Ukrainian Left and the
Canadian State

DONALD AVERY

Between 1914 and 1946 war and social disruption greatly affected the relations between the Ukrainian Left and the Canadian government.[1] Although there had been periodic concern over radical activity among foreign workers before 1914, the war years and the Red Scare of 1919 greatly intensified the fear of the radical alien. Individuals and groups now tended to be deemed loyal or disloyal, law-abiding or revolutionary, according to their conformity to the norms of the Anglo-Canadian middle class. These same attitudes, particularly on the part of Canadian business groups and law enforcement officials, surfaced again during the Great Depression. Renewed efforts to contain the forces of radicalism culminated in August 1931 in the arrest of the major Communist leaders and extensive use of section 41 of the Immigration Act to deport alien radicals. The advent of the Second World War ushered in yet another phase in the continuing struggle between the Left and the Canadian national security state.

During these years the Left was a powerful and distinctive element within the Ukrainian-Canadian community. At the same time, the experience of the Ukrainian Left must be understood within the broader context of the problems that many East European immigrant workers faced, particularly in regions where industrial conflict prevailed. Obviously before 1921 Ukrainian socialists had much in common with Finnish and Jewish socialists, and within the more broadly based Communist movement they often vied for power and influence and shared a common legacy of persecution.[2] These similarities should not, however, obscure the extent to which the experience of the Ukrainian Left was distinctive.

This paper will explore a number of important questions associated with the experiences of the Ukrainian-Canadian Left between 1914 and 1946. How did it develop such resilient cultural and political institutions, and how did it attempt to reconcile ethnic and class loyalties? What role did Ukrainian socialists and pro-Communists assume within the Canadian radical Left? Why did the Ukrainian Left become the special target of Canadian security agencies in both war and peace? And finally, to what extent was the Canadian response to the Ukrainian Left similar during both world wars, and to what extent was it different?

Creating the Ukrainian-Canadian Left, 1900–1914

Before 1914 Ukrainian immigrant workers developed many responses to a Canadian environment that both promised and threatened. Going home was one method of dealing with economic exploitation and social discrimination. This return migration was not confined to sojourners who had accumulated savings and included many who were forced out of Canada by depressed economic circumstances. The lack of unemployment benefits in the Dominion and the existence of ample means to deport public charges and alien radicals further swelled the ranks of the returnees.[3] But for the vast majority of Ukrainian immigrants who remained, a wide variety of cultural and working class institutions helped them to adjust to Canadian society. These ranged from the rather conservative ethnic churches to the more assertive mutual aid societies and political organizations. The transfer of Old World values and ideas was also closely associated with the emergence of a Ukrainian-language press that represented many sides of the ideological spectrum.[4]

Although it is not the intention of this paper to analyse the complex issue of whether ethnic identity is a more effective mobilizing criterion than class issues, some trends can be suggested. For example, recent historical studies have shown how, given the proper economic and political conditions, ethnic and class sentiment can reinforce each other and propel an ethnic group towards forms of militant organization nourished by visions of class emancipation. But when these conditions do not exist (or are undermined by state repression), ethnic and class sentiments may easily become disjointed. And the more these sentiments are disjointed, the more the terrain becomes susceptible for the intervention of conservative ethnic elites, which are able to take advantage of the daily reality of prejudice and discrimination to rally their community towards the vision of ethnic (as opposed to class) emancipation.[5]

In many ways this model applies to the Ukrainian-Canadian community, which was clearly divided into competing groups – a trend most pronounced in western Canada. Before the Great War, the conservatives had a number of advantages in the contest for the loyalty of Ukrainian workers: of these, the most important was a common Old World identification with the Uniate church. This fusion between religious and ethnic identity was kept alive by Nykyta Budka, the first Uniate bishop in Canada, who was able to negotiate successfully with the Manitoba provincial government for Ukrainian cultural rights. By 1914, however, two serious rivals had appeared. One was the group of intellectual nationalists associated with the newspaper *Ukrainskyi holos* (Ukrainian Voice), who were 'distressed by the manner in which Ukrainians were being manipulated by both missionaries and politicians.' The other was the Ukrainian Left.[6]

In 1907 the Winnipeg-based Ukrainian Socialist Labour Committee was created, along with its newspaper *Chervonyi prapor* (Red Flag). Initially the Ukrainian socialists seemed prepared to work within the Socialist party of Canada (SPC), accepting the notion that it was dedicated to uniting 'workers of all nations and faiths.' But even at this early stage Ukrainian socialists argued that the education and mobilization of the '100,000 Ukrainian proletarians' in the three prairie provinces required a Ukrainian Socialist Union within the SPC. In part, this represented a transfer of their Old World experience to Canada; it also demonstrated a practical recognition that ethnic and cultural values would enhance their class appeal and that the socialist hall should be both a political and a social institution. On the negative side, the ethnocentric appeal of the Ukrainian socialists often brought them into conflict with the Anglo-Saxon leadership of the Socialist party, and by 1910 the differences became irreconcilable. As a result, a separate Ukrainian Social Democratic Federation was established with headquarters in Winnipeg and with its own militant newspaper, *Robochyi narod* (Working People). During the next four years, the federation's organizational efforts were enhanced by the presence of such experienced socialists as Matthew Popovich, John Navis (Ivan Navizivsky), and Danylo Lobay, who combined their class message with appeals to Ukrainian nationalism and denunciations of the autocratic tsarist regime.[7] These Ukrainian socialists also played a major role in the formation of the Canadian Social Democratic party (SDP), which was a loose federation of Eastern European and English-speaking socialists.[8]

Ukrainian Workers, the Canadian Left, and State Repression, 1914–1919

The First World War had a enormous impact on Ukrainian workers in Canada. Massive layoffs by resource and industrial companies swelled the ranks of the unemployed, especially in such centres as Montreal,

Toronto, Winnipeg, and Vancouver. Depleted savings and difficulty in obtaining relief created considerable bitterness. Yet another problem was the wave of patriotic dismissals that occurred in many parts of the country, but especially in the resource towns of western Canada.[9]

At the start of the war there was also agitation from prominent western Canadian businessmen and local government officials for the mass internment of all 'idle' and impoverished aliens for humanitarian and security reasons. The Dominion government, however, was not prepared to implement a mass internment policy, largely because of the prohibitive cost of operating internment camps.[10] On the other hand, Dominion security officials did maintain a close watch on potentially dangerous ethnic leaders such as ecclesiastics and newspaper editors. In each major urban centre in the country special registrars of enemy aliens were appointed to monitor the activities of the potentially disloyal. As well, in June 1915 a press censorship branch was created under the auspices of the secretary of state, with a mandate to prevent the publication of 'objectionable' material. In reality, however, censorship applied only to the foreign-language press, a situation that the chief press censor explained in a 1916 circular: 'The reason that editors of Canadian English papers are permitted a broad scope in publishing war news items [is] because they depend on the knowledge and good sense of their English readers to distinguish between official and reliable news and news that comes from suspicious sources.'[11]

Anglo-Canadian hostility towards militant European workers increased after the advent of the 1917 Russian Revolution and the wave of industrial strikes of that year. In some regions, the label 'alien' became synonymous with traitor and revolutionary. The most dramatic official manifestation of the 'hard-line' approach was the order in council of 25 September 1918 prohibiting many enemy-language newspapers and outlawing fourteen 'radical organizations,' among them the Ukrainian Social Democratic party, the Finnish Social Democratic party, the Canadian Social Democratic party, and the Industrial Workers of the World. Nor was this measure merely a warning to the foreign-born population. Magistrates were authorized to impose severe sentences, and Canadian security forces received extensive powers of search and apprehension.[12]

Although the end of hostilities and pressure from such 'progressive' organizations as the Canadian Trades and Labour Congress forced the federal government to adopt a more conciliatory stance towards dissent, the truce was short-lived. The formation of the One Big Union (OBU), the first large-scale Canadian experiment with 'industrial unionism,' the outbreak of the Winnipeg General Strike, and a major confrontation in the Rocky Mountain coalfields turned an already ugly situation into a national crisis.[13]

But why did the Canadian state launch such a campaign against Ukrainian and other immigrant workers who were designated as 'radical aliens'? One explanation would be to regard the nativist sentiment as merely an intensification of pre-war bias. Before 1914 negative stereotypes of east and south European immigrants were widespread. Most notably, reports of the Royal Northwest Mounted Police (renamed the Royal Canadian Mounted Police, or RCMP, in 1919) stressed the tendency of foreign workers in western Canada to take the law into their own hands. During the 1906 Lethbridge coal strike, for example, the district superintendent of the RNWMP insisted upon the maximum deployment of police units to control Slavic and Italian miners: 'These people have been ruled by force for generations ... and in consequence, it now requires force to keep them in order.' The RNWMP was also distressed by its inability to apprehend labour agitators during industrial confrontations, largely because ethnic communities often viewed the law as 'the enemy.'[14]

Anglo-Canadian fear of foreign demagogues was not confined to labour. Before 1914 there were numerous charges that the Canadian political system, especially in the West, was being subverted by such un-Canadian agitators as Bishop Budka of the Uniate church. According to the influential *Manitoba Free Press*, Budka provided the Roblin Conservative government with massive electoral support in return for the expansion of Ukrainian bilingual schools throughout the province. Negative stereotypes of Ukrainian and other Eastern European workers also emanated from the writings of such well-meaning Anglo-Canadian social reformers as J.S. Woodsworth and the Reverend Charles W. Gordon (Ralph Connor), who often equated poverty and folk customs with backwardness and debauchery.[15]

Throughout the First World War there was intense Anglo-Canadian hostility towards all enemy aliens. Yet Ukrainians were much more distrusted than their German counterparts. One reason for this dichotomy was that most of those categorized as 'Austrian' enemy aliens were recent arrivals; in 1911, 60 per cent of the Ukrainians in the prairie provinces were foreign-born, and many of them were of military age and retained their status of reservists in their homeland. This image of divided loyalties was dramatically increased on 27 July 1914, when Bishop Budka issued his celebrated pastoral calling upon his parishioners to remember their duty to the Austro-Hungarian Empire.[16] Anglo-Canadian suspicions had been further aroused when Russophile groups in western Canada charged that Ukrainian nationalists intended to use the war not only to establish a separate homeland in Europe but also 'to organize a Ukrainian nation here in Canada.'[17]

Cultural issues also placed the Ukrainian community in confrontation with Anglo-Canadians: the determined Ukrainian resistance to the abolition of bilingual schools in Manitoba, for example, stirred deep hostility. The western press censor, Fred Livesay, went so far as to interpret the temporary alliance between the *Kanadyiskyi rusyn* (Canadian Ruthenian) and the *Ukrainskyi holos* on the matter of Ukrainian-language rights as part of a German-Austrian conspiracy to disrupt the Canadian war effort.[18] This stereotype of a homogeneous Ukrainian community on the prairies, manipulated by a disloyal and demagogic elite, gained even more credence among Anglo-Canadians during the wartime election of December 1917. It assumed its most insidious form, however, when concern over a global Bolshevik conspiracy gripped the country in 1919.[19]

The Canadian reaction to the Russian Revolution went through several stages. At first there was widespread support for the overthrow of the tsar, in part, at least, because of the belief that the authoritarian character of the imperial government impeded Russia's war effort.[20] By 1918, however, public opinion was distinctly anti-Bolshevik, and the decision to send Canadians troops to Siberia was welcomed. On the whole, however, Anglo-Canadians had little knowledge about the Russian Revolution and what it meant for Canadian Ukrainians.[21]

This reaction is not surprising. Before the war Anglo-Canadians rarely had been able to distinguish between different ideological groupings within the Ukrainian community.[22] With the overthrow of the tsar in March 1917, the situation became even more complicated as the various Ukrainian organizations attempted to redefine their position towards the Russian empire.[23] Thus, in the fall of 1917 the *Robochyi narod* called upon all Ukrainian Canadians to emphasize their common identity and national purpose; now was the time, it argued, to let 'our neighbours in Canada know clearly who and what we are; that we are not "Austrian," or "Galician," or a wild, uneducated people as portrayed by "our own native" undercover agents, who have sold us out and are traitors to our people.' Once the Bolsheviks had seized power in November 1917, the paper adopted a dramatically different editorial stance and vigorously attacked the Ukrainian Central Rada and the prospects of an independent bourgeois Ukraine.[24] As differences between the Ukrainian Social Democratic party and the rest of the Ukrainian-Canadian community became irreconcilable, those opposed to the Bolsheviks often appealed to Canadian security agencies for assistance. In return they were prepared, on occasion, to supply information about subversive activity on the part of the Ukrainian Left. In September 1918, for example, the chief press censor accepted Bishop Budka's claim that a well-organized Bolshevik movement in Canada was seeking to overthrow established authority and that the *Robochyi narod* and *Rabochii narod* were its mouthpieces.[25]

This willingness to provide useful information helped transform Budka's status with Canadian security officials. Not as fortunate were the Ukrainian workers arrested in Winnipeg and other centres of industrial conflict after the defeat of the Winnipeg General Strike who were subject to immediate deportation under section 41 of the Immigration Act.[26] Most of the Ukrainian socialist leaders, however, managed to avoid this fate, and once the Red Scare had subsided they began to rebuild their organizations. They also assumed a major role in the creation of the Communist Party of Canada.[27]

The Ukrainian Left, 1919–1939

Between its formation in July 1921 and its proscription in August 1931, the CPC passed through several stages of development. Initially, it was a secret organization, highly apprehensive of repression by the state. By 1922, however, it came out into the open and engaged in trade-union and political activity. In order to carry out its many tasks the party sponsored a number of specialized bodies: the Workers' Unity League (WUL), the Farmers' Unity League (FUL), the Canadian Labour Defence League, the Friends of the Soviet Union, and the Women's Bureau. The Finnish Organization of Canada (FOC) and the Ukrainian Labour-Farmer Temple Association (ULFTA) were also given special status within the party, and their leaders were included in the permanent executive, or Politbureau.[28]

If the FOC was stronger numerically than the ULFTA, it lacked the latter's diversity.[29] Though primarily a Ukrainian organization, the ULFTA also had support among Poles, Russians, and other Slavic groups. Founded in Winnipeg in 1918, the ULFTA soon expanded to other parts of the Dominion. By 1930 it had about 185 branches with approximately 5,438 members, published the influential *Ukrainski robitnychi visti* (Ukrainian Labour News), and maintained the Workers' Benevolent Society. Its ability to provide essential social services to the Ukrainian community was an important factor in its success. The educational and cultural activities it sponsored, particularly those that evoked the Old

World experience, were very popular. That Matthew Popovich could sing traditional Ukrainian songs at party-sponsored concerts greatly enhanced his prestige as a party organizer.[30]

During the 1920s the language federations assumed an important role in the CPC's attempt to reach foreign workers in the extracting industries and the rapidly expanding factories of central Canada.[31] They also provided a core group of electoral support for Communist candidates during federal, provincial, and municipal elections.[32] Perhaps not surprisingly, it was in working-class north Winnipeg that the CPC achieved its first major success when William Kolisnyk, a prominent member of the ULFTA, was elected to the city council in 1926.[33]

But this harmonious relationship between the Anglo-Canadian members of the CPC executive and the ULFTA would soon change. In 1929 the CPC moved resolutely to carry out the instructions of the Communist International that all workers be organized into factory units. Equally important was the Politbureau's insistence that the progress of communism in North America meant the primacy of the English language and an organizational structure that emphasized occupational and not cultural groups. The Comintern directives were clear: on the factory floor immigrant workers should be made 'to fraternize with other Communists, and hopefully, even with fellow workers who ... did not belong to any ethnic group.' It was expected, therefore, that Ukrainian workers would abandon their language groups and commit themselves to the activities of the newly formed CPC industrial unions, organized under the umbrella of the Workers' Unity League.[34] The ULFTA was bluntly told that it must Canadianize its operation immediately: English classes were to be offered to members, and the *Ukrainski robitnychi visti* would have to discard its narrow focus and 'tie up the struggle of the Ukrainian workers with the general proletarian struggle in Canada.' Instructions were also given for the ULFTA to eliminate most of the Ukrainian folk plays and concerts, which were categorized as being 'extremely empty and often directly harmful.' Not surprisingly, the party's assimilatory policy was strongly resisted. But in the end, there were two choices: either to submit or to leave the party. Most chose the former.[35]

Although this clash of ethnic and ideological loyalties posed a great problem for the leaders of the ULFTA, several factors minimized the disruption. One was the high degree of independence that the local temples enjoyed; another was the extent to which the party centre was dependent on ULFTA financial assistance. In addition, given the hostile political environment of 1931, it was deemed essential to maintain harmony within the Canadian Communist movement at all costs.[36] The

severe economic dislocation, combined with the CPC's aggressive trade-
union and political campaigns, had alarmed many Canadian businessmen and government officials, and there was growing talk of repressive
measures. Throughout 1931 Anglo- and French-Canadian 'patriotic
groups,' as well as various municipal governments, petitioned the government of R.B. Bennett to ban the CPC and deport its adherents. It
also heard from the premiers of Quebec, Ontario, Alberta, and British
Columbia. Arrests and deportations mounted, despite the efforts of the
Canadian Labour Defence League to protect foreign workers. On 11
August 1931 the Bennett government formally declared war on the
Communist party: within a week eight members of the Politbureau were
in custody, charged with seditious conspiracy under section 98 of the
Criminal Code.[37]

Among those imprisoned were two prominent leaders of the ULFTA –
Matthew Popovich and John Boychuk. This targeting of the ULFTA as
a dangerous organization was not surprising given the hostile attitude
of the RCMP and prominent Anglo-Canadian spokesmen. Throughout
the 1920s the Mounties had periodically called for the proscription of
the ULFTA under section 98 and for the deportation of its leaders. Many
Anglo-Canadian newspapers, most notably the *Winnipeg Free Press*,
endorsed this hard-line approach. In December 1923, for example, the
Free Press ran a series of ten articles denouncing all organizations that
carried on 'campaigns for a Soviet Canada, established by violence if
necessary beneath the cloak of "benevolent and educational aims."'
The paper was especially concerned about the operation of some fifty
ULFTA schools, where, it was claimed, the doctrines of communism and
revolution were 'taught to adults and children alike.' Ukrainian radicals,
the *Free Press* warned, 'have placed the little red school house in an
entirely new setting.'[38]

The *Free Press* was also disturbed that Winnipeg had elected the first
Communist to public office in North America. However, the most intense
reaction came from the city's Ukrainian community. Throughout William Kolisnyk's two aldermanic terms (1926–30), the *Ukrainski robitnychi
visti* was forced to defend its champion against the vigorous and vitriolic
attacks of the liberal nationalist *Ukrainskyi holos* and the clerical nationalist *Kanadyiskyi ukrainets* (Canadian Ukrainian).[39] Although the ULFTA
was able to withstand these assaults, a more serious threat emerged
during the thirties. Here the issue was Ukrainian rights in the USSR. By
1935, stories of Stalin's purge of Ukrainian nationalists had filtered back
to Canada; even more shocking was news of the execution of two former
ULFTA organizers, Ivan Sembay and Myroslav Irchan (Andrew Babiuk),

who had gone to the Soviet Union. Soon, such prominent members of
the national executive as Danylo Lobay and Toma Kobzey were in
open revolt. But this grass-roots challenge to the authority of the CPC
hierarchy was ultimately unsuccessful.[40]

One explanation why the CPC was able to hold the allegiance of most
of its Ukrainian members was the ability of the party to expand its trade-
union and political activities after 1935. Moreover, as social and economic
conditions continued to deteriorate, more workers, ethnic and English-
speaking alike, gravitated towards the CPC and its subsidiary organizations, most notably the Workers' Unity League and the National Unemployed Workers' Association. With the advent of the Popular Front
policy, largely in response to the growing threat of fascism, party organizers also assumed an important role in the creation and development
of peace and civil-rights organizations such as the Canadian Youth
Congress, the Canadian League for Peace and Democracy, and the
Committee to Aid Spanish Democracy. On the industrial front, CPC
organizers occupied key positions within such CIO labour unions as
the United Auto Workers, the United Steel Workers, and the United
Electrical Workers. All of this would, however, change in 1939 as the
international Communist movement entered another stage.[41]

The Second World War and the Cold War

The Soviet-German non-aggression pact of August 1939 placed the
ULFTA in a most vulnerable position. Like others within the Canadian
Communist movement, Ukrainian leftists initially had difficulty grasp-
ing the implications of the changes in Soviet strategic policy. On 12
September, for instance, the ULFTA organ *Narodna hazeta* denounced
the Nazi invasion of Poland and exclaimed: 'Destroy Hitlerism! Save
Humanity!'[42] Soon, however, there was a rapid adjustment in the party
line and Canadian Communists stopped describing the war as 'anti-
fascist' and began calling it an 'anti-imperialist' conflict that Canada had
to avoid. This meant that Communist organizations in general, and the
ULFTA in particular, were now legitimate targets under the security
provisions of the Defence of Canada Regulations.

Even before the outbreak of war federal authorities had devised a
variety of measures to deal with groups that might threaten national
security. In a May 1939 memorandum, Norman Robertson, acting in
his capacity as liaison between the RCMP and the cabinet, set forth a
comprehensive list of guidelines to deal with seditious activities. One of
these was the recommendation that immigration and naturalization

regulations be used against Nazis and fascists 'in the same way that police now check the records of persons believed to be of radical or Communist sympathies.' Within the King government, the Communists were viewed with the most intense suspicion, especially by the RCMP. In August 1939, as the international situation became more critical, Commissioner T. Wood recommended that the CPC be outlawed and its leaders interned. Even though moderates such as Norman Robertson and J.F. MacNeill of the Department of Justice argued that this hard-line approach was both undemocratic and inefficient, the RCMP persisted in its long war against the Communists. In January 1940 the round-up of Communists and anarchists began: on 4 June the Communist party and most of its front organizations were proscribed. Under order in council PC 2667 the custodian of enemy property was given control of the property of all banned organizations – including the ULFTA.[43]

In addition, between June 1940 and November 1942, thirty-three leaders of the ULFTA were interned.[44] All endured deprivation and harassment, but for party veterans such as Matthew Popovich renewed imprisonment was devastating.[45] Although the Canadian Civil Liberties Union and its allies had launched a campaign to obtain the immediate release of interned Communists, they could achieve little until June 1941. Even when the Soviet Union became Canada's wartime ally, the King government was slow to release leftist internees or to restore confiscated property despite mounting popular pressure. In October 1942, for example, a massive petition, signed by a large number of 'respectable' Anglo-Canadians, including Premier Mitchell Hepburn of Ontario, was sent to Ottawa calling for the removal of all disabilities. Federal authorities were sufficiently impressed to release the Communists; they did not, however, lift the ban on the movement or agree to restore confiscated property until October 1943. For the ULFTA, return of all its halls would take almost another two years.[46]

Ukrainian Communists were also affected by other wartime measures that the King government implemented. Of particular importance were the activities of two agencies within the newly established Department of National War Services. Both the Nationalities Branch and the Committee on Co-operation in Canadian Citizenship sought to mould public opinion amongst Canada's ethnic groups. What this meant in practical terms was an obligation 'to provide Canadian news for the domestic foreign-language press and to give stories of the activities of the ethnic communities to the French and English newspapers ... [and] to provide the immigrant groups with information about their homelands without reviving nationalistic ambitions or antagonism.' In many ways the creation of these agencies represented a great improvement over the experience of the First World War, when Ottawa adopted a double standard towards the foreign-language press. On the other hand, aspects of Anglo-Canadian condescension and superiority still created problems in communication and understanding. For example, all of the executives within the Nationalities Branch were Anglo-Saxons: the director was Professor George Simpson, an East European specialist with the University of Saskatchewan's history department; his special adviser was Tracy Philipps, a former adviser to the British Foreign Office who had visited and lectured to various Eastern European ethnic communities under the auspices of the Bureau of Public Information.[47] In addition, there was a host of Anglo-Canadian special advisers. One of the most prominent was Professor Watson Kirkconnell of McMaster University, whose 1941 pamphlet *Canadians All* raised the alarm 'that the Soviet Communists along with the German and Italian fascists looked for converts in Canada among the immigrant community.'[48] At this stage, Kirkconnell, Philipps, and other officials of the Nationalities Branch made no excuse either for their anticommunism or for their close association with the newly formed Ukrainian Canadian Committee (UCC).[49]

External events would, however, soon render this type of arrangement unpopular. With the June 1941 German invasion the Soviet Union suddenly became an ally of the British Commonwealth in the struggle against fascism. Canada's Communists in general, and Ukrainian Communists in particular, greatly benefited from this wartime alliance and from stories of Russian heroism. This new pro-Russian sentiment was most evident in the work of the National Council for Canadian-Soviet Friendship, which had branches in eighteen cities across the country and an executive that included such Anglo-Canadian luminaries as Sir Ellsworth Flavelle as president and John David Eaton as vice-president. At the November 1944 congress of the NCSF Flavelle made the following appeal: 'In the past, Canadian public opinion about the Soviet Union has often been distorted by prejudice and misinformation. We know that to a considerable degree misleading information about Russia has been "planted" by those who are now our enemies, and by their willing or unwilling agents in our midst.'[50]

Within the King government, External Affairs officials were especially anxious to establish cordial relations with the USSR. This tendency became even more pronounced in February 1942 when the two countries agreed to exchange ministers. Shortly thereafter Dana Wilgress was sent to the temporary Soviet capital of Kuibyshev as envoy extraordinary and minister plenipotentiary; in September 1942 the Soviet mission

Members of the A. Kotzko Ukrainian Students Society in Edmonton, Alberta, 1922 (G. Dragan Collection, National Archives of Canada)

Student Society of the Brotherhood of Ukrainian Catholics in
Saskatoon, Saskatchewan, 1936–7 (Private collection of
Mrs H. Machuga, Winnipeg)

OPPOSITE

J.E. Tracy Philipps, upon receiving an honorary doctorate from the
University of Durham (Private collection of John Philipps and Lubka
Kolessa, Toronto)

Vladimir J. Kaye-Kysilewsky (Private collection of S. Pawluk and the
Ukrainian Canadian Research Foundation, Toronto)

National executive of the Ukrainian Canadian Committee in Winnipeg, 1946. *Bottom row, left to right:* S. Chwaliboga, J.W. Arsenych, Reverend S.W. Sawchuk, Reverend W. Kushnir, W. Kossar, A. Malofie, A.J. Yaremovich. *Second row, left to right:* M. Pohorecky, M. Stechishin, S. Skoblak, Reverend S. Semczuk, T.D. Ferley, P. Barycky, A. Zaharychuk. *Third row, left to right:* I. Gulay, W. Sarchuk, B. Dyma, E. Wasylyshen, C. Andrusyshen, T. Melnychuk (Ukrainian Canadian Congress Archives, Winnipeg)

OPPOSITE

Headquarters of the Ukrainian Canadian Servicemen's Association, London, England (G.R.B. Panchuk Collection, Archives of Ontario)

Members of the Ukrainian Canadian Servicemen's Association and Central Ukrainian Relief Bureau, London, England, 1946. *Left to right:* F/L G.R.B. Panchuk, Captain Peter Smylski, F/L Joseph Romanow, George Kluchevsky, S.W. Frolick (S.W. Frolick Collection, National Archives of Canada)

Gordon R. Bohdan Panchuk,
MBE, CD, 1945
(G.R.B. Panchuk Collection,
Archives of Ontario)

Captain Stanley W. Frolick, 1945
(S.W. Frolick Collection,
National Archives of Canada)

Ann Crapleve, of the
Ukrainian Canadian Relief Fund,
greeting Anne and Eustace Wasylyshen,
at Bielefeld, Germany, 1 April 1949
(Private collection of Ann Smith, Winnipeg)

Ukrainian Youth Association rally at the Freiman Kasserne Displaced
Persons camp, Munich, Germany, 1948
(Private collection of Danylo Luciuk, Kingston)

Ukrainian-Canadian women modelling traditional folk dress near Vita, Manitoba, 1947 (Western Canada Pictorial Index)

National convention of the Ukrainian Women's Association of Canada, July 1947 (G. Dragan Collection, National Archives of Canada)

Senator John Hnatyshyn and family members, 1959. (G. Dragan Collection, National Archives of Canada)

Canadian Ukrainians greeting Her Majesty Queen Elizabeth II in Kingston, Ontario, May 1959 (Private collection of Danylo Luciuk, Kingston)

Announcement placed by the Ukrainian Canadian Committee and several other East European communities in the national edition of the *Globe and Mail*, 28 September 1985 (Private collection of J.B. Gregorovich, Toronto)

Executive members of the Civil Liberties Commission of the Ukrainian Canadian Committee and of the Lithuanian Canadian Community, in Ottawa, upon the release of the public report of the Commission of Inquiry on War Criminals, 12 March 1987. *Left to right:* Lubomyr Luciuk, J.B. Gregorovich, Ron Vastokas

An abiding concern of many of Canada's Ukrainians – A 'Free Ukraine'
placard displayed at a rally in Toronto
(Private collection of Lu Taskey, Toronto)

arrived in Ottawa.[51] In May 1943 Parliament provided that the Mutual Aid Act would include the USSR, and by the end of the war Canada had supplied the Soviet Union with approximately $167.3 million worth of food, medical supplies, and war material.[52]

Given these wartime commitments, it is not surprising that Canadian diplomats were often impatient and even hostile towards anti-Soviet agitation in Canada. In May 1943 Dana Wilgress told his Ottawa superiors that Soviet authorities had become greatly disturbed over the advocacy of Ukrainian independence by such groups as the UCC. This agitation, Wilgress claimed, would not only seriously complicate Canadian-Soviet relations, but also 'promote disunity' among the Allies.[53] Accordingly, the RCMP was instructed to monitor the activities of all Ukrainian nationalist organizations, and especially the forthcoming UCC Ottawa congress.[54] Although neither the RCMP nor the Nationalities Branch of the Department of National War Services found any evidence of disloyal or disruptive conduct, the federal government increasingly viewed the Ukrainian nationalists as a problem.[55] A June 1943 memorandum that the cabinet considered while trying to decide what to do with the ULFTA properties clearly expressed this point of view: 'Although before June 1941, the Left Wing Ukrainians were undoubtedly a drag on the Canadian war effort insofar as they followed the Communist party line, it is not unreasonable to expect that the Nationalist elements among the Right Wing Ukrainians will become a greater source of embarrassment to the Canadian government insofar as their aspirations center in the creation of an independent Ukraine; we know that this irredentism among Canadian Ukrainians is being closely followed in Moscow and is resented.'[56]

During the last two years of the war, both the nationalists and the Communists sought to convince federal authorities that their vision of a post-war Ukraine was both viable and just.[57] In the end the Communists won – essentially because of external factors. Allied compromises at Yalta and Dumbarton Oaks legitimized Soviet Ukraine and provided for its membership in the United Nations. In keeping with their previous position Canadian diplomats regarded this process as a necessary price for international stability and post-war co-operation. There were, however, those who claimed that UN membership for Ukraine would eventually 'drive from the nationalists' minds the mirage of absolute Ukrainian independence and in this way hasten the process of [Canadian] assimilation.'[58]

By the fall of 1945 this line of reasoning was no longer in vogue as Canada drifted towards the cold war. Throughout the summer and fall of 1945 Canadians had been exposed to an image of the USSR that emphasized its brutal control of Eastern Europe. The millions of refugees fleeing from the Red Army provided additional verification of Soviet repression and imperialism. Even the Anglo-Canadian luminaries of the National Council of Canadian-Soviet Friendship got the message, and soon the NCCSF was nothing more than another embattled Communist front organization.[59] Not surprisingly, the change in the Canadian-Soviet alliance was a signal to the RCMP to renew its long battle against the radical Left. Although its staff was small and poorly trained for counter-espionage, the force threw itself into the work with vigour. The defection of Igor Gouzenko in September 1945 confirmed its worse suspicions about the connection between Communist organizations and Soviet espionage and subversion.[60]

None of the ULFTA's leaders were named as spies by the Royal Commission on Espionage. Nevertheless, many Canadians deemed the organization (called the Association of United Ukrainian Canadians after November 1946) guilty by association. The ULFTA was also accused of divided loyalties on 26 May 1946, when its representative told the Senate Standing Committee on Immigration and Labour that most of the 300,000 Ukrainian displaced persons in Germany were collaborators.[61] The committee not only condemned this spurious allegation, but also recommended that displaced persons of all nationalities 'be admitted to Canada in substantial numbers and commencing as soon as possible.' In the fall of 1946 the Canadian government implemented a relatively generous refugee policy that admitted over 160,000 displaced persons (often called DPs) during the next six years.[62]

Among the DPs were over thirty thousand Ukrainians, most of whom were intensely anti-Communist. Their arrival had many implications for the Ukrainian-Canadian community, not least of which was their ability to expose the ULFTA's myths about the promise of Soviet life. Since many of these Ukrainian DPs were well-educated and politically conscious, they also 'injected new life into and raised the morale of the nationalist camp.' This, in turn, meant more frequent and violent conflict with the Ukrainian Communists.[63] Although each side blamed the other for the violence, the RCMP had no difficulty in identifying the Communists as the culprits.[64] RCMP Commissioner S.T. Wood summed up the situation in a January 1950 memorandum:

Communist functionaries are acutely aware their mass language organizations are losing membership and support because of the factual knowledge being brought to this country by Displaced Persons having actually lived under Soviet

Domination. They foresaw the ultimate repercussions even prior to Displaced Persons immigrating to Canada and did everything in their power to stop it. Unsuccessful in this endeavour, the problem of Displaced Persons is now probably their most important, and exhaustive measures have been taken to counteract the adverse influence. To date their counter measures have been marked with a distinct lack of success.[65]

That the RCMP should have welcomed this support in its campaign against Ukrainian Communists is understandable. Yet surprisingly, Ukrainian anti-Communists received little recognition and few concessions from the government in return. This was most evident in the area of immigration. Throughout the years 1946–50 officials of the newly established Department of Citizenship and Immigration were generally hostile when the Ukrainian Canadian Committee lobbied on behalf of various 'Ukrainian cultural workers and artists.' The government's rationale was simple and familiar: Ukrainian intellectuals would keep an Old World culture alive and thereby impede the Canadianization of the Ukrainian community.[66] Obviously, in the minds of many government officials true loyalty was still equated – as it was in 1914–19 – with unhyphenated Canadianism.[67]

Conclusion

The problem of divided loyalties greatly affected the Ukrainian Left between 1914 and 1946. Throughout this period there was the difficulty of reconciling Marxist principles with Ukrainian nationalism and cultural values; this became even more pronounced after 1921, when the ULFTA became affiliated with the Communist Party of Canada and, by association, with the Communist International. Yet in some ways the association with the Comintern was an asset, especially when Ukrainian Canadians could be convinced that Soviet Ukraine was a dynamic and independent national entity within the USSR. But when this myth was exposed, the problems of reconciling ideological and ethnic loyalties became greatly exacerbated. The Soviet connection also exposed Ukrainian-Canadian Communists to the charge that their primary loyalties were to the USSR. These allegations became particularly menacing when Soviet foreign policy appeared to threaten Canadian national security.

But why did Ukrainian workers join the Left in the first place? Part of the explanation is associated with the exploitation inherent in the Canadian capitalistic labour market – exploitation that had both economic and social consequences. Although many of these workers,

between 1914 and 1946, moved from the uncertainty of frontier employment to more stable industrial jobs, the transition they made was often
from manipulated foreigners to deprived Canadian working class. Moreover, in attempting to inculcate Anglo-Canadian values both government and voluntary agencies, however well-intentioned, often ag-
gravated the immigrants' sense of cultural identification – a pride that
was perhaps their most important asset in dealing with the vicissitudes
of life in a land that at once promised and threatened. Nor was the
performance of the Canadian trade-union movement all that different.
Certainly most unions affiliated with the Trades and Labour Congress
made little effort to draw European immigrant workers into their fold,
largely because of their exclusive craft orientation and their Anglo-
Canadian bias. Shunned or patronized by traditional native institutions,
some alienated immigrant workers turned to groups that sought to
transform Canadian society: the socialist parties, the Industrial Workers
of the World, the One Big Union, and, after 1921, the Communist party.[68]

Yet another factor was the creation of viable ethnocultural class organizations. Although socialists and Communists represented only 5 to 10
per cent of the Ukrainian population of Canada between 1914 and 1946,
they carried on a wide variety of cultural and political activities and
published a number of influential newspapers.[69] Their leaders, especially
those associated with the ULFTA, were often powerful figures within
local Ukrainian communities and were also active at the national level
through the CPC. But being involved did not mean being equal.
Throughout the inter-war years the CPC's Anglo-Canadian leaders
assumed that cultural assimilation by their Ukrainian comrades was a
small price to pay for the proletarian revolution. Nor did they show
much concern for the status of the ULFTA when the party abruptly
altered its policies in September 1939 and again in September 1945. But
even with the advent of the cold war, Ukrainian Communists continued
to operate their various organizations, and in some communities, most
notably Winnipeg's North End, they maintained a political presence
in local government.[70]

Despite, or perhaps because of, its success, the Ukrainian Left became
a favourite target of Canadian security agencies, particularly during
periods of national emergency.[71] During the First World War, for example, Ukrainians of all ideological backgrounds were treated as second-
class citizens, but the leftists suffered most. They were not only labelled
as enemy aliens but were also feared as Bolshevik aliens. The ULFTA's
decision to become a branch of the Communist party further justified
RCMP charges of disloyalty – since it was assumed that all Canadian

Communists owed ultimate loyalty to the Soviet Union. Indeed, justification for the arrest and internment of Ukrainian Communists in June
1940 was very similar to the rationale adopted during previous periods
of repression – September 1918, June 1919, August 1931. The Communists were subversives because they rejected Canadian democratic values; they were potential enemy agents because they slavishly followed
the Comintern line. This similarity between the two wartime situations,
however, ends in June 1941.[72]

The sudden transition of the Soviet Union from Canada's foe to friend
had an enormous impact on the status of the Ukrainian-Canadian Communists. Indeed, for a brief period the ULFTA could claim greater loyalty
and commitment to Canada's war effort than its UCC rivals. This aura
of respectability and legitimacy depended, of course, on continued
Canadian-Soviet friendship – and this would be short-lived. With the
advent of the cold war the Ukrainian Left would once again become
a favourite target of its old foe – the RCMP.

This paper has focused on some aspects of the Ukrainian-Canadian
Left and its relations with the Canadian state between 1914 and 1946. It
has not attempted to explain why some Ukrainians joined the Left and
others did not. Nor has it tried to compare the Ukrainian Left with other
groups – a very difficult task since Canadian scholarship on this topic is
so limited.[73] Indeed, even in its assessment of the response of the national
security state towards Ukrainian leftists this paper has left many questions unanswered, and they may remain so until scholars obtain access
to the voluminous files of the security service of the RCMP and its
successor, the Canadian Security Intelligence Service.[74]

Without Just Cause: Canada's First National Internment Operations

MARK MINENKO

On 30 May 1916 the superintendent in charge of the Regina District of the Royal Northwest Mounted Police (RNWMP) signed a report that stated in part: 'I came to the decision that this man is a subject of the Austro-Hungarian Monarchy and that he was shielding his brother who was crossing and re-crossing the International Boundary line between Canada and the United States.'[1] Philip Marchuk was quickly sent to an internment camp at Brandon, Manitoba, and then to a camp at Banff, Alberta, where he became prisoner number 589. Like many before and after him, he had had a quick and sharp introduction to Canada's new emergency powers legislation, the War Measures Act of 1914 (WMA).[2] While thousands of Ukrainians were fighting and dying for Canada and Great Britain in the trenches of the First World War, tens of thousands of Philip Marchuks were imprisoned in internment camps across Canada or forced to register with the authorities as 'enemy aliens' and to carry a registration card. Pursuant to the new law, hundreds of regulations and orders in council were passed, leading to the internment of 8,759 men and some women and children and the forced registration of over 80,000.[3]

This paper will review the War Measures Act, its regulations, and orders in council as well as the Internment Operations Branch's execution of its mandate to administer the new law. Although many hundreds of regulations were made pursuant to this new authority, only those applicable to the internment of Ukrainians will be reviewed here. But first, some historical background to the wartime legislation and its implementation.

At the turn of the century, Wilfrid Laurier's Liberal government, with

Clifford Sifton as the minister of the interior, planned to settle the Canadian prairies with farmers who would contribute to Canada's wealth.[4] The 1901 census showed Canada's population to be 5,371,315. In 1911 the population jumped to 7,206,643.[5] Many Canadians did not welcome the new immigrants. In 1899 newspapers in Brandon, Manitoba, described the immigrants as 'pampered paupers,' 'foreign scum,' and 'barbarians.' It was felt that they would endanger the democratic process through their willingness to sell their vote.[6] Hugh John Macdonald referred to the Ukrainians as a 'mongrel' race; Manitoba premier Sir Rodmond Roblin called them 'foreign trash.' Many Ukrainians quickly discovered that their traditions and aspirations aroused misunderstanding, suspicion, and censure. Their willingness to accept low pay and poor working conditions on construction gangs and farms threatened the working class.[7]

With the opening of vast stretches of western Canada, wheat production increased from 56 million bushels in 1901 to 231 million bushels in 1911. But by 1907 competition from Russia and Argentina had forced prices lower and made grain farming less profitable. The British, who had steadily invested in Canada, started to withhold some of their investments, causing a downturn throughout the Canadian economy.[8] Immigration continued, but there were fewer jobs. By 1912, the rapid expansion of turn-of-the-century Canada had ebbed. Industrial production and urban development were cut back.[9] The poor prairie wheat crops of 1913 and 1914 contributed to this economic decline.[10]

In Europe, tensions were increasing during the summer of 1914. On 27 July, shortly after the shooting of Archduke Franz Ferdinand of Austria, Bishop Nykyta Budka, the primate of the Ukrainian Catholic church in Canada, issued a statement in which he called upon Ukrainians to be prepared to return to their homeland and fight for their nation. This statement was consistent with the Ukrainian intelligentsia's support of the Habsburgs, who had granted Ukrainians cultural and linguistic rights, economic benefits, and political representation.[11] On 4 August, Great Britain declared war on Austria. Two days later Budka retracted his pronouncement and called on Ukrainians to support their new homeland, but the damage was done and the English press would not let anyone forget his call for support for the Austrians. On 5 August, the *Manitoba Free Press* responded to Bishop Budka's statement by saying that Canada did not ask the newcomer to forget his old home, but that if he did not feel a duty to Canada, he had 'better get out of Canada and keep out.'

The Ukrainian community came out in support of Budka's second letter of 6 August. In an editorial Professor Alex Sushko wrote, 'the Ruthenian Ukrainians of Canada who have settled in this new country are sincerely attached to our New Fatherland, for which we are always ready in case of necessity, to give up our property and blood.' In response the *Free Press* asserted editorially that same day that 'mere lip-service to Canada means nothing when it is belied by the deliberate crusade which is in progress in this Province to establish "the Canadian Ukraine" by the resistance to compulsory education and the effective teaching of English.'[12]

To convince Canadians of their loyalty to the Dominion, over three thousand Ukrainians attended a mass meeting on 9 August, in the hall of the Industrial Bureau. The purpose of the meeting was 'to make clear to the public the attitude of Canadian Ruthenians in the present war.' A resolution that was passed at the meeting read: 'Whereas, the welfare of the British empire is at stake, We, the Ruthenian citizens of Winnipeg, here assembled, hereby express our loyalty to the British flag and declare our readiness to follow the Union Jack when called upon.' By this time, sixty Ukrainians had already volunteered for duty with the 106th Light Infantry in Winnipeg. The *Free Press* commented that although there was no need for Ukrainians publicly to profess their loyalty, there was some question about the loyalty of some of the nationalist and clerical leaders.[13]

Over the next several weeks there was a flurry of letters to the editor of the *Free Press* expressing loyalty to Canada and denouncing Budka's first statement. Nevertheless, on 27 August, the *Free Press* published a letter from Cecil C. Morgan, the secretary of the RNWMP Veterans Association: 'the country is permeated with Austrians and Germans prepared for some act of incendiarism or reprisal ... We are living in a false security, which may any day be fatally dispelled unless we get Martial Law as a remedy and men to enforce it; and as in this city of Winnipeg foreigners who cannot speak a word of English are being sold ammunition by a leading firm it is high time to wake up in the defense of our homes.'

Shortly after Great Britain's declaration of war against Germany and its allies on 4 August 1914, the British Parliament passed the Defence of the Realm Act, 1914 (DRA). It allowed the British government to secure the public safety and to defend the empire and was to be in effect 'during the continuance of the present war.'[14] Instead of introducing similar legislation, the Canadian government dealt with the crisis by passing two orders in council. The first, passed by the cabinet on 7 August 1914, imposed restrictions on German immigrants in Canada.

The second order, passed on 13 August 1914, dealt with Austro-Hungarian immigrants. Both orders stated that as long as persons of these two nationalities pursued 'their ordinary avocations,' they would not be arrested, detained, or interfered with, but German or Austro-Hungarian officers or reservists who attempted to leave Canada would be arrested.[15] In August 1914, the Canadian government passed another order, which broadened the categories of persons who could be arrested and detained. Subjects of enemy countries who were attempting to leave Canada 'with a view of assisting the enemy' as well as anyone who 'engaged or attempt[ed] to engage in espionage or acts of a hostile nature ... or giving or attempting to assist the enemy' could be arrested. No particular evidence of this type of behaviour was required, and reasonable ground was sufficient.[16]

On 19 August 1914, the federal minister of justice introduced a new law into the House of Commons that would grant the cabinet wide powers during the emergency. The reason the government gave for introducing the bill was that 'it is for every man to do that which lies within his power, on behalf of our country whose fate ... is hanging in the balance.' This new law was the War Measures Act of 1914. It was passed with little debate or questions two days later.[17] Royal assent was given on 22 August.

Although it would be reasonable to believe that the Canadian Parliament would have followed the British example, when the Canadian law is compared with its British counterpart a number of differences are evident. Section 1 of the DRA restricted the power of cabinet to the 'continuance of the present war'; section 4 of the WMA provided that the Canadian cabinet's power began with its proclamation of a 'war, invasion or insurrection, real or apprehended.' The powers ended only with the cabinet's proclamation that the war, invasion, or insurrection was over. The WMA was also made retroactive in that it provided for the ratification of acts or omissions of the cabinet, any minister and authority, or person completed since 1 August 1914. By section 5, the period of war declared on 4 August 1914 would continue until the cabinet proclaimed otherwise. Even if such a proclamation was issued, any and all proceedings begun before that proclamation could continue as required. No such provision existed in the DRA.

The greatest difference between the two acts was in the degree of contemplated interference in the lives of the respective countries' citizens. Whereas the DRA was generally limited to a restriction of activities that affected military operations, the Canadian Parliament empowered its cabinet by section 6 of the act to pass regulations on almost every

aspect of Canadian life, including communications, control and transport of persons and things, trading, export, import, manufacture, and
production. This difference was recognized at least by 1915.[18] The Canadian minister of justice was also given a judicial function by virtue of
section 11 of the WMA. His permission was required to release, discharge, or try any person held for deportation, under any regulation
made pursuant to the act, for being an alien enemy (subject of a country
at war with His Majesty) or under suspicion that he was an alien enemy.
On 3 September 1914, the cabinet prohibited the use or possession of
firearms and explosives within Canada by alien enemies.[19] Alien enemies
were given ten days to comply with this order, after which property
that was seized during a search of the person or premises could be
forfeited to the Crown. The police could start a search if they had a
reasonable suspicion of a violation of the order. The onus of proving
oneself not an alien enemy was on the accused.

Section 6 of the WMA was also used to attempt to prevent espionage.
On 12 September 1914, an order was passed preventing people from
being near any railway or bridge 'with intent to do injury thereto' or
selling liquor to soldiers and sailors with the intent of eliciting
information.[20]

On 28 October 1914 the federal minister of justice presented a report
to the cabinet that resulted in the passing of Order in Council 2721.[21]
This cabinet decision led to the creation of an organized system of
detention and internment of thousands of innocent Ukrainians. One of
the factors that was considered by the cabinet before passing the new
order was the prospect of high unemployment that winter. In early
October 1914 correspondence between the federal minister of labour,
T.W. Crothers, and Sir Rodmond Roblin, the premier of Manitoba,
revealed that the federal government was expecting over a hundred
thousand unemployed by early 1915. Although Roblin suggested that
recruiting for the armed forces could be a solution to this problem,
Crothers replied that this would be insufficient and that the three levels
of government would have to address the problem.[22]

On 22 October 1914 Prime Minister Borden sent a message to the
British: 'Situation with regard to Germans and Austrians particularly
Austrians very difficult. From fifty to one hundred thousand will be out
of employment during coming winter as employers are dismissing them
everywhere under compulsion of public opinion. They have been
attracted and indeed invited to Canada by Immigration Department
and now they find themselves without employment, and yet forbidden
to obtain it in United States ... Our inclination is to relax measures

preventing them from entering United States which is a neutral country and specially as there is little probability of their reaching the enemy's country.'[23] The British response was for the Canadians to detain these subjects in Canada. 'This course, in spite of the expense which it will involve, will no doubt prove the most satisfactory and it will preclude the practical certainty of any Germans or Austrians drifting, by way of the United States of America, back to the enemy's firing line.'[24]

Order 2721 authorized the establishment of registration offices in cities to be designated by the minister of justice and the appointment of registrars and assistants. The chief commissioner of the Dominion Police was made responsible for the operation of these offices. Clause 4 ordered the registration of all alien enemies living in or within twenty miles of designated cities. They were to report to the registration centre and answer questions relating to liability and intention as to military service. These people could also apply for exeats to leave Canada. The registrar could issue an exeat if he was satisfied that the registrant could not materially assist the enemy.

According to clause 7, an alien enemy who declared that he had the means to remain in Canada was to be 'permitted his liberty' subject to certain conditions, including monthly reporting. If he did not have the means to live in Canada, then he was to be interned as a prisoner of war. One would also be interned if in the estimation of the registrar it would be against the public safety to release him.

The families of the interned men could accompany them into the camps. Eighty-one women and 156 children were interned during the First World War and were accommodated at Vernon, British Columbia, and Spirit Lake, Quebec.[25] The government provided assistance to those internees whose family members remained behind (including Philip Marchuk's).[26] Forty women and 81 children were provided for in this manner.[27] The military was authorized to put the internees to work as required by clause 10. An internee could be naturalized only if in addition to the other requirements of naturalization he filed a certificate with the government to show that he was registered with the appropriate authorities and if the registrar of his district approved the naturalization.

On 6 November 1914, the cabinet appointed retired Major-General Sir William Dillon Otter to command the internment operations. On 13 November, the deputy minister of justice advised all the registrars that their duties were not merely clerical and that they should make 'due enquiry to ascertain the facts and exercise judgment.' Although they were authorized to issue exeats, 'the Government desire that this authority should not be exercised in any doubtful case.'[28] Less than a month after the order of 28 October 1914 the cabinet amended it to allow registrars to require someone to report more often than once a month and provided a form that was to be signed by the alien enemy who was to remain at large. This order of 20 November 1914 also added a new clause that exempted government employees and Armenian Christians from registering and reporting.

What were the government's motives in passing all of this legislation regarding enemy aliens in Canada? When the federal cabinet passed the order of 28 October 1914 setting up the Internment Operations Branch, it was reacting to growing public pressure. The *Manitoba Free Press* of 29 October described the cabinet order issued the previous day as made 'for relieving the distress of the Austrians and Germans in various parts of the country, who are out of work and unable to support themselves and also for placing under surveillance all who may be considered otherwise likely to cause trouble.' The motives were economic but tinged with nativism, even racism.

At first, registration was slow and created confusion. Many Ukrainian farmers associated the registration with police and military conscription in Austria and, as a result, did not register. Fifteen hundred were interned for this reason.[29] In other cases, the internees' limited English resulted in their internment. Some Ukrainians, when they were asked if they were 'pro-German,' said yes, meaning that they were against Germans as the Ukrainian word *proty* means 'against.'[30] Nonetheless, according to government documents, the most important factor in the internment of many Ukrainians was that they were destitute or unemployed. There is ample evidence that some municipalities used the war as an opportunity to pass the burden for providing relief for the unemployed to the federal government.

In January 1915, General Otter visited the Lakehead to oversee the transfer to his jurisdiction of over eight hundred potential internees designated by the local registrar as 'enemy aliens.' Otter offered this comment to a reporter on the scene: 'Some municipalities are attempting to take advantage of the situation to relieve themselves of the taxations necessary for the relief of the unemployed or destitute foreigners and I think that Port Arthur and Fort William are in this class.'[31] The real reason for the arrest of so many was that Port Arthur and Fort William wanted the alien labour to clear bush adjacent to the two cities. Otter held this belief so strongly that he stated in his final report that 'it is also suspected that the tendency of municipalities to unload their indigent, was the cause of the confinement of not a few.'[32] Of the 8,579 men interned during the First World War, over 5,000 had nothing to do with the war effort and were simply unemployed or destitute.

When someone was arrested by the police, he was first sent to a receiving station, where the initial paperwork was filled out and a decision was made about his final destination. Those arrested in Manitoba and Saskatchewan were first sent to the Brandon exhibition grounds; those from Alberta were initially interned in Lethbridge.[33] After a brief internment at Brandon, many internees were sent to Jasper and Banff (Castle Mountain) to work in the Dominion's parks. Here the internees found themselves clearing the parks at twenty-five cents a day. The work was not voluntary, and the pay was based on the rate of one shilling a day for Imperial soldiers.[34] The rate of pay of a rank-and-file soldier was seventy-five cents a day.[35]

By June 1915 registration centres in Sydney, Ottawa, Toronto, Brandon, Regina, Calgary, and Victoria were closed because many of the offices were doing little except filing nil reports.[36] A report from a Sergeant Fraser to the chief commissioner listed the following for the week of 13 March 1915:

	Average for day [registrations] about
Winnipeg	95
Edmonton	14
Port Arthur	14
Fort William	
Calgary	8
Toronto	5
Montreal	10
Ottawa	7
Brandon	3
Sydney	No returns received since February 16th

By June 1915, 48,500 enemy aliens were registered with the authorities, and 5,088 were interned.[37]

Even though several registration centres had been closed, the government did not relax its requirements with respect to enemy aliens. On 26 June 1915, it passed Order 1501, which augmented the reasons for which an alien enemy could be interned. The minister of justice reported that 'hostility and animosity' towards the alien enemies who were working with others or competing for work with others who belonged to allied nationalities had been 'aroused and excited by the war and the operations of the enemy,' and as a result there was a serious danger of rioting and destruction of work and property. The cabinet therefore passed an order 'to direct the apprehension and internment of aliens of enemy nationality who may be found employed or seeking employment or competing for employment in any community, such aliens of enemy nationality when so interned to be kept and maintained in all respects as prisoners of war, but subject to be released at any time as may be directed by the Minister, whenever it appears that they may be permitted to be discharged with due regard to the public safety.'[38] Thus, while many Ukrainians were being interned for being unemployed others could be arrested for competing with other Canadians or allied nationalities for jobs. Yet by the fall of that year, registration centres in Edmonton, Port Arthur, and Fort William were closed.

Pursuant to the Hague Regulations, prisoners of war could work either for their own comfort, health, and cleanliness (obligatory) or for the advantage of the government (paid).[39] However, as more and more men were required for service overseas, a labour shortage developed in Canada. On 1 January 1916, Borden announced the government's commitment to enlist up to half a million men for active service. The labour shortage had already been acute, especially in farming. After the announcement it became even more critical.

As early as April 1916, selected Ukrainian internees were released into the custody of farmers. The internees were required to sign a 'parole' undertaking loyalty and obedience to the laws of the Dominion as well as agreeing to periodic appearances at the nearest police office.[40] Two conditions were also imposed on the farmers: that they pay the going rate for farm hands and that they file behaviour reports about the released internees every month.[41]

On 7 April 1916, the *Manitoba Free Press* reported that General Otter was to be in Winnipeg the next day to discuss the paroling of internees to work in Manitoba. The internees were to be released on the basis of conduct and cause of internment. On 8 April, representatives of the Canadian Pacific Railway, the Canadian National Railway, the Manitoba Grain Growers Association, and the Canadian Bankers Association agreed with Otter that farmers would pay parolees current wages for at least seven months and cover their transportation costs from the internment camps to their places of employment.

In order to release internees to private industry, Otter also set the following conditions: that (1) other labour was not obtainable; (2) the employment was of a permanent character; (3) wages at current rates would be paid; (4) the cost of transportation from the place of internment would be paid by the firm; (5) the employed would not pay any agency fees. The prisoners were also to be paid twenty cents per hour with fifty cents per day deducted for room and board.[42]

On 1 May 1916 the number of alien enemies interned had risen to 6,061 with some 1,906 troops guarding them in twenty different locations.[43] The greatest numbers of internees were held at Spirit Lake, Quebec (1,144), Kapuskasing, Ontario (1,096), Amherst, Nova Scotia (718), Brandon, Manitoba (465), and Banff, Alberta (428). By the summer of 1916, internees were being released to work on railway construction gangs, in munition and other industrial plants, as well as in coal-mines such as the Crow's Nest Pass Coal Company, places from which many of those interned had been fired. There were many complaints about the release of so many internees to work on the railways, in steel works and coal-mines, and on the farms. In answer to a complaint from the South Vancouver Council, Borden wrote on 20 October 1916 that many of the men had been interned to save them from starving and that the releases were made for the sake of helping Canada's essential industries.[44] In May 1917, there were still 2,336 internees with 103 troops guarding them. The highest concentrations were at Amherst (853), Fort Henry, near Kingston (400), and Vernon (328). By that time Spirit Lake and Brandon were closed.

On 20 September 1916 the cabinet had passed an order requiring all aliens of enemy nationality over the age of sixteen to register with the police in the city, town, or village in which they lived and to report monthly to the police.[45] Applications for homesteads were also affected by the wartime conditions in Canada. On 14 December 1916 the cabinet ordered that applications for homesteads be granted only to British subjects or subjects of an allied or neutral country.[46] The order was amended on 3 April 1917 in recognition of the contribution of thousands of Ukrainians fighting in the Great War. The order allowed those alien enemies who had become naturalized since the beginning of the war and had fought for Canada to be eligible to apply for a homestead. The issue of homesteading once again appeared before the federal cabinet, which on 3 November 1917 passed an order repealing the other two and substituting provisions that required homestead applicants to be British, allied, or neutral subjects at the beginning of the war. But if an alien was naturalized during the Great War and was a member of the Canadian Expeditionary Force or had been honourably discharged from it the previous regulation would not apply.[47]

On 24 February 1917, the cabinet became concerned about the safety of docks, harbours, and ammunition factories and ordered that the chief commissioner of the Dominion Police could require any alien enemy or anyone who formerly was a subject of any nation His Majesty was at war with (undoubtedly to cover those who had become naturalized) 'not to reside, be employed or be in, at or about, or in the vicinity of any ammunition factory, fort, dock, harbour, when in the opinion of the Chief Commissioner the presence of such persons may be prejudicial to the public interest.'[48]

The order requiring alien enemies over the age of sixteen to register was expanded by the cabinet on 5 August 1918. By virtue of this order, Ukrainians were prevented from travelling from their homes without the permission of the local chief of police. If the person was given permission to travel he was required to report to the chief of police at his destination. These restrictions would not apply to those who were (1) maimed or crippled and thereby rendered unfit for military service, (2) 50 years of age or older, (3) Czechs or members of the Bohemian National Alliance, (4) Turkish subjects who are by race Greeks, Armenians, Syrians, or of other community well known as opposed to the Turkish regime and of Christian faith. The order also required an alien enemy to 'submit to reasonable inspection (of his certificate of parole) whenever required by any peace officer or military officer.' The definition of chief of police included constables of the RNWMP or provincial police, the registrar in Montreal and Winnipeg, as well as postmasters where there was no police officer within five miles. Although this order did not appear to impose a heavy burden on an alien enemy, it did greatly increase the chances of apprehension.

Internees were required to deposit with the authorities everything that could facilitate an escape. This included not only maps and knives but also jewellery and cash. These sums were deposited into a 'prisoner of war trust fund,' and ledgers were kept at the local level.[49] By the end of the war, $329,153.17 was deposited. Of this amount, $298,015.44 was returned, leaving $31,137.73 in the hands of the receiver-general.[50] On 1 July 1920 the offices of the Internment Operations Branch of the Department of Justice were closed, and a total of $94,1212.75 was deposited into a special account set up by cabinet directive on 17 March 1920. The figure included not only the cash confiscated by the authorities during the war but also moneys earned by the internees and never paid out to them. On 1 July 1920, the Internment Operations Branch of the Department of Justice, together with its funds and accounts, was transferred to the Department of the Secretary of State. On 30 June 1926 the government still had $32,418.55 in earnings and $3,017.09 in cash in its hands.[51]

Many of those arrested and detained held real and personal property. In a memorandum to the deputy minister of justice on 26 January 1916, the department expressed the opinion that it was not obligated to protect an internee's property. However, 'where control has been voluntarily assumed then an obligation is created not only to provide proper custody but also to apply any storage and other charges which may have been contractually created by reason of its own action.'

It is likely that Canadian citizens as well as enemy aliens were interned during the Great War. From the beginning of the war, the granting of naturalization was a contentious issue. When the cabinet made its order setting up the internment operations, the order included the requirement that to become naturalized an alien had to file a registration certificate. In response to an inquiry from a judge in Kenora, Ontario, regarding the withholding of certificates of naturalization from Ukrainian applicants, the deputy minister of justice said that all they had to do was comply with clause 11 of the October 1914 order. In 1915, 15,758 aliens were naturalized, of whom 2,402 were of enemy origin.[52] Some Canadians were not prepared to grant citizenship as easily as the government had suggested. In a letter to Borden the British Imperial Association of Earlscourt, Toronto, set out the following resolution: 'Resolved, that we, the British Imperial Association do herewith protest against the continuance of naturalization of Austrians and Germans in Canada during the present crisis in Europe, as we believe it is against the best interests of Canada and the Empire.'[53] On 3 February 1916, Otter requested the Justice Department to make a ruling 'as to whether naturalization certificates taken out subsequent to the declaration of war are sufficient grounds in themselves for releasing a Prisoner of War.' A copy of the certificate of a George Y. was enclosed with the letter.[54] The opinion of the acting deputy minister of justice was that because of the requirements of section 11 of the WMA, the consent of the minister was required before someone could be released. This was applicable notwithstanding the fact that George Y. was a naturalized British subject.

Several cabinet orders were also issued under the authority of section 6 of the WMA, which dealt with citizenship. On 17 July 1917 cabinet authorized the secretary of state to revoke a naturalization certificate if it had been issued improperly or as a result of fraud.[55] Any police officer or immigration official could seize the certificate of an alien leaving Canada if he believed that the certificate had been obtained improperly.

This power of seizure was restricted to certificates that had been issued since 1 August 1909. On 13 September 1917, cabinet considered a report from the secretary of state that recommended that because some judges were granting naturalization to alien enemies while others were not and because accurate naturalization records had not been kept before 1902, naturalization certificates should be issued to alien enemies who had lived in Canada for some time and who could show that they were loyal to the United Kingdom and its allies. The cabinet agreed.[56]

Matters relating to citizenship and internment were raised on a number of occasions in court. In *Re: Beranek* (1916), 25 DLR 564, Chief Justice Meredith of the Ontario Supreme Court dismissed an application for discharge from the internment camps. Beranek was a naturalized British subject who argued that only alien enemies could be held in military custody. To this line of argument the court replied that 'in extraordinary times, extraordinary laws' are passed and the rights of prisoners depend on those laws. Under section 11 of the WMA the minister of justice's permission is required before anyone detained as an alien enemy, or upon suspicion that he is one, can be released or tried. Justice Meredith further commented that when 'the law of the land confers upon the court or person any power, this court has no right to interfere with the exercise, in good faith, of that power; it is only when the power conferred is exceeded that this court can interfere; unless some right of appeal to it is also conferred ... in the stress and danger to the like of any nation in war, the courts should be exceeding careful not to hamper the action of those especially charged with the safety of the nation ... It is not a time when the prisoner is to have the benefit of the doubt.' The court refused to release Beranek even if his imprisonment was unlawful. It was for the minister of justice to consider the release, not the courts.

In *Re: Cimonian* (1915), 23 DLR 363, the Ontario Supreme Court considered an application for the naturalization of twelve aliens. Even though no one objected to the issuance of the certificate, Justice Meredith decided to withhold the certificates because Canada was at war with the country from which the applicants originated. The court reviewed the provisions of the Naturalization Act, RSC 1906, c. 77, which said that if no objection was filed, then the court would direct the certificate to be filed. If there was an objection, however, then the court was to hear the matter. The judge ignored the fact that there was no objection and stated that even without opposition a judge could not excuse himself from ensuring that everyone naturalized was carefully considered. The judge decided that the Naturalization Act did not apply to alien enemies. In this case, the court had exceeded its jurisdiction by instituting the inquiry into the matter in the first place and then considering the difference between alien friends and enemies. The court's true intent was to deny naturalization to alien enemies.

The issue of franchise was also raised during the Great War. Were enemy aliens to be allowed to vote while Canadians were fighting and dying in the trenches? The Borden government answered 'no' by passing the Wartime Elections Act, which received royal assent on 20 September 1917.[57] Unlike the WMA, the act was to be in force 'during the present war and until demobilization.' Although it granted women the vote, the Borden government added to the list of those who were to be disqualified from voting. Those disqualified now included: (1) anyone who conscientiously objected to combatant service; (2) Mennonites and Doukhobors, unless they were on active service with the Canadian Expeditionary Force; and (3) persons born in an enemy country and naturalized after 31 March 1902. The possible effect of these changes was that individuals who had lived in Canada for eighteen years might still not be able to vote. The debate in the House of Commons on the act was short. The only MP who objected to it was R. Lemieux (Maisonneuve, Gaspé), who on 22 April 1918 argued that 'Galicians should not be deprived of their right to exercise the franchise' and that this act was 'nothing else but a Hunnish and Kaiser-like measure.'[58]

Of the 8,579 internees listed in Otter's final report, 5,954 were Austro-Hungarians (mostly Ukrainians and some Croats, Slovaks, and Czechs), 99 Bulgarians, 205 Turks, 2,009 Germans, and 312 'miscellaneous.' By 1 June 1918 only 2,087 internees were still detained, of whom 469 were Austro-Hungarians and 1,582 Germans.[59] The release of over 6,000 internees by 1918 lends credence to Otter's statement that the municipalities had been unloading the unemployed on the federal government's doorstep. If these had been truly dangerous saboteurs, the government would not likely have released so many and of predominantly one nationality. Their employment during the war had not pleased everyone. Miss R.C. MacAdams, an MLA from Edmonton, was reported to have said to the *Toronto Telegram* on 27 April 1918 that 'it makes one feel very sad to visit the West now. You see the country being cleared of our fine Anglo-Saxon stock and the alien left to fatten on war prosperity. It is most disheartening. Out there aliens are getting as high as $16 a day. Some of them won't even loan their war earnings to the country. They bury it in the ground rather than do so. It's all very well for people to say that a great number of those aliens will develop into good Canadian citizens. But they should be sharing the sacrifice and service to-day.'[60]

The Ukrainian community's loyalty to the Dominion continued to be questioned throughout the war, and as a result there were numerous public meetings, resolutions, and letters.[61] Were the fears of Canadians justified? A review of RNWMP reports from across western Canada suggests otherwise. The report from the Wood Mountain district reads 'no fear need be entertained regarding [alien Slavs].' Calgary stated that although there were many Austrians and Germans, they had 'caused little trouble ... We have had the usual wild rumours of ... spies ... which on investigation were found to be without foundation.' The Yorkton district reported that aliens were 'behaving themselves.' Numerous investigations had been conducted into suspicious actions of persons of alien nationality, but they had turned out to be 'foolish talk.' The Weyburn district report noted that numerous alarms had been raised, but that 'in every case it was found that there was nothing to the complaint or else that the matter had been greatly exaggerated.'[62] During the five years of war, few if any fires, explosions, or railway accidents were proved to be caused by alien enemies, even though most such occurrences were attributed to them. This had not prevented northern Ontario communities from petitioning the government for mass internment or the miners at the Crow's Nest Pass Coal Company in Fernie, British Columbia, from going on strike until the company fired its German and Ukrainian employees.[63] (After their dismissal, the local internment registrar promptly ordered them interned.)[64]

The internment of Ukrainians in the First World War was a grave injustice against a people who had come to contribute to the opening of western Canada. Hard-working people who came looking for freedom and prosperity found instead a hostile land, not only in physical terms but also in the treatment they received. The attitudes of Canadian society were informed by economic conditions in Canada and political conditions abroad. In spite of the stated intentions for the introduction of the War Measures Act, it soon served as a convenient means for municipalities to clean their streets of the unemployed and for labour organizations to rid themselves and their members of cheap competition. The emergency powers were also used by the police to detain persons whom the existing laws did not encompass.[65] In time of war Canadians should expect certain restrictions on their day-to-day living and movement about Canada. However, the restrictions that were progressively imposed upon all Canadians, and specifically upon Ukrainians, went beyond any measures required to ensure law and order in Canada during the First World War. In times of crisis, it is the responsibility of any government to ensure that the measures it takes do not protect the majority at the expense of a minority.[66]

British-Canadian Intellectuals, Ukrainian Immigrants, and Canadian National Identity

BARRY FERGUSON

To understand the experiences of immigrant peoples it is necessary to appreciate relations between the existing residents, the so-called host peoples, and the waves of immigrants, the new peoples. These relations include the ideas about nationality, ethnicity, and ethnic relations held by the host peoples and the newcomers. The ideas of the host peoples are particularly important in the Canadian case for two reasons. First, Canadian society historically has been characterized by a high degree of social, economic, and political hierarchy. In John Porter's classic formulation, Canada was a 'vertical mosaic' in which a British-Canadian elite dominated, although only by complex alliances with other ethnic, class, and territorial groupings. Thus the views of British Canadians as a distinct cultural group, and not just English-speaking Canadians of any origin, were those of the dominant group in Canadian society during the periods of post-Confederation immigration.[1] Second, Canadian society has never been characterized by a high degree of agreement about its national purposes or even its national identity. As Ramsay Cook has explained, Canadians have continually debated the distinctive purposes of and unifying factors in Canadian society. Unlike such 'predetermined' nations as France or the United States, assured about their mission and identity during the nineteenth and twentieth centuries of nationalism, Canada is a 'self-determined' country that has been involved since 1867 in awkward debates about its purposes and identity.[2] Therefore, the views of the host peoples towards the newer peoples are part of the continuing debate over the content of nationalism in Canada. In sum, the ideas of British Canadians towards Ukrainian Canadians, voluminous and reflective as they are, not only illustrate a minor aspect of the totality of historical experience, the 'climate of opinion,' but lead to the effort of national definition that has characterized Canada and its intelligentsia for so long.

The study of opinions and attitudes is notoriously susceptible to the sample the researcher takes. The subject of British-Canadian attitudes towards Ukrainian Canadians is, therefore, utterly dependent on the sources of British-Canadian views that are used. In this study, British-Canadian opinions are those found among members of the intellectual community of British as opposed to merely English-speaking Canada. It includes the contributions of commentators on political, social, and economic affairs writing in magazines and books during the main period of Ukrainian immigration to Canada, from the 1890s to the 1950s. This body of opinion includes academic and public affairs writing from historians, economists, geographers, sociologists, clergy, literary critics, folklorists, and publicists. The writers are in fact the main group whose views have usually been used to describe Canadian attitudes towards immigrants in the major studies of immigration and nationalist thought in Canada.[3] Almost all the four dozen writers surveyed are men; one-seventh are women: two folklorists, one economist, one historian, and three sociologists. The study excludes fiction and anything approaching popular, mass opinion, including newspaper writing.

The academic and public affairs commentators examined for this essay offered views of Ukrainians in Canada that purported to be informed analyses based on careful observation and logical consideration of issues. Their self-defined purposes were uniformly to explain to their readers both the broad characteristics of immigrant peoples, particularly Ukrainians in our sources, and the ways in which Ukrainians and other 'new Canadians' were adjusting to Canadian society, ways that were both positive and negative. Writer after writer between the age of Laurier and the time of St Laurent contrasted popular opinion, usually said to be critical about Ukrainians, and their informed opinion, always offered as measured and authoritative. This stance is found at the beginning of the period under review in J.S. Woodsworth, writing in 1909 to inform the 'ordinary Canadian' about immigrant peoples, and towards the end, when Young and Reid in 1931 contrasted the ignorant and insular 'man in the street' with their reassuring study of Ukrainian social adaptation to Canada.[4]

The remarkable point here – and it can be found in virtually all the reflective studies commenting on Ukrainian Canadians – is that the tone adopted is a position of mediation and information. The writers surveyed take the position of mediators between the host peoples and the new Canadians, carefully defining their role as identifying the important characteristics of the new peoples and their relations to the resident British-Canadian populace. What emerges in almost all cases, however, is that the writers move from providing a kind of introduction service to defining a 'problem' of new Canadian–old Canadian relations and then to resolving that problem by way of a programme of shaping a new national culture.[5] In moving from description to prescription, of course, the writers reveal, as suggested earlier, much more about their own attitudes and their own British-Canadian society than about the Ukrainian-Canadian society they claim to be examining.[6]

Those commentators whose objections to immigration were very strong virtually never bothered to single out any one group of people for condemnation; they found objections in all peoples based on cultural or class attributes. Critics of immigration like the McGill University medical historian and editor Andrew Macphail or the Queen's University literature professor J.R. Conn attacked British as much as European immigration because it meant the addition of socially and culturally undesirable peoples.[7] Even mere sceptics about immigration like the United College historian Arthur Lower and his mentor, the Queen's economist Adam Shortt, simply took a rigid economic determinist position to argue that cheap immigrant labour drove out dearer native labour.[8] The tendency to criticize all immigration and incidentally immigrants was so pronounced that one federal immigration official, W.D. Scott, argued that there were deficiencies in almost all immigrant groups, including such diverse peoples as the British and the 'Ruthenians,' particularly because of their alleged tendencies to migrate to urban rather than rural locations and thus become sources of public expense.[9]

Such criticism and the distinction between 'preferred' and 'non-preferred' immigrants were, of course, central to Canadian immigration thinking and policy until the seventies. But for every xenophobic critic of immigrants as well as immigration, there was a proponent of both the peoples and the process, however grudging. For every Hugh John Macdonald, a Manitoba Conservative who sat in opposition and railed against the creation of a 'mongrel race' due to Central European immigration, there was a Clifford Sifton, a Manitoba Liberal who shaped government policy and supported, despite his condescension, the 'men in sheepskin coats' as economically and culturally desirable. For each A.J. Hunter, the Presbyterian medical missionary who planned to unseat the Orthodox rite, there was a James Mavor, the Toronto political economist who championed a refugee policy to allow at least some Slavs the chance to enjoy religious liberty in Canada and defended the Galicians as 'important agents' of agricultural settlement.[10]

The point here is not just that critical and favourable commentary should be balanced but that there was something more than simply a set of ethnocentric comments about the European peoples. As one recent study of the British promotional literature on prairie settlement has noted, even before 1914 British observers admitted despite all their self-assurance that they were viewed with unalloyed hostility by large numbers of Canadians. This was due both to prejudice against the working-class and pauper origins of many and to an emergent Canadian national resentment against the British.[11] If selective quotations from historical sources can portray the British as undesirable immigrants, historians should be wary about simply cataloguing bigoted comments and hateful judgments. The task must be to understand the presuppositions and attitudes that lay behind the rather promiscuous opinions that even supposedly informed writers presented.

Still, it must be noted that very few commentators on immigration or immigrant peoples in Canada prior to the Second World War argued against racial barriers based on the tripartite division of people into the more or less preferred white and the completely unpreferred black and yellow, again epitomized by W.D. Scott's 1913 survey of the effects of immigration on the Canadian population.[12] That particular basis for distinction between peoples, however, was virtually never employed against European groups, at least not by the respectable authorities whose books and essays are examined in this paper. Edwin Bradwin alluded to harsher popular opinion in noting that in the labour camps on the mining and forestry frontier in the twenties, there were two groups of workers: 'whites,' meaning Canadian, British, and American employees, and 'foreigners,' meaning all the others.[13] But allusions to popular attitudes aside, whatever hostility and criticism there was towards Ukrainians or other Europeans remained totally different from the suspicion and condemnation of Asians and blacks found among the intelligentsia.

The special place of Ukrainians among the new Canadians was that they were most often referred to in the examinations by British-Canadian commentators of the characteristics of European migration after 1900 and its effects on Canada. While identified as part of a vast shift in the source of Canadian immigrants after 1900 from Western to Central Europe, Ukrainians were the one group most often fastened upon by Canadian commentators as emblematic of the shift in Canada's population. Watson Kirkconnell, the university professor and translator of Ukrainian poetry, casually summed up in 1967 his extended reflections and forty years of attention to Ukrainian Canadians by describing their settlement as a 'typical example' of the immigrant experience.[14] A more passionate contemporary observer, the University of Toronto classicist and United Farmers of Ontario strategist C.B. Sissons, held in 1917 that Ukrainian claims to language rights in Manitoba schools had the effect of making clear the entire issue of all language rights in Canada, including the French-English conflicts that threatened to tear Canada apart.[15]

More recent scholarly observers have followed this course. Elizabeth Wangenheim, in a 1965 study of Canadian nationalism, claimed that the 'Ukrainians' were the 'loudest,' most 'vigorous,' and best 'organized' and therefore the most important of the non-British and non-French peoples in reshaping Canadians' thinking about their nationhood.[16] This opinion is all the more remarkable because it is so typical, finding an echo among historians as otherwise removed chronologically and philosophically as W.L. Morton, who noted in 1957 the 'assertive' and 'aggressive' place of Ukrainians among immigrants, and G.A. Friesen, who was willing in 1985 to grant Ukrainian Canadians almost the entire credit for the emergence of multiculturalism as a Canadian policy since the sixties.[17] In sum, the Ukrainian Canadians emerge as virtually the test-case, and certainly a 'case study' in Young and Reid's 1931 work and in Wangenheim's 1965 usage of the results of the new immigration during the first half of the century.

What was it that led to the distinction of the Ukrainians among the post-1900 European immigrants? This question leads to the three major issues that commentators on Ukrainian and other European immigration focused on in the first half of the twentieth century. First, what were the traits of the society that was hosting these new peoples? Second, what distinguished Ukrainians as a people? Third, how would the new people and the established population interact with one another? These questions are central to the attitudes of British Canadians to Ukrainian Canadians.

In a review of Canadian national life written during the stress of the First World War, the Winnipeg Methodist clergyman J.S. Woodsworth reflected that 'a great wedge of foreigners' had been driven into Canadian community life 'before the French and English had been thoroughly unified.' He elaborated on this in his preface to Sissons's study of the bilingual schools issue that so divided wartime Canada in 1917.

There he noted that the great national problem was 'developing a community life' in Canada.[18]

Perhaps because he assumed that devising some form of common Canadian society was the goal of the French and British in Canada, Woodsworth made clear two presuppositions that permeated British-Canadian commentary on all immigration, particularly Ukrainian immigration, during the period of mass migration. His main assumption was that immigrants should be assimilated into Canadian society. The dimensions of this goal of assimilation received considerable attention from Canadian writers, and it referred variously to cultural as well as economic and political coalescence among the various peoples of Canada. This goal of assimilation, however, was vitiated from the outset by a second presupposition. Canada, Woodsworth and his successors admitted, remained a particularly unformed as well as ill-formed nation. The absence of either the political or cultural traits of autonomy struck Woodsworth during the Great War, and the development of these traits would occupy the attention of most writers in succeeding decades.[19]

It was the tension between their goal of assimilation and their observation that Canadian society was weakly equipped to assimilate Ukrainians or any other peoples that animated most of the writings on the relations between British and Ukrainian Canadians during the period from the 1900s to the 1950s. Lower summarized this inability to assimilate in characteristic British-Canadian fashion in his social history of Canada: 'the foreign immigration of the twentieth century upset a society just nicely getting on its feet and introduced a range of social problems whose settlement would take many decades.'[20] If Lower criticized immigration alone, his fellow historian Edgar McInnis, surveying Canadian history in 1947, also archly referred to the way in which the immigrants emerged in the prairies as a 'conglomeration of racial groups' that may have led to economic success but also to intractable social problems.[21] For his part, W.L. Morton, the doyen of Canadian historians during the mid-twentieth century, referred rather disparagingly in his history of Manitoba to the 'polyglot mosaic of diverse peoples, especially Slavs,' whose presence began a 'testing of Canadian nationality.'[22] This propensity to look to the characteristics of the new peoples as somehow a source of the difficulty of assimilation, manifested by the historians Lower, McInnis, and Morton, was precisely the motivation for dozens of writers to try to identify the peculiar traits of Ukrainians and their place within Canada.

The identification of the Ukrainians and their chief traits led British-

Canadian writers towards two issues. First, they had to try to name
the people and therefore to decide upon criteria for distinguishing
Ukrainians from other Central European people. Second, they isolated
key cultural traits of Ukrainians, a task that usually led them to emphasize two aspects of the Ukrainians in Canada.

By the late fifties, Lower admitted, there was a remarkable religious,
spatial, and even ethnic diversity among Ukrainian Canadians. He noted
that they were 'so diverse that the one feature of which we can be sure
is their mother tongue.'[23] Most observers in the previous half-century
were less observant and less cautious in identifying Ukrainians. Indeed,
agreement on the term 'Ukrainian' did not emerge until after the First
World War, and even then, the historian John Thompson recently noted,
the word was misspelled in the census report of 1921.[24]

Before the Great War, most British Canadians wrote of 'Galicians,'
'Buckovinians,' 'Ruthenians,' or, more rarely, 'Little Russians.' They thus
used a mixture of geographical and linguistic categories to identify a
distinctive people.[25] The means by which a common name was imposed
was not fully explained by post-war writers, but they almost all began
to use 'Ukrainians' as the common term. The tendency of Canadian
writers was, however, to refer to ethnographic work on the 'Slavic'
peoples – basically as a linguistic distinction – to identify the Ukrainian
sub-group. Here the uniqueness of Ukrainians remained muted since, as
W.T. Baumgartner stated in 1930, Ukrainians in Canada were interesting
because they were 'the most typical Slav people.'[26] The sociologist Edwin
Bradwin claimed that they were 'the best type of Slav grouping,' awkward praise but praise nonetheless. But they usually were described as
Ukrainians after 1918.[27]

Even though J.T.M. Anderson, the Saskatchewan educational official,
retained the term 'Ruthenian' in his 1918 study of the 'education of the
new Canadians,' he approached the second issue of British-Canadian
commentators, the identification of the distinctions of the Ruthenians.
In fact, he relied upon a vociferously pro-Slavic study of ethnic adaptation into the United States by Emily Balch, the Wellesley College political
economist, to depict the physical and cultural characteristics of the
Slavic peoples. Balch condemned the American goal of assimilation
and the opposed powerful anti-immigration organizations and their
prominent academic ideologues.[28] Nevertheless her account of Slavic
peoples relied on common clichés about racial traits that conflated individual and group attributes. Anderson's quotation from Balch is worth
reading because it indicated two major features of the description of
Ukrainians and other European immigrant peoples.

The Slavs were, Anderson quoted from Balch, 'short, thick-set and stocky, rather than the reverse; not graceful or light in motion. The face is broad, with wide-set eyes and marked cheek-bones; the nose broad and snub rather than chiselled or aquiline; the expression ranging from sullen to serene, but seldom animated or genial. The eyes are of a distinct shade, grey inclining to blue. One often sees these honest grey eyes in the dark-faced, dark-haired Croatians or Bosnians, as well as in the blonder northerners. The hair ... is light in childhood ... and with added years it turns to a deep brown, darkening gradually through successive ash-brown shades. The whole suggestion is of strength, trustworthiness, and a certain stolidity, until excitement or emotion lights up the naturally rather unexpressive features.'[29]

There are at least two peculiarities to the attributed characteristics of Central Europeans. The first was the tendency to move from a linguistic classification towards a physical and cultural one. The ease with which writers during the entire first half of the twentieth century embraced broad physical as well as cultural criteria to distinguish ethnicity was remarkable. The second peculiarity was the willingness to derive character traits from physical and social traits. Such confident attribution of individual and group behaviour was insulting enough to those being judged, but even more disorienting was the mixture of criticism and praise that the attributions almost invariably involved. This mixture applied, of course, to all peoples, British as well as European.

Both these practices – broad physical and cultural attributions of ethnic identity and judgment of individual behaviour and character in light of the groups' traits – occur in virtually all writings on Ukrainians in Canada at least until the sixties. The persistence of such crude attributions of ethnic and individual identity, however, deserves careful attention in the Ukrainian case because of what it reveals more about the disposition of British Canadians. It was more than simply a form of ethnocentrism or racialism, or Canadian variations of social Darwinism or ethnic nationalism, the point at which most work thus far done seems to stop.[30] What the attributions seem to be more important for is precisely the continuing manifestation of that deep unease about the strength of the society and people who were host to the new residents. The fixation upon the weakness of Canadian identity, therefore, was manifested in the classification and judgment of ethnic groups.

Some writers, including several most sympathetic to the problems and identity of Ukrainians, actually used the racialist categories of such strongly anti-immigration writers in the United States as Madison Grant, although without specific attribution to them. Thus both the translator and professor Watson Kirkconnell and the CPR immigration agent Robert England identified the Ukrainians as part of the 'Alpine' sub-group of Europeans, the other two groups being the 'Nordic' and the 'Mediterranean.' Although neither writer dwelt upon the physical or cultural deficiencies of the 'Alpine' peoples, their effort to delineate broad physical, linguistic, and cultural types was indicative of a tendency to reduce peoples to presumed forms. Kirkconnell and England, it should be remembered, specifically denied special virtues to any of the three peoples as such, whatever their biases were, and these were many.[31]

Two aspects of Ukrainian-Canadian society, however, drew special attention from British-Canadian writers. The first was that Ukrainians were seen as having a propensity to hard work beyond that of other peoples. The second was that Ukrainians were said to have a particular devotion to schooling. Each was central to the reactions of British Canadians.

Writer after writer from the settlement period to today has claimed that a remarkable devotion to hard work characterized Ukrainians. Woodsworth admitted that they were providing 'much of the rough-work of nation-building' even when he criticized an apparent tendency towards crime and drink. He did admit that 'centuries of poverty' in Europe had degraded Ukrainians whereas opportunities in Canada had made them 'ambitious' and 'patient and industrious.' For his part the Anglican clergyman Burgon Bickersteth was amazed at the extraordinary devotion to hard work that 'Galicians' demonstrated in Alberta.[32]

By the thirties, writers emphasized that the Ukrainian settler was, in the words of the folklorist J.M. Gibbon, both an 'excellent pioneer' and a 'great asset to the Dominion.' Even a critical student of prairie settlement, the Brown University historian J.B. Hedges, confidently asserted that the Ukrainians, 'while not the most intelligent farmers in the country ... were industrious and thrifty, and played an important part in the ultimate conquest of the prairie.' He did allow that Ukrainians had an 'essential honesty,' unlike the attribution of criminality that Woodsworth had made. Indeed, almost all authorities in the twenties and thirties, such as Robert England, strongly refuted Woodsworth's charge of criminality.[33]

If Ukrainians were said to work hard, Ukrainian women were seen as especially devoted to labour. Writer after writer noted with astonishment the hard physical labour that Ukrainian women contributed to the household and farm during the settlement period. This characteristic of Ukrainian women, however, was somewhat grudgingly admired. The sociologists quoted economists' work suggesting that the work of

Ukrainian women was much more valuable than any hired labour. Their labour did not indicate the greater autonomy of Ukrainian women, though, because strong patriarchal authority meant that women's labour, particularly gardening, was a contribution to the family income controlled by men. Indeed, several commentators identified Ukrainians as preserving a peculiarly 'European' hierarchy in the relations between men and women, husbands and wives, which apparently contrasted with the equal relations between Canadian men and women.[34]

This intense economic activity meant that Ukrainian women were not seen as the conservators of the folk culture that women usually were in both Ukrainian and other social groups. This of course indicated how economic participation eroded traditional culture and facilitated assimilation. Economic contributions again seemed to exact a price from Ukrainian women, in this case their domestic cultural role, although no study of Ukrainians claimed that women were actually spared household chores. Young women from rural families were said to have migrated to cities in large numbers. There they found work as domestic or clerical workers, furthering their integration into Canada economically and culturally.[35]

Many observers followed the lead of J.W. Dafoe and noted that there was a Ukrainian propensity to avoid the open plains and settle on parkland often less amenable to grain cultivation than to mixed farming. Such prudence would have pleased older economic liberals critical of prairie settlement, writers like Adam Shortt, but it led later commentators to find a degree of economic marginality among Ukrainian and other Central European settlers of the parklands.[36] Thus the sociologist R.W. Murchie from the University of Minnesota noted the Ukrainians' proclivity to settle on bush land and create for themselves even greater labours than other settlers. Murchie did think that the Ukrainians' economic success was the result of their commendable labour, which partly overcame their initial commercial disadvantages in paying too much for and settling upon second-rate land.[37]

However, work by Murchie and a collaborator, the Manitoba economist H.C. Grant, was often cited to prove the extraordinary success Ukrainian settlers made of their settlements. Their hard work on marginal land may have limited their acquisition of capital, but it increased their moral stock with British-Canadian writers like J.M. Gibbon. Curiously, the tendency to group or bloc settlement seldom drew any attention from the reflective British-Canadian writers; bloc settlement was not blamed on the Ukrainians even if it was somewhat regretted, and its effects were usually defended. England recalled of the thirties that some economists had criticized his own defence of bloc settlement as economically as well as socially beneficial to Ukrainians.[38]

Another trait of Ukrainians that pointed to their distinctiveness in Canada was their devotion to education and educational rights. Here both their commitment to education and their willingness to use Manitoba's tolerant pre-1917 language laws to sponsor Ukrainian-language schools drew attention. In 1913, a period in which much popular debate focused on both the weaknesses of the public school system and the tendency of immigrants to avoid compulsory education, Walter Murray, the president of the University of Saskatchewan, praised the enthusiasm for education that Ukrainians demonstrated.[39] Murray had admitted a certain initial resistance among the 'Ruthenians' to public schooling, and later writers often noted the remarkable shift among Ukrainians from an initial hostility to considerable devotion to education for their children. Young and Reid contrasted an initial peasantry's antagonism to schooling with a new settler community's 'hunger' for educational opportunity.[40]

Devotion to education would seem to have been highly desirable, but there was one disadvantage to the Ukrainian love of education. The fact that Ukrainians took full advantage of Manitoba educational policies to establish Ukrainian-language schools was much commented on by British Canadians. Sissons bluntly stated in 1917 that 'in Manitoba the French question meets the Ukrainian question and the Mennonite question.' He then concluded that 'the Red River Valley is the cockpit of the whole language controversy.' In other words, the issue of whether there was going to be one common language and therefore culture not only in Manitoba but elsewhere in English-speaking Canada was the issue that Ukrainian – as well as French and Mennonite – devotion to language led to. Writing at the height of French-English conflict during the Great War, Sissons concluded that English-language education must be paramount everywhere except in Quebec.[41]

Forty years later, W.L. Morton suggested there was a potential for social breakdown in the assertion of non-English-language educational rights. This danger ended only when Manitoba acted to enforce English-language schooling. Foreseeing 'chaos' and discerning ominous ethnic nationalist ambitions for the prairies, Morton argued that a common language was essential to the cultural and educational well-being of Manitoba and the other parts of Canada (presumably excepting Quebec) where non-English speakers had asserted language education rights.[42] Curiously, both Sissons and Morton held that manipulative interests – clerical and European-inspired nationalists – among the Ukrainian peo-

ples actively promoted Ukrainian educational rights. Sissons in particular suggested that only the 'agitators' sought special language rights
whereas the majority of settlers were content with the public English-
language schools.[43] It remained an open question as to whether the
agitators or the masses would triumph even within Ukrainian-Canadian
society.

Regardless of their particular interpretations of minority language
rights and their effects on either the minorities or the majority, writers
like Sissons and Morton had one concern about the tendency of Ukrainians to seek certain educational rights. This concern was that the Ukrainian devotion to education would actually subvert the major purpose
of education, which was its role as an agency of cultural transformation.
To Sissons and Morton, like a number of British-Canadian commentators, English-language education in the public schools was a crucial
force leading to the assimilation of the Ukrainians and all non-English-
speaking people into a new common culture.

But if Ukrainians tended to resist this cultural transformation, if they
were in fact distinguished as a people by a remarkable degree of cultural
self-preservation, were they not subverting the very possibilities of
Canadian society? With this question, then, the main problem of the
interaction of the British and Ukrainian Canadians is at last raised.

One of the most influential examinations of the relations between
British Canadians and new Canadians, particularly Ukrainians (although perhaps notorious is more appropriate a term given its glosses
by historians), was undertaken in 1918 by the Saskatchewan school
administrator J.T.M. Anderson. Anderson's main goal in strengthening
the school system was to make the public school the 'greatest agency in
racial assimilation.' He continued, in perhaps the most significant passage in his book on educating new Canadians, by arguing that the
schools were the 'great melting pot into which must be placed these
diverse racial groups and from which will emerge the pure gold of
Canadian citizenship.'[44]

When Anderson turned to consider the 'Ruthenians' and their disposition towards his goals, he found them to be utterly committed to them.
Ukrainians, he found, 'have settled down with a view to adopting our
system of government and our various educational institutions. They
are satisfied with their new home, and we may anticipate that their
descendants will prove a most valuable contribution to our future Canadian life and citizenship.'[45] Almost every other writer who directly
addressed the issue of assimilation from the twenties to the fifties voiced
similar assurances. Thus, Robert England claimed that the Central Euro-

pean immigrant population was committed to assimilation.[46] The virtual inevitability of assimilation was often explained as a part of the generational experience of immigrants, so that by the third generation, in Kirkconnell's words, Ukrainians were 'almost indistinguishably Canadian.' Or, as Young and Reid put it in identifying a two-generation process, the second generation no longer felt a 'longing' for Europe.[47] The curious aspect of writings like Anderson's or England's that proposed programmes of educational and cultural assimilation was that they were based on the premise that the project was assured given several generations. Whereas writers examined the social conditions of immigrant communities or the schools before 1918 with some fear, the writers who later addressed the situation ended up so optimistic that the problem seemed scarcely to exist.

Why was this so? The answer to this curious situation is found in their understanding of 'assimilation.' First, they saw assimilation as a lengthy historical process. Second, many British-Canadian writers reinterpreted assimilation between the twenties and forties more as a political and economic than as a social and cultural process. The sociologist Eva Younge, heavily influenced by American social scientists tolerant of ethnic differences, noted in 1944 that assimilation more properly referred to political than to cultural adaptation, although earlier writers like the psychologist W.G. Smith understood assimilation to involve both cultural and political change.[48] The result was that many Canadian writers thought that assimilation involved the long-term social and genetic 'blending' of all of Canada's peoples, the equally long-term creation of a similarly blended Canadian culture, and the recognition of how the material environment had already reshaped the political and economic behaviour of all Canadians. The consequences of their interwar reinterpretation of assimilation led to the goal of finding a concept of 'Canadian citizenship' to unite the various peoples of Canada. It was this goal that writers like Anderson, England, Young, and many others sought to achieve between the twenties and the forties.

In the cases of Anderson and England, the demands for cultural change were admitted as taking time and as involving mutual accommodation and changes. In this they were following a line of argument first taken by Woodsworth, whose admission that there was no Canadian culture to which new Canadians might assimilate made it necessary for all residents of Canada, established or new, to work for the creation of a common culture.[49] But rather than lament the absence of a Canadian culture or citizenship, and here there was clear if tacit recognition of a legal as well as a social fact of considerable significance to Canada in the twenties and thirties, British-Canadian writers searched for the grounds to create one.

The celebrated metaphor that J.M. Gibbon used as the theme of his 1938 study of Canadian ethnic cultures, the 'mosaic,' was designed precisely as a model for the future common culture that Canada should evolve. It was most assuredly not an interpretation of cultural relations as merely comprising the sum of the individual pieces or ethnic cultures that made it up, despite Canadian historians' efforts to interpret Gibbon this way.[50]

Gibbon's explanation of his 'mosaic' began with an admission that the Canada of 1938 remained 'a decorated surface, bright with inlays of separate coloured pieces.' But he had already staked a more complete claim to cultural regeneration in explaining that the mosaic was becoming a new amalgamation of the peoples of Canada: 'The Canadian race of the future is being superimposed on the original native Indian races and is being made up of over thirty European racial groups, each of which has its own history, customs and traditions. Some politicians want to see these merged as quickly as possible into one standard type ... Others believe in trying to preserve for the future Canadian race the most worthwhile qualities and traditions that each racial group has brought with it.'[51]

To Gibbon, biological as well as cultural assimilation of all groups of Canadians was already occurring, and the need was to accept the outcome, precisely the demand of Anderson with his goal of a melting pot and England with his goal of mutual accommodation. But above all, for Gibbon as for Anderson and others, there was little doubt that the worry expressed by pre-1918 social scientists and humanists (and especially by inter-war public health commentators and anti-immigration agitators concentrated in medicine, social work, and biology) was abandoned by the post-1918 mainstream of Canadian intellectuals educated in the liberal arts. In other words, the eugenic concern with 'racial purity' was not felt by public affairs writers on immigrant relations.[52]

It is striking that reflective Canadian writers expressed no revulsion against the mingling of the European peoples and even praised the goal of biological hybridization. As the Saskatchewan historian G.W. Simpson described it in 1944, the result of the mingling of peoples was the 'blending' of traditions and the formation of an entirely new population at least in the Canadian prairies. Another historian commented that the same 'blending' had already occurred among the diverse peoples of the Maritimes.[53]

The results of the cultural and demographic blending British Canadians sought were suggested by a most reassuring analogy. Aptly enough, given the history of Canadian suspicion of the United States, Canadians did not use the American model of a 'melting pot,' even though they used the term on occasion. The national model often used was that of the United Kingdom, a state whose ethnic composition probably did not readily strike mid-twentieth-century readers as varied. Yet writer after writer referred to the United Kingdom as an amalgam of peoples. The most tireless exponent of this position was England, who time and again drew upon the many ethnic origins of the modern population of the United Kingdom during the past two thousand years.[54] Kirkconnell thought to add that France was an ethnic pot-pourri and offered both nations as models for the Canada of the future. The demographer Burton Hurd meanwhile reminded Canadians that all races and peoples were the products of considerable 'racial and cultural fusion,' thus making mockery of the notion of a Canadian 'race.'[55]

Adding to the relevance of the British model were similarities between the Ukrainians and two major ethnic groups, indeed nations, in the United Kingdom, the Scots and the Irish. Kirkconnell, England, Young, and Reid compared Ukrainians and Irish with approval for their tenacious commitment to cultural preservation and achievement. Kirkconnell's Ukrainians were the 'Irish of the new world,' while England's Ukrainians were rather like the nineteenth-century Irish of Canada in their cultural distinctiveness. Young and Reid, meanwhile, identified Ukrainians as the 'Irishmen of Russia.'[56] By not elaborating on Irish-Ukrainian similarities, however, the writers seemed content to let readers draw their own conclusions about whether the parallel suggested a happy or a difficult future for Canada.

Comparison with the Scots was also made. Young and Reid did so to draw attention to their common veneration of culture and history. Governor-General Lord Tweedsmuir, a Scot, compared the Ukrainians and the Scots as the leavening peoples in larger federations, the Ukrainians for Canada, the Scots for the United Kingdom.[57] The parallels all suggested that the cultural identity the Ukrainians maintained would be no more worrisome and no less valuable than those of the Irish and the Scots in Canada, a point that Scottish and Irish Canadians at least might have found blunting their worries about Ukrainians.

As for the broader subject of the 'fusion of races,' as Young and Reid put it, the social effects of intermarriage and simple coexistence were foreseen with considerable favour, and contributed to the belief that within two or three generations the basic outlook of Ukrainian Canadians would be Canadian.[58] Ralph Connor, in the preface to his rather infamous novelistic portrait of Ukrainians, *The Foreigner*, wrote tolerantly of his hope that 'out of breeds diverse in tradition, in ideals, in speech, and in manner of life, Saxon and Slav, Teuton, Celt and Gaul, one people is being made.'[59] Woodsworth was more cautious about the pace at which one people was being made, but he did observe in 1917 that 'if ever one type is evolved it will be catholic enough to incorporate in itself the best elements in the various peoples who are making Canada their home.'[60]

Later social scientists offered some data on family structure and fertility patterns if not endogamy and exogamy rates to support their claims. The McMaster demographer and economist Burton Hurd and the McGill sociologist Eva Younge confidently slid into the comfortable view that the change between the first and second generations of Central Europeans was from European to Canadian forms of behaviour. Younge emphasized that this inter-generational change presented a painful enough adjustment for families that was somewhat 'tragic' because of differences between extremely paternalistic fathers and children whose attitudes and goals were almost totally Canadian.[61]

So confident were commentators about the forces of assimilation that W.G. Smith, the author of two guides to immigrant peoples, seemed to plead for the preservation of cultural traits among the immigrants and into the second generation. He argued in 1920 that 'the cultivation of that national spirit which is Canada need not in the slightest interfere with the tender memories that remain in the heart of the new citizen for the land of his birth.'[62] Two years later he honed his point in reflecting upon the special cultural goals of Ukrainians, claiming that 'devotion to [Ukrainian nationalism] is the promise and potency of devotion to [Canadian nationalism].'[63] Others emphasized the theme that the preservation of tradition was a means for the successful adaptation and psychological well-being of Ukrainians. Young and Reid in particular warned that without the preservation of some forms of their cultural identity, Ukrainian Canadians would actually be 'hopelessly handicapped for participation in any form of activity in our society,' an ominous warning indeed, but quite the opposite to the assimilationist position so often attributed to contemporary writers by historians.[64] For his part, England was worried more about the effects on Canadian national development of 'prejudice' against cultural differences than by the differences themselves, again quite the opposite of the alarmed and intolerant nativist position so often identified by historians as predominant.[65] Interestingly enough, Young and Reid, the sociologists, Smith, a psychologist, and England, a teacher, were all chiefly concerned with healthy social adjustment before political and economic integration.

There is another reason than just social adjustment that led some British Canadians to encourage Ukrainian-Canadian culture. By the twenties, a number of British Canadians had completed translations of Ukrainian-language writing and thus realized that the Ukrainian literary culture was extremely large and articulate. Throughout the twenties, both literary critics and, of all people, politicians referred to the rich culture of Ukrainian society, which showed the antiquity, the articulation, and the achievements of Ukrainian peoples. These characteristics were remarkable in themselves and especially so in comparison with an indigenous Canadian literature and culture whose history, size, and quality were limited but increasingly identified as an emergent strength of Canada.[66] As a result, authorities like Gibbon and Kirkconnell drew the conclusion that strands of European culture like the Ukrainian one were going to be important components of the Canadian cultural achievement that would be necessary for a successful national identity and national life. Just as the national identity to which all would contribute was posited in the fusion of all the peoples of Canada, so the cultural life to which all might adhere would have to be built upon the participation of all groups.

Commentators like Kirkconnell who looked to ethnic literary culture were reasonably hopeful about the future cultural development of the nation precisely because of the cultural identity of groups like Ukrainians. Far from just worrying over the existing inadequacies of Canadian cultural life, then, the literary commentators were hopeful for the future growth of Canadian culture because of contributions from both host peoples and new peoples.

British Canadians grew more hopeful for one other reason. They had identified by the forties a form of assimilation that lay outside the cultural and social areas that had been the focus of so much debate until the thirties. In the thirties, geographers, economists, and sociologists completed a considerable body of scientific work on prairie agricultural settlement and had therefore attentively studied the economic and social experience of the settlers. The consistent conclusion of these studies was that the adaptation to the distinctive physical and economic environment had in the most important ways shaped the political and economic behaviour of all the social groups that had settled the prairies.

The key works were social scientific studies of prairie settlement.[67] The Queen's economic historian W.A. Mackintosh explained how well

Ukrainian settlers adapted economically to the 'wooded country' and 'park belt' most familiar to them. Mackintosh remarked on the tendency of all the European groups to form 'cultural islands which have retarded the progress of assimilation,' but he saw this as delaying but not postponing a more essential form of assimilation. This assimilation was to the market economy, which was the only basis of continued viable settlement in the prairies. Integration into the market economy, moreover, led to the political as well as economic integration of all prairie peoples into Canada's liberal capitalist political and economic order.[68]

Sociologists were even more assertive; the McGill professors C.A. Dawson and Eva Younge emphasized that the economic and physical environment greatly altered the ways of immigrants. They did not deny the importance of the new settlers' 'social heritage' to the initial decisions they made, but they argued that behaviour was increasingly shaped by the new environment, including economic needs and relations with other social groups. The result was adoption of and participation in the economic and political organizations necessary for agricultural life. Other aspects of cultural life such as ethnic identity Dawson did not comment on clearly because he thought they were rather marginal indicators of basic behaviour.[69]

Underlining Dawson's and Younge's points were the demographic estimations. Burton Hurd saw a one-generation shift from original European to indigenous Canadian marital and fertility rates. He attributed this shift to the broad environmental factors of urbanization, intermarriage, and material expectations. Younge's later work on Ukrainians in Montreal led her to find considerable inter-generational tension and change. In turn, she noted a pronounced tendency of second-generation women to reject parental patterns of marriage and fertility.[70]

In sum, because their labour had been a source of cultural identity, the Ukrainians' very propensity to hard work had drawn them into the commercial economy and thus integrated them into the economic and political order of the prairies. This integration, based on the material environment, was far more important to economists and sociologists as a sign of assimilation than the adoption of some social mores and cultural forms that other writers, notably historians, had harped on. The environmental factors, in sum, constituted so powerful a body of 'natural forces,' Dawson concluded, that even 'sectarians of whatever type tend to make their peace with the plain facts of the extremely competitive society which has surrounded and invaded their colonies.'[71]

Indeed, only historians remained sceptical about the forces of integration during the thirties – and in reflecting upon ethnic relations between the British and Ukrainian Canadians in subsequent years – so that Lower wondered in the thirties whether any common community would emerge in the agricultural or forest industry frontier. Writing twenty years later, Lower admitted in 1958 that social unity had been rebuilt with remarkable ease, although he claimed that 'every considerable immigrant group ... has had passing dreams of reconstituting its home-land on the new soil' even as he admitted that these groups were 'incomplete societies' in the new setting.[72] His colleague W.L. Morton seemed to remain worried about such autonomist tendencies in arguing that a frustrated nationalism led to cultural preservation by Ukrainians in Manitoba.[73] If it is not clear just what Morton expected of Ukrainian Canadians and others, it seems that the historians were worrying over vague cultural goals and values that were peripheral to the economists and sociologists who fastened upon the primary economic and political participation of Ukrainians and other immigrant groups in prairie life as the only appropriate measures of integration. Finally, it appears that Lower and Morton were more concerned with class attitudes and cultural tastes than with anything more significant in their anguish about culture, but this remains speculation.

Finally, almost all British-Canadian commentators identified contribu-tions to a future Canadian cultural identity and participation in the existing Canadian political economy as the crucial aspects of Ukrainian-Canadian – and other new Canadian – life by the forties. With these two crucial lessons, British Canadians were prepared to proclaim at last that the participation of both old and new Canadians was about to achieve the goal of a new 'common Canadianism' that writers of earlier decades had hoped for. The actual phrase is Queen's political scientist O.D. Skelton's, but the sentiments are those of a range of commentators including Woodsworth, Sissons, Anderson, and Gibbon.[74]

For some writers, like Anderson, assimilation began by sounding like the absorption of 'Anglo-Saxon' cultural goals but ended with the search for a much broader 'new Canadian citizenship.' Once he admitted that Ukrainians had adopted the political and economic goals of Canada, Anderson could look forward, as his reference to the 'pure gold of Canadian citizenship' indicates, to their participation in 'our future Canadian life and citizenship.'[75] Similarly England could only refer to an 'ideal of Canadian citizenship which would accept from all the peo-ples who come to us, methods, customs or habits of life that tend to progress.' He then stated that the only claim the host peoples had was to ask that 'our new Canadians correct their habits of life, and if necessary their language, to make co-operation possible between us.'[76] Even the somewhat harsher advocate of cultural assimilation C.H. Young defined his goal as 'the transition from one cultural world to another,' depicted as the 'transition' from the Old World to the New, a shift Hurd and Younge later thought they had identified.[77]

What Canadian commentators increasingly admitted was that the essential commitment to Canada – participation in the economy, loyalty to the political order – was the important characteristic of Ukrainian Canadians by the thirties and forties. Gibbon's gleeful quotation of Governor-General Lord Tweedsmuir's celebrated 1936 paean to Ukrainian-Canadian political commitment is just one example of this. Tweedsmuir's own intervention was crucial in an establishment response to yet another ground swell of popular grumbling about Ukrainian loyalty. He made the telling point that Ukrainian Canadians 'have accepted the duties and loyalties as you have acquired the privileges of Canadian citizens.' Tweedsmuir also emphasized that only by maintaining their own culture could Ukrainian Canadians become effective participants in Canadian society.[78]

Curiously enough, the citizenship to which Tweedsmuir referred was still a highly dubious one. Canadian politicians and officials were aware in the thirties and forties that there was no consolidated definition of Canadian citizenship despite or because of previous naturalization acts. This had created problems for Canadians abroad and defied resolution at Commonwealth conferences and in Parliament, notably in 1931, when the Bennett government abandoned a bill to create Canadian citizenship. Until 1947, as the diplomat Norman Robertson confessed, there were in fact three categories of Canadian citizens: Canadian-born, naturalized Canadians, and British subjects. Canadian nationality was hardly clear.[79]

When the post-war Mackenzie King government moved to address this problem, the sponsoring minister, Secretary of State Paul Martin, noted that a Canadian citizenship bill would provide at last a definition of citizenship that would be recognized internationally and would unify Canadians domestically. As Martin put it, the goal was to 'establish clearly a basic and definite Canadian citizenship which will be the fundamental status upon which the rights and privileges of Canadians will depend.'[80] When Martin came to define the basis of this new common citizenship, removing the differences between the Canadian-born, British subjects, and naturalized Canadians, he argued that the only criterion was that the individual had 'proved to be good citizen material' by life and work in Canada. He stated that knowledge of French or English was not a criterion and, referring to European nationalism, denied that the bill was designed to encourage the 'selfish introversion' of 'nationalism.'[81] In short, Canadian citizenship was a legal definition of status that was based on political rights and political and economic participation in Canadian life.

What is so remarkable about Martin's statement is that he totally abandoned the kind of cultural tests that had been worried over for so many years by British Canadians. To the Liberals of 1946, neither language nor fervent 'nationalism' was part of the test of citizenship. It is as if Martin had been briefed by those social scientists who had offered such reassuring evidence in the thirties about the fundamental commitments of Ukrainian Canadians and other prairie settlers to the economic and political structure of Canada, never mind their cultural ways. In a way, Martin had been so advised in two ways. First, he had been an executive member of the major social scientific organizations whose members had written the assured studies of political and economic assimilation during the thirties. Second, the leading designers of the post-1945 reconstruction programme of government were these same social scientists, including above all W.A. Mackintosh, who had co-ordinated the research and publication of major works done in the thirties.[82]

However he had arrived at his conclusion, and clearly contemporary public attitudes were central to the political decision to act, Martin's Canadian Citizenship Act of 1947 was a rejection of the crude goal of cultural assimilation and cultural conformity similar to the rejection that the British-Canadian intelligentsia had long since made.

When the Canadian Citizenship Act was declared on 3 January 1947, a ceremony was held in Ottawa, and certificates of Canadian citizenship were issued. Appropriately enough, Certificate No. 1 was awarded to Mackenzie King, the prime minister. But if that award was fitting, so, too, was the award of Certificate No. 2 not to another prominent person or to a French Canadian or a native Canadian but to Wasyl Eleniak, one of the first two Ukrainians to settle the prairies.[83] After fifty years, it can only be seen as appropriate that the new citizenship based on working in Canada embraced a representative of one group that had never fitted the old citizenship based on cultural conformity.

The attitudes of British-Canadian intellectuals towards Ukrainian Canadians led away from existing interpretations of the relations between the host peoples and new peoples in the first half of the twentieth century. The British-Canadian attitudes towards Ukrainians were not particularly prone to the forms of ethnic nationalism described as 'nativism' that Canadian historians have often taken from American historical writing. Although popular Canadian opinion might well be said to reflect the 'Anglo-Saxon' sense of superiority that American nativism is said to consist of,[84] reflective Canadian opinion accommodated the presence of non-British peoples in Canada with remarkable ease. Similarly, far from abandoning the very possibility of a Canadian identity in the amorphous conception of a mosaic or non-national identity, British Canadians were convinced that the mixture of historic peoples and new peoples, epitomized by their reading of the place of Ukrainians in Canada, was leading towards a unique and strong identity for Canada.[85]

However worried about the relations between the host society and the new peoples and however uneasy about their own culture's strengths, by the twenties British Canadians were remarkably confident about the amicable result of ethnic relations between the branches of the European peoples. The Canadian writers believed that assimilation meant the blending of both host and new peoples. They also were confident that cultural assimilation was far less important than economic and political assimilation. This indicates that their own nationalism was very confident as an expression of political and economic goals and that the political and economic integration of all the peoples of Canada did not unduly disturb British-Canadian students of ethnic relations by the end of the Second World War.

The implications here about relations between the 'charter' groups of French and British are also suggestive. Canadian ideas of nationalism in the mid-twentieth century surely had changed as a result of the discussion of the place of Ukrainian Canadians. For instance, the British-Canadian opinion that had sneered at Henri Bourassa's vision of a bicultural Canada and sought out the First World War conscription crisis would seem to have shifted significantly in the twenties, thirties, and forties.[86] The British-Canadian encounter with European immigrants therefore suggests accommodations that also made way for the re-examination of the place of French Canadians within Canada that began during the forties and fifties.

Tracy Philipps and the Achievement of Ukrainian-Canadian Unity

N. FRED DREISZIGER

One of the most perplexing and difficult issues facing the Canadian government on the home front during the Second World War was its relations with the country's Ukrainian community. The reasons for the existence of a 'Ukrainian question' in Canada during the war were complex and numerous. Canada's Ukrainians constituted the most influential immigrant ethnic group in the country. Numbering over three hundred thousand, demographically they were well ahead of other immigrant groups, with the exception of people of German ancestry, who had little political influence at the time. The Ukrainian group, moreover, was made up mainly of recent arrivals who were largely untouched by the process of assimilation. In the prairie provinces, they tended to live in compact settlements, which made them a factor to contend with during provincial and federal elections. More importantly, theirs was a highly politicized community, with strong feelings about Poland and the USSR. The Ukrainians' powerful attachment to their homeland was no doubt shaped in part at least by the momentous events that had taken place there during the First World War and the inter-war decades. Not surprisingly, during the Second World War, the Canadian government found the country's Ukrainian community to be emotion-charged, energetic, and vocal, determined to make its voice heard on issues – both domestic and international – related to Ukrainian national interests.

The highlight of the Ukrainian-Canadian community's wartime evolution was the establishment, in November 1940, of the Ukrainian Canadian Committee (UCC), a co-ordinating body and lobby for the vast majority of Ukrainian organizations in the country. The UCC is a controversial organization in the eyes of students of the Ukrainian-Canadian experience. O.W. Gerus calls the creation of the UCC a 'most significant event' that 'transformed the fractionalized nationality into a cohesive ethnic community, thereby helping to preserve the Ukrainian identity in its new homeland.'[1] J. Balan, in assessing the UCC's performance over the decades, is less categorical. He admits that the UCC's effectiveness has often been limited by the compromises it has had to make to please all of its components; nevertheless, he stresses the value of the organization's work 'over the years ... in both unifying and representing Ukrainian Canadians.'[2] Other students of Ukrainian-Canadian history, however, take a different view. B.S. Kordan and L.Y. Luciuk deem the establishment of the UCC to be a premature attempt at Ukrainian-Canadian unity that left a lasting legacy of ineffective community leadership.[3] Despite the importance (positive or otherwise) attributed to the birth of the UCC, little research has been done on this event. No one has explored in depth the political forces at work – especially those emanating from outside the community – that made for the establishment of this supra-community organization. Not even the events leading to its proclamation in November 1940 have been told in detail. In fact, some accounts of the UCC's creation offer a confused picture, listing as causal factors in its creation circumstances that obtained only after 1940.

The basic outlines of the UCC's founding have been known ever since 1940. They have been told in numerous government memoranda during the war. According to these, in early November 1940, the most influential of the non-Communist Ukrainian-Canadian organizations united, mainly on the prompting of a handful of non-Ukrainian individuals.[4] Aside from further comments on the organizations that came together in the UCC, these government sources offer little information on the reasons for the committee's establishment or on the negotiations that preceded its birth. The secondary literature, although in some cases more detailed than the official and semi-official wartime accounts, is equally laconic on these questions. It is particularly unclear on the role that the Canadian government played in the affair.

The UCC's origins receive fairly detailed treatment in most accounts of the committee's history.[5] Gerus, among others, devotes considerable space to the story of the various organizations that coalesced into the UCC. He stresses the tradition in Ukrainian-Canadian circles of responding to crises affecting Ukrainians – both in their homeland and in their adopted country – by 'drawing together temporarily in order to meet specific short-term objectives.'[6]

The crises that Gerus sees as being catalytic to Ukrainian-Canadian unity in the early part of the Second World War did not.happen in Ukraine itself but in Ukrainian-populated areas of East Central Europe. The first of these came in September 1938 when the government of Poland launched a campaign against the Orthodox church in a Ukrainian district of that country. Ukrainians in Canada, both Orthodox and Catholics, reacted to the news of this development by organizing protest demonstrations. Other events in Central Europe soon overshadowed the problem in Poland. The Sudeten crisis threatened the very existence of multinational Czechoslovakia. Indeed, Ukrainians in Subcarpathian Ruthenia, the easternmost province of Czechoslovakia, could hope for the possible establishment of a Ukrainian state there. The prospect of the birth of a 'Ukrainian Piedmont' threw Ukrainian-Canadian organizations into frenzied activity, but this activity did not lead to effective united action.[7]

The obstacle to unity was not the lack of effort. Ukrainian-Canadian leaders expended much effort to establish co-ordinating organizations; however, they could not achieve such a body, incorporating all or at least most of Canada's Ukrainians. In fact, during the winter of 1939–40, two competing umbrella organizations emerged. These soon engaged in a bitter war of words that lasted until early November 1940, when their leaders met in Winnipeg and agreed to unite in the UCC.

Historians of the UCC attribute this dramatic turn of events to the intervention of outside forces, notably the Canadian government. Gerus describes the committee's birth in this way: 'The Federal Government assumed the role of arbitrator ... The Department of National War Services ... saw the lack of unity among Ukrainians ... as inimical to the war effort.'[8] The persons in the 'employ' of the Department of National War Services who had a hand in implementing the department's decision are identified as Professor George Simpson of the University of Saskatchewan, Professor Watson Kirkconnell of McMaster University, Dr Vladimir Kaye, 'a Ukrainian official of the Citizenship Branch,' and a certain 'British East-European specialist, Tracy Philipps.'[9]

This story is, with some variations, the 'received version' of the UCC's birth. It has been accepted in such works of synthesis as the most recent survey of the history of Canadian ethnic groups.[10] Unfortunately, there are several problems with this version. First, there seems to be an inconsistency between the official and the historical accounts of the UCC's birth. The former tend to stress that the initiative for the committee's establishment came from private individuals; the latter emphasize the Canadian government's involvement in the matter. The second problem with the received version is that none of the accounts explain satisfactorily the reasons for the suddenness of this important turn of events in Ukrainian-Canadian organizational efforts. Lastly, the 'facts' given in the most prominent historical accounts are inaccurate. Watson Kirkconnell and George Simpson, for example, in November 1940 had no official connections to the Canadian government.[11] True, they – and others – played important roles in the UCC's establishment, but only as private individuals. The government's sole agent, if one can call him such, was that certain 'British expert,' Tracy Philipps. His intervention was pivotal, yet it has not been explored – no doubt in part because the relevant government files and private collections did not become open to researchers until the 1980s. The general purpose of this paper is to fill some of the gaps in our knowledge of the birth of a remarkable ethnic organization and to throw light on the complex relations that developed between the Canadian state and ethnic groups in wartime. A more specific objective of this inquiry is to re-examine Philipps's role in this story.

The politics of the Ukrainian-Canadian community during the early phases of the Second World War can be understood only through an examination of its political and social circumstances and organizational make-up. The most important characteristic of the group was its recentness. In 1939 the oldest Ukrainian colonies in Canada were not quite fifty years of age. Like most immigrant communities of recent vintage, the Ukrainian Canadians of the inter-war period were largely untouched by the processes of immigrant integration and assimilation and remained intensely concerned about developments in their homeland.

Another circumstance that is important about Canada's inter-war Ukrainian community is the fact that the vast majority of its members hailed from East Central Europe rather than Eastern Europe. The peace settlements at the end of the First World War had ignored the aspirations of Europe's forty million Ukrainians.[12] The peace-makers had claimed to have united and emancipated East Central Europe's downtrodden nationalities through the break-up of the Habsburg, Hohenzollern, and – in part at least – the Romanov empires. But while the Poles were liberated and the Romanians and South Slavs were united in their respective countries, others were divided more than ever before in this process. Among those who ended up – or remained – separated from their co-nationals were the Ukrainians. When the peace making was over, they found themselves in four different countries: Poland, Romania, Czechoslovakia, and the Soviet Union. They began their lives in lands that had been, with some exceptions, devastated by four years of war and under governments that were jealously protective of their countries' newly won independence and territories. These circumstances assured the exodus of Ukrainians from these Ukrainian lands, particularly from Poland, following often in the footsteps of Ukrainians who had come to Canada from Galicia and Bukovyna before the First World War.

The fact that most Ukrainians in Canada had come from East Central Europe explains their keen interest in the national and international politics of the region. Moreover, developments there – as well as in Soviet Ukraine – during the 1930s were dramatic enough to grab and retain the attention of most Ukrainian Canadians. First to arouse the concerns of these people was the news of the sufferings of the people of Ukraine itself inflicted by Iosif Stalin's vicious collectivization campaigns of the early 1930s. The general revulsion in all Ukrainian communities of the world against Stalin's deeds could have been used by governments in Poland and Romania, for example, to unite public opinion against a common enemy (i.e. Soviet communism) and thereby lessen inter-ethnic tensions, but the opportunity was missed.[13]

The country that most concerned Ukrainian Canadians was probably not Soviet Russia but Poland. As has been mentioned, most of Canada's Ukrainians had come from there. Unlike Stalin's Russia, Poland was not a totalitarian state, and news from there could freely travel across the Atlantic. Alas, much of this news was unfavourable. The Ukrainians of Poland were an underprivileged minority.[14] They were underrepresented in the country's parliament; their access to higher education and public careers was limited; and they were subjected to pressure to abandon their traditional Ukrainian culture. They responded to these policies with a vigorous defence of their institutions and culture, agitation against the Polish state and its agents, political organization, and, occasionally, open defiance and even violence. As a result, by the 1930s Polish-Ukrainian relations deteriorated into intermittent 'quasi-guerrilla' warfare.[15] Overseas Ukrainians viewed this situation with keen concern. Particularly vehement was the Ukrainian-Canadian echo of the efforts of the Polish government in the late 1930s to Polonize the country's Eastern Orthodox dioceses. By then, however, events were taking place elsewhere in East Central Europe that were to evoke even stronger emotions among Ukrainians overseas.

In the wake of the Munich Agreement, what was left of Czechoslovakia (from then on known as Czecho-Slovakia) was reorganized. Slovakia and Ruthenia received their autonomy. In the case of the latter, this was the realization of an expectation that had been held ever since the early days of the Czechoslovak republic, but could not be attained earlier as the Czechs had preferred to run that part of the country in the manner of a benevolent dictatorship.[16] But in the restructuring of 1938, Czech rule was exchanged for German influence. And the Germans, for the time being, preferred to allow the local authorities to stress the Ukrainian character of Carpatho-Ukraine. Not surprisingly, Ukrainian became the region's official language, and the Ukrainian national colours were 'hoisted everywhere.'[17] Ukrainian Canadians saw in this experiment a harbinger of the rebirth of an independent Ukraine. They considered Carpatho-Ukraine a potential Piedmont from which the struggle for the self-determination of all Ukrainians could begin.[18] According to Gerus, Ukrainians in Canada held 'mass rallies' and collected 'relief funds' to promote the cause of the Carpatho-Ukrainian experiment.[19] Unfortunately for Ukrainian Canadians, an independent Ukrainian state in the Carpathians was not about to come into existence. When the whole experiment started, Hitler was anxious to cause mischief for both Poland and Soviet Russia. A few months later he must have realized the possible need to make a deal with Stalin. Under the changed circumstances, the idea of a Ukrainian Piedmont lost much of its validity. Accordingly, when the *Führer* made his mind up to dismember the rest of Czecho-Slovakia, he decided to let the region revert to Hungary. On 15 March 1939, Hungarian troops entered Carpatho-Ukraine. Soon there would be celebrations in Budapest, sighs of relief in Warsaw (probably also in Moscow), and profound disappointment in Ukrainian-Canadian circles.[20]

The events of 1938–9 in East Central Europe did have some impetus towards Ukrainian-Canadian organizational unity. In the wake of these developments, Ukrainian-Canadian institutions coalesced into two coordinating committees, the Representative Committee of Ukrainian Canadians (RCUC)[21] and a rival federation, the Ukrainian Central Committee of Canada (UCCC).[22] The emergence of the two committees reflected long-standing divisions within the community. The most prominent of these divisions during the inter-war years, the split between Communist and nationalist Ukrainians, was not an important factor in 1939–40, as the former had no direct role to play in the political process that led to the creation of the UCC. In the early phases of the Second World War, Ukrainian-Canadian Communists were placed under surveillance and sporadically harassed by the RCMP for their opposition to the Canadian war effort.[23] Partly as a result of this, they were a discredited group with little influence in ethnic affairs. Other divisions within Ukrainian-Canadian society, however, were important factors in the efforts at political unity. Conflicts between monarchists and republicans, between followers of the Ukrainian Catholic and Orthodox churches, as well as differences relating to the place of origin of the immigrants, all had their impact. Added to these were personality clashes among community leaders and suspicions and rivalries among residents of the major Ukrainian-Canadian centres, such as Winnipeg, Saskatoon, and Regina.

The full story of the feuding that went on between the UCCC and the RCUC during the spring and summer of 1940 need not concern us here.[24] Gerus suggests that the UCCC's 'slanderous' newspaper campaign against its rival prompted more responsible leaders within the RCUC to counsel moderation and unity.[25] Unity, however, would elude the Ukrainian community for a few more months, and when it came, it resulted from the intercession of outsiders – foremost among them Tracy Philipps. To understand these developments, we have to look at the wider context of ethnic politics in Canada in 1940.

The problem of ethnic minorities in Canada was an important concern for the country's government as war clouds gathered on the horizon and especially when war broke out in September 1939. The most tangible manifestations of these concerns were the provisions of the Defence of Canada Regulations (DOCR) concerning enemy aliens. These regulations were drawn up before the war and were put into effect at its outbreak. Though the paragraphs regarding unnaturalized immigrants to Canada affected mainly recent arrivals, the letter of the law, and the way officials tended to interpret the regulations, had implications for the whole of the country's immigrant ethnic community. It might be added that in September 1939 some Canadian officials wanted to move against Italian-Canadian sympathizers of Mussolini and were restrained only when they were reminded that Italy had not entered the war yet.[26]

During the winter of 1939–40 there was a gradual reaction in some Ottawa circles against the government's negative approach to its dealings with the country's European immigrant community. Suggestions were made for the taking of positive steps to counterbalance the police measures that were embodied in the approach represented by the DOCR. It was urged that the government embark on a propaganda campaign to explain Canada's position in the war to the immigrant masses in the country and establish an office that would keep in touch with the leaders of immigrant communities.[27] The government of Prime Minister Mackenzie King was slow to implement these recommendations. Nevertheless, an important start was made in the summer of 1940 when the Department of National War Services was created. The officials of the department embraced the idea of establishing contacts with immigrant groups and began to think about setting up a section or branch within their ministry to handle relations with them.

Ottawa's new approach to wartime ethnic politics resulted in the involvement of new people in the administration and even the formulation of the government's policies towards immigrant ethnics. Some of these people were not new on the Ottawa scene, but their new responsibilities allowed them to make a significant impact on the handling of the 'enemy alien issue.' Others had been involved with immigrant populations on the local and provincial scene, but now assumed an important role on the national level. Still others were newcomers. A book would be needed to analyse their attitudes; in a paper such as this one, a few generalizations must suffice. The names of these people are familiar to students of Canadian ethnic history: Watson Kirkconnell, George Simpson, Robert England, and Murray Gibbon. Kirkconnell and Simpson were academics. England and Gibbon worked at CNR and CPR headquarters respectively and were authors of books about Canada's immigrants. Kirkconnell, who spoke or at least read the languages of most of Canada's European immigrants, cultivated the friendship of the Ukrainian National Federation (one of the two organizations making up the RCUC). Simpson often acted as an adviser to the Ukrainian Self-Reliance League (the chief organization within the UCCC).[28]

The most important of the Ottawa mandarins to become connected with the work concerning immigrant ethnics was Norman Robertson, in 1939 the assistant under-secretary of state for external affairs. Robertson became a member of two wartime inter-departmental committees dealing with 'enemy aliens' and their property. In handling this work, he demonstrated a genuine sympathy for immigrants to Canada as well as an understanding for the emotional, economic, and social impact the war was having on them. J.F. MacNeill, a high-ranking official of the Department of Justice, developed a similar approach to the problem during the early months of the war.

In 1939, in the cabinet itself, no one was specifically responsible for dealing with the country's ethnic minorities. In the summer of 1940 this situation was remedied to some extent when James G. Gardiner was appointed minister responsible for the new Department of National War Services. Although he retained his previous portfolio (agriculture), he dedicated much of his time to the work of his new department. The fact that Gardiner had a deep-rooted sympathy and understanding for immigrants meant that their cause would have a spokesman in the highest organ of decision-making. Also important was the fact that

Thomas C. Davis, a former Saskatchewan politician who had ideas similar to Gardiner's, became one of the deputy ministers of the new ministry. As he was to have an important impact on developments, it may be worth outlining his background and ideas.

Thomas C. Davis was called to Ottawa in July 1940 from the Higher Court of Saskatchewan. Earlier he had been the attorney general of his province. He was an energetic, competent man in whom Canada's immigrants found a true friend. He had developed respect and trust for immigrants in Saskatchewan, where their proportion in the population was high and where they were more readily accepted as Canadian citizens equal in status to native-born Canadians than in eastern Canada. Davis expressed his sympathies for the 'enemy alien' immigrants who fell victim to anti-alien feelings in the Canada of 1940 in a letter he wrote soon after his arrival in Ottawa. He explained that persons with German or Italian names were 'set upon by the people in their communities and they are more or less harassed and persecuted unjustly and unwisely.'[29] Once established in his Ottawa office, Davis began formulating a policy that would counterbalance the treatment immigrants were receiving from the Canadian public. One of his first measures was the arranging of a lecture tour of some of the ethnic communities of the West. The man whom Davis selected for this task was the main protagonist of our story, Tracy Philipps.

James Erasmus Tracy Philipps, MC, DCL, FRIA, came from an old, upper-class English family, many of whose members had served Britain with distinction as soldiers, scholars, or civil servants. He had had a most interesting career. He had studied at Oxford and had served in the First World War in Africa, after which he had been in the service of the British government on various assignments. Philipps had travelled in Africa, the Middle East, and Eastern Europe. He had published in scholarly and semi-scholarly journals and had a honorary doctorate from the University of Durham. He prided himself on his linguistic skills: he spoke French, German, and Italian and claimed some knowledge of Turkish as well as of thirteen African languages.[30]

Philipps was a man of determination, energy, and ambition. He gained the admiration of some people and the hostility of others. On the occasion of his impending Canadian visit, his sponsors designed a flyer that gave information on his purpose as well as his qualifications and background. By the time the ink had dried on the first drafts of this announcement, it was out of date, as Hitler had struck in the West and not in the Mediterranean as the announcement implicitly predicted. Nevertheless, the flyer's text appears to have been revised to accommodate the latest developments, as it went to great lengths to explain why, at a time of crisis in Europe, attention had to be paid to the problems of the Near East. A look at this flyer's statements is important for anyone who wants to understand the man who would become central to the story of Canada's attempts to deal with her immigrant ethnic population during the war.[31]

Philipps himself probably drafted the announcement of his visit by the National Council of Education of Canada. Its cumbersome and pretentious prose spoke of its author's high self-esteem and of his propensity for unabashed exaggeration. On the first page of the flyer Philipps was shown 'seated at the Edge of EUROPE, on the battlements of Istambul looking towards England,' to use the exact words of the publication – themselves taken from a letter Philipps had received from 'an old friend, a distinguished Turkish diplomat.' 'He is visiting the Dominion,' the text continued, 'at a momentous hour, and when the situation in the Mediterranean is giving rise to anxiety.' Philipps's 'addresses,' the flyer proclaimed, would be 'supported by a scientific and intimate knowledge' and would be 'welcomed by many people in their efforts to appraise what is happening in Eastern Europe and the Near East.' 'On such questions,' the flyer promised, 'Tracy Philipps can speak out of rich experience, from a long and scientific study.'[32]

The announcement then turned to Philipps's personal background. He came 'of a family deeply rooted in England's history, which contains records associating the family name with Vortigen and Coeur de Lion. Herein, possibly, lies the subconscious reason why, after leaving the University of Oxford and being commissioned to the Regular Army Reserve, he set out, in 1913, to travel extensively in Eastern Europe and the Near East.'[33]

The following seventeen paragraphs outlined Philipps's exploits as a soldier, civil servant, diplomat, colonial administrator, scientist, explorer, war correspondent, League of Nations official, and writer on academic subjects in 'Comparative Religion, Anthropology, Zoology, and on certain aspects of Bird Migration.' The last part of the flyer was devoted not to Philipps, but to his wife. 'Mr. Philipps,' the statement announced, 'will be accompanied by his wife, who is among Europe's women pianists of the very first rank.' Mrs Philipps, the statement went on, was the daughter of 'a great Slavonic savant.' Under her maiden name Lubka Kolessa she had 'given concerts to delighted audiences in all the capitals of Europe.'[34]

Philipps came to Canada on a 'dollar-a-year' basis, to serve the cause of the Allies by explaining various aspects of the war to Canadians. Once in Canada, Philipps was handed over to the Association of Canadian Clubs, which became the sponsor of his lectures by the fall of 1940. At first, ethnic groups were not singled out as targets for Philipps's oratory; however, in the autumn it was arranged that Philipps should repeat his tour of Canada, talking this time not to English and French Canadians, but to members of certain foreign-language groups. The new tour was initiated by the Department of National War Services. To avoid linking Philipps to the government, his expenses continued to be covered by the Association of Canadian Clubs.

One of the groups that Philipps was directed to pay special attention to was the Ukrainian. For his work among them, Philipps had a collaborator, Vladimir J. Kysilewsky. Kysilewsky, who would be known to students of Canadian ethnic history as 'Dr Kaye,' was well-qualified for his assignment. He knew the Canadian West as he had lived there after he came to Canada for the first time in 1924. Later he enrolled in the University of London's School of Slavonic and East European Studies. After the outbreak of the war he became a journalist and worked for the BBC.[35] In the spring of 1940, he decided to return to Canada, motivated no doubt in part at least by Philipps's plans to go there. The two men were close friends: when Kysilewsky had married not long before their departure from England, Philipps was his best man.

The fact that the Ukrainians were singled out as prime targets for Philipps's attention indicates that the Canadian government considered them to be an especially important ethnic minority. Actually, the beginnings of Ottawa's approach to the 'Ukrainian problem' pre-dated the involvement of Philipps and Davis in Canadian ethnic affairs. The Canadian government had a 'Ukrainian policy' as early as the spring of 1940, and we have a description of it from O.D. Skelton himself, who was then the under-secretary of external affairs.

The occasion that prompted Skelton to commit his government's policy to paper was a visit to External Affairs by Wasyl Swystun in late April 1940.[36] Swystun, who had formerly headed the Ukrainian Self-Reliance League (USRL), came to Ottawa on behalf of the RCUC to lobby for a free Ukraine. He explained to Skelton and Robertson that the obstacle to Ukrainian-Canadian unity was the opposition of his organization to the demand of the USRL that a group described as 'a small Trotskyist fraction' be included in any umbrella organization of non-Communist Ukrainian Canadians. Next, Swystun outlined his plans to visit London, and possibly Paris and Washington, to promote his organization's views.

Skelton and Robertson's response could not have pleased Swystun.

They told him that the Canadian government appreciated the importance of the Ukrainian problem but could not give 'official approval to the movement for an independent Ukrain[e] in view of the fact that such a country would have to be carved out of the territories of the U.S.S.R. and ... Poland.' They also told Swystun that Ottawa could not accept his suggestion that the RCUC's memorandum should be transmitted to the governments of Britain and France, as such an act would create the impression that Canada was endorsing the RCUC's views.[37]

Although the Canadian government's attitude to the issue of a 'free Ukraine' is well documented, its view on the inability of Ukrainian Canadians to achieve unity is not. There is an ex-post-facto claim by Judge Davis that this unity was achieved in early November at the instigation of his department, but it dates from 1943, and documents originating from the autumn of 1940 that would corroborate this claim have not been found.[38] Philipps's own attitudes towards the Ukrainian problem, however, are known to us in detail. It may be worth outlining them and explaining how they were preserved for the historical record.

Soon after Ukrainian-Canadian unity had been achieved in November 1940, Philipps went to Prince Albert to address a gathering of Ukrainians. He talked about similarities in English and Ukrainian history and the long struggle of the two nations for freedom. According to him, 'both races valued freedom above life itself, and this is what [made] Britain and Ukraine natural allies in the present world struggle.' Not surprisingly, Philipps was enthusiastically received. Following the meeting, Philipps chatted with one William Burianyk, who offered to take him to Saskatoon the next morning by car. Philipps accepted. During their journey, Burianyk and the Englishman talked about the Ukrainian question in Canada and, especially, in Europe. As Burianyk turned out to be a private informer for Saskatchewan premier W.J. Patterson, we have a record of their conversation.[39]

In their discussion, Burianyk and Philipps concentrated on the Ukrainian problem in Europe and the approach taken by the British government to it. According to Philipps, the officials of the Foreign Office were not 'big enough' to see the potentialities of the 'Ukrainian factor' in Eastern Europe. The Foreign Office was a 'collection of old fogies' bound by 'tradition and precedent' and unable to look for new allies even in times of 'dire peril' to the Empire. In particular, the Russian experts in the Foreign Office, many of whom were of pre-war 'vintage,' were hostile to the Ukrainian movement because it was working for the break-up of Russia. These people were still 'foolishly' hoping for an alliance with Russia, 'too blind to see that now Stalin is a chore-boy of Hitler.'

Philipps's own views were very different. In his opinion the Ukrainian factor was of 'profound importance to Great Britain.' In fact, 'the very salvation and preservation' of the British Empire depended on 'the proper understanding and utilization of the Ukrainian factor.' Such understanding could be achieved only if the fossilized attitudes in the Foreign Office were changed, and the only agency that could change them was the Canadian government. England was 'now wholly dependent on Canada, therefore any wish that the Canadian Government may express in connection with the Ukrainian ... matter will be given closest attention.' When Burianyk asked Philipps why he did not present his views directly to Ottawa, the Englishman explained that such an initiative had better not come from a private citizen.[40] Obviously, it would be the task of a powerful lobby to get Ottawa to try to influence London.

Philipps's views of the Ukrainian question in Europe place his approach to the Ukrainian problem in Canada in a different perspective. Obviously he considered his work among Ukrainian Canadians not only as the performance of a task assigned to him by the Canadian government, but also as the fulfilment of a personal mission. This fact puts the events in Winnipeg of 6 and 7 November 1940 in a new light.

Philipps's itinerary for his tour of the Ukrainian communities of the Canadian West had been arranged in the early autumn of 1940. It was drawn up largely by the Ukrainian Catholic bishop Ladyka, on the recommendation of the officials of the CPR's Colonization Department in Winnipeg. Ladyka was in turn advised by his chancellor, the Reverend Wasyl Kushnir, and Swystun. The result was that the trip became monopolized by the Ukrainian Catholic faction of the Ukrainian-Canadian community. In early November Philipps began his lectures in Winnipeg. He first addressed the Ukrainian Educational Institute, where he shared the platform with Kushnir and Swystun. Here it became obvious to Philipps that his intention to promote Ukrainian-Canadian unity was being compromised by his 'sponsors.' The next day he visited Father Kushnir and Swystun separately and explained to them what a disservice they were doing to their community. He also proposed to cancel his tour and to publish his reasons for doing so, unless Kushnir and Swystun convened a meeting of Ukrainian-Canadian leaders for the purpose of ending all feuding and establishing a single Ukrainian national organization.[41]

Confronted with the choice of being denounced for their mischief by Philipps or complying with his ultimatum, Kushnir and Swystun opted for the lesser of two evils. Swystun immediately phoned the RCUC's

Wladimir Kossar and Professor T.K. Pavlychenko in Saskatoon. He asked them to come to Winnipeg and to bring with them Professor George Simpson (who had good ties with the RCUC's rivals) as a possible intermediary. When the RCUC's leaders, Simpson, and others arrived in Winnipeg, both Philipps and Simpson talked to those present before the official opening of the deliberations.[42] They pointed out the advantages that unity offered to Ukrainian Canadians.

At first it seems that the admonitions were in vain. By the second day of the conference a deadlock had developed. Many of the Ukrainian leaders present opposed the leadership aspirations of Father Kushnir, deeming him to be 'too recent' an arrival to be suitable for high office. Even more serious seemed to be the objections to Swystun, who was seen as a 'trouble-maker' on the basis of his record of about-faces and fratricidal politics. At this stage Philipps and Simpson were asked to arbitrate. Philipps, who realized that a 'dynamic if domineering' personality such as Swystun had better not be left out of the new organization, argued for the inclusion of the Kushnir-Swystun duo in the proposed committee's executive. The suggestion was accepted, and a united committee was agreed to. Its president was to be Kushnir, and its two vice-presidents Swystun and the Ukrainian Orthodox priest S.W. Sawchuk.[43]

The story of the UCC's birth tells us much about both the politics of ethnic groups in Canada and the approach of the Canadian government to these groups. It is an understatement to say that Canadian ethnic groups have difficulties in attaining even a limited degree of political unity. The residents of a county, borough, or town are compelled by geographic circumstances and municipal law to work within a united local government; the members of an ethnic group have nothing to prevent them from setting up myriad organizations. Personalities often play an important role in the proliferation of these. When an aspiring leader finds himself outnumbered and outvoted in an ethnic organization, he can set up a rival body more in tune with his political goals.

One might suppose that a highly politicized ethnic group such as the Ukrainian one during the Second World War would be more likely to achieve unity as a result of its greater appreciation of the need for effective action. This is not necessarily the case, as divisions tend to be sharper and more deep-rooted among members of politicized groups. Though the experience of the Ukrainian-Canadian community may not illustrate a general trend, it still suggests that politically conscious ethnic groups will not achieve a significant degree of political unity without some outside intervention. The UCC was certainly not the first or the last Canadian ethnic umbrella organization that has come about as a result of outside pressure.[44]

Although the conditions within the Ukrainian-Canadian community during the early years of the war were not conducive to the quick achievement of organizational unity, the situation outside the group was ripening for intervention in the community's political affairs. Before the war, few people in Canada and especially in Britain cared much about the politics of Ukrainian Canadians, and some of those who did were hostile to immigrants from Eastern Europe. Within the government, only the tiny intelligence establishment inside the RCMP maintained a professional and covert interest in this group, particularly its leftist organizations. When the war broke out and especially when the 'Phony War' turned into a real war in the spring of 1940, the government embarked on a programme of reaching out to the ethnic groups and, in certain cases, of intervening in their affairs.

Several factors rendered the realization of the Canadian government's new plan difficult. Canadian bureaucrats, especially those in External Affairs, were extremely reluctant to take any measures that would offend other powers or be out of step with those taken by Great Britain. Moreover, few people in Ottawa had an adequate knowledge of the problem. In short, in 1940 Ottawa was not yet ready or able to provide leadership on this question.

While the Canadian authorities were still groping in the dark, others took the initiative. The most important of these was Philipps, who, while acting with the presumed authorization of his masters in Ottawa, took matters in his own hands and coerced the appropriate Ukrainian-Canadian leaders to initiate decisive action. In doing so, he nominally furthered the wishes of the Department of National War Services, but in reality served the purposes of his own personal mission to promote the interests of Great Britain. The UCC's birth, then, was part of a greater scheme of things, an attempt by an Englishman to further the idea of a British-Ukrainian alliance against the danger that Europe's dictators had posed since September 1939 to free men everywhere.

All this places the UCC's emergence in a somewhat different light and requires us to qualify the existing historical accounts. The story told in wartime official and semi-official documents that the committee's birth was the result of the initiative of private individuals (i.e. 'outsiders') should be augmented by an explanation about why Philipps was so eager to assume the initiative. At the same time, the historical interpretations stressing the role of the Canadian government in the UCC's creation should be stripped of the emphasis on Ottawa's contribution.

Aside from Philipps, none of those involved was an agent for Ottawa, and none – not even Philipps – was in the 'employ' of the government. Philipps acted mainly out of his own strong convictions, though those convictions coincided with his Canadian masters' expectations. The committee's birth was above all Philipps's achievement, and a greater knowledge of his attitudes and actions allows us to have a better understanding of those events in Winnipeg in early November 1940.

Philipps's scheme for the alliance of two of Europe's large nations against the dictators was dashed just about the time the UCC was born, when Hitler gave the go-ahead for the preparation of a German invasion of the USSR. Not surprisingly, within a few months of the start of that invasion, both Philipps and the UCC were in danger. In 1942 the UCC began to be overshadowed by a resurgent Ukrainian-Canadian Left and its national organization, the Ukrainian Labour-Farmer Temple Association, now renamed the Association of United Ukrainian Canadians. In the same year Philipps's position (by then within the Canadian public service) also began to weaken, and by 1943 he was under attack not only from the Left, but also from sections of the Ottawa bureaucracy, especially the Department of External Affairs.[45] The UCC (and, until 1944, even Philipps) managed to survive this post-1942 political onslaught. How effectively they performed their tasks or served their respective constituencies thereafter is a question that is beyond the scope of this paper; however, it is one that deserves the attention of future historians.

Ukrainian-Canadian Politics

NELSON WISEMAN

For a long time our understanding of Ukrainian-Canadian politics was clouded, rather than clarified, because much of the literature was written by partisans engaged in internecine ideological battles. Just as Vera Lysenko's *Men in Sheepskin Coats* ignored the anti-Communist national movement, so Paul Yuzyk's anticommunism detracted from his otherwise scholarly *The Ukrainians in Manitoba*.[1] On both sides of this ideological divide the early literature was self-laudatory, coming from the school of ethnic boosterism, celebrating Ukrainian-Canadian advances. It sought to highlight what Ukrainians had in common rather than their differences. Authors were keen to demonstrate the loyalty of Ukrainians as Canadians and the magnitude of their contribution. Recently, however, we have gained access to more sophisticated, mature, and reputably documented research. Thomas Prymak, for example, has uncovered archival data that challenge the oft-repeated but undocumented claim that thirty-five thousand to forty thousand Ukrainians served in the Canadian armed forces in the Second World War.[2] Bohdan Kordan and Lubomyr Luciuk have assembled an impressive collection of primary documents that cast light on the Ukrainian-Canadian political experience.[3] There is now a deeper understanding of how Anglo-Canadians have perceived Ukrainians and how Ukrainians have responded, of the politics of right-wing and left-wing Ukrainians, of the divisions between the Ukrainian churches, and of the tensions within Ukrainian fraternal organizations around the national question.

A new generation of scholars, most of them Ukrainian-Canadian, has illuminated the past and is confronted by the conclusion that Ukrainians have been acculturated, assimilated, and successfully integrated into the political system, but they now have less influence politically as an organized and ethnically conscious group. This is not to say, of course, that individual Ukrainians have not done well in Canadian politics. They have, but this is not because of their identity or ethnic support. Increasingly they have succeeded as individuals who happen to be of Ukrainian background. The achievements of individual Ukrainians in government and politics are particularly noteworthy. As the nineties begin a Ukrainian serves as the queen's representative at the apex of Canada's constitutional order. One serves on the Supreme Court, another serves as a lieutenant-governor, and yet another (who is also part Romanian) serves as a premier.

The Canadian political system has been transformed from one in which Ukrainians were initially excluded and manipulated by race-proud Anglo-Saxons to one in which Ukrainians and others have been welcomed, accommodated, and integrated. Today, the 'ethnic' label insofar as Ukrainians are concerned carries neither stigma nor benefit. Ukrainian Canadians have gone from being a suspect and criticized 'alien' force to becoming an integral component in Canada's multicultural mosaic. Often referred to as representing the 'third force' or 'third element' in Canadian society, Ukrainians, arguably more than any other ethnic group, are responsible for pioneering the concept of multiculturalism in Canada.[4] The concept is now entrenched in the Constitution of Canada and reflects a redefinition of Canada (from the one in the British North America Act) and what it means to be Canadian.[5] An expression of the Ukrainian 'fact' in Canada's external relations was the prime minister's 1989 visit to Soviet Ukraine and the planned opening of a Canadian consulate in Kiev.

Ukrainian Canadians, whatever their subjective ethnic attachments, have become more like Canadians in general. As a group their average income is near the national average and exceeds those of some others, including the French-Canadian charter group and Canada's native peoples. When Ukrainians first came to Canada they were a visible and sometimes vocal minority. Most settled on the land, many in bloc colonies on the prairies. Now they are as urbanized as Canadians in general; in post-secondary educational institutions they are overrepresented, and they are more dispersed geographically than in the past.

Over time distinct ethnic identity has become more difficult to maintain. Ukrainian neighbourhoods have been undermined by rural-urban migration and by movements within cities – from ethnic enclaves to undifferentiated suburbs. It is no longer possible to locate – as it was as late as the forties in north Winnipeg – an individual census district where those having Ukrainian as a mother tongue make up 57 per cent of all residents and where 93 per cent of Ukrainians report that Ukrainian is their mother tongue.[6] Today nearly 90 per cent are Canadian-born, and fewer use Ukrainian in the home as older generations of immigrants pass away. Ukrainians make up a smaller percentage of the total population than they did half a century ago and have dropped from the fourth to the fifth largest ethnic group.

Anglo-Canadian Perceptions

Until Canada's recent embrace of 'multiculturalism' and 'equality' as constitutional principles, Anglo-Canadian attitudes provided the context for Ukrainian political participation. When Ukrainians first arrived in substantial numbers a century ago, the mythic expanse of British imperialism and the popularly distorted logic of Darwin's *Origin of Species* – published just thirty years earlier – led British Canadians to see themselves atop a racial pecking order. Next in this hierarchy were northern and central Europeans such as Scandinavians, Dutch, and Germans and the longer-established French Canadians. Ukrainians and other Slavs were more alien recent arrivals and lower down the ethnic totem-pole, but ahead of southern Europeans, blacks, Arabs, and the Chinese, who were imported to build the railroad rather than to homestead.

Resentment of Ukrainians was widespread. In the Manitoba provincial election of 1899, Conservatives characterized Ukrainians 'as a race unfit to participate in Canadian politics.'[7] Alberta's Frank Oliver, a future minister of the interior who, ironically, would preside over the settling of even more Ukrainians, declared in the House of Commons in 1901 that he resented 'the idea of having the millstone of this Slav population hung around our necks in our efforts to build up, beautify and improve our country.'[8] Temperance-driven Anglo-Saxon Protestants looked upon Ukrainian weddings as debased orgies.[9] Even well-intentioned social reformers like J.S. Woodsworth depicted Slavs as ignorant, unskilled, dirty, and prone to crime and drunkenness.[10] The story of Ukrainian internment and disenfranchisement during the First World War is well known and needs little retelling: Ukrainians went from being characterized as alien supporters of Austria and Germany in 1914–15 to being labelled Bolsheviks and Soviet fellow travellers after 1917.[11] Canadian immigration policy was driven by the desire to keep Canada British, but it was modified by economic and political concerns that the West be settled and kept out of American grasp. As late as 1922 the railroads clamoured for more immigration from the 'non-preferred' countries of Central and Eastern Europe by pointing to the thirty-four million acres of vacant land within fifteen miles of prairie railroad tracks.[12]

Some politicians who benefitted directly from Ukrainian voting support – like Charles Dunning, the Liberal premier of Saskatchewan in the twenties and Mackenzie King's minister of finance in the thirties – had contemptuous disdain for Ukrainians. 'Upon the whole he [Dunning] is not very friendly to immigration from Central Europe,' wrote John W. Dafoe, the influential editor of the *Manitoba Free Press*, to Clifford Sifton, the former immigration minister. 'He says the country doesn't want any Poles at all. Ruthenians are a good deal better but he seems to think that they deteriorate in this country particularly if they are educated. He says they can be educated all right but that they cannot be civilized, at least not in one generation; and that the educated Ruthenian is a menace to his own countrymen and to the community.'[13]

Dafoe himself, in the aftermath of the Winnipeg General Strike of 1919, which was led by British-born immigrants, called for restricting new immigration to Britons and northern Europeans. Like many others, he demanded the government 'clear the aliens out of this community and ship them back to their happy homes in Europe which vomited them forth a decade ago.'[14] His *Free Press* propagated the notion that most Ukrainians were Communists by noting that Winnipeg's main Ukrainian Labour Temple was larger than any Ukrainian church in its vicinity, that Ukrainian Canadians were visiting the Soviet Union under the Labour Temple's sponsorship, and that 'a very considerable proportion of resident Ukrainians are now open or secret adherents of Bolshevism and are extending every effort to turn Canada into a communist nation, modelled on Soviet Russia.'[15] Judge Hugh John Macdonald, a former premier and the son of the first prime minister, recommended deporting Ruthenians, Russians, Poles, and Jews.[16] It was a comment on official sensitivity that when the Dominion Bureau of Statistics first acknowledged 'Ukrainians' as a distinct group in the 1921 census, every column referring to them had them misspelled as 'Ukranians.' The Department of External Affairs preferred that Ukrainians from Galicia be described as Galicians.[17]

Anglo-Canadian attitudes, of course, were not exclusively ignorant and bigoted. Frances Swyripa has traced ably how Anglo-Canadian sentiments towards minorities shifted from prescribing conformity to embracing ethnic diversity.[18] One might compare Charles H. Young's *Ukrainian Canadians: A Study in Assimilation* (1931) with Robert England's study *The Central European Immigrant in Canada* (1929). The former was sympathetically well-informed and depicted Ukrainians as a distinct cultural group to which Canadian government and politics were extraneous forces that contributed to assimilation and social disorganization. The latter reeked with paternalism and contrasted the Ukrainian's preference for gambling and alcohol with the Anglo-Saxon's proclivity for service, courtesy, and humaneness. Mixed feelings towards Ukrainians abounded. At the 1922 convention of the United Farmers of Manitoba – an organization that did not exclude Ukrainians but had no Ukrainian officers even in heavily Ukrainian districts like Dauphin – a public school teacher complained that 'it is no use talking to these people in terms of higher Canadianism, and to think [of them] in terms of Bohunk.'[19] Governor-General Lord Tweedsmuir expressed sympathetic support, in a since much-repeated quote, when he told Ukrainians in 1936 that 'you will be better Canadians, for being also good Ukrainians.'[20] Manitoba's lieutenant-governor declared at the first Ukrainian-Canadian congress in 1943 that 'your record is one of the finest in this country, your contributions are not excelled by those of any Anglo-Saxons.'[21]

Nevertheless, stereotypical images of Ukrainians persisted and were disseminated. The Slav as a dangerous revolutionary found his way into French-Canadian novels in the thirties, where the Jew already had an established role as money-lender.[22] None of Winnipeg's large banks, trust companies, or insurance firms would knowingly hire Ukrainians, Poles, or Jews, and Slavic and Jewish applicants to the University of Manitoba's medical school were restricted by arbitrary quotas as late as the forties.[23] An example of the generally negative portrayal of Ukrainians in the media was a *Toronto Daily Star* front-page headline in 1938. It boldly shouted 'Slavs to Swallow up Britishers, Germans Is a 100-Year Prediction' and cited as its authority an unidentified British 'noble lord and great demographer' who, lamenting the demise of the British Empire, asserted that 'a century from now the race will have gone to the strong, to the Slavs and Mongolians, to the people who are still willing to breed.'[24] During the depression Ukrainians and other immigrants were convenient scapegoats. 'When times are hard, and the native is forced by economic pressure to compete with the immigrant for any kind of work,' wrote an observer in the intellectual *Canadian Forum*, then the immigrant 'becomes a "Dirty Wop," a "Hunky," or a "Dago," and is regarded as an interloper who is trying to take the bread out of the honest mouths of our Native Sons.'[25]

Even in provinces and political parties that were relatively receptive to Ukrainian participation in public affairs, Ukrainians found themselves discriminated against and looked down upon well into mid-century. Consider the social-democratic melting pot that has been Saskatchewan where a Ukrainian is currently vying for the premiership as leader of the New Democratic party. In 1929 the Ku-Klux Klan contributed to the Conservatives' election by stirring up resentment against Ukrainian immigration.[26] The American sociologist Seymour Martin Lipset noted as late as 1950 that in Saskatchewan 'there is considerable prejudice against non-Anglo-Saxon groups, especially those from central and eastern Europe.' Ukrainians were made to feel inferior. They were underrepresented in rural community organizations and as convention delegates and in leadership posts in the governing Co-operative Commonwealth Federation, the NDP's forerunner. All the while, however, they were 'among the strongest supporters of the CCF' in Saskatchewan and were the only predominantly Catholic group whose support for the CCF was commensurate with that of the general population.[27] An ungenerous assessment of the political motivations of Ukrainians came from a long-time Manitoba MLA and senior CCF official: 'I have sensed that Ukrainians in particular are very interested in political positions,' wrote Donovan Swailes in 1956. 'Not that they want to advance any particular social principles, but just to enjoy the prestige of being in office. They are proud of anyone who holds a public position, whether he be Liberal, Tory, Social Credit, CCF or Communist.'[28] In the fifties Ukrainians had to make do with the appellation DP (for 'displaced person'), which was used loosely and pejoratively and as a reminder of inferior status.

Since the late fifties and early sixties, Canadian public opinion has come to look upon ethnic minorities more with pride and less with prejudice. Governor-General Ed Schreyer included some phrases in Ukrainian – along with English, French, German, and Polish – in his 1979 inaugural address. Ukrainians as a group are now viewed by others and themselves as established rather than as recent Canadians. That is what they are. They are seen now not as a threat or disquieting force, but as a valued component of a rich multicultural national fabric.

Political Participation

Anglo-Canadian perceptions of Ukrainians have evolved, been redefined, and have never been monolithic. Similarly, Ukrainian perceptions of their place in the Canadian political system have changed, and there has never been a single Ukrainian-Canadian political viewpoint. Much of the story of Ukrainian-Canadian political participation unfolds on the prairies and especially in Manitoba, for it was the primary receptacle for Ukrainians until after the Second World War. Winnipeg was the organizational and spiritual capital for Ukrainian Canadians. Five Ukrainian weeklies were published there by 1919. It is the only large Canadian city that has consistently, since 1911, elected Ukrainians to public office, including the mayoralty. Between 1908 and the early 1960s, more than seventy Ukrainians became reeves and mayors of Manitoba municipalities.[29] Since the forties, Ukrainians have been over-represented, relative to their population, in the Manitoba legislature. They made up one-quarter of the 1981 NDP cabinet.

In the early years, initiation into political life was carried out by the Liberals and Conservatives, who recognized and courted potential bloc votes. This led J.S. Woodsworth to describe 'a wholesale trade in "Galician" votes.' As in the dominant Anglo community, a small socialist group, the Ukrainian Social Democratic party, emerged and drew on European antecedents. After 1917, Ukrainian socialists were inspired by the Russian Revolution whereas Anglo-Canadian socialists continued to look to Fabianism, Methodism, and the British Labour party. Socialists, however, were a minority among Ukrainians as they were among Anglos.

Canadian government and politics for most Ukrainians was something still best left to and controlled by the dominant Anglos. The war had painfully underlined the tenuous status offered by citizenship granted through naturalization. For the established parties Ukrainians were a group to be manipulated at election time. The *Kanadiiskyi farmer* summed up how many Ukrainians perceived their political role on the eve of Manitoba's 1922 election:

both the Conservatives and Liberals never tried to enlighten the Ukrainians in political matters, but rather demoralized them during election campaigns by lavishing money rewards, by offering strong drink and by promising to build roads, etc. for their votes. This ... caused Ukrainians to consider elections as opportunity for making a little money or getting some other rewards. They were granted naturalization papers without being educated as to the real value and importance of these papers; they were told that the papers entitled them to a vote – although the parties bribed their votes. In short, our settlers, until comparatively recent times, were fine political instruments in the hands of the Anglo-Saxons; whichever party expended more money on buying their votes, that party prided in its victories and glories in its domination ...; neither government cared to inform the Ukrainians of their political rights and duties.[30]

In the inter-war years Ukrainians voted for Ukrainian and other candidates representing a variety of parties. For the most part, however, they continued to practise the politics of deference to the established parties and governments, especially in rural areas. The *Kanadiiskyi farmer* rationalized the logic of deferential behaviour in 1932: 'Canadian Ukrainians do not have any influence. We are poor and need political help. Ukrainian farmers and workers depend for their livelihood on the more powerful. This forces us to support a politically influential party. Affiliation with small radical parties brings us Ukrainians only discredit and ruin.' The *Ukrainskyi holos* forwarded a similar argument: 'We have to elect candidates put forward by the governing party ... Candidates from parties making strange and impossible promises will bring us no advantage, only national dishonour.'[31]

Despite these submissive sentiments, a goodly number of Ukrainians in Winnipeg voted for the 'strange and impossible' Communists. The Communist vote – whatever the ethnicity of the candidate – increased directly in proportion to the number of Ukrainians in each poll, a pattern unbroken between the thirties and the fifties.[32] The bond that existed between Ukrainian voters and the Communist party is revealed in table 1. It offers a matrix of correlations based on ethnic and voting data for Winnipeg North's multi-member constituency in the 1953 provincial election. Unsurprisingly and like the British and Jews, the percentage vote for Ukrainian candidates in the polls increased as the percentage of Ukrainian voters increased. All three ethnic groups tended to prefer candidates of their own ethnic background (correlations of 0.85, 0.76, and 0.90 respectively for the British, Jews, and Ukrainians). But this is where the similarity ended. Whereas the percentage vote for the Conservative, Liberal, and Social Credit candidates increased as the numbers of British voters increased (0.38, 0.84, and 0.51 respectively) and whereas the percentage vote for the CCF increased as the numbers of Jewish voters increased (0.74), support for the Communist Labour-Progressives increased only as the number of Ukrainian voters increased (0.87). Four of the twelve candidates were Ukrainian, and one each represented the Conservative, Liberal, CCF, and Communist parties. Although the collective vote totals for the non-Communist Ukrainians exceeded those for the Ukrainian Communist party leader, W.A. Kardash, he fared the best by far among Ukrainian voters and garnered more than twice as many votes on the first ballot (in a transferable ballot voting system) as any of his three Ukrainian rivals. Clearly, then, much of the Ukrainian vote in Winnipeg was neither deferential, anti-Communist, nor mainstream.

The decline of political deference among Ukrainians in the rural

TABLE 1
Correlations among ethnic and voting indicators for Winnipeg North in 1953

	Residents' ethnic origin		
	British Isles	Jewish	Ukrainian
Voting for candidates			
Anglo-Saxon candidates	0.85	−0.38	−0.59
Jewish candidates	0.18	0.76	−0.69
Ukrainian candidates	−0.59	−0.42	0.90
Voting for parties			
Conservatives	0.38	−0.07	−0.23
Liberals	0.84	−0.34	−0.63
CCF	−0.02	0.74	−0.46
Social Credit	0.51	−0.38	−0.37
Labour Progressives (Communist)	−0.78	−0.13	0.87

Source: Adapted from Nelson Wiseman and K.W. Taylor, 'Class and Ethnic Voting in Winnipeg during the Cold War,' *Canadian Review of Sociology and Anthropology* 16 (1979).

areas helps explain why the Saskatchewan CCF succeeded in the forties after having failed in the depression-ridden thirties, when one would have expected a stronger, more successful socialist party. Rural Ukrainians were one decade more Canadianized by the forties. As each year passed, more and more of them were second- and third-generation and felt more secure in voting for a socialist party. In rural Saskatchewan, unlike any of the other provinces, there were enough British socialists to make the CCF a viable political force. With the support of Ukrainians, the CCF broke the long-standing Liberal hold on the 'ethnic' vote. At the same time Ukrainian-Canadian leaders increasingly defined themselves as Anglo-Canadians had done, referring to themselves as 'British citizens,' 'British subjects,' and even 'British Ukrainians.'[33]

In the post-war era, Ukrainians shattered more barriers by attaining symbolically and politically important positions: in the fifties Michael Starr of Oshawa was selected for the first Diefenbaker cabinet, and two Ukrainians were appointed to the Senate. All the political parties became more receptive to Ukrainian membership and leadership. In the early years of the century the Liberals and Conservatives had organized partisan Ruthenian clubs, and the socialists and Communists had Ukrainian wings in the form of the Ukrainian Social Democratic party and the Ukrainian Labour-Farmer Temple Association. The concept of ethnic affiliates lost attraction for both Ukrainians and the political parties as time passed. In 1959 a Ukrainian Progressive-Conservative Club of

Manitoba was formed but it was not taken seriously and was disbanded by 1963.[34]

In this era Ukrainian Canadians became more energetic in asserting their group rights as an element of the Canadian mosaic. The RCMP had noted in the forties that some Ukrainian leaders were suggesting raising the status of the Ukrainian language to that of French.[35] If demography and pioneer settlement dictated English-French bilingualism in Quebec, reasoned many Ukrainians, why not English-Ukrainian bilingualism on the prairies? Paul Yuzyk used his maiden speech in the Senate in the sixties to denounce the tradition of having English and French Canadians alternate as the mover and seconder of the address in reply to the Speech from the Throne. This was discrimination, he noted (perhaps confusing the English-speaking with the ethnically British), against those who were neither English nor French in origin.[36] As a member of the Royal Commission on Bilingualism and Biculturalism, J.B. Rudnyckyj proposed a multilingual constitution that would entrench Ukrainian as a 'regional language.'[37] Editorials in the *Ukrainskyi holos* in the seventies and eighties argued for the recognition of Ukrainians' 'natural rights to language and culture' and for a public network of multilingual radio stations.[38] Such hopes were dashed in the exclusively bilingual language provisions for education and government services that emerged in the Constitution Act, 1982. This led some Ukrainians to argue that their language had been condemned to 'second-class status' and that they must 'rise as one in defence of their language' and 'mobilize politically and demand the resources needed to develop their Ukrainian-Canadian identity.'[39]

In terms of the Canadian national question, the French fact has reinforced rather than weakened the Ukrainian argument for bilingual education and multiculturalism. After the turn of the century French and Ukrainian Canadians were Catholic allies on the issue of bilingual schools, pursuing common cause in the face of an Anglicizing British Protestantism. Bilingual schools and special training schools for Ukrainian teachers were established but disappeared in the unilingual backlash unleashed by the First World War. Although an unofficial, sporadic, and informal type of bilingual education re-emerged in Manitoba, where Ukrainian was taught in some high schools after regular hours, the practice faded by the late thirties as there was a shortage of Canadian-born Ukrainians with a sufficient knowledge of the language to teach it competently.[40] Since the sixties, the language of individual and minority group rights has gained currency in Canada. As the status of the French language was recognized in Canada's revised constitution in the eighties, so too was the multicultural perspective so long lobbied for by Ukrainian-Canadian organizations. The courts are now directed explicitly to interpret the Charter of Rights and Freedoms 'in a manner consistent with the preservation and enhancement of the multicultural heritage of Canadians.' Moreover, the equality provisions of the charter now prohibit discrimination on the basis of national or ethnic origin.

Left and Right

Ukrainian Canadians have never been an ideologically homogeneous group. In fact, more than most other Canadian ethnic groups they have produced a variety of bitterly antagonistic parties and factions. The ideological spectrum of Ukrainian-Canadian politics has been remarkably wide and polarized. It has contained liberals and democrats, chauvinists and reactionaries, monarchists and republicans, Communists, socialists, and social democrats. Some political group activity has been worldly and has involved pursuing practical goals such as improving the economic lot and cultural status of Ukrainian Canadians. Other aspects of political group activity have been utopian and otherworldly. In the inter-war years, for example, there was the Communist pie-in-the-sky vision of proletarian internationalism. There was also the Hetmanite dream of an independent Ukraine headed by a monarch. In considering the fortunes of left and right organizations, one needs always to remember that many members were politically unsophisticated and joined more for the social and cultural facilities that they offered than because of a strong ideological predisposition.

The religious spectrum has also been broadened. Some of the Catholics were won over to the Orthodox church after 1918. The Presbyterians, the United Church, evangelical fundamentalists, Anglicans, and others also made inroads, and today fewer than half of Ukrainian Canadians claim an affiliation with the Ukrainian Catholic and Orthodox churches. In the inter-war years religious differences reinforced political differences: the Communists were anti-clerical atheists; most Hetmanites were Catholic and Conservative; the Ukrainian Self-Reliance League was Orthodox and primarily Liberal. Organized religion and religious differences have become weaker forces in Ukrainian-Canadian politics, and the ideological spectrum has narrowed as those on the periphery (Communists, monarchists, and inveterate nationalists keen on returning to a liberated Ukraine) have faded away or moved towards the centre.

Socialism, of both the Communist and social democratic varieties, was more popular in the pioneer wave of Ukrainians than in the inter-war and cold-war waves of immigrants. It may be suggested that Canada's 'exploitative working conditions [meant that] socialism could be expected to have widespread appeal.'[41] However, the rather small Ukrainian socialist organizations that were successful in community organizing were so despite, rather than because of, their critique of property relations and capitalism. What won Ukrainians over to the ULFTA was the cultural programmes: lectures, theatre, and music and language classes. Canada's 'exploitative working conditions' were not sufficient to explain the strong link between communism and Ukrainians in Canada, for the same 'exploitative conditions' were experienced by other ethnic groups that proved less susceptible to Communist organizations. Moreover, in comparative perspective, Canada's economic conditions were never all that bad: no Ukrainian Canadian has starved to death, not even in the depths of the depression in the thirties – quite a contrast to conditions in Soviet Ukraine at the same time.

As part of the Ukrainian-Canadian community, Communists have been few; as part of the Communist party of Canada, however, Ukrainians have been many. This tells us more about the Communist party than about Ukrainians. Nevertheless, reviewing their experience in the CP reveals their distinctive and powerful influence as a group. Accounts vary, but Finns, Ukrainians, and Jews made up the overwhelming majority of the CP when it was a nascent force in Canadian politics in the thirties and forties. Anglos dominated the CP's leadership, but the other three groups made up an estimated 90 per cent of the party. John Kolasky, a former Communist, suggested that about a thousand of the CP's twenty-five hundred members in the early thirties were Ukrainians. Others claim that Ukrainians were the single largest group.[42] Matthew Popovich – urbane, educated, and talented – was one in a Canadian delegation of two to the plenum of the Comintern in 1926, and John Navis (Navizivsky) was one of four Canadians at the Comintern's sixth congress in 1928. Both of them came from Galicia and settled in Canada in 1911–12. Tim Buck, the CP's British-born leader, recalled how in Winnipeg the party was overwhelmingly Ukrainian and Jewish.[43] North Winnipeg's Ukrainians elected Bill Kolisnyk as an alderman in 1926, making him the first Communist office holder in North America.

The substantial size and influence of the ULFTA in the CP was itself an issue in the history of Canadian communism. In the twenties the ULFTA felt that the party insufficiently recognized its efforts while the party leadership felt that some Ukrainian comrades were political opportunists.[44] One side stressed national identity and national struggle, the other class identity and class struggle. The Comintern came down on the side of the Anglo leadership and insisted that the party 'Bolshe-vize' itself by eliminating party affiliation based on language group-ings.[45] The Canadian CP was told to offer English classes to Ukrainian members and to adopt English as its common language outside of Que-bec. The ULFTA was directed to reorient its newspaper and programmes so that they de-emphasized Ukrainian cultural activities and stressed the common struggle of Ukrainian workers and the international proletariat. The ULFTA resisted CP directives, however, and on two occasions the Comintern sent representatives to Canada to mediate.[46]

What was remarkably absent on the Ukrainian-Canadian Left for a long time after the First World War was a non-Communist socialist or social democratic tendency like the one represented by the USDP in the years before the war. One such group, the Ukrainian Workers' League, emerged in the mid-thirties after irrepressible reports of famine and persecution in Soviet Ukraine. It joined the Ukrainian Canadian Com-mittee in 1940. None of this, however, was of much expense to the ULFTA, whose national membership nearly doubled from eight thou-sand to fifteen thousand during the thirties.[47]

The weakness of social democracy and the strength of communism among Ukrainians until after the Second World War are reflected in Ivan Avakumovic's parallel studies of Canadian socialism and commu-nism. His book on the CCF-NDP contains not a single reference to Ukrainians in the inter-war years; his book on the CP is replete with them.[48] Although the Manitoba CCF produced a Ukrainian translation of the Regina Manifesto, hired a Ukrainian organizer, and briefly printed a Ukrainian version of its newspaper, these efforts bore little fruit.[49] There were virtually no Ukrainian members of the Manitoba CCF before the mid-forties. As we have seen, significant social democratic gains among Ukrainians came in Saskatchewan beginning in 1944. To a lesser and later extent they also came in Manitoba in 1969 when Ukrainians voted disproportionately for the NDP in an election characterized as an 'ethnic revolt.'[50] David Orlikow, who served as an elected school trustee, alderman, MLA, and MP for north Winnipeg for forty-four consecutive years, in 1972 offered this insight into Ukrainian voting behaviour in his constituency: 'Both the Communists and the anti-Communists ... had their politics determined by the Russian Revolution. You were pro-Bolshevik or anti. As time has gone along that generation of people is disappearing. Their children, on both sides, don't care ... I would say, in a general way, that Ukrainian people forty-five and younger take their politics from work and not from the church or from the fraternal organi-zations. A very large percentage of them work in the packing houses, the steel plants, and the railways. And those unions are sympathetic to the NDP, so they, the workers, are sympathetic to the NDP.'[51]

Nevertheless, the Ukrainian influence in the now tiny CP persists; in the eighties half of the financial contributors to the Manitoba CP were Ukrainians.[52] The ULFTA's successor is the Association of United Ukrainian Canadians. It claims to have launched a critical review of its history and denies that it is any longer a 'direct transmission belt' for the CP.[53] It continues to provide the same language and analyses, however, as the CP and the CPSU: that the Soviet Union is undergoing a process of 'reconstruction, openness, and democratization,' that Stalin's era was one of errors and Brezhnev's one of 'stagnation.'

Our understanding of right-wing Ukrainian-Canadian politics has been underdeveloped in comparison with what we know of left-wing Ukrainian politics, although recent work is helping to level this imbalance.[54] While some Anglo-Canadians saw Ukrainians as radical Communists, others saw them as reactionary nationalists, calling them 'Fascists' and 'militants.' The second wave of Ukrainian immigrants, those of the late twenties, included proud and bitter war veterans of Ukraine's brief flirtation with national independence. Although Paul Yuzyk claimed that the inter-war immigrants were 'mainly' veterans of the Ukrainian armies, there were only 585 members of the Ukrainian War Veterans' Association in Canada in 1930.[55] Nevertheless, these Old World warriors became the nucleus of the fiercely anti-Communist Ukrainian National Federation, the strongest and most vocal Ukrainian-Canadian nationalist organization, whose leaders the Canadian government considered to be in wartime contact with the terrorist, European-based Organization of Ukrainian Nationalists (OUN).[56] By the outbreak of the Second World War, the UNF boasted 145 branches,[57] but its popular following was never the size of the ULFTA's. Whereas the latter was a mass organization that consciously appealed to large numbers of Ukrainians, the UNF was a cadre organization built around a few leaders.

Unlike the Left, the Ukrainian Right was highly fragmented and incessantly quarrelsome. There were competing churches, lay organizations, and newspapers. Less militant on the national question and more driven by religious conviction than the UNF was the Ukrainian Self-Reliance League, which, when it appeared in the twenties, stressed the organic interrelationship of the Ukrainian nation, Ukrainian culture, and the Ukrainian Orthodox church. Rather than class struggle, the USRL pursued 'the harmonizing of class differences.'[58] Its vehicle was the *Ukrainskyi holos*, which had helped popularize the term 'Ukrainian' before the First World War.

A colourful, conservative, and militaristic organization was the Sitch, which also sprang up in the twenties. It claimed five hundred uniformed members divided into twenty-one companies, marched in a parade celebrating Canada's diamond jubilee, and participated in annual military exercises at Camp Hughes.[59] The Sitch was organized with the support of Canada's Ukrainian Catholic bishop, Nykyta Budka, and represented a form of 'born again' Catholicism. In the thirties the Sitch became the United Hetman Organization and claimed fifty branches. The Hetmanites created a League of British Ukrainians and prescribed a monarchal, independent Ukraine with a form of responsible government as practised in the British Empire. Their programme called for a 'good neighbourly ... political and economic relationship between the two Monarchal Governments – British and Ukrainian.'[60] The high point for Hetmanism in Canada was the 1938 visit of *Hetmanych* Danylo Skoropadsky, the son of the hetman who had ruled Ukraine briefly in 1918. He was greeted by leading Canadian politicians and lauded as a 'prince' and heir to the Ukrainian throne by his supporters. Ukrainian Communists and Orthodox church supporters, in contrast, compared the title *hetman* to *Führer* and *duce*, pointed to Skoropadsky's German residence, and denounced him as Hitler's agent.[61] The death of Skoropadsky in 1957 extinguished the Hetmanite flame.

Today the ideological politics of Ukrainian Canadians more than half a century ago seem distant, quaint, and impossibly polarized. In their day, however, they paralleled ideological divisions within Europe, if not Canada, and were symptomatic of their times. It was the extremes in the Ukrainian-Canadian political spectrum that led to systematic surveillance by the RCMP and occasional special attention by the Department of External Affairs and American intelligence services.

Ukrainian-Canadian voting behaviour has been, increasingly since the fifties, like that of the general population. Ukrainian Canadians have voted for Ukrainian and non-Ukrainian candidates of the major parties, and there cannot be said to be, as once there could be, a bloc vote in specific ridings. In federal politics on the prairies, where most Ukrainian Canadians continue to reside, they have voted generally like their neighbours: against the Liberals. They have preferred the Conservatives and, secondarily, the NDP. They have also become more receptive to provincial Conservative parties that were historically antipathetic to them but have opened up to Ukrainian leaders and members. The Russian Revolution and the Sovietization of Ukraine are, with each passing year, that much more removed from and less relevant to Ukrainian Canadians. That generation has largely passed away, and there has been hardly any immigration of Ukrainians for nearly forty years. Public education and generational replacement have reduced the deep ideological differences. Ukrainian-Canadian politics has become more like mainstream Canadian politics: moderate, bunched near the centre, and driven by middle-class values.

The National Question

Once upon a time the national question was at the heart of Ukrainian consciousness. Relative to its population, Canada received more Ukrainian immigrants than any other non-European state. They helped sustain the dream of Ukrainian independence. Since the First World War the wish for a non-Communist homeland has driven many Ukrainian Canadians and their organizations, especially those formed by the émigrés, war veterans, and intellectuals of the second and third waves of migration. A difference between the pioneer and the inter-war waves was that some of the latter were critical of the former's established organizations, like the Orthodox-inspired USRL, which they considered too 'Canadian,' too preoccupied with Ukrainian-Canadian institutions, and insufficiently zealous in support of an independent Ukraine.

The competing ideologies of the Ukrainian-Canadian Left and Right reflected, as we have seen, different visions of how society generally and a Ukrainian state specifically ought to be structured. For the always minoritarian and now disoriented and minuscule Communist tendency, Ukrainian independence was a non-issue, for it defined Ukraine as the USSR defined it: a constitutionally independent, politically 'progressive' socialist republic within the Soviet federation. The divisions between the Ukrainian Left and Right in Canada were at times reflected in parallel efforts around the same European cause, as in the late twenties, when nationalists and Communists organized competing relief committees to aid victims of a devastating flood in Galicia. Sometimes the Left and Right clashed physically. In the late forties, a mêlée broke out at a meeting organized by the Association of United Ukrainian Canadians, the pro-Soviet group. Recent DPs disrupted the proceedings, shouted anti-Communist and anti-Semitic obscenities, and the ensuing fracas left several people injured.[62]

Ukrainian consciousness in the New World was blurred initially by the lack of an independent European homeland. The absence of a clear sense of ethnic group coherence among immigrants was evident in their describing themselves by various regional terms such as Galician and Bukovynian or by the older national designation Ruthenian (*rusyn*). The

Ukrainian National Republic's brief life (1917–21) helped to galvanize Ukrainian identity in Canada. It was a source of pride and hope. It represented the first time in the modern history of Ukrainians that their political elite strove to unite and that they possessed such national symbols as a government and an army.

The remarkably strong links between Ukrainian Canadians and the struggle for a 'liberated,' independent Ukraine now run back over seven decades to the days of the UNR. The Ukrainian Canadian Citizens' League beseeched Prime Minister Borden in 1919 to recognize the Ukrainian government but to no avail.[63] Two Ukrainian Canadians attended the Paris Peace Conference at the end of the First World War, and the Ukrainian Canadian Committee lobbied the Paris Peace Conference at the end of the Second World War in support of international recognition of the sovereign rights of an independent Ukraine.[64] In the early twenties ten thousand Ukrainians marched on Winnipeg's Polish consulate to protest that government's policies in Galicia; it was a congregation of Ukrainian Canadians unrivalled until the dedication of Taras Shevchenko's statue on the grounds of the Manitoba legislature in the sixties. Ukrainian Canadians were in the forefront of international support for the Galician (or Western Ukrainian National Republic) government-in-exile, but their hopes were dashed in 1923 when the Council of Ambassadors of the allied powers recognized all of Galicia as part of Poland and no longer as merely territory under Polish military occupation.

The Canadian government's position on Ukraine has never favoured independence and has had more in common with the Communist view than with that offered by nationalist Ukrainian Canadians. In the interwar years Mackenzie King's government saw Canada as a 'fireproof house' that was best kept that way by remaining silent on European issues and avoiding European entanglements. After the outbreak of the Second World War, the government banned the ULFTA and the CP. Ottawa actively encouraged the other Ukrainian organizations to join a united front – the Ukrainian Canadian Committee – whose purposes were to aid the Canadian war effort and repress any contrary inclinations. More than any other ethnic group, the Ukrainian-Canadian group was suspected by the RCMP and other government authorities like the Nationalities Branch of the War Department of containing 'radical leftists' and unsympathetic sentiments vis-à-vis the war effort.[65] The results of the conscription referendum of 1942 reinforced these views. Whereas Anglo districts voted overwhelmingly in favour, Ukrainian, French, and German districts were much less supportive and in some cases were opposed.[66] This led the then influential *Winnipeg Free Press* to supplement its older view of Ukrainians as Communists with the charge that they were now also 'potential fifth columnists' with fascistic, pro-Hitler proclivities.

Thus, in both wars, Ukrainian Canadians had to contend with being depicted as siding with Canada's enemy. When the Soviet Union entered the war on the allied side, the ULFTA and the CP were decriminalized. They promptly denounced the UCC as a fascist agent of Germany. The Canadian government now saw Ukrainian-Canadian aspirations for an independent Ukraine as being inconsistent with British policy at a time when Britain counted for more in Canadian calculations than it did later and as an unwelcome challenge to its new and strategically vital Soviet ally, with whom it established diplomatic relations in 1942.

The Canadian government actively discouraged broaching the issue of Ukrainian independence. To External Affairs the concept was a 'mirage,' an idea that had to be driven out of the minds of Ukrainian Canadians in order to 'hasten the process of their assimilation.'[67] Thus, when the UCC made proposals on this score, they were judged 'presumptuous' and 'unacceptable.' Although the government was willing to agitate for the liberation of Soviet satellites like Poland and Hungary after the war, it steadfastly refused to extend the principle to Ukraine and considered it to be neither economically nor politically viable even if the USSR shed communism.[68] As for the Soviet government, it viewed the anti-Communist Ukrainian-Canadian community as the major obstacle to improved Soviet-Canadian relations since it was so persistent and vociferous in challenging the very legitimacy and integrity of the USSR.

Despite their efforts the nationalists never budged Ottawa – even in the sympathetic Diefenbaker years – from the position that Ukraine ('the' Ukraine to External Affairs and the Canadian media generally) is a constituent republic of the USSR.[69] Throwing even more cold water on the idea that Canada might consider stressing Ukraine's 'political individuality,' External Affairs pointed to the success of such 'Ukrainians' as Khrushchev in the central government.[70] Like many countries, Canada has lived with the contradiction of recognizing Ukraine as a voting member of the United Nations but not as a separate sovereign state.

After the Second World War Ukrainian Canadians lobbied to maintain a hard anti-Soviet stance in Canadian foreign policy and cautioned Ottawa against being seduced by Moscow's assurances of 'peaceful coexistence.' Leading the anti-Soviet assault were those in the third

wave of immigration from whom were drawn many of the leaders of
the Canadian League for the Liberation of Ukraine. Formed in the late
forties, it initially operated outside the UCC umbrella, but in the fifties
it came to terms with its Canadianism and the reality that the condition
of diaspora was permanent rather than temporary. It then joined the
UCC as did many other post-war organizations.[71] Concerned that the
agenda of the UCC might become more driven by recent immigrants
with European rather than Canadian interests, the government maintained its surveillance.[72] The last wave's impact was muted, however,
because it was smaller and more widely dispersed than the earlier waves.
Most of it gravitated to southern metropolitan Ontario. where older
organizations – the UNF, for example – had also transferred their headquarters after the war, but where the Ukrainian presence was less concentrated, less noticeable, and, as time passed, less distinct than it had
been on the prairies.

Even before *glasnost* and *perestroika* worked their way into Soviet-
Canadian relations, the zeal for a liberated Ukraine had mellowed
among Ukrainian Canadians as more and more of them were Canadian-
born. Manoly Lupul has lamented their 'indifference to the fate of
Ukraine.'[73] Nevertheless, mistrust of the USSR continued to be reflected
in the eighties in the vigorous protests by Ukrainian organizations
against the mandate of the Deschênes commission on war criminals and
the recognition by Canadian courts of documents provided by the Soviet
government. Suspicion, however, is giving way as the world changes:
Ukrainian-Canadian businessmen are reaching out to Soviet Ukraine,
where they can now deal directly with local authorities.[74] Increased trade
with and direct investment in Ukraine represent new entrepreneurial
challenges for Ukrainian Canadians. Conversely, Soviet Ukrainians now
have more access to information about and interest in Ukrainian Canadians and their now century-old heritage.

The Future of Ukrainian-Canadian Politics

Over the past century, Ukrainian Canadians have expressed themselves
dually: as a strong, organized, and consciously distinct cultural group
and as a group exhibiting many features of assimilated behaviour.
Although most Ukrainians are not affiliated with any Ukrainian organization and the Ukrainian Canadian Congress is not as inclusive as it
was in the past, more than most ethnic groups Ukrainian Canadians
have been concerned with publicizing their image and claiming public
recognition and assistance for the cause of perpetuating their culture.

Organizational efforts, such as the successful campaign for bilingual schools in the seventies and eighties, have been testimony to the importance of Ukrainian Canadians as a political force even though most Ukrainians have not been associated with these efforts.

Reciprocal influence has pervaded the Ukrainian-Canadian experience. Canadianization has changed Ukrainians, but Ukrainians have helped transform Canada. Dual identity has entailed a loss of language and customs among many Ukrainians. Simultaneously more of them have succeeded in politics, an avocation once the preserve of the British and French charter groups. Although Ukrainian-Canadian organizations were in the forefront of those demanding official multiculturalism, more Ukrainians in recent years have criticized the concept. Many on the prairies especially regard it now as benefiting primarily the newer and visible waves of immigrants – from Asia, the Caribbean, Latin America, and southern Europe – who have tended to settle in central Canada.[75]

Ukrainian immigration to Canada since the fifties has been no more than a trickle. The prospect of a new wave is dim. Religion, moreover, is neither the unifying force for Ukrainians nor the divisive force for Canadians that it once was. As assimilation, intermarriage, and acculturation proceed, a distinctive Ukrainian-Canadian political influence will be less discernible even while Ukrainian Canadians attain high political office and their organizations and cultural institutions flourish. Unforeseeable political developments in Ukraine may feed a revitalized Ukrainian consciousness in Canada as they have in the past. But that is problematic as Ukrainian Canadians lose their otherness. Ukrainian separateness is more a feature of the past than of the present. As for the future, Ukrainian Canadians will become even more deeply entrenched in the mainstream of Canadian political life. They have permanently left the periphery of the political system.

Looking for the Ukrainian Vote

BOHDAN HARASYMIW

One of the enduring myths and mysteries of Canadian politics is the ethnic bloc vote. It is the Big Foot – or, if you prefer, the Ogopogo – of political lore in Canada. No one has seen it, except for an infrequent and fleeting shadow, but everyone believes it exists. Politicians in particular are prone to pay homage to it in victory and to blame it in defeat.[1] The hundredth anniversary of the settlement of Ukrainian immigrants in Canada, therefore, provides an appropriate – some would say compulsory – opportunity to re-examine this myth as it applies to these immigrants and their descendants, the Ukrainian Canadians.

The tendency for Ukrainian Canadians to vote as a bloc was noted on the prairies in the 1920s and 1930s.[2] One way for parties to court this vote was to field candidates of the same ethnic group. The voters generally responded, or so it was thought. 'Almost invariably Ukrainians in Manitoba, as elsewhere, voted for Ukrainian candidates, regardless of party affiliation.'[3] In Saskatchewan, token Ukrainian candidates were expected to attract votes to the party throughout the province.[4] In Alberta, the United Farmers and Social Credit parties encouraged ethnic political participation, and 'Ukrainian candidates for the UFA and Social Credit parties were largely successful because they could count upon a bloc of Ukrainian votes.'[5] The 'bloc vote' phenomenon was not treated with much credibility by the early 1980s.[6]

It is not possible to retrieve from the written record of Canadian political history, from public opinion surveys, or from interviews with the participants the voting habits of Ukrainians in Canada over the better part of the last hundred years, yet the question of a tendency to vote en bloc, especially for a fellow ethnic or compatriot, remains an intriguing one. If during at least some part of their experience in Canada these Ukrainian Canadians have felt an identity with certain political parties or have expressed their solidarity through voting, then this ought to have manifested itself in the fate of Ukrainian candidates for elective office. Although the motives of Ukrainian-Canadian voters cannot be retrospectively reconstructed, the results of elections where Ukrainians were candidates may provide a way to assess the plausibility of the ethnic bloc vote. If there has been bloc voting, and if Ukrainians do prefer 'their own' candidates, then this should have made a difference in the results of elections contested by Ukrainians.

Starting from this line of reasoning, this study undertakes to conduct an experiment so as to do three things:

1 to ascertain whether there has been a clearly identifiable Ukrainian vote, by which is meant a vote by Ukrainians for a Ukrainian candidate that thereby enhanced that candidate's chances for success;

2 to identify the exact political colouring of the Ukrainian vote in Canadian federal and provincial elections and to specify its particular partisan orientation in given times and places; and

3 to test the commonly held assumption that competition among Ukrainian candidates splits the Ukrainian vote and thereby prevents these candidates from obtaining an electoral victory.

These objectives are here pursued not by observing the voting of Ukrainians for Ukrainian candidates directly, but by interpreting the outcomes of elections. It is assumed that there may be a Ukrainian vote in constituencies where there has been a Ukrainian candidate; the fate of the candidate may be decided by that ethnic Ukrainian vote – if not, then for all practical purposes, as far as this study is concerned, that vote does not exist because it makes no difference. No ethnic tie, in other words, no ethnic vote.

The study attempts to analyse the problem systematically by exploring the following four hypotheses:

1. *If there is a Ukrainian vote, as defined here, then the chances of candidates with Ukrainian names being elected should be independent of the number of such Ukrainians seeking office.* That is, if the ability of Ukrainian candidates to pull in the votes of their kinsmen is real, then their likelihood of winning elections cannot be based on their proportion of candidates, but must be due to something else (i.e., this Ukrainian vote). Since it is usually assumed that Ukrainian voters will rally behind one of their compatriots, then Ukrainian candidates should have done better at winning election in those cases where there were fewest of them – preferably one – per constituency. When there is more than one ethnic candidate,

so the conventional thinking (which this study regards critically and tries to put to the test) goes, the vote is split and there is less likelihood of a Ukrainian victory. If the percentage of Ukrainian candidates as a proportion of all candidates in those contests in which Ukrainians choose to do electoral battle varies proportionately (i.e., correlates) with the percentage of Ukrainians victorious in such contests, then the hypothesis is nullified.

2. *If there is a Ukrainian vote, then two or more Ukrainian candidates will usually split that vote and neither or none will win, provided they are not the sole candidates.* The conventional wisdom thus holds that since Ukrainians vote for Ukrainians, competition is bad for the objective of obtaining representation and consolidation is preferable. Competing Ukrainian candidates, it says, will lose out to their non-Ukrainian competitors. This assumes the primacy of the ethnic over the partisan tie in electoral politics, which is questionable.

3. *If there is a Ukrainian vote, then its partisan tendency should be ascertainable, at least in part, from the results of elections in those constituencies where all candidates were Ukrainians.* In this instance, ethnicity is held constant and the partisan proclivity of the group is apparent. This political coloration of Ukrainian Canadians will vary according to time and place.

4. *If there is a Ukrainian vote, then, in cases where a Ukrainian incumbent steps down or is defeated or replaced by a non-Ukrainian and there is another Ukrainian in a subsequent race, votes of Ukrainian electors should be seen to 'migrate' to the other Ukrainian candidate rather than remaining loyal to the former's party.* In other words, while a shift of voters cannot be documented without survey data, the net effect of such a shift should be visible, and a party's loss of its Ukrainian candidate should also entail its loss of Ukrainian voters. Ukrainian voters should be the first to defect once they no longer have a candidate of 'their own.'

In these various ways, then, the presumed ethnically motivated voting of Ukrainian voters should be seen to make a critical difference to the success of Ukrainian-Canadian candidates.

Method

Based on the monumental compendium on Ukrainians in Canada compiled some years ago by William Darcovich and the late Senator Paul Yuzyk, supplemented by more up-to-date materials,[7] this chapter reports the results of this modest but novel experiment. Lists were drawn up of the election results (including by-elections) spanning the period from 1904 at the earliest down to 1990 at the latest in all of those federal

TABLE 1
Summary results of elections contested by Ukrainian candidates, federal and four provinces

Jurisdiction	No. of constituencies contested	Total candidates	Ukrainians	No. of Ukrainian winners
Federal (1904–88)	332	1,561	426	87
Ontario (1945–90)	95	369	98	23
Manitoba (1914–88)	224	879	312	98
Saskatchewan (1912–86)	135	465	166	48
Alberta (1913–89)	208	915	302	104
Total	994	4,189	1,304	360

and provincial constituencies where the name of at least one candidate was known or thought to be Ukrainian.[8] In selecting only these contests, it was assumed that other constituencies probably did not have significant concentrations of Ukrainian settlement or political activism. These lists were then subjected to an analysis that produced the following findings relevant to the stated hypotheses.

Findings

First Hypothesis

For the entire period, 1904 to 1990, for the elections and by-elections to the House of Commons and the legislatures in the provinces of Ontario, Manitoba, Saskatchewan, and Alberta, there were 994 contests in which at least one of the candidates' names was Ukrainian (see table 1).[9] There were 4,189 candidacies in all of these contests, or an average of 4.2 each. A total of 1,304 of these carried Ukrainian names, or 1.3 per contest. Thus candidates with Ukrainian names in all of these elections represented 31.1 per cent of all the candidacies; they were successful in 360 (or 36.2 per cent) of the contests. If Ukrainian candidates have managed to capture a larger proportion of seats than their percentage of candidacies, then they must historically have had something going for them: perhaps it was the ethnic Ukrainian vote that gave them the edge.

When this large aggregate is broken down into its federal and individual provincial components, the first hypothesis receives its first real test. The breakdown shows that competition is actually good, rather than bad, for Ukrainian candidates. Alberta and Manitoba, with averages of

1.5 and 1.4 Ukrainian candidacies respectively per contest, also have the highest success rates for Ukrainians winning these contests – 50.0 and 43.8 per cent, respectively. Ontario, with an average of only 1.0 Ukrainian candidacy – or one per constituency per election – fares worst with a success rate of only 24.2 per cent. (The House of Commons and Saskatchewan fall in between with averages of 1.3 and 1.2 and percentages of 26.2 and 35.6, respectively.) The more the merrier, seems to be the slogan here – the more competition in contesting elections, the more likelihood of Ukrainians capturing seats instead of vice versa.

Further disaggregation of the data places the first hypothesis more into doubt. Using each election and by-election in each jurisdiction – federal, Ontario, Manitoba, Saskatchewan, and Alberta – as an event, and the string of these as a series, the percentage of Ukrainian candidacies was correlated with the percentage of Ukrainian victories (data not shown). This produced the following values of r (the Pearson product-moment correlation coefficient): Federal $+0.3643$, Ontario $+0.6474$, Manitoba $+0.0462$, Saskatchewan $+0.1202$, Alberta $+0.3492$ – which is to say, values ranging from slightly to negligibly significant indicating a positive relationship between the two variables and challenging, if not yet overturning, the hypothesis about Ukrainian voting being channelled to Ukrainian candidates in some special (non-mechanical) way.

Using the longitudinal time-series, another correlation was carried out, looking for the relationship between the competitiveness among Ukrainian candidates and their likelihood of electoral victory. Competitiveness was measured as the ratio between (a) the number of constituencies contested by Ukrainians, in this study the number of 'contests,' and (b) the number of Ukrainian candidates. The value of this ratio was equal to unity if there was only one candidate per contest; less than unity if there were more. According to the conventional wisdom, the percentage of victories should have been greatest when competitiveness was at or approaching 1.0. The measurement of the correlation coefficient for the five jurisdictions does not at all support such a conclusion. The values of r were, in fact: Federal -0.3033, Ontario -0.3702, Manitoba -0.2569, Saskatchewan -0.1699, Alberta $+0.0328$.

Not only are these rather insignificant, but all of the signs are in the wrong direction except one. What this means is that there is, according to this measure, which looks at the whole historical experience of the past century, no significant relationship in an overall ecological sense between the intraethnic competition among Ukrainian candidates and their ability to pull in the supposedly all-important Ukrainian vote that helps them gain a seat in Parliament or a provincial legislature. If anything, it is the opposite of what is popularly assumed.

The first hypothesis, therefore, if not entirely laid to rest, should at least be given a rest in further discussions of how ethnic voting works in Canada.

Second Hypothesis

According to the second hypothesis, competition, not just in the aggregate but down at the grass roots in the actual riding, is the path to perdition as far as hopes of translating Ukrainian votes into Ukrainian seats are concerned. To test this, let us look at all of the contests where there was more than one Ukrainian name among the candidates, but not all of the candidates were Ukrainian – that is, two or more, but not all – and at whether a Ukrainian won the contest or not. We thus discover some remarkable characteristics about these particular contests (as opposed to those where there was only one Ukrainian was the sole candidate, or where only Ukrainians were contestants). In federal politics, where there were fifty-three such contests, this in-group ethnic competition made no difference at all to the outcome in terms of a Ukrainian victory. Almost exactly half of these cases (50.9 per cent) resulted in a win for a Ukrainian candidate; half (49.1) did not. In Manitoba, of forty-two cases, the corresponding percentages were exactly 50.0. In Saskatchewan and Alberta, the likelihood of a Ukrainian victory despite competition from fellow Ukrainians was even greater: 60.0 per cent (but $N = 20$ in Saskatchewan) and 63.0 ($N = 46$). Again, the more the merrier seems to be the rule here, not the fewer the better.

Taking a closer look at those who won and those who lost these contests where Ukrainians struggled among themselves in the great political arena of elections, what becomes apparent is that party affiliation made an extremely significant difference as to whether these candidates won or lost. If party affiliation had made no difference, then the same proportion of candidates for each of the parties should have fallen on either side of the great divide. This was not the case. In federal politics, between 1935 and 1988, only a single one of the twenty-eight attempts by a Ukrainian to carry the banner of the CCF or the NDP into the House of Commons succeeded; none of the forty-six attempts by those of the LPP, CP, MLP, Green, Libertarian, Reform, or Independent persuasion was successful. Only two out of twenty-five Liberal attempts succeeded. On the other hand, twenty-seven out of forty Progressive

Conservative standard-bearers were victorious, and five out of twenty-nine Social Crediters.[10]

In Manitoba (1922–88), the relationship is not as strong, chiefly because the Liberal and Conservative candidates fit the overall pattern of wins and losses exactly. The CCF, NDP, and others are the nonconformists. The value of chi-squared is 11.29 with three degrees of freedom such that $p = 0.01$, which is still a significant relationship. In Saskatchewan (1921–86), there were too few cases in too many cells for a statistical test. On eight out of fourteen occasions when a Ukrainian ran as a CCF or NDP candidate the result was a victory; only two out of twelve Liberal standard-bearers and only one out of six Conservatives were successful. This means that party affiliation is more significant than ethnicity in Saskatchewan as well.

In Alberta (1915–89), where chi-squared for the relationship in question was 29.70 with df $= 2$ and $p < 0.001$, Social Credit and Progressive Conservative candidates tended to win, reflecting the dominance of those two parties historically on the provincial political scene. The Ukrainian candidates who, in competition with their fellow ethnics, tended to lose (only five out of fifty-six attempts successful) belonged to what in that province, if not elsewhere in the country, counts as the flaky fringe – CCF, NDP, LPP, CP, UFA, Independent, Representative, Western Canada Concept, and Liberal. Out of twenty-five attempts at public office on behalf of the Social Credit party, fourteen were successful despite the ethnic competition, as were eleven out of nineteen on behalf of the Conservatives.

If the conventional wisdom holds that competition is bad for garnering those ethnic votes and getting elected to office, then the corollary to this must be that the lone Ukrainian candidate ought to do comparatively better than those in the competitive situation. In fact, this is not so. Lone Ukrainian candidates are more likely to lose than are those in competition with fellow Ukrainians. In federal elections and by-elections between 1904 and 1988, 80.4 per cent of such ethnically unopposed candidacies were unsuccessful (as compared to 50 per cent for the competitive ones), or just taking the three major parties into account, 72.1 per cent (see table 2). In Ontario (1945–90), the figure was 66.1 per cent; in the three prairie provinces, the corresponding percentages were: 65.4 in Manitoba (1914–88); 73.1 in Saskatchewan (1912–86); and 65.9 in Alberta (1913–89), or just 61.7 counting only those parties with a chance of winning historically like Social Credit, Progressive Conservative, Farmer, Liberal, and CCF or NDP (see tables 3–6). In all four arenas (except Manitoba), party affiliation makes a significant difference in the outcome. In federal

TABLE 2
Lone Ukrainian candidates in federal electoral contests, by party and outcome, 1904–88

Party	Won	Lost	Total
Liberal	5	34	39
Conservative and Progressive Conservative	42	30	72
UFA, CCF, NDP	6	58	64
Total	53	122	175

$Chi^2 = 45.76$; df $= 2$; $p < 0.001$

TABLE 3
Lone Ukrainian candidates in Ontario electoral contests, by party and outcome, 1945–90

Party	Won	Lost	Total
Liberal	6	14	20
Progressive Conservative	14	16	30
CCF and NDPL	3	18	21
Total	23	48	71

$Chi^2 = 6.00$; df $= 2$; $p = 0.05$

politics, the Conservatives and their successors, the Progressive Conservatives, have been disproportionate winners; the CCFers, NDPers, Socreds, LPPs, Communists, Marxist-Leninists, and Independents disproportionate losers. In Saskatchewan, on the other hand, CCFers and NDPers have been favoured; others (but not Liberals) have suffered. Socreds and Progressive Conservatives have been beneficiaries of fortune in Alberta; Liberals, CCFers, and NDPers with Ukrainian names in that period (1913–89) won only four out of fifty-two contests. Lone Ukrainian candidates are not likely to have been the lightning rods for Ukrainian votes, for they have fared worse than their more competitively situated colleagues, and their fortunes are probably determined more by their political stripe than by their appeal to ethnic sentiment.

Third Hypothesis

The third hypothesis gives us a chance to look at a category of contest that we have so far neglected: the exclusively Ukrainian slate, the contest in which all of the candidates have Ukrainian names. These contests should tell us about the specific partisan tendencies of Ukrainian voters, assuming that the ethnic link between voters and each of the candidates

TABLE 4
Lone Ukrainian candidates in Manitoba electoral contests, by party and outcome, 1914–88

Party	Won	Lost	Total
Independent	6	11	17
Liberal	8	24	32
CCF and NDP	23	33	56
Other	16	30	46
Total	53	98	151

Chi^2 = 2.31; df = 3; p = 0.50

TABLE 5
Lone Ukrainian candidates in Saskatchewan electoral contests, by party and outcome, 1912–86

Party	Won	Lost	Total
Liberal	4	24	28
CCF and NDP	22	16	38
Other	3	39	42
Total	29	79	108

Chi^2 = 28.77; df = 1; p < 0.001

TABLE 6
Lone Ukrainian candidates in Alberta electoral contests, by party and outcome, 1913–89

Party	Won	Lost	Total
Liberal	1	18	19
Conservative and Progressive Conservative	30	18	48
Social Credit and Independent SC	16	9	25
CCF and NDP	2	25	27
Other	2	19	21
Total	51	89	140

Chi^2 = 46.57; df = 2; p < 0.001

is equal so that the pull of kinship is in these cases 'controlled for,' leaving aside other factors such as the candidates' personalities. The available cases lead to the unremarkable conclusion that, using this test, Ukrainians on the whole vote like other Canadians.

For the House of Commons, there has only been one instance in which Ukrainian candidates squared off against each other. This was in the constituency of Vegreville (Alberta) in 1949, when John Decore for the Liberals faced and defeated incumbent Anthony Hlynka of the Social Credit Party. At the time, this failure to rally behind the sitting member was regarded as quite shocking.[11] Two things are of interest here. One is that the voters did not automatically support the incumbent, who normally has this reservoir of inertia to defend himself against a challenger. The second is that although these voters returned a Liberal to Ottawa, they preferred at the same time a Social Credit member (Ponich) in Edmonton, thus conforming to the well-established Canadian tradition of splitting votes between the federal and provincial arenas. What this illustrates is that the Ukrainian electorate cannot be stereotyped into a particular partisan mould.

In the three prairie provinces, there have been no fewer than forty-eight such contests (including acclamations of a single nominee), and although the candidates have represented virtually everything under the sun, the winners have been completely predictable to anyone familiar with prairie politics. The choices offered the voters in these all-Ukrainian contests have, in fact, been the entire panoply of prairie political parties from the second decade of this century to the present time: United Farmers of Manitoba, Conservatives, Liberals, Social Credit, Liberal Progressives, CCF, LPP, Progressive Conservative, NDP, United Farmers of Alberta, and Communist party. The voters' preferences in these contests, however, are identical with the well-known political dynasties that have historically existed on the prairies: in fifteen instances (31.3 per cent) the winner was the candidate for the CCF or NDP; in twelve (25.0), a Liberal or Liberal Progressive; in eleven (22.9), a Social Crediter; and in four (8.3), a Farmers' party representative. These four partisan groupings account for forty-two of the forty-eight cases (87.5 per cent). Incumbents were returned in only twenty-five (52.1 per cent) of these contests. Ukrainian voters on the prairies are not unlike any other voters, it would seem, nor are they adverse to change.

The congruity between this Ukrainian vote and the general norm is even more remarkable when the results of the forty-eight all-Ukrainian contests are separated into individual provincial sets, and still more so into particular constituencies. In Manitoba, there have been twenty-one such contests in the period 1922–69, and in twelve instances (57.1 per cent) incumbents have been returned. The lion's share (nine out of twenty-one, or 42.9 per cent) of winners has been Liberal Progressives or Liberals; the next largest category, CCF or NDP (six cases, or 28.6 per cent). Only six such contests have taken place in Saskatchewan (1948–78), all of them triumphs for the CCF or NDP, not surprisingly, and three of them returning the incumbent. The percentage of incumbents re-elected has been lowest in Alberta (ten out of twenty-one contests, or 47.6), which may indicate a lesser degree of loyalty to sitting members and therefore to incumbent parties. For Alberta, the lion's share of winnings in such contests has gone to the Social Credit (ten); the Liberals, Farmers, and CCF and NDP managed to take only three each (14.3 per cent). Ukrainian voters on the prairies, therefore, do not appear to differ radically from the rest of the electorate in their province in general.

A few constituencies with relatively long histories of sponsoring all-Ukrainian provincial electoral contests illustrate the likelihood that the Ukrainian electorate shifts its allegiances with the prevailing political mood of the country or the province. In Manitoba, in the riding of Ethelbert, where the UFM candidate, N. Hryhorczuk, was acclaimed in 1922, and returned in the next two elections (1927 and 1932) under the banner of the Government Coalition, he was overturned in 1936 by a Social Crediter, W. Lisowsky. Hryhorczuk regained the seat in 1941 (as a Liberal Progressive), but was beaten in 1945 by the CCF candidate, M. Sawchuk. The Whitford constituency in Alberta was represented by a Liberal, A. Shandro, up to 1922, when it was taken over by the Farmers, in the person of M. Chornohus. Isidore Goresky retained it for the UFA in 1930, but in 1935 William Tomyn took it over for the Social Credit movement under the leadership of the legendary 'Bible Bill' Aberhart. Tomyn continued to hold the riding, renamed Willingdon, until 1952, when he was unseated by N. Dushenski for the CCF. In 1963, when it was called Willingdon–Two Hills, N. Melnyk recaptured it for the Socreds. Redwater, also in Alberta, saw three all-Ukrainian contests, in 1948, 1959, and 1967, each of them returning a Social Credit candidate. This continuity was abruptly broken in 1971, the same year that the Progressive Conservatives under Peter Lougheed upset the Socreds provincially, with a win by a PC candidate, G. Topolnisky. By then, the riding bore the name Redwater-Andrew. It saw its most recent all-Ukrainian contest in 1989, when Steve Zarusky, then the incumbent, retained it for the Progressive Conservatives, still the governing party. The tendency for Ukrainian voters on the prairies, using this measure, would seem to be to support the government unless swept along on a broader wave of social or political protest – Ukrainian voting is not done in isolation from its wider context, and an incumbent Ukrainian MLA cannot count on its undying loyalty.

It should be pointed out that the all-Ukrainian slate is becoming rare. Although in evidence in Alberta as recently as 1989, it has not been seen in Saskatchewan since 1978. In Manitoba, there has not been an all-

Ukrainian provincial electoral contest since 1969. As a phenomenon it belongs to history and is not likely to serve as an indirect way of studying the Ukrainian vote in the future.

To the extent, therefore, that Ukrainian electors are drawn to vote especially for Ukrainian candidates, the political complexion of that part of the Canadian electorate is as distinctly multicoloured as that of the rest of the voting public in Canada. Characterizing the entire ethnic group in terms of its partisan inclinations, without taking into consideration time and place, is distinctly hazardous. Ukrainians, according to this methodology, are much like other Canadians in similar circumstances.

Conventional historical accounts of Ukrainian voting from the beginning of this century to the present day emphasize its multifarious nature. Reacting to various incentives and disincentives, Ukrainian Canadians have voted for almost every imaginable formation on the political spectrum at one time or another. Discriminated against by the Conservatives in Manitoba before the First World War, they tended to support the Liberals until that party betrayed their trust by abolishing bilingual schools. The Conservatives then actively sought out the Ukrainian vote, competing for it with the Liberals by using liquor and money. Disgust with the two parties' corruption led to the emergence of independent candidates who promoted the community's interests instead of corralling votes on behalf of the parties.[12] In Saskatchewan, however, the Liberals were apparently successful in courting and holding the Ukrainian vote in that same prewar period. The Alberta Liberals, meanwhile, at first attracted but then also alienated the Ukrainian voters by taking away educational concessions.[13]

During the war their treatment as 'enemy aliens' further estranged Ukrainians from the two major parties, especially at the federal level, and encouraged the emergence of a radical strain. 'By 1923, the six Ukrainian MLAs on the prairies were either Independents or third-party representatives, while none of the candidates who had contested federal seats had run on a Liberal or Conservative ticket.'[14] During the rest of the inter-war period, owing to their economic circumstances, Ukrainians were drawn to supporting the various protest movements on the prairies: Farmers, Social Credit, CCF, and Communist.[15] Yet, especially in Saskatchewan, they still voted for Liberal candidates.[16]

Following the Second World War and the influx of a new wave of immigrants, Ukrainians began to be drawn to the Progressive Conservative party, thanks to the Diefenbaker phenomenon. Otherwise, there has been a differentiation of the group along regional and social class lines, so that rural voters support the Tories while urbanites back the

Liberals and NDP; in provincial politics, Ukrainians will eventually support the governing party. Thus the political orientations of Ukrainian Canadians vary from place to place and time to time and are now not much different from those of other Canadians in similar socio-economic situations.[17]

Fourth Hypothesis

The fourth hypothesis of the present study states that if Ukrainians are drawn primarily to 'their own' candidates, then one of the tests of this comes when a choice needs to be made between partisan and ethnic loyalties. When a Ukrainian incumbent is replaced as his party's representative by a non-Ukrainian, the theory – or folklore – of Canadian ethnic voting would have it that the votes hitherto accorded that candidate naturally pass to another Ukrainian candidate at the next contest. Unfortunately for the theory, this does not appear at all to be the truth.

Some cases will illustrate the reason for entertaining scepticism about a supposed 'migration' of Ukrainian votes from the camp of a recently departed compatriot to the camp of another who happens to be present (and is assiduously, no doubt, courting that vote). First, here are five from Canadian federal politics:

1. In Edmonton East (Alberta) in 1953, Ambrose Holowach, a Ukrainian, won the riding for the Social Credit party with 8,802 votes. In 1958, he was defeated by William Skoreyko for the Progressive Conservatives by a vote of 15,236 to 6,441. In the next election, in 1962, Holowach dropped out and was replaced for the Socreds by a man named Maynard. Maynard garnered 7,657 votes, which was higher than Holowach's most recent showing. Certainly there was no net 'migration' here of supposedly Ukrainian Socred votes; if there was any, it was at Skoreyko's expense (9,291 votes in 1962) and to the benefit of the Liberal candidate, John Decore (6,771).

2. In the Ontario federal riding of Ontario (Oshawa-Whitby) in 1965, Michael Starr, the PC incumbent, defeated his Liberal rival by 22,752 votes to 20,515. At the next general election, the PC candidate was Muirhead, and the Liberal candidate, Norman Cafik, won. But Cafik's total was only 13,483, which makes nonsense of any notion of masses of ex-PC Ukrainian voters deserting and going over to the Liberals just because their candidate happened, like Starr, to be Ukrainian.

3. In Marquette (Manitoba), in 1965, Nicholas Mandziuk held the seat for the PCs with a total of 10,613 votes. In 1968, Mandziuk was replaced

by Stewart, who did even better despite not having a Ukrainian name, racking up a total of 12,706 votes. No mass desertion here, either.

4. In the riding of High Park (Toronto), in 1968, Walter Deacon, a Ukrainian Liberal, came out on top with 16,260 votes; he beat out McKay of the PCs, who received 10,743 votes. In 1972, Deacon improved his tally to 16,426, but nevertheless lost to Otto Jelinek, the PC candidate, whose total was 18,329. In 1979, the Liberals replaced Deacon with Jesse Flis, a Pole, who won the election with 15,281 votes. Second place was taken by a new PC candidate, the Ukrainian Yuri Shymko. Shymko's vote was only 15,207, considerably less than for either Jelinek or Deacon before him, so he did not appear to be the beneficiary of Deacon's departure, as per the hypothesis.

5. In Dauphin (Manitoba) in 1980, Laverne Lewicky of the NDP was elected MP with 12,960 votes. At the next election in 1984, he slipped to second place with 10,219 votes. In 1988, Eric Irwin, Lewicky's replacement, again failed to recapture the seat for the NDP, but increased the vote to 11,876, which was obviously better than Lewicky's total in the previous election. Clearly, Lewicky's Ukrainian supporters did not desert their party just because of the candidate's ethnicity.

In the three prairie provinces, there were fourteen analogous cases in Manitoba (1927–88), i.e., a reduction of the number of Ukrainian candidates in a given riding from one general election to the next; eleven in Saskatchewan (1952–86); and nine in Alberta (1921–89). In the majority (twenty) of these thirty-four cases, there was definitely no net migration of votes (which presumably would have been Ukrainian) to the benefit of the Ukrainian candidate(s) remaining in the race after one or more had dropped out. Indeed, in a few cases, the remaining Ukrainian candidate had the astonishing effect of actually frightening away votes as compared to the previous election. Specifically, when there is only one Ukrainian left in the race, he often does more poorly than he did when there were other Ukrainians in the race as well. In the remaining cases, there is an apparent migration of votes, but it is not always clear that the surviving Ukrainian is the beneficiary. It is frequently ambiguous and qualified. Often the migration of votes is ideological (i.e., to a party proximate to one's own on the political spectrum, as Liberals to NDP and vice versa) rather than ethnic in coloration.

The evidence examined here, indirect though it is, clearly points away from the notion that there is a homogeneous, stable, and solid Ukrainian vote, which gives Ukrainian candidates an edge in federal or provincial elections in Canada. The Ukrainian vote is not something that adheres like velcro to any passing political candidate who happens to be Ukrainian or to have a recognizable Ukrainian name. It is as complex and multifaceted as the careers of Ukrainian candidates and politicians, as much a part of the fabric of Canadian politics and history as anything else. No wonder that the Ukrainian vote is paid attention to, or given lip service, only at election times. Because it is diffuse rather than discrete, the Ukrainian vote does not become translated into a voice, an expression of interests, for who knows what it means. All we can say for certain at the end of this excursion is that it really is ephemeral, the stuff that dreams are made of, and here are the statistics to prove it.

Still Coming to Terms: Ukrainians, Jews, and the Deschênes Commission

MORRIS ILYNIAK

From February 1985 to September 1987, the Ukrainian and Jewish communities in Canada were involved in a heated dispute over the identification of alleged Nazi war criminals and the means of bringing them to justice. Though the bitterness between the two sides has subsided, the conflict has revealed the importance of historical consciousness and the use of history to advance the goals of the two diaspora communities. But how did the issue of Nazi war criminals bring these goals into conflict?

Joseph Mengele, the notorious 'Angel of Death' who had performed cruel experiments on the inmates of Auschwitz, was one of the most important Nazi war criminals to have escaped the Nuremberg-style prosecutions that had netted thousands of other war criminals and collaborators after the Second World War. Despite the efforts of various 'Nazi-hunters,' all trails leading to Mengele had grown cold. But in the winter of 1984–5 the hunt for the fugitive Nazi suddenly resumed as reports about rumoured sightings made international headlines. The trail had been found again. It was, however, a false trail. Forensic experts who examined Mengele's unearthed remains confirmed that he had died in Brazil six years earlier.[1]

In the midst of the extensive publicity surrounding the Mengele affair, the *New York Times* reported in January 1985 that Mengele may have tried to enter Canada during the 1960s en route to his South American havens.[2] Information about Mengele's putative journey to Canada was discovered in American government files and brought to light by Sol Littman, a semi-retired journalist and the Canadian representative of the Simon Wiesenthal Center for Holocaust Studies in Los Angeles. The

Canadian news media subsequently disseminated the story along with an announcement by Prime Minister Brian Mulroney that he had ordered an investigation. On 29 January, Littman and Rabbi Abraham Cooper, the associate dean of the Wiesenthal Center, met with the federal solicitor-general to discuss the Mengele case and a proposal that Canada establish a Nazi-hunting agency modelled on the Office of Special Investigations (OSI) in the United States.[3] On 7 February the Canadian government announced that it was establishing a 'Commission of Inquiry on War Criminals' to be headed by the retired Quebec chief justice, Jules Deschênes. Despite its name, the commission had the purpose of investigating the presence of only Nazi war criminals in Canada and the legal options for bringing them to justice.[4]

After nearly four decades of government inaction on Nazi war criminals, both Canadian Jews and many other people were surprised when the Deschênes commission was announced. It was equally odd that the government would respond in such a hasty fashion to an allegation based, as more careful scrutiny later revealed, on one man's flimsy conjecture. This was the scathing conclusion that Justice Deschênes reached, as Littman himself admitted.[5] But as far as many Jews were concerned, the Mengele case was symbolic of the legal and political impunity that thousands of other Nazi war criminals enjoyed in Canada and the United States. Although there were many guesses about the actual number of fugitive Nazi war criminals, for most Jews one was too many.[6] The Deschênes commission would not actually prosecute anyone, but it was a start towards reversing what critics have labelled as Canada's traditional 'do nothing' policy on war criminals. At least the government finally appeared to be listening, even though, it seems, it had badly miscalculated the subsequent political fall-out.

Deschênes was no stranger to controversy. During his ten years as Quebec's chief justice he had frequently become embroiled with the separatist Parti Québecois government, both on and off the bench. Apparently, however, neither he, nor the Jewish-Canadian community, nor the Mulroney government anticipated that the commission would cause such rancour among Canada's Eastern European communities, especially the Ukrainians.

Throughout the two years in which the Deschênes commission was conducting its investigation, the Ukrainian community denounced what it called 'selective justice' and protested against the way in which war criminal suspects of Ukrainian background were incriminated. Claiming that the allegations were part of a 'witch-hunt' instigated by the Soviet Union in league with Jewish Nazi-hunters and left-wing appeasers, community spokesmen expressed fear that the reputation not only of individuals but of all Ukrainian Canadians would be slandered.[7] Groups from the Lithuanian, Latvian, Estonian, Croatian, and Slovenian communities shared this fear. Together they formed a loose-knit coalition to defend their reputation as organized communities and to oppose bringing suspected war criminals to justice according to the terms proposed by Jewish organizations. But it was the Ukrainian community – the largest, best organized, and most influential of the nationalist and anti-Soviet Eastern European communities in Canada – that undertook the lead role in mounting an organized 'antidefamation' campaign.[8]

At the same time, a related, though perhaps even more protracted dispute between Jewish and Eastern European groups was taking place in the United States. There the reaction was directed at the activities of the OSI. Most of the active cases involved suspects of Eastern European origin who were accused of having entered the United States as political refugees on fraudulent grounds. The strongest reaction came from Baltic and Ukrainian Americans, resulting in a major rift between them and the Jewish-American community. The confrontation came to a head over the case of John Demjanjuk, a Soviet soldier who was captured by the Germans and alleged by the OSI to be 'Ivan the Terrible,' a sadistic guard who had operated the gas ovens at the Treblinka death camp. In 1986 he was extradited to stand trial in Israel, where he was convicted two years later.[9] Demjanjuk claimed that he was a victim of a wrongful and malicious accusation and that the Soviet secret police had forged an identity card that linked him to a Nazi guard training camp. Many Ukrainians in Canada and the United States believed him and identified his fate with that of their community. Some thought that the Jerusalem court had put a whole nation on trial and contemptuously denounced its proceedings as a theatrical farce.[10]

When the Deschênes commission was first announced, however, most Ukrainians in Canada did not make a connection between their community and the hunt for Nazi war criminals. Few were aware, as most are now, of the battles between the OSI and the Ukrainian and other Eastern European communities in the United States. And although accusations that Ukrainian nationalists had participated in the Holocaust were a sore point for Ukrainians for many years, before February 1985 the community had had no organization with the aim of defending individuals or the community against such accusations. Perhaps Ukrainians complacently believed that an official inquiry would never be launched in Canada and that no Canadian government would ever extradite a war criminal suspect to the Soviet Union.

The controversy began not with the formation of the commission itself but with a front-page article that appeared on 10 February 1985 in the *Toronto Star*. Linked to the main story about the commission, as is common news practice, the article stated that '218 former Ukrainian officers of Hitler's SS (elite guard) which ran death camps in Eastern Europe are living in Canada.'[11] The allegation emanated from an interview given by Simon Wiesenthal on Israeli radio and distributed by an international news agency. The Toronto *Globe and Mail* published a similar report the next day.[12] As part of a 'local angle,' both articles cited Sol Littman as saying that the 218 former Ukrainian SS officers belonged to an unidentified organization campaigning for the 'emancipation of "captive nations"' with thirteen chapters across Canada. He also claimed that the identities of fourteen suspects, obtained from an abridged list of twenty-eight suspects that Wiesenthal had provided to the federal solicitor-general in December 1984, were confirmed by checking telephone directories in the Toronto area.

Wiesenthal and Littman were referring to former officers of the 'Galicia Division,' a volunteer Ukrainian military unit formed in 1943 as part of the Waffen SS by the Germans and the Melnyk faction of the Ukrainian nationalists. For the Germans, the division was a last-ditch attempt to enlist support against the Soviet march towards Germany. For the Ukrainians, however, the division was the nucleus of a future army of national liberation.[13] In 1950, after extensive lobbying by the Ukrainian Canadian Committee (or UCC, now called the Ukrainian Canadian Congress), the first of approximately one thousand veterans of the Galicia Division were permitted to enter Canada.[14] In time, most of the veterans faded into Canada's multicultural fabric, not to be thought of or heard from for many years. Now they had suddenly become front-page news. Yet none of the published reports provided any background on the division and its veterans' organization or on its political and historical significance for the nationalist Ukrainian community in Canada. No effort was made to solicit an official comment from the Ukrainian side. The media were oblivious to Ukrainian sensitivities and to the long-standing feud between Wiesenthal and Littman on one side and the Ukrainians on the other.[15] They did not even question how Littman had been able to confirm the identities of fourteen suspects simply by looking in a telephone directory.

The news stories about the '218 former Ukrainian SS' almost immediately triggered an alarm within the Ukrainian community. It believed that the very close timing of the Deschênes commission announcement, the allegations, and a B'Nai Brith proposal to permit the prosecution of war criminals in Canada was more than a coincidence.[16] This was the beginning of a co-ordinated campaign, which, if not in its aims then at least in its consequences, would seriously damage the public image of the Ukrainian community.

In particular, Littman and Wiesenthal appeared to the Ukrainians to be exploiting for their own ends or the ends of the Jewish community the general lack of understanding of Eastern European history during the Second World War and to be relying upon unceasing Soviet attempts to villify émigré Ukrainian nationalists as 'Nazi collaborators' and 'war criminals' who had fled from justice in their homeland. Indeed, the Soviet accusations would occasionally make their way to strategic or receptive destinations in the West through various publications as well as through lists of war criminals supplied by Soviet embassies.[17] Only several months before the formation of the Deschênes commission, the Soviet embassy in Ottawa had circulated lists of Nazi war criminal suspects to the press. One enterprising journalist from a Winnipeg daily began knocking on doors with a list in hand. A leaflet asking 'Do war criminals live on your street?' appeared in several Winnipeg neighbourhoods. On it was a picture from a 1943 recruitment poster for Ukrainians to join the Galicia Division. Both Littman and Wiesenthal acknowledge that they have used Soviet sources in forming their own lists and allegations against Ukrainian and Baltic émigré nationalists.

The national executive of the UCC in Winnipeg responded with a news conference on 14 February in Toronto. In a statement read by Orest Rudzik, the UCC carefully avoided criticizing the Deschênes commission or the Jewish community's efforts to bring Nazi war criminal fugitives to justice. Indeed, the UCC supported the commission, with the proviso that its mandate be extended to cover all war criminals regardless of their ethnic, religious, or racial origin or of the place and time at which they had committed their crimes. At the same time, however, it attacked Littman's and Wiesenthal's comments (though never identifying the two men by name) and the news media for publishing them. Calling the reports about alleged Ukrainian war criminals 'erroneous and inflammatory,' the UCC claimed that the good name of all Canadians of Ukrainian descent had been slandered, that the memory of the Ukrainians who had died in Nazi concentration camps had been besmirched, and that the allegations of anti-Semitism were promoting 'social and ethnic intolerance among Canadians.' The UCC also explained that 'the Ukrainian Division was never a Nazi SS unit in the true sense of the word and that its members considered themselves serving Ukrainian national interests and not those of Nazi Germany.'

Furthermore, it denied that the division was ever involved 'in any capacity with respect to the Jews.'[18] Rudzik, a former president of the UCC Toronto branch, said that the news reports were giving the public the false impression that Ukrainians as a rule are anti-Semitic and had collaborated with the Nazis during the war. That impression, he said, was a stigma on people like him and even his children, who were born in Canada.[19]

Anxiety in the Ukrainian community intensified as more articles about the Galicia Division and other alleged war criminals appeared in the press in the spring and summer of 1985. Consequently, the daily press was flooded with letters to the editor, claiming, as one put it, that Ukrainians were 'getting sick and tired of being singled out as being the world's criminals.'[20] Ukrainian newspapers were also replete with polemical articles on the Deschênes commission and Jewish-Ukrainian relations. A symposium on Ukraine during the Second World War, held in Toronto in March 1985, turned out to be a badly needed sensitization session. About 660 people, mostly first-generation Canadian-born Ukrainians, came to obtain inspiring and reassuring answers about their nation's history, which they had been taught to revere, and about their parents' past.[21] This meeting, as well as an earlier one organized by Toronto's Lithuanian community at which an appeal was made to hold a 'Nuremberg II' for Soviet war crimes,[22] was a signal to the media, the federal government, and the Jewish community that Eastern European groups were poising for a 'counter-offensive.'

The hearings of the Deschênes commission, at which testimony would be heard publicly, were scheduled to begin in Ottawa on 10 April. If Ukrainians were to get more public exposure for their side of history, it would have to be at the hearings of the commission. Thus, organized preparations for appearances before the commission and a broad anti-defamation campaign were begun in earnest. At a series of informal UCC meetings held in Toronto and Winnipeg, an ad hoc group of community activists was created. At a general meeting of the UCC in Winnipeg on 15 March, the group was formally voted into existence as the Civil Liberties Commission (CLC).[23] Headed by the Toronto lawyer John Gregorovich, the CLC was to be the front-line educational and lobbying group that would mobilize the Ukrainian community to take a public stand 'against slanderous allegations which have resulted in the defamation of all Canadians of Ukrainian descent.'[24]

The CLC was originally slated to have sixty members with representation from all major Ukrainian communities across Canada. In reality, the group never expanded beyond its twenty-member executive, and for the most part it was controlled by a core of seven or eight individuals, though 'community action committees' attracted volunteers in Toronto, Montreal, Winnipeg, Saskatoon, and Edmonton.[25] Only a handful of executive members were from outside Toronto, partly reflecting the fact that the issue was of much less concern to Ukrainians in western Canada than in Ontario and Quebec, where most of the strongly nationalist 'third-wave' immigrants had settled after the war. In April 1985, a coalition of Ukrainian, Lithuanian, Latvian, Estonian, Croatian, German, and Slovenian groups formed 'Canadians for Justice,'[26] though it was always acknowledged that the CLC would play the dominant role in the antidefamation campaign.

During 1985, the Deschênes commission received eighteen submissions and testimony from forty-two witnesses at public hearings in Ottawa-Hull, Winnipeg, Montreal, and Toronto. In addition, the commission ordered a number of legal and historical studies, and its team of lawyers and historians culled for investigation 776 prima facie cases out of more than 1,800 submitted names of suspects.[27] Commission investigators also travelled to West Germany, Austria, the Netherlands, the United States, and Israel. The suspects were interviewed in camera, some more than once. Though the commission's rules of practice and procedure explicitly stated that there were 'no contesting parties,'[28] the granting of legal status – and the power to cross-examine witnesses during the public hearings – to only two Ukrainian (the CLC and the Brotherhood of Veterans of the Ukrainian National Army, First Division) and two Jewish organizations (the League of Human Rights of B'Nai Brith Canada and the Canadian Jewish Congress) exacerbated tensions between the two communities and made it appear that the search for Nazi war criminals in Canada was a Jewish-Ukrainian issue.[29] The hearings often degenerated into heated confrontations. 'The antagonism was quickly evident at the inquiry's public hearings,' reported David Vieanneau of the *Toronto Star*, 'where often their respective lawyers could barely disguise their contempt for the other side. Most of their public spokesmen did not even attempt to mask their hatred.'[30]

Yet the Ukrainians did not express any principled objection to the idea of prosecuting war criminals. On this point they even agreed with the Jews. But they did disagree on the scope of the inquiry (the Ukrainians demanded that all and not only Nazi war criminal suspects be investigated) and on the identities of the suspects (the Ukrainians denied that they had any knowledge of Nazi war criminals among the thousands of Ukrainian post-war immigrants). They opposed the use of Soviet and Eastern bloc evidence and proposals for a Canadian counter-

part to the OSI. They also took exception to some of the legal remedies
proposed by Jewish spokesmen, such as extradition and deportation.
War criminal suspects, said John Sopinka in the submission to the commission that he wrote for the UCC, should be brought to trial in Canada
under Canadian criminal law.[31]

Outside of the commission, the dispute simmered in newspapers,
public forums, and demonstrations. A few minor ugly incidents were
reported, including the defacement of two Ukrainian monuments and
the storefront of a Ukrainian newspaper, a bomb threat against a Ukrainian family, some name-calling, and the mailing of scurrilous literature
by a tiny band of anonymous Ukrainian zealots. Organizers of one
Jewish meeting on the war-criminals issue threatened to 'name names,'
knowing full well that this would only fan enmity with the Ukrainians.
Fortunately, cooler heads prevailed. Meanwhile, hundreds of Ukrainian
demonstrators paraded on Parliament Hill in Ottawa, angrily denouncing the use of evidence from Soviet sources. The antidefamation campaign, led primarily by the CLC, included frequent news conferences
and community forums (sometimes sponsored jointly with Jewish
organizations). Letters and petitions were sent en masse to Parliament.
Students converged on federal politicians during a 'lobbying blitz' of
Ottawa. English and French full-page advertisements with pictures of
innocent-looking children were placed in daily newspapers. A campaign
to raise one million dollars to pay for the expensive legal counsel and
the required background studies was organized. The mainstream press
commissioned articles on Ukrainians during the war and published a
constant stream of letters to the editor.

But most of the Ukrainian fury was vented at Sol Littman, whose
allegations about Mengele had prompted the formation of the
Deschênes commission. There was no love lost between Littman and
the Ukrainians. He was well known by the community for previous
newspaper and magazine articles as well as for a television documentary
that alluded to former members of the Galicia Division as possible war
criminal suspects now living a comfortable life in Canada.[32] In his submission to the Deschênes commission, Littman called the militant Organization of Ukrainian Nationalists (OUN) 'the most pernicious of
collaborators.'[33] The confidential list of 475 names that he submitted to
the commission undoubtedly included a large number of Ukrainian
nationalists. 'I insist that there were in every country incipient fascist
parties, fascist in ideology and programme, and almost universally fascist
in anti-Semitism,' Littman explained later in an interview. 'The OUN
was definitely a fascist organization.'[34] Although it privately dissociated

itself from Littman and his remarks, the Canadian Jewish Congress would not agree to the UCC's request to issue a public condemnation.

Generally, the Jewish-Canadian community expressed surprise at the Ukrainian reaction. 'Our main concern was to bring war criminals to justice after forty years. We couldn't conceive of any group not supporting it,' said Ellen Kaychuk, director of public affairs for B'Nai Brith Canada.[35] Why would anyone want to defend, for example, a Ukrainian Waffen SS unit? How could anyone even remotely associated with Hitler's elite combat troops be considered a 'liberator' or a hero? Rabbi Gunther Plaut could not understand why the organized Ukrainian community was so sensitive about the Nazi war crimes accusations.[36] It was not, after all, the Ukrainian community that was under investigation, but certain individuals, who, as it happened, were its members.

In a country that prides itself on having a 'mosaic' of ethnocultural communities living in harmony, the open expression of Jewish-Ukrainian enmity over the issue of Nazi war criminals was a disturbing affair. But opinions on radio talk shows and in newspaper editorials varied. Many people were unprepared for the visceral reaction of the Ukrainians. To a large extent, the media and the public did not comprehend what the controversy was about or why it was happening in Canada. Resentment was expressed over how the Canadian political process and public resources were being utilized by ethnic lobbies to further political agendas far removed from present-day Canadian society.

Although the contrary positions of the two parties to the issue were apparent, there was no clear-cut confrontation of the underlying interests of particular social groups as is typical in most social conflict situations. Ukrainians and Jews in Canada were not in direct competition for resources or economic advantage. Neither did the war-criminals issue directly impinge on the valiant efforts made by both communities to preserve their cultural distinctiveness within a multicultural milieu. As an editorial in an English-language Ukrainian newspaper put it, 'No one proposes, of course, to strip us of our Easter eggs or dancing troupes.'[37] Social prejudice was also not a major cause of the conflict, though it may have become more important in the later stages. The mostly Canadian-born activists on both sides of the issue generally disassociated themselves from the lingering Old World hates of some of their elders. If anything, the Ukrainians had a stronger case to present that the civil liberties of individuals were potentially at risk, and quite rightly, their concerns were addressed by the Deschênes commission. Both groups, however, argued that the war-criminals issue was one of doing justice in their particular case, and in the general case of Canadian society. The Ukrainians further argued that doing justice according to the demands made by the Jews would do injustice to them as a group. But what kind of injustice?

From an analysis of their ideologies, what emerges foremost is that both groups perceived their historical interests to be at stake in the issue. These interests may be defined as the bonds which link a people to its own sense of history and from which it derives its collective identity and self-worth and justifies its political aspirations. The Jewish and Ukrainian communities are strikingly similar in that they derive their raison d'être not only from a sense of common cultural descent but also from historical images of victimhood, which, in turn, supply the ideological premises for their respective political goals.

In Jewish historical memory the Holocaust represents the culmination of centuries of persecution. It not only helps Jews define themselves as a people, but also gives force to their emotional identification with Israel as the spiritual and cultural Jewish homeland. Hence, Jews have made a supreme effort to chronicle, study, theologize, and even, in the words of Robert Alter, to 'market' the Holocaust to the world and to evoke it in the defence of Israel.[38]

Thus, Jews saw the campaign to bring Nazi war criminals to justice, and its partial realization through the Deschênes commission, as an affirmation of their historical victimhood, in particular, the Holocaust and the West's indifference to the fate of European Jews escaping the Nazi cauldron. 'The existence of barriers to Jewish refugees that did not exist for Nazi war criminals is more than just an historical irony,' argued David Matas while representing B'Nai Brith Canada before the Deschênes commission. 'It helps explain why Nazi war criminals were able to enter.'[39] The Mengele affair in the winter of 1984–5, which included a mock trial in Jerusalem involving emotional testimony by witnesses,[40] was also an attempt to draw the world's attention, on the eve of the fortieth anniversary of the Allied victory over Nazi Germany, to the thesis that the Jews were Hitler's primary victim. The emergence of a virulent 'Holocaust denial' movement made the defence of this historical self-image even more urgent. Irwin Cotler, a McGill University law professor who represented the Canadian Jewish Congress before the Deschênes commission, put forth a simple argument. If there was a crime, he reasoned, then there must also be criminals. Conversely, if there are no criminals to be found, then it may be contended that there was no crime.[41]

But it is also true that the process of identifying and prosecuting someone for a Nazi war crime is more than an indictment of a single person. Accusing individuals who donned uniforms in the service of a national cause draws attention to the fact that many other people shared what the moral philosopher Michael Walzer calls 'similar offices and circumstances.'[42] As whole groups and societies are drawn into accounting for their role in Nazi war crimes, the question of who should be prosecuted as a Nazi war criminal ultimately becomes a historical question of how far moral responsibility for the Holocaust should be extended.

The Holocaust has emerged as a moral benchmark of exceptional significance in world history. It has become the archetypal genocide, the standard by which all other mass abuses of human rights are measured, yet with proprietary claims to its application laid exclusively by the Jews. Consequently, as a moral benchmark in history, the Holocaust demarcates a line between good and evil, victim and victimizer. How is this line to be drawn, by whom, and under what circumstance? Many non-Jewish groups resent what they perceive to be a concerted effort by Jews to push them into coming to terms with a role in the Holocaust.[43] The problem is not simply short memory or the denial of an unwanted past. Rather, it is one of collective moral judgments: when people don't like what they see in the looking-glass of history. And it seems to be particularly bad when they see themselves in the context of the Holocaust.

How people view themselves in history is very much a part of how they see themselves, and would like to be seen by others, as a people in the present. Every national community wants to be persuaded – and to persuade other people – of the moral rectitude of its existence and of its collective ends. What every national community wants, in short, is to have 'good history.'[44] For Ukrainians in the diaspora this objective is of extreme importance. At the core of the Ukrainian historical consciousness exists a set of images of a victim-nation, of Ukraine as Golgotha, the site of crucifixion by one foreign subjugator after another. It is these images that supply the historical premises for promoting the Ukrainian case for independence and unite Ukrainians around the world. Yet most Ukrainians are painfully aware that their cause is politically marginalized in the West.[45] It simply does not have the same degree of political or moral rectitude as, say, the national liberation movement in South Africa. Moreover, the Ukrainian community is envious of the Jewish diaspora's success in achieving moral and political legitimacy for its cause. But there is also resentment over how the Jewish success has overshadowed and, in the view of many Ukrainians, devalued the legitimacy of the Ukrainian cause in the West, even though the two causes are not fundamentally antagonistic. Their own historical experience of victimhood and resistance to oppression, when it is acknowledged at all, is often cast in doubt by the curse of 'traditional anti-Semitism.'[46]

Over the past four decades, numerous Ukrainian groups and intellectuals have engaged in a polemical dialogue with Jews on the Holocaust and on historical relations in Ukraine.[47] But in many cases the Jewish-Ukrainian dialogues, if they can even be called that, were transformed into negotiating strategies for listing conditions and demands about recognizing who did what to whom.[48] This form of historical debate has also been a feature of dialogues between Jews and other groups.[49] What is really happening in these so-called dialogues is that the various parties are attempting to 'negotiate history.' The objective of these negotiations, at least for the non-Jewish groups that tend to initiate them, is not so much to come to terms with their relationship to Jews in the past as to settle 'moral accounts' with them.

From the Ukrainian perspective, the key motive in negotiating history with the Jews has been to correct the moral judgment of Ukrainians and to offset the 'displacement effect' of Jewish accounts in the mass media, which tend to emphasize the historical image of Ukrainians, and other Eastern European groups, as victimizers rather than as victims. Yet despite the many symposia, round-table discussions, and meetings between religious and political leaders that have taken place, the two sides have failed to agree on the historical facts. The quarrels over what happened during the seventeenth-century Cossack rebellions, the revolutions and civil wars of 1917–21, and the Second World War seem almost anachronistic. Yet Ukrainians and Jews simply do not see eye-to-eye on their common past in Eastern Europe, a past that stretches back at least a thousand years.

The asymmetry of interest in Jewish-Ukrainian relations compounds the disagreement. Howard Aster and Peter Potichnyj observe that although 'certain individuals within the Jewish community may wish to engage in consideration of this subject, there does not appear to be the same sense of urgency on a community basis to do so. Indeed, one might claim that there is a reluctance on the part of most segments within the Jewish community to undertake a consideration of Jewish-Ukrainian relations.'[50]

When people and groups are said to 'come to terms' with their past, it generally means that they have taken a courageous stand to face, to acknowledge, and perhaps even to atone for uncomfortable and often heretofore denied aspects of their history. Psychologically, the process of coming to terms with the past can be healthy.[51] But who should come to terms with the past, in what way, and on whose terms is another matter. The Ukrainian antidefamation campaign during the Deschênes commission arose because the two diaspora communities failed to come to terms with their common past following years of 'negotiation.' This failure supplied the fuse for the ensuing conflict, and the allegation of Ukrainian war criminals was the spark that ignited it. Though it was not the role of Deschênes to resolve conflicting historical claims in the case of Jews and Ukrainians, neither he nor, if the past is a reliable guide, any future war-crimes prosecution can avoid dealing with a Pandora's box of historical issues.

Deschênes submitted his report (in two parts, one public and one confidential) to the cabinet on 31 December 1986, exactly a year after the original deadline. The 966-page public part was released only in March 1987 after additional editing by the prime minister's office. No Ukrainians were known to be on the secret list of 20 Nazi war criminal suspects submitted by Deschênes for immediate prosecution (though it is less certain whether the list of 105 suspects requiring 'further investigation' contained any Ukrainian names).[52] On the basis of Deschênes's recommendations, a bill was submitted to the House of Commons in June 1987 to amend the Criminal Code and statutes covering immigration and citizenship to give the federal government broad powers to prosecute Canadian citizens and residents suspected of having committed 'war crimes' and 'crimes against humanity.'[53] The bill became law only in September 1987, after a delay caused in part by two Conservative backbenchers of Ukrainian descent.[54] The following year, Canada signed agreements on the gathering of evidence against war criminal suspects with the Soviet Union, Israel, and the Netherlands. Thus far, only three suspects have been charged with war crimes and crimes against humanity, of whom only one has gone to trial. None of them is Ukrainian. However, the head of the federal war crimes unit has said that forty-five 'high priority' cases are under investigation.[55] It is not known whether any of these suspects are Ukrainian.

The new issues and priorities that arose out of the political changes taking place in the Soviet Union under Mikhail Gorbachev have reduced the intensity of the confrontational relations between Jews and Ukrainians in Canada. With the end of the Deschênes commission, media attention faded, and Jewish-Ukrainian relations, in the words of one Jewish spokesman, have reverted to a 'relatively quiescent mode.'[56] Spokesmen for Canada's Ukrainian and Baltic communities called for 'a time for healing,' a sentiment their Jewish-Canadian counterparts echoed.[57]

Notes

Part 1

Hryniuk: 'Sifton's Pets'

1 See, for example, Paul Yuzyk, *The Ukrainians in Manitoba: A Social History* (Toronto: University of Toronto Press, 1953), 26–8, Pierre Berton, *The Promised Land: Settling the West 1896–1914* (Toronto: McClelland and Stewart, 1984), 42–3, Jars Balan, *Salt and Braided Bread: Ukrainian Life in Canada* (Toronto: Oxford University Press, 1984), 4–7; Jaroslav Petryshyn, *Peasants in the Promised Land: Canada and the Ukrainians, 1891–1914* (Toronto: James Lorimer, 1985), 27–41.
2 See the various works of Tadeusz Pilat, the chief crownland statistician, such as 'Der landtäflicher Grundbesitz in Galizien,' *Statistische Monatschrift* 18 (1892); and Z. Ludkiewicz, *Kwestia Rolna w Galicji* (Lviv: Gubrynowicz i Syn, 1910). In a similar vein, but bitterly critical of the Polish gentry, was S. Szczepanowski, *Nędza Galicyi w cyfrach i program energicznego rozwoju gospodarstwa krajowego* (Lviv: Gubrynowicz i Schmidt, 1888).
3 See Ivan Franko, *Tvory v dvadtsiaty tomakh* (Kiev: Derzhlitvydav Ukrainy, 1950–6) xix; and Mykhailo Pavlyk, *Tvory* (Kiev: Derzhavne vydavnytstvo khudozhnoi literatury, 1959).
4 A.M. Kraut, *The Huddled Masses: The Immigrant in American Society, 1880–1914* (Arlington Heights, Ill.: Harlan Davidson, 1982), 4.
5 Two exceptions are W. Pruski, *Hodowla zwierząt gospodarskich w Galicji w latach 1772–1918*, 2 vols. (Wroclaw, 1975), and Stella M. Hryniuk, 'Peasant Agriculture in East Galicia in the Late Nineteenth Century,' *Slavonic and East European Review* 63 (April 1985): 228–43.
6 R.F. Kaindl, *Geschichte von Czernowitz von der ältesten Zeiten bis zur Gegenwart* (Chernivtsi: Universitäts-Buchhandlung, 1908), 201.

7 For the foregoing see especially I. Konta, *Geschichte der Eisenbahnen der oesterreichisch-ungarischen Monarchie* (Vienna: Karl Prochaska, 1898) I, pt. 2, passim; K. Bachinger, 'Das Verkehrswesen,' in A. Wandruschka and P. Urbanitsch, eds., *Die Habsburgermonarchie* (Vienna: Verlag der Österreichischen Akademie der Wissenschaften, 1980) I: 287–319; S. Hryniuk, *Peasants with Promise: Ukrainians in Southeastern Galicia, 1880–1900* (Edmonton: Canadian Institute of Ukrainian Studies, forthcoming), 55–7, and footnotes thereto.

8 A. Sirka, *The Nationality Question in Austrian Education: The Case of the Ukrainians in Galicia 1867–1914* (Frankfurt am Main: Peter D. Lang, 1980), passim. In Bukovyna, many schools were unilingual, but others used two or three of German, Ukrainian, and Romanian as languages of instruction; k.k. Statistische Central-Kommission, *Schematismus der allgemeinen Volksschulen und Bürgerschulen in den im Reichsrathe vertretenen Königreichen und Ländern auf Grund der statistischen Aufnahme vom 15. Mai 1900* (Vienna: Alfred Hölder, 1902), 749–69. For the educational experiences of Ukrainian settlers in Manitoba before the First World War see Stella Hryniuk and N. McDonald, 'The Schooling Experience of Ukrainians in Manitoba, 1896–1916,' in D.C. Jones et al, eds., *Schools in the West: Essays in Canadian Educational History* (Calgary: Detselig, 1986), 155–73.

9 In contrast to Western Galicia, where 61 per cent of the elementary schools had one teacher.

10 In Kolomyia county of Eastern Galicia, 40 per cent of children of school age attended school in 1890, and 66.1 per cent did so in 1900. In Terebovlia county the percentages were 44.4 and 66.8. The immigration agent in Dauphin, Manitoba, thought in 1900 that 'fully 35 per cent of the male adult Galicians can read and write their own language, and many of these can also read and write Polish' and that 'nearly all' of the children who had attended school 'in the old country' for any length of time were literate. *Dauphin Weekly Herald*, cited in A. Baran et al, eds., *The Jubilee Collection of the Ukrainian Free Academy of Sciences* (Winnipeg: Ukrainian Free Academy of Sciences, 1976), 363.

11 A. Rom, 'Der Bildungsgrad der Bevölkerung Österreichs und seine Entwicklung seit 1880 in den im Reichsrathe vertretenen Königreichen und Ländern,' *Statistische Monatschrift* 19 (1893): 634–5.

12 In 1899, forty needy school students were being maintained by the Narodnyi Dim in Chernivtsi. *Hromadskyi holos*, 1 May 1899. Also in Chernivtsi, 'many working people' hired one or more persons to teach them to read and write and themselves paid for such service from their own small wages, but it was difficult to recruit such persons to give instruction after working hours or on Sundays. *Hromadskyi holos*, 15 July/1 August 1899.

13 On Prosvita see Hryniuk, *Peasants with Promise*, 90–3; for the Kachkovsky Society see ibid., 93–5, and P.R. Magocsi, 'Cultural Organizations as an

Instrument of National Revivals: The Kachkovs'kyi Society in 19th Century Eastern Galicia,' *Harvard Ukrainian Studies* (forthcoming).

14 Hryniuk, *Peasants with Promise*, 95. By 1898 the Narodna Torhivlia had 15 warehouses (one in each of its affiliate towns) and 549 associated village shops. *Svoboda*, 10 November 1898.

15 Volodymyr Kubijovyč, ed., *Encyclopedia of Ukraine* (Toronto: University of Toronto Press, 1984) I: 318–19; *Batkivshchyna*, 20 April and 27 July 1888. On Soiuz, which at times was plagued by rivalries between Ukrainophile and Russophile students, see W. Denesczuk, 'Rechtliche Stellung der Ukrainer (Ruthenen) in der Bukowina von 1774–1918' (PhD dissertation, University of Innsbruck, 1972), 71–4.

16 P. Melnyk, 'Das ukrainische landwirtschaftliche Genossenschaftswesen in Galizien' (dissertation, University of Vienna, 1944), 11.

17 Hryniuk, *Peasants with Promise*, 195–7.

18 Ivan L. Rudnytsky, 'The Role of Ukraine in Modern History,' in Ivan L. Rudnytsky, *Essays in Modern Ukrainian History*, ed. Peter L. Rudnytsky (Edmonton: Canadian Institute of Ukrainian Studies, 1987), 23.

19 Hryniuk, *Peasants with Promise*, 99, 125–7, 140, 153, and 179–80.

20 Ibid., 129–30.

21 Varfolomii Ihnatiienko, *Bibliohrafiia ukrainskoi presy, 1816–1916* (Kharkiv, 1930; rpt., State College, Pa.: Ukrainska nova knyha, 1968), 20ff.

22 John-Paul Himka, *Galician Villagers and the Ukrainian National Movement in the Nineteenth Century* (Edmonton: Canadian Institute of Ukrainian Studies, 1988), 68.

23 Ibid., 71.

24 Himka, *Galician Villagers*, 80–4; Hryniuk, *Peasants with Promise*, 97–101.

25 *Batkivshchyna*, 19 June 1886.

26 Hryniuk, *Peasants with Promise*, 103–4.

27 Ibid., 91–2, 93–5, and 102.

28 *Batkivshchyna*, 24 August 1886.

29 Hryniuk, *Peasants with Promise*, 107.

30 Ibid., 106–7.

31 *Batkivshchyna*, 2 April 1886; *Chytalnia*, 6 July 1895.

32 Hryniuk, *Peasants with Promise*, 104–6; Himka, *Galician Villagers*, 86–92. Activists associated with Prosvita were also instrumental in establishing the Ukrainian insurance company Dnister, which in 1900 underwrote 84,765 policies in over 3,000 Galician communes, as well as some in Bukovyna (*Podręcznik statystyki Galicyi*, VIII, pt. 2: 258).

33 Himka, 92–7; Hryniuk, *Peasants with Promise*, 104–5.

34 Hryniuk, *Peasants with Promise*, 101–7; Himka, *Galician Villagers*, 97–104.

35 J. Martin and W. Leonard, *Principles of Field Crop Production*, 2d ed. (New York: Macmillan, 1967), 5.

36 *Hospodar i promyshlennyk*, no. 2, 1886.

37 *Istorychno-memuarnyi zbirnyk Chortkivskoi okruhy: Povity Chortkiv, Kopy-chyntsi, Borshchiv, Zalishchyky*, Ukrainskyi arkhiv, XXVI (New York, 1974), 628.

38 Hryniuk, *Peasants with Promise*, 129–30.

39 Ibid., 129–30 and 195.

40 See, for example, the letters from Raranchi, Chernivtsi county, Bukovyna, *Batkivshchyna*, 9 March 1888; and from Terebovlia county, Eastern Galicia, *Svoboda*, 29 April and 23 December 1897.

41 By way of comparison it may be noted that in France the minimum area planted with subsistence crops that was required to sustain a family of five declined from about five hectares in 1815 to two hectares in 1892. See E. Labrousse, 'The Evolution of Peasant Society in France from the Eighteenth Century to the Present,' in E.M. Acomb and M.L. Brown, eds., *French Society and Culture since the Old Regime* (New York: Holt, Rinehart and Winston, 1966), 58.

42 See Franciszek Bujak, *Galicya* (Lviv: H. Altenberg, 1908–10) I: 240 and 420–3; Wincenty Stys, *Rozdrąbnienie gruntów chłopskich w byłym zaborze austrjackim od roku 1787 do 1931* (Lviv: Gubrynowicz i Syn, 1934), 54–5; and Hryniuk, *Peasants with Promise*, 120–1.

43 Bujak, *Galicya*, I: 240; and John-Paul Himka, 'The Background to Emigration: Ukrainians of Galicia and Bukovyna, 1848–1914,' in Manoly R. Lupul, ed., *A Heritage in Transition: Essays in the History of Ukrainians in Canada* (Toronto: McClelland and Stewart, 1982), 15.

44 *Oesterreichische Statistik*, 83, no. 1.

45 See, for example, *Hospodar i promyshlennyk*, no. 13, 1880, no. 2, 1884, and nos. 1, 2, 3, and 22, 1885; and *Batkivshchyna*, 13 February and 14 March 1890. By 1913, only 5 per cent of Galician land was being left fallow; Pruski, *Hodowla zwierząt gospodarskich*, II: 27.

46 W.T.R. Preston, 'Report of Inspector of Agencies in Europe,' Canada, *Sessional Papers*, no. 13, 1900: 12–19.

47 See the annual volumes of *Statistisches Jahrbuch des k.k. Ackerbau-Ministeriums* (Vienna, 1875–); also *Hromadskyi holos*, 10 May 1898.

48 Hryniuk, 'Peasant Agriculture,' 235.

49 Bujak, *Galicya*, I: 309–10.

50 Mr W. Michalchyshyn, Winnipeg, interviewed on 29 December 1983, stated that the following were grown in his family's garden in Bychkivtsi, Chortkiv county, Eastern Galicia, around 1913–14: cabbages, cucumbers, small melons, various sorts of beans, peas, beets, parsnips, turnips, cauliflower, potatoes, maize, celery, onions, garlic, dill, parsley, raspberries, strawberries, gooseberries, currants, and loganberries. Although his mother did not plant tomatoes or spinach, he had heard of people growing these. Few people grew raspberries or strawberries because they took up much space. People with large gardens sometimes grew hemp.

51 For these practices in the Southern Podillia region of Eastern Galicia see Hryniuk, *Peasants with Promise*, 141–2.

52 See the annual data in *Statistisches Jahrbuch des k.k. Ackerbau-Ministeriums* from 1884 onwards. On the growing of clover, also as a second crop, see *Hospodar i promyshlennyk*, no. 22, 1885; *Nauka*, 31 January and 28 February 1890; and *Batkivshchyna*, 13 February 1890.

53 The correlation of size of landholding and numbers of farm animals is derived from the agricultural census of 1902, *Oesterreichische Statistik*, 83.

54 Bujak, *Galicya*, I: 313. Western Ukrainian peasants thus shared in the general Austrian 'transition from the "keeping of animals" to the "breeding of animals."' K. Dinklage, 'Die Landwirtschaftliche Entwicklung,' in Wandruszka and Urbanitsch, *Die Habsburgermonarchie*, I: 427.

55 *Oesterreichische Statistik*, 60, no. 3, pt. 2.

56 Ibid.

57 Pruski, *Hodowla zwierząt gospodarskich*, I: 372–4.

58 For a Ukrainian pig-marketing co-operative in Stanyslaviv see *Svoboda*, 22 December 1898; for dairy co-operatives, especially in the first decade of the twentieth century, see A. Kachor, *Ukrainska molocharska kooperatsiia v Zakhidnii Ukraini* (Munich, 1949), I. Vytanovych, *Istoriia ukrainskoho kooperatyvnoho rukhu* (New York: Naukove tovarystvo im. Shevchenka, 1964), 150–2; and Melnyk, 'Das ukrainische landwirtschaftliche Genossenschaftswesen,' 12–17. For sizes of businesses and general occupational data in Galicia and Bukovyna in 1902 see *Oesterreichische Statistik*, 75, pts. 11 and 12.

59 Hryniuk, *Peasants with Promise*, 171–87.

60 Stella M. Hryniuk, 'The Peasant and Alcohol in Eastern Galicia in the Late Nineteenth Century: A Note,' *Journal of Ukrainian Studies* 11 (Summer 1986): 75–85.

61 See, for example, *Hromadskyi holos*, 1 May 1899, for shortages of work and low wages in Bukovyna.

62 For work stoppages in 1900 at Babyntsi, Borshchiv county, Eastern Galicia, and at Onut, Kitsman county, Bukovyna, see *Hromadskyi holos*, 1 April and 15 May 1900. In the former case the village reeve was arrested for siding with the villagers.

63 Z. Daszynska-Golinska, 'Neuere Literatur über galizisches Agrarwesen,' *Archiv für Sozialwissenschaft und Sozialpolitik* 20 (1904): 729. The real history of the 1902 agrarian strikes remains to be written.

64 For example, *Hromadskyi holos*, 1 October 1898, reported that the elections to the Bukovynian Landtag had been held 'without bayonets, noise, or agitation.'

65 As used in this essay, the term 'Western Ukraine' applies to Eastern Galicia and Bukovyna and does not encompass Transcarpathia (which

was part of the Kingdom of Hungary and which did not contribute to any great extent to the emigration to Canada).

66 Hryniuk, *Peasants with Promise*, 107–202.

67 *Svoboda*, 14 October 1897.

68 For accounts of assemblies in Borshchiv, Chortkiv, and Zalishchyky counties, Eastern Galicia, see *Svoboda*, 21 January, 25 November, and 23 December 1897, and 10 and 24 February, 3 and 24 March, 28 April, 27 November, and 23 December 1898. For an assembly at Chernivtsi, Bukovyna, attended by three hundred or four hundred people (compared to about a thousand two or three years earlier), see *Hromadskyi holos*, 6 and 20 September 1900.

69 For the first assembly see *Viche*, vol. 1, no. 1, and *Prolom*, 9 January 1882; for harassment by gendarmes see, for instance, *Batkivshchyna*, 10 December 1886, and 7 January and 4 March 1887.

70 *Svoboda*, 18 and 25 November and 30 December 1897.

71 In addition to evidence already presented, the following contemporary descriptive comment deserves to be cited: 'Our grandfathers had twenty or more morgs but didn't have as much from it as the grandsons now get from four or six morgs. From one morg of field they got two wagons of bad hay; today we get ten-fifteen wagons of clover.' *Batkivshchyna*, 8 March 1889.

72 A.M. Shlepakov, *The Emigration of Ukrainians to Canada: Reasons and Circumstances* (Toronto, 1981), 11. His much longer work is *Ukrainska trudova emihratsiia v SShA i Kanadi: Kinets XIX–pochatok XX st.* (Kiev: Akademiia nauk Ukrainskoi RSR, 1960).

73 Zonia Keywan and Martin Coles, *Greater than Kings: Ukrainian Pioneer Settlement in Canada* (Montreal: Harvest House, 1977), preface.

74 This and similar sentiments were expressed to the author in interviews she conducted between 9 and 20 July 1979 with persons who came from Western Ukraine or whose families came from there and who were residing in the Stuartburn area of Manitoba: Mrs K. Chubaty, Mr J. Horobec, Mrs L. Salamandyk, Mr M. Sokolyk, and Mr J. Storoschuk. It is nevertheless quite possible that there were some poor people among the immigrants.

75 *Hromadskyi holos*, 1 May 1899.

76 Hryniuk, *Peasants with Promise*, 205.

77 V.J. Kaye, *Early Ukrainian Settlements in Canada, 1895–1900: Dr. Josef Oleskow's Role in the Settlement of the Canadian Northwest* (Toronto: University of Toronto Press for the Ukrainian Canadian Research Foundation, 1964), 3–44.

78 Petryshyn, *Peasants in the Promised Land*, 22.

79 Typical was the circular of the governor of Galicia to all Galician county officers (*starosty*) of May 1889, chastising them, as well as reeves, clergymen, and teachers, for not working hard enough to stop emigration.

Fond 146, op. 4, spr. 2451, Tsentralnyi derzhavnyi istorychnyi arkhiv URSR u Lvovi (Central State Historical Archive of the Ukrainian SSR in Lviv, or TsDIAL). In 1887 a fifteen-year-old boy was accused of acting as an agent for distributing a pamphlet entitled *Manitoba*. He was acquitted by a court in Kolomyia because he had received the brochures without having ordered them. Report of the Sniatyn County Officer, 30 October 1887, fond 146, op. 4, spr. 2446, TsDIAL.

80 S. Kacharaba, 'Ukrainska trudova emihratsiia iz skhidnoi Halychyny i pivnichnoi Bukovyny v kintsi XIX–na pochatku XX st. (1890–1914 rr.)' (candidate's dissertation, Lviv State University, 1990).

81 'That they often lacked bread and salt, they did not tell us; we found that out when we came to Canada.' Quoted in Kaye, *Early Ukrainian Settlements*, 363.

82 Ibid., xiv.

83 *Hromadskyi holos*, 1 May 1899.

84 It is noteworthy that John-Paul Himka's 'Cultural Life in the Awakening Village in Western Ukraine' in M.R. Lupul, ed., *Continuity and Change: The Cultural Life of Alberta's First Ukrainians* (Edmonton: Canadian Institute of Ukrainian Studies, 1988), 10–23, although based largely on materials from the mid-1880s, is very different in tone and substance from his 1982 essay cited in note 43.

85 J. Harriss, 'General Introduction,' in J. Harriss, ed., *Rural Development: Theories of Peasant Economy and Agrarian Change* (London: Hutchinson, 1982), 21.

86 Rudnytsky, 'The Role of Ukraine,' 23.

87 P. Taylor, *The Distant Magnet: European Emigration to the U.S.A.* (New York: Harper and Row, 1972), 49.

Petryshyn: Sifton's Immigration Policy

1 From the approximately six hundred who came in 1896 Ukrainian immigration continued to increase so that by 1900 over twenty-seven thousand Ukrainians had settled in Manitoba and the Northwest. By 1905 this figure had grown to more than seventy thousand.

2 See, for example, Donald Avery, 'Canadian Immigration Policy and the Alien Question in Canada, 1896–1919: The Anglo-Canadian Perspective' (PhD dissertation, University of Western Ontario, 1973), 141–2; John Campbell Lehr, 'Ukrainian Rural Settlement in the Prairie Provinces, 1891–1914' (PhD dissertation, University of Manitoba, 1978), 54–8; David J. Hall, *Clifford Sifton* (Vancouver: University of British Columbia Press, 1981–5) I: 261–2, II: 65, 69; Michael H. Marunchak, *The Ukrainian Canadians: A History* (Winnipeg: Ukrainian Free Academy of Sciences, 1970), 28–38; and Jaroslav Petryshyn, *Peasants in the Promised Land: Canada and the Ukrainians, 1891–1914* (Toronto: James Lorimer, 1985), 19–26.

Notes to pages 18–20

3 This paper uses 'Ukrainian' interchangeably with 'Galician' and 'Bukovynian,' the nomenclature used by most Canadian commentators of the
  period.
4 Osyp (Iosyf) Oleskiv was born on 28 September 1860 to a priest's family
  in the village of Nova Skvariava in Galicia. He completed secondary
  school in Lviv and proceeded to the University of Lviv, where he received
  a doctorate, specializing in natural sciences, chemistry, and geology. He
  continued studies in botany and agriculture in Erfurt, Germany, then
  returned to Galicia and lectured at the agricultural college in Dubliany,
  near Lviv. After completing examinations, he was appointed imperial
  and royal professor at the teachers' seminary in Lviv. Oleskiv was a
  director of the Prosvita Society and a friend of Ivan Franko.
5 Emigration was a fact of life in Galicia and Bukovyna long before Canada
  was discovered to be an attractive land for settlement. Brazil was the
  first overseas destination. During the second half of the nineteenth century the rapidly expanding coffee-growing industry in Brazil experienced a scarcity of labour. Plantation owners sent agents to Austria-
  Hungary and Germany to entice peasants with promises of a prosperous future. Most of the peasants who went to Brazil were taken to coffee
  plantations in Sao Paolo to provide essentially free labour. Ill-adapted
  to plantation work, hundreds perished. See Emilio Willems, *Brazil: The
  Positive Contribution by Immigrants* (New York: United Nations Educational, Scientific and Cultural Organization, 1955).
6 Vladimir J. Kaye, *Early Ukrainian Settlements in Canada, 1895–1900: Dr. Josef
  Oleskow's Role in the Settlement of the Canadian Northwest* (Toronto: University of Toronto Press for the Ukrainian Canadian Research Foundation, 1964), 385. But see also the number cited on p. 7 above.
7 For an itinerary of Oleskiv's trip through Canada see Kaye, *Early Ukrainian Settlements*, 387–9.
8 Oleskiv to the Department of the Interior, 6 September 1896, RG 76, vol.
  110, file 31442, NAC.
9 Ibid.
10 Concern was expressed that Oleskiv would not be able to procure the
  necessary operating licence from the government in Vienna. Canadian
  officials were also dubious about his abilities to obtain a franchise from
  one of the steamship companies doing business on the continent. See
  Kaye, *Early Ukrainian Settlements*, 89.
11 Oleskiv to the Department of the Interior, 9 December 1896, RG 76, vol.
  110, file 32880, NAC. Cited in Kaye, *Early Ukrainian Settlements*, 90.
12 The official Department of the Interior figures of Galician arrivals were
  4,010 for 1898 and 6,700 for 1899. Canada, Parliament, Sessional Paper
  No. 25, 3–4 Edward VII, 1904, xxx.
13 James Mavor to Sifton, June 1900, 'Report No. 2,' James Mavor Papers,
  University of Toronto Archives.

14 Ibid.

15 Canada, Parliament, Select Standing Committee on Agriculture and Colonization, 'Immigration to Canada' (hereafter cited as SSCAC-IC), 63 Victoria, Appendix 1, 18 April 1900, 328, 420.

16 Mavor Papers.

17 Kaye, *Early Ukrainian Settlements*, 122.

18 In his report to Sifton Mavor states at one point: 'Oleskow struck me as likely to be a rather vindictive person.' The context of this remark, however, is obscure. Mavor Papers.

19 Ibid.

20 The government and Oleskiv did reach a satisfactory agreement on payment. See Kaye, *Early Ukrainian Settlements*, 131.

21 William F. McCreary to Sir Clifford Sifton, 20 April 1899, Sir Clifford Sifton Papers, MG 27 II D15, vol. 66, 48222, NAC.

22 Ibid., 48224.

23 Ibid., 48224–5.

24 Sifton to James A. Smart, 26 April 1899, Sir Clifford Sifton Papers, MG 27 II D15, vol. 232, 163, NAC.

25 It may be of interest to note that Sifton's oft-quoted statement, 'I think a stalwart peasant in a sheepskin coat, born on the soil, whose forefathers have been farmers for 10 generations, with a stout wife and a half dozen children is a good quality immigrant,' was made in the heated context of the 1904 federal election campaign when his opponents again criticized his supposed 'open-door' immigration policies and referred to Galicians as 'Sifton's pets.'

26 SSCAC-IC, 63 Victoria, Appendix 1, 18 April 1900, 313.

27 Ibid. It appears that the government of Austria-Hungary did take an interest in how the Galicians and Bukovynians were faring in Canada. Certainly Edward Schultze, the Austro-Hungarian consul in Montreal, wrote a number of favourable reports to Vienna. See, for example, Kaye, *Early Ukrainian Settlements*, 121.

28 SSCAC-IC, 63 Victoria, Appendix 1, 18 April 1900. The testimony of Frank Pedley, superintendent of immigration, 532.

29 W.T.R. Preston (1851–1942), a journalist, Liberal party organizer in Ontario, and librarian to the Legislature of Ontario before his appointment by Sifton, had a reputation as a political scoundrel. Twice defeated in his bid for the House of Commons, he was implicated in a bribe attempt and election fraud. It seemed that because of his reputation Preston was unemployed when Laurier urged Sifton to provide a place for him. Laurier, in turn, had received pressure from Ontario liberals, who were anxious that Preston be rewarded for his party work in the province. A.S. Hardy to Sir Wilfrid Laurier, 20 July 1898; Laurier to Hardy, 25 July 1898, Sir Wilfrid Laurier Papers, MG 26 G1(a), vol. 81, NAC.

30 According to Preston, Sifton's instructions were that he 'should leave no

stone unturned with a view of solving the difficulties connected with emigration which had been in an unsatisfactory state for so many years on the continent.' SSCAC-The North Atlantic Trading Company (hereafter cited as SSCAC-NATC) 6 Edward VII, Appendix 2, 1906, 323.

31 See Preston's report on restrictive emigration in European countries, SSAC-IC, 63 Victoria, Appendix 1, 18 April 1900, 309–13.

32 Ibid., 324.

33 Ibid., 285, 289–90, 293.

34 Ibid., 283. See also W.T.R. Preston, *My Generation of Politics and Politicians* (Toronto: D.A. Rose Publishing Co., 1927), 260.

35 Canada, House of Commons, *Debates* (hereafter cited as *Debates*), 20 April 1906, col. 1796.

36 SSCAC-NATC, Testimony of James A. Smart, 300.

37 Ibid. The information given to agents by many immigrants upon landing at Canadian ports regarding the amount of money they possessed often did not correspond with statements furnished by the company from the exchange offices at the ports of debarkation where these same immigrants exchanged their money. Report of the Committee of the Privy Council, 20 September 1904, Sir Wilfrid Laurier Papers, MG 26 G1(a), vol. 336, 89665–9, NAC.

38 *Debates*, 1 May 1906, vol. 2330–1.

39 Ibid.

40 SSCAC-NATC, 300.

41 In private letters Preston referred to the NATC as a 'gold mine' from which he made a large sum of money. See ibid., The Testimony of Alfred F. Jury, Emigration Agent at Liverpool, 402–10.

42 Canada, Senate, *Debates*, 13 June 1906, 692.

43 James A. Smart (1856–1942) knew Sifton from their Brandon days when they sat in the Manitoba legislature. Sifton summoned Smart to Ottawa in 1897 to become deputy minister of the interior and deputy superintendent of Indian affairs.

44 SSCAC-NATC, 491.

45 Ibid., 337.

46 Ibid., 402–10.

47 *Debates*, 20 April 1906, col. 1809.

48 Ibid., 30 April 1906, col. 1833.

49 When the contract was cancelled on 3 November 1906, the government had paid the company a total of $367,245.85. *Debates*, 4 December 1907, col. 770.

50 SSCAC-NATC, 339.

51 Sifton to Laurier, 11 January 1906, Sir Wilfrid Laurier Papers, MG 26 D1(a), vol. 350, 93603–5, NAC. See also David J. Hall, 'Clifford Sifton: Immigration and Settlement Policy, 1896–1906,' in H. Palmer, ed., *The Settlement of the West* (Calgary: University of Calgary Press, 1977), 72.

52 Cited in Avery, 'Canadian Immigration Policy,' 142.
53 Ivan L. Rudnytsky, 'The Ukrainians in Galicia under Austrian Rule,' *Austrian History Yearbook* 3, pt. 2 (1967): 418.
54 See J. Zubrzycki, 'Patterns of Peasant Migration with Special Reference to Eastern Europe,' *Research Group for European Migration Problems Bulletin* 4 (October–December 1956), 73–87.
55 Ivan Franko, *Tvory v dvadtsiaty tomakh* (Kiev: Derzhlitvydav Ukrainy, 1950–6) XIX: 311. (Editors' note: For a different view of Galician conditions, see Stella Hryniuk's contribution to this volume.)
56 Eleniak remained in Canada, hiring himself out locally, while Pillipiw returned to Galicia to gather their families for emigration. In June 1892, twelve families from Pillipiw's village emigrated to Gretna, Man. Eleniak's family arrived some years later and settled in Chipman, Alta.
57 Between two hundred thousand and three hundred thousand Ukrainians had come to the United States in the last three decades of the 1800s. The presence of this community encouraged Ukrainians to emigrate to Canada. See Petryshyn, *Peasants in the Promised Land*, 43–50.
58 SSCAC-NATC, 304, 476. See also *Debates*, 26 April 1906, col. 2368.
59 SSCAC-NATC, 304.
60 Ibid., 331.
61 Ibid., 411.
62 See Kaye, *Early Ukrainian Settlements*, 103–31.
63 It was believed that Galicia was overpopulated by two to three million. Kaye, *Early Ukrainian Settlements*, 119.
64 SSCAC-NATC, 319.

Lehr: Peopling the Prairies with Ukrainians

1 Ukrainians were for a long time a subject people, politically fragmented under a variety of alien administrations. By the end of the nineteenth century they replaced the ancient names of 'Rus'' and 'Rusyn' with 'Ukraine' and 'Ukrainian,' but in Canada 'Ukrainian' was not officially recognized until 1930. Before then, in Canadian governmental correspondence, Ukrainians were described variously according to their national origin as Austrians or Russians, as Ruthenians (the Latin form of Rusyn), or as Galicians and Bukowinians after their provinces of origin. The Canadian government favoured the latter terms before 1914. The practice of expanding the term 'Galician' to embrace all Ukrainians regardless of province of origin created further confusion. For a discussion of the problems of the ethnic name see G.W. Simpson, 'The Names "Rus'," "Russia," "Ukraine," and Their Historical Background,' *Slavistica: Proceedings of the Institute of Slavistics of the Ukrainian Free Academy of Science* 10 (1951), 1–24; E.D. Wangenheim, 'Problems of Research on Ukrainians in Eastern Canada,' in Yar Slavutych, ed., *Slavs in Canada: Proceedings of the First National Conference on Slavs, Banff, Alberta, 1965* (Edmonton: Inter-

University Committee on Canadian Slavs, 1966) I: 44–53; and Vladimir
J. Kaye, *Early Ukrainian Settlements in Canada, 1895–1900: Dr. Josef Oleskow's
Role in the Settlement of the Canadian Northwest* (Toronto: University of
Toronto Press for the Ukrainian Canadian Research Foundation, 1964),
xxiii–xxvi.

2 Hansgeorg Schlictmann, 'Ethnic Themes in Geographical Research in
Western Canada,' *Canadian Ethnic Studies* 9 (1977): 10–14; C.A. Dawson,
Group Settlement: Ethnic Communities in Western Canada (Toronto: Macmil-
lan, 1936).

3 This claim is most common in left-wing Ukrainian-Canadian historiogra-
phy. See, for example, Charles H. Young, *The Ukrainian Canadians: A
Study in Assimilation* (Toronto: Thomas Nelson and Sons, 1931), 57; Vera
Lysenko, *Men in Sheepskin Coats: A Study in Assimilation* (Toronto: Ryer-
son Press, 1947), 33; Petro Kravchuk, *Na novii zemli* (Toronto: Tovarystvo
obiednanykh ukrainskykh kanadtsiv, 1958), 82–5; William Harasym,
'Ukrainian Values in the Canadian Identity,' in *Proceedings of the Special
Convention of United Ukrainian Canadians* (Winnipeg: Association of
United Ukrainian Canadians, 1966), 67; and Helen Potrebenko, *No Streets
of Gold* (Vancouver: New Star Books, 1977), 38–9. Some right-wing
historians – for example, Michael H. Marunchak, *The Ukrainian Canadians:
A History* (Winnipeg: Ukrainian Free Academy of Sciences, 1970), 87 –
also subscribe to this view.

4 William Darcovich and Paul Yuzyk, eds., *A Statistical Compendium on the
Ukrainians in Canada, 1891–1976* (Ottawa: University of Ottawa Press,
1980), 500–2.

5 There have been three major immigrations of Ukrainians into Canada,
each having distinct characteristics in terms of the socio-economic character of the immigrants, their motives for emigration, and their destinations in Canada. See Vladimir J. Kaye, 'Three Phases of Ukrainian
Immigration,' in Slavutych, *Slavs in Canada*, I: 36–43.

6 Emily Greene Balch, 'Slav Emigration at Its Source,' *Charities and the
Commons* 16 (May 1906): 179.

7 A.M. Shlepakov, *Ukrainska trudova emihratsiia v SShA i Kanadi: Kinets XIX–
pochatok XX st.* (Kiev: Akademiia nauk Ukrainskoi RSR, 1960), 23.

8 Peter F. Sugar, 'The Nature of the Non-Germanic Societies under Habsburg Rule,' *Slavic Review* 22 (1963): 17; Shlepakov, *Ukrainska trudova
emihratsiia*, 29.

9 Stella M. Hryniuk, 'A Peasant Society in Transition: Ukrainian Peasants
in Five East Galician Counties 1880–1920' (PhD dissertation, University
of Manitoba, 1985), offers a comprehensive review of conditions in Galicia
at the time of emigration. She argues that conditions were not as poor
as has often been claimed and that the Galician peasantry was entering
a stage of rapid change and improved economic conditions.

10 Henry J.T. Dutkiewicz, 'Main Aspects of the Polish Peasant Immigration

to North America from Austrian Poland between the Years 1863 and 1910' (MA thesis, University of Ottawa, 1958), 58.

11 W.L. Scott, 'Catholic Ukrainian Canadians,' *Dublin Review* 202 (1938): 283; Hans Kohn, 'The Viability of the Habsburg Monarchy,' *Slavic Review* 22 (1963): 38–9: Nicholas Andrusiak, 'The Ukrainian Movement in Galicia,' *Slavonic and East European Review* 14 (1935–6): 163–75, 372–9; and Ivan L. Rudnytsky, 'The Ukrainians in Galicia under Austrian Rule,' *Austrian History Yearbook* 3, pt. 2 (1967): 394–429.

12 Although poor, social and political conditions in the part of Ukraine administered by Austria were far better than those endured under Russian rule. See Ivan L. Rudnytsky, 'The Intellectual Origins of Modern Ukraine,' *Annals of the Ukrainian Academy of Arts and Sciences in the U.S.* 6 (1958): 1381–1405.

13 John Paul Himka, 'The Background to Emigration: Ukrainians of Galicia and Bukovyna, 1848–1914,' in Manoly R. Lupul, ed., *A Heritage in Transition: Essays in the History of Ukrainians in Canada* (Toronto: McClelland and Stewart, 1982), 16–18.

14 Rudnytsky, 'The Ukrainians in Galicia,' 418; Balch, 'Slav Emigration,' 177.

15 For a fascinating personal account of migration to Brazil, remigration to Canada, and return to Brazil by an emigrant from Galicia, see Michael Ewanchuk, *Pioneer Settlers: Ukrainians in the Dauphin Area, 1896–1926* (Winnipeg: Privately printed, 1988), 33–5, 107–15, and 129–32.

16 Iosyf Oleskiv, *O emigratsii* (Lviv: Obshchestvo Mykhaila Kachkovskoho, 1895), 35; and Isidore Goresky, 'Early Ukrainian Settlement in Alberta,' in Editorial Committee, *Ukrainians in Alberta* (Edmonton: Ukrainian Pioneers' Association of Alberta, 1975), 17–19.

17 Ivan Pylypiw, 'How We Came to Canada,' in Harry Piniuta, trans. and ed., *Land of Pain, Land of Promise: First Person Accounts by Ukrainian Pioneers, 1891–1914* (Saskatoon: Western Producer Prairie Books, 1978), 27–35. For an assessment of the role of emigration propaganda in generating immigration to Canada, see John C. Lehr, 'Propaganda and Belief: Ukrainian Emigrant Views of the Canadian West,' in Jaroslav Rozumnyj, ed., *New Soil – Old Roots: The Ukrainian Experience in Canada* (Winnipeg: Ukrainian Academy of Arts and Sciences in Canada, 1983), 1–17.

18 For a popular account of this initial phase see James G. MacGregor, *Vilni Zemli – Free Lands: The Ukrainian Settlement of Alberta* (Toronto: McClelland and Stewart, 1969). A more scholarly treatment is found in Goresky, 'Early Ukrainian Settlement,' 17–38.

19 Oleskiv, *O emigratsii*, 41. Oleskiv noted that the Ukrainians in Winnipeg did 'not live too badly.' Some were saving money to buy a farm; others had become accustomed to city life and intended to remain in town.

20 Dr R.H. Mason, Saltcoats, Assiniboia, to James A. Smart, Ottawa, 12 July 1899, Record Group 76, vol. 144, file 34214, pt. 1, National Archives of Canada, Ottawa (hereafter cited as NAC). Mason noted that in the Salt-

coats colony he found 'several clever carpenters and wagon makers,' an expert shoemaker, and 'a musician who constructed a very good violin and played selections from Mozart.'

21 See, for example, William F. McCreary, Winnipeg, to James A. Smart, Ottawa, 20 May 1897, RG 76, vol. 144, file 34214, pt. 1, NAC.

22 On the Ukrainian community in Sydney, see John Huk, *Strangers in the Land: The Ukrainian Presence in Cape Breton* (Sydney, NS: Privately printed, 1986).

23 Government of Canada, Records of Homestead Entry for Alberta, 1891–6.

24 This fallacy led the Department of the Interior to engage interpreters proficient in German to deal with 'Austrian' immigrants as late as 1897. William F. McCreary, the commissioner of immigration at Winnipeg, went to considerable pains to convince his superiors in Ottawa that interpreters conversant in Ukrainian, not German, were required. William F. McCreary, Winnipeg, to James A. Smart, Ottawa, 24 May 1897, RG 76, vol. 144, file 34214, pt. 1, NAC.

25 Oleskiv's role in the settlement of Ukrainians in Canada has been examined in detail in Kaye, *Early Ukrainian Settlements*. Oleskiv's first letter to the Canadian Department of the Interior was received on 1 April 1895. Dr Joseph Oleskow, Lemberg (Lviv), Austria, to the Department of the Interior, Ottawa, 16 March 1895, translation from the German by Miss Mercer, Department of the Interior, RG 76, vol. 109, file 21103, pt. 1, NAC.

26 Osyp Oleskiv, *Pro vilni zemli* (Lviv: Tovarystvo Prosvita, 1895).

27 Józef Olesków, *Rolnictwo za Oceanem a Przesiedlna Emigracja* (Karlsbad: Basilian Fathers, 1896). Accounts of the circumstances surrounding Oleskiv's visit to western Canada are given in Vladimir J. Kaye, 'Dr. Josef Oleskow's Visit to Canada, August–October 1895,' *Revue de l'Université d'Ottawa* 32 (1962): 30–44; and idem, *Early Ukrainian Settlements*, 3–43.

28 Oleskiv, *O emigratsii*, 39.

29 Ibid., 30–1.

30 Michael Ewanchuk, *Pioneer Profiles: Ukrainian Settlers in Manitoba* (Winnipeg: Privately printed, 1981), 13; Gus Romaniuk, *Taking Root in Canada: An Autobiography* (Winnipeg: Columbia Press, 1954), 37; Ol'ha Woycenko, *The Ukrainians in Canada* (Winnipeg: Trident Press, 1967), 38; Young, *Ukrainian Canadians*, 55; MacGregor, *Vilni Zemli*, 117; and E. Shlanka, 'Krydor Community No. 13, Interviews of Pioneers,' April 1944 (typewritten ms.), 11, G.W. Simpson Papers, Archives of Saskatchewan, Saskatoon.

31 William F. McCreary, Winnipeg, to James A. Smart, Ottawa, 14 May 1897, RG 76, vol. 144, file 34214, pt. 1, NAC.

32 S. Dymianiw, ed., *Land of Dreams Come True* (Gorlitz, Sask.: Ukrainian School Division No. 972, 1955), 11–12.

33 See John C. Lehr, 'The Rural Settlement Behaviour of Ukrainian Pioneers

in Western Canada, 1891–1914,' in B.M. Barr, ed., *Western Canadian Research in Geography: The Lethbridge Papers*, B.C. Geographical Series, No. 21, Occasional Papers in Geography (Vancouver: Tantalus Research, 1975), 51–66; and idem, 'The Process and Pattern of Ukrainian Rural Settlement in Western Canada, 1891–1914' (PhD dissertation, University of Manitoba, 1978), 129–65.

34 T.R. Weir, 'Pioneer Settlement of Southwest Manitoba, 1874 to 1901,' *Canadian Geographer* 8 (1964): 66–9.

35 Canada, Parliament, Sessional Papers, 'Department of the Interior,' 1896, Report of E.F. Stephanson, Winnipeg Land Agent, 12–13; J.R. Burpé, Commissioner of Dominion Lands, Winnipeg, Report to the Secretary, Department of the Interior, Ottawa, 27 August 1896, RG 76, vol, 110, file 21103, pt. 2, NAC. For a comprehensive history of the Star bloc settlement see Orest T. Martynowych, *The Ukrainian Bloc Settlement in East Central Alberta, 1890–1930: A History* (Edmonton: Historic Sites Service, Alberta Culture and Multiculturalism, 1985).

36 For a more detailed discussion of the question of coercion in directing immigrants to various locales, see John C. Lehr, 'Government Coercion in the Settlement of Ukrainian Immigrants in Western Canada,' *Prairie Forum* 8 (1983): 179–94.

37 Frank Pedley, Winnipeg, to CPR Agent, New York, n.d., RG 76, vol, 144, file 34214, pt. 3, NAC; and P. Doyle, Quebec City, to the Secretary, Department of the Interior, Ottawa, 30 May 1898, RG 76, vol. 144, file 34214, pt. 2, NAC.

38 William F. McCreary, Winnipeg, to James A. Smart, Ottawa, 20 May 1898, RG 76, file 34214, pt. 2, NAC.

39 John C. Lehr and D. Wayne Moodie, 'The Polemics of Pioneer Settlement: Perspectives on Ukrainian Immigration from the Winnipeg Press, 1896–1905,' *Canadian Ethnic Studies* 12 (1980): 88–101.

40 Clifford Sifton, 'The Immigrants Canada Wants,' *Maclean's Magazine*, 1 April 1922, 16, 33. For a discussion of the government's attitudes towards Ukrainian settlers see John C. Lehr, 'Government Perceptions of Ukrainian Immigrants to Western Canada, 1896–1902,' *Canadian Ethnic Studies* 19 (1987): 1–12.

41 See, for example, *Winnipeg Telegram*, 7 July and 2 November 1899. The attacks of the *Telegram* appear restrained in comparison with those of other Canadian newspapers. The *Belleville Intelligencer* called the Ukrainians 'disgusting creatures' and wondered how 'beings having human form could have sunk to such a bestial level'; *Halifax Herald*, 18 March 1899. For even more extreme views see Clive Phillips Wolley, 'Mr. Sifton's Anglo-Saxondom,' *Anglo-Saxon* 12 (June 1899): 1–4.

42 *Winnipeg Telegram*, 11 June 1898, 1 August 1899, and 14 July 1900; *Kingston News*, 23 June 1899.

43 *Nor'Wester*, 20 July 1897.

44 *Winnipeg Telegram*, 3 February 1899.
45 *Winnipeg Tribune*, 21 July 1909; *Daily Sun*, St John, NB, 31 July 1899.
46 *Winnipeg Telegram*, 10 August 1899.
47 Lehr and Moodie, 'The Polemics of Pioneer Settlement,' 93–8.
48 Established in 1872, the *Manitoba Free Press* was connected with Canadian
   Pacific Railway interests until its purchase in 1898 by Clifford Sifton
   and a business associate. Ramsay Cook, *The Politics of John W. Dafoe and
   the Free Press* (Toronto: University of Toronto Press, 1963), 15.
49 RG 76, vol. 144, file 34214, NAC.
50 See, for example, *Nor'Wester*, 10 March 1897 and 21 January 1898; *Winnipeg
   Telegram*, 9 June 1899.
51 *Manitoba Free Press*, 16 October 1901.
52 William F. McCreary, Winnipeg, to James A. Smart, Ottawa, 13 May 1897,
   RG 76, vol. 144, file 34214, pt. 1, NAC.
53 Canada, Parliament, Sessional Papers, 1899, 'Department of the Interior,'
   113.
54 William F. McCreary, Winnipeg, to James A. Smart, Ottawa, 26 May 1898,
   RG 76, vol. 144, file 34214, pt. 2, NAC.
55 William F. McCreary, Winnipeg, to James A. Smart, Ottawa, 18 May 1898,
   ibid.
56 The many applications for work entered with the Edmonton colonization
   agent were an important factor in the decision to curtail the growth of
   the Star settlement by establishing other nodes of Ukrainian settlement.
   The Strathclair–Shoal Lake area was selected for settlement by Ukrainians partly because of the employment potential of the Riding Mountain
   Timber Reserve lumbering camps and the opportunity to employ settlers
   on fire protection work if extra employment was found to be necessary.
   For an extended discussion of this question see John C. Lehr, 'The
   Government and the Immigrant: Perspectives on Ukrainian Bloc Settle-
   ment in the Canadian West,' *Canadian Ethnic Studies* 9 (1977): 48–9.
57 D. McIntosh, Roadmaster, CPR, Prince Albert, to William F. McCreary,
   Winnipeg, 25 July 1898, RG 76, vol. 178, file 60868, pt. 1, NAC; James
   Mavor, *Report to the Board of Trade on the North-West of Canada with Special
   Reference to Wheat Production for Export* (London: HMSO, 1904), 57.
58 William F. McCreary, Winnipeg, to James A. Smart, Ottawa, 27 June 1900,
   RG 76, vol. 144, file 34214, pt. 4, NAC; J.S. Crerar, Yorkton, to William
   F. McCreary, Winnipeg, 7 July 1900, RG 76, vol. 178, file 60868, pt. 1, NAC;
   Todor Kutzak, pioneer of the Sirko district, Manitoba, interview with
   author, 15 September 1975; Peter Humeniuk, *Hardships and Progress of
   Ukrainian Pioneers: Memoirs from Stuartburn Colony and Other Points*
   (Steinbach, Man.: Derksen Printers, 1979), 56–8.
59 William F. McCreary, Winnipeg, to James A. Smart, Ottawa, 27 June 1900,
   RG 76, vol. 144, file 34214, pt. 4, NAC; C.W. Speers, Winnipeg, to Frank
   Pedley, Ottawa, 22 May 1899; 'Report of Thomas McNutt, Strathclair–
   Shoal Lake Colonization Scheme,' ibid., pt. 3, NAC.

60 Canada, Parliament, Sessional Papers, 'Department of the Interior,' 1896, 118.

61 Oleskiv, *O emigratsii*, 39.

62 J. Obed Smith, Winnipeg, to the Minister of Public Works, Manitoba, 7 January 1902, RG 76, vol. 238, file 141288 (1), NAC. The map accompanying this letter shows proposed routes for colonization roads to be built in Manitoba during 1902. Over 420 miles of colonization roads were planned for that year in Manitoba alone.

63 Under pressure of circumstances beyond their control Canadian immigration officials occasionally ignored and sometimes even promoted squatting ahead of the survey, if by doing so they could attain contiguity of group settlement. In some instances the local land guides simply had no surveyed land upon which to locate the settlers under their charge. Petition to Clifford Sifton, Minister of the Interior, Ottawa, from Basil Barawatski et al., Fork River, Man., 2 January 1905; Fred Lacey, Fork River, Man., to Clifford Sifton, Ottawa, 2 January 1902; J.A. Mitchell, Pakan, Alta, to Frank Oliver, MP, Ottawa, 4 March 1903, John W. Thompson, Minnedosa, Man., to M.E. Darby, Ottawa, 10 September 1902; and D.T. Wilson, Justice of the Peace, Asessippi, Man., to the Minister of the Interior, Ottawa, 24 December 1904, RG 15, B-1a (224) 410595, pts. 2–3, NAC. This practice was not confined to settlement of Ukrainians. In 1901 a Norwegian colony of forty families was established ahead of the survey in Manitoba's Interlake district. J. Obed Smith, Winnipeg, to Frank Pedley, Ottawa, 5 June 1901, RG 76, vol. 238, file 141288, pt. 1, NAC.

64 Map accompanying memorandum from C.W. Speers, Winnipeg, to E.L. Newcombe, Ottawa, 24 January 1901, RG 76, vol. 179, pt. 1, NAC.

65 In *O emigratsii* and *Rolnictwo za Oceanem* Oleskiv may have contributed to an erroneous view of southeastern Manitoba as a settlement location. In 1895 he visited the prairie margins east of Dominion City, Man., but as far as can be ascertained he did not inspect the area as far east as Stuartburn, where the first Ukrainians chose their homesteads. He probably endorsed the area as suitable for settlement on the assumption that the country did not change greatly east of Dominion City. Unfortunately, land quality declines rapidly east of the area viewed by Oleskiv as fertile Red River clays give way to gravelly beach ridges, areas of impeded drainage, and thin stony soils. Oleskiv, *O emigratsii*, 31; idem, *Rolnictwo za Oceanem*, 10. The first party of Ukrainian immigrants to settle in the Stuartburn district assessed the land in late July, at the driest time of the year. Many areas then dry became virtual swamps during the following spring thaw. J.R. Burpé, Secretary to the Commissioner of Dominion Lands, Winnipeg, to the Secretary, Department of the Interior, Ottawa, 30 November 1896, RG 76, vol. 110, file 21103, pt. 2, NAC.

66 John W. Wendelbo, Winnipeg, to H.H. Smith, Winnipeg, 8 August 1896, RG 15, B-1a (224), file 410595, pt. 1, NAC.

67 Canada, Parliament, Sessional Papers, 'Department of the Interior,' 1900,

Report of E.F. Stephanson, Winnipeg Land Agent, 12–13; Hugo Cars-
tens, Winnipeg, to H.H. Smith, Winnipeg, 25 November 1896, RG 76, vol.
110, file 21103, pt. 2, NAC.

68 Canada, Parliament, Sessional Papers, 'Department of the Interior,' 1900,
Report of E.F. Stephanson, Winnipeg Land Agent, 12–13.

69 Kaye, *Early Ukrainian Settlements*, 180–5.

70 Alfred Akherlindh, Winnipeg, to Frank Pedley, Ottawa, 3 May 1898, RG
76, vol. 144, file 34214, pt. 2, NAC.

71 William F. McCreary, Winnipeg, to Frank Pedley, Ottawa, 4 May 1898,
RG 76, vol. 144, file 34214, pt. 2, NAC.

72 C.W. Speers, Saskatoon, telegram to William F. McCreary, Winnipeg, 19
May 1898, ibid.

73 William F. McCreary, Winnipeg, to James A. Smart, Ottawa, 20 May 1898,
ibid.

74 William A. Czumer, *Recollections about the Life of the First Ukrainian Settlers
in Canada*, trans. Louis T. Laychuk (Edmonton: Canadian Institute of
Ukrainian Studies, 1981), 38.

75 Ewanchuk, *Pioneer Profiles*, 128; Anne B. Woywitcka, 'Homesteader's
Woman,' *Alberta History* 24 (1976): 20.

76 Wasyl Mihaychuk, 'Mihaychuk Family Tree' (typewritten), n.p. Stefan
Yendik, Frazerwood, Man., interview with author, 12 November 1974.
Ewanchuk, *Pioneer Profiles*, 130–1. Declarations of Abandonment, Records
of Homestead Entry, SE 1/4 Section 18, Township 57, Range 18, West of
the 4' meridian; NE 10, T. 59, R. 17, W. 4; SE 22, T. 59, R. 17, W. 4; NW 30,
T. 57, R. 16, W. 4, Provincial Archives of Alberta, Edmonton.

77 Kaye, *Early Ukrainian Settlements*, 139; Ewanchuk, *Pioneer Profiles*, 13;
Woycenko, *Ukrainians in Canada*, 39; N. Wagenhoffer, 'Some Socio-
economic Dynamics in Southeastern Manitoba with Particular Reference
to the Farming Communities within the Local Government Districts of
Stuartburn and Piney' (MA thesis, University of Manitoba, 1972), 55.

78 Canada, Parliament, Sessional Papers, 'Department of the Interior,' 1897,
Report of John W. Wendelbo, 127.

79 The role of kinship and 'old-country' linkages in determining the new
social geography of homestead settlement established by Ukrainian
immigrants is discussed in detail in John C. Lehr, 'Kinship and Society in
the Ukrainian Pioneer Settlement of the Canadian West,' *Canadian Geographer* 24 (1985): 207–19.

80 Donald R. Taft and Richard Robbins, *International Migrations: The Immigrant and the Modern World* (New York: Ronald Press, 1955), 111.

81 Michael Hrushevsky, *A History of Ukraine* (New Haven: Yale University
Press, 1941; np: Archon Books, 1970), 469–71.

82 Lehr, 'Process and Pattern,' 249–85. See also Thomas McNutt, 'Galicians
and Bukowinians,' in John Hawkes, ed., *The Story of Saskatchewan and
Its People* (Chicago-Regina: S.J. Clarke Publishing Co., 1924), 731–2; Paul

Yuzyk, *The Ukrainians in Manitoba: A Social History* (Toronto: University of Toronto Press, 1953), 42; Kaye, *Early Ukrainian Settlements*, 142; idem, *Canadians of Recent European Origin: A Survey* (Ottawa: Citizenship Division of the Department of National War Services, 1945), 46; Timothy C. Byrne, 'The Ukrainian Community in North Central Alberta' (MA thesis, University of Alberta, 1937), 31; MacGregor, *Vilni Zemli*, 157; Young, *Ukrainian Canadians*, 75; Iuliian Stechyshyn, *Istoriia poselennia ukraintsiv u Kanadi* (Edmonton: Ukrainian Self-Reliance League, 1975), 242–7; Mykhailo Ivanchuk, *Istoriia ukrainskoho poselennia v okolytsi Gimli* (Winnipeg: Trident Press, 1975), 24–8; and Petro Zvarych, 'Do pytannia rozvytku i postupu v materiialnii kulturi ukrainskykh poselentsiv u Kanadi,' in *Zbirnyk na poshanu Zenona Kuzeli* (Paris: Shevchenko Scientific Society, 1962), 151; Goresky, 'Early Ukrainian Settlement in Alberta,' 17–38; Joseph M. Lazarenko, 'Rusiw Pioneers in Alberta,' in *Ukrainians in Alberta*, 38–41; and Alexander Royick, 'Ukrainian Settlements in Alberta,' *Canadian Slavonic Papers* 10 (1968): 278–97.
83 William F. McCreary, Winnipeg, to James A. Smart, Ottawa, 15 May 1897, RG 76, vol. 144, file 34214, pt. 1, NAC.
84 C.W. Speers, Winnipeg, to William F. McCreary, Winnipeg, 9 July 1897, ibid. See also Thomas McNutt, 'Galicians and Bukowinians,' in Hawkes, *The Story of Saskatchewan*, 731–2.
85 John C. Lehr, '"The Peculiar People": Ukrainian Settlement of Marginal Lands in Southeastern Manitoba,' in David C. Jones and Ian MacPherson, eds., *Building beyond the Homestead* (Calgary: University of Calgary Press, 1985), 29–46.
86 The data upon which the following discussion of kinship linkages in settlement is based were compiled from Vladimir J. Kaye, *Dictionary of Ukrainian Canadian Biography: Pioneer Settlers of Manitoba 1891–1900* (Toronto: Ukrainian Canadian Research Foundation, 1975), 120–98; and Homestead General Registers, Department of Lands, Government of Manitoba. These data were supplemented by information contained in John Panchuk, *Bukowinian Settlements in Southern Manitoba* (Battle Creek, Mich.: Privately printed, 1971), and by field research in southeastern Manitoba.
87 Ties of marriage accounted for the presence and initial close settlement of settlers from Galicia and Bukovyna in the Stuartburn area. Stefan Storeschuk, Gardenton, Man., interview with author, 21 July 1975.
88 Kaye, *Early Ukrainian Settlements*, 273–6.
89 C.W. Speers, Brandon, to Frank Pedley, Ottawa, 4 April 1899, RG 76, vol. 144, file 34214, pt. 3, NAC.

Darlington: The Ukrainian Impress on the Canadian West

1 By far the most prolific writer on the various aspects of the Ukrainian-

Canadian landscape is John C. Lehr. See, for example, 'Ukrainian Houses in Alberta,' *Alberta Historical Review* 21 (1973), 9–15; 'Ukrainian Vernacular Architecture,' *Canadian Collector* 11 (1976), 66–70; 'The Log Buildings of Ukrainian Settlers in Western Canada,' *Prairie Forum* 5 (1980): 183–96; 'Colour Preferences and Building Decoration among Ukrainians in Western Canada,' *Prairie Forum* 6 (1981): 203–6; 'The Landscape of Ukrainian Settlement in the Canadian West,' *Great Plains Quarterly* 2 (1982): 94–105; 'The Ukrainian Sacred Landscape: A Metaphor of Survival and Acculturation,' *Material Culture Bulletin* 29 (1989): 3–11; and 'Preservation of the Ethnic Landscape in Western Canada,' *Prairie Forum* 15 (1990): 263–76. Others have also reported on the Ukrainian presence in the prairie provinces: Cathy Chorniawy, *Commerce in the Country* (Edmonton: Historic Sites Service, Alberta Culture and Multiculturalism, 1989); James W. Darlington, 'The Evolving Ukrainian-Canadian Landscape: A Driving Tour of the Dauphin Block Settlement Region of Manitoba,' *Proceedings of the Prairie Division of the Canadian Association of Geographers 1990* (forthcoming); Lubomyr Y. Luciuk and Bohdan S. Kordan, *Creating a Landscape: A Geography of Ukrainians in Canada* (Toronto: University of Toronto Press, 1989); Edward M. Ledohowski, *Ukrainian Farmsteads in Manitoba: A Preliminary Investigation* (Winnipeg: Manitoba Culture, Heritage and Recreation, Historic Resources Branch, 1987); and Basil Rotoff et al., *Monuments to Faith: Ukrainian Churches in Manitoba* (Winnipeg: University of Manitoba Press, 1990).

2 Miriam Elston, 'The Russian in Our Midst' (journal and date unknown), as cited in John C. Lehr, 'Changing Ukrainian House Styles,' *Alberta History* 23 (1975): 26–7.

3 C.A. Dawson, *Group Settlement: Ethnic Communities in Western Canada* (Toronto: Macmillan, 1936).

4 Hansgeorg Schlichtmann, 'Ethnic Themes in Geographical Research in Western Canada,' *Canadian Ethnic Studies* 9 (1977): 10–14; Dawson, *Group Settlement*.

5 According to one survey, 50 per cent of the Ukrainians arrived in western Canada penniless, and another 42 per cent had less than five hundred dollars. See J.S. Woodsworth, 'Ukrainian Rural Communities,' Report of Investigation by Bureau of Social Research, Governments of Manitoba, Saskatchewan, and Alberta (Winnipeg, 1917), 73–94. One copy of the report is at the National Archives of Canada, Ottawa (hereafter cited as NAC).

6 Lehr, 'The Landscape of Ukrainian Settlement,' 94.

7 See, for example, the correspondence between William F. McCreary of the Immigration Office in Winnipeg and James A. Smart, Ottawa, 14 May 1897, RG 76, vol. 144, file 34214, pt. 1, NAC; and the telegram from C.W. Speers, Saskatoon, 19 May 1898, ibid.

8 John C. Lehr, 'The Government and the Immigrant: Perspectives on

Ukrainian Block Settlement in the Canadian West,' *Canadian Ethnic Studies* 9 (1977): 42–52.

9 Roman Fodchuk, 'Building the Little House on the Prairies: Ukrainian Technology, Canadian Resources,' *Material History Bulletin* 29 (1989): 89–97.

10 The prospect of seasonal employment in the lumber camps located in the Riding Mountain Timber Reserve was one of the reasons for the establishment of the Shoal Lake–Strathclair bloc settlement south of what is now Riding Mountain National Park. C.W. Speers, Winnipeg, to Frank Pedley, Ottawa, 10 June 1899, RG 76, vol. 144, file 34214, pt. 3 (83911), NAC. For non-agricultural sources of income see John C. Lehr, "'The Peculiar People": Ukrainian Settlement of Marginal Lands in Southeastern Manitoba,' in David C. Jones and Ian MacPherson, eds., *Building beyond the Farmstead* (Calgary: University of Calgary Press, 1985), 34.

11 See, for example, James M. Richtik, 'The Agricultural Frontier in Manitoba: Changing Perceptions of the Resource Value of Prairie and Woodland,' *Upper Midwest History* 3 (1983): 55–61.

12 J. Wreford Watson, 'The Role of Illusion in North American Geography: A Note on the Geography of North American Settlement,' *Canadian Geographer* 13 (1969): 16.

13 For figures on Galician farm acreage see Emily Greene Balch, 'Slav Emigration at Its Source,' *Charities and the Commons*, 16 (May 1906): 179; for Bukovynian farm size see A.M. Shlepakov, *Ukrainska trudova emihratsiia v SShA i Kanadi: Kinets XIX–pochatok XX st.* (Kiev: Akademiia nauk Ukrainskoi RSR, 1960), 23.

14 See, for example, N. Wagenhoffer, 'Some Socio-economic Dynamics in Southeastern Manitoba with Particular Reference to the Farming Communities within the Local Government Districts of Stuartburn and Piney' (MA thesis, University of Manitoba, 1972), 55; and Kaye, *Early Ukrainian Settlements*, 139.

15 John C. Lehr, 'The Rural Settlement Behaviour of Ukrainian Pioneers in Western Canada, 1891–1914,' in B.M. Barr, ed., *Western Canadian Research in Geography: The Lethbridge Papers*, BC Geographical Series, No. 21, Occasional Papers in Geography (Vancouver: Tantalus Research, 1975), 59.

16 Kaye, *Early Ukrainian Settlements*, 203.

17 Ibid., 201–3.

18 Iosyf Oleskiv, *O emigratsii* (Lviv: Obshchestvo Mykhaila Kachkovskoho, 1895), 39.

19 For one such example see Kaye, *Early Ukrainian Settlements*, 179.

20 John C. Lehr, 'Kinship and Society in the Ukrainian Pioneer Settlement of the Canadian West,' *Canadian Geographer* 29 (1985), 207–19; see also Luciuk and Kordan, *Creating a Landscape*, map 4, 'District, village, and kinship ties in Manitoba, 1901.'

21 Lehr, 'Kinship and Society,' 216–17.
22 For an analogous situation in coal-mining communities see Ben Marsh, 'Continuity and Decline in the Anthracite Towns of Pennsylvania,' *Annals of the Association of American Geographers* 77 (1987), 337–52.
23 Kaye, *Early Ukrainian Settlements*, 184–8.
24 Department of the Interior, 'Plan of Township 26 Range 20 West of First Meridian,' Department of the Interior, Topographic Surveys Branch, 1891, NAC.
25 Kaye, *Early Ukrainian Settlements*, 185–6.
26 The three ships were the SS *Scotia*, docked in Halifax 30 April 1897 with thirty-five single men or families bound for Dauphin, the SS *Arcadia*, docked in Quebec City 2 May 1897 with thirty-five single men or families bound for Dauphin, and the SS *Prussia*, docked in Halifax 22 May 1897 with fifty-nine single men or families bound for Dauphin. Vladimir J. Kaye, *Dictionary of Ukrainian Canadian Biography: Pioneer Settlers of Manitoba 1891–1900* (Toronto: Ukrainian Canadian Research Foundation, 1975), 2–118.
27 J. Obed Smith, Commissioner of Immigration, Winnipeg, to the Secretary, Department of the Interior, Ottawa, 1 February 1901, Reports on Immigration Operations, NAC.
28 W.A. Ehrlich et al., *Report of Reconnaissance Soil Survey of Grandview Map Sheet Area*, Soils Report No. 9, Manitoba Soil Survey, 1959.
29 *The Maksymetz Family Reunion* (Np: Privately printed, 1982), 12.
30 Dmytro Romanchych, 'Ukrainski kolonii v okruzi Dauphin, Manitoba,' in Semen Kovbel, comp., and Dmytro Doroshenko, ed., *Propamiatna knyha Ukrainskoho narodnoho domu u Vynypegu* (Winnipeg: Ukrainskyi narodnyi dim, 1949), 514–16; and Kaye, *Early Ukrainian Settlements*, 203.
31 Luciuk and Kordan, *Creating a Landscape*, map 4, 'District, village, and kinship ties in Manitoba, 1901.'
32 Michael Ewanchuk, *Pioneer Settlers: Ukrainians in the Dauphin Area, 1896–1926* (Winnipeg: Privately printed, 1988), 28.
33 Lehr, 'Kinship and Society,' 214.
34 Township 28, Range 20 W, is a standard township containing thirty-six sections; Township 27, Range 20 W, is a modified township of only twenty-four sections. Both were surveyed according to the Third Dominion Land Survey system. See John L. Tyman, *By Section, Township and Range: Studies in Prairie Settlement* (Brandon: Assiniboine Historical Society, 1972), 12.
35 Ibid., 160–1.
36 Ledohowski, *Ukrainian Farmsteads in Manitoba*, 9. Kaye, *Early Ukrainian Settlements*, 139, provides a description of the construction of a dug-out in the Stuartburn region of Manitoba. See also Andriy Nahachewsky, *Ukrainian Dug-out Dwellings in East Central Alberta* (Edmonton: Historic Sites Service, Alberta Culture and Multiculturalism, 1985).

37 Ibid., 186.
38 Fodchuk, 'Building the Little House on the Prairies,' 93.
39 *Khata* refers both to a house and to the rooms within it. Thus *velyka khata* can be translated as 'big house' or 'big room,' and *mala khata* as 'little house' or 'little room.'
40 Thomas Young, Forest Ranger, Dauphin, to E.F. Stephenson, Winnipeg, 18 June 1898, Immigration, Dominion Lands Branch, file 480870, NAC, as quoted in Kaye, *Early Ukrainian Settlements*, 206–8.
41 Thirteen petitioners from Township 23, Range 20 W, to Thomas Young, Homestead Inspector, Dauphin, Man., 10 March 1901, Immigration, Dominion Lands Branch, file 621566, NAC, as quoted in Kaye, *Early Ukrainian Settlements*, 216–17.
42 C.W. Speers, General Colonization Agent, Portage la Prairie, to Frank Pedley, Superintendent of Immigration, Ottawa, 27 March 1899, Reports on Immigration Operations, file 78733, NAC, as quoted in Kaye, *Early Ukrainian Settlements*, 187–8.
43 9 April 1902, Reports on Immigration Operations, file 198189, NAC, as quoted in Kaye, *Early Ukrainian Settlements*, 188.
44 *Maksymetz Family Reunion*, 12–14.
45 See *Cummins Rural Directory: Manitoba: 1923*.
46 Michael H. Marunchak, *The Ukrainian Canadians: A History* (Winnipeg: Ukrainian Free Academy of Sciences, 1970), 352.
47 Charles H. Young, *The Ukrainian Canadians* (Toronto: Thomas Nelson, 1931), 97.
48 Personal communication with Stephen Negrych, son of the original owner, September 1990.
49 Report of the Department of Education of Manitoba for 1900, 31–2, Provincial Archives of Manitoba, Winnipeg.
50 The figures were compiled from Kaye, *Dictionary of Ukrainian Canadian Biography*.
51 Ibid.
52 The important role that the Greek Catholic church played in the Ukrainian community is discussed in John-Paul Himka, 'The Greek Catholic Church and Nation-Building in Galicia, 1772–1918,' *Harvard Ukrainian Studies* 8 (December 1984): 426–52; and Paul Yuzyk, 'Religious Life,' in Manoly R. Lupul, ed., *A Heritage in Transition: Essays in the History of Ukrainians in Canada* (Toronto: McClelland and Stewart, 1982), 143–72. The church was important in the life of other immigrant groups as well. See, for example, Robert C. Ostergren, 'The Immigrant Church as a Symbol of Community and Place in the Upper Midwest,' *Great Plains Quarterly* 1 (1981): 225–38.
53 Lehr, 'Landscape of Ukrainian Settlement,' 99.
54 Marunchak, *The Ukrainian Canadians*, 103.
55 The numbers and dates are provided by *Ukrainian Churches of Manitoba:*

A Building Inventory (Winnipeg: Manitoba Culture, Heritage and Recreation, Historic Resources Branch, 1987). See also Basil Rotoff et al., *Monuments to Faith*.

56 *Of the 451 families that settled in the Dauphin region and are listed in Kaye,* *Dictionary of Ukrainian Canadian Biography,* *only two gave Bukovyna as their home province; the rest named Galicia.*

57 Yuzyk, 'Religious Life,' 147–52; and Orest T. Martynowych, '"Canadianizing the Foreigner": Presbyterian Missionaries and Ukrainian Immigrants,' in Jaroslav Rozumnyj, ed., *New Soil – Old Roots: The Ukrainian Experience in Canada* (Winnipeg: Ukrainian Academy of Arts and Sciences in Canada, 1983), 33–57.

58 Yuzyk, 'Religious Life,' 155–6.

59 Field-work by the author.

60 Bohdan Medwidsky, 'Ukrainian Grave Markers in East-Central Alberta,' *Material History Bulletin* 29 (1989), 72–5. See also A.M. Kostecki, 'Crosses of East Slavic Christianity among Ukrainians in Western Canada,' *Material History Bulletin* 29 (1989): 55–8.

61 Luciuk and Kordan, *Creating a Landscape*, map 16, 'The Religious Landscape in Manitoba.'

62 Paul Yuzyk, *The Ukrainians in Manitoba: A Social History* (Toronto: University of Toronto Press, 1953), 144–5.

63 Frances Swyripa, 'The Ukrainians and Private Education,' in Lupul, *A Heritage in Transition*, 245.

64 Marunchak, *The Ukrainian Canadians*, 120–1.

65 Ibid., 166–7; and Luciuk and Kordan, *Creating a Landscape*, map 17, 'Prosvitas.'

66 C.W. Speers to Frank Pedley, 27 March 1899, Reports on Immigration Operations, file 78733, NAC, as quoted in Kaye, *Early Ukrainian Settlements*, 187.

67 Orest T. Martynowych, *The Ukrainian Bloc Settlement in East Central Alberta, 1890–1930: A History* (Edmonton: Historic Sites Service, Alberta Culture and Multiculturalism, 1985), 225.

68 Marunchak, *The Ukrainian Canadians*, 236.

69 The Western Canada Fire Underwriters' Association, 'Fire Insurance Plan for Sifton, Man.' (Winnipeg, 1919).

70 Dominion Bureau of Statistics, *Census of Manitoba, 1936: Population and Agriculture* (Ottawa, 1938).

71 Lehr, 'Changing Ukrainian House Styles,' 28; and Ledohowski, 'Ukrainian Farmsteads in Manitoba,' 19.

72 Ledohowski, 'Ukrainian Farmsteads in Manitoba,' 20.

73 William J. Carlyle, 'The Relationship between Settlement and the Physical Environment in Part of the West Lake Area of Manitoba from 1878 to 1963' (MA thesis, University of Manitoba, 1965), 172, has identified the

mid-1940s as the end of the economic transition period for the Ukrainian settlement immediately to the east of Riding Mountain.

74 Lehr, 'Kinship and Society,' 217.

75 In this respect the Ukrainian settlers behaved like most other immigrants in North America. See Robert C. Ostergren, 'A Community Transplanted: The Formative Experience of a Swedish Immigrant Community in the Upper Middle West,' *Journal of Historical Geography* 5 (1979): 208.

76 D. Aidan McQuillan, 'Territory and Ethnic Identity: Some New Measures of an Old Theme in the Cultural Geography of the United States,' in James R. Gibson, ed., *European Settlement and Development in North America: Essays on Geographical Change in Honour and Memory of Andrew Hill Clark* (Toronto: University of Toronto Press, 1978), 136–69.

77 John G. Rice, 'The Role of Culture and Community in Frontier Prairie Farming,' *Journal of Historical Geography* 3 (1977): 155–75; and Ostergren, 'A Community Transplanted,' 189–212.

78 Two such arrangements exist in the Dauphin area. The more ambitious project is located south of Dauphin at Selo Ukraina, the site of the Canadian National Ukrainian Festival. The second site involves several buildings that have been incorporated into a roadside picnic area at Terembowla. The same approach to preservation has also been followed in Alberta at the Shandro Historical Living Village and Pioneer Museum at Willingdon and the Ukrainian Cultural Heritage Village at Elk Island.

79 Lehr, 'Preservation of the Ethnic Landscape,' discusses this idea more thoroughly.

Osborne: 'Non-Preferred' Peoples

This paper is an outgrowth of my research into two related topics: the role of the Canadian National Railway's Colonization and Agriculture Department in 1919–60 and the emergence of the concepts of 'scientific settlement' and 'social engineering' in Canada between the wars. The following consideration of the Ukrainian experience has been much informed by Myron Gulka-Tiechko, 'Inter-war Ukrainian Immigration to Canada, 1919–1939' (MA thesis, University of Manitoba, 1983); other references include Lubomyr Y. Luciuk and Bohdan S. Kordan, *Creating a Landscape: A Geography of Ukrainians in Canada* (Toronto: University of Toronto Press, 1989), and Michael H. Marunchak, *The Ukrainian Canadians: A History* (Winnipeg: Ukrainian Free Academy of Sciences, 1970).

1 William Darcovich and Paul Yuzyk, eds., *A Statistical Compendium on the Ukrainians in Canada, 1891–1976* (Ottawa: University of Ottawa Press, 1980).

2 Ibid.

3 Ibid.

4 Minutes of the Federal-Provincial Conference on Immigration, Ottawa, 14 and 15 November 1923, 171, quoted in Gulka-Tiechko, 'Inter-war Ukrainian Immigration,' 24.

5 CNR Annual Report, 1921, Western Ontario, Manitoba, Saskatchewan region, ibid., 24.

6 Myron Momryk, *A Guide to Sources for the Study of Ukrainian Canadians* (Ottawa: Public Archives Canada, 1984), 5.

7 Jane Brooks, 'Immigration Policy and the Railways: The Formation of the Railway Agreement' (MA thesis, Concordia University, 1977), 2–3; Vernon C. Fowkes, *Canadian Agricultural Policy: The Historical Pattern* (Toronto: University of Toronto Press, 1946), 1978 ed., 180.

8 Robert England, *The Colonization of Western Canada: A Study of Contemporary Land Settlement (1896–1934)* (London: P.S. King and Son, 1936), 95.

9 Brooks, 'Immigration Policy,' 8.

10 C.A. Stewart, *Canadian Annual Review*, 1922, quoted in ibid., 12–14.

11 Ibid.

12 John R. Commons, *Races and Immigrants*, cited in W.G. Smith, *A Study in Canadian Immigration* (Toronto: Ryerson Press, 1920), 201.

13 Freda Hawkins, *Critical Years in Immigration: Canada and Australia Compared* (Montreal: McGill-Queen's University Press, 1989), 17.

14 Ibid., 17.

15 Brooks, 'Immigration Policy,' 10.

16 Blair to P.M. Butler, 10 November 1920, RG 76, vol. 611, file 902168, National Archives of Canada, Ottawa (hereafter cited as NAC), cited in Brooks, 'Immigration Policy,' 10.

17 Irving Abella and Harold Troper, *None Is Too Many: Canada and the Jews of Europe, 1933–1948* (Toronto: Lester and Orpen Dennys, 1983), xii.

18 *Manitoba Free Press*, 12 September 1923, quoted in Brookes, 'Immigration Policy,' 19.

19 J.B. Hedges, *Building the Canadian West: The Land and Colonization Policies of the Canadian Pacific Railway* (New York: Russell and Russell, 1939), 357; see also John A. Eagle, *The Canadian Pacific Railway and the Development of Western Canada* (Montreal: McGill-Queen's University Press, 1989).

20 *Canadian Annual Review*, 1922, 494, in Brooks, 'Immigration Policy,' 25.

21 CNR Annual Report for 1923, RG 30, NAC.

22 Department of Immigration and Colonization, Annual Reports, 1924–5, RG 76, NAC.

23 The Deputy Minister to W.J. Black, 10 February 1925, RG 76, vol. 253, file 193745, NAC.

24 Department of Immigration and Colonization, Annual Reports, 1924–5, 1925–6, RG 76, NAC, in Brooks, 'Immigration Policy,' 37.

25 Gulka-Tiechko, 'Inter-war Ukrainian Immigration,' 95–105.

26 Major J. Barnett to W.J. Egan, 24 April 1924, RG 276, vol. 232, file 135361, NAC, quoted in ibid.

27 Gulka-Tiechko, 'Inter-war Ukrainian Immigration,' 102.
28 Darcovich and Yuzyk, *A Statistical Compendium.*
29 Brooks, 'Immigration Policy,' 41–64.
30 Ibid., 110–11.
31 Ibid.
32 F.C. Blair, 'Memo for filing,' RG 276, vol. 262, file 216882, NAC.
33 Details of the CPR and CNR colonization operations are derived from
   Testimony of J.N.K. Macalister, Assistant Commissioner, Department of
   Colonization and Development, CPR, and Dr W.J. Black, Director, Colonization, Agriculture, and Natural Resources, CNR, before the House of
   Commons, Select Standing Committee on Agriculture and Colonization,
   Immigration Inquiry, 21 March 1928.
34 W.J. Egan to W.R. Little, 16 September 1925, RG 30, vol. 5625, NAC.
35 Black to Johnson, 28 November 1933, RG 30, vol. 8337, file 3070–31, NAC.
36 CNLSA Annual Report, 1928, RG 30, vol. 5571, NAC.
37 J.S. McGowan, interdepartmental memo, 23 November 1929, RG 30, vol.
   5625, NAC.
38 Darcovich and Yuzyk, *A Statistical Compendium.*
39 Brooks, 'Immigration Policy,' 110–11.
40 See testimony of J.N.K. Macalister and W.J. Black before the Select Standing Committee on Agriculture and Colonization, Immigration Inquiry,
   21 March 1928.
41 Hedges, *Building the Canadian West,* 346–86.
42 Gulka-Tiechko, 'Inter-war Ukrainian Immigration,' 190–2.
43 CNLSA Annual Report, 1927, RG 30, vol. 5570, NAC.
44 Gulka-Tiechko, 'Inter-war Ukrainian Immigration,' 82–4.
45 CNR Western Lines, Annual Report of the Colonization and Development Department, 1924, RG 30, NAC.
46 CNLSA Annual Report, 1928, RG 30, vol. 5571, NAC.
47 Report of Western Canada Office and US Organization, Department of
   Colonization and Development, CPR, 1 December 1926–30 November
   1927, Box 72, folio 615, CPR Archives, Glenbow-Alberta Institute, Calgary.
   See Gulka-Tiechko, 'Inter-war Ukrainian Immigration,' for further discussion of this.
48 Craigmyle UFWA to Robert Forke, Minister of Immigration, 13 April 1928,
   RG 30, vol. 5629, NAC. The CNR's sensitivity to fears such as this is
   demonstrated by an exchange between two of its colonization officers
   regarding the photographs of immigrant settlers in a report produced
   to demonstrate the advancement of settlement in the St Paul–Cold Lake
   District of Alberta: 'The photographs are generally excellent. We would
   suggest, however, that in future it would be a good idea to have the
   women remove the head shawls before taking the photographs. Mode
   of dress is responsible for much of the criticism of newcomers as "foreigners" and in our photographs it is well to have them look as "Canadian" as

possible.' F.J. Freer, Superintendant of Land Settlement, to N.S. McGuire, Edmonton, 1 December 1928, RG 30, vol. 5608, file 11,101, NAC. McGuire explained the circumstances in his reply: 'In extentuation of our lack of good judgment in photographing the Continental ladies with their head-shawls on, we may say that both Mr. Kirkwood and Mr. Smolyk did everything in their power to do as you have suggested, but the only condition on which they would allow us to take their picture, was in full continental regalia. We are very sorry, therefore, that we were unable to get just what we wanted in this respect.' Ibid., 5 December 1928.

49 Gulka-Tiechko, 'Inter-war Ukrainian Immigration,' 217.

50 RCMP Commissioner Cortland Sterne to W.J. Eagan, 7 November 1927, RG 76, vol. 299, file 274585, NAC, quoted in ibid., 210.

51 The presidents of the CPR and CNR to W.S. Gordon, Minister of Immigration and Colonization, 1 October 1930, RG 30, vol. 8337, file 3070–31, NAC.

52 Dr W.J. Black to D.M. Johnson, 2 February 1931, RG 30, vol. 8337, file 3070–31, NAC.

53 Dr W.J. Black to D.M. Johnson, 24 February 1931, ibid.

54 See Gulka-Tiechko, 'Inter-war Ukrainian Immigration,' for a detailed discussion of this theme.

55 W.A. Gordon to Sir Henry Thornton, 31 October 1930, RG 30, vol. 8337, file 3070–31, NAC.

56 Ibid.

57 England, *The Colonization of Western Canada*, 116–35.

58 CNR Grande Prairies Office, Devlin Papers, RG 30, vol. 5572, 1930, NAC.

59 England, *The Colonization of Western Canada*, 126.

60 W. Smoluck to McGuire, RG 30, vol. 5651; McGowan to Black, 1930, RG 30, vol. 5647, NAC.

61 For more details see Barbara Roberts, *Whence They Came: Deportation from Canada, 1900–1935* (Ottawa: University of Ottawa Press, 1988); and Donald Avery, *'Dangerous Foreigners': European Immigrant Workers and Labour Radicalism in Canada, 1896–1932* (Toronto: McClelland and Stewart, 1979).

62 England, *The Colonization of Western Canada*, 86–7.

63 Black to Johnson, 28 November 1933, RG 30, vol. 8337, file 3070–31, NAC.

64 Gulka-Tiechko, 'Inter-war Ukrainian Immigration,' 256.

65 England, *The Colonization of Western Canada*, 87.

66 Maria Tippett, *Making Culture: English-Canadian Institutions and the Arts before the Massey Commission* (Toronto: University of Toronto Press, 1990), 19–20.

67 England, *The Colonization of Western Canada*, 183.

68 Tippett, *Making Culture*, 57.

69 Ibid., 118.

70 W.J. Black to R. Kutylowski, Director, Gdynia-American Line, 21 August 1937, RG 30, vol. 8337, file 3070–31, NAC.

71 F.C. Blair to the Polish Consul General, 27 October 1937, RG 76, NAC.

72 Darcovich and Yuzyk, *A Statistical Compendium.*

73 W.J. Black to D.M. Johnson, 26 January 1938, vol. 8337, file 3070–31, RG 30, NAC.

74 CNSLA Annual Report, 1939, vol. 5581, RG 30, NAC.

75 J.S. Woodsworth, *Strangers within Our Gates: Or Coming Canadians* (Toronto: University of Toronto Press, 1972), 109–14.

76 England, *The Colonization of Western Canada*, 215.

77 V.J. Kaye, *Canadians of Recent European Origin: A Survey* (Ottawa: Citizenship Division of the Department of National War Services, 1945), 2.

78 Ibid., 45.

79 Terence Corcoran, 'Xeconophobia versus free immigration,' *Globe and Mail*, 27 October 1990.

Luciuk: 'This Should Never Be Spoken or Quoted Publicly'

1 'Statement submitted by B. Panchuk in connection with administrative and financial report of the Central Ukrainian Relief Bureau, period of August 1, 1945 to December 31, 1945,' G.R.B. Panchuk Collection, Archives of Ontario, Toronto (hereafter cited as GRBPC). See also G.R.B. Panchuk, *Heroes of Their Day: The Reminiscences of Bohdan Panchuk*, ed. L.Y. Luciuk (Toronto: Multicultural History Society of Ontario, 1983). The CURB's operational records begin on 17 September 1945 and end on 9 December 1948, after which a Ukrainian Canadian Relief Fund office was maintained in Bielefeld, Germany, first by Ann Crapleve and then, between 1949 and 1950, by Eustace and Anne Wasylyshyn. After their departure Crapleve took over the UCRF office until 1951. For more on the bureau see 'A Troubled Venture: Ukrainian-Canadian Refugee Relief Efforts, 1945–1951,' in W. Isajiw, Y. Boshyk, and R. Senkus, eds., *The Refugee Experience: Ukrainian Displaced Persons after World War II* (forthcoming).

2 Panchuk reasserted this point in a letter to the United Ukrainian American Relief Committee, 14 April 1947, GRBPC.

3 'Ukrainian Canadian Relief Fund, Report and Outline of Achievements, February 15, 1945 to June 1, 1946,' GRBPC.

4 On the origins of the Ukrainian Canadian Committee see Bohdan S. Kordan, 'Disunity and Duality: Ukrainian Canadians and the Second World War' (MA thesis, Carleton University, 1981), and N.F. Dreisziger's paper in this volume. On Ukrainian-Canadian society in the late interwar period and Ukrainian-Canadian participation in the war effort see Thomas M. Prymak, *Maple Leaf and Trident: The Ukrainian Canadians during the Second World War* (Toronto: Multicultural History Society of Ontario, 1988). For an overview of the Ukrainian experience in Canada see Lubomyr Y. Luciuk and Bohdan S. Kordan, *Creating a Landscape: A Geography of Ukrainians in Canada* (Toronto: University of Toronto Press, 1989).

5 See Lubomyr Yaroslav Luciuk, 'Searching for Place: Ukrainian Refugee Migration to Canada after World War II' (PhD dissertation, University of Alberta, 1984).

6 See B.N. Stein, 'The Refugee Experience: Defining the Parameters of a Field of Study,' *International Migration Review* 15 (1981): 320–30.

7 This paper is based on ' "Trouble All Around": Ukrainian Canadians and Their Encounter with the Ukrainian Refugees of Europe, 1943–1951,' *Canadian Ethnic Studies* 21 (1989): 36–54.

8 See Document No. 28 in Bohdan S. Kordan and Lubomyr Y. Luciuk, eds, *A Delicate and Difficult Question: Documents in the History of Ukrainians in Canada, 1899–1962* (Kingston: Limestone Press, 1986), 74–6. Special Royal Canadian Mounted Police Constable Michael Petrowsky reported that many leading Ukrainian Canadians were motivated by a 'fear of the barbed wire fence.' MG 30 E-3So, file 14, 25–31 August 1941, National Archives of Canada (hereafter cited as NAC). Memories of the 1914–20 internment operations, which grievously affected the Ukrainian-Canadian community, played no small role in reminding the delegates of what might happen to them if they appeared disloyal. On the internment operations during the First World War see Frances Swyripa and John Herd Thompson, eds., *Loyalties in Conflict: Ukrainians in Canada during the Great War* (Edmonton: Canadian Institute of Ukrainian Studies, 1983); Lubomyr Y. Luciuk, *A Time for Atonement: Canada's First National Internment Operations and the Ukrainian Canadians, 1914–1920* (Kingston: Limestone Press, 1988); and the review of the booklet by V.O. Buyniak, *Prairie Forum* 14 (1989): 273–5.

9 Between 2.5 and 3.0 million Ukrainians became refugees during the Second World War. See Ihor Stebelsky, 'Ukrainian Population Migration after World War II' (paper delivered at conference, The DP Experience: Ukrainian Refugees after World War II, Toronto, November 1983), and his contribution in this volume.

10 'Notes on the Immigration of Ukrainian Refugees and DPs,' 8 October 1946, GRBPC. Anthony Yaremovich, a member of the CURB, expanded on the theme of hard-working pioneers when he lobbied Canadian government officials and politicians. In a letter to W.A. Tucker, MP, Yaremovich pointed out that Canada's experience of Ukrainians as pioneers who came 'with no funds whatsoever, yet managed to become good farmers today' should be kept in mind when decisions were made about allowing for an immigration of Ukrainian refugees. They, too, he claimed, would prove themselves to be good settlers and citizens. A.Y. Yaremovich to W.A. Tucker, 15 June 1948, MG 28 v9, vol. 15, NAC.

11 Report by G.R.B. Panchuk, 30 January 1946, MG 28, v9, vol. 17, NAC.

12 Ibid.

13 'Minutes of the first day of a conference held in London, England, Central

Ukrainian Relief Bureau and representatives of Ukrainian Relief Committees, February 7, 8, 1946,' private collection of S.W. Frolick, National Archives of Canada (hereafter cited as SWFPC). For Frolick's account of this period see *Between Two Worlds: The Memoirs of Stanley Frolick*, ed. Lubomyr Y. Luciuk and Marco Carynnyk (Toronto: Multicultural History Society of Ontario, 1990).

14 See, for example, CURB, 'Report on a visit to the War Office,' 2 February 1946, and 'Report on a conference with British Foreign Office,' 18 November 1946, GRBPC.

15 The Organization of Ukrainian Nationalists (OUN) was formed in 1929 to wage an armed struggle for independence. In 1940 it split into the OUN-revolutionary (OUN-r) faction under Stepan Bandera and the OUN-solidarist (OUN-s) faction under Andrii Melnyk. See John Armstrong, *Ukrainian Nationalism*, 3d ed. (Englewood, Colo.: Ukrainian Academic Press, 1990); and Alexander J. Motyl, *The Turn to the Right: The Ideological Origins and Development of Ukrainian Nationalism, 1919–1929* (Boulder: East European Monographs, 1980). On the evolution of the movement's ideology see Peter J. Potichnyj and Yevhen Shtendera, eds., *Political Thought of the Ukrainian Underground, 1943–1951* (Edmonton: Canadian Institute of Ukrainian Studies, 1986).

16 'Minutes of the first day of a conference held in London, England, Central Ukrainian Relief Bureau and representatives of Ukrainian relief committees, February 7–8, 1946,' SWFPC.

17 P. Shteppa to S.W. Frolick, 5 February 1948, SWFPC.

18 A small booklet on the Ukrainian DPs was released at this time: M.I. Mandryka, *Ukrainian Refugees* (Winnipeg: Canadian Ukrainian Educational Association, 1946). The back cover listed eleven relief organizations, including the CURB, the UCRF, the United Ukrainian American Relief Committee, and groups organized by bureau personnel in Belgium, France, Italy, Argentina, Brazil, and Switzerland.

19 The acting high commissioner of Canada in the United Kingdom reported on 9 August 1946 that the UCC and its London representatives had decidedly influenced British policy towards the Ukrainian DPs. File 8296–40C, Department of External Affairs, Ottawa (hereafter cited as DEA).

20 G.R.B. Panchuk to the UCC, 20 October 1946, Ukrainian Canadian Committee Archives, Winnipeg.

21 Frolick, *Between Two Worlds*, 150–1.

22 T. Datskiw to G.R.B. Panchuk, 26 October 1946, Ukrainian Canadian Committee Archives, Winnipeg.

23 See the introduction to Kordan and Luciuk, *A Delicate and Difficult Question*, 1–12.

24 Norman A. Robertson to George Pifher, 15 November 1944, file 2514–40, DEA.

25 Dana Wilgress to Norman A. Robertson, 25 January 1945, ibid.

26 Ibid.
27 Norman A. Robertson to G. Pifher, 15 November 1944, ibid. The Soviet ambassador to Canada made it clear that his government considered the establishment of a Ukrainian-Canadian relief fund to be 'a question of particular importance.' File 2514–40C, 30 May 1945, DEA.
28 'Memorandum for Mr Robertson,' initialled by 'JER,' file 2514– 40, 15 May 1945, DEA.
29 On the history of the Ukrainian-Canadian Left see John Kolasky, *The Shattered Illusion: The History of Ukrainian Pro-Communist Organizations in Canada* (Toronto: PMA Books, 1979). Curiously, Reg Whitaker in *Double Standard: The Secret History of Canadian Immigration Policy* (Toronto: Lester and Orpen Dennys, 1987) pays little attention to the Left's agenda on immigration issues, possibly because of his preference for the thesis that government officials actively impeded the immigration into Canada of those 'fleeing the oppression of our side' and encouraged those 'fleeing Communist oppression.' Whitaker has also written approvingly about Sol Littman, whose specious allegations had much to do with inflaming public opinion and bringing about the formation of the Commission of Inquiry on War Criminals. See Reg Whitaker, 'Canada used loose screen to filter Nazi fugitives,' *Globe and Mail*, 1 March 1985. In his book Whitaker misrepresents other scholars' treatment of this issue. See, for example, his jaded speculation about the article by Ron Vastokas and Lubomyr Luciuk, 'Soviet villains omitted: A flaw in Canada's search to uncover war criminals,' *Globe and Mail*, 4 March 1986. As for Littman see Nikolai Tolstoy, *Trial and Error: Canada's Commission of Inquiry on War Criminals and the Soviets* (Toronto: Justinian Press, 1986).
30 Cited in the correspondence between P.J. Lazarowich and the UCC, 9 and 12 February 1945, UCC Archives, Winnipeg. I have not been able to locate the article in the *Edmonton Journal*.
31 Ibid.
32 Accusations that the Ukrainian-Canadian community was sheltering 'war criminals' erupted again in February 1985, and the federal government established the Commission of Inquiry on War Criminals, headed by Justice Jules Deschênes, to investigate. The commission reported that allegations about Nazi war criminals in Canada made by Sol Littman and others had been 'grossly exaggerated' and recommended that the government accept the Ukrainian-Canadian community's position that *any* war criminals found in Canada, regardless of their ethnic, religious, or racial origin or the period or place in which they committed war crimes or crimes against humanity, be brought to trial in Canada under Canadian criminal law. See Commission of Inquiry on War Criminals, *Report. Part I: Public* (Ottawa: Minister of Supply and Services Canada, 1986), 249–61; and Morris Ilyniak's paper in this volume. A rather prepossessed view of the entire episode is provided in Harold Troper and Morton Weinfeld,

Old Wounds: Jews, Ukrainians and the Hunt for Nazi War Criminals in Canada (Markham, Ont.: Viking, 1988), for a critique of which see my review, *Canadian Ethnic Studies* 21 (1989): 136–9.

33 V.J. Kaye to G.R.B. Panchuk, 28 November 1946, GRBPC.

34 Ibid.

35 Ibid.

36 G.R.B. Panchuk to J. Karasevich, 21 December 1946, GRBPC.

37 Ibid.

38 See 'Report on the U.S. Area of Control, Germany, as submitted by Ann Crapleve, period April 30 to 31 July 1947,' private collection of A. Smith (Crapleve), Winnipeg.

39 See, for example, G.R.B. Panchuk to J. Choma, 18 June 1948, and G.R.B. Panchuk to D. Gerych, 10 September 1948, GRBPC.

40 V.J. Kaye to G.R.B. Panchuk, 30 January 1949, GRBPC. Indicative of what other Canadians expected of the Ukrainian community is the editorial 'Divided Loyalties Refutation of Good Canadian Citizenship,' *Windsor Daily Star*, 20 April 1948. The writer chided those Ukrainian Canadians who believed in Lord Tweedsmuir's adage that 'to be a good Canadian one must first be a good Ukrainian.' This was a 'strange, foolish and dangerous fallacy' because no one with 'divided loyalties' could ever be a 'good Canadian.'

41 G.R.B. Panchuk to D. Gerych, 16 February 1949, GRBPC.

42 W. Wenger to G.R.B. Panchuk, 20 April 1949, GRBPC.

43 G.R.B. Panchuk to Miss Hanson, British Ministry of Labour, 30 April 1949, GRBPC.

44 See P. White and R. Woods, eds., *The Geographical Impact of Migration* (London: Longman, 1980).

45 See L.Y. Luciuk, 'Unintended Consequences in Refugee Resettlement: Post-war Ukrainian Refugee Immigration to Canada,' *International Migration Review* 20 (1986): 467–82.

46 A.J. Yaremovich to E. Wasylyshen, 2 July 1949, private collection of Eustace and Anne Wasylyshen, Winnipeg.

47 A.J. Yaremovich to G.R.B. Panchuk, 6 November 1949, GRBPC.

48 *Third All-Canada Congress of Ukrainian Canadians* (Winnipeg: Ukrainian National Publishing Co., 1959).

49 See, for example, M.I. Mandryka to E. Wasylyshen, 14 November and 7 December 1949, private collection of Eustace and Anne Wasylyshen, Winnipeg.

50 G.R.B. Panchuk to T. Philipps, 18 February 1950, GRBPC.

51 E. Kunz, 'Exile and Resettlement: Refugee Theory,' *International Migration Review* 15 (1981): 42–52.

52 Inter-Allied Psychological Study Group, 'Psychological Problems of Displaced Persons,' 1945, Archives of the Hoover Institution on War, Revolution, and Peace, Stanford, Calif.

53 A survey of post-war Ukrainian refugee immigrants to Canada found that nearly 90 per cent claimed they would have returned to Ukraine shortly after resettlement if their homeland had achieved independence. Even after the passage of some forty years 46 per cent still maintain that they would return to Ukraine under such circumstances. The survey is found in Luciuk, 'Searching for Place,' 531–55.

54 In Panchuk's estimate some fifty thousand Ukrainian DPs resettled in Canada after the Second World War. See G.R.B. Panchuk to A. Crapleve, 28 February 1951, GRBPC. Panchuk had concerns about Canadian immigration policy at this time, particularly about the collaboration between British and Canadian officials in discriminating against Ukrainian DPs. See his letter to P.R. Rhodes of Montreal, 9 March 1949, GRBPC, in which he noted that he had received information from a 'very dependable source' in Alberta to the effect that there was 'some form of understanding between our own Canadian Immigration authorities and the British authorities, to the effect that certain people from the U.K. should NOT be admitted to Canada too soon from the U.K. in order that they might "serve out their dues" to H.M.G. for having brought them from Germany to the U.K.' This, in Panchuk's opinion, constituted 'plain economic exploitation.' For comparative purposes the study by Milda Danys, DP: Lithuanian Immigration to Canada after the Second World War (Toronto: Multicultural History Society of Ontario, 1986), is useful.

55 For an interpretation of the resulting nature of Ukrainian society in Ontario see Lubomyr Y. Luciuk and Iroida L. Wynnyckyj, 'A Distinct Constituency – The Ukrainians of Ontario,' Ukrainians in Ontario, special issue of Polyphony 10 (1988): 3–10.

56 'Report on the U.S. Area of Control, Germany as submitted by Ann Crapleve, period April 27 to 31 July, 1947,' private collection of A. Smith (Crapleve), Winnipeg.

57 D.G. Roussow of Montreal made the observation in a letter to P. Shteppa, February 1949, GRBPC.

Stebelsky: Resettlement of Ukrainian Refugees

1 O.W. Gerus and J.E. Rea, The Ukrainians in Canada (Ottawa: Canadian Historical Association, 1985), 16–18. For more details, see William Darcovich and Paul Yuzyk, eds., A Statistical Compendium on the Ukrainians in Canada, 1891–1976 (Ottawa: University of Ottawa Press, 1980), and Michael H. Marunchak, The Ukrainian Canadians: A History, 2d ed. (Winnipeg: Ukrainian Free Academy of Sciences, 1982).

2 V. Maruniak, 'Ukraintsi v Nimechchyni,' in Atanas M. Milianych et al., eds., Ukrainski poselennia: Dovidnyk (New York: Ukrainskyi Sotsiolohichnyi Instytut, 1980), 149.

3 Accounts of this military unit are offered in R. Landwehr, *Fighting for Freedom: The Ukrainian Volunteer Division of the Waffen-SS* (Silver Spring, Md.: Bibliophile Legion Books, 1985) and P. Shandruk, *Arms of Valor*, intro. by R. Smal-Stocki, trans. by R. Olesnicki (New York: Robert Speller and Sons, 1959). A brief assessment is in B. Dmytryshyn, 'The Nazis and the SS Volunteer Division "Galicia,"' *American Slavic and East European Review* 15 (1956): 1–10.

4 M.J. Proudfoot, *European Refugees, 1939–52: A Study in Forced Population Movement* (Evanston, Ill.: Northwestern University Press, 1956), 159, 207–20.

5 J. Vernant, *The Refugee in the Post-War World* (New Haven: Yale University Press, 1953), 86–7.

6 L. Luciuk, '"Trouble All Around": Ukrainian Canadians and Their Encounter with the Ukrainian Refugees of Europe, 1943–1951,' *Canadian Ethnic Studies* 21 (1989): 37–54.

7 I. Stebelsky, 'Ukrainians in the Displaced Persons Camps of Austria and Germany after World War II,' Parts 1, 2. *Ukrainskyi istoryk* 23 (1986), no. 1–2: 55–64; no. 3–4: 44–57.

8 *Plight of Ukrainian DP's* (New York: Ukrainian Congress Committee of America, [1945]). In State Department Decimal File, 800.4016 DP/12–1945, RG 59, National Archives, Washington, DC.

9 Stebelsky, 'Ukrainians in the Displaced Persons Camps,' no. 1–2: 58. Protests by Ukrainian Canadians included 'Immigration,' a memorandum by the Ukrainian Catholic Council of Canada to J.L. Glen, Minister of Mines and Natural Resources (October 1946), MG 31, D69, vol. 47, file 5, National Archives of Canada, Ottawa (hereafter cited as NAC).

10 Samples of such documents are contained in the Ukrainian Red Cross Collection, box 1, file 2, Archives of the Ukrainian Cultural and Educational Centre, Winnipeg.

11 International Refugee Organization, Office of Statistics and Operational Reports, *Statistical Report on PCIRO Operations, November, 1947* (Seneca: PCIRO, 1947), 7.

12 Memorandum by G.R.B. Panchuk to PCIRO, 12 September 1947, RG 76, vol. 856, file 554–3, NAC.

13 V. Maruniak, 'V 25ty-littia ukrainskoi emihratsii v Nimechchyni ta Avstrii po druhii svitovii viini: 1943–1951–1967' (PhD dissertation, Ukrainian Free University, Munich, 1968), 47–51. For the UNRRA view of grouping displaced persons by nationality, see UNRRA, *Report of the Director General to the Council for the Period 1 January 1947 to 31 March 1947* (Washington, DC.: UNRRA, 1947), 53.

14 K. Pankivsky, *Vid komitetu do Derzhavnoho Tsentru* (New York: Kliuchi, 1986), 153.

15 Maruniak, 'V 25ty-littia ukrainskoi emihratsii,' 63.

16 V. Kubijovyč, 'Ukrainian Political Refugees and Emigrants after 1945,' in Volodymyr Kubijovyč, ed., *Ukraine: A Concise Encyclopaedia* (Toronto: University of Toronto Press, 1963) I: 914–15.
17 Central Ukrainian Relief Bureau, 'Material for CURB Commemorative Book, 1945–1952,' 34, MG 28 V9, vol. 17, NAC.
18 International Refugee Organization, General Council, *Migration from Europe* (Geneva, n.d.).
19 Vernant, *The Refugee in the Post-War World*, 259, 298, 305–7.
20 E. Zahachevsky, *Beliariia – Rimini – Anhliia* (Munich: Biblioteka 'Lystky Chervonoi Kalyny,' 1968), 292.
21 Vernant, *The Refugee in the Post-War World*, 365.
22 Organizations in Europe, North America, South America, Asia and Africa, extending relief to Ukrainian refugees, displaced persons and victims of war, RG 76, vol. 856, file 554-33, NAC.
23 H.F. Eckerson and G. Krichefsky, 'Displaced Persons in the United States,' *Monthly Review of the U.S. Immigration and Naturalization Source* 6 (September 1948): 33–6.
24 Myron B. Kuropas, *The Ukrainians in America* (Minneapolis: Lerner Publications Co., 1972), 43; V. Bandera, 'Ukraintsi v ZSA,' in Milianych, *Ukrainski poselennia*, 259.
25 Oleh Volovyna, Ihor Hordiiv, and Liubov Hordiiv, 'Ukraintsi v Avstralii,' in Milianych, *Ukrainski poselennia*, 327–38.
26 For a description of the valiant efforts of the director of CURB, see G.R.B. Panchuk, *Heroes of Their Day: The Reminiscences of Bohdan Panchuk*, ed. L.Y. Luciuk (Toronto: Multicultural History Society of Ontario, 1983).
27 Department of Mines and Resources, Immigration Branch, Statistical Unit, Annual Summary Tables of Immigrants Arriving from Ocean Ports, RG 26, vol. 53, NAC.
28 Maruniak, 'V 25ty-littia ukrainskoi emihratsii,' 189. See also 'Material for CURB Commemorative Book,' 42, MG 28 V9, vol. 17, NAC.
29 See correspondence between government officials and the Ukrainian Canadian Committee in RG 76, vol. 856, file 554-33, NAC.
30 'Immigration into Canada,' *International Labour Review* 55 (May 1947): 449–50; 'Progress of Immigration into Canada,' *International Labour Review* 56 (November–December 1947): 609–10.
31 According to V.J. Kaye, Ukrainian refugees resided in 1955 as follows: 7,520 in Austria (2,244 of whom lived in camps and settlements registered as refugees), about 22,000 in the Federal Republic of Germany, about 500 in Italy, and about 50 in Trieste. V.J. Kaye to the Deputy Minister, Department of Citizenship and Immigration, 27 December 1955, MG 31 D69, vol. 12, file 17, NAC; V.J. Kaye, 'Report on a Visit to Germany, Austria, Trieste and Italy, November 14 to December 14, 1955,' RG 26, vol. 110, NAC.

32 Bohdan S. Kordan, 'Ukrainians in Ontario and the 1981 Canada Census: A Research Note,' in Lubomyr Y. Luciuk and Iroida L. Wynnyckyj, eds., *Ukrainians in Ontario*, special issue of *Polyphony: Bulletin of the Multicultural History Society of Ontario* 10 (1988): 14.

33 Examples on which this general statement is based are drawn from personal observations (1949–55) in Surrey, BC, a formerly rural, now suburban area southwest of Vancouver.

34 I.M. Myhul, 'Ethnic Minorities and the Nationality Policy of the Parti Québecois,' in Manoly R. Lupul, ed., *Ukrainian Canadians, Multiculturalism, and Separatism: An Assessment* (Edmonton: Canadian Institute of Ukrainian Studies, 1978), 38.

35 Olga M. Kuplowska, 'Language Retention Patterns among Ukrainian Canadians,' in W. Roman Petryshyn, ed., *Changing Realities: Social Trends among Ukrainian Canadians* (Edmonton: Canadian Institute of Ukrainian Studies, 1980), 157–8.

36 For an elaboration on the process by which one such organization, the Bandera faction of the Organization of Ukrainian Nationalists, extended its network from West Germany to Canada, see Lubomyr Yaroslav Luciuk, 'Searching for Place: Ukrainian Refugee Migration to Canada after World War II' (PhD dissertation, University of Alberta, 1984), 339–40, 352–70.

37 For details, see ibid., 377–86.

38 Ibid., 375–6.

39 Much of the factual material is summarized in V. Kysilevsky, 'Social and Political Life,' in Kubijovyč, *Ukraine: A Concise Encyclopaedia*, II: 1168–71; Ol'ha Woycenko, 'Community Organizations,' in Manoly R. Lupul, ed., *A Heritage in Transition: Essays in the History of Ukrainians in Canada* (Toronto: McClelland and Stewart, 1982), 187–90. More details, notably about organizations centred in Ontario, may be found in various articles in Luciuk and Wynnyckyj, eds., *Ukrainians in Ontario*.

40 V.J. Kaye, 'Ukrainian Scientists in Canada,' MG 31 D69, vol. 15, file 31, NAC.

41 Oleh Wolowyna, 'Trends in the Socio-economic Status of Ukrainians in Canada, 1921–1971,' in Petryshyn, *Changing Realities*, 62, 65.

42 A. Kachor, *Muzhi idei i pratsi: Andrii Palii i Andrii Mudryk – tvortsi Maslosoiuzu i modernoi ukrainskoi molocharskoi kooperatsii v Zakhidnii Ukraini* (Winnipeg-Toronto-Cleveland: Bratstvo Maslosoiuznykiv u Kanadi i ZSA, 1974).

43 Wsevolod W. Isajiw, 'Participation of Ukrainians in Business Occupations in Canada,' in Petryshyn, *Changing Realities*, 101–2.

Part 2

Gerus: Consolidating the Community

1 As yet there is no comprehensive central USRL archive. Primary sources

are fragmentary and scattered. There seems to be precious little on the inter-war period.

2 For an overview of the Ukrainian experience in Canada see O.W. Gerus and J.E. Rea, *The Ukrainians in Canada* (Ottawa: Canadian Historical Association, 1985). Pioneer history is readily available in English: Vladimir J. Kaye, *Early Ukrainian Settlements in Canada, 1895–1900: Dr. Josef Oleskow's Role in the Settlement of the Canadian Northwest* (Toronto: University of Toronto Press for the Ukrainian Canadian Research Foundation, 1964); Michael H. Marunchak, *The Ukrainian Canadians: A History*, 2d ed. (Winnipeg: Ukrainian Free Academy of Sciences, 1982); Paul Yuzyk, *The Ukrainians in Manitoba: A Social History* (Toronto: University of Toronto Press, 1953); Peter Humeniuk, *Hardship and Progress of Ukrainian Pioneers* (Steinbach, Man.: Privately printed, 1977); William A. Czumer, *Recollections about the Life of the First Ukrainian Settlers in Canada*, trans. Louis T. Laychuk (Edmonton: Canadian Institute of Ukrainian Studies, 1981); Jaroslav Petryshyn, *Peasants in the Promised Land: Canada and the Ukrainians, 1891–1914* (Toronto: James Lorimer, 1985).

3 John-Paul Himka, *Socialism in Galicia: The Emergence of Polish Social Democracy and Ukrainian Radicalism (1860–1890)* (Cambridge: Harvard Ukrainian Research Institute, 1983); Ivan L. Rudnytsky, ed., *Mykhailo Drahomanov: A Symposium and Selected Writings*, special issue, *Annals of the Ukrainian Academy of Arts and Sciences in the US* 2 (Spring 1952); O.I. Dei, *Ukrainska revoliutsiino-demokratychna zhurnalistyka: Problema vynyknennia i stanovlennia* (Kiev: Akademiia nauk Ukrainskoi RSR, 1959).

4 John-Paul Himka, 'Sheptyts'kyi and the Ukrainian National Movement before 1914,' in Paul Robert Magocsi, ed., *Morality and Reality: The Life and Times of Andrei Sheptyts'kyi* (Edmonton: Canadian Institute of Ukrainian Studies, 1989), 29–46.

5 On efforts to establish a Ukrainian Catholic church in Canada see M. Marunchak, *Orhanizatsiini pochatky Ukrainskoi Katolytskoi Tserkvy v Kanadi i Amerytsi* (Winnipeg: Ukrainska vilna akademiia nauk v Kanadi, 1978); P. Yuzyk, 'The History of the Ukrainian Greek Catholic (Uniate) Church in Canada' (MA thesis, University of Saskatchewan, 1948); Paul Yuzyk, 'Religious Life,' in Manoly R. Lupul, ed., *A Heritage in Transition: Essays in the History of Ukrainians in Canada* (Toronto: McClelland and Stewart, 1982), 143–50; B. Kazymyra, 'Metropolitan Andrew Sheptytskyj and the Ukrainians in Canada,' *Canadian Catholic Historical Association, Study Sessions* (1957): 75–86.

6 I. Bodrug, 'Spomyny pastora Ivana Bodruga,' *Ievanhelska pravda* 18 (1957) and 19 (1958); Vivian Olender, 'The Canadian Methodist Church and the Gospel of Assimilation, 1900–1925,' *Journal of Ukrainian Studies* 7 (Fall 1982): 61–74.

7 A new account of Budka is provided by Stella Hryniuk, 'Pioneer Bishop, Pioneer Times: Nykyta Budka in Canada,' *Canadian Catholic Historical*

Association, *Historical Studies* 54 (1988): 21–41. For an Orthodox perspective on Budka see Iu. Mulyk-Lutsyk, *Istoriia Ukrainskoi Hreko-Pravoslavnoi Tserkvy v Kanadi* (Winnipeg: Ecclesia, 1987) III: 162–84.

8 J. Rea, 'Welcome to Western Canada: Ethnic Minorities and Prairie Regionalism,' in O. Gerus et al., eds., *The Jubilee Collection of the Ukrainian Free Academy of Sciences* (Winnipeg: Ukrainian Free Academy of Sciences, 1976), 431–42.

9 B. Bilash, 'Bilingual Public Education in Manitoba, 1897–1916' (MEd thesis, University of Manitoba, 1960); M. Ewanchuk, 'Development of Education among the Early Settlers in Manitoba,' in Gerus et al., *The Jubilee Collection*, 379–401.

10 On the history of the Ukrainian press see M. Borowyk, 'The Ukrainians in Canada and Their Press' (PhD dissertation, University of Ottawa, 1968).

11 Aspects of the history of the *Ukrainskyi holos* can be found in the fiftieth anniversary almanac of the paper, *Iuvileinyi almanakh 'Ukrainskoho holosu,' 1910–1960* (Winnipeg, 1960). The paper began the practice of highlighting Ukrainian success stories in Canada with special emphasis on achievements in education. The issue for 9 November 1910, for example, praised the twenty graduates of the Ruthenian Training School as role models.

12 Wasyl Kudryk (1880–1963) arrived in Canada in 1903 and taught bilingual school in rural Manitoba. A moralist and a fervent anti-Catholic, he was ordained in the Ukrainian Greek Orthodox church in 1923, served in Saskatchewan, and later edited the church's organ, the *Vistnyk* (Herald), in Winnipeg.

13 Taras Ferley (1882–1947) arrived in Canada in 1903 and then briefly lived in the Honcharenko Cossack commune in California. Later he taught Ukrainian at the Ruthenian Training School in Brandon. In 1907 he helped to organize the bilingual teachers and served as their president. In 1915 Ferley was the first Ukrainian to be elected to the Manitoba legislature, where he vigorously but vainly defended bilingual schools. In 1933 he was elected alderman in Winnipeg.

14 Jaroslav Arsenych (1887–1953) arrived in 1904, taught school in Manitoba and Saskatchewan, and in 1917 became the first Ukrainian lawyer in Canada. Active in the Orthodox church, he was appointed the first Ukrainian judge (Dauphin district, Man.) in 1947.

15 *Ukrainskyi holos*, 27 September 1910; Iuliian Stechyshyn, *Istoriia poselennia ukraintsiv v Kanadi* (Edmonton: Soiuz ukraintsiv samostiinykiv, 1975), 68–92.

16 *Ukrainskyi holos*, 26 July 1911, 20 March 1912, 6 August, 13 August, and 16 November 1913, 15 April 1914, 17 October and 27 December 1917, 2 January and 3 July 1918.

17 The innovative objectives of the institute were stated in the memorandum

of the initiative committee: 'To promote, establish, maintain, and manage institutions for students of Ukrainian descent, both male and female, of any religious denomination, in those Saskatchewan centres inhabited by Ukrainian people, for the purpose of furnishing board and lodgings to said students at a moderate charge, or entirely free of charge ... whereby the said students may be able by means of such assistance to pursue courses of study in public schools, high schools, collegiate institutes, normal schools and universities.' H. Udod, *Julian W. Stechishin: His Life and Work* (Saskatoon: Mohyla Institute, 1978), 21; Iu. Stechyshyn, ed., *Iuvileina knyha Ukrainskoho Instytuta im. P. Mohyly v Saskatuni, 1916–1941* (Winnipeg: P. Mohyla Ukrainian Institute, 1945), 63–98. In its first term the institute accommodated twenty-three Catholic, six Protestant, four Orthodox, and two Roman Catholic students.

18 *Ukrainskyi holos*, 3 July 1918.

19 Mulyk-Lutsyk, *Istoriia Tserkvy*, III: 344–58; Paul Yuzyk, *The Ukrainian Greek Orthodox Church of Canada, 1918–1951* (Ottawa: University of Ottawa Press, 1981), 75.

20 S. Sawchuk. 'Osnovni zasady Ukrainskoi Hreko-Pravoslavnoi Tserkvy v Kanadi,' convocation address, St Andrew's College, Winnipeg, 28 April 1950. Sawchuk (1895–1983) arrived in Canada in 1898, became a teacher, and in 1920 was ordained a priest in the UGOC. An outstanding church organizer, he was a dominant force in the USRL and the UCC.

21 Stechyshyn, *Iuvileina knyha*, 192.

22 Stechishin, who had flirted with socialism as the editor of *Robochyi narod*, worked as the secretary of the diplomatic mission of the Ukrainian People's Republic in Washington and in 1921 became editor of the *Ukrainskyi holos*, a position he held until his death in 1947.

23 Stechyshyn, *Iuvileina knyha*, 193.

24 *Ukrainskyi holos*, 4 January 1928. The following accounts of the USRL are written from its point of view: Myroslav Stechyshyn, *Soiuz ukraintsiv samostiinykiv v Kanadi i obiednannia ukrainskoho narodu* (Winnipeg: SUS, 1933); V. Batytsky, *Shcho ie Soiuz ukraintsiv samostiinykiv ta ioho soiuzni organizatsii?* (Winnipeg: SUS, 1942); P.I. Lazarovych, *Soiuz ukraintsiv samostiinykiv i ukrainska vyzvolna sprava* (Winnipeg: Trident Press, 1951); Iu. Stechyshyn, *Mizh ukraintsiamy v Kanadi* (Saskatoon: SUS, 1953), 25–47; K. Telychko, *Nashi zavdannia* (Edmonton: SUS, 1961); W. Burianyk, *SUS: Its Meaning and Significance* (Toronto: USRL, 1967). N. Kohuska produced a useful account of the Ukrainian Women's Association of Canada, *Chvert stolittia na hromadskii nyvi, 1926–1951* (Winnipeg: Soiuz ukrainok Kanady, 1952), and of the Ukrainian Canadian Youth Association, *Iuvileina knyha Soiuzu ukrainskoi molodi Kanady, 1931–1956* (Winnipeg: Soiuz ukrainskoi molodi Kanady, 1956). Although statistical data are elusive, it appears that in 1939 the USRL operated twenty-five fully integrated locals, over three hundred women's and youth groups, and nearly one

hundred community centres. In addition, there were incomplete locals, that is, with women's and youth branches but without the men's. Regional conventions drew hundreds of participants and were highly popular social outings (dinners, concerts, contests, softball games) for rural Ukrainians.

25 The original executive consisted of W. Swystun, president, J. Arsenych, vice-president, M. Stechishin, secretary, P. Woycenko, treasurer, and Father S. Sawchuk, General V. Sikevych, and N. Bachynsky, members.

26 There also existed a small conservative group dedicated to the ideals of Ukrainian monarchism as formulated by Viacheslav Lypynsky. Established in Canada as Sitch in 1924, it became the Soiuz hetmantsiv-der-zhavnykiv, or United Hetman Organization, in 1934. The UHO considered Hetman Pavlo Skoropadsky, who had ruled Ukraine with German help in 1918, to be the future monarch of Ukraine.

27 Vasyl Svystun, *Nova khvylia chervonoho teroru na Ukraini* (Winnipeg: Soiuz ukraintsiv samostiinykiv, 1930). The USRL was so effective in denouncing Polish abuses in Western Ukraine that it caused serious concern in the Polish ministry of foreign affairs. A. Zieba, 'Polish Diplomacy and Its Attitude towards Ukrainians in Canada, 1919–1939' (unpublished paper, 1989).

28 'Ukrainians are not beggars who arrived here with empty hands. They are children of a highly cultured nation with a glorious history. They brought with them a rich cultural heritage that they will happily contribute to the collective cultural treasury of Canada. Ukrainians do not seek special favours from others. They only want neighbourliness and understanding from their fellow citizens.' Stechyshyn, *Iuvileina knyha*, 308.

29 V. Svystun, 'Nasha ideolohiia,' and M. Stechyshyn, 'Politychni kombina-tsii,' in *Soiuz ukraintsiv samostiinykiv v Kanadi i obiednannia ukrainskoho narodu*, 7–20.

30 M. Stechyshyn, 'Politychni kombinatsii,' 8.

31 Iu. Stechyshyn, *Mizh ukraintsiamy v Kanadi*, 30–1.

32 *Ukrainskyi holos*, 11 February 1931.

33 T. Pavlychenko, 'Ukrainski vorony' (unpublished paper, nd), 6, Pavlychenko file, Ukrainian Cultural and Educational Centre, Winnipeg (hereafter cited as UCEC).

34 Z. Knysh, 'Ukrainska Striletska Hromada v Kanadi,' in Z. Knysh, ed., *Za chest, za slavu, za narod: Zbirnyk na zolotyi iuvilei Ukrainskoi Striletskoi Hromady v Kanadi, 1928–1978* (Toronto: Vydannia Holovnoi Upravy Ukrainskoi Striletskoi Hromady, 1978), 19.

35 On the OUN see Alexander J. Motyl, *The Turn to the Right: The Ideological Origins and Development of Ukrainian Nationalism, 1919–1929* (Boulder: East European Monographs, 1980), 129–52; John Armstrong, *Ukrainian Nationalism*, 3d ed. (Englewood, Colo.: Ukrainian Academic Press, 1990); V. Martynets, *Ukrainske pidpillia vid UVO do OUN* (Winnipeg: Novyi

shliakh, 1949); *Prohrama vykhovannia v Orhanizatsii ukrainskykh natsionalistiv* (Prague: Orhanizatsiia ukrainskykh natsionalistiv, 1930); *U.V.O.* (np:
Vydannia Propagandyvnoho viddilu Ukrainskoi viiskovoi orhanizatsii,
1929), 28–42.

36 Entitled 'Conversations with Colonel Evhen Konovalets,' who was assassinated in 1938, the accounts disclosed for the first time the details of the confidential discussions. *Ukrainskyi holos*, 7 June, 28 June, and 5 July 1939.

37 Ibid., 28 June 1939.

38 Ibid., 5 July 1939.

39 Ibid., 7 June 1939

40 Ibid.

41 Ibid.

42 In 1935 the Ukrainian War Veterans' local in Edmonton consisted of fifty-seven members, but only two were employed. Knysh, 'Ukrainska Striletska Hromada v Kanadi,' 287.

43 Stechyshyn, *Iuvileina knyha*, 222–36; Semen Kovbel, comp., and Dmytro Doroshenko, ed., *Propamiatna knyha Ukrainskoho narodnoho domu u Vynypegu* (Winnipeg: Ukrainskyi narodnyi dim, 1949), 582.

44 Tymish Pavlychenko (1892–1958) was born in central Ukraine, belonged to the Orthodox church, and participated in the Ukrainian Revolution as a member of the Central Rada. He emigrated to Czechoslovakia, where he continued his studies. In Canada, in addition to his UNF work, he developed a respectable scientific career as a plant ecologist. He held a doctorate from the University of Nebraska and a professorship at the University of Saskatchewan.

45 'Ukrainske natsionalne obiednannia i vyzvolna borotba ukrainskoi natsii,' draft ms, 1932, Pavlychenko file, UCEC.

46 *Ukrainskyi holos*, 22 October 1930.

47 'Pochatky "Novoho shliakhu,"' *New Pathway Jubilee Book, 1930–1955* (Winnipeg: Novyi shliakh, 1956).

48 Paul Yuzyk (1913–86) was born in Pinto, Saskatchewan, and excelled as a youth organizer for the UNF. He was the first president of the Young Ukrainian Nationalists. His pioneering interest in Ukrainian-Canadian studies led to a reputable academic career at the University of Manitoba and later at the University of Ottawa. A pillar of Ukrainian-Canadian society, he was appointed to the Senate of Canada in 1963.

49 Wolodymyr Kossar (1890–1970) was an officer in the Ukrainian Galician Army and a refugee in Czechoslovakia, where he obtained a degree in agricultural engineering. He was a member of the Ukrainian Military Organization and upon his arrival in Canada became a prominent nationalist organizer. A longtime president of the UNF, he was a co-founder of the largest Ukrainian cultural repository outside of Ukraine, the Ukrainian Cultural and Educational Centre in Winnipeg. Ironically,

he deposited his own papers at the National Archives of Canada in Ottawa.

50 Knysh, 'Ukrainska Striletska Hromada v Kanadi,' 437.

51 The BUC organ *Buduchnist natsii* (Future of the Nation) is probably the best source of information on the BUC.

52 'Fashyzm i Ukraina,' *Ukrainskyi holos*, 6 September 1933; 'UNO: ideolohiia, tsil i taktyka,' *Novyi shliakh*, 17 October 1933.

53 Pavlychenko, 13, UCEC.

54 *Novyi shliakh*, 15 February, 5 December 1938.

55 The *Novyi shliakh* accused the USRL of moral cowardice, of representing 'a form of Austro-Ruthenian patriotism which they adapted to Canada and which is based on the fear of detention camps and on toadying to the authorities.' *Novyi shliakh*, 6 April 1938. Stechishin was villified as 'the champion of slanderous criticism and false allegations.' *Novyi shliakh*, 21 November 1938. Stechishin replied in kind, labelling Pohorecky a Hitlerite and a former Communist. *Ukrainskyi holos*, 24 February 1937, 7 July 1938.

56 *Novyi shliakh*, 17 October 1933.

57 As early as 1933, Myroslav Stechishin criticized the Germanophile streak among the Ukrainian nationalists and reaffirmed that the USRL 'does not belong to those who pin their hopes on Hitler as the saviour of Ukraine.' *Ukrainskyi holos*, 26 July 1933. When the polemical war with the *Novyi shliakh* intensified in 1938, the *Ukrainskyi holos* featured stories that characterized UNF organizational activities as 'Nazi terror in Canada.' *Ukrainskyi holos*, 8 March, 6 April, 29 April 1938. Stechishin continued to attack the UNF for its alleged political arrogance and authoritarian inclinations: 'It is difficult to find any Ukrainian who would not be a politician; and every Ukrainian politician is first of all a world politician, and a Ukrainian politician only insofar as one can attach Ukrainian politics to that of the entire world ... As long as Ukrainians live under foreign rule, only democracy is good for them ... Ukrainians must firmly support democracy in those countries in which they live, because therein they find the only possibility of enjoying their rights. It is not at all practical for Ukrainians to be hostile to democracy, even if the "wise German" is against democracy. Lack of democracy may be an insignificant matter to a German; but lack of democracy in the countries in which the Ukrainians have been included would be deadly to them ... We must look at the world not with German eyes, but with Ukrainian eyes.' *Ukrainskyi holos*, 14 August 1938.

58 For the Swystun-UGOC conflict see Yuzyk, *The Ukrainian Greek Orthodox Church of Canada*, 143–83; Mulyk-Lutsyk, *Istoriia Tserkvy*, IV: 699–747. There is little doubt that Swystun's personality and attitude were the major causes of his alienation from the Ukrainian community. During the church crisis Myroslav Stechishin drew Swystun's attention to his

egocentricity: 'In your eyes everyone is fallible but you. No one under-
stands anything; no one knows what he should do; only you are
infallible, and you alone know everything and do everything well. The
[church] council is "illegal and unlawful" because it did not decide the
matter in accordance with your wishes; the Consistory is so and so
because it does not act in accordance with your wishes. In fact, all those
who are not in agreement with you are necessarily "fallible" and "know
nothing." Who, then, considers himself an infallible pope?' 'Reply of the
Consistory to the Letter of Mr. Swystun,' 21 May 1936, No. 9259,
Archives of the Ukrainian Orthodox Church of Canada, Winnipeg.

59 *Ukrainskyi holos*, 16 July 1938. Swystun's baffling propensity to change
sides would continue. In 1946 he abandoned Ukrainian nationalism in
favour of a pro-Soviet position, which he maintained until his death and
from which he attacked the Ukrainian Canadian Committee. See his
'Ukrainskyi patriotyzm' v Kanadi na slovakh i na dili (Winnipeg: Nakladom
Tovarystva kulturnoho zviazku z Ukrainoiu, 1957). But even there he
was unhappy, and he died a bitter outcast from the Ukrainian-Canadian
society that he had so profoundly influenced. His personal papers are still
inaccessible to researchers.

60 D. Doroshenko, *History of the Ukraine*, translated and abridged by Hanna
Keller, edited and with an introduction by G.W. Simpson (Edmonton,
1939); revised and updated by O.W. Gerus as *A Survey of Ukrainian History*
(Winnipeg: Trident Press, 1975).

61 *Winnipeg Tribune*, 6 January 1937.

62 *Novyi shliakh*, 30 October 1939.

63 *Ukrainskyi holos*, 5 December 1938.

64 M. Kamianetsky, *Nimtsi i Ukraina: Vidnosyny nimtsiv do ukraintsiv v protiahu
istorii* (Winnipeg: Ukrainska vydavnycha spilka v Kanadi, 1940).

65 The *Novyi shliakh* estimated that there were as many as three hundred
fund-raising groups in Canada. *Novyi shliakh*, 5 December 1938.

66 The *Ukrainskyi holos* even accused the *Novyi shliakh* of diverting public
funds for personal use because 'the employees of the *Novyi shliakh* drive
cars to work while the employees of the *Ukrainskyi holos* have no cars.'
Ukrainskyi holos, 21 August 1938.

67 Diary of Andrew Pawlyk, 4 August 1938, excerpts in author's possession.

68 Wasyl Kushnir (1893–1979) was a Catholic priest and theologian who
arrived in Winnipeg in 1934 and became one of the leading members
of the Ukrainian community. He was president of the UCC for twenty-
six years and twice president of the World Congress of Free Ukrainians,
which he helped to found.

69 *Ukrainskyi holos*, 30 February 1939.

70 Ibid., 5 October 1939.

71 Ibid., 1 August 1938.

72 The Saskatoon executive of the RCUC consisted of T. Pavlychenko, presi-

dent, J. Stechishin, vice-president, A. Gregorovich, secretary, and Father M. Pelech, treasurer. Pavlychenko file, UCEC.

73 *Vistnyk*, 1 March 1940.

74 Wasyl Burianyk (1895–1985) arrived in Canada in 1912 and served in the Canadian army during the First World War. A teacher and USRL organizer, he wrote his rambling memoirs in 1981. They touch on the formation of the UCC and will be published in 1991. Relevant events in Burianyk are corroborated by S. Sawchuk's and A. Pawlyk's diaries. Excerpts in author's possession.

75 Burianyk ms, pt. 1, 14; Sawchuk dairy, 15 June and 13 July 1939.

76 Sawchuk diary, 14 July 1939.

77 Burianyk ms, pt. 2, 19.

78 The USRL was paying Kaye one hundred dollars a month for his service. 'V spravi predstavnytstva Soiuzu ukraintsiv samostiinykiv v Londoni,' Pavlychenko file, UCEC.

79 The USRL spared no words in demonstrating its loyalty and readiness to serve Canada: 'On behalf of the Ukrainian Self-Reliance League of Canada we are happy to be able to assure everyone that all those many thousands of Canadian citizens of Ukrainian descent who are members of, or are in sympathy with, the League and its affiliated organizations in Canada have never wavered in their loyalty and devotion to Canada and their faith in the democratic institutions and that therefore all of them will without hesitation respond to the earnest appeal of their King and their Government and will faithfully serve and defend the vital interests of Canada and the British Empire side by side with all Canadian citizens by all means at their disposal and in any manner that may be demanded of them.' *Ukrainskyi holos*, 6 August 1939. The UNF was less verbose but equally patriotic: 'We stand without hesitation in a united and voluntary defence of our adopted fatherland.' *Novyi shliakh*, 9 August 1939.

80 Sawchuk dairy, 4 October 1939.

81 Ibid., 19 November 1939.

82 Pavlychenko to the members of the initiative committee of the RCUC, 31 October 1939; Pavlychenko's notes (in English) on his visit with J. Stechishin, 31 January 1940; P. Lazarowich to Pavlychenko, 26 October 1939, Pavlychenko file, UCEC; Sawchuk diary, 23 December 1939.

83 *Ukrainskyi holos*, 29 January 1940.

84 The USRL resolution ridiculed the RCUC as a committee of 'private individuals without public support at large and thus it is self-appointed and does not represent anybody except the individuals of whom it is composed.' *Ukrainskyi holos*, 10 January 1940.

85 Sawchuk diary, 6 March 1940.

86 Ibid., 1 March 1940.

87 It seems that Datskiw's switch of support from the RCUC to the USRL

was motivated by his publisher, a Czech businessman, who judged that a UNF connection would be bad for business.

88 W. Kushnir and W. Kossar, *Pratsia i pravda peremozhe* (Saskatoon: RCUC, 1940), 17. The UNF's lingering suspicion of the Left was, in part, based on the ULFTA confidential brochure on the methods of infiltration of nationalist organizations by 'progressive' elements, *Rozhornim udarnyi nastup na zhovtoblakytnykiv* (Winnipeg: Todovyrnazu, 1937).

89 Sawchuk diary, 7 March 1940.

90 Pavlychenko to Kushnir, 18 March 1940, Pavlychenko file, UCEC.

91 Ibid.

92 Sawchuk diary, 25 March 1940.

93 Ibid., 24 May 1940.

94 RCUC file, 1939–40, box no. 188, UCEC.

95 Sawchuk diary, 7 May 1940; *Ukrainskyi holos*, 15 May 1940.

96 For example, Semen Kovbel, a respected member of the Ukrainian National Home and a long-time USRL supporter, publicly chastised Stechishin for his irresponsible journalism, which was preventing unity. *Novyi shliakh*, 20 October 1940.

97 Thomas M. Prymak, *Maple Leaf and Trident: The Ukrainian Canadians during the Second World War* (Toronto: Multicultural History Society of Ontario, 1988).

98 Sawchuk diary.

99 Burianyk's contact in Ottawa was James G. Gardiner, the former Liberal premier of Saskatchewn. Burianyk ms.

100 'Perehovory v spravi zluky dvokh tsentralnykh orhanizatsii Ukrainskoho tsentralnoho komitetu i Representatsiinoho komitetu ukraintsiv Kanady,' Archives of the Ukrainian Canadian Committee, UCEC.

101 Sawchuk diary.

102 'Perehovory,' 9.

103 'Protokoly ekzekutyvnykh ta skladovykh orhanizatsii KUK,' Archives of the Ukrainian Canadian Committee, UCEC.

104 *Ukrainskyi holos*, 13 October 1940

105 *Novyi shliakh,* 21 October 1940.

106 For the post-formation history of the UCC, see Gerus, 'The Ukrainian Canadian Committee,' in Lupul, *A Heritage in Transition*, 195–214.

107 John Syrnick, secretary-general of the UCC and editor of the *Ukrainskyi holos*, composed 'My Credo,' which in 1967 became the ideology of the World Congress of Free Ukrainians, a global association of Ukrainians in the diaspora.

108 In July 1990 the Ukrainian Orthodox church finally broke with the USRL tradition and accepted the ecclesiastical jurisdiction of the Ecumenical Patriarchate of Constantinople.

109 M. Hykawy, the future editor of the *Kanadiiskyi farmer* and the *Ukrainskyi holos*, noted in 1942 that at the USRL conventions 'we always see the

same people, year after year. Don't we have anybody else besides the same people? If we really don't, then we will perish because of the lack of leadership. If we do, then why don't we see or hear them?' Hykawy diary, UCEC.

Carynnyk: Swallowing Stalinism

1 'Rezoliutsiia Plenumu TOUK po perehliadu nashoi istorii,' *Zhyttia i slovo*, 18 December 1989; 'Review of History Launched,' *Ukrainian Canadian*, December 1989, 13–14.
2 Geoffrey York, 'Canadian Communist, 77, struggles with his beliefs as horror stories emerge,' *Globe and Mail*, 8 January 1990.
3 Rosie DiManno, 'Communist bit red-faced by big changes,' *Toronto Star*, 10 January 1990.
4 Transcribed from an audiotape of Krawchuk's comments. After the conference Krawchuk was quoted as saying that 'the truth about the famine in Ukraine was concealed for a very long time, and even today it has not been fully revealed. Some archives continue to preserve their secrets. Today we know that in fact this was a real genocide against the peasantry, which was forcibly driven into the collective farms and subjected to repression ... Thank God that Ukrainian scholars now have the opportunity to research their history on the basis of documents and testimony, so that our children and grandchildren will know the truth about this terrible national tragedy when they study the history of Ukraine.' Iurii Valuiev, 'Petro Kravchuk: "Zustrichi, iaki matymut dobri naslidky,"' *Visti z Ukrainy*, no. 40, September 1990.
5 Dozens of writers have discussed Stalin and Stalinism. See, for example, 'Toward a Theory of Stalinism' in Irving Howe and Lewis Coser, *The American Communist Party: A Critical History* (New York: Frederick A. Praeger, 1962), 500–54; Robert C. Tucker, ed., *Stalinism: Essays in Historical Interpretation* (New York: W.W. Norton, 1977); G.R. Urban, ed., *Stalinism: Its Impact on Russia and the World* (London: Maurice Temple Smith, 1983); Roy Medvedev, *Let History Judge: The Origins and Consequences of Stalinism*, rev. ed., ed. and trans. George Shriver (New York: Columbia University Press, 1989); Robert C. Tucker, *Stalin in Power: The Revolution from Above, 1928–1941* (New York: W.W. Norton, 1990); and Walter Laqueur, *Stalin: The Glasnost Revelations* (New York: Charles Scribner's Sons, 1990). Several studies of Stalinism and its consequences for Ukraine have recently appeared, among them Dmytro Tabachnyk and Vitalii Roztalny, 'Stalinskyi teror: Ukraina naprykintsi trydtsiatykh,' *Kyiv*, February 1989, 140–57; M.F. Buhai, 'Deportatsii naselennia z Ukrainy: 30–50-ti roky,' *Ukrainskyi istorychnyi zhurnal*, 1990, no. 10: 32–8, no. 11: 20–6; Iu.I. Shapoval, 'Stalinizm i Ukraina,' *Ukrainskyi istorychnyi zhurnal*, 1990, no. 12: 47–59, 1991, no. 2: 20–30, no. 4: 43–54; and O.S.

438   Notes to pages 189–90

Rublov and Iu.A. Cherchenko, 'Stalinshchyna i dolia zakhidnoukrainskoi intelihentsii: 20-ti–40-vi roky XX st.,' *Ukrainskyi istorychnyi zhurnal*, 1991, no. 1: 3–12, no. 2: 10–20, no. 3: 3–15; no. 4: 30–43. Our present purposes will be served if we keep in mind the definition offered by *News from Ukraine* in 1988. 'Stalinism is not just a "personality cult,"' the newspaper wrote. 'It means deformation of the Party beyond recognition. Stalinism is wholesale terror, assassination of millions of innocent victims and devaluation of human life ... Stalinism is an outrage on the basic principles of democracy, skillfully disguised beneath eloquent rhetoric about human rights; it is the absence of a legal state system, extreme intolerance of all dissidents, distortion of the Leninist nationality policy, arbitrary policy in respect of religion, church and believers. Stalinism is estrangement of working people from property and the end results of work; it is forced labor of millions of people, based on primitive technology; it is misappropriation of human and natural resources of the country. Stalinism is social parasitism and injustice owing to broad wage leveling combined with privileges granted to "chosen" sections of the population. It is an ever expanding spiritual enslavement of man, subordination to the dictator's will; it is inculcation of suspiciousness, baseness, servility, hypocrisy, destruction of people's self-respect, it is bringing word and deed far apart from each other, it is theft and alcoholism. Stalinism is state-level deception; fabrication of "traitors to the Motherland"; it is falsification of the results of the collectivization, of the First Five-Year Plan and those of the all-Union census of the population; falsification of the Party's, USSR's and world's history.' 'Stalinism,' *News from Ukraine*, no. 38, September 1988.

6 A.W. Kliefoth to the Secretary of State, 11 October 1928, General Records of the Department of State, Record Group 59, 861.5017 Living Conditions/11, National Archives, Washington, DC (hereafter cited as NA).

7 Barton Hall to the Secretary of State, 13 October 1928, RG 59, 861.48 Famine 1928/12, NA.

8 Louis Sussdorff, Jr., to the Secretary of State, 3 December 1928, RG 59, 861.00B/554, NA.

9 H.E. Carlson to Louis Sussdorff, Jr., 18 December 1928, RG 59, 861.5017 Living Conditions/25, NA.

10 R.H. Hanson (American Export Lines, New York), 'Report on Trip to Russia, May 4th–July 15th, 1929,' RG 59, Office of Eastern European Affairs, Box 5, Reports of Visitors to Russia 1928–30, NA. This and the four previously cited documents will appear in Marco Carynnyk, ed., *Foggy Bottom and the Famine: The United States and Ukraine, 1928–1935* (forthcoming).

11 *Farmerske zhyttia*, 31 December 1930, as translated in John Kolasky, comp., *Prophets and Proletarians: Documents on the History of the Rise and Decline*

of Ukrainian Communism in Canada (Edmonton: Canadian Institute of Ukrainian Studies, 1990), 223.

12 *Ukrainski robitnychi visti*, 19 October 1933, as translated in Kolasky, *Prophets and Proletarians*, 222. The British Foreign Office, which was receiving almost daily reports on famine conditions from its embassy in Moscow, was taken aback by Herriot's naîvety. His 'visit was well stage-managed and his eulogies of everything Soviet must surely have come up to the most optimistic expectations of his hosts,' minuted one Whitehall official. 'M. Herriot seems surprisingly gullible. He even informed journalists, after he had left Russia, that the reports of famine in the Ukraine were gross libels (though this is no doubt largely explained by the methods of deception practised on him ...),' wrote another official. Marco Carynnyk, Lubomyr Y. Luciuk, and Bohdan S. Kordan, eds., *The Foreign Office and the Famine: British Documents on Ukraine and the Great Famine of 1932–1933* (Kingston: Limestone Press, 1988), 301–2.

13 *Farmerske zhyttia*, 25 April 1934, as translated in Kolasky, *Prophets and Proletarians*, 224.

14 Petro Kravchuk and Pylyp Lysets, *Zavzhdy z ridnym narodom: Uchast kanadskykh ukraintsiv v borotbi za vyzvolennia Zakhidnoi Ukrainy* (Toronto: Kraiovyi komitet po vidznachenniu 20-richchia vyzvolennia i vozziednannia Zakhidnoi Ukrainy z Radianskoiu Ukrainoiu, 1959), 107–11.

15 *Komu pomahaty?* (Winnipeg: Todovyrnazu, 1934), [2].

16 *Het okupantiv i UVO iz Zakhidnoi Ukrainy* (Winnipeg: Todovyrnazu, 1935), 5.

17 Petro Kravchuk, *Odyn z pershykh: Biohrafichnyi narys* (Toronto: 'Ukrainske Zhyttia,' 'Ukrainske Slovo,' and 'Ukrainian Canadian,' 1963), 3–12.

18 Lita-Rose Betcherman. *The Little Band: The Clashes between the Communists and the Political and Legal Establishment in Canada, 1928–1932* (Ottawa: Deneau, nd), 10.

19 Kravchuk, *Odyn z pershykh*, 44.

20 In 1928 Navis attended the Sixth Congress of the Comintern in Moscow, where he became friendly with Dmytro Manuilsky, the secretary of the Communist International, and travelled to Kharkiv and Kiev to meet Ukrainian political and cultural leaders. Ibid., 23; Petro Kravchuk, *Matvii Popovych: Ioho mistse v istorii ukrainskykh kanadtsiv* (Toronto: Kobzar, 1986), 91; Peter Krawchuk, *Matthew Popovich: His Place in the History of Ukrainian Canadians* (Toronto: CSULR, 1987), 86. Ian Angus, *Canadian Bolsheviks: The Early Years of the Communist Party of Canada* (Montreal: Vanguard Publications, 1981), 310, mentions that Navis went to Moscow in the autumn of 1930 but gives no details of the trip.

21 Betcherman, *The Little Band*, 168.

22 Kravchuk, *Odyn z pershykh*, 31–2.

23 Record Group 4, Records of the Ministry of the Attorney-General, MS

367, Records of the Communist Party of Canada, 30 L 0756, Archives of Ontario, Toronto.

24 John Hladun, 'They Taught Me Treason,' *Maclean's*, 1 November 1947, 21.

25 Ibid., 52. Hladun gives a similar account in two Ukrainian translations of the *Maclean's* series, 'Vony vchyly mene zrady,' *Ukrainski visti*, 21, 24, 28, and 31 January, 4, 7, 14, 18, 21, 25, and 28 February, and 6 March 1948, and *Mene vchyly zrady* (Winnipeg: Ukrainska vydavnycha spilka v Kanadi, 1948), and in a recently published autobiography: Ivan Hladun, *Inkoly i odyn u poli voin* (Mississauga, Ont.: Hoverlia, 1990).

26 'Z kanadskoiu delehatsiieiu po Radianskii Ukraini.' Cited in Petro Krav-chuk, *Lysty z Kanady* (Kiev: Radianskyi pysmennyk, 1976), 128.

27 D. Lobai, *Za diisne vyiasnennia polozhennia na Radianskii Ukraini* (Winnipeg-New York: Privately printed, 1935), 1–2; Danylo Lobai, 'Komunistychnyi rukh sered ukraintsiv Kanady,' in Semen Kovbel, comp., and Dmytro Doroshenko, ed., *Propamiatna knyha Ukrainskoho narodnoho domu u Vyny-pegu* (Winnipeg: Ukrainskyi narodnyi dim, 1949), 755–9.

28 Lobai, *Za diisne vyiasnennia*, 5.

29 Ibid., 11.

30 Ibid., 12, 37.

31 Hladun, 'They Taught Me Treason,' *Maclean's Magazine*, 1 November 1947, 54.

32 An editorial in *Pravda* that discusses the role of Pavel Postyshev, appointed by Stalin to run the Communist Party of Ukraine in 1933, in the events of the famine years is translated in Bohdan S. Kordan and Lubomyr Y. Luciuk, *A Delicate and Difficult Question: Documents in the History of Ukrainians in Canada, 1899–1962* (Kingston: Limestone Press, 1986), 65–6.

33 Avakumovic, *The Communist Party in Canada*, 120.

34 *Pysmennyky Radianskoi Ukrainy, 1917–1987: Biobibliohrafichnyi dovidnyk* (Kiev: Radianskyi pysmennyk, 1988), 245.

35 Kravchuk, *Lysty z Kanady*, 114–28.

36 Kravchuk, *Matvii Popovych*, 112–13.

37 Peter Krawchuk, 'I. Sembay – A Victim of Stalinism,' *Ukrainian Canadian*, November 1989, 13–15.

38 Petro Kravchuk, 'Spilka revoliutsiinykh pysmennykiv "Zakhidna Ukraina,"' *Literaturna Ukraina*, 14 December 1989.

39 In 1963, for example, Mykola Hrynchyshyn, an activist of the AUUC and editor of the *Ukrainske slovo* who had spent a year at the Higher Party School in Kiev, published an editorial in which he called the famine 'imaginary' and a 'slander against Ukraine.' '"Famine" for dirty politics,' *Ukrainske slovo*, 23 October 1963, as translated in Kolasky, *Prophets and Proletarians*, 371–2.

40 See, for example, Peter Boychuck, 'Nazi big lie about Ukraine grows

bigger,' *Canadian Tribune,* 6 June 1983; Kolasky, *Prophets and Proletarians,*
372–4.

41 An Englishman who visited the Soviet Union in 1929 and 1931 described
the system of restrictions on the taking of photographs: 'The Soviet is
averse to the photography of beggars and food-queues, and lest the
tourist should take views that meet with official disapproval, the expor-
tation of undeveloped films is prohibited. This creates a problem of
considerable difficulty for the tourist, as there are no photographic
chemists or dark-rooms anywhere. I partially solved the difficulty by
developing in my bedroom, frequently without running water and in
the pitch dark. The Intourist takes upon itself the development of photographic films; some of our films were duly handed over to the Moscow
office in September and only reached us at the end of December. I only
received a part of those I sent.' Archibald Forman, *From Baltic to Black
Sea: Impressions of Soviet Russia To-day* (London: Sampson, Low, Marston,
[1931]), 326–7. Carveth Wells, an American travel lecturer who visited
the Soviet Union in July 1932, was warned not to take photographs of
railways, bridges, military sites, or government buildings. The real purpose of the prohibition became apparent when his train stopped at a
station in Ukraine and he got out to walk through the near-by market.
When Wells returned to the station, two soldiers ordered him to follow
them to the station commandant's office. His camera had been found
in the carriage, and he was suspected of taking photographs from the
train window. 'The accusation was absolutely false,' Wells wrote.
'While I would dearly have liked to photograph some of the sights I had
seen from the train, especially the freight cars full of Kulaks and the
children eating grass and the miles of weeds, I had given Olga [Wells's
Intourist guide] my word of honor not to break that law of the Soviets
which prohibits photographs in the neighborhood of railway stations.
After protesting my innocence, the offending camera, which was lying
on the Commandant's desk, was opened and the unexposed roll of film
destroyed.' Carveth Wells, *Kapoot: The Narrative of a Journey from Leningrad
to Mount Ararat in Search of Noah's Ark* (New York: Robert M. McBride,
1933), 74 and 128–9. Humphrey Mitchell, a Canadian MP who visited
the Soviet Union in September 1932, noted in his diary that a soldier
ordered him not to take pictures when he visited a village near Kharkiv.
Foreign Office 371/16339 N 6741, Public Record Office, London. And
Claude Arthur Rowley, a newspaper publisher in northern Ohio who
toured the Soviet Union in the summer of 1933, wrote in his travel diary:
'we have to leave all our films at the customs house in Odessa for development by the Russian government. No films of any kind are supposed to
be taken out of the Soviet until they have been censored by the border
officials who are of the G.P.U. Or we can leave our undeveloped films
with the Intourist office which will have them developed and sent to

us in America. It is said that the reason for this is to prevent photographs of military importance leaving the country, and further to hold up pictures which will give the Bolsheviks unfavorable publicity.' C.A. Rowley, *Russia: A Country Upside-Down* (Painesville, Ohio: Painesville Telegraph, [1933]), 178–9 and 188.

42 In the spring of 1922, for example, the Ukrainian Red Cross in Kharkiv sent a collection of seventeen photographs to newspapers in Europe and North America. No North American newspapers published them, but they did appear in newspapers in Western Ukraine and in Comité international de secours à la Russie, Haut Commissariat du Dr Nansen, *Information*, no. 22, 30 April 1922. Other relief organizations, including the American Red Cross, the YMCA, and the American Relief Association, also circulated photographs, many of which are now in the Prints and Photographs Division of the Library of Congress in Washington, DC. (See in particular lots 2916, 3052, 3147, 9952, and 9953.)

43 Thomas Walker, '6 Million Peasants Die as Soviet Hoards Grain,' *New York Evening Journal*, 18 February 1935; 'Children starve among Soviet dead,' 19 February 1935; 'Bodies of Soviet famine victims robbed,' 21 February 1935; 'Soviet drafts men, starves women,' 25 February 1935; 'Starvation wipes out Soviet villages,' 27 February 1935.

44 Louis Fischer, 'Hearst's Russian "famine,"' *Nation*, 13 March 1935, 296–7. See also the reply by William Henry Chamberlin, the Moscow correspondent of the *Manchester Guardian* and *Christian Science Monitor*, who did report the famine, 'The Ukrainian Famine,' *Nation*, 29 May 1935, 629, and the response by Fischer in the same issue, 629–30.

45 In his contribution to *The God That Failed: Six Studies in Communism* (London: Hamish Hamilton, 1950), 199–229, in which he described the brutal methods used to collectivize agriculture and then wrote that once the peasants had joined the collectives, 'many sulked or sabotaged the co-operative effort as a protest against excessive taxes or because they still hoped the government would abandon the collectives as failures. In the Ukraine these circumstances produced the famine of 1931–2 which killed several million people. The price of Bolshevik haste and dogmatism was enormous.'

46 'Ukraine famine secrets disclosed by tourist's camera. Risked life for pictures,' *Daily Express*, 6 August 1934; 'Starving Ukraine. More secrets from the hidden camera,' 7 August 1934; 'Ukraine village wiped out. Famine worse next autumn. No medical aid,' 8 August 1934.

47 Vienna: Wilhelm Braumüller, 1935.

48 It now appears that the genuine and authentic photographs in Ammende's book were taken by Alexander Wienerberger. See his *Hart auf Hart: 15 Jahre Ingenieur in Sowjetrußland* (Salzburg: Verlag Anton Pustet, 1939), which contains many of the photographs in Ammende's book, and the collection of photographs from Cardinal Theodor Innitzer's archives in

Vienna published in *The 1933 Original Photographs from Kharkiv, Ukraine* (Toronto: World Congress of Free Ukrainians, nd).

49 *Human Life in Russia* (London: George Allen & Unwin, 1936; Cleveland: John T. Zubal, 1984).

50 See, for example, A. Laubenheimer, *Und du Siehst die Sowjets Richtig: Berichte von deutschen und ausländischen 'Spezialisten' aus der Sowjet-Union* (Berlin: Nibelungen-Verlag, 1935). Laubenheimer's *Die Sowjetunion am Abgrund* (Berlin-Halensee: Verlag Volkswirtschaftsdienst, 1933) also contains photographs of hungry and bedraggled peasants.

51 Robert Conquest, *The Harvest of Sorrow: Soviet Collectivization and the Terror-Famine* (London: Century Hutchinson; New York: Oxford University Press; Edmonton: University of Alberta Press in association with the Canadian Institute of Ukrainian Studies, 1986). The photographs, it should be noted, disappeared from later reprints of the book.

52 D. Tottle, 'Holocaust,' *Winnipeg Free Press*, 10 February 1984.

53 Toronto: Progress Books, 1987.

54 'Hearst forges pictures to rouse war fever against U.S.S.R. Joins Hitler in notorious forgeries on "starvation" in the Soviet Union – Thousands prepare to fight war growing menace,' *Daily Worker*, 21 February 1935; Vern Smith, 'Hearst's anti-Soviet "authority" never was in the U.S.S.R,' 26 February 1935; idem, 'Aide admits Hearst is liar: Chief of publisher's bureau in Moscow says toilers prosper,' 27 February 1935; 'Hearst's "freedom of press" is freedom to slander worker,' 1 March 1935; Vern Smith, 'Nazi papers with Hearst. Hitler is increasing flood of anti-Soviet propaganda,' 1 March 1935. See also the editorial comment in the *Nation*, 6 March 1935, 263.

55 Douglas Tottle, 'Anti-Semitism and the Ukrainian 1933 famine-genocide hoax,' *Outlook*, June 1987, 5–6, 14; *Ukrainian News*, 2–9 July 1987.

56 *Ukrainian Canadian*, April 1988, 22–4.

57 P. Krawchuk and W. Harasym, 'Teaching unit on Ukrainian famine is just political axe-grinding' [letter to the editor], *Villager* (Toronto), January 1984, 5.

58 One of the most prolific writers is the historian Stanislav Kulchytsky. His numerous publications, which focus on the demography of the famine, include *1933: Trahediia holodu* (Kiev: Tovarystvo 'Znannia' Ukrainskoi RSR, 1989). A group of scholars headed by R.Ia. Pyrih has published a collection of interpretive essays and documents: *Holod 1932–1933 rokiv na Ukraini: Ochyma istorykiv, movoiu dokumentiv* (Kiev: Vydavnytstvo politychnoi literatury Ukrainy, 1990). The young writer Oleksandr Mishchenko has published an excellent oral history based on eyewitness accounts that he collected in the Poltava region: *Bezkrovna viina: Knyha svidchen* (Kiev: Molod, 1991). And the journalist Volodymyr Maniak announced in 1989 the publication of a collection of eyewitness accounts and documents entitled *33ii: Holod*. See, for example, Volodymyr

Maniak, 'Narodovi povertaietsia istoriia, a istorii – pravda,' *Literaturna Ukraina*, 27 July 1989; idem, 'Iak ne my, to khto?' *Literaturna Ukraina*, 17 May 1990; and Volodymyr Maniak and Lidia Kovalenko, 'Pamiat ne proshchaie,' *Literaturna Ukraina*, 2 August 1990.

59 One small irony of the recent Soviet interest in the famine is that the photographs that the pro-Communist Canadians disputed so fiercely in the early 1980s have been reprinted in the Soviet press. See, for example, Mykola Shudria, 'Stezhkamy boliu i muk,' *Ukraina*, no. 12, 19 March 1989, 14–16; no. 13, 26 March 1989, 22–3; no. 14, 2 April 1989, 22–3; no. 15, 9 April 1989, 20–[21]; no. 16, 16 April 1989, [18]–[19]; no. 17, 23 April 1989, 20–1. This collection of eyewitness accounts of the famine of 1933 is illustrated with eleven photographs, three of which are from 1921–2 and one of which was taken by Wienerberger.

60 Betcherman, *The Little Band*, 216.

61 'Ethnicity on Trial: The Italians of Montreal and the Second World War,' in Norman Hillmer, Bohdan Kordan, and Lubomyr Luciuk, eds., *On Guard for Thee: War, Ethnicity, and the Canadian State, 1939–1945* (Ottawa: Canadian Committee for the History of the Second World War, 1988), 77.

Krawchuk: Between a Rock and a Hard Place

1 Archbishop Langevin to Metropolitan Sheptytsky, 31 March 1901, f. 358, op. 2, spr. 69, Tsentralnyi derzhavnyi istorychnyi arkhiv URSR u Lvovi (Central State Historical Archive of the Ukrainian SSR in Lviv, hereafter cited as TsDIAL).

2 Of the 11,345 Catholic immigrants from Europe who landed in Quebec between 28 April and 1 June 1912, 6,559 (58 per cent) were Galician Ruthenians. P.H.D. Cosgrain, Secretary, Catholic Immigration Association of Canada, to the editor of the *Tablet*, 15 June 1912, f. 358, op. 2, spr. 73, TsDIAL.

3 J.A. Sabourin, 'Un imitateur de Chiniquy' (dated Sifton, 24 January 1911), clipping from *Le Devoir*, f. 358, op. 2, spr. 72, TsDIAL.

4 A. Delaere, CSSR, to Sheptytsky, 28 December 1901, f. 358, op. 2, spr. 72, TsDIAL.

5 Sabourin to Sheptytsky [summer 1906], f. 358, op. 2, spr. 72, TsDIAL.

6 Ibid. Sabourin's attempts to be admitted to the Ruthenian College were unsuccessful, at least in the following academic year. By May 1907 he was still writing to Sheptytsky from the Canadian College in Rome. F. 358, op. 2, spr. 72, TsDIAL.

7 Sabourin (Rome) to Langevin, 31 March 1907, f. 358, op. 2, spr. 72, TsDIAL.

8 A. Delaere, CSSR, 'Rapport de la réunion des quelques prêtres du Rite Ruthène à l'Archevêche de Saint Boniface, le 4 Janvier, 1910,' ms copy by N. Demchuk, f. 358, op. 2, spr. 75, TsDIAL.

9 Langevin to Sabourin, 28 January 1911, f. 358, op. 2, spr. 69, TsDIAL. With the consent of Metropolitan Sheptytsky and the Ukrainian Greek Catholic bishop of the United States, Soter Ortynsky, who was also in Montreal for the eucharistic congress in September 1910, Archbishop Langevin gave instructions for the three priests to travel to Galicia.

10 Langevin to Sabourin, 28 January 1911, f. 358, op. 2, spr. 69, TsDIAL.

11 In a signed but undated (probably ca. 1910) statement, a copy of which is in the papers of Metropolitan Sheptytsky (f. 358, op. 2, spr. 72, TsDIAL), Sabourin mentioned that he had baptized and confirmed 436 children.

12 Delaere, Yorkton, to Sheptytsky, 17 August 1910, f. 358, op. 1, spr. 248, TsDIAL.

13 See, for example, Sabourin's letter to Sheptytsky, from Sifton, 25 January 1912: 'Vous le savez, Excellence, je me suis donné tout entier au ministère au milieu des Ruthènes. Je ne désire rien de plus que leur bien spirituel,' f. 358, op. 1, spr. 339, TsDIAL; and Delaere (Brandon) to Sheptytsky, n.d.: 'j'ai à coeur l'intérêt des Galiciens ici parsemés dans le Canada'; f. 358, op. 1, spr. 248, TsDIAL.

14 On the suspended Reverend Krochmalny see Sabourin, 'Un imitateur'; Sabourin to Sheptytsky, 3 April 1911, f. 358, op. 1, spr. 248, TsDIAL; and the letter of M. Zaporozan, *Winnipeg Free Press*, 9 June 1911.

15 About the Ukrainians in Shoal Lake, Delaere wrote: 'quelques mauvais esprits veulent soulever le peuple à abonder [abandoner?] l'église et à bâtir une cerkiew et à exiger à grand cris un prêtre Ruthène.' F. 358, op. 1, spr. 248, TsDIAL.

16 Sabourin's signed but undated statement, f. 358, op. 2, spr. 72, TsDIAL.

17 Copy of a letter from Delaere, Montreal, to Sabourin, 6 March 1910, f. 358, op. 2, spr. 75, TsDIAL. Emphasis added.

18 See, for example, 'je serais le premier à me rejouir de l'arrivée d'un prêtre ... je suis tout-à-fait disposé ... de ceder la place et l'église au premier bon prêtre qui serait envoyé'; Delaere (Brandon) to Sheptytsky, f. 358, op. 1, spr. 248, TsDIAL; and 'je suis bien convaincu que Monseigneur veut réelement avoir [au Canada] des bons prêtres ruthènes de Galicie,' Sabourin to Sheptytsky, 25 January 1912, f. 358, op. 1, spr. 339, TsDIAL.

19 Sabourin statement, f. 358, op. 2, spr. 72, TsDIAL.

20 Delaere, Montreal, to Sabourin, 6 March 1910 (copy), f. 358, op. 2, spr. 75, TsDIAL.

21 'Consul Schwegel Discusses Clergy,' *Free Press Evening News Bulletin* (Winnipeg), 30 August 1910, clipping in f. 358, op. 2, spr. 73, TsDIAL.

22 Quoted in Langevin to Sabourin, 28 January 1911 (copy), f. 358, op. 2, spr. 69, TsDIAL.

23 Letter from Winnipeg, signed 'Sisters of the church,' to Sheptytsky, 15 October 1910, f. 358, op. 2, spr. 75a, TsDIAL. Nor were Ukrainians alone in the perception that French priests were being imposed on them. On

similar feelings among Hungarians in Kaposvar, Sask., see 'Consul Schwegel discusses clergy.'

24 Sabourin to Sheptytsky, 3 April 1911, f. 358, op. 1, spr. 248, TsDIAL.

25 'Sisters of the church' to Sheptytsky. Sabourin also wrote to Sheptytsky in October 1910 to thank him for his visit to Sifton; in this letter he also mentioned the boycott of his ministry and hinted that it might be linked to Ukrainian suspicions that he opposed Sheptytsky's visits to Ukrainian settlements. Sabourin assured Sheptytsky that such suspicions were unfounded; Sabourin to Sheptytsky (in St Albert, Alta), 23 October 1910, f. 358, op. 2, spr. 72, TsDIAL.

26 Sister Ambrose [Lypkevych] SSMI, Winnipeg, to Sheptytsky, 9 December 1912, f. 358, op. 2, spr. 75a, TsDIAL.

27 Delaere to Langevin, 21 August 1911, f. 358, op. 1, spr. 248, TsDIAL. Delaere further remarked that 'it would take only a few unscrupulous priests from Galicia to mobilize the people against the Latin bishops and those who have passed into the Ruthenian rite to completely destroy our work.' Ibid. As for priests from Galicia who came to Canada and accepted the jurisdiction of a French bishop, Delaere believed that they would be 'suspected of selling out their people.' He cited the example of the Basilians, who were highly regarded in Galicia but were not trusted in Canada precisely 'because they are under the jurisdiction of the Latin bishop.' Ibid.

28 Ibid. Ukrainian opponents of the Latin rite in Canada also appealed to the authority of Bishop Ortynsky in the United States when it suited them; Sabourin statement, f. 358, op.2, spr. 72, TsDIAL.

29 Sabourin statement, f. 358, op. 2, spr. 72, TsDIAL.

30 Delaere to Langevin, 21 August 1911, f. 358, op. 1, spr. 248, TsDIAL.

31 Ibid.

32 Sabourin statement, f. 358, op. 2, spr. 72, TsDIAL.

33 Sabourin to Sheptytsky, ibid.

34 Langevin to Nuncio Stagni, 28 July 1911 (copy), f. 358, op. 1, spr. 248, TsDIAL.

35 Delaere to Langevin, 21 August 1911 (copy), f. 358, op. 1, spr. 248, TsDIAL. Delaere recommended the Basilian protohegumen Platonid Filas for the position, indicating also that Sheptytsky agreed that Filas was the best man for the job. Ibid. In his letter to Nuncio Stagni, Langevin gave his support to the proposal of the Reverend Filas, as one who was 'very favourable towards the Latin priests who had transferred to the Ruthenian rite.' Langevin to Stagni, ibid. In fact it was not Filas but Nykyta Budka, the prefect of the theological seminary in Lviv, who was consecrated as the Greek Catholic bishop of Canada. See Stella Hryniuk, 'Pioneer Bishop, Pioneer Times: Nykyta Budka in Canada,' Canadian Catholic Historical Association, *Historical Studies* 54 (1988): 21–41.

36 Delaere to Langevin, 21 August 1911, f. 358, op. 1, spr. 248, TsDIAL.

37 Ibid.
38 Ibid. The Ukrainian-American newspaper *Svoboda* attacked those who accepted the authority of the Roman Catholic bishop as 'traitors to their nation.' Ibid.
39 'Sisters of the church' to Sheptytsky, f. 358, op. 2, spr. 75a, TsDIAL.
40 Sabourin to Sheptytsky, 27 April 1912, f. 358, op. 2, spr. 73, TsDIAL.
41 F. 201, op. 4v, spr. 1331, ark. 1–80, TsDIAL.
42 Delaere to Langevin, 21 August 1911, f. 358, op. 1, spr. 248, TsDIAL; and Delaere, 'L'Evêque Ruthène,' ms, nd (ca. January 1910), f. 358, op. 2, spr. 75, TsDIAL.
43 A. Delaere, 'L'Evêque Ruthène,' f. 358, op. 2, spr. 75, TsDIAL.
44 Of the fears of Latinization among Ukrainians, Delaere wrote that 'those fears are for the most part pretexts rather than real convictions; but they are cherished [as a means] to get a bishop of their own nationality.' Ibid.
45 Vasyl Ladyka to Sheptytsky, 4 November 1909, f. 358, op. 2, spr. 75, TsDIAL. Ladyka was consecrated as the Ukrainian Catholic bishop of Canada in 1929.
46 Petro Kamenetsky to Sheptytsky, 28 June 1913, ibid.
47 Joseph Poitras, 'Rapport de la réunion de quelques prêtres du rite Ruthène à l'Archevêché de Saint Boniface le 4 janvier, 1910,' St Boniface, 21 January 1910, copy in f. 358, op. 2, spr. 75, p. 94, TsDIAL.
48 Ibid., p. 96.
49 Ibid., p. 99.
50 Ibid., p. 89.
51 Ibid., pp. 87 and 90–2.
52 For missions visited by a priest, the monthly rate was to be twenty-five cents per family; for a parish where a priest resided, it was suggested that a somewhat higher fee be asked. Baptisms were free of charge, but if people volunteered a contribution, the suggested donation was one dollar. Ibid., pp. 90–2.
53 Ibid., p. 90.
54 Ibid., p. 93.
55 Ibid., p. 99.

McGowan: 'A Portion for the Vanquished'

1 Sheptytsky quoted in 'On Ruthenians,' 1 July 1920, Neil McNeil Papers, Extension File, Archives of the Roman Catholic Archdiocese of Toronto (hereafter cited as ARCAT).
2 Oscar Handlin, *The Uprooted* (New York: Grosset and Dunlap, 1951), 137–8.
3 The Reverend J. Schweitzer to O'Connor, 12 April 1907, Denis O'Connor Papers, ARCAT.

4 P.J. Kenedy, *American Catholic Directory* (New York: P.G. Kenedy and Sons, 1910–12).

5 In 1908 Archbishop Paul Bruchesi reported that he had three hundred Ukrainian families in the city and suburbs of Montreal. Bruchesi to Sbarretti, 31 July 1908, Apostolic Delegates' Correspondence, 184.6, Archivio Segreto Vaticano (hereafter cited as ASV).

6 Sbarretti to Gotti, 29 June 1905, Apostolic Delegates' Correspondence, 184.2, ASV. The letter reiterates the opposition of the French bishops to a Ukrainian bishop: one cannot have two bishops in one territory.

7 Roberto Perin, *Rome in Canada* (Toronto: University of Toronto Press, 1990), 168–71.

8 Raymond Huel, 'Gestae Dei Per Francos: The French Catholic Experience in Western Canada,' in Benjamin Smillie, ed., *Visions of the New Jerusalem: Religious Settlement on the Prairies* (Edmonton: NeWest Press, 1983), 39–54.

9 Stella Hryniuk, 'Pioneer Bishop, Pioneer Times: Nykyta Budka in Canada,' Canadian Catholic Historical Association, *Historical Studies* 54 (1988): 24–5. See also Perin, *Rome in Canada*, 173–4.

10 Perin, *Rome in Canada*, 179.

11 Jean, SE, 'Adelard Langevin, Archevêque de St Boniface, et les Ukrainiens,' SCHEC *Rapport* 12 (1944–5): 103.

12 Alfred E. Burke, 'Need of a Missionary College,' in Francis C. Kelley, ed., *The First American Catholic Missionary Congress* (Chicago: J.S. Hyland, 1909), 84. The precise number of Ukrainian Catholics in Canada in this period is subject to debate. Estimates by recent scholars tend to make Burke's figure of 150,000 appear exaggerated. See William Darcovich and Paul Yuzyk, eds., *A Statistical Compendium on the Ukrainians in Canada, 1891–1976* (Ottawa: University of Ottawa Press, 1980), 165–211.

13 Boels to McEvay, 13 October 1909, CCES Papers, ARCAT.

14 Zaporzan to Sbarretti, 27 May 1910, Apostolic Delegates' Correspondence, 184.32, ASV.

15 Memorandum of Leo Sembratowicz, 22 October 1909, CCES Papers, ARCAT.

16 Gerald Stortz, 'Thomas Joseph Dowling: The First "Canadian" Bishop of Hamilton, 1889–1924,' CCHA *Historical Studies* 54 (1987): 100; McEvay to Ortynsky, 25 January 1912, Fergus McEvay Papers, ARCAT.

17 For a general discussion of O'Connor's activities in Toronto see Mark G. McGowan, 'The Catholic "Restoration": Pius X, Denis O'Connor, and Popular Catholicism in Toronto, 1899–1908,' CCHA *Historical Studies* 54 (1987): 69–92.

18 *Register*, 16 September 1909.

19 Circular letter of Bishop Thomas Joseph Dowling, Hamilton, Feast of the Purification of the BVM, 1910, Apostolic Delegates' Correspondence, 184.22, ASV.

20 *Register*, 12 November 1908.

21 Copy of letter from McEvay to Archbishop Bégin of Québec, 27 September 1910, Charles Fitzpatrick Papers, vol. 12, p. 5816, National Archives of Canada, Ottawa (hereafter cited as NAC); Burke to the Duke of Norfolk, 9 April 1909, Fitzpatrick Papers, vol. 82, pp. 45453–4. For more detail see Mark G. McGowan, 'Religious Duties and Patriotic Endeavours: The Catholic Church Extension Society, French Canada and the Prairie West, 1908–1916,' CCHA *Historical Studies* 51 (1984): 107–20.

22 *Register*, 24 June 1915. See also 31 December 1908 and 16 September 1909. Fitzpatrick Papers, 13, McEvay to Bégin, 27 December 1910, p. 5816, NAC. George Daly, CSSR, *Catholic Problems in Western Canada* (Toronto: Macmillan, 1921), 85.

23 Langevin to Thomas Dauson, 24 October 1912; Langevin to Archbishop Bégin, 21 August 1908; Langevin to Arthur Beliveau, 20 September 1909; Report on 'The Canadian Catholic Church Extension Society,' 31 January 1913, Langevin Papers, AASB. Langevin made his feelings known directly to Fergus McEvay, objecting to the fact that the CCES had been founded to work in the West without his knowledge or approval. Langevin to McEvay, 16 January 1909, CCES Papers, ARCAT.

24 J.T. Roche to Burke, August 1909, Apostolic Delegates' Correspondence, 184.18, ASV. Himself an expert at playing clandestine games, Burke politely offered to withdraw all funds from St Boniface if Archbishop Langevin wanted nothing to do with the Extension Society. Burke to Langevin, 3 October 1909, Apostolic Delegates' Correspondence, 184.18, ASV.

25 Catholic Church Extension Society (Toronto), Minute Book, 1908–9; Bishop P.T. Ryan (Auxiliary-Pembroke) to McNeil, 26 February 1913, McNeil Papers, ARCAT.

26 Sembratowicz to Burke, 27 June 1909; 'Memorandum of Father Leo Sembratowicz,' 22 October 1909, CCES Papers, ARCAT.

27 Copy of letter from Achille Delaere to Bruchési, 7 June 1910, CCES Papers, ARCAT.

28 Burke to McEvay, 28 October 1909, CCES Papers, ARCAT.

29 Roche to Burke, 30 August [1909] and [August 1909], Apostolic Delegates' Correspondence, 184.18, ASV. Both priests were impressed by the absence of a daily breviary to recite and the loosened dress code on the prairies.

30 'Memorial to the First Plenary Council on the Ruthenian Catholics of Western Canada,' 1 October 1909, Ruthenian and Ukrainian Papers, ARCAT. *Register*, 24 October 1912.

31 The Annual Meeting of the Archbishops of Canada, 6 November 1911, Ruthenian and Ukrainian Papers, ARCAT.

32 Statistics vary from source to source. See 'Statement of Facts Submitted by Right Reverend Nicetas Budka,' 30 September 1919, Ruthenian and Ukrainian Papers, ARCAT; copy, 'Memorandum on the Status and

Improvement of the Ruthenian People in Canada,' Nicetas Budka, 31
January 1914, Fitzpatrick Papers, vol. 15, pp. 6716–18, NAC.

33 Paul Yuzyk, 'Religious Life,' in Manoly Lupul, ed., *A Heritage in Transition:
Essays in the History of Ukrainians in Canada* (Toronto: McClelland and
Stewart, 1982), 150. His powers are spelled out in *Les Cloches de Saint-
Boniface* 11 (October 1912).

34 Langevin to Josaphat Jean, 4 August 1913, ASB. In all fairness to Langevin,
Les Cloches de Saint-Boniface 11 (15 September 1912) included a short
note of welcome to Budka in addition to a short biography of the new
Uniate bishop.

35 Josaphat Jean to Langevin, 10 August 1913, ASB.

36 'Statement of Facts Submitted by Right Reverend Nicetas Budka for the
Information of Our Committee,' 30 September 1919, Ruthenian and
Ukrainian Papers, ARCAT.

37 'Record of Donations Sent to Dioceses from March 1, 1919 to March 1,
1928,' nd, McNeil Papers, Extension File, ARCAT.

38 Bulletin on the Ruthenian Situation, 1916, McNeil Papers, Extension File,
ARCAT.

39 *Register*, 6 April and 6 July 1916.

40 Ibid., 4 December 1919.

41 Ibid.

42 'Memorandum – Catholic Immigrants,' 22 December 1926, Ruthenian and
Ukrainian Papers, ARCAT; Ella Zinck, SOS, 'Church and Immigration:
The Sisters of Service, English Canada's First Missionary Congregation
of Sisters, 1920–1930,' CCHA *Study Sessions* 43 (1976): 23–38.

43 *Register*, 25 July 1918; *Kanadyiskyi rusyn*, 29 January 1919.

44 Secretary's Report, Minutes of the Annual Meeting, 1916, Holy Name
Society Papers, ARCAT.

45 For an example of this see John Zucchi, 'Church and Clergy and the
Religious Life of Toronto's Italian Immigrants, 1900–1940,' CCHA *Study
Sessions* 50 (1983): 545–64. Zucchi's comments on the Italians are equally
applicable to the Ukrainian Catholics of the city in terms of Holy Name.
Neither Italian nor Ukrainian branches survived.

46 *Register*, 4 March 1920.

47 Ibid., 19 March 1914.

48 Edward Jackman et al., *The People Cry – Send Us Priests: The First Seventy-
Five Years of St Augustine's Seminary of Toronto, 1913–1988* (Toronto: St
Augustine's Seminary Alumni Association, 1988), 41.

49 'One of Our Needs for the Church in Canada,' 2 January 1926, McNeil
Papers, ARCAT. See also CCES Papers, *Annual Reports of the Catholic
Church Extension Society of Canada, 1923–30*.

50 Stella Hryniuk, 'The Bishop Budka Controversy: A New Perspective,'
Canadian Slavonic Papers 23 (June 1981): 162.

51 J.S. Foran to John Tomich, 14 April 1919, Apostolic Delegates' Correspondence, 130.1, ASV.
52 Paul Yuzyk, *The Ukrainian Greek Orthodox Church of Canada* (Ottawa: University of Ottawa Press, 1981), 84.
53 Yuzyk, 'Religious Life,' 166.
54 Confidential Report, 1923, Ukrainian and Ruthenian Papers, ARCAT.
55 Yuzyk, 'Religious Life,' 156.
56 CCES, Minutes Book, 16 January 1923 and 25 April 1928; *Register*, 3 May 1928; Malone, Malone, and Montgomery, Solicitors, to McNeil, 3 January 1922, Extension Papers, ARCAT.
57 'Memorandum on the Western Provinces by Neil McNeil,' 13 January 1926, McNeil Papers, Reports File, ARCAT.
58 Report of the Canadian Catholic Conference, 20 July 1962, Ruthenian and Ukrainian Papers, ARCAT. This report cites 200,000 Ukrainian Catholic faithful. Paul Yuzyk's more conservative figure is about 160,000. See Yuzyk, 'Religious Life,' 157.
59 Yuzyk, 'Religious Life,' 157.
60 Joseph H. O'Neill, 'Archbishop McGuigan of Toronto and the Holy Name Society: Its Role as a Force against Canadian Communism,' CCHA *Historical Studies* 55 (1988): 65.
61 Jeanne Beck, 'Henry Somerville and Social Reform: His Contribution to Canadian Catholic Social Thought,' CCHA *Study Sessions* 42 (1975): 91–108.
62 Notes on Friendship House, nd, compiled for *The Catholic Worker*; Report on Activities, March 1 to May 1, 1934; de Hueck to McNeil, 1 July 1934, McNeil Papers, APo2.01, ARCAT.
63 After the death of McNeil in Toronto, de Hueck found it difficult to substantiate claims to diocesan administrator Francis Carroll that the late archbishop actually sanctioned her work for a hostel. Although her soup-kitchen and reading-room remained intact, she was not permitted to expand her operations. Archbishop McGuigan, McNeil's successor, never gave de Hueck approval for her mission. De Hueck to Carroll, 24 June, 17 September, 1 October, 16 October, and 2 March 1934, McNeil Papers, ARCAT; James Cardinal McGuigan Papers, McGuigan to Father Paul, 15 August 1936, and 'Report on Communist Activities – Saint Patrick's Parish, 4 November 1936'; Archives of the Archdiocese of Ottawa (AAO), Guillaume Forbes Papers, Friendship House, L6/18/10, de Hueck to Forbes, 20 July 1936; L151/136, de Hueck to Forbes, 21 July 1936; L151/164, de Hueck to Forbes, 26 October 1936. Perhaps the best sources on de Hueck's work are Shane Carmody, 'Catherine de Hueck and Catholic Action in Toronto, 1930–1936' (unpublished master's paper, Department of History, University of Toronto, 1985) and Jeanne R. Beck, 'Contrasting Approaches to Social Action: Henry Somerville, the Educator, and

Catherine de Hueck, the Activist' (unpublished paper, CATO-150 – the
Catholic Archdiocese of Toronto over 150 Years Historical Conference,
June 1990).
64 Carmody, 'Catherine de Hueck and Catholic Action in Toronto,' 28–31.
65 The Reverend M. Olenchuk to McNeil, 10 May 1934; Mr Windron, Dominion Bank to McNeil, 27 May and 22 July 1929, Oriental Churches, vol.
   20, ARCAT.
66 Ladyka to Carroll, 24 January 1934, Oriental Churches, vol. 20, ARCAT.
67 Carroll to Ladyka, 2 February 1935, Oriental Churches, vol. 20, ARCAT.
68 Toronto Telegram, 12 February 1935; Toronto Star, 13 February 1935.
69 Toronto Star, 13 February 1935.
70 Ibid.

Swyripa: Wedded to the Cause

The themes and arguments raised in this paper are developed more fully
in my doctoral dissertation, 'From Princess Olha to Baba: Images, Roles
and Myths in the History of Ukrainian Women in Canada' (University of
Alberta, 1988).
1 Beth Light and Veronica Strong-Boag, *True Daughters of the North: Canadian Women's History, An Annotated Bibliography* (Toronto: Ontario
   Institute of Studies in Education, 1980), 1–8; Ruth Pierson, 'Women's
   History: The State of the Art in Atlantic Canada,' *Acadensis* 7 (Autumn
   1977): 121–31; Margrit Eichler, 'Sociology of Feminist Research in Canada,' *Signs* 3 (Winter 1977): 409–22; Alison Prentice, 'Writing Women
   into History: The History of Women's Work in Canada,' *Atlantis* 3 (Spring
   1978): 72–83; *Canadian Woman Studies* 3 (1981), on woman as nation
   builder, especially the editorial by Beth Light; Alison Prentice and Ruth
   Pierson, 'Feminism and the Writing and Teaching of History,' *Atlantis* 7
   (Spring 1982): 37–46; and Eliane Silverman, 'Writing Canadian Women's
   History, 1970–1982: An Historiographical Analysis,' *Canadian Historical
   Review* 63 (December 1982): 513–33.
2 Nancy M. Sheehan, '"Women Helping Women": The WCTU and the
   Foreign Population in the West, 1905–1930,' *International Journal of Wom-
   en's Studies* 6 (November–December 1983): 395–411, is a good example of
   the subordination of ethnics (male and female) to mainstream concerns.
   Eliane Leslau Silverman's *The Last Best West: Women on the Alberta Frontier,
   1880–1930* (Montreal and London: Eden Press, 1984) both downplays
   differences among women and makes the mistake of generalizing from
   the middle-class Anglo-Canadian experience. To treat the Industrial
   Revolution and myth of the Victorian lady as common immigrant baggage leaves no room for Ukrainian peasants with serfdom in their
   background.
3 For example, Light and Strong-Boag, *True Daughters of the North*, were

careful to balance region, period, and English-French dualism but made no provision for women of other national origins, and the few items relating to ethnic women stressed 'mainstream' topics. The decision to include an article on the Ursulines in Quebec and not works like *To Serve Is to Love* (Toronto: Sisters Servants of Mary Immaculate, 1971), a history of the Ukrainian Sisters Servants of Mary Immaculate in Canada, also implies that the activities of French nuns eclipse in value those of their ethnic sisters.

4 Gerda Lerner's seminal articles were republished as *The Majority Finds Its Past: Placing Women in History* (New York: Oxford University Press, 1979).

5 Pierson, 'Women's History,' 123. For improving women's position in society as the goal of Canadian women's history, see Prentice and Pierson, 'Feminism and the Writing and Teaching of History,' 37–46; Light and Strong-Boag, *True Daughters of the North*, 6; Silverman, 'Writing Canadian Women's History,' 513–33; and Margaret Andrews, 'Review Article: Attitudes in Canadian Women's History, 1945–1975,' *Journal of Canadian Studies* 12 (Summer 1977): 69–78.

6 Andrews, 'Attitudes in Canadian Women's History,' 69.

7 In her 'Henri Bourassa and the Woman Question,' *Journal of Canadian Studies* 10 (November 1975): 3–11, and 'Les femmes dans l'oeuvre de Groulx,' *Revue d'histoire de l'Amerique française* 32 (December 1978): 385–98, Susan Mann Trofimenkoff began with the oppression and moulding of women to ensure a certain type of society and not with the needs of the French-Canadian nation, perceived or actual. Groulx's image of women was an essential component of his nationalism, for example, not vice versa.

8 Criticism of the negative impression created by illiterate and 'uncivilized' Ukrainian peasants, too fond of the tavern and poolroom, appeared frequently in the pioneer Ukrainian-Canadian press. See, for example, *Kanadiiskyi farmer*, 7 February 1908, 29 December 1909, 17 May 1912, 16 July 1913, 26 February 1916; *Kanadyiskyi rusyn*, 3 June 1911, 9 December 1911, 23 June 1915, 16 August 1916; and *Ukrainskyi holos*, 12 and 26 October 1910, 16 August 1916, 4 September 1918.

9 Prentice, 'Writing Women into History,' 78.

10 The historian William L. Morton used the phrase to explain why Ukrainian Canadians campaigned so vigorously for the idea of Canada as a mosaic; see 'The Historical Phenomenon of Minorities: The Canadian Experience' (mimeographed paper presented to the Fourteenth International Congress of Historical Sciences, San Francisco, 22–29 August 1975), 20.

11 See, for example, Leonid Biletsky, *Ukrainski pionery, 1891–1951* (Winnipeg: Komitet ukraintsiv Kanady, 1951); Paul Yuzyk, *The Ukrainians in Manitoba: A Social History* (Toronto: University of Toronto Press, 1953); Iuliian

Stechyshyn, *Istoriia poselennia ukraintsiv u Kanadi* (Edmonton: Ukrainian Self-Reliance League, 1975); Michael H. Marunchak, *The Ukrainian Canadians: A History*, 2d ed. (Winnipeg: Ukrainian Free Academy of Sciences, 1982); and Jaroslav Petryshyn, *Peasants in the Promised Land: Canada and the Ukrainians, 1891–1914* (Toronto: James Lorimer, 1985).

12 See, for example, Marjorie Harrison, *Go West! Go Wise! A Canadian Revelation* (London: Edward Arnold, 1930), 80–1.

13 Stechyshyn, *Istoriia poselennia ukraintsiv u Kanadi*, 217.

14 Helen Potrebenko, *No Streets of Gold: A Social History of Ukrainians in Alberta* (Vancouver: New Star Books, 1977), 46. See also Vera Lysenko, *Men in Sheepskin Coats: A Study in Assimilation* (Toronto: Ryerson Press, 1947), 241–2; and Myrna Kostash, *All of Baba's Children* (Edmonton: Hurtig, 1977), 71.

15 On Grescoe, see Lysenko, *Men in Sheepskin Coats*, 272; Yuzyk, *Ukrainians in Manitoba*, 106–7; Marunchak, *The Ukrainian Canadians*, 456; and for community press commentary, *Opinion*, November 1947. For the treatment of Ukrainian-Canadian women in economics, politics, and the arts in the major surveys, see Yuzyk, *Ukrainians in Manitoba*, 52–7, 140–1, 166–9, 201, 204; Marunchak, *The Ukrainian Canadians*, 120, 529, 669–74, 690–8, 705, 709–10, 756–9, 772–87, 803–4, 859–67; Ol'ha Woycenko, *Ukrainians in Canada*, 2d ed. rev. (Winnipeg and Ottawa: Canada Ethnic Press Federation, 1968), 33–4, 42, 52, 95–6, 155–6, 177–9; Biletsky, *Ukrainski pionery v Kanadi*, 65–8, 75–94; and Semen Kovbel, comp., and Dmytro Doroshenko, ed., *Propamiatna knyha Ukrainskoho narodnoho domu u Vynypegu* (Winnipeg: Ukrainskyi narodnyi dim, 1949), 605–27.

16 Woycenko, *Ukrainians in Canada*, 155–6.

17 For the treatment of Ukrainian-Canadian women in organizational and community life, see Yuzyk, *Ukrainians in Manitoba*, 82–8, 104, 118, 122, 204; Woycenko, *Ukrainians in Canada*, 97, 190, 192, 210; and Marunchak, *The Ukrainian Canadians*, 104, 134–6, 151–3, 164, 167, 188, 194–207, 218, 255–6, 333, 376, 381, 390–2, 411–17, 443–5, 462–3, 481–2, 487–90, 496, 500–1, 513, 524, 529, 532, 539, 546, 564, 601–2, 641, 662–79, 693–9, 761–71, 805–24.

18 Continuing language loss has sometimes been buried under the triumphs of Ukrainian-language studies at Canadian universities and publicly funded bilingual education programmes since the Second World War; Marunchak, *The Ukrainian Canadians*, 625–31, 717–21, 742–55, 868–71.

19 In the major standard histories, see: Yuzyk, *Ukrainians in Manitoba*, 45–6, 84, 122, 151, 160–2, 170–3; Woycenko, *Ukrainians in Canada*, 23, 27–34, 177; and Marunchak, *The Ukrainian Canadians*, 95, 458.

20 E. Sitnyk, 'Zavdannia ukrainskoho zhinotstva v Kanadi v systemi diialnosty KUK,' in Komitet ukraintsiv Kanady, *Tretii vse-kanadiiskyi kongres ukraintsiv Kanady* (Winnipeg: Komitet ukraintsiv Kanady, [1950]), 86–90.

21 Nataliia L. Kohuska, *Pivstolittia na hromadskii nyvi: Narys istorii Soiuzu*

ukrainok Kanady (Edmonton and Winnipeg: Soiuz ukrainok Kanady, 1986), 655–6.

22 In addition to the Communist press, particularly the inter-war journals *Holos robitnytsi* and *Robitnytsia,* see Petro Kravchuk, comp., *Zhinochi doli* (Toronto: Kobzar, 1973); and Petro Prokopchak, ed., *Almanakh: Piatdesia-tyrichchia zhinochykh viddiliv Tovarystva obiednanykh ukrainskykh kanadtsiv, 1922–1977* (Toronto: Kobzar, 1976).

23 The UWAC maintained a women's page in *Ukrainskyi holos* until it began publishing its own magazine, *Promin,* in 1960. There are several organizational histories, including Soiuz ukrainok Kanady, *Iuvileina knyzhka Soiuzu ukrainok Kanady z nahody 10-litnoho isnovannia, 1926–1936* (np: Soiuz ukrainok Kanady, 1937); Natalka L. Kohuska, *Chvert stolittia na hromadskii nyvi, 1926–1951: Istoriia Soiuzu ukrainok Kanady* (Winnipeg: Soiuz ukrainok Kanady, 1952); Kohuska, *Pivstolittia na hromadskii nyvi*; and Saveliia Stechyshyn, *Pivstorichchia (1923–1973) Zhinochoho tovarystva im. Olhy Kobylianskoi v Saskatuni, Saskachevan, pershoho viddilu Soiuzu ukrainok Kanady* (Saskatoon: Zhinoche tovarystvo im. Olhy Kobylianskoi, 1975).

24 Eparchial histories of the UCWL include Iryna Pavlykovska, ed., *Dlia Boha, tserkvy i narodu: Liga ukrainskykh katolytskykh zhinok edmontonskoi ieparkhii v 1944–1964 rokakh, pochatky i diialnist* (Edmonton: Ieparkhiialna uprava LUKZh v Edmontoni, [1966]); Vira Buchynska, ed., *Slidamy diiakonis: 25 rokiv pratsi Ligy ukrainskykh katolytskykh zhinok Kanady u Manitobi* (Winnipeg: Arkhyeparkhiialna uprava LUKZh, 1973); and Iaroslava Vynnytska, ed., *Nacherk istorii Ligy ukrainskykh katolytskykh zhinok Kanady torontskoi eparkhii, 1945–1975* (Toronto: Torontska eparkhiialna uprava LUKZh, 1975). The UCWL launched its own magazine, *Nasha doroha,* in 1970.

25 *Zhinochyi svit* has served as the official organ of the UWOC since 1950; before that, it maintained a page in *Novyi shliakh,* the mouthpiece of the male Ukrainian National Federation. Iryna Knysh, ed., *Na sluzhbi ridnoho narodu: Iuvileinyi zbirnyk Orhanizatsii ukrainok Kanady im. Olhy Basarab u 25-richchia vid zaisnuvannia, 1930–1955* (Winnipeg: Orhanizatsiia ukrainok Kanady im. Olhy Basarab, 1955), and a second volume published to mark the UWOC's golden anniversary (Toronto: Orhanizatsiia ukrainok Kanady im. Olhy Basarab, 1984), are the best historical sources.

26 *Robitnytsia,* 1 September 1926, 15 February 1928, 15 March–1 April 1929, 1 June 1931, 1 July 1931, 15 January 1936.

27 Knysh, *Na sluzhbi ridnoho narodu,* 68, 213, 288, 383; Kohuska, *Pivstolittia na hromadskii nyvi,* 803, 823, 828, 839, 852, 864, 949; and Olha Boichuk, comp., *Zolotyi vinets pivstolittia ukrainok Kanady u Kanori, Saskachevan, 1926–1976* (Canora: Viddil Soiuzu ukrainok Kanady im. Marii Markovych u Kanori, 1981), 198.

28 See, for example, 'Liga ukrainskykh katolytskykh zhinok/Ukrainian Cath-

olic Women's League,' in *Iuvileina knyha ukraintsiv katolykiv Saskachevanu, 1905–1955* (Saskatoon: Ukrainian Catholic Council of Saskatchewan, 1955), 63–79.

29 See the comments of Stephanie Sawchuk (UWOC) in Ukrainian Canadian Committee, *First All-Canadian Congress of Ukrainians in Canada* (Winnipeg: Ukrainian Canadian Committee, 1943), 79. Delegates from women's organizations participated in the founding congress through the male organizations represented in the superstructure.

30 *Robitnytsia*, 1 March 1937, August 1937; Soiuz ukrainok Kanady, *Iuvileina knyzhka*, 89–93; and *Novyi shliakh*, 6 July 1937.

31 William Darcovich and Paul Yuzyk, eds., *A Statistical Compendium on the Ukrainians in Canada, 1891–1976* (Ottawa: University of Ottawa Press, 1980), series 20.63–80, pp. 41–4; and *Robitnytsia*, August 1937.

32 Pavlykovska, *Dlia Boha, tserkvy i narodu*, 77; and E. Iankivska, comp., *Liga ukrainskykh katolytskykh zhinok Kanady: Vira – nadiia – liubov* (Toronto: Kraieva uprava LUKZh, 1985), 193, 272, 280, 288.

33 Oleh Romanyshyn, 'The Canadian League for the Liberation of Ukraine and Its Women's Association,' in Lubomyr Y. Luciuk and Iroida L. Wynnyckyj, eds., *Ukrainians in Ontario*, special issue, *Polyphony: Bulletin of the Multicultural History Society of Ontario* 10 (1988): 164.

34 Prokopchak, *Almanakh*, 52–109.

35 For branch activities between 1956 and 1980, see *Na sluzhbi ridnoho narodu*, II: 110–417. In February 1985, *Zhinochyi svit* reported sixteen branches with approximately five hundred members in Ontario, but did not identify them by location.

36 From the recent UCWL press alone, see *Nasha doroha*, January–March 1978, October–December 1984, January–March 1987. Traditional responses have been the establishment of junior and English-speaking branches, cooking and embroidery classes to attract new members, and courses to improve Ukrainian-language skills.

37 See, for example, *Novyi shliakh*, 17 May 1932, 11 December 1934, 19 and 26 February 1935, 10 November 1936, 28 December 1937, 17 April 1941, 10 November 1945; N. Kohuska, 'Woman's Part in the Life of a Nation,' in Ukrainian Canadian Committee, *First All-Canadian Congress of Ukrainians in Canada*, 156–60; Kohuska, *Pivstolittia na hromadskii nyvi*, 605; and *Nasha doroha*, January–February 1973, July–September 1977.

38 *Ukrainskyi holos*, 5 December 1928, 12 June 1929, 27 November 1929, 3 May 1933.

39 Stephanie Sawchuk, 'Our Women in Ukrainian and Canadian Life,' in Ukrainian Canadian Committee, *First All-Canadian Congress of Ukrainians in Canada*, 162; and *Novyi shliakh*, 17 May 1932, 5 June 1934, 11 December 1934, 19 and 26 February 1935, 10 November 1936, 23 March 1937, 12 October 1937, 28 December 1937, 17 April 1941, 10 November 1945.

40 Savella Stechishin, quoted in Kohuska, *Pivstolittia na hromadskii nyvi*, 605.

41 On the role of women and the home in raising Ukrainian youth in Canada, see *Ukrainskyi holos*, 22 December 1915, 16 February 1916, 8 March 1916; and *Kanadyiskyi rusyn*, 26 August 1911, 5 September 1914, 7 and 14 October 1914, 7 April 1915, 4 September 1918.

42 Possibly the best statement on motherhood, both as a manual for the masses and as an example of organizational thinking, is the UWAC booklet *Na storozhi kultury* (Winnipeg: Soiuz ukrainok Kanady, 1947), intended as an inspirational and practical guide 'to help the home raise youth as worthy citizens of Canada and true children of the Ukrainian people' (3).

43 See, for example, *Ukrainskyi holos*, 16 July 1919 (reprinted in *Kanadiiskyi ukrainets*, 10 July 1929).

44 See the many UWAC branch histories in Kohuska, *Pivstolittia na hromadskii nyvi*; their authors nevertheless point out that state schools would not provide the Ukrainian atmosphere necessary to create a politicized national consciousness.

45 See, for example, *Nasha doroha*, April–June 1983 and October–December 1984; and *Promin*, December 1961. This sense of organized women's centrality to community growth and progress exists in Communist circles as well; *Ukrainian Canadian*, 1 April 1957 and 15 May 1962.

46 The 'Second Wreath,' a loose group of Ukrainian-Canadian women interested in the issues of ethnicity and feminism, has sponsored two conferences, the first in Edmonton in 1985 to mark the hundredth anniversary of the Ukrainian women's movement, the second in Toronto in 1988.

47 *Nasha doroha*, October-December 1984.

48 Ukrainian Community Development Committee, Prairie Region, *Building the Future: Ukrainian Canadians in the 21st Century, A Blueprint for Action* (Edmonton: Ukrainian Community Development Committee, Prairie Region, 1986), 14–15, 33–4. See also Sonia Maryn, 'Ukrainian-Canadian Women in Transition: From Church Basement to Board Room,' *Journal of Ukrainian Studies* 10 (Summer 1985): 89–96.

Isajiw: The Changing Community

1 Alex Simirenko, *Pilgrims, Colonists, and Frontiersmen: An Ethnic Community in Transition* (New York: Free Press of Glencoe, 1964); Vladimir C. Nahirny and J.A. Fishman, 'Ukrainian Language Maintenance Efforts in the United States,' in J.A. Fishman et al, eds., *Language Loyalty in the United States* (The Hague: Mouton, 1966), 318–57; C.W. Hobart et al., *Persistence and Change: A Study of Ukrainians in Alberta* (Toronto: Ukrainian Canadian Research Foundation, 1978); Renata M. Sharan-Olearchyk, *Types of Ethnic Identification and Generational Position: A Study of the Ukrainian Immigrant Group in the U.S.A.* (London: Association of Ukrainians in Great Britain, 1971); Roma Chumak-Horbatsch, 'Language in the

Ukrainian Home: Its Use in Ten Toronto Families Attempting to Preserve
Their Mother Tongue' (PhD dissertation, Ontario Institute for Studies
in Education, 1984).

2 Vsevolod Isaiv, 'Druhe pokolinnia imigrantiv v amerykanskii diisnosti,'
Suchasnist, September 1964, 102–10; 'Vplyv dovkillia na ukrainsku
molod na emigratsii,' *Plastovyi shliakh,* July 1967, 8–17; 'Vykhovni napri-
amky i podviine dovkillia,' *Suchasnist,* November 1972, 111–17.

3 Nadia H. Skop, 'Ethnic Singlehood as a Sociological Phenomenon' (PhD
dissertation, University of Toronto, 1988).

4 Wsevolod W. Isajiw, 'Ethnic Identity Retention,' in R. Breton et al., *Ethnic
Identity and Equality: Varieties of Experience in a Canadian City* (Toronto:
University of Toronto Press, 1990), 45–9.

5 Alexander I. Roman, 'Ethnic Identity among the Ukrainian Canadians:
An Assessment of Generational Change' (PhD dissertation, York University, 1988).

6 Peter C. Pineo, 'The Social Standing of Ethnic and Racial Groupings,'
Canadian Review of Sociology and Anthropology 14 (May 1977): 147–57.

7 Norbert J. Hartmann and Wsevolod W. Isajiw, 'Ethnicity and Occupation:
An Assessment of the Occupational Structure of Ukrainian Canadians
in the 1960s,' *Canadian Ethnic Studies* 12 (1980): 55–73.

8 Wsevolod W. Isajiw and Norbert J. Hartmann, 'Changes in the Occupational Structure of Ukrainians in Canada: A Methodology for the Study
of Changes in Ethnic Status,' in W.E. Mann, ed., *Social and Cultural Change
in Canada* (Vancouver: Copp Clark Publishing Co., 1970) I: 96–112.

9 Norbert J. Wiley, 'The Ethnic Mobility Trap and Stratification Theory,'
Social Problems 15 (1967): 147–59; John Porter, *The Vertical Mosaic: An
Analysis of Social Class and Power in Canada* (Toronto: University of Toronto
Press, 1965), 60–103.

10 Breton et al., *Ethnic Identity and Equality,* particularly 45–9.

11 Ibid., 87.

12 Wsevolod W. Isajiw and Leo Driedger, 'Ethnic Identity: Resource or
Drawback for Social Mobility?' (Paper delivered at the Eighty-second
Annual Meeting of the American Sociological Association, Chicago, Ill.,
18 August 1987), 1–31.

13 The estimate is based on information supplied in 1990 by the Ukrainian
Immigrant Aid Society in Toronto.

Part 3

Avery: Divided Loyalties

1 Reference to the Ukrainian Left in this paper will mean the pro-Communist Left and not the Ukrainian social democrats.

2 Between 1910 and 1930 all three groups were influenced by a range of

socialist organizations and newspapers. For example, before the Great War Finnish-American newspapers such as *Tyomies* (Worker), *Raivannja* (Pioneer), and *Toveri* (Comrade) helped Canadian Finns adjust to North American mores and at the same time advanced socialist principles. Although *Aika* (Time), a utopian socialist newspaper founded in British Columbia in 1901, and *Tyokansa* (Working People), established by Port Arthur Finns in 1907, lacked the resources of their American counterparts, they, too, launched an active socialist educational campaign.

3 Bruno Ramirez, *On the Move: French-Canadian and Italian Migrants in the North Atlantic Economy* (Toronto: McClelland and Stewart, 1990); Donald Avery, *'Dangerous Foreigners': European Immigrant Workers and Labour Radicalism in Canada, 1896–1932* (Toronto: McClelland and Stewart, 1979), 1–60.

4 Between 1900 and 1982 about 549 Ukrainian publications were produced in Canada, mainly in Winnipeg (205), Toronto (157), and Edmonton (60). Before 1914 most of the newspapers were weeklies located in western Canada. Some of the more important were commercial publications such as the *Kanadiiskyi farmer* (Canadian Farmer), the Catholic *Kanadyiskyi rusyn* (Canadian Ruthenian), and the nationalist *Ukrainskyi holos* (Ukrainian Voice). Although socialists accounted for only about 5–10 per cent of the Ukrainian population of the country before 1939, they carried on a wide range of cultural and political activities and published a variety of influential newspapers. Before 1918 the list included *Chervonyi prapor* (Red Flag) and *Robochyi narod* (Working People) in Winnipeg, *Nova hromada* (New Society) in Edmonton, and *Robitnyche slovo* (Workers' Word) in Toronto. Yuri Daschko, 'The Ukrainian Press in Canada,' in Manoly R. Lupul, ed., *A Heritage in Transition: Essays in the History of Ukrainians in Canada* (Toronto: McClelland and Stewart, 1982), 263–80.

5 Bruno Ramirez and I have presented this argument in a forthcoming joint article entitled 'European Immigrant Workers in Canada and the Transfer of Plebeian Culture.' In showing the range of ethnic responses to class issues Ramirez makes particular reference to the adjustment of Canadian Italians. He also demonstrates that the appeal of ethnic, not class solutions, was strongly influenced by external events such as the First World War and the advent of fascism in Italy. See also his article 'Ethnicity on Trial: The Italians of Montreal and the Second World War,' in Norman Hillmer, Bohdan Kordan, and Lubomyr Luciuk, eds., *On Guard for Thee: War, Ethnicity, and the Canadian State, 1939–1945* (Ottawa: Canadian Committee for the History of the Second World War, 1988).

6 In Galicia and Bukovyna there had been reading clubs or Prosvita societies, as well as various populist and socialist political organizations. Ol'ha Woycenko, 'Community Organizations,' in Lupul, *A Heritage in Transition*, 173; Orest T. Martynowych and Nadia Kazymyra, 'Political Activity in Western Canada, 1896–1923,' ibid., 85–107.

7 After 1910 the moderate socialists, such as Myroslaw Stechishin and Paul Crath (Pavlo Krat), who had founded the Winnipeg-based Ukrainian labour movement, were replaced by 'younger, more radical men.' Martynowych and Kazymyra, 'Political Activity,' in Lupul, *A Heritage in Transition*, 97.

8 Avery, *'Dangerous Foreigners,'* 1–60. The links between nationalism and socialism were equally visible elsewhere. Finnish social democrats, for example, appealed just as strongly to their countrymen's ethnic consciousness and nationalist aspirations. Arja Pilli, *The Finnish-language Press in Canada 1901–1939: A Study in the History of Ethnic Journalism* (Turku, 1982); Mauri Jalava, 'The Finnish-Canadian Cooperative Movement in Ontario,' ibid., 93–100; Douglas Ollila, Jr., 'From Socialism to Industrial Unionism (I.W.W.): Social Factors in the Emergence of Left-Labor Radicalism among Finnish Workers of the Mesabi, 1911–1919,' in Michael Karni et al, eds., *Finnish Experience in the Western Great Lakes Region: New Perspectives* (St Paul: University of Minnesota Press, 1975), 170.

9 Nor were Anglo-Canadian workers impervious to this wartime hysteria, and Canadian unions often demanded that enemy aliens be fired and interned. In the Rocky Mountain mining districts, for example, this nativist sentiment seriously weakened the working-class solidarity that the UMWA had achieved before the war. Moreover, throughout the war Anglo-Canadian newspapers and patriotic groups argued that enemy aliens were profiting from wartime prosperity while 600,000 Canadians were fighting overseas. Andrij Makuch, 'Ukrainian Canadians and the Wartime Economy,' in Frances Swyripa and John Herd Thompson, eds., *Loyalties in Conflict: Ukrainians in Canada during the Great War* (Edmonton: Canadian Institute of Ukrainian Studies, 1983), 69–77.

10 See Lubomyr Luciuk, *A Time for Atonement: Canada's First National Internment Operations and the Ukrainian Canadians, 1914–1920* (Kingston: Limestone Press, 1988); Peter Melnycky, 'The Internment of Ukrainians in Canada,' in Swyripa and Thompson, *Loyalties in Conflict*, 1–24; and Lubomyr Luciuk and Bohdan Kordan, 'And who says time heals all?' *Globe and Mail*, 28 October 1988. Although the Ukrainian Canadian Congress is lobbying to secure acknowledgment from the federal government that the internments were 'unwarranted and unjust' and is seeking symbolic redress, there has been criticism of this position from within the Ukrainian-Canadian community. See Orest Martynowych, 'Re: internment of Ukrainian Canadians,' *Ukrainian Weekly*, 9 April 1989, and the replies by E.E. Forbes Mitchell, 'About excuses for internment,' and J.B. Gregorovich, 'Internment was unjustified act,' *Ukrainian Weekly*, 28 May 1989.

11 'Secret Memorandum for Foreign Newspaper Publishers,' 11 February 1916, Chief Press Censor Papers, vol. 157, 195-2, National Archives of Canada, Ottawa (hereafter cited as NAC). Not surprisingly, Chief Press

Censor Colonel Ernest Chambers and his associates were drawn from the ranks of the major English-language dailies.

12 Ibid.; Avery, *'Dangerous Foreigners,'* 40–90.

13 Avery, *'Dangerous Foreigners,'* 70–115; A. Ross McCormack, *Reformers, Rebels, and Revolutionaries: The Western Canadian Radical Movement 1899–1919* (Toronto: University of Toronto Press, 1977), 90–160; Gregory Kealey, '1919: The Canadian Labour Revolt,' *Labour/Le Travailleur* 13 (Spring 1984): 11–44.

14 Inspector E.J. Camies to J.O. Wilson, Supt. K Division, 7 April 1906, file 790, Royal Canadian Mounted Police Records, NAC. See also the annual reports by Commissioner A. Bowen Perry in the Sessional Papers for 1904, 1910, 1912, and 1914.

15 *Manitoba Free Press*, 5 March 1914; Murray Donnelly, *Dafoe of the Free Press* (Toronto: Macmillan of Canada, 1968), 57, 71; James S. Woodsworth, *Strangers within Our Gates* (Toronto: F.C. Stephenson, 1909); Charles W. Gordon, *The Foreigner: A Tale of Saskatchewan* (Toronto: Westminster Co., 1909).

16 What is often overlooked is that on 6 August Budka issued a second pastoral letter 'renouncing his previous statement and urging support for the Canadian war effort.' Paul Yuzyk, 'Religious Life,' in Lupul, *A Heritage in Transition*, 153.

17 *Edmonton Bulletin*, 22–28 September, 6 October 1914; *Vegreville Observer*, 23 September 1914. According to Frances Swyripa, Russophile organs such as the *Russkii holos* in Edmonton hoped that the war would make it possible 'to unite Hapsburg Ukrainian territories with the Russian empire ... [and] exploited the opportunity provided by the war to expose the traditional anti-Russian bias of most Austrian Ukrainians and to label them a danger to Canada.' Frances Swyripa, 'The Ukrainian Image: Loyal Citizen or Disloyal Alien,' in Swyripa and Thompson, *Loyalties in Conflict*, 47–68.

18 In March 1916, charges were made in the Manitoba legislature that Bishop Budka of the Uniate church was an Austrian spy. Significantly, Dominion military authorities supported these allegations, claiming that Budka had received guarantees for an independent Ukrainian state from the Austrian consul in St Paul, Minn. Donald Avery, 'Canadian Immigration Policy and the Alien Question in Canada, 1896–1919: The Anglo-Canadian Perspective' (PhD dissertation, University of Western Ontario, 1973), 400–5. For a different explanation of Budka's loyalty to Canada, see Stella Hryniuk, 'The Budka Controversy: A New Perspective,' *Canadian Slavonic Papers* 23 (June 1981): 154–65.

19 Donald Avery, 'Ethnic and Class Tension in Canada, 1918–1920,' in Swyripa and Thompson, *Loyalties in Conflict*, 79–98; D. Mitchell, *1919: Red Mirage* (New York: Macmillan, 1970).

20 That did not mean that Canadian security authorities had been prepared to countenance criticism of their Russian ally by Ukrainian nationalist

organizations such as the Society for an Independent Ukraine (founded in July 1914). Indeed, between 1914 and 1917 the chief press censor on numerous occasions warned the *Kanadyiskyi rusyn* and the *Ukrainskyi holos* about offensive editorials. Even influential nationalist organizations, such as the Ukrainian Canadian Citizen's Committee and the Ukrainian National Council (both formed in 1917), had to observe the censorship guidelines. Melnycky, 'Internment of Ukrainians,' in Swyripa and Thompson, *Loyalties in Conflict*, 1–24; Swyripa, 'The Ukrainian Image,' ibid., 47–68.

21 J. Swettenham, *Allied Intervention in Russia, 1918–1919, and the Part Played by Canada* (London: Allen and Unwin, 1967).

22 Before 1914 one of the major divisions was ideological: socialists versus non-socialists. But in addition, there were bitter feelings between the Ukrainian Greek Catholic church and its various rivals: the Russian Orthodox church, the Ukrainian Orthodox church, and the Independent Greek church, which was secretly subsidized by the Presbyterian church of Canada. In 1919 an even more formidable opponent appeared with the formation of the Ukrainian Greek Orthodox church. Included in its ranks were many of the leading members of the Ukrainian lay elite in western Canada, men such as Wasyl Swystun, Jaroslav Arsenych, and Myroslaw Stechishin. Woycenko, 'Community Organizations,' in Lupul, *A Heritage in Transition*, 180–1. According to one historian, the formation of the Ukrainian Greek Orthodox church 'became a watershed in the history of Ukrainian Canadians, causing a deep ferment in most communities, bitter controversies over church rituals and calendar changes, and a religious tension that occasionally exploded into violence.' Yuzyk, 'Religious Life,' in Lupul, *A Heritage in Transition*, 156.

23 During these years neither Canadian newspapers nor politicians showed much awareness of, or concern for, the Ukrainian National Republic and the Western Ukrainian National Republic. Moreover, despite concerted lobbying from the Ukrainian Canadian Citizens' Committee and the Ukrainian National Council, the Borden government made little effort to convince British authorities to advance the cause of an independent Ukraine. Nadia Kazymyra, 'Ukrainian Canadian Response to the Paris Peace Conference, 1919,' in Swyripa and Thompson, *Loyalties in Conflict*, 125–41; Oleh Gerus, 'Ukrainian Diplomatic Representation in Canada, 1920–3,' ibid., 143–57.

24 Nestor Makuch, 'The Influence of the Ukrainian Revolution on Ukrainians in Canada, 1917–22,' *Journal of Ukrainian Graduate Studies* 4 (Spring 1979): 44, 49.

25 Budka's troubles, however, were not entirely over: in February 1919 he was also the subject of an inquiry by Canadian veterans' organizations. Donald Avery, 'The Radical Alien and the Winnipeg General Strike of 1919,' in Carl Berger and Ramsay Cook, eds., *The West and the Nation:*

Essays in Honour of W.L. Morton (Toronto: McClelland and Stewart, 1976), 209–31.

26 Most of the 'foreigners' arrested during the riots in Winnipeg on 21 June were sent to the internment camp at Kapuskasing for 'safe keeping.' By the fall of 1919 approximately two hundred 'anarchists and revolutionaries' were scheduled for deportation. Avery, *'Dangerous Foreigners,'* 86–8.

27 In the competition between the three main radical organizations in the country, the Communist Party of Canada (CPC) was most successful in recruiting foreign workers. There are several reasons for its succcess. Whereas the OBU and IWW were determinedly North American, the CPC had a strong European orientation. It was easier for foreign radicals to obtain leadership positions in it than in either the OBU or the IWW. The party was popular with immigrant workers because of the emphasis it placed on industrial organization and its interest in the unemployed. Finally, the party's advocacy of mass demonstrations and picket-line confrontations was often more appealing than the more cautious and 'respectable' tactics of the craft unions and the social democratic Independent Labour party. Avery, *'Dangerous Foreigners,'* 60–90.

28 William Rodney, *Soldiers of the International: A History of the Communist Party of Canada, 1919–1929* (Toronto: University of Toronto Press, 1968); Ian Angus, *Canadian Bolsheviks: The Early History of the Communist Party of Canada* (Montreal: Vanguard Publications, 1981); *Canada's Party of Socialism: History of the Communist Party of Canada, 1921–1976* (Toronto: Progress Books, 1982); Norman Penner, *The Canadian Left: A Critical Analysis* (Scarborough: Prentice-Hall of Canada, 1977).

29 Between 1921 and 1931 the FOC provided over half of the CPC's membership. Some Finnish Communists had fought on the 'Red' side during the Finnish Civil War, but most moved into the CPC as a result of their Canadian experiences. For its part, the FOC required all of its members 'automatically to take out a card in the [Communist] Party or be blacklisted or expelled.' The growth of the FOC in the 1920s far exceeded that of the CPC membership as a whole; by 1930 the organization had seventy-four branches and over six thousand members. It also published a weekly newspaper, *Vapaus*, and maintained a variety of cultural and social programmes. Ivan Avakumovic, *The Communist Party in Canada: A History* (Toronto: McClelland and Stewart, 1975), 15–95; Edward W. Laine, 'Finnish Canadian Radicalism,' in Jorgen Dahlie and Tissa Fernando, eds., *Ethnicity, Power and Politics in Canada* (Toronto: Methuen, 1981), 94–113.

30 The founding and growth of the ULFTA were largely the work of four men: Matthew Popovich, John Navis, Matthew Shatulsky, and John Boychuk. All had come from Galicia before 1914; all became important functionaries of the Canadian Communist party. During the 1920s two other groups emerged. One was composed of post-1918 immigrants such

as Myroslav Irchan, Peter Prokop, Peter Krawchuk, Ivan Sembay, and Stepan Macievich. The other group had grown up within the ULFTA fold and included John Weir, Andrew Bilecki, Mary Kardash, and John Boyd. John Kolasky, *The Shattered Illusion: The History of Ukrainian Pro-Communist Organizations in Canada* (Toronto: PMA Books, 1979), 6–12.

31 The CPC also attempted to reach women workers through organizations such as the Women's Labour Leagues (WLL). Founded in 1923, largely through the efforts of Florence Custance, a British-born member of the Politbureau, the WLL actively campaigned against the grim situation faced by many Canadian women – low wages, economic insecurity, meagre social welfare benefits, and sexual harassment. Joan Sangster, *Dreams of Equality: Women on the Canadian Left, 1920–1950* (Toronto: McClelland and Stewart, 1989).

32 Rodney, *Soldiers of the International*, 17–106; Penner, *Canadian Left*, 79–90.

33 Avakumovic, *The Communist Party in Canada*, 15–120; Donald Avery, 'Ethnic Loyalties and the Proletarian Revolution: A Case Study of Communist Political Activity in Winnipeg, 1923–1936,' in Dahlie and Fernando, *Ethnicity, Power and Politics*, 68–93.

34 Sangster, *Dreams of Equality*, 26–115; Avery, *'Dangerous Foreigners,'* 120–30; Kolasky, *Shattered Illusion*, 1–30.

35 Avery, *'Dangerous Foreigners,'* 126–33; Rodney, *Soldiers of the International*, 62–130.

36 Avery, 'Ethnic Loyalties,' 78–81.

37 Lita-Rose Betcherman, *The Little Band: The Clashes between the Communists and the Political and Legal Establishment in Canada, 1928–1933* (Ottawa: Deneau, nd), 171–212.

38 Avery, 'Ethnic Loyalties,' 68–93.

39 The ULFTA was fortunate that its anti-Communist adversaries were themselves divided into warring factions. In part, the conflict was along religious lines, and throughout the twenties the Ukrainian Catholic church maintained a steady barrage against its main rival, the Ukrainian Greek Orthodox church. In addition, there was serious rivalry between the liberal nationalists associated with the Ukrainian Self-Reliance League of Canada (SUS) and monarchist-militarist groups such as the Canadian Sitch Organization. Woycenko, 'Community Organizations,' in Lupul, *A Heritage in Transition*, 178–86.

40 Ibid.; Kolasky, *Shattered Illusion*, 1–26.

41 During the late thirties the FOC and the ULFTA began to lose much of their influence in determining party policy. In part this was attributed to the fierce controversy over Bolshevization. Even more important was the impact of Soviet policies. In the case of the FOC, for example, some of its most resolute members went off in a futile search for a new socialist paradise in Soviet Karelia or enlisted in the Mackenzie-Papineau battalion during the Spanish civil war. For the ULFTA the major trauma was

Stalin's brutal collectivist policies in Ukraine, and in 1935 a number of prominent ULFTA members repudiated their Communist affiliation. Avakumovic, *The Communist Party in Canada*, 20–90.

42 Thomas M. Prymak, *Maple Leaf and Trident: The Ukrainian Canadians during the Second World War* (Toronto: Multicultural History Society of Ontario, 1988), 37.

43 Donald Avery, 'Canada's Response to European Refugees, 1939–1945: The Security Dimension,' in Norman Hilmer, Bohdan Kordan, and Lubomyr Luciuk, eds., *On Guard for Thee: War, Ethnicity, and the Canadian State, 1939–1945* (Ottawa: Canadian Committee for the History of the Second World War, 1988), 179–216.

44 Although the federal government had warrants for the arrest of many more members of the Communist party, only ninety-eight were interned. The reason for this disparity is that CP leaders such as Tim Buck and Fred Rose initially eluded arrest and surfaced only when the movement was no longer illegal. Although the ULFTA leaders expected that some would be detained, they apparently did not anticipate such a large-scale round-up. But why did the ULFTA become the only Communist front group treated in such a harsh manner? Unfortunately, RCMP records on this subject still remain closed. John Kolasky, however, offers a plausible explanation: 'Not only was it the most active and the most militant of the pro-Communist language organizations, but the country of origin of its members constituted an integral part of the USSR which had a pact with Germany with whom Canada was at war.' Kolasky, *Shattered Illusion*, 28.

45 Peter Krawchuk, *Matthew Popovich: His Place in the History of Ukrainian Canadians* (Toronto: Canadian Society for Ukrainian Labour Research, 1987), 64–119.

46 On 8 September 1942, J.L. Cohen, a prominent labour lawyer, began the process of recovering the ULFTA halls and their contents by submitting a brief to Dr E.H. Coleman, Under-Secretary of State, Custodian of Alien Enemy Property. Although most of the 108 properties were returned after 14 October 1943, when Order in Council P.C. 8022 lifted the ban on the ULFTA, the final settlement did not occur until the spring of 1945. At issue were the 17 halls, valued at $269,270.82, which had been sold by the Custodian of Enemy Property for only $38,176.33, or 14 per cent of their worth. To make matters worse, many of these halls had been sold to the Ukrainian National Federation, a decision that was denounced not only by the ULFTA, but also by the Civil Liberties Association of Toronto. Cohen to Coleman, 6 September 1942, J.L. Cohen Papers, file 2893, NAC; ibid., John Boychuk, Central Executive Committee, ULFTA, to N.A. McLarty, Secretary of State of Canada, 12 June 1944, file 3148, NAC. *An Appeal for Justice: The Case of the Seized Properties of the Ukrainian Labour-Farmer Temple Association* (Toronto: Civil Liberties Assocation of

Toronto, 1944). See also Kolasky, *Shattered Illusion*, 26–88; and William and Kathleen Repka, *Dangerous Patriots: Canada's Unknown Prisoners of War* (Vancouver: New Star Books, 1982).

47 The team also included Vladimir J. Kaye (Kysilewsky), a Ukrainian civil servant in the Citizenship Branch. N.F. Dreisziger, 'The Rise of a Bureaucracy for Multiculturalism: The Origins of the Nationalities Branch, 1939–1941,' in Hillmer, Kordan, and Luciuk, *On Guard for Thee*, 1–22; William R. Young, 'Chauvinism and Canadianism: Canadian Ethnic Groups and the Failure of Wartime Information,' ibid., 38–9.

48 Young, 'Chauvinism and Canadianism,' 36–46. The wartime careers of both Tracy Philipps and Watson Kirkconnell are extremely controversial. According to Young, they were part of an anti-Communist element within the Canadian government that 'set about on a disastrous course of trying to "help" ethnic groups – the Ukrainians for example – settle ideological conflicts between anti- and pro-Communist sympathizers.' (38) In contrast, Bohdan Kordan and Lubomyr Luciuk have lamented that Philipps's 'astute prescription for nation-building was all but ignored,' a decision that 'hampered and handicapped Ukrainians well into the postwar period.' Bohdan S. Kordan and Lubomyr Y. Luciuk, 'A Prescription for Nationbuilding: Ukrainian Canadians and the Canadian State, 1939–1945,' in Hillmer, Kordan, and Luciuk, *On Guard for Thee*, 97.

49 The Ukrainian Canadian Committee was created at a conference in Winnipeg in November 1940 as an attempt 'to provide a faction-ridden community with an umbrella organization that could speak for the community while helping to preserve its identity.' All major groups except the pro-Communists were included. Gerus, 'The Ukrainian Canadian Committee,' in Lupul, *A Heritage in Transition*, 195–205.

50 Donald Avery, 'Canadian Communism and Popular Front Organizations, 1935–1945' (paper delivered at a meeting of the Canadian Political Science Association, Vancouver, June 1983).

51 Denis Smith, *Diplomacy of Fear: Canada and the Cold War 1941–1948* (Toronto: University of Toronto Press, 1988), 25–72.

52 Donald Avery, 'Secrets between Different Kinds of Friends: Canada's Wartime Exchange of Scientific Military Information with the United States and the USSR, 1940–1945,' Canadian Historical Association, *Historical Papers* (1986): 231.

53 Wilgress was particularly critical of the self-determination sections of the Atlantic Charter, which prompted groups such as the Ukrainians to submit territorial claims. Prymak, *Maple Leaf*, 91. In April 1941 George Glazebrook of the Department of External Affairs expressed concerns that many Ukrainian Canadians would become 'disillusioned' if Canada did not insist that the Soviet Union accept the principles of the Atlantic Charter. Smith, *Diplomacy of Fear*, 33.

54 The major speeches in favour of Ukrainian independence came not from the UCC organizers, but from Dr Watson Kirkconnell, a long-term critic of the Ukrainian Left, and General Sikevych, a spokesman of the anti-Communist grass roots of the UCC. Prymak, *Maple Leaf*, 92.

55 In his reports on the UCC, Commissioner Wood was quite favourable and rejected any allegations that it was disruptive. Tracy Philipps, the primary investigator for the Nationalities Branch, was even more open in his support of the Ukrainian nationalists and his criticism of the Ukrainian Left. In this instance, however, Norman Robertson and his External Affairs colleagues carried the day. Prymak, *Maple Leaf*, 87, 92.

56 'Restoration of Property of Ukrainian Farmer Labour [sic] Temples: Basic Considerations which should determine government Policy,' 7 June 1943, cited in Prymak, *Maple Leaf*, 96. The return of ULFTA property was begun in October 1943, but the process was not completed until September 1945. Krawchuk, *Popovich*, 90–117; Kolasky, *Shattered Illusion*, 36–47.

57 One of the most strident leftist attacks was by the experienced Communist propagandist R.A. Davies. In his book *This Is Our Land: Ukrainian Canadians against Hitler* (Toronto: Progress Books, 1943), 100, Davies defended the ULFTA's record as being 'progressive and anti-fascist,' and again accused the various nationalist organizations of 'harboring pro-German sympathies.' The most influential rebuttal to these charges came from Watson Kirkconnell in his 1944 publication *Seven Pillars of Freedom*.

58 Secret Memo for the Prime Minister, 4 July 1944, cited in Prymak, *Maple Leaf*, 121. There was also a hostile response by External Affairs officials when it was suggested that Ukrainian Canadians should send a delegation to the San Francisco founding of the United Nations. Ibid.

59 The ULFTA was able to maintain its high profile and confidence throughout 1945 for a number of reasons. One was the popularity of its Soviet Ukraine rallies and concerts. On 30 June 1945, for example, over a thousand performers entertained an audience of fifteen thousand at Maple Leaf Gardens in Toronto. The concert ended with speeches from the Soviet ambassador and three delegates of the Ukrainian SSR who were on their way to the United Nations conference in San Francisco. Another reason was the sudden defection of the prominent nationalist Wasyl Swystun from the UCC on 18 February 1945. On this occasion he claimed that within the USSR 'the Ukrainian nation lives and will continue to live ... and will continue to develop its state.' Kolasky, *Shattered Illusion*, 51, 78.

60 Donald Avery, 'Canadian Communism and Popular Front Organizations' (unpublished article); Smith, *Diplomacy of Fear*, 74–136.

61 In November 1945 and again in January 1946 pro-Communist Ukrainian organizations sent petitions to Prime Minister King charging that most of the Ukrainian displaced persons were either war criminals or Nazi

collaborators. Kolasky, *Shattered Illusion*, 94–8. At the Senate hearing
John Boychuk, John Navis, George Krenz, Peter Prokop, and Stepan
Macievich represented the ULFTA and presented its brief. Significantly,
some days earlier, Polish and Yugoslav diplomats in Ottawa had
informed External Affairs that many, if not most, of their nationals who
now sought sanctuary in Canada had either served in the Waffen SS or
in concentration camps. Senate Standing Committee on Immigration
and Labour Minutes of the Proceedings and Evidence 1946 (Ottawa,
1946). Prymak, *Maple Leaf*, 126.
62 Gerald Dirks, *Canada's Refugee Policy: Indifference or Opportunism?* (Montreal: McGill-Queens's University Press, 1974), 99–175, 273.
63 The propaganda war was primarily conducted in the rival Ukrainian-
   language newspapers. In some communities, however, pitched battles
   between the two sides also erupted. One of the worst incidents was a
   bombing attack on a Ukrainian labour temple in Toronto on 8 October
   1950. Kolasky, *Shattered Illusion*, 100–10.
64 Kolasky, *Shattered Illusion*, 64–107; Woycenko, 'Community Organizations,' in Lupul, *A Heritage in Transition*, 186–93; Gerus, 'The Ukrainian
   Canadian Committee,' ibid., 195–214.
65 Commissioner Wood to A. MacNamara, Deputy Minister of Labour, 23
   January 1950, Immigration files, vol. 856, file 555–13, NAC.
66 Immigration authorities were even more determined to exclude members
   of the Ukrainian 'Galicia Division,' which had been resettled in Great
   Britain. It was only in the spring of 1950 that Canada reversed its position
   on the matter of enemy aliens. Donald Avery, 'Canadian Immigration
   Policy towards Europe, 1945–1952: Altruism and Economic Self-Interest,'
   Zeitschrift der Gesellschaft für Kanada-Studien 6 (1986): 38–56.
67 The practice of excluding or restricting the entry of ethnic spokesmen
   was not confined to Ukrainians. In her book *DP: Lithuanian Immigration
   to Canada after the Second World War* (Toronto: Multicultural History Society of Ontario, 1986), Milda Danys describes the difficulties encountered
   by Lithuanian professionals, artists, and priests.
68 Avery, *'Dangerous Foreigners,'* 95–180; Kolasky, *Shattered Illusion*, 140–76.
69 In its September 1942 appeal to the custodian of enemy property for the
   return of its halls, the ULFTA emphasized the range of its cultural
   activities among Ukrainian Canadians: 'Over two hundred orchestras –
   mandolin, string and wind – over 150 choirs, and many dramatic
   circles, gymnastics and dancing groups, literary societies and reading
   groups functioned in these buildings advancing the cultural life of the
   people and helping to integrate them as useful Canadians contributing
   to the social and cultural growth of the whole Dominion.' Cohen Papers,
   file 2893, NAC.
70 Avery, 'Ethnic Loyalties,' 68–91; Kolasky, *Shattered Illusion*, 125–40.
71 During this period, most Anglo-Canadian security officials were insensi-

tive to the complexities of and differences among the country's diverse ethnic cultures. At best, they considered ethnic identities as problems that had to be addressed on occasion. During war and social turmoil, the officials adopted various strategies to control ethnic communities: creating co-operative and co-opting structures, using coercion, or intensifying differences within the community.

72 Reg Whitaker, 'Official Repression of Communists during World War II,' *Labour/Le Travail* 17 (1986): 135–66; Kolasky, *Shattered Illusion*, 1–47; Krawchuk, *Popovich*, 65–119.

73 Between 1914 and 1946 the Canadian government did not have a security policy directed exclusively at the Ukrainian Left. Rather it regarded alien radicalism as a general problem requiring a complex response. Thus, an understanding of the broader aspects of this topic requires comprehensive studies of the Finnish-Canadian Left, the Jewish-Canadian Left, the Italian-Canadian Left, etc. It would also require an analysis of how the Canadian security agencies treated each of these groups.

74 William Kaplan, 'The Access to Information Act: A 1988 Review,' *Labour/ Le Travail* 22 (1988): 181–98.

Minenko: Without Just Cause

1 Royal Northwest Mounted Police, RG 18, 1794, Annual Reports, 1915, National Archives of Canada, Ottawa (hereafter cited as NAC).

2 *War Measures Act*, 1914, SC, 1915, c. 2.

3 For more on the internments see Peter Melnycky, 'The Internment of Ukrainians in Canada,' in Frances Swyripa and John Herd Thompson, eds., *Loyalties in Conflict: Ukrainians in Canada during the Great War* (Edmonton: Canadian Institute of Ukrainian Studies, 1983), 1–24; Lubomyr Luciuk, *A Time for Atonement: Canada's First National Internment Operations and the Ukrainian Canadians, 1914–1920* (Kingston: Limestone Press, 1988); and J.B. Gregorovich, ed., *Ukrainian Canadians in Canada's Wars: Materials for Ukrainian Canadian History* (Toronto: Ukrainian Canadian Research Foundation, 1987), which contains the full text of General W.D. Otter's final report to the government on the internments.

4 Pierre Berton, *The Promised Land* (Toronto: McClelland and Stewart, 1984), 14.

5 Desmond Morton, *Years of Conflict 1911–1921* (Toronto: Grolier, 1983), 9.

6 W. Leland Clark, *Brandon's Politics and Politicians* (Altona, Man.: Friesen Printers, 1981), 37.

7 Desmond Morton, *The Canadian General: Sir William Otter* (Toronto: Hakkert, 1944), 325.

8 Morton, *Years of Conflict*, 12.

9 Nadia O.M. Kazymyra, "Aspects of Ukrainian Opinion in Manitoba dur-

ing World War I,' in Martin L. Kovacs, ed., *Ethnic Canadians: Culture and Education* (Saskatoon: Modern Press, 1978), 120.

10 Morton, *Years of Conflict*, 22.

11 Kazymyra, 'Aspects of Ukrainian Opinion,' 122. Both of Bishop Budka's letters are reprinted in Bohdan S. Kordan and Lubomyr Y. Luciuk, eds., *A Delicate and Difficult Question: Documents in the History of Ukrainians in Canada, 1899–1962* (Kingston: Limestone Press, 1986). For an interpretation of this event that is favourable to Budka see Stella Hryniuk, 'The Bishop Budka Controversy: A New Perspective,' *Canadian Slavonic Papers* 23 (1981): 154–65.

12 *Manitoba Free Press*, 7 August 1914.

13 Ibid., 10 August 1914.

14 Defence of the Realm Act, 1914, 4–5 George V, c. 29.

15 Privy Council Orders, RG 2, 844, NAC.

16 Ibid.

17 Canada, House of Commons, *Debates*, CXVIII, 20–1, 42.

18 W. Kent Power, 'Rights of Individuals in Peace and War' (1917). 37 Canadian Law Times, 33 at 45.

19 Privy Council Orders, RG 2, 850, NAC.

20 Ibid.

21 Ibid.

22 MG 13, G. NAC.

23 RLB 673–674 (2).

24 Borden Papers, NAC.

25 Morton, *The Canadian General*, 333.

26 Roach to Officer Commanding, Weyburn Detachment, 17 July 1916, Royal Northwest Mounted Police, Correspondence, NAC. Roach had supplied Mary Marchuk with flour, sugar, rice, coffee, tea, salt, soap, oatmeal, lard, and peas.

27 Morton, *The Canadian General*, 43.

28 Draft Letter, Deputy Minister to Registrars, 13 November 1914, Department of Justice Papers, NAC.

29 Myrna Kostash, *All of Baba's Children* (Edmonton: Hurtig Publishers, 1977), 47.

30 Kazymyra, 'Aspects of Ukrainian Opinion,' 125.

31 Morton, *The Canadian General*, 334.

32 Ibid.

33 Ibid., 336.

34 Memorandum to Comptroller, 16 January 1935, RG 6, H1, 819, NAC.

35 *Manitoba Free Press*, 3 August 1914.

36 Memorandum, Chief Commissioner of Police to Deputy Minister, 18 March 1915, Department of Justice Papers, NAC.

37 C.H. Cahan, KC, to the Minister of Justice, C4334, RG 26, H1(c), vol. 104, NAC.

38 Privy Council Orders, RG 2, 866, NAC.

39 Sir William Otter, *Internment Operations 1914–1920* (Ottawa: King's Printer, 1921), 19.
40 Ibid., 13.
41 Morton, *The Canadian General*, 341.
42 Otter to Fritch, 10 May 1916, and Otter to Hungerford, 20 September 1918, RG 6, 753, 3194(1), NAC.
43 6–759–3473, NAC. For a map illustrating these internment operations see Lubomyr Luciuk and Bohdan Kordan, *Creating a Landscape: A Geography of Ukrainians in Canada* (Toronto: University of Toronto Press, 1989), map 20.
44 *Canadian Annual Review* (1916): 432.
45 Report by C.H. Cahan to the Minister of Justice, 14 September 1918, Borden Papers, 56666, NAC.
46 RG 2/1, vol. 913, NAC.
47 RG 2/1, vol. 930, NAC.
48 Privy Council Orders, RG 13, 237, NAC.
49 Otter, *Internment Operations*, 12.
50 Ibid.
51 A.H. Mathieu, Assistant Deputy Custodian, Statement of Earnings, RG 6, 819, NAC. (Editors' note: Efforts were made to trace the owners.)
52 *Canadian Annual Review* (1917): 436.
53 Russell to Borden, 2 November 1914, Borden Papers, 106273, NAC.
54 Name excluded by paragraph 8 (2)(j), *Privacy Act*, RSC 1984, c. 110.
55 RG 2/1. 921, NAC.
56 Ibid.
57 Wartime Elections Act, SC, 1917, c. 39.
58 Canada, House of Commons, *Debates*, CXXXI, 1917, 5416–17. Canadian newspapers also editorialized against the War Time Elections Act. For example, the *Daily British Whig* in Kingston wrote on 8 September 1917: 'It is very probable that if this proposal becomes law the "alleged" foreigners and hitherto "naturalized" Canadians will bear their reproach meekly, but they will have sown in their hearts the seeds of a bitterness that can never be extirpated. The man whose honour has been mistrusted, and who has been singled out for national humiliation, will remember it and sooner or later it will have to be atoned for.'
59 Cahan to Borden, 14 September 1918, Borden Papers, 56666, NAC.
60 *Canadian Annual Review* (1918): 580.
61 Ibid., 581.
62 RNWMP, Annual Reports, 1915, RG 18, vol. 1794, NAC.
63 Ibid.
64 Morton, *The Canadian General*, 338.
65 RNWMP Annual Reports, RG 18, vol. 1794, NAC. On 4 June 1915, Petro Petryk escaped while he was on his way to an internment camp. When Petryk was found by the police (on the basis of information provided by Russian informants), he was once again taken into custody. The three men

who were with him at the time of his arrest were also arrested and
charged with assisting an escaped alien enemy. One other man, J.
Gawlylyk, was also charged with this offence, although he was not
arrested until later. The three were found guilty of the offence, and
one was sentenced to four months, the other two to two months in jail.
'The accused Gawlylyk was discharged on account of the fact that he
was not present in the house at the time Petryk was arrested ... He was
interned as a Prisoner of War.'

66 A prime example was the concern over the civil liberties of Arab and
Muslim Canadians during the Gulf war of 1991. See Desmond Morton,
'Canada at war: Dissent, human rights take a back seat,' and Lubomyr
Luciuk's reply, 'Support for tolerance and dissent,' *Ottawa Citizen*, 13
February 1991. The Civil Liberties Commission of the Ukrainian Canadian
Congress has set up a redress committee. For a statement of the case for
acknowledgment and redress see Lubomyr Y. Luciuk and Bohdan S.
Kordan, 'And who says time heals all?' *Globe and Mail*, 28 October 1988.

Ferguson: Canadian National Identity

1 John Porter, *The Vertical Mosaic: An Analysis of Social Class and Power in
Canada* (Toronto: University of Toronto Press, 1965), passim.
2 Ramsay Cook, *Canada, Quebec and the Uses of Nationalism* (Toronto: Macmillan, 1986), 184–7. Cook has discussed the ideology of Canadian nationalisms in *The Maple Leaf Forever* (Toronto: Macmillan, 1977), 96–122 and
123–47, and E.J. Hobsbaum has illustrated the shaping of European
nationalisms in *The Invention of Tradition*, ed. T. Ranger and E. Hobsbaum
(Cambridge: Cambridge University Press, 1983), 263–307, and *Nations
and Nationalism since 1780* (Cambridge: Cambridge University Press, 1990).
3 Allan Smith, 'Metaphor and Nationality,' *Canadian Historical Review* 51
(1970): 247ff; Howard Palmer, 'Reluctant Hosts: Anglo-Canadian Views
of Multiculturalism in the Twentieth Century,' in R.D. Francis and D.B.
Smith, eds, *Readings in Canadian History* (Toronto: Holt, Rinehart and Winston, 1982) II: 123–39.
4 James S. Woodsworth, *Strangers within Our Gates* (Toronto: University of
Toronto Press, 1972, original edition 1909), 9; Charles H. Young and H.
Reid, *The Ukrainian Canadians: A Study in Assimilation* (Toronto: Thomas
Nelson and Sons, 1931), 5.
5 E.g., Robert England, *The Central European Immigrant in Canada* (Toronto:
Macmillan, 1929), 9. This position is typical of the 'professional'
approach that arose among twentieth-century intellectuals. Canadian
historians dance around the subject, but 'professionalization' lies at the
centre of the authority of social science and humanities writing in the
twentieth century.
6 This is a common enough observation by historians of attitudes and

values. Readers who would use sources such as those I have used to find out about Ukrainian Canadians and their experiences in Canada would have to read them very carefully indeed. On the problem of studies of attitudes see S.F. Wise and R.C. Brown, *Canada Views the United States: Nineteenth Century Attitudes* (Seattle: University of Washington Press, 1967), esp. 95–7 and 121–2; George M. Frederickson, *The Black Image in the White Mind* (New York: Harper and Row, 1971), preface.

7 Andrew Macphail, 'Immigration,' *University Magazine* 19 (1920): 133ff; J.R. Conn, 'Immigration,' *Queen's Quarterly* 8 (1900): 117–31.

8 Adam Shortt, 'Some Observations on the Great North-West,' *Queen's Quarterly* 3 (1895): 11ff; Arthur Lower, 'The Case against Immigration,' *Queen's Quarterly* 37 (1930), quoted in his *History and Myth*, ed. W.H. Heick (Waterloo: Wilfrid Laurier University Press, 1974), 251–63.

9 W.D. Scott, 'Immigration and Population,' *Canada and Its Provinces* (Toronto: Publishers' Association, 1914) VII: 555, 558.

10 David J. Hall, *Clifford Sifton* (Vancouver: University of British Columbia Press, 1981) I: 264–6; D.C. Corbett, *Canada's Immigration Policy* (Toronto: University of Toronto Press, 1957), 134; Stella Hryniuk, 'Pioneer Bishop, Pioneer Times: Nykyta Budka in Canada,' Canadian Catholic Historical Society, *Historical Studies* 54 (1988): 27.

11 R.G. Moyles and Doug Owram, *Imperial Dreams and Colonial Realities* (Toronto: University of Toronto Press, 1988), 115–39, especially 134ff.

12 Scott, 'Immigration and Population,' 517ff.

13 E.W. Bradwin, *The Bunkhouse Man* (Toronto: University of Toronto Press, 1972, original edition 1928), 92. Woodsworth notes this usage in *Strangers within Our Gates*, 9.

14 Watson Kirkconnell, *A Slice of Canada: Memoirs* (Toronto: University of Toronto Press, 1967), 281.

15 C.B. Sissons, *Bilingual Schools in Canada* (Toronto: J.M. Dent & Sons, 1917), 156.

16 Elizabeth Wangenheim, 'The Ukrainians: A Case Study of the "Third Force,"' in Peter Russell, ed., *Nationalism in Canada* (Toronto: McGraw-Hill, 1965), 89–90.

17 W.L. Morton, *Manitoba: A History* (Toronto: University of Toronto Press, 1957), 309, 409; G.A. Friesen, *Canadian Prairies: A History* (Toronto: University of Toronto Press, 1985), 265.

18 J.S. Woodsworth, 'Nation-Building,' *University Magazine* 17 (1917): 86; preface to Sissons, *Bilingual Schools in Canada*, 3.

19 J.S. Woodsworth, 'Some Aspects of Immigration,' *University Magazine* 14 (1915): 189–93.

20 Arthur Lower, *Canadians in the Making* (Toronto: Longmans, Green, 1958), 372.

21 Edgar McInnis, *Canada: A Social and Political History* (Toronto: Rinehart, 1947), 375.

22 Morton, *Manitoba*, 308.

23 Lower, *Canadians in the Making*, 385.

24 John Thompson, *Canada 1922–1939* (Toronto: McClelland and Stewart, 1986), 7.

25 Scott, 'Immigration and Population,' 558; Woodsworth, *Strangers within Our Gates*, 110.

26 F.W. Baumgartner, 'Central European Immigration,' *Queen's Quarterly* 38 (1930): 190, 189.

27 Bradwin, *The Bunkhouse Man*, 106. The word 'Ukraine' was only defined by Charles Young and Helen Reid in their 1931 sociological study, and they noted the political, economic, and cultural bases of Ukrainian identity in Canada and its links to Europe. So did the CPR publicist and self-taught folklorist J.M. Gibbon, and it is telling that he, like Young and Reid, used at least some Ukrainian-Canadian sources for his work. Writing in the fifties, W.L. Morton speculated that the rise of Ukrainian nationalism directly affected Ukrainian Canadians and that this nationalism 'turned the zeal of their nationalism to the preservation of their group in Manitoba' after the First World War. But however archly and belatedly linked by British-Canadian authorities, it remains notable that the adoption of the term Ukrainian and the state of Ukraine emerged simultaneously at the end of the Great War. See Young and Reid, *Ukrainian Canadians*, 14–15; J.M. Gibbon, *Canadian Mosaic: The Making of a Northern Nation* (Toronto: McClelland and Stewart, 1938), 83–5; Morton, *Manitoba*, 409.

28 Mercedes M. Randall, ed., *Beyond Nationalism: The Social Thought of Emily Greene Balch* (New York: Twayne, 1972), passim.

29 Quoted by James T.M. Anderson, *The Education of the New Canadian: A Treatise on Canada's Greatest Educational Problem* (Toronto: J.M. Dent & Sons, 1918), 51.

30 Palmer, 'Reluctant Hosts,' and his *Patterns of Prejudice: A History of Nativism in Alberta* (Toronto: McClelland and Stewart, 1982). See also Francis Swyripa, *Ukrainian Canadians: A Survey of Their Portrayal in English-language Works* (Edmonton: Canadian Institute of Ukrainian Studies, 1978); and Terrence Craig, *Racial Attitudes in English-Canadian Fiction 1905–1980* (Waterloo: Wilfrid Laurier University, 1987).

31 Watson Kirkconnell, *Canadians All* (Ottawa: Director of Public Information, 1941), 8ff; England, *The Central European Immigrant*, 42ff.

32 Woodsworth, *Strangers within Our Gates*, 110, 112; Burgon Bickersteth, *Land of Open Doors* (Toronto: University of Toronto Press, 1976, original edition 1914), 161–2.

33 Gibbon, *Canadian Mosaic*, 291; J.B. Hedges, *Building the Canadian West: The Land and Colonization Policies of the Canadian Pacific Railway* (New York: Macmillan, 1939), 132; Robert England, *The Colonization of Western Canada: A Study of Contemporary Land Settlement (1896–1934)* (London: P.S. King & Son, 1936), 205.

34 Young and Reid, *Ukrainian Canadians*, 68, 71, 169–72; England, *The Central European Immigrant*, 89–90; Eva Younge, 'Population Movements and the Assimilation of Alien Groups in Canada,' *Canadian Journal of Economics and Political Science* 10 (1944): 376–9.

35 Young and Reid, *Ukrainian Canadians*, 122–3, 169–72; Younge, 'Population Movements,' 379.

36 J.W. Dafoe, 'Economic History of the Prairie Provinces,' *Canada and Its Provinces* XIX: 305; Shortt, 'Some Observations,' passim.

37 Robert Murchie, *Agricultural Progress on the Prairie Provinces* (Toronto: Macmillan, 1936), 148–9, 190–1; Gibbon, *Canadian Mosaic*, 292–2.

38 Robert England, *Living, Learning, Remembering* (Vancouver: Center for Continuing Education, University of British Columbia, 1980), 60–1.

39 Walter Murray, 'History of Education in Saskatchewan,' *Canada and Its Provinces* XIX: 459–60.

40 Young and Reid, *Ukrainian Canadians*, 178.

41 Sissons, *Bilingual Schools in Canada*, 156, 184, 213–14.

42 Morton, *Manitoba*, 311.

43 Sissons, *Bilingual Schools in Canada*, 127.

44 Anderson, *The Education of the New Canadian*, 114.

45 Ibid., 53.

46 England, *The Central European Immigrant*, 1ff, 165ff.

47 Kirkconnell, *A Slice of Canada*, 281; Young and Reid, *Ukrainian Canadians*, 175.

48 Younge, 'Population Movements,' 372; Smith, *A Study in Canadian Immigration*, 381; Marlene Shore, *The Science of Social Redemption* (Toronto: University of Toronto Press, 1987), 246.

49 Woodsworth, 'Some Aspects of Immigration,' 192–3.

50 Smith, 'Metaphor and Nationality'; Palmer, 'Reluctant Hosts.'

51 Gibbon, *Canadian Mosaic*, viii, vii.

52 Cf. Angus McLaren, *Our Own Master Race: Eugenics in Canada, 1885–1945* (Toronto: McClelland and Stewart, 1990), passim.

53 G.W. Simpson, 'The Blending of Traditions,' *Canadian Historical Association Annual Report* (1944): 46–52; R.G. Trotter, 'Discussion,' 53.

54 England, *The Central European Immigrant*, 66; *Colonization of Western Canada*, 305, 308.

55 Kirkconnell, *A Slice of Canada*, 181; W.B. Hurd, 'Is There a Canadian Race?' *Queen's Quarterly* 35 (1928): 615–28.

56 Kirkconnell, *Canadians All*, 47; England, *The Colonization of Western Canada*, 297; Young and Reid, *Ukrainian Canadians*, 31.

57 Young and Reid, *Ukrainian Canadians*, 130–1; Tweedsmuir quoted in Gibbon, *Canadian Mosaic*, 307; Arthur Hawkes, *The Birthright* (Toronto: J.M. Dent & Sons, 1919), 182.

58 Young and Reid, *Ukrainian Canadians*, 348.

59 Ralph Connor, *The Foreigner: A Tale of Saskatchewan* (Toronto: Westminster Co., 1909).

60 J.S. Woodsworth in Sissons, *Bilingual Schools in Canada*, 3.
61 W.B. Hurd, 'The Decline of the Canadian Birth-Rate,' *Canadian Journal of Economics and Political Science* 3 (1937): 40–57; Younge, 'Population Movements,' 372–80.
62 William G. Smith, *A Study in Canadian Immigration* (Toronto: Ryerson Press, 1920), 382.
63 William G. Smith, *Building the Nation: The Churches' Relation to the Immigrant* (Toronto: Ryerson Press, 1922), 111, quoted in Francis Swyripa, *Ukrainian Canadians*, 32.
64 Young and Reid, *Ukrainian Canadians*, 173–4, quote 131.
65 England, *The Colonization of Western Canada*, 215.
66 Florence Livesay, 'Three Poems from the Ukrainian,' *University Magazine* 14 (February 1915); her 'Making the Boundary,' *University Magazine* 17 (April 1918); her novel translation, *Marusia* (New York: E.P. Dutton, 1940); and her poetry translation *Songs of Ukraine* (New York: E.P. Dutton, 1938). See also Gibbon, *Canadian Mosaic*, 282ff; Kirkconnell, *A Slice of Canada*, 274–81; Young and Reid, *The Ukrainian Canadians*, 173. The cultural nationalism of the twenties and thirties is best described and explained in Cook, *The Maple Leaf Forever*, 158–79, and his *Canada, Quebec and the Uses of Nationalism*, 119–42.
67 Foreshadowings of this new approach were found in such disparate sources as Adam Shortt, the Queen's economist, and Victoria Hayward, the American folklorist and travel writer. Shortt had warned that prairie geographical and economic conditions would make certain that no unfit or inferior settlers would survive and that western Canada would be 'preserved from the overflow of southern Europe' and their American equivalents. (Shortt, 'The Great North-West, II,' 14.) Hayward simply noted in her 1922 travel guide to Canada that wheat growing and marketing shaped the entire prairies even as she foresaw the emerging 'mosaic of vast dimensions and great breadth' formed by the new peoples. Victoria Hayward, *Romantic Canada* (Toronto: Macmillan, 1922), 185, 187.
68 W.A. Mackintosh, *Prairie Settlement: The Geographical Setting* (Toronto: Macmillan, 1934), 103–4; W.A. Mackintosh, *Agricultural Co-operation in Western Canada* (Kingston: Jackman Press, 1924), 88–9; also his introduction to C.A. Dawson, *Group Settlement: Ethnic Communities in Western Canada* (Toronto: Macmillan, 1936), ix.
69 C.A. Dawson and E. Younge, *Pioneering in the Prairie Provinces* (Toronto, 1940), 123–4, 286–7; C.A. Dawson, *Settlement of the Peace River Country* (Toronto: Macmillan, 1934) passim.
70 Hurd, 'The Decline of the Canadian Birth-Rate,' 40–57, esp. 50–1; Younge, 'Population Movements,' 378–9.
71 Dawson, *Group Settlement*, 380, xvii.
72 Arthur Lower, *Settlement and the Forest Frontier* (Toronto: Macmillan, 1936), 149–50; Lower, *Canadians in the Making*, 376.
73 Morton, *Manitoba*, 409.

74 O.D. Skelton, 'The Language Issue in Canada,' *Queen's Quarterly* 24 (1917): 468.
75 Anderson, *Education of the New Canadian*, 56, 53.
76 England, *Central European Immigrant*, 169.
77 Young and Reid, *Ukrainian Canadians*, 7.
78 Gibbon, *Canadian Mosaic*, 307.
79 Canada, House of Commons, *Debates*, 27 May 1931, 2021ff; 'Memorandum: Constitutional Questions,' 24 April 1937, *Documents on Canadian External Relations* (Ottawa: Information Canada, 1967–77) VI (1936–9): 144–50; N.A. Robertson to W.L.M. King, 19 April 1946, ibid., XII (1946): 1357–60.
80 Canada, House of Commons, *Debates*, 2 April 1946, 503.
81 Ibid., 507, 510.
82 Doug Owram, *The Government Generation* (Toronto: University of Toronto Press, 1986), 285–334.
83 Paul Martin, *A Very Public Life: Memoirs* (Ottawa: Deneau, 1983) I: 445–53.
84 Cf. Palmer, *Patterns of Prejudice*, passim. Palmer is guided by the American historical experience found in John Higham, *Strangers in the Land: Patterns of American Nativism 1860–1925* (New York: Atheneum, 1963).
85 Cf. Smith, 'Metaphor and Nationality.' Smith is guided by the American experience and norms developed by Louis Hartz, *The Founding of New Societies* (New York: Harcourt, Brace & World, 1964).
86 Cf. Michael Behiels, *Prelude to Quebec's Quiet Revolution* (Montreal: McGill-Queen's University Press, 1986), which examines the Quebec debate during the thirties, forties, and fifties without considering any changes in or influences from the rest of Canada. Ramsay Cook has examined nationalist opinion in *Canada and the French Canadian Question* (Toronto: Macmillan, 1966), passim. Finally, Susan Bellay has examined 'English-Canadian' views of French Canadians during the period of Imperialist nationalism in 'The Image of the French Canadian in English Canada, 1880–1920' (MA thesis, University of Manitoba, 1990).

Dreisziger: The Achievement of Ukrainian-Canadian Unity

This paper is based on research that the author has done with the help of grants and fellowships from the Social Science and Humanities Research Council of Canada, the Department of Multiculturalism and Citizenship, and the Department of National Defence of Canada.
1 Oleh W. Gerus, 'Ethnic Politics in Canada: The Formation of the Ukrainian Canadian Committee,' in O.W. Gerus et al., eds., *The Jubilee Collection of the Ukrainian Free Academy of Sciences in Canada* (Winnipeg: Ukrainian Free Academy of Sciences, 1976), 467.
2 Jars Balan, *Salt and Braided Bread: Ukrainian Life in Canada* (Toronto: Oxford University Press, 1984), 82.
3 Bohdan S. Kordan and Lubomyr Y. Luciuk, 'A Prescription for Nation-

building: Ukrainian Canadians and the Canadian State, 1939–1945,' in
Norman Hillmer, Bohdan Kordan, and Lubomyr Luciuk, eds., *On Guard
for Thee: War, Ethnicity, and the Canadian State, 1939–1945* (Ottawa: Canadian Committee for the History of the Second World War, 1989), 126–51.

4 See, for example, the memorandum from Norman A. Robertson to Dana
Wilgress of 28 May 1943, RG 25, G 1, vol. 1896, file 165, National Archives
of Canada, Ottawa (hereafter cited as NAC), printed in Bohdan S. Kordan
and Lubomyr Y. Luciuk, eds., *A Delicate and Difficult Question: Documents
in the History of Ukrainians in Canada, 1899–1962* (Kingston: Limestone
Press, 1986), 94–100. The RCMP's account of the UCC's formation offers
a similar interpretation. See the RCMP Intelligence Bulletin for 23 December 1940 in Gregory S. Kealey and Reg Whittaker, eds., *R.C.M.P. Security
Bulletins: The War Series, 1939–1941* (St John's: Committee on Canadian
Labour History, 1989), 318f.

5 Two earlier studies of the UCC's origins are by O.W. Gerus. One is
entitled 'The Ukrainian Canadian Committee' and can be found in
Manoly R. Lupul, ed., *A Heritage in Transition: Essays in the History of
Ukrainians in Canada* (Toronto: McClelland and Stewart, 1982), 195–214;
the other study has been cited in n. 1. Another work dealing with the
UCC's gestation and establishment in some detail is Bohdan S. Kordan,
'Disunity and Duality: Ukrainian Canadians and the Second World War'
(MA thesis, Carleton University, 1981), especially 38–47. A document
relating to the subject can be found in Kordan and Luciuk, *A Delicate and
Difficult Question*, 74–6. T.M. Prymak has also dealt with the UCC's
background but not with the details of its establishment. See Thomas M.
Prymak, *Maple Leaf and Trident: The Ukrainian Canadians during the Second
World War* (Toronto: Multicultural History Society of Ontario, 1988), 44–6.

6 Gerus, 'Ethnic Politics,' 471. Gerus cites examples of Ukrainian-Canadian
umbrella organizations that came into existence during the First World
War to promote the cause of Ukraine's struggle for independence.

7 Ibid., 472f.

8 Ibid., 476; Gerus, 'The Ukrainian Canadian Committee,' 197f. Kordan's
account is less problematic. Kordan, 'Disunity and Duality,' 46f.

9 Gerus, 'Ethnic Politics,' 476f.

10 Jean R. Burnet with Howard Palmer, *'Coming Canadians': An Introduction
to a History of Canada's Peoples* (Toronto: McClelland and Stewart, 1988),
190f.

11 Furthermore, the minister of national war services in 1940 was not J.T.
Thorson but J.G. Gardiner, and Kaye was not with the Citizenship
Branch (which would be established only in 1944) and was not even a
civil servant. See Gerus, 'Ethnic Politics,' 476f.

12 Estimates of the Ukrainian population in Europe at various times in the
first half of the twentieth century vary a great deal. One Ukrainian-
Canadian source put the figure (based on data from the 1930s) at

55,164,000. Memorandum of the Representative Committee of Ukrainian Canadians to the Right Honourable W.L. Mackenzie King (1940). A copy of this printed memo can be found in RG 25, vol. 1896, file 165–39c, NAC. In referring to Europe's Ukrainian population in 1900, Balan gives the figure of 20,700,000. Balan, *Salt and Braided Bread*, 4.

13 Joseph Rothschild, *East Central Europe between the Two World Wars* (Seattle and London: University of Washington Press, 1974), 43.

14 They had, for centuries, composed the lowest class (i.e. the peasantry) in these regions. Jars Balan gives a dramatic summary of the poverty that was the lot of peasants in the Ukrainian-populated provinces of Austria at the turn of the century. Balan, *Salt and Braided Bread*, 4. A more positive view of the socio-economic conditions in Galicia at the turn of the century can be found in Stella M. Hryniuk, 'A Peasant Society in Transition: Ukrainian Peasants in Five East Galician Counties 1880–1900' (PhD dissertation, University of Manitoba, 1984). These views are given in capsule form in Stella M. Hryniuk, 'Health Care in Rural Eastern Galicia in the Late Nineteenth Century: The Role of Women,' in John Komlos, ed., *Economic Development in the Habsburg Monarchy and in the Successor States* (Boulder: East European Monographs, 1990), 1–2.

15 Rothschild, *East Central Europe*, 43. See also C.A. Macartney and A.W. Palmer, *Independent Eastern Europe: A History* (London: Macmillan, 1962), 276; and Edward D. Wynot, 'Poland's Christian Minorities, 1919–1939,' *Nationalities Papers* 13 (1985): 214–28.

16 Macartney and Palmer, *Independent Eastern Europe*, 197.

17 Ibid., 390f.

18 Some Ruthenians did not identify with the emergent Ukrainian national cause in Carpathian Ruthenia. Certain organizations of Ruthenians in the United States, for example, felt that the leaders of Carpatho-Ukraine stood for pan-Ukrainian, as opposed to local Ruthenian, national culture. Paul Robert Magocsi, *Our People: Carpatho-Rusyns and Their Descendants in North America* (Toronto: Multicultural History Society of Ontario, 1984), 84.

19 Gerus, 'Ethnic Politics,' 472.

20 Hitler, who had virtually forbidden the Hungarians to move into Sub-Carpathia during the fall of 1938, suddenly changed his mind in March 1939 and encouraged them to do so. On this see a letter by Otto von Erdmannsdorf to J.F. Montgomery, 12 September 1954. A copy of this letter was enclosed in a letter by Montgomery to the Hungarian émigré politician Tibor Eckhardt, 8 January [1955], Tibor Eckhardt Papers, Box 2, Hoover Institution Archives, Stanford University. (Erdmannsdorf and Montgomery were the German and American ministers in Budapest at one time or another during the war.) Hitler even allowed the Hungarians to maintain the impression that the invasion was undertaken on Hungarian initiative and not at the bidding of a great power. The Hungarian govern-

ment received the bill for these favours a short time later when the Germans confronted it with demands for further economic concessions. See Nandor A.F. Dreisziger, *Hungary's Way to World War II* (Toronto: Helicon, 1968), 97–9, 109–11.

21 The most important component of the RCUC, the Ukrainian National Federation (UNF), was an organization of Ukrainians who had come relatively recently and mainly from the territories that before 1918 had belonged to Austria. Many leading members of the UNF were veterans of the Ukrainian struggle for independence at the end of the war against the White and Red armies in Russia, as well as against Poland and Romania. They were staunchly anti-Communist and anti-monarchist and had little sympathy for the democratic tendencies that they felt were prevailing in other Ukrainian-Canadian organizations. Since Germany had been a supporter of Ukrainian independence at the end of the war, many Ukrainian émigré soldiers felt affinity for Germans, a fact which gave rise to wartime accusations that some UNF members were 'pro-Nazi.' The other major organization within the RCUC was the Brotherhood of Ukrainian Catholics (BUC). Although it had a large membership, it played a low-key role in Ukrainian-Canadian political life. Many of its leaders also held positions in the UNF, which made direct BUC involvement in political controversy unnecessary. Prymak, *Maple Leaf and Trident*, 27f; Gerus, 'Ethnic Politics,' 469–70; and W. Burianyk, 'Confidential Report on the Ukrainian Situation in Canada,' mss (ca. November 1940), copy enclosed in T.C. Davis to Norman A. Robertson, 18 November 1940, RG 25, vol. 1896, file 165–39c, pt. II, NAC. William Burianyk was a prominent member and an ideologue of the Ukrainian Self-Reliance League (USRL) and, as such, not the most reliable source on the rival UNF; however, his charges that the UNF had anti-democratic tendencies are echoed in the RCMP intelligence report of 23 December 1940. See Kealey and Whittaker, *R.C.M.P. Security Bulletins*, 316–18.

22 The organizations that formed the UCCC were the USRL, the United Hetman Organization (UHO), and the League of Ukrainian Organizations (LUO). Of the three, the USRL was the largest and most influential. It was the political arm of the Ukrainian Greek Orthodox Church in Canada. Though its membership was smaller than that of the BUC, it had the reputation of a large, well-run organization with a dedicated following. Its members tended to be 'nationally conscious,' 'anti-Catholic,' and intolerant of other Ukrainian viewpoints. Prymak, *Maple Leaf and Trident*, 18. Furthermore, some of the league's leaders were considered to be political manipulators and were accused of harbouring in their ranks the 'worst Polonophobes' among all the Ukrainian organizations. (Watson Kirkconnell to Norman Robertson, 14 December 1940, RG 25, vol. 1896, file 165–39c, pt. II, NAC.) The United Hetman Organization consisted of the supporters of a conservative monarchist form of govern-

ment for an independent Ukraine. Most of the UHO's leaders were post-war arrivals, and some of them had served under Hetman Pavlo Skoro-padsky of 1918 fame. The LUO was made up of people who had broken with the Ukrainian Communists (and their organization, the Ukrainian Labour-Farmer Temple Association, or ULFTA) over the issue of Moscow's treatment of its Ukrainians, and had become one of the ULFTA's bitterest critics. W. Burianyk, Confidential Report on the Ukrainian Situation in Canada [November 1940], enclosed in T.C. Davis to Norman Robertson, 18 November 1940, RG 25, vol. 1896, file 165–39c, pt. II, NAC. See also the UCC to O.D. Skelton, 11 December 1940, RG 25, vol. 1896, file 165–39c, pt. II, NAC.

23 Many Ukrainian-Canadian 'enemy alien' leftists were interned during the fall of 1939. See William Repka and Kathleen M. Repka, *Dangerous Patriots: Canada's Unknown Prisoners of War* (Vancouver: New Star Books, 1982).

24 Gerus, 'Ethnic Politics,' 474–6.

25 Ibid., 476.

26 In the summer of 1940 the DOCR's provisions regarding enemy aliens were amended so as to make them apply against a large portion of Canada's immigrant ethnic community, even thousands of people who had become naturalized in the 1920s and 1930s. Most of those interned at this time were Italians. For a discussion of Canadian governmental attitudes towards Italian Canadians during the war see my paper, 'The Evolving Status of Italian "Enemy Aliens" in Canada, 1939–1945,' given at a conference on Italy and Canada in the two world wars, at the University of Pisa, in 1988. The proceedings of this conference were published in L. Bruti-Liberati, ed., *Il Canada e la Guerra dei Trent'anni* (Milan: Guerini, 1989).

27 N.F. Dreisziger, 'The Rise of a Bureaucracy for Multiculturalism: The Origins of the Nationalities Branch, 1939–1941,' in Hillmer, Kordan, and Luciuk, *On Guard for Thee*, 3–6.

28 Watson Kirkconnell, *A Slice of Canada: Memoirs* (Toronto: University of Toronto Press, 1967), 275. For information on Simpson's relations with Ukrainians see Thomas M. Prymak, 'George Simpson, the Ukrainian Canadians and the "Pre-History" of Slavic Studies in Canada,' *Saskatchewan History* 41 (1988): 53–66. For Kirkconnell's contacts with them see his memoirs, especially the chapter on 'The New Canadians'; also N.F. Dreisziger, 'Watson Kirkconnell and the Cultural Credibility Gap between Immigrants and the Native-Born in Canada,' in *Ethnic Canadians: Culture and Education* (Regina: Canadian Plains Research Center, 1978), 87–96.

29 Copy of letter, T.C. Davis to Harry Hereford, Commissioner, Unemployment Relief Branch, Department of Labour, 12 October 1940, RG 44, vol. 36, NAC.

30 Pamphlet of the National Council of Education of Canada, 15 May 1940, on the forthcoming lecture tour by Tracy Philipps. Philipps Papers, vol. 2, NAC. Philipps's own explanation of the origins of his mission can be found in an unsigned memo, dated January 1941, Philipps Papers, vol. 1, f. 16, NAC.

31 Pamphlet of the National Council of Education of Canada.

32 Ibid.

33 Ibid.

34 Ibid.

35 By early 1940 Kaye had taken on another responsibility, the directorship of the Ukrainian Press Bureau.

36 After abandoning the USRL, this dynamic and volatile lawyer became a leader of the rival UNF.

37 Memorandum by O.D. S[kelton], 23 April 1940, RG 25, vol. 1896, file 165–39c, pt. II, NAC. The RCUC's memorandum, addressed to Prime Minister MacKenzie King, can be found in the same file.

38 T.C. Davis, writing from Canberra, to Norman Robertson, 21 May 1943, RG 25, vol. 1896, file 165–39c, pt. III, NAC. Kordan cites another government document that makes a similar claim (Kordan, 'Disunity and Duality,' 37, n. 17). Regrettably that document, too, dates from a later period, September 1942.

39 Copy of letter, W. Burianyk to W.J. Patterson, 17 November 1940, enclosed in T.C. Davis to Norman Robertson, 2 December 1940, RG 25, vol. 1896, file 165–39c, pt. II, NAC. Another record of the Burianyk-Philipps conversation exists in: copy of letter, 'Bill' [Burianyk] to Walter [Brockington], 22 November 1940, also enclosed in the above letter [?]. Brockington acted as adviser to the PMO at the time.

40 Ibid.

41 Copy of letter, T. Philipps to Colonel James Mess, President, Association of Canadian Clubs, 14 November 1940, enclosed in T.C. Davis to Norman Robertson, 2 December 1940 [?], RG 25, vol. 1896, file 165–39c, pt. II, NAC. See also copy of letter, 'Bill' [Burianyk] to Walter [Brockington], 22 November 1940, cited above. Burianyk was a USRL supporter, and his account has an anti-RCUC flavour. Nevertheless, in its most important aspects, Burianyk's account of the UCC's birth coincides with Philipps's.

42 Among other non-Ukrainians present, according to Kirkconnell, were Edgar Tarr and Victor Sifton (the latter from the *Winnipeg Free Press*). Kirkconnell, *A Slice of Canada*, 276.

43 Copy of letter, Philipps to Mess, 14 November 1940, enclosed in Davis to Robertson, 2 December 1940 [?], RG 25, vol. 1896, file 165–39c, pt. II, NAC. In his letter Philipps paid tribute to the preparatory work that had been done for Ukrainian-Canadian unity by Kaye during his earlier tour of the West.

44 Hungarian Canadians, after a trouble-plagued start in 1928, managed to

set up a promising umbrella organization of their own in the following year. They did so after Baron Zsigmond Perényi, an emissary of the Hungarian government, mediated among their various factions. Towards the end of the Second World War they managed to establish a non-partisan committee to aid war victims in Hungary only after Ottawa told them that it would recognize only a united Hungarian aid organization. And during the early 1950s, when Prime Minister St Laurent told the Hungarians that they should lobby Ottawa not in the name of local co-ordinating committees but as a united group, they established the Hungarian Canadian Federation, which exists to this day. N.F. Dreisziger, 'In Search of a Hungarian-Canadian Lobby: 1927–1951,' *Canadian Ethnic Studies* 12 (1980): 85–90.

45 For more details see Dreisziger, 'The Rise of a Bureaucracy,' 20–1, and Kordan and Luciuk, 'A Prescription,' 90–6, passim.

Wiseman: Ukrainian-Canadian Politics

1 Vera Lysenko, *Men in Sheepskin Coats: A Study in Assimilation* (Toronto: Ryerson Press, 1947); Paul Yuzyk, *The Ukrainians in Manitoba: A Social History* (Toronto: University of Toronto Press, 1953), chapter 7, 'The Ukrainian-Communist Delusion.'

2 Thomas M. Prymak, *Maple Leaf and Trident: The Ukrainian Canadians during the Second World War* (Toronto: Multicultural History Society of Ontario, 1988), appendix A, 131–2. The former estimate is in the *Toronto Star Weekly*, 12 November 1943; *Winnipeg Free Press*, 2 June 1943; and Paul Yuzyk, *The Ukrainian Greek Orthodox Church in Canada, 1918–1951* (Ottawa: University of Ottawa Press, 1981), 186. The latter estimate is from Paul Yuzyk, Canada, Senate, *Debates*, 3 March 1964, 53.

3 Bohdan S. Kordan and Lubomyr Y. Luciuk, eds., *A Delicate and Difficult Question: Documents in the History of Ukrainians in Canada, 1899–1962* (Kingston: Limestone Press, 1986).

4 Elizabeth Wangenheim, 'The Ukrainians: A Case Study of the "Third Force,"' in Peter Russell, ed., *Nationalism in Canada* (Toronto: McGraw-Hill, 1966), 72–91.

5 Constitution Act, 1982, Section 27.

6 *Census of the Prairie Provinces, 1946* (Ottawa, 1949) I, tables 33, 99, and *Census of Canada, 1941* (Ottawa, 1950) IV: 266–7.

7 Peter Melnycky, 'Political Reaction to Ukrainian Immigrants: The 1899 Election in Manitoba,' in Jaroslav Rozumnyj, ed., *New Soil – Old Roots: The Ukrainian Experience in Canada* (Winnipeg: Ukrainian Academy of Arts and Sciences in Canada, 1983), 30–1.

8 Canada, House of Commons, *Debates*, 12 April 1901. Reproduced in Harold Troper, *Only Farmers Need Apply* (Toronto: Griffin House, 1972), 22; and in Kordan and Luciuk, *A Delicate and Difficult Question*, 20.

9 J.E. Rea, 'The Roots of Prairie Society,' in David P. Gagan, ed., *Prairie Perspectives: Papers of the Western Canadian Studies Conference* (Toronto: Holt, Rinehart and Winston, 1970), 51.

10 James S. Woodsworth, *Strangers within Our Gates* (Toronto: F.C. Stephenson, 1909), 125, 135–6.

11 Lubomyr Luciuk, *A Time for Atonement: Canada's First National Internment Operations and the Ukrainian Canadians, 1914–1920* (Kingston: Limestone Press, 1988); and Frances Swyripa and John Herd Thompson, eds., *Loyalties in Conflict: Ukrainians in Canada during the Great War* (Edmonton: Canadian Institute of Ukrainian Studies, 1983).

12 Myron G.G. Gulka-Tiechko, 'Inter-war Ukrainian Immigration to Canada, 1919–1939' (MA thesis, University of Manitoba, 1983), 21, 138.

13 Ramsay Cook, ed., *The Dafoe-Sifton Correspondence, 1919–1927* (Winnipeg: Manitoba Record Society, 1966), 13 January 1923, 137.

14 *Manitoba Free Press*, 22 May 1919 and 15 February 1922. See also Donald Avery, 'The Radical Alien and the Winnipeg General Strike of 1919,' in Carl Berger and Ramsay Cook, eds., *The West and the Nation* (Toronto: McClelland and Stewart, 1976), 209–31.

15 *Manitoba Free Press*, 18, 19, 20, 21, 22, 24, 25, 27, 28, and 29 December 1923.

16 Donald H. Avery, 'Ethnic and Class Tensions in Canada, 1918–20: Anglo Canadians and the Canadian Worker,' in Swyripa and Thompson, *Loyalties in Conflict*, 90. See Macdonald's letter to Arthur Meighen, 3 July 1919, in Kordan and Luciuk, *A Delicate and Difficult Question*, 43–5.

17 W.H. Walker, Department of External Affairs, to the Governor-General, 15 June 1922, in Kordan and Luciuk, *A Delicate and Difficult Question*, 45–6.

18 Frances Swyripa, *Ukrainian Canadians: A Survey of Their Portrayal in English-language Works* (Edmonton: University of Alberta Press, 1978).

19 Quoted in Gerald E. Panting, 'A Study of the United Farmers of Manitoba to 1928' (MA thesis, University of Manitoba, 1954), 170. For the UFM's list of officers see Board of Directors Minutes, 1919–39, and Executive Committee Minutes, 1919–39, UFM Papers, Provincial Archives of Manitoba, Winnipeg.

20 Yuzyk, *The Ukrainians in Manitoba*, 211.

21 Kordan and Luciuk, *A Delicate and Difficult Question*, 126.

22 B.Z. Shek, 'The Portrayal of Canada's Ethnic Groups in Some French-Canadian Novels,' in Cornelius J. Jaenen, ed., *Slavs in Canada* (Toronto: Inter-University Committee on Canadian Slavs, 1969) III: 270.

23 James Gray, *The Winter Years* (Toronto: Macmillan, 1966), 126–7; and Henry Trachtenberg, 'The Winnipeg Jewish Community and Politics: The Inter-war Years' (paper delivered at the Annual Joint Meeting of the Jewish Historical Society of Western Canada and the Manitoba Historical Society, 12 December 1978), 30.

24 *Toronto Daily Star*, 31 October 1938.

25 J.F. White, 'Deportations,' July 1932, in J.L. Granatstein and Peter Stevens, eds., *Forum: Canadian Life and Letters, 1920–70* (Toronto: University of Toronto Press, 1972), 102.

26 William Calderwood, 'The Rise and Fall of the Ku Klux Klan in Saskatchewan' (MA thesis, University of Saskatchewan, 1968).

27 Seymour Martin Lipset, *Agrarian Socialism: The Cooperative Commonwealth Federation in Saskatchewan* (1950; rpt., Garden City, NY: Doubleday, 1968), 52, 208–9, 226, 232.

28 Donovan Swailes to Mrs E. Lyon, 26 January 1956, CCF Papers, Provincial Archives of Manitoba.

29 Murray S. Donnelly, *The Government of Manitoba* (Toronto: University of Toronto Press, 1963), 83.

30 Reproduced in *Manitoba Free Press*, 24 May 1922.

31 *Kanadiiskyi farmer*, 8 June 1932, and *Ukrainskyi holos*, 22 July 1936. Quoted in Thomas Peterson, 'Manitoba: Ethnic and Class Politics,' in Martin Robin, ed., *Canadian Provincial Politics*, 2d ed. (Scarborough, Ont.: Prentice-Hall, 1978), 84.

32 Nelson Wiseman and K.W. Taylor, 'Ethnic vs. Class Voting: The Case of Winnipeg, 1945,' *Canadian Journal of Political Science* 7 (1974): 314–28; 'Class and Ethnic Voting in Winnipeg during the Cold War,' *Canadian Review of Sociology and Anthropology* 16 (1979): 60–76; 'Voting in Winnipeg during the Depression,' *Canadian Review of Sociology and Anthropology* 19 (1982): 215–36; and K.W. Taylor and Nelson Wiseman, 'Class and Ethnic Voting in Winnipeg: The Case of 1941,' *Canadian Review of Sociology and Anthropology* 14 (1977): 174–87.

33 W. Kossar, President of the Ukrainian National Federation, to O.D. Skelton, Under-Secretary of State for External Affairs, 9 June 1939, and V.J. Kaye, Director of the Ukrainian Bureau, London, to the Ukrainian Self-Reliance League, 18 February 1940, in Kordan and Luciuk, *A Delicate and Difficult Question*, 67–70, 71–3.

34 Olha Woycenko, *The Ukrainians in Canada* (Winnipeg: Trident Press, 1968), 117–18.

35 Kordan and Luciuk, *A Delicate and Difficult Question*, 111–13.

36 Canada, Senate, *Debates*, 3 March 1963, 56–7.

37 *Report of the Royal Commission on Bilingualism and Biculturalism* (Ottawa: 1967) I: 155–69.

38 Editorials, 11 August 1971, 28 June 1972, and 7 January 1981, reproduced in Isydore Hlynka, *The Other Canadians* (Winnipeg: Trident Press, 1981), 6, 9, and 236.

39 W. Roman Petryshyn, 'Political Dimensions of Ukrainian Canadian Culture,' in Manoly R. Lupul, ed., *Visible Symbols: Cultural Expression among Canada's Ukrainians* (Edmonton: Canadian Institute of Ukrainian Studies, 1984), 178–98.

40 Yuzyk, *The Ukrainians in Manitoba*, 147.

41 Jaroslav Petryshyn, *Peasants in the Promised Land: Canada and the Ukrainians, 1891–1914* (Toronto: James Lorimer, 1985), 210.
42 Ivan Avakumovic, *The Communist Party in Canada: A History* (Toronto: McClelland and Stewart, 1975), 35; Ian Angus, *Canadian Bolsheviks: The Early Years of the Communist Party of Canada* (Montreal: Vanguard Publications, 1981), 291; John Kolasky, *The Shattered Illusion: The History of Ukrainian Pro-Communist Organizations in Canada* (Toronto: PMA Books, 1979), 17; Charles H. Young, *The Ukrainian Canadians: A Study in Assimilation* (Toronto: Thomas Nelson and Sons, 1931), 146.
43 Avakumovic, *The Communist Party in Canada*, 94.
44 Communist Party of Canada, 1929 Convention Report, cited in Angus, *Canadian Bolsheviks*, 295; William Rodney, *Soldiers of the International: A History of the Communist Party of Canada, 1919–1929* (Toronto: University of Toronto Press, 1968), 86; see also Statements of the CPC, 1929 and 1930, in Kordan and Luciuk, *A Delicate and Difficult Question*, 53–9.
45 Rodney, *Soldiers of the International*, 159–60.
46 Angus, *Canadian Bolsheviks*, 301–2, 310.
47 Avakumovic, *The Communist Party in Canada*, 120.
48 Compare Avakumovic, *The Communist Party in Canada*, with Ivan Avakumovic, *Socialism in Canada* (Toronto: McClelland and Stewart, 1978).
49 Nelson Wiseman, *Social Democracy in Manitoba: A History of the CCF-NDP* (Winnipeg: University of Manitoba Press, 1983), 15, 20.
50 Donald Swainson, 'Ethnic Revolt: Manitoba's Election,' *Canadian Forum*, August 1969, 98–9.
51 Interview with author, April 1972.
52 'Return for Contributions to a Political Party,' for 1985. File for the Communist Party of Canada (Manitoba Section), Office of the Chief Electoral Officer, Winnipeg.
53 *Ukrainian Canadian*, December 1989.
54 For example, Prymak, *Maple Leaf and Trident*.
55 Yuzyk, *The Ukrainians in Manitoba*, 85; and Gulka-Tiechko, 'Inter-war Ukrainian Immigration,' 3 and 315.
56 Department of External Affairs memo, 28 May 1943, in Kordan and Luciuk, *A Delicate and Difficult Question*, 94–100.
57 Lubomyr Y. Luciuk and Bohdan S. Kordan, *Creating a Landscape: A Geography of Ukrainians in Canada* (Toronto: University of Toronto Press, 1989), map 18.
58 Programme of the Ukrainian Self-Reliance League, December 1927, in Kordan and Luciuk, *A Delicate and Difficult Question*, 48–50.
59 Press release, 'Ukrainians Loyal to King and Canada,' 11 August 1927, Box 23, D.M. Elcheshen Papers, Ukrainian Cultural and Education Centre, Winnipeg; and Yuzyk, *The Ukrainians in Manitoba*, 87–8.
60 W. Bossy and D.M. Elcheshen to the editor, *Whitehall Gazette and St James Review*, 4 February 1931.

61 *Winnipeg Free Press*, 13 and 14 December 1937 and 3 January 1938; *Winnipeg Evening Tribune*, 3 January 1938.
62 *Winnipeg Tribune*, 17 October 1949.
63 Kordan and Luciuk, *A Delicate and Difficult Question*, 42–3.
64 Nadia O.M. Kazymyra, 'Ukrainian-Canadian Response to the Paris Peace Conference, 1919,' in Swyripa and Thompson, *Loyalties in Conflict*, 127–9; Kordan and Luciuk, *A Delicate and Difficult Question*, 142–6.
65 Leslie A. Pal, 'Identity, Citizenship, and Mobilization: The Nationalities Branch and World War Two,' *Canadian Public Administration* 32 (1989): 411, 414.
66 Prymak, *Maple Leaf and Trident*, 72–3; and Luciuk and Kordan, *Creating a Landscape*, map 22.
67 Secret Memorandum for the Prime Minister, 4 July 1944, in Kordan and Luciuk, *A Delicate and Difficult Question*, 115.
68 Ibid., 156–66.
69 Samuel J. Nesdoly, 'Changing Perspectives: The Ukrainian-Canadians' Role in Canadian-Soviet Relations,' in Aloysius Balawyder, ed., *Canadian-Soviet Relations, 1939–1980* (Oakville: Mosaic Press, 1981), 107–27.
70 Kordan and Luciuk, *A Delicate and Difficult Question*, 171–3.
71 Ukrainian Canadian Committee, *United Community* (Winnipeg, 1960?).
72 Confidential Memo, Department of Citizenship and Immigration, May 1958, in Kordan and Luciuk, *A Delicate and Difficult Question*, 168–9.
73 'Ukrainian-Jewish Relations in Canada,' in Peter J. Potichnyj and Howard Aster, eds., *Ukrainian-Jewish Relations in Historical Perspective* (Edmonton: Canadian Institute of Ukrainian Studies, 1988), 467.
74 'Winnipeg firms hope for bonanza in Ukraine,' *Globe and Mail*, 26 June 1989.
75 David Smith, 'Political Culture in the West,' in David Jay Bercuson and Phillip A. Buckner, eds., *Eastern and Western Perspectives* (Toronto: University of Toronto Press, 1981), 173–4.

Harasymiw: Looking for the Ukrainian Vote

1 See, for instance, 'Ethnic vote makes it tough to limit immigration,' *Calgary Herald*, 7 August 1974; 'Liberals, NDP humiliated in Ontario by the Tories,' *Globe and Mail*, 24 May 1979; and 'Tories' dreams of ethnic empire turn to nightmare,' *Globe and Mail*, 8 November 1986.
2 Rose T. Harasym, 'Ukrainians in Canadian Political Life, 1923–45,' in Manoly R. Lupul, ed., *A Heritage in Transition: Essays in the History of Ukrainians in Canada* (Toronto: McClelland and Stewart, 1982), 116. For a review of the immediately preceding period, see Orest T. Martynowych and Nadia Kazymyra, 'Political Activity in Western Canada, 1896–1923,' in Lupul, *A Heritage in Transition*, 85–107.
3 Harasym, 'Ukrainians in Canadian Political Life,' 117.

4 Ibid., 119.
5 Ibid., 121–2.
6 Bohdan Harasymiw, 'Political Participation of Ukrainian Canadians since 1945,' in Lupul, *A Heritage in Transition,* 129.
7 William Darcovich and Paul Yuzyk, eds., *A Statistical Compendium on the Ukrainians in Canada, 1891–1976* (Ottawa: University of Ottawa Press, 1980), section 33, 'Political Participation.' In addition, this study utilizes the serial publications *Canadian Parliamentary Guide* (1945–90) and *Report of the Chief Electoral Officer on Federal By-Elections* (1945–81), the relevant issues of the *Globe and Mail, Edmonton Journal, Calgary Herald, Canadian News Facts, Ukrainskyi holos,* and *Ukrainski visti,* and personal knowledge.
8 There is obvious potential for error in this technique, but since voters, too, may make a mistake in identifying their ethnic kinsmen, it will have to be tolerated.
9 A small number of seats have been contested by Ukrainians in British Columbia, which by reason of this comparative insignificance is omitted from the analysis here.
10 In federal politics, for multicandidate Ukrainian (but not exclusively so) contests, the value of chi-squared for electoral outcome as compared to party affiliation (reduced for the sake of simplicity to PC, Socred, and other) is 73.73; with 2 degrees of freedom, this is significant at $p < .001$.
11 Harasymiw, 'Political Participation,' 129.
12 Martynowych and Kazymyra, 'Political Activity in Western Canada,' 90–4.
13 Ibid., 94–6.
14 Ibid., 96.
15 Ibid., 100–2; Harasym, 'Ukrainians in Canadian Political Life,' 109–13.
16 Harasym, 'Ukrainians in Canadian Political Life,' 116–23.
17 Harasymiw, 'Political Participation,' 128–30.

Ilyniak: Still Coming to Terms

This paper is based on 'Coming to Terms: Jewish-Ukrainian Relations and the Hunt for Nazi War Criminals in Canada,' a master of journalism thesis, Carleton University, 1990. The author is grateful to the Civil Liberties Commission of the Ukrainian Canadian Congress for financial assistance received towards completion of the thesis.
1 Oakland Ross, '"Angel of Death" elusive as ever,' *Globe and Mail,* 13 March 1985; 'Israel still has doubts Josef Mengele is dead,' *Toronto Star,* 7 September 1985. A summary of the pursuit of Mengele in 1984–5 can be found in *Response* (newsletter of the Simon Wiesenthal Center), March 1985.
2 Ralph Blumenthal, 'Records indicate Mengele sought Canadian visa,' reprinted in the *Ottawa Citizen,* 23 January 1989. See also 'Ottawa

reported hiding Nazis,' *Toronto Star*, 27 January 1985; Jock Ferguson, 'Mengele did not enter Canada,' *Globe and Mail*, 16 February 1985.

3 *Response*, March 1985: 5–6; Harold Troper and Morton Weinfeld, *Old Wounds: Jews, Ukrainians and the Hunt for Nazi War Criminals in Canada* (Toronto: Viking, 1988), 140–2. For a critique of *Old Wounds* see L. Luciuk, *Canadian Ethnic Studies* 21 (1989): 136–9.

4 Order No. 1985–348 of the Privy Council for Canada, 7 February 1985.

5 Commission of Inquiry on War Criminals, *Report. Part I: Public* (Ottawa: Supply and Services Canada, 1986), 82; 'Conclusions about Mengele lacked support, inquiry told,' *Globe and Mail*, 6 December 1985.

6 See, for example, B'Nai Brith Canada, League for Human Rights, *One Is Too Many: An Information and Action Booklet* (undated).

7 Jock Ferguson, 'Ukrainians fear witch hunt for war criminals,' *Globe and Mail*, 4 March 1985.

8 This was not the first time that the Ukrainian community launched an anti-defamation campaign. In the late 1930s several Ukrainian organizations in Canada and the United States were the subject of government investigations for 'fifth columnist' ties to Nazi Germany and Fascist Italy. See August Raymond Ogden, *The Dies Commission (1945)* (New York: Greenwood Press, 1984), 130. In 1939–40, The *Hour*, a small but influential newsletter edited by Albert Kohn, published a series of articles alleging connections between Ukrainian-American organizations and the Nazis.

9 Hugh Schofield, 'Israeli court sentences Demjanjuk to be hanged for Nazi war crimes,' *Globe and Mail*, 26 April 1988; Susan Reid, 'Demjanjuk trial in Israel unfair Canadian backers say after verdict,' *Toronto Star*, 19 April 1988.

10 A view shared by Willem Wagenaar, *Identifying Ivan: A Case Study in Legal Psychology* (Cambridge: Harvard University Press, 1988).

11 'Nazi hunter Wiesenthal says Ottawa ignored his 28 suspects,' *Toronto Star*, 10 February 1985.

12 'Ottawa assailed on hunt for Nazis,' *Globe and Mail*, 11 February 1985.

13 See Basil Dmytryshyn, 'The Nazis and the SS Volunteer Division "Galicia",' *American Slavic and East European Review* 15 (1956): 1–10; Myroslav Yurkevich, 'Galician Ukrainians in German Military Formations and in the German Administration,' in Yury Boshyk, ed., *Ukraine during World War II: History and Its Aftermath* (Edmonton: Canadian Institute of Ukrainian Studies, 1986), 67–88.

14 David Matas with Susan Charendoff, *Justice Delayed: Nazi War Criminals in Canada* (Toronto: Summerhill Press, 1987), 45f.

15 See, for example, Myron Kuropas, 'The Wiesenthal shotgun,' *Ukrainian Weekly*, 4 May 1986.

16 'B'Nai B'rith wants new laws to hit ex-Nazis in Canada,' *Globe and Mail*, 11 February 1985.

17 The publications include Michael Hanusiak, *Lest We Forget* (Toronto: Progress Books, 1976); Vladimir Molchanov, *There Shall Be Retribution: Nazi War Criminals and Their Protectors* (Moscow: Progress Publishers, 1981); *Condemned by History* (Kiev: Dnipro Publishers, 1982); V. Styrkul, *The SS Werewolves* (Lviv: Kamenyar Publishers, 1982); *Their True Face* (Kiev: Ukraina Society, 1982); V. Styrkul, *We Accuse* (Kiev: Dnipro Publishers, 1984); Marko Terlytsia, *Here Is the Evidence* (Toronto: Kobzar Publishing Co., 1984); *When the Statute of Limitations Doesn't Apply* (Lviv: Kamenyar Publishers, 1985); and Pavlo Kowalchuk, *Brown Shadows of the Past* (Toronto: Kobzar Publishing Co., 1986). Anti-émigré articles appeared regularly in *Visti z Ukrainy* and its English-language counterpart, *News from Ukraine*, which until 1991 were available only outside the Soviet Union.

18 Ukrainian Canadian Committee, National Executive, 'Press Release,' 14 February 1985; 'Historical Note on the Ukrainian Division,' UCC News Conference, 14 February 1985.

19 Regina Hickl-Szabo, 'Ukrainian community leaders fear effects of Nazi reports,' *Globe and Mail*, 15 February 1985.

20 Ostap Hawaleshka, *Winnipeg Free Press*, 19 May 1985.

21 Most of the papers were published in Boshyk, *Ukraine during World War II*.

22 Regina Hickl-Szabo, 'Expose Soviet war crimes, professor urges,' *Globe and Mail*, 18 February 1985.

23 Agenda of the Civil Liberties Commission (CLC) meeting, 15 March 1985; Executive Reports of the CLC to the Fifteenth Congress of the UCC, 10–13 October 1986, Winnipeg, 3–4; CLC Executive Committee Minutes, 9 April 1985, item 15.

24 *In Defence of Ukrainian Canadians*, leaflet issued by the Civil Liberties Commission, April 1985.

25 Membership lists of the CLC Executive Committee, 25 March 1985; 6 February 1986; other undated lists of the various subcommittees.

26 'Canadians for Justice,' agenda of first meeting, 21 April 1985.

27 Commission of Inquiry on War Criminals, *Report*, 262–74.

28 Ibid., 33.

29 The first public hearings of the commission were held in Ottawa on 10–11 April 1985. Against the advice of his two counsel, Yves Fortier and Michael Meighen, Justice Deschênes granted standing to the Canadian Jewish Congress. The Canadian press widely reported that the CJC had been accorded the right not only to cross-examine witnesses but also to call individuals before the commission. Concerned about this development, representatives of a number of ethnocultural organizations applied for similar privileges. Justice Deschênes granted standing to the League for Human Rights of B'Nai Brith Canada, the Ukrainian Canadian Commit-

tee, and the Brotherhood of Veterans of the First Division of the Ukrainian National Army.

30 David Vieanneau, 'Nazi report a ticking bomb,' *Toronto Star*, 23 November 1986.

31 Ukrainian Canadian Committee, *Submission to the Commission of Inquiry on War Criminals* (Toronto: Justinian Press, 1986). A complete list of submissions is found in Commission of Inquiry on War Criminals, *Report*, 857.

32 See, for example, Sol Littman, 'Trail grows cold in Canada's hunt for war criminals,' *Toronto Star*, 8 June 1980; and idem, 'Agent of the Holocaust: The Secret Life of Helmut Rauca,' *Saturday Night*, July 1983, 11–23. After complaints by the Brotherhood of Veterans of the Ukrainian National Army, First Division, the *Star* published a rare apology and retraction. In November 1983, two former Division officers filed a libel suit against Littman and *Saturday Night*.

33 Sol Littman, *Report on the Presence of War Criminals in Canada (Submission to the Commission of Inquiry on War Criminals)*, 24 April 1985, 10.

34 Sol Littman, interview with author, 14 May 1986.

35 Ellen Kaychuk, interview with author, 21 May 1986.

36 Gunther Plaut, 'War criminal hunt a sore point for Jews, Ukrainians,' *Globe and Mail*, 20 November 1985.

37 'The End of Multiculturalism?' *Ukrainian Echo*, 25 September 1985.

38 Robert Alter, 'Deformations of the Holocaust,' *Commentary*, February 1981: 48–54.

39 David Matas, *Submission of the League for Human Rights of B'Nai Brith Canada to the Commission of Inquiry on War Criminals*, 22 May 1985.

40 Thomas L. Friedman, 'Jerusalem listens to the victims of Mengele,' *New York Times*, 3 February 1985.

41 Debbie Raicek, 'Bringing Nazi War Criminals to Justice: An Issue of Human Rights,' *Quid Novi* (McGill University Faculty of Law), 13 November 1985, 2–4.

42 Michael Walzer, *Just and Unjust Wars: A Moral Argument with Historical Illustrations* (New York: Basic Books, 1977), 287–316.

43 'When Jews insist on recalling the Holocaust,' writes Anne Roiphe, 'when Jews express their anger and their pain about the Holocaust, they are directly or indirectly accusing others of not being good and these implicit or explicit accusations cause terrible anger. When people feel guilty they feel vastly uncomfortable and then they become angry with the group or person who has made them feel guilty. In the last forty years the Jews have made many people feel guilty and many people feel angry.' Anne Roiphe, *A Season for Healing: Reflections on the Holocaust* (New York: Summit Books, 1988), 26f.

44 'Every people has used its history to justify itself in its own eyes and in

the eyes of the world and every people has enlisted its historians to
that end.' Lucy Dawidowicz, *The Holocaust and the Historians* (Cambridge:
Harvard University Press, 1981), 142.

45 Some of the efforts and frustrations of Ukrainians to present their case
are documented in Lubomyr Y. Luciuk and Bohdan S. Kordan, eds.,
*Anglo-American Perspectives on the Ukrainian Question, 1938–1951: A Docu-
mentary Collection* (Kingston: Limestone Press, 1987) and Bohdan S.
Kordan and Lubomyr Y. Luciuk, *A Delicate and Difficult Question: Documents in the History of Ukrainians in Canada, 1899–1962* (Kingston: Limestone Press, 1986). See also 'The Pious Abandonment of Ukraine and
Other Captive Nations' (editorial), *Ukrainian Quarterly* 20 (Autumn
1964): 197–204; and Roman Rakhmanny, *In Defense of the Ukrainian Cause*
(North Quincy, Mass.: Christopher Publishing House, 1979). Ukrainians
have been especially frustrated in attempting to present their case that
the famine of 1932–3, in which an estimated seven million Ukrainians
died, was a genocidal action aimed at destroying the Ukrainian nation.
See Marco Carynnyk, 'The Famine the "Times" Couldn't Find,' *Commentary*, November 1983, 32–40; Mykhailo H. Marunchak, *Natsiia v borotbi za
svoie isnuvannia: 1932 i 1933 v Ukraini i diiaspori* (Winnipeg: Ukrainska vilna
akademiia nauk v Kanadi, 1985); and Marco Carynnyk, Lubomyr Y.
Luciuk, and Bohdan S. Kordan, eds., *The Foreign Office and the Famine:
British Documents on Ukraine and the Great Famine of 1932–1933* (Kingston:
Limestone Press, 1988). See also Jeff Coplon, 'In Search of a Soviet
Holocaust: A 55-Year-Old Famine Feeds the Right,' *Village Voice*, 12 Janu-
ary 1988, which calls the famine a 'fraud.'

46 See, for example, 'Again, Revisionist History,' *Ukrainian Weekly*, 4 October
1981; 'Again, "Ukrainian Anti-Semitism,"' *Ukrainian Weekly*, 13 December 1981; and Sviatoslav Karavansky, 'What Ruins Jewish-Ukrainian Relations?' *Ukrainian Quarterly* 42 (Spring–Summer 1986): 81–6.

47 A good overview of the history of meetings between Ukrainians and Jews
is provided in Iosyf L. Likhten (Josef L. Lichten), 'Ukrainsko-zhydivski
stosunky v nedavnomu mynulomu ta ikh perspektyvy na maibutnist,'
Ukrainskyi samostiinyk, Summer 1975, 22–34. Lichten is a former activist
with the Anti-Defamation League. Howard Aster and Peter J. Potichnyj,
Jewish-Ukrainian Relations: Two Solitudes (Oakville: Mosaic Press, 1983),
14–15, give a more up-to-date, though very brief, description of the
meetings. Troper and Weinfeld, *Old Wounds*, 64–110, provide a Canadian context for the dialogues on Jewish-Ukrainian relations, especially
in describing the efforts of Alexander Epstein. In 1979, a group of former
prisoners of Zion in Israel formed the Society for Ukrainian-Jewish Relations. By 1986 it claimed to have four hundred members, who were
almost evenly divided between Ukrainians and Jews. In 1983, the Society
began publishing, in Ukrainian and Russian, the journal *Diialohy* (Dia-

logues). Some ten double issues of the journal were issued, the last in 1988.

48 See, for example, the conditions listed by Shimon Redlich for a Jewish-Ukrainian understanding in 'Efforts to block anti-Ukrainian backlash ... despite history of mutual mistrust,' *Jerusalem Post*, 20 March 1987.

49 On Jewish-Catholic and Jewish-Polish relations see Michael Lerner, 'Memory and Anger,' *Tikkun*, September–October 1987, 41–6; Shimon Frost, 'Reclaiming the Past of the Jews in Poland,' *American Jewish Congress Monthly*, September–October 1983, 6–7; and Alexander Smolar, 'Jews as a Polish Problem,' *Daedulus* 116 (Spring 1987): 31–73.

50 Aster and Potichnyj, *Jewish-Ukrainian Relations*, 16. In contrast, Jews have expressed far greater interest in Jewish-Polish relations. An institute for Polish-Jewish studies has been established at Oxford University, and the American Foundation for Polish-Jewish Studies has branches in Toronto, Montreal, New York, Boston, Chicago, and Miami. (*Canadian Jewish News*, 9 February 1989.)

51 Theodor W. Adorno, 'What Does Coming to Terms Mean?' in Geoffrey Hartman, ed., *Bitburg in Moral and Political Perspective* (Bloomington: Indiana University Press, 1986), 114–29.

52 Commission of Inquiry on War Criminals, *Report*, 13–14. Deschênes also concluded that 'between 1971 and 1986, public statements by outside interveners concerning alleged war criminals residing in Canada have spread increasingly large and grossly exaggerated figures as to their estimated number.' Ibid., 249. He singled out Sol Littman for his 'loose language and careless public statements.' Ibid., 246. Deschênes also exonerated the former members of the Galicia Division of charges of war crimes and misrepresentation or fraudulent immigration claims. Ibid., 261.

53 Bill C-71, 'An Act to Amend the Criminal Code, the Immigration Act 1976 and the Citizenship Act,' Thirty-third Parliament, Second Session, 35–36 Elizabeth II, 1986–7.

54 Richard Cleroux, 'Ottawa introduces bill to prosecute war criminals,' *Globe and Mail*, 24 June 1987; idem, 'Two Tory backbenchers plan to stall Nazi bill,' *Globe and Mail*, 27 June 1987; idem, 'Hnatyshyn withdraws war crimes legislation,' *Globe and Mail*, 1 July 1987. By proposing amendments, the two Ukrainian MPs prevented Bill C-71 from receiving unanimous consent, and the bill died on the order paper because of the House's summer recess.

55 David Vieanneau, '45 war crimes cases probed,' *Toronto Star*, 27 May 1990; Krishna Rau, 'Finta acquittal sparks concern about future of war-crimes cases,' *Globe and Mail*, 28 May 1990; Rudy Platiel, 'Several trials needed to test war-crimes law,' *Globe and Mail*, 28 May 1990.

56 Paul Lungen, 'Jewish-Ukrainian relations in "quiescent mode,"' *Canadian Jewish News*, 17 May 1990.

57 Ron Vastokas and Lubomyr Luciuk, 'The Deschênes Report: A Time for Healing,' in *On the Record: The Debate over Alleged War Criminals in Canada* (Toronto: Justinian Press, 1987), 49–50.

Notes on Contributors

Donald Avery is a professor in the Department of History at the University of Western Ontario in London, Ontario.

Marco Carynnyk is an associate of the Chair of Ukrainian Studies at the University of Toronto.

James Darlington teaches in the Department of Geography at Brandon University in Brandon, Manitoba.

N. Fred Dreisziger is a professor in the Department of History at the Royal Military College of Canada in Kingston, Ontario.

Barry Ferguson teaches in the Department of History at the University of Manitoba in Winnipeg.

Oleh Gerus is a professor in the Department of History at the University of Manitoba in Winnipeg.

Bohdan Harasymiw is a professor in the Department of Political Science at the University of Calgary in Calgary, Alberta.

Stella Hryniuk is a Canada Research Fellow and teaches in the Department of History at the University of Manitoba in Winnipeg.

Morris Ilyniak is a communications specialist with interests in conflict resolution and environmental affairs who works as an adviser in the Ontario Ministry of the Environment.

Wsevolod Isajiw is a professor in the Department of Sociology at the University of Toronto.

Andrii Krawchuk is a research associate at the Harvard Ukrainian Research Institute.

John C. Lehr is a professor in the Department of Geography at the University of Winnipeg.

Lubomyr Luciuk teaches in the Department of Politics and Economics at the Royal Military College of Canada in Kingston, Ontario, and is an adjunct assistant professor in the Department of Geography at Queen's University.

Mark McGowan teaches in the Department of Religion at the University of Ottawa.

Paul R. Magocsi is the holder of the Chair of Ukrainian Studies at the University of Toronto and the director of the Multicultural History Society of Ontario.

Mark Minenko, LLB, is a private scholar from Winnipeg, Manitoba.

Brian Osborne is a professor in the Department of Geography at Queen's University in Kingston, Ontario.

Jaroslav Petryshyn teaches history at Grande Prairie Regional College in Alberta.

Ihor Stebelsky is a professor in the Department of Geography at the University of Windsor.

Frances Swyripa is a Canada Research Fellow and teaches in the Department of History at the University of Alberta in Edmonton.

Nelson Wiseman is a professor in the Department of Political Science at the University of Toronto.

Index

Bickersteth, Burgon, 312
Black, W.J., 82, 90, 96, 99, 100, 101
Blair, F.C., 89
B'Nai Brith Canada: 380, 385, 386;
League of Human Rights, 383
Boels, Rev. Henrich, 222
Borden, 292, 297, 301, 358, 296
Borecky, Isidore (bishop of Toronto),
233
Borshchiv, Galicia, Ukrainian
immigration from, 61
Bossy, Volodymyr, 232
Bourassa, Henri, 325
Boychuk, John, 191, 279
Bradwin, Edwin, 306, 310
Brazil: Ukrainian emigration to, 14,
33, 35, 392 n.5; post-war
Ukrainian emigration to, 135
British Imperial Association, 299
Brotherhood of Ukrainian Catholics
(BUC), 149, 170, 181, 183
Brotherhood of Veterans of the
Ukrainian National Army, First
Division, 383
Bruchesi, Paul (bishop of Montreal),
225
Buck, Tim, 192, 198, 353
Budka, Bp Nykyta, 88, 92, 159, 161,
226, 228, 229, 230, 232, 236, 273,
275, 277, 289, 356
Buduchnist (credit union), 148
Buduchnist natsii (Future of the
Nation, magazine), 178
Building the Future, 253
Bujak, Franciszek, 12
Burianyk, Wasyl (William), 167, 175,
181, 185, 337, 435 n.74, 436 n.99
Burke, Rev. Alfred E., 209, 223–5

Cafik, Norman, 374
Canada, post-war Ukrainian
emigration to, 123–54
Canadian Bankers Association, 296
Canadian Citizenship Act, 1947, 324

Canadian Civil Liberties Union, 281
Canadian Colonization Association,
91
Canadian Expeditionary Force, 297
Canadian Forum, 346
Canadian Jewish Congress, 383, 385,
386
Canadian Labour Defence League,
277, 279
Canadian League for Peace and
Democracy, 280
Canadian League for Ukraine's
Liberation, 148; Women's
Association of, 247, 249
Canadian National Land
Association, 91
Canadian National Railway (CNR):
88–9, 296; Department of
Colonization and Agriculture, 82;
Department of Colonization and
Development, 87
Canadian Pacific Railway (CPR): 63,
86, 88–9, 296; Department of
Colonization and Development,
86–7, 338
Canadian Relief Mission for Ukrai-
nian Victims of War (CRM), 103,
111
Canadian Security Intelligence Ser-
vice, 287
Canadian Sitch Organization, 232,
247, 356, 431 n.26. See also United
Hetman Organization
Canadians All (Kirkconnell), 282
Canadians for Justice, 383
Canadian Social Democratic party
(SDP), 273, 274
Canadian Trades and Labour Con-
gress, 274, 286
Canadian Ukrainian Youth Associa-
tion, 149
Canadian Youth Congress, 280
Canning, Rev., 226
Carpatho-Ukraine, 173

Ukrainian Canadian Centennial Committee, Inc.